The PATHOLOGY of DRUG ABUSE

Second Edition

Steven B. Karch, M.D.

Medical Director
Department of Fire Services
City of Las Vegas
Assistant Medical Examiner
City and County of San Francisco

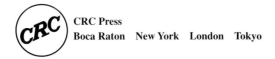

CRC Press
Boca Raton   New York   London   Tokyo

Acquiring Editor: Paul Petralia
Project Editor: Erica Orloff
Direct Marketing Manager: Becky McEldowney
Marketing Manager: Susie Carlisle
Typesetter: Pamela Morrell
Cover Designer: Shayna Murry
Manufacturing: Sheri Schwartz
Pre Press: Kevin Luong

Library of Congress Cataloging-in-Publication Data

Karch, Steven B.
  The pathology of drug abuse / Steven B. Karch. — 2nd ed.
      p. cm.
  Includes bibliographical references and index.
  ISBN 0-8493-9464-3 (alk. paper)
  1. Drug abuse—Pathophysiology. I. Title.
  [DNLM: 1. Substance Abuse—physiopathology. 2. Substance Abuse-
-history. 3. Cocaine—adverse effects. 4. Designer Drugs—adverse
effects. 5. Narcotics—adverse effects. 6. Anobolic Steroids-
-adverse effects. WM 270 K18p 1996]
  RM316.K37 1996
  615'.78—dc20
  DNLM/DLC
  for Library of Congress   96-14757
                                                                                    CIP

Dedication

For my wife, Donna, and for our friends from Kalimantan.
And for Sam.

Preface to first edition

Physicians deal with the consequences of drug abuse on a daily basis, but information about the basic pathology of abused drugs is hard to come by. Hundreds of papers have been published describing the effects of drug abuse on brain neurochemistry, but practitioners are hard pressed to find out how cocaine affects blood vessels or how heroin affects the lungs. I hope this book supplies the information they need. While far from encyclopedic, I think the book does provide answers to most of the questions physicians ask when they are confronted with cases of drug-related death or disability.

In the course of writing the sections on heroin, I was surprised to discover that more than twenty years have elapsed since the first papers were published by Milton Helpern, Charles Wetli, and Michael Baden. Since that time, our government has done little to foster research into the pathology of abused drugs, and knowledge has advanced very little. With the advent of the great HIV pandemic, there may be a price to pay for this lack of knowledge, and for the failure to foster meaningful research. Perhaps with changing government priorities this situation will some day be rectified.

Finally, readers of the book will notice two important omissions: alcohol and marijuana. The reason for not dealing with the former is that alcohol requires its own book. The reason for not discussing the latter is that there isn't enough good anatomic pathology to write about, although recently there have been some interesting studies dealing with marijuana toxicology. I hope this subject can be added in future editions.

Steven B. Karch, M.D.
Berkeley, California
November, 1992

Preface to second edition

Nearly 900 new references have been added since the first edition. The large increase in number is explained partly by the addition of new subjects, such as solvent abuse. Most of the increase is simply due to increased interest in drug abuse, which is reflected by an increase in the number of papers being published. This increase became apparent late in 1991, and already seems to have peaked. This edition contains 233 new references from 1993, 224 from 1994, and 110 from the first six months of 1995.

There have been some major advances since the first edition was published, but most of these have been in the fields of molecular biology and neurochemistry. The characterization of receptor changes in agitated delirium and the cloning of opiate receptors come quickly to mind. By comparison, advances in the field of pathology have been pitifully few. Fewer than 2% of the new references added to this edition have anything to do with anatomy or pathology. Whether this dismal finding reflects a lack of interest among pathologists, or simply is a function of the fact that pathologists have no voice on the various panels that control drug abuse research funding, is not clear. I suspect, however, it is the latter.

I was gratified by the response to the first edition, and pleased that so many have found the book to be useful. I have tried to make this version even better. Perhaps there will be some new pathology to describe in the next edition.

Steven B. Karch, M.D.
Berkeley, California
July 31, 1995

Acknowledgments

All of my teaching files were lost in the Oakland Hills Wildfire of 1991. If it were not for the generous assistance of the contributors listed below, this book would have had a lot fewer illustrations!

Dr. Margaret Billingham, Department of Cardiovascular Surgery, Stanford University School of Medicine

Dr. Rosario Barroso-Moguel, Instituto Nacional De Neurologia Y Neurocirogia, Mexico City

Dr. Arthur K. Cho, Department of Pharmacology, UCLA School of Medicine

Dr. Agnes Fogo, Vanderbilt University Medical Center, Nashville, Tennessee

Dr. Jacques Gilloteaux, Department of Anatomy, College of Medicine, Northeastern Ohio Universities

Dr. François Gray, Department of Pathology, Hôpital Henri Mondor, Creteil, France

Dr. Peter S. Hersh, Chairman, Department of Ophthalmology, Bronx-Lebanon Hospital

Dr. Robert Kloner, Hospital of the Good Samaritan, Los Angeles

Dr. Russell Kridel, University of Texas, Health Sciences Center, Houston

Dr. David A. Krendel, Section of Neurology, The Emory Clinic, Atlanta

Professor M. Maillet, Hôpital Lariboisère, Paris

National Library of Medicine, Bethesda, Maryland

Marilyn Masek, Laboratory of Cardiovascular Pathology, Stanford University School of Medicine

Dr. Morton A. Meyers, Department of Radiology, SUNY at Stony Brook, NY

Dr. José Peña, Facultad De Medicina, Universidad De Cordoba

Dr. Giuseppe G. Pietra, Director, Division of Anatomic Pathology, Hospital of the University of Pennsylvania

Dr. N. G. Ryley, University of Oxford, Nuffield Department of Pathology and Bacteriology, Oxford, England

Stephen M. Roberts, University of Florida, Center for Environmental and Human Toxicology

Dr. J. M. Soares, Faculty of Sport Sciences, University of Porto, Portugal

Dr. P. Som, Medical Department, Brookhaven National Laboratory, Upton, New York

Dr. Randall L. Tackett, Head, Department of Pharmacology and Toxicology, University of Georgia

U.S. Department of Justice, Drug Enforcement Administration

Dr. Renu Virmani, Chairman, Department of Cardiovascular Pathology, Armed Forces Institute of Pathology

Dr. E. Ch. Wolters, Department of Neurology, Academisch Zickenhuis, Amsterdam, the Netherlands

I also wish to thank *Professor Henry Urich* of the London Hospital, and *Professor Margaret Billingham* of Stanford University, for their years of patient instruction. A special thanks also to Drs. *Hardwin Mead* and *Roger Winkle*. Without their help this book would not have been written. Thanks also to *William Keach* and to *Sara A. Morabito* for her invaluable help with manuscript corrections and encouragement.

The Pathology of Drug Abuse, 2nd Edition

by Steven B. Karch, M.D.

Dedication iii

Preface to the first edition.. iv

Preface to the second edition v

Acknowledgments, second edition.. vi

Chapter 1   Cocaine...1
  1.1   History 1
  1.2.   Prevalence of cocaine-related morbidity...........................10
  1.3   Cultivation and manufacture...11
      1.3.1   Cultivation and crop yields.....................................11
      1.3.2   Cocaine paste production 13
  1.4   Drug constants...17
  1.5   Routes of administration 18
      1.5.1   Leaf chewing...18
      1.5.2   Snorting 18
      1.5.3   Surgical application 20
      1.5.4   Intravenous use 21
      1.5.5   Genital application...22
      1.5.6   Dermal absorption 22
      1.5.7   Inhalation...23
      1.5.8   Gastrointestinal absorption 25
      1.5.9   Maternal/fetal considerations 27
  1.6   Metabolism..34
      1.6.1   Cocaine disposition..34
          1.6.1.1   General considerations.............................34
          1.6.1.2   Benzoylecgonine and ecgonine
                 methyl ester..36
          1.6.1.3   Cocaethylene...39

      1.6.1.4 Anhydroecgonine methyl ester
             (methylecgonidine) 42
      1.6.1.5 Norcocaine...42
  1.6.2 Fetal metabolism 43
1.7 Interpreting cocaine blood levels 48
1.8 Cocaine tissue disposition 51
  1.8.1 Brain 52
  1.8.2 Heart..54
  1.8.3 Liver 55
  1.8.4 Kidneys...56
  1.8.5 Adrenals..56
  1.8.6 Hair..57
  1.8.7 Fat 58
  1.8.8 Biofluids..58
      1.8.8.1 Saliva 58
      1.8.8.2 Vitreous humor..59
      1.8.8.3 Spinal fluid 60
      1.8.8.4 Breast milk..60
      1.8.8.5 Urine...60
      1.8.8.6 Amniotic fluid..61
1.9 Cocaine's effects on catecholamine metabolism...........64
  1.9.1 General considerations..64
  1.9.2 Mechanisms of catecholamine toxicity...............67
  1.9.3 Histopathology of catecholamine toxicity 70
  1.9.4 Contraction band necrosis and sudden death 73
1.10 Epidemiologic data..77
1.11 External markers of cocaine abuse 78
  1.11.1 Perforated nasal septum 79
  1.11.2 Cocaine "tracks"..79
  1.11.3 "Crack keratitis"...80
  1.11.4 Dental erosions 81
  1.11.5 "Crack thumb" 81
  1.11.6 "Crack hands" 81
  1.11.7 Evidence of terminal seizures...............................81
1.12 Toxicity by organ system..82
  1.12.1 Intugement..82
  1.12.2 Cardiovascular system 83
      1.12.2.1 Coronary artery disease 84
      1.12.2.2 Coronary artery spasm...........................90
      1.12.2.3 Myocardial diseases...............................92
      1.12.2.4 Valvular heart disease 99
      1.12.2.5 Aorta and peripheral vessels 100
      1.12.2.6 Sudden cardiac death...........................102
             1.12.2.6.1 Acute anesthetic-related
                  effects 106

1.12.2.6.2 Acute catecholamine-related effects 107
1.12.2.6.3 Chronic cocaine effects.........................108
1.12.2.6.4 Relationship between seizures and sudden death 109
1.12.2.6.5 Agitated delirium and the neuroleptic malignant syndrome 110
1.12.3 Pulmonary disease...124
1.12.3.1 Local inflammation 125
1.12.3.2 Barotrauma..126
1.12.3.3 Parenchymal disease...............................127
1.12.3.4 Vascular adaptations...............................130
1.12.4 Gastrointestinal disorders......................................135
1.12.4.1 Ischemic injuries.....................................135
1.12.4.2 Hepatic disease..137
1.12.5 Neurologic disorders..142
1.12.5.1 Psychiatric syndromes............................143
1.12.5.2 Cerebral infarction 144
1.12.5.3 Cerebral vasculitis...................................146
1.12.5.4 Subarachnoid and intraventricular hemorrhage 148
1.12.5.5 Seizures 150
1.12.5.6 Movement disorders...............................151
1.12.6 Renal disease..156
1.12.7 Hematologic abnormalities 161
1.12.8 Hormonal alterations...163
1.12.9 Immune system abnormalities...............................165
1.12.10 Pregnancy interactions 168
1.13 When is cocaine the cause of death?.................................171

Chapter 2   Other naturally occurring stimulants.......................177
2.1 Absinthe..177
2.1.1 History 177
2.1.2 Clinical and autopsy studies..................................179
2.2 Caffeine..180
2.2.1 History 180
2.2.2 Chemical constants and tissue disposition............183
2.2.3 Clinical studies of caffeine....................................184
2.2.4 Blood levels..186
2.2.5 Autopsy findings..187
2.3 Khat 190
2.3.1 History 190
2.3.2 Chemistry and clinical studies 192
2.4 Ephedrine 194
2.4.1 History 194

2.4.2   Chemistry and metabolism 196
2.4.3   Clinical studies 196

Chapter 3   Synthetic stimulants..199
3.1   Amphetamine and methamphetamine 199
  3.1.1   History 199
  3.1.2   Illicit manufacture..203
  3.1.3   Chemistry 205
  3.1.4   Routes of administration 205
  3.1.5   Metabolism...205
  3.1.6   Tissue disposition..208
  3.1.7   Interpreting amphetamine levels 210
  3.1.8   Toxicity by organ system..212
    3.1.8.1   Cardiovascular...213
    3.1.8.2   Pulmonary toxicity......................................216
    3.1.8.3   Central nervous system 218
    3.1.8.4   Renal disease...220
    3.1.8.5   Hepatic disease..221
3.2.   Phenylpropanolamine 230
  3.2.1   Historical aspects 230
  3.2.2   Chemistry 231
  3.2.3   Metabolism...232
  3.2.4   Toxicity by organ system..233
    3.2.4.1   Neurologic disease......................................233
    3.2.4.2   Cardiac disease..234
    3.2.4.3   Pulmonary disease......................................234
    3.2.4.4   Renal disease...234
    3.2.4.5   Gastrointestinal disorders..........................234
3.3   Fenfluramine..237
  3.3.1   Historical aspects 237
  3.3.2   Drug constants...238
  3.3.3   Metabolism...238
  3.3.4   Blood and tissue levels 238
  3.3.5   Toxicity by organ system..239
    3.3.5.1   Cardiopulmonary..239
    3.3.5.2   Neurological...239

Chapter 4   Hallucinogens..241
4.1   Phenylethylamine derivatives...241
  4.1.1   Mescaline..241
    4.1.1.1   Historical aspects 241
    4.1.1.2   Drug constants and drug preparation.................243
    4.1.1.3   Metabolism and tissue levels.....................244
    4.1.1.4   Clinical syndromes 244
    4.1.1.5   Pathologic findings 244
  4.1.2.   Other 2-carbon phenethylamine derivatives..................245

4.2 Substituted amphetamines (phenylisopropylamines) 245
    4.2.1 TMA (2,4,5-trimethoxyamphetamine) 245
    4.2.2 DOM (methyl-2,5-dimethoxyamphetamine) 245
    4.2.3 PMA (paramethoxyamphetamine) 246
    4.2.4 DOB (4-bromo-2,5-dimethoxyamphetamine, also called bromo-DMA) 246
    4.2.5 Nexus (4-bromo-2,5-dimethoxyphenethylamine), 2-C-B...247
    4.2.6 MDA (3,4-methylenedioxyamphetamine) "The love drug" 247
    4.2.7 MDMA (3,4-methylenedioxymethamphetamine; other names include XTC, Adam, MDM).........................249
    4.2.8 MDEA (3,4-methylenedioxyethamphetamine), Eve 253
    4.2.9 4-MAX (4-methylaminorex) 253
    4.2.10 Other MDMA homologs 255
    4.2.11 "KAT" 255
4.3 Phenylalkylamines 260
    4.3.1 Simple tryptamines 260
        4.3.1.1 DMT (N,N-dimethyltryptamine) 260
        4.3.1.2. Bufotenine (5-hydroxy-N,N-dimethyl-dryptamine) 261
        4.3.1.3 Psilocybin (4-phosphoryl-N,N-dimethyl-tryptamine)...262
            4.3.1.3.1 History 262
            4.3.1.3.2 Chemical constants 263
            4.3.1.3.3 Metabolism and tissue levels.............263
            4.3.1.3.4 Clinical findings 264
    4.3.2 Beta carbolines...264
        4.3.2.1 Harmaline..264
    4.3.3 Alpha-methyltryptamines 265
        4.3.3.1 5-MeO-DMT (5-methoxy-N,N-dimethyl-tryptamine)..265
        4.3.3.2 α-Ethyltryptamine..265
    4.3.4 Ergolines 267
        4.3.4.1 Lysergic acid diethylamine................................267
            4.3.4.1.1 History 267
            4.3.4.1.2 Chemical constants and drug manufacture 268
            4.3.4.1.3 Tissue levels and metabolism.............269
            4.3.4.1.4 Clinical syndromes 269
            4.3.4.1.5 Detection...270
4.4 Other agents..270
    4.4.1 Phencyclidine..270
        4.4.1.1 Historical aspects 270
        4.4.1.2 Physical constants 272

4.4.1.3 Clandestine laboratories..272
4.4.1.4 Routes of administration 272
4.4.1.5 Metabolism...273
4.4.1.6 Tissue levels 274
4.4.1.7 Interpreting blood and tissue levels 274
4.4.1.8 Toxicity by organ system 275
        4.4.1.8.1 Neurologic disorders.............................275
        4.4.1.8.2 Renal disorders.......................................275
4.4.2 Dextromethorphan...275

Chapter 5 Narcotics 281
5.1 Introduction 281
    5.1.1 Prevalence of opiate-related morbidity.............281
    5.1.2 Classification of narcotics agents.......................281
5.2 History of opiate abuse..284
    5.2.1 Origins in antiquity 284
    5.2.2 Introduction to Europe and Asia 285
    5.2.3 Invention of the hypodermic syringe................288
    5.2.4 Synthesis of heroin..290
    5.2.5 The first pathology studies..................................291
5.3 Cultivation and manufacture......................................293
    5.3.1 Botanic considerations 293
    5.3.2 Manufacture..295
    5.3.3 Sample analysis..296
5.4 Individual narcotic agents 298
    5.4.1 Morphine..298
        5.4.1.1 General considerations.............................298
        5.4.1.2 Absorption and routes of administration 302
                5.4.1.2.1 Intravenous 302
                5.4.1.2.2 Subcutaneous........................302
                5.4.1.2.3 Oral...302
                5.4.1.2.4 Rectal.......................................303
                5.4.1.2.5 Intranasal................................303
                5.4.1.2.6 Inhalation 304
                5.4.1.2.7 Skin...304
                5.4.1.2.8 Maternal/Fetal 305
        5.4.1.3 Tissue Disposition 305
                5.4.1.3.1 Blood...306
                5.4.1.3.2 Brain..307
                5.4.1.3.3 Liver..307
                5.4.1.3.4 Lymph nodes..........................308
                5.4.1.3.5 Other biofluids.......................308
                5.4.1.3.6 Urine 309
        5.4.1.4 Excretion and detectability 309
    5.4.2 Heroin 309
        5.4.2.1 Tissue distribution.....................................310
        5.4.2.2 Excretion and detectability 311

5.4.3   Codeine...312
      5.4.3.1   General considerations..............................312
      5.4.3.2   Routes of administration 313
      5.4.3.3   Role of genetic polymorphism..................314
      5.4.3.4   Codeine tissue disposition........................315
      5.4.3.5   Excretion and detectability.......................315
5.4.4   Methadone..315
      5.4.4.1   General considerations..............................316
      5.4.4.2   Routes of absorption and
                 pharmacokinetics 317
      5.4.4.3   Autopsy findings......................................318
      5.4.4.4   Tissue levels 318
      5.4.4.5   Maternal-fetal considerations....................319
5.4.5   Propoxyphene...319
      5.4.5.1   General considerations..............................319
      5.4.5.2   Tissue distribution....................................320
      5.4.5.3   Excretion and detectability.......................321
      5.4.5.4   Mechanisms of toxicity 321
5.4.6   Fentanyl and other synthetic agents....................322
      5.4.6.1   General considerations..............................322
      5.4.6.2   Routes of absorptions................................323
      5.4.6.3   Metabolism and excretion 324
      5.4.6.4   Tissue levels 325
5.4.7   Other opiates..326
      5.4.7.1   Hydromorphone (Dilaudid®).....................327
      5.4.7.2   Hydrocodone (Hycodan®, Tussend®,
                 Tussionex®) 328
      5.4.7.3   Oxycodone (Tylox®, Percodan®) 328
      5.4.7.4   Oxymorphone (Numorphan®).....................329
      5.4.7.5   Meperidine (Demerol®, Pethidine®).............329
      5.4.7.6   Pentazocine (Talwin®)...............................330
5.5   Interpreting tissue and blood levels 342
  5.5.1   Introduction 342
  5.5.2   Clinical profile of opiate abusers...........................342
  5.5.3   Testing urine 343
  5.5.4   Testing blood..344
  5.5.5   Interpreting test results...345
5.6   Dermatologic sequelae of opiate abuse..........................348
  5.6.1   Fresh puncture sites..348
  5.6.2   Atrophic scarring 348
  5.6.3   Abscess and ulcerations...349
  5.6.4   "Track" marks...349
  5.6.5   Tattoos...350
  5.6.6   "Puffy" hands...350
  5.6.7   Necrotizing fascitis 350
  5.6.8   Histamine-related urticaria 350

	5.6.9	Fungal lesions	352
	5.6.10	Miscellaneous cutaneous abnormalities	353
5.7	Cardiovascular disorders		355
	5.7.1	Introduction	355
	5.7.2	Pathology associated with HIV infection	357
	5.7.3	Endocarditis	357
	5.7.4	Other myocardial disorders	361
	5.7.5	Miscellaneous disorders	362
5.8	Pulmonary disorders		365
	5.8.1	Noninfectious complications	365
		5.8.1.1 Respiratory failure and pulmonary edema	365
		5.8.1.2 Emphysema	367
		5.8.1.3 Needle and mercury emboli	367
		5.8.1.4 Foreign body granulomas	367
		5.8.1.5 Injuries of the great vessels	369
	5.8.2	Infectious complications	370
		5.8.2.1 Aspiration pneumonia	370
		5.8.2.2 Community-acquired pneumonia	370
		5.8.2.3 Fungal pneumonia	370
		5.8.2.4 Tuberculosis and melioidosis	371
		5.8.2.5 Septic pulmonary emboli	371
		5.8.2.6 Anterior mediastinitis	372
5.9	Gastrointestinal disorders		375
	5.9.1	Introduction	375
	5.9.2	Bowel disease	375
	5.9.3	Liver disorders	376
		5.9.3.1 Porta hepatis adenopathy	376
		5.9.3.2 Non-specific alterations	377
		5.9.3.3 Hepatitis	378
		5.9.3.4 HIV infection and AIDS	378
		5.9.3.5 Hepatic amyloidosis	379
5.10	Renal disorders		381
	5.10.1	Introduction	381
	5.10.2	Acute renal failure due to nontraumatic rhabdomyolysis	382
	5.10.3	Secondary amyloidosis	382
	5.10.4	Heroin-associated nephropathy (HAN) and other glomerular disorders	383
	5.10.5	Necrotizing angiitis	384
5.11	Neuropathology		386
	5.11.1	Introduction	386
	5.11.2	Hypoxic encephalopathy	388
	5.11.3	Infectious diseases	389
		5.11.3.1 Complications of endocarditis	389
		5.11.3.2 Complications of HIV infection	389
		5.11.3.3 Primary phycomycosis	390

        5.11.3.4 Spongiform leukoencephalopathy 391
        5.11.3.5 Transverse myelitis 392
        5.11.3.6 Peripheral neuropathy..............................393
        5.11.3.7 Rhabdomyolysis 393
        5.11.3.8 Stroke..394
        5.11.3.9 Necrotizing angiitis..............................395
        5.11.3.10 Parkinsonism......................................396
  5.12 Hormonal and immune alterations 401
  5.13 Bone and soft tissue disorders.....................................405
      5.13.1 Introduction 405
      5.13.2 Bone and joint infection..................................405
      5.13.3 Soft tissue infections....................................407
      5.13.4 Fibrous myopathy of pentazocine abuse 407

Chapter 6 Anabolic steroids 409
  6.1 Introduction 409
  6.2 Pharmacology 412
      6.2.1 Synthesis and metabolism................................412
      6.2.2 Black market steroids and steroid contaminants 413
  6.3 Legitimate clinical indications 414
  6.4 Steroid-related disorders...414
      6.4.1 Liver disease 414
           6.4.1.1 Peliosis hepatis 414
           6.4.1.2 Cholestasis....................................415
           6.4.1.3 Hepatic tumors...............................416
      6.4.2 Cardiovascular disease....................................416
      6.4.3 Neurologic disorders......................................419
      6.4.4 Musculoskeletal disease...................................420
      6.4.5 Detecting steroid abuse....................................422

Chapter 7 Organic solvent and aerosol abuse 431
  7.1 General considerations...431
  7.2 Absorption and tissue disposition 432
  7.3 Clinical syndromes 433
      7.3.1 Neurologic disorders......................................433
      7.3.2 Renal disease..434
      7.3.3 Gastrointestinal disease....................................434
      7.3.4 Cardiovascular disease....................................435

Appendix 439

chapter one

Cocaine

1.1 History

The word "coca" comes from the Aymara "khoka," meaning "the tree." Coca has nothing to do with the chocolate-producing nut called cocoa, and its only relation to the kola nut is phonetic. Although it is claimed that measurable quantities of cocaine and nicotine have been detected in 3,000-year old Egyptian mummies (Balabanova et al., 1992), both of these chemicals are derived from New World plants. How they came to be used in Africa remains a mystery. Even if these plants were known to the ancient Egyptians, Europeans did not hear about them until the Spanish colonized South America. When the Spanish took Peru in the 1500s, they encountered Indians who had been chewing coca leaf for thousands of years. The experience of the Indians with coca was recounted in Nicolas B. Monardes' monograph, *Joyfulle News out of the New Founde Worlde, wherein is declared the Virtues of Herbs, Treez, Oyales, Plantes, and Stones.* Monardes' book was reprinted many times after first being published in Barcelona sometime in the early 1560s. In 1599, a translation by an English merchant was published in London. Monardes' book contained accurate descriptions of many New World plants, including tobacco and coca. Monardes was fascinated by the fact that coca appeared to allow users to go without food, but he also was aware that coca had undesirable side effects. He observed, "Surely it is a thyng of great consideration, to see how the Indians are so desirous to bee deprived of their wittes, and be without understanding" (Guerra, 1974).

For a long time the medical community remained unimpressed with coca. Boerhave favorably mentioned coca in his textbook on medicinal plants, published in 1708 (Mortimer, 1901); however, more than 100 years elapsed before the first illustration of coca appeared in an English publication. An article on coca by Sir William Hooker, then curator of the Royal Botanical Gardens at Kew, appeared in 1835. In addition to illustrations of the coca plant, the article also contained Hooker's translation of a book by the German explorer and naturalist, Edward Poeppig. Poeppig thought that coca chewers were very much like opium addicts and warned against coca's immoderate use (Poeppig, 1835). Other travelers and explorers had more positive impressions, but coca's potential for toxicity was known even before it became widely available in Europe.

Johan von Tschudi was one of the early explorers of the Amazon. He was a prolific writer, and his travel books were widely read in Europe and the United States. He, too, was impressed with coca's apparent ability to increase endurance, but he was concerned that Europeans might develop a "habit." His book "Travels in Peru," first published in 1852, contains the first accurate description of cocaine "binging" (von Tschudi, 1854). The term describes the tendency of cocaine users to consume, in one session, all the drug in their possession. According to von Tschudi, "They give themselves up for days together to the passionate enjoyment of the leaves. Then their excited imaginations conjure up the most wonderful visions...I have never yet been able to ascertain correctly the conditions the Coquero passes through on returning to his ordinary state; it, however, appears that it is not so much a want of sleep, or the absence of food, as the want of coca that puts an end to the lengthened debauch."

In 1857, von Tschudi persuaded a professor of chemistry at the University of La Paz, Enrique Pizzi, to try isolating coca's active principle. Pizzi thought he had succeeded and gave von Tschudi a sample to take home to Europe. Returning to Göttingen, von Tschudi gave the sample to his friend, Carl Wöhler, the chemist who had first synthesized urea. Wöhler gave the sample to Albert Niemann, his graduate student. Niemann found that the sample contained only gypsum. Wöhler remained curious, and when he heard that Archduke Ferdinand was sending a frigate on an around the world training cruise, he approached Carl von Scherzer, chief scientist of the expedition, and asked him if he could bring back enough leaves to analyze (Scherzer, 1861). von Scherzer returned three years later with 60 pounds of leaves and gave them to Wöhler, who again gave them to Niemann. Given an adequate supply of leaf, purification of cocaine proved relatively simple. Niemann published his Ph.D. thesis, "On a New Organic Base in the Coca Leaves" in 1860 (Niemann, 1861). Even after the purification of cocaine, interest in its therapeutic applications remained slight, and reports in journals were still mostly anecdotal.

A *Lancet* editorial published in 1872, twelve years after cocaine had been purified, stated that "There is considerable difference of opinion as to its effects upon the human subject, and the published accounts are somewhat conflicting; but we think that there is a strong evidence in favor of its being a stimulant and narcotic of a peculiar kind, and of some power" (Anon, 1872). Coca-containing wines became popular in France and Italy during the late 1860s. The most famous of these was manufactured by Angelo Mariani. It contained 6 mg of cocaine per ounce and was advertised as a restorative and tonic; that seems to be how it was used. Satisfied customers endorsing "Vin Mariani" included Thomas Edison, Robert Louis Stevenson, Jules Verne, Alexandre Dumas, and even Pope Leo XIII. Within ten years of its introduction in Paris, Mariani's wines were in much demand throughout the United States (Mariani, 1872). The amount of cocaine contained in these products was modest. It is now known that when alcohol and cocaine are combined, a new metabolite called cocaethylene is formed. It has the same affinity for the dopamine receptor as cocaine itself, which means that it should be just as psychoactive. Since it has a half-life that is many times longer than that of cocaine, combinations of alcohol and cocaine may be quite intoxicating.

In the early 1880s, Parke Davis and Company began marketing a fluid extract containing 0.5 mg/mL of semipurified cocaine. At about the same time, physicians began prescribing elixirs containing cocaine for a variety of ailments, including alcohol and morphine addiction. In spite of the inappropriate use of these mixtures, reports of toxicity and cocaine-related disease were rare. Concurrent with the increased dispensing by physicians, patent medicine manufacturers began adding cocaine extract to nearly all of their products. One such promoter was John Styth Pemberton. He went into competition with Mariani and began selling "French Wine Cola." His initial marketing efforts were not very successful. In what proved to be a wise marketing move, Pemberton dropped the wine from the product, and added a combination of cocaine and caffeine. The reformulated product was named "Coca-Cola®."

Two events occurred in 1884 that significantly changed the pattern of cocaine use in the United States and Europe. The first was the publication of Freud's paper, Über Coca (Freud, 1884; Andrews and Solomon, 1975). The second was Köller's discovery that cocaine was a local anesthetic (Noyes, 1884). By the time Freud sat down to write his paper, American physicians had already published over a dozen papers recommending cocaine in the treatment of morphine addiction (Bently, 1880). Freud enthusiastically accepted this American notion and even elaborated on it, recommending cocaine as a remedy for a host of conditions that are not recognized as diseases today. Köller's discovery was probably even more important. The availability of an effective local anesthetic had tremendous impact. Cocaine was propelled into the limelight, and physicians around the world were soon experimenting with the use of cocaine in a wide range of conditions. Some of the applications, such as eye and hemorrhoid surgery (Anon, 1886c), were quite appropriate. Other applications, such as the treatment of hay fever, were more questionable (Anon, 1886a). Still other uses were bizarre and potentially dangerous (Anon, 1886b).

The first reports of cocaine toxicity appeared less than one year after Köller's and Freud's papers were published. An article in the British Medical Journal described the toxic reactions associated with cocaine use in ophthalmologic surgery (Anon, 1885b). About the same time, reports of cocaine-related death started to appear in the popular press (Anon, 1885a). The first cocaine-related cardiac arrest was reported in 1886 (Thompson, 1886), as was the first stroke (Catlett, 1886). In 1887, Mattison reviewed 50 cases of cocaine toxicity, four of which were fatal. Each of the fatalities had the characteristics associated with cardiac arrhythmias (Mattison, 1887a; Mattison, 1887b). The following year Mattison published data on an additional 40 cases, including two more fatalities (Mattison, 1888).

None of these negative reports appeared to have much impact. Patent medicine manufacturers continued to cash in on the popularity of coca by replacing low-concentration cocaine extracts with high concentrations of refined cocaine hydrochloride. Thousands of cocaine-containing patent medicines flooded the market, some with truly enormous amounts of cocaine. Dr. Tucker's Asthma Specific, for instance, contained 420 mg of cocaine per ounce and was applied directly to the nasal mucosa. Absorption was nearly total. As the cocaine content of the products increased, so did the number of reported medical complications. The situation rapidly deteriorated when users learned they could "snort" cocaine. Until the early 1900s, cocaine had been taken mainly by mouth or by injection. The fact that the first cases of septal perforation and collapse (saddle nose deformity) were not reported until 1904 suggests that "snorting" had only became popular a year or so earlier (Maier, 1926).

The first histologic studies of cocaine toxicity were published in 1888. Vasili Zanchevski of St. Petersburg studied the acute and chronic effects of cocaine in dogs. After a single lethal dose (24 mg/kg), the animals had changes typical of acute asphyxia. Smaller daily doses given for several weeks caused a "marked hyperemic condition of the central nervous system, in contrast to the rest of the organs, which were anemic." There were focal degenerative changes in the spinal ganglia, heart, and liver. In some cases, the myocytes had "lost their striae and (were) intensely granular" (Zanchevski, 1888). Although illustrations are lacking, Zanchevski's descriptions suggest that he was the first to observe a form of contraction band necrosis occurring as a result of cocaine toxicity.

French researchers were the first to systematically study cocaine's psychological effects, largely because cocaine and morphine addiction were such a major problem in Paris. In 1889, at a meeting of the Biological Society of Paris, Magnon presented three cases which illustrated that cocaine users were subject to tactile hallucinations. The symptom complex became known as "Magnon's symptom." In 1914, Georges Guillain contrasted the differences between cocaine and alcoholic hallucinations, commenting on how variable the effects of a given dose of cocaine could be (Maier, 1926).

One psychiatric disorder that has only recently been rediscovered is cocaine-associated agitated delirium. It was first described by an American, Edward Williams, in 1914 (Williams, 1914). The syndrome consists of multiple components, including wildly irrational behavior and feats of near superhuman strength that culminate in sudden death.

Because Williams' writings were patently racist, and because he observed the syndrome only in blacks, later historians wrote off his observations as racist hysteria (Kennedy, 1985). New reports of the syndrome began to appear again at the start of the current pandemic. Although the disorder has nothing to do with race, it is quite real (Wetli and Fishbain, 1985).

The first human autopsy study of a cocaine-related death was published in 1922. Bravetta and Invernizzi described a 28-year old man who had been sniffing cocaine regularly for some months before his death. He neither drank nor used other drugs (Bravetta and Invernizzi, 1922). Hyperemia of the brain, lungs, and adrenals was noted and the heart was described as "flaccid"

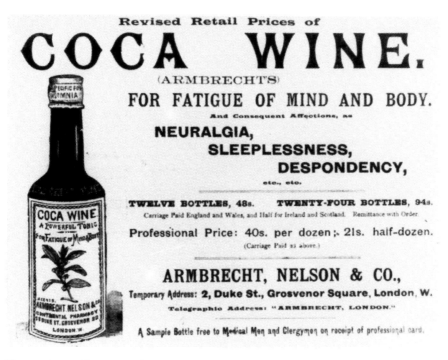

Figure 1.1.1 Coca containing wines. These wines became popular during the 1860's. The most famous was Vin Mariani, but there were many competitors. The average product contained 5 to 10 mg of cocaine per ounce. From the National Library of Medicine.

(cardiomyopathy?). The accompanying illustrations show lesions similar to those described by Zanchevski. Animal studies by the same authors confirmed the autopsy findings and also demonstrated widespread endothelial injuries. These studies were reprinted in Maier's classic text on cocaine abuse, published in 1926 (Maier, 1926).

Cocaine's tissue disposition was studied at an even earlier date. In 1887, a German chemist, Helmsing, published his technique for the detection of cocaine in urine and tissues. The technique was fairly sensitive, and Helmsing was able to detect cocaine in urine from a cat that had been given 8 mg of cocaine (Anon, 1887). In 1951, Woods et al. developed a calorimetric technique capable of detecting levels of cocaine as low as 500 ng/mL (Woods et al., 1951). A quarter century later, Jatlow and Bailey used gas chromatography to lower the limits of detection down to 5 ng/mL (Jatlow and Bailey, 1975).

Shortly after Maier's text was published, case reports simply stopped appearing. Between 1924 and 1973, there was only one reported fatality, and it involved a surgical misadventure. In 1977, Suarez first described the "body packer" syndrome, where death results from the rupture of cocaine-filled condoms in the smuggler's intestines (Suarez et al., 1977). The absence of case reports no doubt reflected a decline in use, but the decline itself is difficult to explain. Certainly the outlawing of cocaine (The Pure Food and

Figure 1.1.2   Indonesian coca production. During the 1920s, Indonesian plantations exported more coca leaf than producers in South America. This photograph, taken in 1927, shows workers sorting coca leaf. Courtesy of the Tropen Museum Photo Bureau, Amsterdam.

Drug Act of 1906 and the Harrison Narcotic Act of 1914) had a great deal to do with it, but other factors were involved (McLaughlin, 1973). Perhaps the most important factor may have been the introduction of the amphetamines. Although amphetamines share important mechanisms of toxicity with cocaine, the former appear to have a higher therapeutic index. In addition to being less toxic than cocaine, amphetamines are also cheaper, easier to obtain, and more socially acceptable.

Significant toxicity from the use of coca leaf and coca extract was never a problem in Europe or the United States. Toxicity only emerged when purified cocaine became readily available and individuals could increase their dosage by an order of magnitude. The small amounts of cocaine in "Vin Mariani" were apparently harmless, but the huge amounts in Dr. Tucker's formula were occasionally lethal. With the appearance of crack cocaine in 1986, another order of magnitude increase in dosage occurred (Jekel et al., 1986). That cocaine-related illness is now a significant cause of morbidity and mortality should not be surprising. It is not just that more people are using the drug. They are using more of it and using it more effectively.

The number of reported cocaine-related deaths rose rapidly during the late 1980s and continued to rise during the early 1990s. From 1990 to 1992 the number of deaths increased by nearly 25% (2,408 to 3,220), but the process now appears to have plateaued. In 1994, the most recent year for which

Cocaine   **5**

THE OPHTHALMOLOGICAL CONGRESS IN
HEIDELBERG.
(From our Special Correspondent.)

MURIATE OF COCAINE AS A LOCAL ANÆSTHETIC TO THE
CORNEA—NO RADIATING MUSCULAR FIBRES IN THE
IRIS—ACTUAL CAUTERY IN SUPERFICIAL CORNEAL UL-
CERATIONS—OPTICO-CILIARY NEURECTOMY—IS CATA-
RACT THE RESULT OF CHRONIC BRIGHT'S DISEASE?—
PROFESSOR ARLT AND HIS RECENT WORK IN GLAU-
COMA.

KREUZNACH, GERMANY. September 19, 1884.

SIR : The usual Ophthalmological Congress in Heidelberg
has just closed its session, and a few cursory notes at
this early date may interest some readers. At this meeting elaborate papers are not read, but condensed state-
ments are presented of the subjects introduced. The
notable feature of this Society is that only new things
or new phases of old topics are presented. This is
not from any expressed rule, but is from the tacit understanding which controls men who are so diligently investigating the unknown in science as are these eager
workers. These men have no patience with mere reiter-
ations. Perhaps the most notable thing which was presented was the exhibition to the Congress upon one of
the patients of the Heidelberg Eye Clinic, of the extra-
ordinary anæsthetic power which a two per cent. solution
of muriate of cocaine has upon the cornea and conjunctiva when it is dropped into the eye. Two drops of the
solution were dropped into the eye of the patient at the
first experiment, and after an interval of ten minutes it
was evident that the sensitiveness of the surface was below the normal, then two drops more were instilled and
after waiting ten minutes longer there was entire absence
of sensibility, a probe was pressed upon the cornea until
its surface was indented, it was rubbed lightly over the
surface of the cornea, it was rubbed over the surface of
the conjunctiva bulbi, and of the conjunctiva palpebrarum ;
a speculum was introduced to separate the lids and they
were stretched apart to the uttermost ; the conjunctiva
bulbi was seized by fixation forceps and the globe moved
in various directions. In all this handling the patient declared that he felt no unpleasant sensation, except that
the speculum stretched the lids so widely asunder as to
give a little discomfort at the outer canthus. Before the
experiment his eye was shown to possess the normal
sensitiveness, and the other eye, which was not experi-
mented on, was in this respect perfectly normal. The
solution caused no irritation of any kind, nor did it at
all influence the pupil. The anæsthetic influence seemed
to be complete on the surface of the eye, and it lasted for
about fifteen minutes and the parts then resumed their
usual condition. This first experiment was done in the
presence of Professor Arlt and the clinical staff, of Dr.
clinical staff, of Dr. Ferrer of San Francisco, of some
other physicians, and of the writer. The next day the
same experiment was performed on the same patient in
the presence of the Congress and with the same results.
This application of the muriate of cocaine is a discovery
by a very young physician, or he is perhaps not yet a
physician, but is pursuing his studies in Vienna, where he
also lives. His name is Dr. Koller, and he gave to Dr.
Brettauer, of Trieste, a vial of the solution, to be used in
the presence of the Congress by Dr. Brettauer. Dr.
Koller had but very recently become aware of this notable effect of cocaine, and had made but very few trials
with it. These he had been led to make from his knowl
edge of the entirely similar effect which it has for some
year or more been shown to have over the sensibility of
the vocal cords, and because of which laryngologists pen-
cil it upon their surface to facilitate examinations.

The future which this discovery opens up in ophthalmic
surgery and in ophthalmic medication is obvious. The
momentous value of the discovery seems likely to prove
to be in eye practice of more significance than has been
the discovery of anæsthesia by chloroform and ether in
general surgery and medicine, because it will have thera-

peutic uses as well as surgical uses. It remains, however, to investigate all the characteristics of this substance, and we may yet find that there is a shadow side
as well as a brilliant side in the discovery. Professor
Kühne, who in the Heidelberg Physiological Laboratory
worked out the details of Boll's discovery of the visual
purple of the retina, received the news of this new discovery with the liveliest interest. We may, perhaps, get
from him a further investigation into its properties. The
substance makes a clear solution, and is found in Merck's
catalogue.

Another notable statement came from Dr. Eversburch,
of Munich, as the result of very exact and elaborate
studies, to the effect that there are no radiating muscular
fibres in the iris ; in other words, that the dilator iridis
has no existence in man. It is found, he says, in some
animals, and especially in those which have oblong pupils,
whether vertical or horizontal, and in the form of fasciculi
at the extremities of the slit. He absolutely denies the
existence of such fibres in the human eye, and asserts
that the fibres hitherto described under this name are
nerve-fibres. These revolutionary assertions were received with respect and attention, because the investi-
gator was known to be a careful and competent anato-
mist. If his declarations should be confirmed, and they
will not be lightly accepted, we must find out a new
theory for the active dilatation of the pupil. A good deal
of physiology will have to be cast into a new form. It
is true that the anatomical discussion has not been closed
on this point, but in favor of the existence of the dilator
stand the names of Merkel, Henle, and Iwanoff among recent investigators. Eversburch has in his possession the
preparations of Iwanoff, who died a few years ago, and
he knows the nature of the contest into which he enters.

The uses of the actual cautery in superficial forms of
corneal ulceration and in some other superficial processes, especially in those of micrococcic origin, were discussed both here and in Copenhagen. There seems to
be a general consensus as to the usefulness of this treatment in selected cases of superficial corneal disease, viz.,
in ulcus rodens, in superficial suppurative processes, in
atonic ulcers, and by Nieden in xerophthalmus. Nieden
will shortly announce his views in full in an article in the
Archives for Ophthalmology. He presented a most
delicate and elegant form of galvano-cautery which he
had devised, and to which he had applied a very delicate
and promptly acting key invented by Professor Sattler.
Another form of cautery is in use in the Heidelberg Eye
Clinic, which has been devised by Professor Becker, and
is a very small and utilizable Paquelin cautery. Both
these instruments can be handled with nicety and deli-
cacy, and without frightening the patient, and also in
most cases without giving him any pain. This treatment,
as well as the scraping of such ulcers by a sharp spoon,
as does Meyer, of Paris, is founded on the micrococcic
theory of the pathology of these processes, and marks
another forward step in ophthalmic therapeutics.

Optico-ciliary neurectomy as a preventive of sympathetic ophthalmia has not passed out of practice, as to a
considerable degree has become the case among us. So
able an observer and logical a reasoner as Professor
Schweigger, of Berlin, recommends its performance and
holds it in higher esteem than enucleation. He divides
the internal rectus muscle to gain easy approach to the
nerve, and he lifts it from its bed by a sharp double
hook and excises 10 mm. of it. He is said to be extremely skilful in this proceeding, and the very small disturbance which he causes in the structures of the orbit
may perhaps explain the success which he has had and
the confidence which he expresses in its prophylactic
virtue. Among more than a hundred cases which furnished
the material for his conclusions, in two cases he saw occur
in the opposite eye an acute neuro-retinitis, with opalescent
infiltration, etc. There was no reduction of vision either
central or peripheral. In two weeks the appearance

Figure 1.1.3   Cocaine as a local anesthetic. The discovery that cocaine was a potent
local anesthetic revolutionized surgery. It was first reported at an ophthalmology
congress in Heidelberg. Shortly thereafter an account appeared in the *Medical Record*
of October 11, 1884. From the Medical Library at the University of California, San
Francisco.

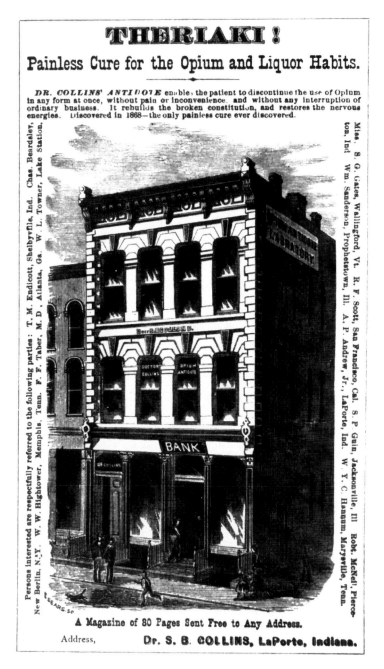

Figure 1.1.4   Cocaine as a treatment for morphine addiction. Opiate addiction was a major problem during the 1870s. The principal ingredient in Theriaki, like most proprietary cures for addiction, was cocaine. From the National Library of Medicine.

complete statistics are available, medical examiners reported 3,981 cocaine-related deaths, up only slightly from the 3,220 reported in 1992 (Substance Abuse and Mental Health Services Administration, 1995). Since the medical examiners participating in the DAWN (Drug Abuse Warning Network) survey perform only 60% of all autopsies done in the United States, the total of all cocaine-releated deaths in 1993 would have been well over 6,500.

References

Andrews, G. and Solomon, D. (Eds.). (1975). The coca leaf and cocaine papers (1st ed.). New York and London: Harcourt Brace Jovanovich.

Anon (1872). Coca. Lancet (May 25): 746.

Anon (1885a). Cocaine's terrible effect. The New York Times, Vol 35(10): 684.

Anon (1885b). Toxic action of cucaine. Br Med J: (November 21), 983.

Anon (1886a). Cucaine in hay-fever. Br Med J: (May 8), 893.

Anon (1886b). Cucaine in nymphomania. Br Med J: (March 20), 564.

Anon (1886c). Cucaine in painful defecation. Br Med J: (March 27), 614.

Anon (1887). The detection of cocaine in the animal body. Therapeutic Gazette, 185.

Balabanova, S., Parsche. F., and Pirsig, W. (1992). First identification of drugs in Egyptian mummies. Naturwissenschaften, 79: 358.

Bently, W. (1880). Erythroxylon Coca in the opium and alcohol habits. Therapeutic Gazette, i: 253.

Bravetta, E. and Invernizzi, G. (1922). Il Cocainismo. Osservazione cliniche. Ricerche sperimentali e anatomo-patoligiche. Note Riv Psichiatr, 10: 543.

Catlett, G. (1886). Cocaine: what was its influence in the following case? Medical Gazette (February 6): 166.

Freud, S. (1884). Über coca. Wien Centralblatt für die ges Therapie, 2: 289–314.

Guerra, F. (1974). Sex and drugs in the 16th century. Br J Addict Alcohol, 69(3): 269–290.

Jatlow, P. and Bailey, D. (1975). Gas-chromatographic analysis for cocaine in human plasma, with use of a nitrogen detector. Clin Chem, 21: 918–1921.

Jekel, J., Allen, D., Podlewski, H. et al., (1986). Epidemic freebase cocaine abuse: case study from the Bahamas. Lancet, 1: 459–462.

Kennedy, J. (1985). Coca Exotica: The illustrated story of cocaine (1st ed.). New York: Fairleigh Dickinson University Press and Cornwall Books.

Maier, H. W. (1926). Der Kokainismus (O.J. Kalant from the German 1926 edition, Trans.). Toronto: Addiction Research Foundation.

Mariani, A. (1872). La coca du Pérou. Rev de thérap méd chir Paris: 148–152.

Mattison, J. (1887a). Cocaine dosage and cocaine addiction. Pacific Med and Surg J and Western Lancet, XXX(4): 193–213; also Listed in the Index Medicus as Med Reg Phil, 1887, i: 125–133.

Mattison, J. (1887b). Cocaine habit. Lancet, 1: 1024.

Mattison, J. (1888). Cocaine toxemia. Am Pract and News: Louisville, n.s.v. 10–15.

McLaughlin, G. (1973). Cocaine: The history and regulation of a dangerous drug. Cornell Law Rev, 58: 537–573.

Mortimer, W. G. (1901). Peru: history of coca, the "divine plant" of the Incas: with an introductory account of the Incas and of the Andean Indians of today (reprint ed.). New York: J. H. Vail, reprinted by AMS Press in 1978.

Niemann, A. (1861). Über eine neue organische Base in den Cocablättern. Göttingen: E. A. Huth, Inaug.-diss.

Niemann, A. (1861). On the alkaloid and other constituents of coca leaves. Am J Pharmacy, 33 [Third series, 9 (reprinted in)]: 123–127.

Noyes, H. (1884). Murate of cocaine as a local anaesthetic to the cornea; The ophthalmological Congress in Heidelberg. Med Record (October 11): 417–418.

Poeppig, E. (1835). Reise in Chile, Peru, und auf dem Amazonen Ströme während der Jahre 1827–1832 (republished in Stuttgart, Brockhaus in 1960 ed.). Leipzig: F. Fleischer.

Scherzer, K. (1861). Narrative of the circumnavigation of the globe by the Austrian Frigate Novara. London: Saunders, Otley, and Company.

Suarez, C., Arango, A., and Lester, J. (1977). Cocaine-condom ingestion. JAMA, 238, 1391–1392.

Substance Abuse and Mental Health Services Administration. (1995). Annual Medical Examiner Data. Data from the Drug Abuse Warning Network. Statistical Series, Number 13–B. Rockville, MD. U.S. Department of Health and Human Services.

Thompson, A. (1886). Toxic action of cucaine. Br Med J (January 9), 67.

von Tschudi, J. J. (1854). Travels in Peru (Thomasina Ross, Trans.). New York: A.S. Barnes and Co.

Wetli, C. and Fishbain, D. (1985). Cocaine-induced psychosis and sudden death in recreational cocaine users. J Forensic Sci, 30(3): 873–888.

Williams, E. (1914, February 8). Negro cocaine "fiends" are a new southern menace. New York Times, p. 1.

Woods, L., Cochin, J., Fornefeld, E. et al. (1951). The estimation of amines in biological materials with critical data for cocaine and mescaline. J. Pharmacol Exp Ther, 101(2): 188–199.

Zanchevski, V. (1888). Effects of acute and chronic cocaine-poisoning. Lancet, i (May 26): 1041.

1.2   Prevalence of cocaine-related morbidity

According to the 1995 edition of the federally sponsored DAWN (Drug Abuse Warning Network) Survey, 3,981 cocaine-related deaths occurred in 1994. During that same period, cocaine abuse necessitated 134,000 emergency room visits (National Institute on Drug Abuse, 1995). Both numbers underestimate the severity of the problem. DAWN data collection procedures do not routinely incorporate toxicology testing results and, because of the way data is abstracted for the DAWN survey, cocaine-related injuries are generally underreported (Brookoff et al., 1993).

The World Health Organization (WHO) sponsored an international survey on the natural history of cocaine use, and attempted to profile use patterns in different countries. Remarkably similar patterns were seen in most countries. Users are most likely to be young males, under 30 years of age, from lower socio-economic classes, and members of ethnic minorities (Lewis and Wagner, 1995). Even though most users are under 30 years of age, fatalities occur more often in older age groups. According to the 1994 DAWN survey, 47% of cocaine-related deaths occurred in men over age 35 (National Institute on Drug Abuse, 1995). There were 4.5 male fatalities for every one female.

References

Brookoff, D., Campbell, E., and Shaw, L. (1993). The underreporting of cocaine-related trauma: Drug Abuse Warning Network reports vs. hospital toxicology tests. Am J Pub Health, 83(3): 369–371.

Lewis, D. and Wagner, E. (1995). WHO global cocaine project. In Problems of Drug Dependence 1995: Proceedings of the 57th Annual Scientific Meeting, the College on Problems of Drug Dependence, Inc. National Institutes on Drug Abuse, Rockville, MD.

National Institute on Drug Abuse. (1994). Annual Medical Examiner Data. Data from the Drug Abuse Warning Network, Statistical Series I, Number 13-B.

1.3   Cultivation and manufacture

1.3.1   Cultivation and crop yields

Coca leaf has grown in the Andean sub-region for thousands of years. Early explorers found it all along the eastern curve of the Andes, from the Straits of Magellan to the borders of the Caribbean. Coca grows best on the moist, warm, slopes of mountains ranging from 1,500 to 5,000 feet. Coca shrubs grow to heights of 6–8 feet. The trunk of the plant is covered by rough, somewhat glossy bark that has a reddish tint. Its flowers are small, and usually white or greenish yellow. Leaves are elliptical, pointed at the apex, and dark green in color. All cultivated coca is derived from two closely related species that grow naturally only in South America, *Erythroxylum coca Lam* and *Erythroxylum novogranatense Hieron*. Each species has one distinct variety designated as *E. coca var. ipadu Plowman* and *E. coca novogranatense var. truxillense (Rusby) Plowman* (Plowman, 1985). All four types are cultivated, although the alkaloid content of the different plants varies considerably (Plowman and Rivier, 1983b). *E. coca ipadu* is cultivated only in the Amazon valley of Brazil, Colombia, and Peru. Of all the cultivated varieties, ipadu contains the least alkaloid, less than 0.5%, and very little of that is cocaine. *E. novogranatense* is cultivated more widely and is better adapted to growth in hotter, drier climates. Although there is some controversy, it seems likely that novogranatense was the variety cultivated in Java, Ceylon, India, and Taiwan. This variety may contain anywhere from 1 to 3% total alkaloid, with cocaine constituting as much as half of the total alkaloid present (Lee, 1981; Bohm et al., 1982; Plowman and Rivier, 1983a; Plowman, 1985; Schlesinger, 1985). A strain of novogranatense cultivated in the desert coast region of Peru, near Trujillo, is the plant that is used to flavor Coca Cola® and other cola beverages.

Major growing areas in Bolivia share many characteristics. Yungas, which is close to La Paz, has an average annual rainfall of 45.7 inches. Chaparé, which is close to Cochabamba, has an annual rainfall of 102 inches. The plantations in Yungas can be harvested three times a year. Each harvest yields from 2 to 2.7 tons per hectare per year. Chaparé leaf contains, on average, 0.72% cocaine. It is estimated that the currently used refining techniques are only 45% effective (e.g., less than half the cocaine is actually

TAB.XXI.

Erythroxylon Coca.

Figure 1.3.1   The first illustrations of cocaine. The first illustration of coca to appear in an English magazine was published in 1836. It was drawn by Sir William Hooker, then director of the Royal Botanical Gardens at Kew, and appeared in the *Companion to the Botanical Magazine*. From the library at the Royal Botanical Gardens at Kew, England.

recovered from the leaf). As a result, 390 kilograms of Chararé leaf are required to produce 1 kilogram of cocaine base. The alkaloid content varies from area to area, depending on the local conditions and the strain cultivated. Leaf from Youngas, for example, has an alkaloid content of 0.85% (Drug Enforcement Administration, 1991).

The average coca plantation will produce for about 20 years, but after the 10th year, its yield steadily declines. Yields throughout South America are comparable. Both the yield per acre, and the alkaloid content of leaf, were much higher in the Southeast Asian plantations (at one time Indonesia exported more leaf than Peru). More than 60% of all coca leaf is grown in Peru, with another 22% coming from Bolivia and 15% from Colombia. Minor amounts come from Ecuador. When processed, 400 pounds of leaf will yield between 1 to 2 kg of coca paste, depending on the quality of the leaf and how efficiently the coca is extracted (Abruzzese, 1989).

It is estimated that in 1994, Andean coca producers had 201,700 hectare under cultivation, with more than half in Peru. This acreage would have produced 291,000 metric tons of leaf, yielding 820-850 tons of refined cocaine (Drug Enforcement Administration, 1991).

1.3.2   Cocaine paste production

Cocaine extraction is a two or three step process, carried out in a series of laboratories. The first steps occur on site. Immediately after harvesting, leaves are placed in a shallow pit lined with heavy plastic. The leaves are then soaked in a dilute solution of water and strong alkali, like lime, for three or four days. An organic solvent, i.e., gasoline, kerosene, or even acetone, depending on availability, is then added to the mixture. In this way, the nitrogenous alkaloids are extracted.

The extracted coca leaf is discarded and sulfuric acid is added to the extract, dissolving a complex mixture of alkaloids in the aqueous layer. If the alkaloid content of the leaves is very high (as in Bolivia), hydrochloric acid may be used instead of sulfuric. The organic solvent, usually kerosene, is then removed and the remaining aqueous solution is made alkaline by the addition of lime, ammonia, or the equivalent, causing the more basic alkaloids to precipitate out. This crude form of cocaine, called coca paste, is allowed to dry in the sun. The site where the initial steps occur is referred to as a "paste lab." Laborers, called pisacocas, keep the alkali-coca leaf mulch mixed by stirring it with their hands and walking through it with their bare feet. The fluid is quite corrosive and the workers quickly develop large extremity ulcers. The pisacocas tolerate the ulcers only because they are given a constant supply of coca paste to smoke (Weatherford, 1988).

The dried product is a mixture of cocaine, cis- and trans- cinnamoylcocaine, tropine, tropacocaine, hygrine, cuscohygrine, ecgonine, benzoylecgonine, methylecgonine, and isomers of truxillines. The mixture also contains a host of soluble organic plant waxes and benzoic acid. Depending on the alkaloid content of the leaves and on how the leaves were processed, it takes between 100 and 150 kilograms of dry leaf to produce 1 kilogram of paste (Montesinos, 1965; Brewer and Allen, 1991).

Once the paste is prepared, the clandestine manufacturer has two options. The paste may be further purified at a base lab, or the producer may go directly to a crystal lab. At base labs, paste is dissolved in dilute sulfuric acid. Potassium permanganate is added until the solution turns pink, thereby destroying the cinnamoylcocaine isomers present as impurities in the paste. The isomers of cinnamoylcocaine are converted to ecgonine and, since ecgonine is very water soluble, it is easy to separate from the cocaine. The job of the clandestine chemist is to stop the oxidation process (usually by adding ammonia or some other alkali) before the cocaine starts to oxidize, and the yield drops. Analysis of impounded samples suggests that permanganate oxidation is used only about 60% of the time.

The reddish-pink solution is allowed to stand, then it is filtered and the filtrate is made basic with ammonia. Cocaine base precipitates out. The precipitate is filtered, washed with water, and then dried. Finally, it is dissolved in diethyl ether or acetone. After filtering, concentrated hydrochloric acid and acetone are added, causing purified cocaine hydrochloride to precipitate out (United Nations, 1986). This final step may be done on site, or the semi-purified cocaine may be transported to a "crystal lab," usually located in one of the larger Colombian cities, although some drug producers have begun to set up labs in the United States. As much as 50 kg may be processed at one time (Lee, 1981). The semipurified cocaine is dissolved in a solvent, often ether. Hydrochloric acid is then added, along with a bridging solvent such as acetone, and white crystals precipitate out. The crystals are collected by filtration. Traces of the solvent remain and their presence can sometimes be used to identify the origin of cocaine samples. In producing countries there is a significant market for the semi-purified paste itself. Paste is smoked, rolled up in pieces of newspaper or packed into cigarettes. Many of the ingredients introduced during manufacture are still present in the paste and are inhaled as pyrolysis products. Coca paste smoking is a major cause of morbidity in coca-producing countries, but there is a paucity of scientific data about it (Paly et al., 1980).

When permanganate is added during the refining process, cocaine's N-methyl group is oxidized, leading to the formation of N-formyl cocaine. Hydrolysis of N-formyl cocaine leads to the formation of norcocaine. The presence of the last two compounds can have forensic and clinical significance. Since N-formyl cocaine is a product of permanganate oxidation, it is not present in paste. Accordingly, the presence of this compound may yield valuable information about how, and possibly where, the cocaine sample was produced (Brewer and Allen, 1991). Norcocaine is potentially hepatotoxic. Analysis has shown norcocaine concentrations in illicit samples ranging from 0.01% to 3.70% (Kumar, 1991).

As may be expected, chemical analysis of paste has disclosed the presence of all the elements used during its manufacture, including benzoic acid, methanol, kerosene, sulfuric acid, cocaine sulfate, and other coca alkaloids (Jeri, 1984; Jeri et al., 1978; Moore and Casale, 1994). Impurities may constitute from 1% to 40% of a given paste sample. Paste can be broken down into neutral, acidic, and basic fractions. Gasoline residues are particularly common in the neutral fraction (ElSohly et al., 1991). Unlike amphetamines, which may be contaminated with lead during the course of manufacture, analysis of paste samples shows them to be lead-free. However, paste can contain large amounts of manganese, and the amount of manganese present is a marker for where the paste was produced. Colombian paste is manganese-rich while Peruvian is not (ElSohly et al., 1991). Limited studies of blood levels suggest that the results of paste smoking are not much different than "crack" smoking (Paly et al., 1980a; Paly et al., 1982; Paly et al., 1980b).

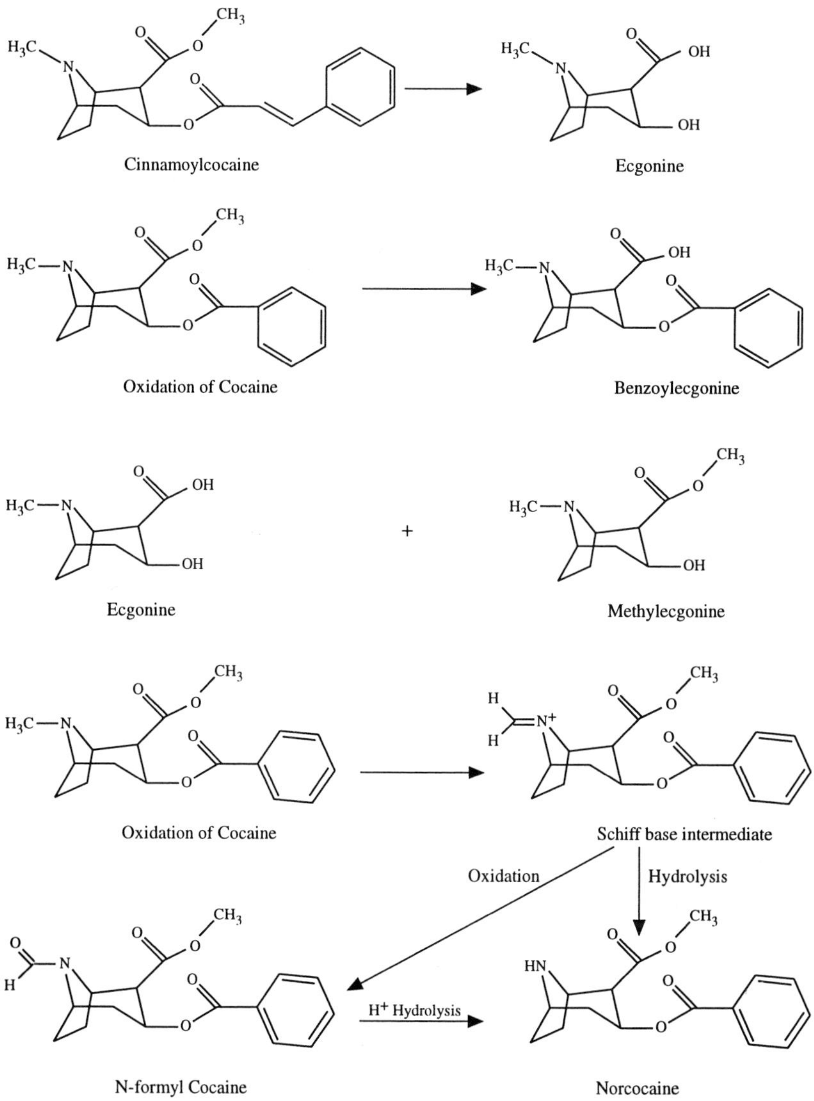

Figure 1.3.2.1   Cocaine refining. Cocaine refiners often add potassium permanganate to remove impurities. Cinnamoylcocaine is converted to ecgonine which is water soluble and easy to separate from cocaine. If the process is allowed to continue for too long, the cocaine itself is degraded and the yield drops. Norcocaine, which may be hepatotoxic, is formed at the same time.

The total synthesis of cocaine is possible, and clandestine cocaine laboratories have been confiscated. The process is, however, a great deal more demanding than the synthesis of amphetamine, and has never been attempted on a large scale. The synthetic origin of the cocaine will be evident from the contaminants found along with the cocaine. Diastomers of cocaine, such as pseudococaine, allococaine, and the *dl*- form (which

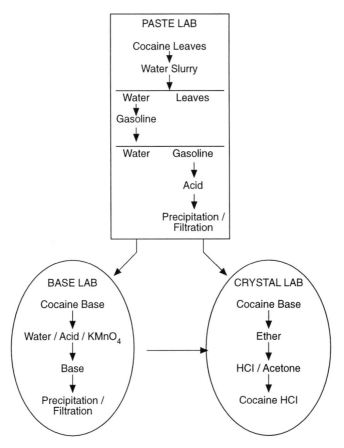

Figure 1.3.2.2   Flow chart of illicit cocaine processing. The preparation of purified cocaine from leaf, adapted from WHO bulletin.

does not occur in nature) of cocaine are not found in cocaine refined from leaf (Soine, 1989).

The purity of confiscated cocaine is considered to be a good general indicator of availability. At wholesale levels, kilogram quantities that had been averaging 80% purity during 1990, increased to 87% purity during 1991. There is no recent indication that these purity levels are declining. At the retail level, ounce-sized specimens, which had been only 58% pure in 1990, had increased to 70% purity by 1991. The purity of the gram-sized samples sold on the street increased by only 2% during the same period. From 1990 through the first nine months of 1991, the price in the U.S. for kilogram quantities ranged from $11,000 to $40,000 (Drug Enforcement Administration, 1992).

References

Abruzzese, R. (1989). Coca-leaf production in the countries of the Andean subregion. Bull Narc, 41 (1 and 2): 95–98.

Bohm, B., Ganders, F., and Plowman, T. (1982). Biosystematics and evolution of cultivated coca (Erythroxylaceae). Systematic Botany, 7(2): 121–133.

Brewer, L. and Allen, A. (1991). N-formyl cocaine: a study of cocaine comparison parameters. J Forensic Sci, 36(3): 697–707.

Drug Enforcement Administration. (1992). Illegal drug price/purity report. United States, calendar years 1988 through September 1991. U.S. Department of Justice, DEA-92015, Washington, DC.

ElSohly, M., Brenneisen, R., and Jones, A. (1991). Coca paste: chemical analysis and smoking experiments. J Forensic Sci, 36(1): 93–103.

Jeri, F. (1984). Coca-paste smoking in some Latin American countries: a severe and unabated form of addiction. Bull Narc, 36(2): 15–31.

Jeri, F., Sanchez, C., del Pozo, T. et al. (1978). Further experience with the syndromes produced by coca paste smoking. Bull Narc, 30: 1–11.

Kumar, A. (1991). Identification and quantitation of norcocaine in illicit cocaine samples. Annual Meeting of the American Academy of Forensic Sciences. Anaheim: AAFS, 73.

Lee, D. (1981). Cocaine handbook. Berkeley: And/Or Press.

Montesinos, F. (1965). Metabolism of cocaine. Bull Narc, 17(2): 11–17.

Moore, J. and Casale, J. (1994). In-depth chromatographic analyses of illicit cocaine and its precursor, coca leaves. J Chromotography A, 674: 165–205.

Paly, D., Jatlow, P., Van Dyke, C. et al. (1980). Plasma levels of cocaine in native Peruvian coca chewers. F. Juri (Ed.), Cocaine 1980, Proceedings of the Interamerican Seminar on Coca and Cocaine. Lima: Pacific Press, 86–89.

Paly, D., Jatlow, P., Van Dyke, C. et al. (1982). Plasma cocaine concentrations during cocaine paste smoking. Life Sci, 30(9): 731–738.

Paly, D., Van Dyke, C., Jatlow, F., and Byck, R. (1980). Cocaine: plasma levels after cocaine paste smoking. In F. Jeri (Eds.), Cocaine: Proceedings of the Interamerican seminar on medical and sociological aspects of coca and cocaine. Lima, Peru, 106–110.

Plowman, T. (1985). Coca and cocaine: effects on people and policy in Latin America. D. Pacinie and C. Franquemont (Eds.), The coca leaf and its derivatives — biology, society and policy. Ithaca, NY: Cultural Survival, Inc.

Plowman, T. and Rivier, L. (1983b). Cocaine and cinnamoylcocaine of Erythroxylum species. Ann Botany, 51: 641–659.

Schlesinger, H. (1985). Topics in the chemistry of cocaine. Bull Narc, 37(1): 63–78.

Soine, W.H. (1989). Contamination of clandestinely prepared drugs with synthetic by-products. Proceedings of the 50th Annual Scientific Meeting, The Committee on Problems of Drug Dependence, published as NIDA Research Monograph 95: 44–50.

Weatherford, J. (1988). Indian givers: the drug connection. New York: Crown, 198.

1.4 Drug constants

The freebase has the formula $C_{17}H_{21}NO_4$ with a molecular weight of 303.4. It contains 67.31% carbon, 6.98% hydrogen, 4.62% nitrogen, and 21.10% oxygen. Pure cocaine forms colorless crystals or white crystalline powder. It is odorless and has a bitter taste. Its melting point is 98°C. However, it becomes volatile at temperatures over 90°C. Aqueous solutions are alkaline to litmus. The pK_a at 15°C = 5.59. One gram dissolves in 600 mL of water,

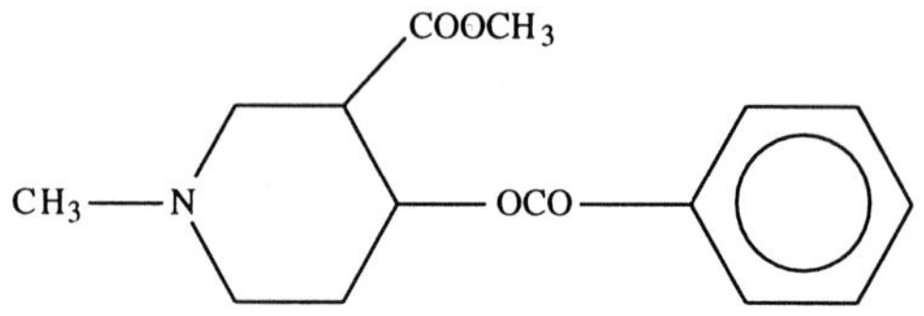

Figure 1.4.1   Cocaine, m.w. = 300.4.

6.5 mL of alcohol, 0.7 mL of chloroform, 3.5 mL of ether, or 12 mL of olive oil. It is also soluble in acetone and ethyl acetate.

Cocaine hydrochloride, referred to in the older literature as cocaine muriate, has the formula $C_{17}H_{22}ClNO_4$. Its composition is 60.08% carbon, 6.53% hydrogen, 4.12% nitrogen, and 10.43% chloride. Its molecular weight is 339.81. Either powdery, crystalline, or granular, it is water soluble and has a slightly bitter taste. The pK_a is 8.6 and the melting point of pharmaceutical grade material is 195°C. One gram dissolves in 0.4 mL of water or 3.2 mL of cold alcohol. It is also soluble in chloroform (one gram in 12.5 mL), glycerol, and acetone. It is insoluble in ether or oils. When heated in solution, it will decompose. Cocaine hydrochloride, stored in a tightly closed container at room temperature, will not decompose for at least five years. Solutions are stable for at least 21 days, provided the temperature is below 24°C and the pH is below 4.0. Above that pH, hydrolysis rapidly occurs (Muthadi and Al-Badr, 1986).

Reference

Muthadi, F. and Al-Badr, A. (1986). Cocaine Hydrochloride. Analyt Profiles of Drug Substances, 15: 151–230.

1.5   Routes of administration

1.5.1   Leaf chewing

Coca has been chewed for over 3,000 years, but the pharmacodynamics of the process have only been partially characterized. Habitual users chew an average of 12 to 15 grams of leaf three or four times a day. Depending on the quality of the leaf, the alkaloid content is usually less than 0.5%. Thus, the total amount consumed at any one time is unlikely to amount to more than 75 mg. In one experiment, novice chewers who spit out their saliva had average peak blood levels of 38 ng/mL at one hour. Experienced users, who swallow their saliva, had mean values of 249 ng/mL; however, the range was from 130 to 859 ng/mL (Paly et al., 1980; Holmstedt et al., 1979). These levels probably lie towards the lower end of the spectrum of levels attained when the drug is snorted.

1.5.2   Snorting

Variable levels result when cocaine is snorted. In general, peak plasma concentrations are proportional to the amount of cocaine ingested (Wilkinson

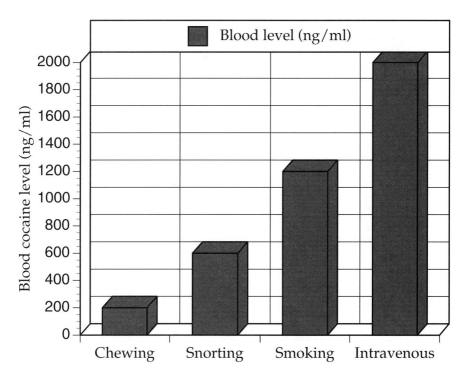

Figure 1.5.1 Blood levels and routes of administration. The route of ingestion determines cocaine blood levels. Crack smokers may have blood levels three or four times as high as leaf chewing Indians. Levels after snorting are intermediate.

et al., 1980). Because cocaine is a vasoconstrictor, it inhibits its own absorption, and the time it takes to reach peak concentration gets longer as the dose gets larger. One hundred milligrams, which is approximately the equivalent of two to three "lines," will produce a blood level of 50–100 ng/mL, sufficient to cause transient increases in pulse and blood pressure (Javaid et al., 1978; Javaid et al., 1983; Fischman, 1983; Foltin et al., 1988). Scanty data suggests that the "average" cocaine snorter will have blood levels not that much different from experienced leaf chewers. In one study, intranasal application of 1.5 mg/kg (which would be 90 mg in a 60-kilo man, or roughly the amount of cocaine found in 15 grams of leaf) produced peak levels of 120–474 ng/mL within 30–60 minutes afterward (Van Dyke et al., 1976). In a more recent study, a dose of 2 mg/kg (which amounted to between 100 and 255 mg total) produced peak levels ranging from 131 ng/mL up to 1,012 ng/mL, with an average of 370 ng/mL at 30 minutes. The average level fell to 295 ng/mL at 60 minutes, and 223 ng/mL at 90 minutes (Brogan et al., 1992). Actual levels in abusers have not been quantitated. Clinical experience suggests that the use of a gram or more at one time is not uncommon, but ethical and safety considerations generally prohibit administration of such large doses in a laboratory setting.

1.5.3   Surgical application

Blood levels after intranasal application in recreational users are generally much lower than those seen in patients undergoing surgical procedures. Otorhinolaryngologists and plastic surgeons still use combinations of epinephrine and cocaine to maintain a dry operative field, although as the dangers of this practice have become more apparent, cocaine/epinephrine combinations are used much less often. Different mixtures have been employed. The surgical application of even small amounts of cocaine will cause patients to have positive urine tests for as long as three days. In one study, patients undergoing lacrimal duct surgery were anesthetized with less than 3 mL of topical 4% cocaine hydrochloride. In almost every instance, urine specimens obtained 24 hours later exceeded the 300-ng NIDA cutoff, and some still exceeded it at 48 hours. In some patients, cocaine was still detectable 72 hours later, though at levels less than 300 ng/mL (Cruz et al., 1991).

Topical cocaine may be combined with submucous injections of lidocaine/epinephrine. Because pH has a significant effect on local anesthetic activity, bicarbonate is occasionally mixed with the cocaine to increase its efficacy (Sollman, 1918). Cocaine mixed with an epinephrine solution is referred to as "paste." When a mixture of cocaine and epinephrine is used, with or without the addition of bicarbonate, the resultant plasma levels can be quite high. Concentrations of over 2,000 ng/mL have been observed (Lips et al., 1987; Bromley and Hayward, 1988).

Injected epinephrine is, of course, absorbed along with the cocaine, and this may lead to toxicity (Taylor et al., 1984). Cocaine's toxic effects on the heart are at least partly mediated by catecholamine excess, and the potential for the occurrence of an untoward event is quite real when cocaine is combined with epinephrine. Myocardial infarction (Chiu et al., 1986; Meyers, 1980; Littlewood and Tabb, 1987; Ross and Bell, 1992; Ashchi et al., 1995) and cardiac arrest have both been described as complications of cocaine and cocaine/epinephrine anesthesia. Such complications were much more common in older literature, presumably because much larger amounts of cocaine were used (Mayer, 1924). When infarction occurs in this setting, it is nearly impossible to determine the etiology.

Malpractice suits have alleged that either too much epinephrine or too much cocaine had been given, but the probability is that both agents combined to cause coronary artery spasm (Karch, 1989; Flores et al., 1990; Wilkerson et al., 1990; Ascher et al., 1988; Flores, 1990; Wilkerson, 1990). Both cocaine and epinephrine can also induce lethal cardiac arrhythmias (Kabas et al., 1990; Laster et al., 1990; Schwartz et al., 1988). Catecholamine measurements at autopsy are not possible, and even measurements made during life, especially in the post arrest state, are impossible to interpret. Some individuals with uncomplicated infarction will have higher catecholamine levels than others with cardiac arrest who have been given exogenous epinephrine (Worstman, Frank, and Cryer, 1984). Similarly, cocaine levels, in and of themselves, do not appear to correlate with the probability of developing coronary artery spasm, and infarction can occur when there is only metabolite present (Del Aguila and Rosman, 1990; Levine and Nishikawa, 1991). If preexisting lesions can be demonstrated, then at least there is a plausible mechanism for infarction. Cocaine and epinephrine increase oxygen consumption. Previous asymptomatic lesions can suddenly become symptomatic if the demand for increased blood supply becomes too great.

The use of cocaine as a local anesthetic also carries with it the risk that the surgeon may inadvertently contaminate himself and test positive for cocaine (see also Section 1.5.6). One study considered several possible scenarios for exposure (Bruns et al., 1994). The study involved 22 patients who had routine nasal surgery, and their surgeons. The surgeons participating in the study used their fingers to mix 4 cc of 4% cocaine into cotton pledgets which were then inserted into the patient's nostrils. The surgeons wore masks at all times. In six cases they also wore gloves, and in six cases they did not. In order to test for cumulative effects, a separate experiment was done; a single physician handled cocaine on Day 1 once every two hours for six hours, and on Day 2, once every hour for six hours. Cotton-soaked pledgets were prepared as if surgery was to be performed. The cotton was handled for two minutes; 15 minutes were allowed to pass, and then the surgeon washed his hands.

When surgeons wore gloves, no cocaine metabolite was detected. When the surgeons did not wear gloves, benzoylecgonine appeared in their urine, although at levels well below NIDA or DOD cutoffs, either for screen assays or GC/MS confirmation. Mean BEG concentration was 30.1 ng/mL at 8 hours and 18.8 ng/mL at 24 hours. The highest level recorded was 53 ng/mL. However, much higher levels were observed where one surgeon handled the cocaine-soaked cotton for the two-day study, and a cumulative effect was definitely observed. Twelve hours after the first exposure (once every two hours for six hours) BEG levels were approximately 90 ng/ml. Eighteen hours after the second exposure, levels measured by GC/MS had risen to 245 ng/mL, a positive result by either military or civilian standards.

1.5.4   Intravenous use

Significantly higher levels than chewing or snorting occur after intravenous use. Kumor et al. found that a 40-mg intravenous bolus given to a human volunteer resulted in blood levels of between 204 and 523 ng/mL at 10 minutes (Kumor et al., 1988). Chow et al. gave a 32-mg dose to volunteers and observed peak levels of approximately 250 ng/mL with a maximum increase in heart rate at 7.3 minutes (Chow et al., 1985). Barnett observed levels of 700–1,000 ng/mL, five minutes after injecting 100 mg. The levels exceeded 2,500 ng/mL after 200 mg were injected (Barnett et al., 1981). One important aspect of intravenous cocaine use is that it requires multiple frequent injections to get "high." Narcotic users, by comparison, inject infrequently. The increased number of injections places the cocaine user at greater

risk for HIV infection and for all the other infectious complications of intravenous drug use.

1.5.5   Genital application

Genital and rectal application serves two purposes. Absorption is prompt
and relatively complete, so high blood levels are reached very quickly. In
addition, cocaine used in this manner also acts as a local anesthetic. For
obvious reasons, rectal application has become popular among homosexual
abusers. Fatalities have been reported after both rectal and vaginal application. Except for a pregnant woman who died of air embolism after her
partner blew crack smoke into her vagina (Collins et al., 1994), the clinical
histories in these patients suggest that death was due to arrhythmia but,
interestingly, reported blood levels have not been high (Doss and Gowitt,
1988; Ettinger and Stine, 1989; Burkett et al., 1990). Occasionally, genital
application may be inadvertent. There are two reports in the literature of
women using their vaginas to smuggle drugs. In one instance, the woman
was found dead with two plastic bags, each containing 85 grams of cocaine,
in her vagina (Mebanex and De Vito, 1975; Benjamin et al., 1994). The external
genitals were necrotic. In a second case, a woman detained by customs agents
was found to have a 16 × 10 × 1 cm elliptical packet of cocaine wedged so
tightly in her vagina that obstetric forceps were required for removal.

1.5.6   Dermal absorption

Cocaine adheres to the skin and can be absorbed through it. Cocaine can be
recovered from the skin of individuals who have handled crack cocaine,
even after thorough hand washing, although in most cases, it is quite unlikely
that anyone will have recoverable cocaine on their skin simply because they
have been in contact with cocaine-contaminated objects (as opposed to handling pieces of crack cocaine or bulk cocaine) (Maloney et al., 1994).

Even very small amounts of cocaine applied to the skin can cause cocaine
metabolite to appear in the urine. The levels following dermal exposure are
generally far too low to produce symptoms, but the fact that measurable
levels appear in the blood at all is troublesome, especially for individuals,
such as customs agents and physicians, whose work brings them into contact
with cocaine.

Several studies have addressed this problem, but a number of questions
still remain to be answered. In one study, cocaine dissolved in alcohol was
painted on the forearm skin of a volunteer, and the urine was then tested
intermittently over a 96-hour period. Absorption of both freebase and
cocaine hydrochloride occurred. Maximal urinary benzoylecgonine concentration after the application of 5 mg of freebase was 55 ng/mL at 48 hours.
Much less of the cocaine hydrochloride was absorbed, with a peak urine
level of only 15 ng/mL at 48 hours (Baselt et al., 1990). The more complete
absorption of the freebase can probably be accounted for by the fact that

weak bases, such as cocaine, are not very lipid soluble. Freebase, on the other hand, is lipophilic and is readily absorbed.

Unpublished data, cited in the study mentioned above, described what happened when five laboratory workers had 2 mg of cocaine hydrochloride, dissolved in water, placed on their palms. Urine collected three hours later tested with the EMIT® d.a.u. assay was positive in all five participants. In one case, the resultant blood level was above the 300 ng/mL cutoff (Baselt et al., 1990, in the study cited above). A third study, done with cocaine paste, yielded much the same result (ElSohly, 1991).

The risk that medical personnel might test positive because of innocent contact was assessed in two other studies. Neither the placing of 2 drops of 4% cocaine on the skin, nor breathing deeply when spraying a patient with 4% cocaine aerosol, nor squeezing cocaine-soaked cotton pledgets between the fingers caused any of 11 volunteers to test positive (Zieske, 1992). In a 1994 study, three different scenarios were tested; physicians' urines were tested after they had soaked cottonoid pledgets in a 4% cocaine solution and then inserted them into the patient's nares. The physicians wore masks for all the trials, but wore gloves for only six. No metabolite was found in the urine of physicians wearing gloves, and only low levels of benozoylecgonine were detected in the six who wore no gloves (mean concentration of 30.1 ng/mL at 8 hours, 18.8 ng/mL at 24 hours). In the third scenario, a single physician handled cocaine-soaked cottonoids three times a day for two days, then washed his hands fifteen minutes later. After the first day of testing, urine levels were below 100 ng/mL, but after the second day, urine levels rose to 245 ng/mL on GC/MS testing (Bruns et al., 1994).

Given that skin contact can, in some situations, result in significant urinary benzoylecgonine concentrations that persist for some time, extreme caution is warranted when interpreting low-level urine drug-testing results. This is especially true when these results fall below the commonly accepted immunoassay and GC/MS limit for benzoylecgonine of 300 and 150 ng/mL, respectively.

1.5.7   Inhalation

The extraction of cocaine freebase with volatile solvents, popular in the early 1980s, and referred to as "freebasing," gave way entirely to "crack" smoking by 1986 (Washton and Gold, 1986). The origins of this practice are not entirely clear. It was first observed in Jamaica in 1983 (Jekel et al., 1986). The first mention of usage in the U.S. came from New York City in 1985 (Gross, 1985). When freebase cocaine is smoked, peak blood levels comparable to those achieved with intravenous use are rapidly attained.

There have been limited clinical studies accessing plasma levels in intoxicated "crack" smokers. "Crack" prepared on the streets contains very large amounts of bicarbonate and other contaminants. For clinical experiments, "crack" is prepared by mixing cocaine hydrochloride with an equal weight of sodium bicarbonate in sterile water and heating in a boiling waterbath. Cocaine base precipitates out and forms small pellets or "rocks" when the water is cooled. When prepared in this manner, smoking 50 mg of base delivers between 16 and 32 mg of cocaine to the subject (Perez-Reyes et al., 1982; Foltin, 1991; Paly et al., 1980; Paly et al., 1982; Jeffcoat et al., 1989). The potency of smoked cocaine is about 60% of intravenous cocaine, at least in regard to the production of cardiovascular effects (Foltin, 1991).

In one study, plasma levels 6–12 minutes after smoking one 50-mg dose ranged from 250–350 ng/mL. In a second study, from the same laboratory, two 50-mg doses of freebase, smoked 14 minutes apart, produced a peak level of 425 ng/mL four minutes after the last dose (Foltin, 1991). Smoking a 50-mg dose every 14 minutes, for a total of four doses, produced a level of over 1,200 ng/mL in one subject. To closely simulate the actual smoking patterns of crack users, volunteers smoked two 35-mg doses at intervals of 15, 30, and 45 minutes. When the doses were 15 minutes apart, plasma levels were on the order of 800 ng/mL. When the doses were 30 minutes apart, peak levels were only half as high, approximately 400 ng/mL. When 45 minutes elapsed between doses, the level rose to only 200 ng/mL (Hatsukami et al., 1993). There is, however, a great deal of variation between experimental subjects. After smoking a 50-mg dose, peak effects on blood pressure occur 2–6 minutes after inhalation and return to baseline within 30 minutes after a single dose (Foltin and Fischman, 1991; Jeffcoat et al., 1989). In a 1991 study, smoking 50 mg results in blood levels ranging anywhere from 80 to 460 ng/mL. If a second 50-mg dose was smoked 14 minutes after the first, then resultant blood levels would range from 200 to 600 ng/mL (Isenschmid et al., 1992). In both man and experimental animals, changes in heart rate and blood pressure are dose-dependent and correlate temporally with peak cocaine plasma concentrations (Boni et al., 1991).

Sidestream exposure to cocaine can cause measurable quantities of cocaine metabolite to appear in the urine. In one experiment, a 73-kg adult male was exposed to 200 mg of freebase that was volatilized in a confined space about the size of a closet. Serial urine specimens collected over 24 hours contained 10–50 ng/mL of urine (Baselt et al., 1991). Environmental exposure to cocaine is a real hazard for inner city children. Nearly 2.5% of children attending a metropolitan emergency department tested positive for cocaine or cocaine metabolite. The number would probably have been higher, but children with signs of cocaine toxicity, or history of cocaine exposure, were specifically excluded from the survey (Kharasch et al., 1991).

When attempting to interpret the significance of low cocaine and benzoylecgonine levels, especially in children, it is important to remember that cocaine smoke, just like cigarette smoke, can be passively absorbed. The process has been described in children and can produce transient neurologic syndromes (Bateman and Heagarty, 1989). Whether or not such exposure can lead to serious consequences is not clear, but it certainly can lead to positive urine, blood, and hair tests. If parents use cocaine, then it will be in the home environment and, no matter what their wishes, it will end up in their children. In a recent study, 85% of the children living with cocaine-using parents had detectable levels of cocaine in their hair (Smith and Kidwell, 1994). Whether the positive tests were a result of inhaled cocaine being deposited within hair, or environmental cocaine being deposited on hair, has not been determined. In the absence of a definitive answer to the question, courts have tended to rule that the presence of detectable amounts of cocaine, or cocaine metabolite, is proof of willful child endangerment. Breastfeeding mothers of SIDS babies have actually been charged with murder because low blood levels of cocaine and/or methamphetamine (under 50 ng/mL) have been detected at autopsy, even though such levels may well have come from environmental sources, and not from the mother.

The case for such child endangerment and murder charges is supported by very little evidence. One of the most frequently cited studies was reported from Philadelphia. Sixteen children who had cocaine or metabolite in their blood were identified over a two-year period. The authors of the study suggested that the presence of the cocaine might have contributed to their deaths. Scene investigations documented that shortly before death, these infants had been exposed to "crack" smoke. Most of the infants were under three months of age, none had revealing autopsy findings, and their average cocaine blood level was 76 ng/mL, just barely over the level required to produce any measurable physiologic effects (Mirchandani et al., 1991). On the basis of this evidence alone, and in the absence of any plausible mechanism, sudden infant death syndrome would appear to be the more likely diagnosis in these particular cases. (Sudden infant death syndrome has been alleged to be a complication of maternal cocaine use; however, proof is lacking.) In fact, the low levels of cocaine could have had their origin from other sources in the child's environment. Sidestream intake of volatilized cocaine could also occur in innocent mothers. Cocaine and its metabolite would then appear in the infant, although the mother herself was not a cocaine user. The identification of cocaine in the infant is not, necessarily, proof of abuse by the mother.

1.5.8 Gastrointestinal absorption

A significant proportion of the cocaine found in the blood of coca leaf chewers comes from gastrointestinal absorption. Chewers who swallow their saliva have higher cocaine levels than those who do not. While it is widely believed that cocaine is not absorbed from the gastrointestinal tract, quite the opposite is true (Wilkinson et al., 1980; Jenkins and Cone, 1995), at least for the hydrochloride salt. The absorption of "crack" pellets has never been systematically studied, but clinical experience suggests that it is not very good. "Crack" dealers who swallow their inventory in order to avoid arrest seldom become symptomatic. Since dealers are often users as well, tolerance may afford a degree of protection.

Gastrointestinal absorption assumes particular importance in the "body packer" syndrome. This syndrome can be lethal (Bednarczyk et al., 1980; Fishbain and Wetli, 1981; McCarron and Wood, 1983; Caruana et al., 1984; Beck and Hale, 1993; Hierholzer et al., 1995; Meyers, 1995). The practice was first described in 1972 (Suarez et al., 1972). Low level smugglers ("mules") swallow packets containing hundreds of grams of cocaine. The drug to be

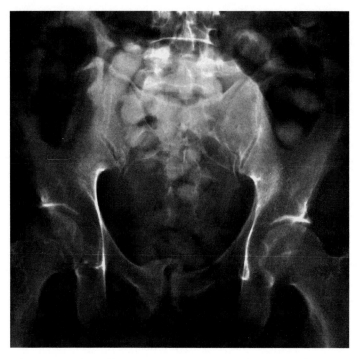

Figure 1.5.8.1 "Body packer" syndrome. Drug couriers can be diagnosed with plain abdominal x rays, although occasionally CT scanning is required. This plain film clearly demonstrates cocaine-containing packets. Courtesy of Dr. M. Meyers, State University of New York, Health Sciences Center. From Abd Imaging, 20: 339, 1995, with permission.

smuggled is wrapped either in a condom, plastic bag, or aluminum foil. Packets generally contain 3–6 grams of drug. The radiodensity of cocaine is very close to that of stool, and that can make detecting smugglers difficult (Wetli and Mittleman, 1981; Karhunen et al., 1991). If a packet should rupture, the smuggler will quickly absorb a very large amount of drug. Seizures commonly result and appear to be the mechanism of lethality in experimental animals given huge amounts of cocaine (Catravas et al., 1978; Catravas and Waters, 1981). But humans may also develop pulmonary edema and heart failure. Even a massive overdose is not necessarily fatal (Bettinger, 1980). Blood levels in these cases have ranged from 3 to 11 mg/L. Such levels are well in excess of levels normally seen after intravenous abuse. Tolerance occurs, and levels as high as 30 mg/L or more may be recorded as incidental findings (Howell and Ezell, 1990).

Even if the cocaine-containing packets do not rupture, small amounts of cocaine may still appear in the urine, and urine testing may be diagnostic for the syndrome (Gherardi et al., 1988). Other diagnostic techniques that have been advocated included plain x-ray films, barium contrast studies, and CT scanning. As the smugglers have become more sophisticated, they have improved their packing techniques to prevent leakage. They have also attempted to avoid x-ray detection by ingesting mixtures of oil which will

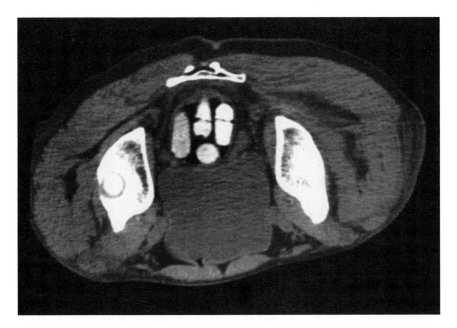

Figure 1.5.8.2 "Body packer" syndrome. This syndrome was first described in 1972. Smugglers who swallow multiple, rubber coated, packets of drugs are at grave risk for massive overdose. Courtesy of Dr. M. Meyers, State University of New York, Health Sciences Center. From Abd Imaging, 20: 339, 1995, with permission.

reduce the contrast difference between the packets and the surrounding bowel contents (Gherardi et al., 1990; Pinsky et al., 1978; Sinner, 1981; Revuelta et al., 1995).

1.5.9   Maternal/fetal considerations

In pregnant ewes, fetal blood concentrations five minutes after a maternal infusion are only 12% of the values seen in the mother (Moore et al., 1986). In near-term Macaque monkeys, 1 mg/kg injected intramuscularly in the mother, yielded peak plasma concentrations of 132–312 ng/mL 10–20 minutes after injection. Fetal levels lagged behind, peaking at from 30 minutes to two hours later, but peak levels were the same (18–329 ng/mL) (Paule et al., 1991; Binienda et al., 1993).

Cocaine pharmacokinetics have also been studied in pregnant and lactating rats (Wiggins et al., 1989). From 30 minutes to three hours after injection, cocaine levels are 3–4 times higher in the brain and 3–5 times higher in the liver than in the blood. During the period from 30 minutes to 90 minutes after injection, fetal brain concentrations were 50% to 90% of the mothers' and 1.5 times as high as the blood concentration of either. Injected cocaine also appeared in the milk of lactating mothers in fairly high concentrations.

In vivo human data is extremely limited, although a number of *in vitro* studies with human placenta have been published. One interesting study measured cocaine, benzoylecgonine, cotinine, and caffeine in cord blood. Seven of 11 newborn infants with benzoylecgonine detectable in their cord blood also had cocaine detected. All of the infants had caffeine detected, and in more than half, cotinine was also present. Cocaine levels ranged from 9–77 ng/mL with benzoylecgonine levels ranging from 55–2,540 ng/mL. Caffeine levels were much higher, ranging from 80–10,000 ng/mL (Dempsey et al., 1993).

Human placenta has high affinity binding sites for cocaine (Ahmed et al., 1990). In isolated perfused cotyledons of normal term human placenta, cocaine is passively, but rapidly transported without undergoing metabolic transformation. The same holds true for cocaethylene and norcocaine. In this *in vitro* model, the direction of transport depends entirely upon the relative concentration of cocaine in the mother and fetus; when fetal levels are higher than maternal levels, equally rapid transport back across the placenta occurs (Schenker et al., 1993). The results of other studies done with perfused human cotyledons suggest that the placenta may, under appropriate circumstances, act as a depot, initially absorbing, then slowly releasing, both cocaine and benzoylecgonine into the fetal circulation (Simone et al., 1994). Whether that occurs *in vivo* is not known, nor is it clear whether such an action would be harmful or beneficial. If the placenta acts as a buffer, then it may keep the infant from being exposed to large doses of cocaine taken as an intravenous bolus. On the other hand, storage and slow release by the placenta probably would also ensure that the fetus is chronically exposed to low levels of drug.

There appears to be a great deal of individual variability in placental handling of cocaine. The results of animal studies suggest that high maternal/fetal cocaine ratios occur in humans as well as animals. In a case described by Mittleman, the maternal/fetal ratio was 9:1 (13,700 ng/mL to 1,500 ng/mL) (Mittleman et al., 1989). The high ratio may reflect cocaine-induced vasospasm and reduced flow to the uterus, or it may simply mean that woman and child were not in equilibrium when the mother expired. However, there is now some very good evidence that maternal use may not guarantee fetal exposure.

A paper published in 1994 described the case of a 26-year old woman who bore a four pound infant at 32 weeks of gestation (Potter et al., 1994). The mother was an admitted intravenous cocaine user who injected herself daily throughout the course of her pregnancy. She also used hashish on a weekly basis during the first trimester of the pregnancy, drank an occasional beer, and smoked 1–2 packs of cigarettes a day throughout the pregnancy. Hair samples from the mother obtained two months after delivery contained nicotine, cotinine, and benzoylecgonine (concentrations in various segments ranged from 0.8 to 2.3 ng/mg hair). Urine from the child was negative for benzoylecgonine and cannabinoids, and only cannabinoids were detected in the meconium. Hair samples obtained from the child at birth were negative for cocaine and benzoylecgonine, but did contain nicotine and cotinine. Thus the presence of cocaine, or one of its metabolites, in a neonate does not necessarily prove that the drugs came from the mother.

Women have been tried and convicted for child endangerment and abuse because trace amounts of drug were found in infants who would otherwise have been diagnosed as crib deaths. The presumption of the courts has been that the presence of drug proves a maternal role in the exposure. In fact, the presence of drug just proves that there is drug in the environment. Environmental exposure is now a well recognized explanation for positive drug tests in children. Laboratory studies have shown conclusively that exposure to sidestream crack cocaine vapor results in the presence of detectable levels of cocaine metabolite in the urine (Goldberger and Cone, 1994), even if only at levels well below NIDA cutoffs. In some inner city hospitals, 10–20% of children presenting for medical treatment (unrelated to drug use or exposure) have tested positive (Bhushan et al., 1994). In another study, which utilized hair testing, 85% of the children of drug-using parents had drug detected in their hair, sometimes in even greater concentrations than those found in the hair of the parents (Smith and Kidwell, 1994).

Because cocaine is a weak base and a small molecule, it diffuses freely across the placenta. That is not the case for benzoylecgonine, which is highly ionized at physiological pH ranges, and which hardly crosses the placenta. The situation is very similar to cocaine metabolism in the brain. Benzoylecgonine (BEG) does not cross the blood-brain barrier, so all the BEG found in the brain is produced by the metabolism of cocaine in the brain. All the BEG in the fetus is derived from cocaine metabolized in the fetus. Because the fetus cannot clear BEG as quickly as the mother, maternal/fetal ratios are just the opposite of the case with cocaine, the parent metabolite. In Meeker's autopsy study, the ratio in six cases was 2.44, with a range of 1.17–6.80 (Meeker and Reynolds, 1990).

Neonates that have been exposed to drug *in utero*, including cocaine, marijuana, and opiates, will have measurable amounts of these drugs detectable in their meconium, where levels can be determined using minimally modified standard immunoassays for at least several days after birth (Maynard et al., 1991; Ostrea et al., 1992). Compared to cord blood, meconium has a greater number of cocaine metabolites and a higher concentration of cocaine and cocaine metabolites, including norcocaine and benzoylecgonine derivatives (Konkol et al., 1994). These same drugs can also be detected in the neonates' hair (Graham et al., 1989; Forman et al., 1992) and, if available, brain.

In cases of fetal demise, it is useful to quantitate drug levels in brain homogenates (Hernandez et al., 1994). High benzoylecgonine levels, in conjunction with low or absent cocaine levels, suggest a pattern of long-term exposure during pregnancy, but no recent drug use by the mother. High cocaine levels, with low benzoylecgonine levels, suggest cocaine ingestion shortly before death. The presence of cocaethylene indicates that the mother was also consuming alcohol, and, since cocaethylene has a much longer half-life than cocaine, no cocaine may be detected, even though other cocaine metabolites will be present. Laboratory reports indicating that only cocaine, or only cocaethylene, was present probably reflect laboratory error.

References

Ahmed, M., Zhou, D., Maulik, D., and Elderfrawi, M. (1990). Characterization of cocaine binding sites in human placenta. Life Sci, 46: 553–561.

Ascher, E., Stauffer, J., and Gaash, W. (1988). Coronary artery spasm, cardiac arrest, transient electrocardiographic Q waves and stunned myocardium in cocaine-associated acute myocardial infarction. Am J Cardiol, 11: 939–941.

Ashchi, M., Wiedmann, H., and James, K. (1995). Cardiac complication from use of cocaine and phenylephrine in nasal septoplasty. Arch Otolaryngol Head Neck Surg, 121: 681–684.

Barnett, G., Hawks, R., and Resbick, R. (1981). Cocaine pharmacokinetics in humans. J Ethnopharm, 3: 353–366.

Baselt, R., Chang, J., and Yoshikawa, D. (1990). On the dermal absorption of cocaine. J Anal Toxicol, 14(6): 383–384.

Baselt, R., Yoshikawa, D., and Chang, Y. (1991). Passive inhalation of cocaine. Clin Chem, 37(12): 2160–2161.

Bateman, D. and Heagarty, M. (1989). Passive freebase cocaine ("crack") inhalation by infants and toddlers. Am J Dis Child, 143: 25–27.

Beck, N. and Hale, J. (1993). Cocaine "body packers." Br J Surg, 80: 1513–1516.

Bednarczyk, L., Gressman, E., and Wymer, R. (1980). Two cocaine-induced fatalities. J Anal Tox, 4 (September/October): 263–265.

Benjamin, F., Guillaume, J., Chao, L. et al. (1994). Vaginal smuggling of illicit drug: a case requiring forceps for removal of drug container. Am J Obstet Gynecol, 171: 1385–1387.

Bettinger, J. (1980). Cocaine intoxication: massive oral overdose. Ann Emerg Med, 8: 429–430.

Binienda, Z., Bariley, J., Duhart, H. et al. (1993). Transplacental pharmacokinetics and maternal/fetal plasma concentrations of cocaine in pregnant macaques near term. Drug Metab Disp, 21(2): 364–368.

Boni, J. P., Barr, W. H., and Martin, B. R. (1991). Cocaine inhalation in the rat — pharmacokinetics and cardiovascular response. J Pharmacol Exp Ther, 257(1): 307–315.

Brogan, W., Lange, R., Glamann, B., and Hillis, D. (1992). Recurrent coronary vaso-constriction caused by intranasal cocaine: possible role for metabolites. Ann Intern Med, 116(7): 556–561.

Bromley, L. and Hayward, A. (1988). Cocaine absorption from the nasal mucosa. Anesthesia, 43: 356–358.

Bruns, A., Zieske, L., and Jacobs, A. (1994). Analysis of the cocaine metabolite in the urine of patients and physicians during clinical use. Otolaryngol Head Neck Surg, 111: 722–726.

Burkett, G., Bandstra, E. S., Cohen, J. et al. (1990). Cocaine-related maternal death. Am J Obstet Gynecol, 163(1): 40–41.

Caruana, D., Weinbach, B., Goerg, D. et al. (1984). Cocaine packet ingestion. Diagnosis, management, and natural history. Ann Intern Med, 320: 73–74.

Catravas, J. and Waters, I. (1981). Acute cocaine intoxication in the conscious dog: studies on the mechanism of lethality. J Pharm and Exp Ther, 217: 350–356.

Catravas, J., Waters, I., Waiz, M. et al. (1978). Acute cocaine intoxication in the conscious dog: pathophysiologic profile of acute lethality. Arch Int Pharmacodyn Ther, 235: 328–340.

Chiu, Y., Brecht, K., Das Gupta, M. et al. (1986). Myocardial infarction with topical cocaine anesthesia for nasal surgery. Arch Otolaryngol Head Neck Surg, 112: 988–990.

Chow, M., Ambre, J., Ruo, T. et al. (1985). Kinetics of cocaine distribution, elimination, and chronotropic effects. Clin Pharmacol Ther, 38: 318–324.

Collins, K., Davis, G., and Lantz, P. (1994). An unusual case of maternal-fetal death due to vaginal insufflation of cocaine. Am J Forensic Med Pathol, 15: 335–339.

Cruz, O., Patrinely, J., Reyna, G., and King, J. (1991). Urine drug screening for cocaine after lacrimal surgery. Am J Ophthalmol, 111(6): 703–705.

Del Aguila, C. and Rosman, H. (1990). Myocardial infarction during cocaine withdrawal. Ann Intern Med, 112(9): 712.

Dempsey, D., Rowbotham, M., Dattel, B., and Partridge, J. (1993). Neonatal blood cocaine concentrations. Am Soc Clin Pharm Ther, February, 150.

Doss, P. and Gowitt, G. (1988). Investigation of a death caused by rectal insertion of cocaine. Am J Forensic Med and Pathol, 9(4): 336–338.

ElSohly, M. A. (1991). Urinalysis and casual handling of marijuana and cocaine. J Anal Toxicol, 15(1): 46.

Ettinger, T. and Stine, R. (1989). Sudden death temporally related to vaginal cocaine abuse. Am J Emerg Med, 7(1): 129–130.

Fischman, M. W., Schuster, C. R., and Rajfer, S. (1983). A comparison of the subjective and cardiovascular effects of cocaine and procaine in humans. Pharmacol Biochem Behav, 18: 711–716.

Fishbain, D. and Wetli, C. (1981). Cocaine intoxication, delirium, and death in a body-packer. Ann Emerg Med, 10(10): 531–532.

Flores, E. D., Lange, R. A., Cigarroa, R. G., and Hillis, L. D. (1990). Effect of cocaine on coronary artery dimensions in atherosclerotic coronary artery disease — enhanced vasoconstriction at sites of significant stenoses. J Am Coll Cardiol, 16(1): 74–79.

Foltin, J. F., Fischman, M., Pedroso, J., and Pearlson, G. (1988). Repeated intranasal cocaine administration: lack of tolerance to pressor effects. Drug and Alcohol Dependence, 22: 169–177.

Foltin, R. W. and Fischman, M. W. (1991). Smoked and intravenous cocaine in humans — acute tolerance, cardiovascular and subjective effects. J Pharmacol Exp Ther, 257(1): 247–261.

Forman, R., Schneiderman, J., Klein, J. et al. (1992). Accumulation of cocaine in maternal and fetal hair — the dose response curve. Life Sci, 50(18): 1333–1341.

Forman, R., Klein, J., Barks, J. et al. (1994). Prevalence of fetal exposure to cocaine in Toronto, 1990–1991. Clin Invest Med, 17(3): 206–211.

Gherardi, R., Baud, F., Leporc, P., and Marc, B. (1988). Detection of drugs in the urine of body-packers. Lancet, 1(May 14): 1076–1078.

Gherardi, R., Marc, B., Alberti, X. et al. (1990). A cocaine body packer with normal abdominal plain radiograms. Am J Forensic Med and Pathol, 11(2): 154–157.

Goldberger, B. and Cone, E. (1994). Confirmatory tests for drugs in the workplace by gas chromatography-mass spectrometry. J Chromotograph A, 674: 73–86.

Graham, K., Koren, G., Klein, J. et al. (1989). Determination of gestational cocaine exposure by hair analysis. JAMA, 262(23): 3328–3330.

Grant, T., Brown, Z., Callahan, C. et al. (1994). Cocaine exposure during pregnancy: improving assessment with radioimmunoassay of maternal hair. Obstet Gynecol, 83: 524–531.

Gross, J. (1985). New purified form of cocaine causes alarm as abuse increases. New York Times, November 29, p. 1.

Hatsukami, D., Pentel, P., Glass, J. et al. (1994). Methodological issues in the administration of multiple doses of smoked cocaine-base in humans. Pharmacol Biochem Behav, 47: 531–540.

Hernandez, A., Andollo, W., and Hearn, L. (1994). Analysis of cocaine and metabolites in brain using solid phase extraction and full-scanning gas chromatography/ion trap mass spectrometry. Forensic Sci Int, 65: 149–156.

Hierholzer, J., Cordes, M., Tantow, H. et al. (1995). Drug smuggling by ingested cocaine-filled packages: conventional x-ray and ultrasound. Abdom Imaging, 20: 333–338.

Holmstedt, B., Lindgren, J., Rivier, L., and Plowman, T. (1979). Cocaine in blood of coca chewers. J Ethnopharm, 1: 69–78.

Howell, S. and Ezell, A. (1990). An example of cocaine tolerance in a gunshot wound fatality. J Analyt Toxicol, 14: 60–61.

Isenschmid, D., Fishman, M., Foltin, R., and Caplan, Y. (1992). Concentration of cocaine and metabolites in plasma of humans following intravenous administration and smoking cocaine. J Analyt Toxicol, 16: 311–314.

Javaid, J., Fischman, M., Schuster, C. et al. (1978). Cocaine plasma concentrations: relation to physiological and subjective effects in humans. Science, 202: 227–228.

Javaid, J., Musa, M., Fischman, M. et al. (1983). Kinetics of cocaine in humans after intravenous and intranasal administration. Biopharm Drug Dispos, 4: 9–18.

Jeffcoat, A., Perez-Reyes, M., Hill, J. et al. (1989). Cocaine disposition in humans after intravenous injection, nasal insufflation (snorting) or smoking. Drug Metab. Dispos, 17(2): 153–159.

Jekel, J., Allen, D., Podlewski, H. et al. (1986). Epidemic freebase cocaine abuse: case study from the Bahamas. Lancet, 1: 459–462.

Jenkins, A. and Cone, E. (1995). Urinary excretion of cocaine metabolites following oral cocaine administration. Read at the Annual Meeting, American Academy of Forensic Science, Seattle, February 15, 1995.

Kabas, J., Blanchard, S., Matsuyama, Y. et al. (1990). Cocaine-mediated impairment of cardiac conduction in the dog: a potential mechanism for sudden death after cocaine. J Pharmacol and Exp Ther, 252(1): 185–191.

Karch, S. (1989). Coronary artery spasm induced by intravenous epinephrine overdose. Am J Emerg Med, 7(5), 485–488.

Karhunen, P. J., Suoranta, P. J., Penttilä, A., and Pitkäranta, P. (1991). Pitfalls in the diagnosis of drug smuggler's abdomen. J Forensic Sci, 36(2): 397–402.

Kharasch, S. J., Glotzer, D., Vinci, R. et al. (1991). Unsuspected cocaine exposure in young children. Am J Dis Child, 145(2): 204–206.

Konkol, R., Murphey, L., Ferriero, D. et al. (1994). Cocaine metabolites in the neonate: potential for toxicity. J Child Neurol, 9: 242–248.

Kumor, K., Sherer, M., Thompson, L. et al. (1988). Lack of cardiovascular tolerance during intravenous cocaine infusions in human volunteers. Life Sci, 42: 2063–2071.

Laster, M., Johnson, B., Eger, E., and Taheri, S. (1990). A method for testing for epinephrine-induced arrhythmias in rats. Anesth Analg, 70: 654–657.

Levine, M. and Nishikawa, J. (1991). Acute myocardial infarction associated with cocaine withdrawal. Can Med Assoc J, 144(9): 1139–1140.

Lips, F., O'Reilly, J., Close, D. et al. (1987). The effects of formulation and addition of adrenaline to cocaine for haemostasis in intranasal surgery. Anesth Intensive Care, 15: 141–146.

Littlewood, S. and Tabb, H. (1987). Myocardial ischemia with epinephrine and cocaine during septoplasty. J LA State Med Soc, 139(5): 15–18.

Maloney, B., Barbato, L., Ihm, B. et al. (1994). The qualitative determination of trace amounts of cocaine obtained through casual contact. Microgram, 27(6): 185–187.

McCarron, N. and Wood, J. (1983). The cocaine "body packer" syndrome — diagnosis and treatment. JAMA, 250: 1417–1420.

Mayer, E. (1924). The toxic effects following the use of local anesthetics. An analysis of the reports of forty-three deaths submitted to the Committee for the Study of Toxic Effects of Local Anesthetics of the American Medical Association. JAMA, 82(11): 876–885.

Maynard, E., Amoruso, L. P., and Oh, W. (1991). Meconium for drug testing. Am J Dis Child, 145(6): 650–652.

Mebanex, C. and De Vito, J. (1975). Cocaine intoxication — a unique case. J Fla Med Assoc, 62: 19–20.

Meeker, J. E. and Reynolds, P. C. (1990). Fetal and newborn death associated with maternal cocaine use. J Anal Toxicol, 14(6): 379–382.

Meyers, E. (1980). Cocaine toxicity during dacryocystorhinostomy. Arch Opthalmol, 98: 842–843.

Meyers, M. (1995). Editorial commentary: The inside dope: cocaine, condoms, and computed tomography. Abdom Imag, 20: 339–340.

Mirchandani, H. G., Mirchandani, I. H., Hellman, F. et al. (1991). Passive inhalation of freebase cocaine ('crack') smoke by infants. Arch Pathol Lab Med, 115(5): 494–498.

Mittleman, R., Cofino, J., and Hearn, W. (1989). Tissue distribution of cocaine in a pregnant woman. J Forensic Sci, 34(2): 481–486.

Moore, T., Sorg, J., Miller, L., and Key, T. (1986). Hemodynamic effects of intravenous cocaine on the pregnant ewe and fetus. Am J Obstet Gynecol, 155: 883–888.

Ostrea, E., Brady, M., Gause, S. et al. (1992). Drug screening of newborns by meconium analysis: a large scale, prospective, epidemiologic study. Pediatrics, 89: 107–113.

Paly, D., Jatlow, P., Van Dyke, C. et al. (1980). Plasma levels of cocaine in native Peruvian coca chewers. In F. Juri (Ed.), Cocaine 1980, Proceedings of the inter-american seminar on coca and cocaine. Lima: Pacific Press, 86–89.

Paly, D., Jatlow, P., Van Dyke, C. et al. (1982). Plasma cocaine concentrations during cocaine paste smoking. Life Sci, 30: 731–738.

Paly, D., Van Dyke, C., Jatlow, P., and Byck, R. (1980). Cocaine: plasma levels after cocaine paste smoking. In F. Juri (Ed.), Cocaine 1980, Proceedings of the inter-american seminar on coca and cocaine. Lima: Pacific Press, 106–110.

Paule, M., Bailey, J., Fogle, C. et al. (1991). Maternal and fetal plasma disposition of cocaine in near-term Macaque monkeys. Problems of drug dependence 1991: Proceedings of the 53rd Annual Scientific Meeting of the Committee on Problems of Drug Dependence, Inc. National Institute on Drug Abuse Monograph Series, Rockville, MD.

Perez-Reyes, M., Guiseppi, S., Ondrusek, G. et al. (1982). Freebase cocaine smoking. Clin Pharmacol Ther, 32: 459–465.

Pinsky, M., Ducas, J., and Ruggere, M. (1978). Narcotic smuggling: the double condom sign. J Can Assoc Radiol, 29(2): 78–81.

Potter, S., Klein, J., Vallante, G. et al. (1994). Maternal cocaine use without evidence of fetal exposure. J Peds, 125(4): 652–654.

Revuelta, E., Hedouin, V., Desurmont, M. et al. (1995). Intra rectal body concealment of drugs: problems for the diagnosis. Read at the Annual Meeting, American Academy of Forensic Sciences, Seattle, February 15, 1995.

Ross, G. and Bell, J. (1992). Myocardial infarction associated with inappropriate use of topical cocaine as treatment for epistaxis. Am J Emerg Med, 10: 219–222.

Schenker, S., Yang, Y., Johnson, R. et al. (1993). The transfer of cocaine and its metabolites across the term human placenta. Clin Pharm Ther, 53: 329–339.

Schwartz, A., Boyle, W., Janzen, D., and Jones, R. (1988). Acute effects of cocaine on catecholamines and cardiac electrophysiology in the conscious dog. Can J Cardiol, 4(4): 188–192.

Simone, C., Derewlany, L., Oskamp, M. et al. (1994). Transfer of cocaine and benzoylecgonine across the perfuse human placental cotyledon. Am J Obstet Gynecol, 150(5, Part I): 1404–1410.

Sinner, W. (1981). The gastrointestinal tract as a vehicle for drug smuggling. Gastrointest Radiol, 198(6): 319–323.

Smith, F. and Kidwell, D. (1994). Cocaine in children's hair when they live with drug dependent adults. Presented at the SOFT conference on drug testing in hair, Tampa, FL, October 29, 1994.

Sollmann, T. (1918). Comparative activity of local anesthetics. II. Paralysis of sensory nerve fibers. J Pharm and Exp Ther, 11(1): 1–7.

Suarez, C., Arango, A., and Lester, L. (1972). Cocaine-condom ingestion. Surgical treatment. JAMA, 238(13): 1391–1392.

Taylor, S., Achola, K., and Smith, G. (1984). Plasma catecholamine concentrations. The effect of infiltration with local analgesics and vasoconstrictors during nasal operations. Anesthesia, 39: 520–523.

Van Dyke, C., Barash, P., Jatlow, P., and Byck, R. (1976). Cocaine: plasma concentrations after intranasal application in man. Science, 191: 859–861.

Washton, A., Gold, M., and Pottash, A. (1986). "Crack": early report on a new drug epidemic. Postgrad Med, 89(5): 52–58.

Wetli, C. and Mittleman, R. E. (1981). The "body packer" syndrome — toxicity following ingestion of illicit drugs packaged for transportation. J Forensic Sci, 26(3): 492–500.

Wiggins, R., Rolsten, C., Ruiz, B., and Davis, C. (1989). Pharmacokinetics of cocaine: basic studies of route, dosage, pregnancy, and lactation. Neurotoxicology, 10(3): 367–381.

Wilkerson, R., Franker, T. et al. (1990). Cocaine-induced coronary-artery spasm. N Engl J Med, 322(17): 1235.

Wilkinson, P., Van Dyke, C., Jatlow, P. et al. (1980). Intranasal and oral cocaine kinetics. Clin Pharmacol Ther, 27: 386–394.

Worstman, J., Frank, S., and Cryer, P. (1984). Adrenomedullary response to maximal stress in humans. Am J Med, 77: 779–784.

Zieske, L. A. (1992). Passive exposure of cocaine in medical personnel and its relationship to drug screening tests. Arch Otolaryngol Head Neck Surg, 118: 364.

1.6   Metabolism

1.6.1   Cocaine disposition

1.6.1.1   General considerations

Cocaine is rapidly cleared from the blood stream (Inaba, Stewart, and Kalow, 1978; Chow, et al., 1985; Javaid et al., 1983; Kumor et al., 1988; Barnett et al., 1981). Cocaine has a steady-state volume of distribution of 2 L/kg. Elimination clearance is 2.0 L per minute. The half-life of the drug in humans is variously

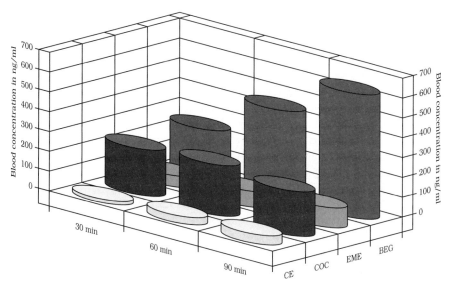

Figure 1.6.1.1 Blood concentrations of cocaine and its metabolites in humans. Average blood concentrations of cocaethylene (CE), cocaine (COC), ecgonine methyl ester (EME), and benzoylecgonine (BEG) in 8 subjects given 2 mg/kg of intranasal cocaine and 5 mL/kg of 10% ethanol. Data adapted from Pirwitz et al., Arch Intern Med, 155: 1186–1191, 1995.

reported as being between 0.5 and 1.5 hours (Jatlow, 1987; Chow et al., 1985; Kumor et al., 1988).

The difficulty with all of the physiological measurements is that they have been made in volunteers, usually chronic cocaine users admitted to detoxification programs, who have been given relatively small doses of cocaine, often on the order of 20–50 mg. In each one of these studies, enrollment was conditional on the individual being drug-free at the time of the study. But, both animal and human studies suggest that cocaine is stored, that its rate of excretion changes as cocaine accumulates (Weiss and Gawin, 1988; Nahas et al., 1995), and that the amount of cocaine consumed by crack smokers is measured in multiple gram quantities, not milligrams (Gossop et al., 1994). If that is the case in humans, and the evidence strongly suggests that it is, then none of the earlier kinetic studies validly describe the situation in chronic abusers.

Nor has it ever been determined whether results from individuals can be extrapolated to the population at large. Extrapolation from animal experiments is equally difficult, since half-life and elimination clearance differ markedly from species to species. In the rat, for instance, the plasma half-life is only 18 minutes. The half-life of inhaled cocaine in ewes, which are often used as an experimental model for maternal/fetal distribution studies, is only 1.6 ± 0.5 minutes and 3.4 ± 0.9 minutes when injected intravenously (Burchfield et al., 1991).

It had generally been believed that only a very small percentage of cocaine was excreted unchanged in the urine, and that it was only detectable there for three to six hours (Jatlow, 1988). More recent studies suggest that is not the case. In one study, 104 postmortem urine specimens testing positive for cocaine metabolite (either benzoylecgonine or ecgonine methyl ester, or both) were reanalyzed for cocaine. Cocaine was detected in 66% of the specimens in concentrations ranging from 0.07–78 mg/L. When benzoylecgonine concentration was greater than 2.0 mg/L, cocaine was detected in 83% of the specimens, but the detection rate dropped to only 30% when benzoylecgonine levels were under 2.0 mg/L (Ramcharitar et al., 1995).

More than a dozen different breakdown products have been identified, but the other metabolites are rarely measured. Most laboratories use commercial immunoassays designed to detect only benzoylecgonine, so other metabolites remain undetected and unstudied. However, techniques now exist for the simultaneous measurement of cocaine, cocaethylene, their metabolites, and even pyrolysis products, using gas chromatography-mass spectrometry (Cone et al., 1994). More information may become available in the near future, but for the moment, at least in humans, it appears that there are only two important cocaine metabolites: benzoylecgonine and ecgonine methyl ester. There is little evidence that either exerts toxicity in its own right.

1.6.1.2   Benzoylecgonine and ecgonine methyl ester

In the absence of alcohol, cocaine's principal metabolites are benzoylecgonine (BEG) and ecgonine methyl ester (EME). Estimates of the proportions formed have varied widely. In one study of drug-free volunteers given 20 mg of cocaine intravenously, 15–34% of a given dose appeared in the urine as BEG (Cone et al., 1989), but others have reported that 85–90% is converted to BEG (Jatlow, 1988).

Neither of the metabolites is believed to be pharmacologically active, although the results of *in vitro* studies suggest that benzoylecgonine is inherently cytotoxic (Lin and Leskawa, 1994), and that it may cause spasm of coronary and/or cerebral vessels (Erzouki et al., 1993; Covert et al., 1994; Schreiber et al., 1994). Cocaine-related spasm is thought to be the result of its adrenergic effects. Even though BEG is not an adrenergic agent, the possibility exists that it could cause spasm via some other mechanism, such as altering calcium flux and calcium channel regulation (Madden et al., 1995). The notion of BEG-induced vasospasm is particularly attractive because of its long half-life; many patients with stroke or myocardial infarction only develop symptoms hours after drug use, at a time when only benzoylecgonine is detectable. In spite of animal and *in vitro* studies which suggest that BEG might be the culprit, clinical support for the idea is entirely lacking.

Depending on the circumstances, variable amounts of each metabolite may be detected. Some researchers even question whether EME is a major *in vivo* metabolite of cocaine in humans (Isenschmid et al., 1992). The traditional view held that cocaine spontaneously hydrolyzed to BEG, while EME formation required enzymatic hydrolysis by hepatic esterases and plasma cholinesterase (Stewart et al., 1979; Stewart et al., 1977; Inaba et al., 1978). The most recent data suggests that the situation is much more complex (Brzezinski et al., 1994).

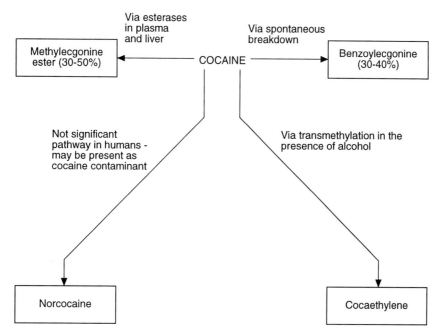

Figure 1.6.1.2 Metabolic fate of cocaine. In the absence of alcohol, benzoylecgonine (BEG) and ecgonine methyl ester (EME) are cocaine's principal breakdown products. Cocaine is converted to EME by hepatic esterases and by plasma cholinesterase. Benzoylecgonine forms spontaneously. In cases of cholinesterase deficiency, more cocaine is shunted via the BEG route. There is very little evidence, however, that cholinesterase levels affect toxicity.

The half-life of both BEG and EME is much longer than the half-life of cocaine. EME has a half-life of about four hours, while BEG's is closer to six hours. As a consequence, BEG is likely to still be detectable in plasma 24 hours after ingestion (Javaid et al., 1983; Jatlow, 1987). How much will be detected, and in what proportions EME and BEG will be present, seems to depend on how the cocaine is administered. When 2 mg/kg doses of cocaine were given intranasally to individuals with no prior history of cocaine use, 60 minutes later, cocaine levels averaged 295 ng/mL, the EME level was 209 ng/mL, and the BEG level was 621 ng/mL (Brogan et al., 1992; Farré et al., 1993). Other researchers have obtained conflicting results, finding that after cocaine was smoked or given intravenously, EME levels amounted to less than 5% of BEG levels (Isenschmid et al., 1992). Still others have found that BEG concentrations were 50% higher after intranasal intake, than after smoking or intravenous routes of administration (Cone et al., 1994).

BEG is stable in frozen specimens, but cocaine is not (Dugan et al., 1994), and the amount of BEG and EME measured in urine will vary depending on how the specimen is stored. EME is stable for as long as three years in urine samples with pH ranges of 3–5, but at pH 9, 100% will have disappeared in 30 days (Vasiliades, 1993). Under alkaline conditions EME will hydrolyze to form ecgonine, and thus will not be detected (Vasiliades, 1993).

Most postmortem urine samples contain more BEG than EME (Howell and Ezell, 1990; Clark and Hajar, 1987), but changes in sample acidity can also lead to the measurement of inaccurately high ratios of EME/BEG in postmortem blood samples. During life, EME circulating in the blood is rapidly converted to ecgonine and levels remain quite low. But after death, anaerobic metabolism continues and the pH of serum gets progressively lower. As a result, conditions are not suitable for spontaneous hydrolysis and the conversion of cocaine to BEG, and EME to ecgonine, stops. At the same time, enzyme-mediated hydrolysis continues, albeit at a slower rate, and EME continues to accumulate. The resultant high EME levels and relatively low BEG levels will give a false impression of the situation before death (Logan and Peterson, 1994).

In a recent study of postmortem urine specimens screening positive for either EME or BEG, 90% were positive for both, 4% were positive for EME and negative for BEG, and 7% were positive for BE and negative for EME. Screening for BE with an immunoassay (at the HHS recommended cutoff of 300 ng/mL) would have identified 96% of the cocaine users, while screening for EME with gas chromatography (50 ng/mL cutoff) would have been 93%.

Spontaneous hydrolysis of cocaine to BEG certainly accounts for much of the BEG detected in blood or urine, but it is now clear that humans possess two distinct hepatic cocaine carboxylesterases; one catalyzes the conversion of cocaine to EME, the other catalyzes the hydrolysis of cocaine's methyl ester group to form BEG and, in the presence of alcohol, this same enzyme has the ability to transesterify cocaine to form cocaethylene (Dean et al., 1991; Brzezinski et al., 1994; Boyer and Petersen, 1992). What remains to be determined are the relative roles played by carboxylesterase systems, by plasma cholinesterase, and by spontaneous hydrolysis.

The role of plasma cholinesterase has been the subject of much speculation, particularly in regard to EME production. If cocaine is given intravenously to pigs treated with plasma cholinesterase inhibitors, the amount of EME produced is not affected (Kambam et al., 1992). In that same model, if the liver is also removed, then substantial decreases in EME production occur, but production is not entirely eliminated (Kambam et al., 1994). This means that, in the pig at least, other enzymes, in other organs, besides those located in the liver and the plasma, are involved in EME production. Data from the hepectomized pig suggests that other sites must also be involved in the conversion of cocaine to BEG, since BEG levels rise after hepatectomy and stay elevated even after plasma cholinesterase inhibitors are given (Kambam et al., 1994). The extrahepatic transformation of cocaine is also evident in dogs, where hepatic blood flow amounts to only about one-quarter of total body clearance (Garrett et al., 1994).

A number of authors have suggested that low plasma cholinesterase levels might explain many cases of cocaine toxicity (Jatlow et al., 1979; Handler et al., 1991; Kump et al., 1994; Morishima et al., 1993; Om et al., 1993; Hoffman et al., 1990; Konkol et al., 1994), but there is very little evidence to support this notion. Normal plasma cholinesterase levels vary tremendously from individual to individual, and are subject to change depending on the physiologic state of the individual. In one study purporting to show that "complications" were more common in individuals with low PCE levels, some of the individuals with "complications" had higher PCE levels than controls (Om et al., 1993). A more recent study compared plasma pseudocholinesterase levels in cocaine abusers and controls and found no differences. Clearly, individuals with genetic defects and atypical forms of cholinesterase, as indicated by low dibucaine numbers, will metabolize cocaine more slowly than individuals without that defect. This does not prove that they are more likely to become toxic, even though one cocaine abuser believed strongly enough in this relationship to take an organophosphate insecticide in hopes of prolonging his high (Herschman and Aaron, 1991).

Arguments that decreased cholinesterase activity can result in prolonged elevation of cocaine levels and increased toxicity are weakened by the absence of evidence that the occurrence of any particular complication of chronic cocaine use is dose-related (Smart and Anglin, 1986; Karch and Stephens, 1991; Karch, 1995). Nor would a cholineserase deficiency explain episodes of acute toxicity. Cocaine is only partially metabolized by plasma cholinesterases; substantial amounts are metabolized in the liver. Even if plasma cholinesterase activity were completely absent, cocaine metabolism would continue, only more slowly. Massive cocaine overdose can certainly be fatal, but it is hard to see how a blood level of 40,000 ng/mL would be any more toxic than a blood level of 30,000 ng/mL, and levels that high have been measured in individuals who were devoid of symptoms (Howell and Ezell, 1990). The phenomena of tolerance could render either level harmless. Unfortunately, there is no way to access tolerance at autopsy.

1.6.1.3   Cocaethylene

Other cocaine metabolites are potentially toxic. One of them, cocaethylene, is unique in that it is produced only in the presence of ethyl alcohol (De La Torre et al., 1991; Hearn et al., 1991; Jatlow et al., 1991). Cocaethylene is synthesized in the liver by a transesterification reaction which adds an extra methyl group to cocaine. The reaction occurs in the microsomal fraction, and is catalyzed by a non-specific carboxylesterase that not only catalyzes the transesterification of cocaine to cocaethylene, but also converts cocaine to benzoylecgonine (Brzenzinski et al., 1994).

Evidence also exists for a second route of cocaethylene formation. The enzyme fatty acid ethyl ester synthetase, which normally esterifies ethanol with fatty acids, may also use cocaine as a substrate and produce cocaethylene (Heith et al., 1995). This enzyme has a wider distribution in the body than does the non-specific carboxylesterase, but its relative role in cocaethylene production is not known.

Homogenates of human liver are capable of transesterifying cocaine with other molecules, such as n-propyl alcohol (Bailey, 1995). In some experimental animals, there is evidence for the presence of similar esterases in the kidney (Boyer and Peterson, 1992), but the only human tissue capable of producing cocaethylene appears to be the liver (Bailey, 1994).

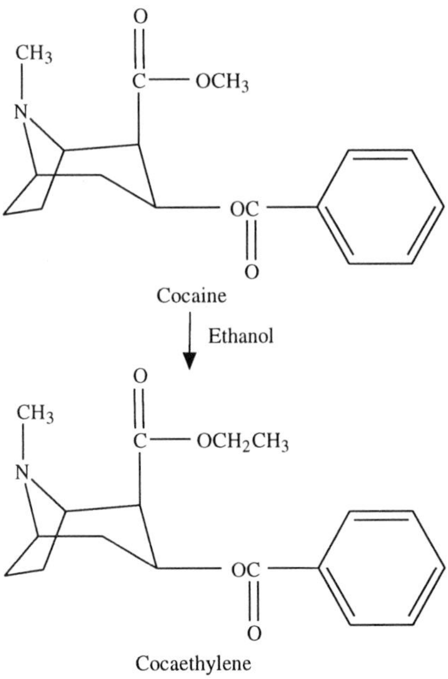

Figure 1.6.1.3   Cocaethylene formation. Cocaethylene is formed in the liver by a transesterification reaction which adds an extra methyl group to cocaine. Cocaethylene has a much longer half-life than cocaine, but cocaethylene binds to the dopamine receptor with the same affinity as cocaine.

Animals treated with cocaine and alcohol convert 2–10% of a given dose of cocaine to cocaethylene (Dean et al., 1992; Miller et al., 1994; Levine and Tebbett, 1994) and other, potentially toxic, N-demethylated cocaine metabolites (Dean et al., 1992); however, there may be a greater degree of conversion in humans. Once formed, cocaethylene can be further metabolized to benzoylecgonine, norcocaethylene, and ecgonine methyl ester (Cone et al., 1994).

Because cocaethylene is a nonpolar molecule, it crosses the blood-brain barrier easily, and its concentration in the brain equals that of cocaine. In 1979, traces of cocaethylene were first detected in the urine of an individual using both alcohol and cocaine. The observation was repeated again five years later, but the possibility that cocaethylene itself might be metabolically active was not considered. Newer studies suggest that not only does cocaethylene contribute to the psychological effects produced by cocaine, it may also contribute to the toxicity (Foltin and Fischman, 1989; Lynn et al., 1991; Farré et al., 1990; Woodward et al., 1991). In animal studies, cocaethylene is just as effective at blocking dopamine reuptake as cocaine, and it produces the same behavioral alterations (Jatlow et al., 1991; Hearn et al., 1991).

In one autopsy study, 231 cases of cocaine-associated death were retrospectively analyzed, and 124 were found to have both alcohol and cocaine in their blood. More than half (62%) of those with alcohol and cocaine in their blood also had easily detectable levels of cocaethylene in their blood, livers, and brains. Those without alcohol, or with very low alcohol levels, had no cocaethylene present (Hearn et al., 1991). In a second autopsy study, postmortem blood measurements were made in a series of seven patients whose blood alcohols ranged from 20 to 190 mg/dL. Blood cocaine levels were between 34 to 4,370 ng/mL, while cocaethylene levels were between 73 and 1,447 ng/mL. In half the cases, the cocaethylene level was higher than the cocaine level (Jatlow et al., 1991). In contrast to the findings in animal studies, mean cocaethylene levels in a series of 10 trauma patients, measured at the time of hospital admission, were at least half as high as the cocaine levels (cocaine = 138 ng/mL with cocaethylene = 86 ng/mL) (Bailey, 1993).

The relationship between cocaine and alcohol has now been evaluated in several studies using healthy volunteers (Farré et al., 1993; McCance-Katz et al., 1993). In the first studies, individuals with a history of recreational drug use were given cocaine alone or a drink containing 1 gm/kg of vodka followed by a 100-mg dose of cocaine hydrochloride (snorted). Cocaethylene was detected only in the samples from the alcohol-pretreated group. The peak cocaethylene concentration was 55 ± 8 ng/mL, and serial blood measurements were consistent with a half-life of 109 minutes. Norcocaine levels were also much higher in the group that had been pretreated with alcohol. An observation difficult to explain was that the alcohol group had higher peak cocaine levels than those who had used cocaine alone (352 ± 111 ng/mL vs. 258 ± 115 ng/mL). It may be that spontaneous conversion to benzoylecgonine, the normal route by which 40% of a given dose of cocaine would be metabolized, is, in some way, inhibited by alcohol-induced pH shifts. With less of a given dose being metabolized to benzoylecgonine, more is available for hepatic metabolism, leading to increased norcocaine formation.

In a different group of patients with clinical signs of cocaine intoxication and positive alcohol screening tests, cocaine concentrations ranged from 50 ng/mL to 4,360 ng/mL, and blood alcohol levels ranged from 0.09 to 0.84 g/dL. The mean cocaethylene level was 710 ng/mL $\pm$ 0.100 (Mash et al., 1991). Cocaethylene does not appear in the bloodstream until 20 to 30 minutes after cocaine and alcohol are ingested (McCance-Katz et al., 1993), so the time of specimen collection may make some difference. In studies using tracer quantities of C^{11}-labeled cocaine, no cocaethylene could be detected until ten minutes after the simultaneous administration of alcohol and intravenous cocaine (Fowler et al., 1992).

In another controlled, double-blind experiment, healthy human volunteers were treated with various combinations of 1 g/kg of ethanol and 100 mg of intranasal cocaine. As might be expected, alcohol alone impaired psychomotor performance, but cocaine alone produced, in addition to euphoria, improved reaction times. When the alcohol and cocaine were taken together, the degree of cocaine euphoria increased, but the psychomotor impairment induced by the alcohol was substantially reversed in the presence of cocaine. Heart rate and blood pressure increases were greater when cocaine was taken with alcohol than when it was taken alone. Plasma cocaine levels were higher when cocaine was taken with alcohol (225 ng/mL vs. 344 ng/mL), and norcocaine levels doubled (1.5 ng/mL vs. 3.5 ng/mL); however, alcohol ingestion had no measurable effect on benzoylecgonine or ecgonine methyl ester production. The peak plasma cocaethylene level was 53 ± 12 ng/mL, or roughly 15% of the parent compound level (Farré et al., 1993).

In a different human study utilizing nearly the same doses of cocaine and alcohol, cocaethylene was first detected in plasma 30 minutes after the cocaine was given. The initial concentration was 10 ng/mL and the peak level was 62 ng/mL, reached at two hours. The peak cocaethylene level was 20% of the peak cocaine level, but both levels were equal after six to seven hours had elapsed (McCance-Katz et al., 1993). The calculated half-life in this study was 148 ± 15 minutes, which is generally in agreement with earlier measurements. Cocaine and preformed cocaethylene have been given to volunteers in controlled studies (Perez-Reyes et al., 1994). With the volunteers acting as their own controls, cocaethyelene had a longer elimination half-life (1.68 vs. .67 hours), but, on a weight for weight basis, produced less of a "high."

The detection of cocaethylene in tissue, blood, or hair samples is not, as previously believed, proof positive of cocaine use. It is, instead, proof of exposure. When ethanol is used for refluxing, cocaethylene can be generated as a by-product during the extraction of cocaine from coca leaf (Turner et al., 1979). Cocaethylene can be found in street samples of illicitly prepared drug and even in samples of pharmaceutical grade cocaine (Casale and Moore, 1994).

Finally, the pharmacologic properties of cocaethylene and cocaine, though largely similar, do differ in some important aspects. The results of *in vitro* studies suggest that cocaethylene is a more potent blocker of the inward sodium channel than the parent compound (Xu et al., 1994). If that is the case in humans, then high levels of cocaethylene would be more likely to produce cardiac conduction abnormalities than would high levels of cocaine. There is also evidence that cocaethylene decreases myofilament Ca^{2+} responsiveness and may produce more severe negative inotropic effects than cocaine (Qiu and Morgan, 1993).

1.6.1.4   Anhydroecgonine methyl ester (methylecgonidine)

Another metabolite of forensic interest, anhydroecgonine methyl ester (AEME), is a pyrolysis product of cocaine. It is excreted only in the urine of crack smokers. Its identification may be of some forensic significance (Jacob et al., 1990), but its pharmacology has never been studied. Structurally, AEME shares features with other chemicals, such as anatoxin and arecoline that have cholinergic properties, raising the possibility that this compound may be toxic in its own right, and studies in animals confirm that AEME inhalation decreases airway conductance (Chen et al., 1995). However, the preliminary data suggest that AEME-induced bronchoconstriction has more to do with its physical properties than with any cholinergic effect.

1.6.1.5   Norcocaine

In animals, cytochrome P450 and flavin adenine dinucleotide containing monooxygenase metabolize cocaine to norcocaine. Further enzymatic breakdown yields N-hydroxynorcocaine and norcocaine nitroxide (Shuster et al.,

1983). Norcocaine nitroxide, once thought to be a highly reactive free radical, is now known to be stable. However, further oxidation to the norcocaine nitrosodium ion produces a compound that is highly reactive with glutathione. If glutathione stores fall below a certain level, lipid peroxidation is unopposed and cocaine metabolites bind to hepatic proteins, eventually leading to cell death (Evans, 1983; Kloss et al., 1984). In humans, only minute amounts of cocaine undergo oxidative metabolism, which may explain why liver lesions have only rarely been reported in cocaine users. The higher levels of norcocaine seen when alcohol use is combined with cocaine are yet to be explained.

1.6.2 Fetal metabolism

The human placenta has cholinesterase activity and metabolizes cocaine, possibly affording the fetus a degree of protection (Roe et al., 1990). Nonetheless, in animal studies, newborns develop higher blood levels than adults receiving the same dose, and their plasma and tissue levels decline more slowly than adults (Morishima et al., 1990). Infants born to cocaine-using mothers may have persistently elevated cocaine levels for days (Chasnoff et al., 1986). However, a causal relationship between persistently elevated levels and the occasional case reports of perinatal stroke and intraventricular hemorrhage in the newborn has not been demonstrated.

The fetus handles BEG differently than the mother. Since BEG is excreted primarily in the urine, and since both renal blood flow and glomerular filtration rate double in pregnant women, mothers clear metabolite much more quickly than their fetus, but there have been too few studies to make any further generalizations. In one study where BEG concentrations were measured in mother and child shortly after birth, the mother's BEG concentration was nearly 20–30 times that of the fetus (12.2 ng/mL vs. 240 ng/mL and 10.8 ng/mL vs. 378 ng/mL) (Meeker and Reynolds, 1990). Though unproven, the possibility also exists that the enzymatic pathway for conversion of cocaine to methylecgonine may not be fully developed in the newborn.

References

Bailey, D. (1993). Plasma cocaethylene concentrations in patients treated in the emergency room or trauma unit. Am J Clin Pathol, 99: 123–127.

Bailey, D. (1994). Studies of cocaethylene (ethylcocaine) formation by human tissues *in vitro*. J Analyt Toxicol, 18: 13–15.

Bailey, D. (1995). Cocapropylene (propylcocaine) formation by human liver *in vitro*. J Analyt Toxicol, 19: 1–5.

Barnett, G., Hawks, R., and Resbick, R. (1981). Cocaine pharmacokinetics in humans. J Ethnopharm, 3: 353–366.

Boyer, C. and Petersen, D. (1992). Enzymatic basis for the transesterification of cocaine in the presence of ethanol: evidence for the participation of microsomal carboxylesterases. J Pharm Exp Ther, 260: 939–946.

Brogan, W., Lange, R., Glamann, D. et al. (1992). Recurrent coronary vasoconstriction caused by intranasal cocaine — possible role for metabolites. Ann Intern Med, 116(7): 556–561.

Brzezinski, M., Abraham, T., Stone, C. et al. (1994). Purification and characterization of a human liver cocaine carboxylesterase that catalyzes the production of benzoylecgonine and the formation of cocaethylene from alcohol and cocaine. Biochem Pharm, 48(9): 1747–1755.

Burchfield, D., Abrams, R., Miller, R., and DeVane, C. (1991). Inhalational administration of cocaine in sheep. Life Sci, 48(22): 2129–2136.

Casale, J. and Moore, J. (1994). An in-depth analysis of pharmaceutical cocaine: cocaethylene and other impurities. J Pharm Sci, 83(8): 1186.

Chasnoff, I., Bussey, M., Savich, R., and Stack, C. (1986). Perinatal cerebral infarction and maternal cocaine use. J Pediatrics, 108: 456–459.

Chen, L., Graefe, J., Shojale, J. et al. (1995). Pulmonary effects of cocaine pyrolysis product, methylecgonidine in guinea pigs. Life Sci, 56: 7–12.

Chow, M., Ambre, J., Ruo, T. et al. (1985). Kinetics of cocaine distribution, elimination, and chronotropic effects. Clin Pharmacol Ther, 38: 318–324.

Clark, D. and Hajar, T. (1987). Detection and confirmation of cocaine use by chromatographic analysis for methylecgonine in urine. Clin Chem, 33: 118–119.

Cone, E., Menchen, S., Paul, B. et al. (1989). Validity testing of commercial urine cocaine metabolite assays: 1. Assay detection times, individual excretion patterns, and kinetics after cocaine administration in humans. J Forensic Sci, 34: 15–31.

Cone, E., Hillsgrove, M., and Darwin, W. (1994). Simultaneous measurement of cocaine, cocaethylene, their metabolites, and "crack" pyrolysis products by gas chromatography. Clin Chem, 40(7): 1299–1305.

Covert, R., Schreiber, M., Tebbett, I. et al. (1994). Hemodynamic and cerebral blood flow effects of cocaine, cocaethylene and benzoylecgonine in conscious and anesthetized fetal lambs. J Pharm and Exp Ther, 270: 118–126.

Dean, R., Christian, C., Samplle, R. et al. (1991). Human liver cocaine esterases: ethanol-mediated formation of ethylcocaine. FASEB J, 5: 2735–2739.

Dean, R., Harper, N., Dumaual, N. et al. (1992a). Effects of ethanol on cocaine metabolism: formation of cocaethylene and norcocaethylene. Tox and Appl Pharm, 117: 1–8.

De La Torre, R., Farré, M., Ortuño, J. et al. (1991). The relevance of urinary cocaethylene as a metabolite of cocaine under the simultaneous administration of alcohol. J Analyt Toxicol, 15: 223.

Dugan, S., Bogema, S., Schwartz, R. et al. (1994). Stability of drugs of abuse in urine samples stored at –20°C. J Analyt Toxicol, 18: 391–393.

Erzouki, H., Baum, I., Goldberg, S. et al. (1993). Comparison of the effects of cocaine and its metabolites on cardiovascular function in anesthetized rats. J Cardiovasc Pharm, 22: 557–563.

Estevez, V., Ho, B., and Englert, L. (1979). Metabolism correlates of cocaine-induced sterotypy in rats. Pharmacol Biochem Behav, 10: 267–271.

Evans, M. A. (1983). Role of protein binding in cocaine-induced hepatic necrosis. J Pharmacol Exp Ther, 224(1): 73–79.

Farré, M., Llorente, M., Ugena, X. et al. (1990). Interaction of cocaine with ethanol. Problems of drug dependence 1990: Proceedings of the 52nd Annual Scientific Meeting of the Committee on Problems of Drug Dependence, Inc., Harris, L. (Ed.), National Institute on Drug Abuse, Rockville, MD, 570–571.

Farré, M., De La Torre, R., Llorente, M. et al. (1993). Alcohol and cocaine interactions in humans. J Pharm Exp Ther, 266(3): 1364–1373.

Foltin, R. and Fischman, M. (1989). Ethanol and cocaine interactions in humans: cardiovascular consequences. Pharmacol Biochem Behavior, 31(4): 877–883.

Fowler, J., Volkow, N., Logan, J. et al. (1992). Alcohol intoxication does not change (^{11}C)Cocaine pharmacokinetics in human brain and heart. Synapse, 12: 228–235.

Garrett, E., Eberst, K., and Maruhn, D. (1994). Prediction of stability in pharmaceutical preparations. XXI: The analysis and kinetics of hydrolysis of a cocaine degradation product, ecgonine methyl ester, plus the pharmacokinetics of cocaine in the dog. J Pharm Sci, 83(2): 269–272.

Gossop, M., Burton, M., and Molla, M. (1994). High dose cocaine use in Bolivia and Peru. Bull Narc, XLVI(2): 25–34.

Handler, A., Kistin, N., Davis, F. et al. (1991). Cocaine use during pregnancy: perinatal outcomes. Am J Epidemol, 2: 221–223.

Hearn, W. L., Flynn, D., Hime, D. et al. (1991). Cocaethylene — a unique cocaine metabolite displays high affinity for the dopamine transporter. J Neurochem, 56(2): 698–701.

Heith, A., Morse, C., Tsujita, T. et al. (1995). Fatty acid ethyl ester synthatase catalyzes the esterification of ethanol to cocaine. Biochem Biophys Res Comm, 208: 549–554.

Herschman, Z. and Aaron, C. (1991). Prolongation of cocaine effect. Anesthesiology, 74(3): 631–632.

Higgins, S., Bickel, W., Hughes, J. et al. (1991). Behavioral and cardiovascular effects of cocaine and alcohol combination in humans. NIDA Research Monograph, 105: 501.

Hoffman, R., Henry, G., Weisman, R. et al. (1990). Association between plasma cholinesterase activity and cocaine toxicity. Ann Emerg Med, 19(4): 467.

Howell, S. and Ezell, A. (1990). An example of cocaine tolerance in a gunshot wound fatality. J Analyt Toxicol, 14: 60–61.

Inaba, T., Stewart, D., and Kalow, W. (1978). Metabolism of cocaine in man. Clin Pharmacol Ther, 23: 547–552.

Isenschmid, D., Fischman, M., Foltin, R., and Caplan, H. (1992). Concentration of cocaine and metabolites in plasma of humans following intravenous administration and smoking of cocaine. J Analyt Toxicol, 16: 311–314.

Isenschmid, D., Levine, B., and Caplan, Y. (1992). The role of ecgonine methyl ester in the interpretation of cocaine concentrations in postmortem blood. J Anal Toxicol, 16: 319–324.

Jacob, P., Lewis, E., Elias-Baker, B., and Jones, R. (1990). A pyrolysis product, anhydroecgonine methyl ester (methylecgonidine), is in the urine of cocaine smokers. J Anal Toxic, 14(6): 353–357.

Jatlow, P., Barash, P.,Van Dyke, C. et al. (1979). Cocaine and succinylcholine sensitivity: a new caution. Anesth Analg, 58: 235–238.

Jatlow, P. (1987). Drug abuse profile: cocaine. Clin Chem, 33(11B): 66B–71B.

Jatlow, P. (1988). Cocaine: analysis, pharmacokinetics, and metabolic disposition. Yale J Biol and Med, 61: 105–113.

Jatlow, P., Elsworth, J. D., Bradberry, C. et al. (1991). Cocaethylene — a neuropharmacologically active metabolite associated with concurrent cocaine-ethanol ingestion. Life Sci, 48(18): 1787–1794.

Javaid, J., Musa, M., Fischman, M. et al. (1983). Kinetics of cocaine in humans after intravenous and intranasal administration. Biopharm Drug Dispos, 4: 9–18.

Kambam, J., Naukam, B., Paris, W. et al. (1990). Inhibition of pseudocholinesterase (PCHE) activity protects from cocaine-induced cardiorespiratory toxicity (CICT) in rats. Anesthesiology, 73(3A): A581.

Kambam, J., Mets, B., Hickman, R. et al. (1992). The effects of inhibition of plasma cholinesterase and hepatic microsomal enzyme activity on cocaine, benzoylecgonine, ecgonine methyl ester, and norcocaine blood levels in pigs. J. Lab Clin Med, 120(2): 323–328.

Kambam, J., Franks, J., Mets, B. et al. (1994). The effect of hepatectomy and plasma cholinesterase inhibition on cocaine metabolism and cardiovascular responses in pigs. J Lab Clin Med, 124(5): 715–722.

Karch, S. (1996). Cardiac arrest in cocaine users. Am J Emerg Med, in press.

Karch, S. and Stephens, B. (1991). When is cocaine the cause of death? [editorial]. Am J Forensic Med Pathol, 12(1): 1–2.

Kloss, M., Rosen, G., and Rauckman, E. (1984). Cocaine-mediated hepatotoxicity: a critical review. Biochem Pharmacol, 33: 169–173.

Konkol, R., Murphey, L., Ferriero, D. et al. (1994). Cocaine metabolites in the neonate: potential for toxicity. J Child Neurol, 9: 242–248.

Kumor, K., Sherer, M., Thompson, L. et al. (1988). Lack of cardiovascular tolerance during intravenous cocaine infusions in human volunteers. Life Sci, 42: 2063–2071.

Kump, D., Matulka, R., Edinboro, L. et al. (1994). Disposition of cocaine and norcocaine in blood and tissues of B6C3F1 mice. J Analyt Toxicol, 18: 342–345.

Levine, B. and Tebbett, I. (1994). Cocaine pharmacokinetics in ethanol-pretreated rats. Drug Metab Disp, 22(3): 498–500.

Lin, Y. and Leskawa, K. (1994). Cytotoxicity of the cocaine metabolite benzoylecgonine. Brain Res, 643: 108–114.

Logan, B. and Peterson, K. (1994). The origin and significance of ecgonine methyl ester in blood samples. J Analyt Toxicol, 18: 124–125.

McCance-Katz, E., Price, L., McDougle, C. et al. (1993). Concurrent cocaine-ethanol ingestion in humans: pharmacology, physiology, behavior, and the role of cocaethylene. Psychopharmacology, 111: 39–46.

Mash, D., Ciarleglio, A., Tanis, D. et al. (1991). Toxicology screens for cocaethylene in emergency department and trauma admissions associated with cocaine intoxication. In Problems of drug dependence 1991: Proceedings of the 53rd Annual Scientific Meeting of the Committee on Problems of Drug Dependence, Inc. National Institute on Drug Abuse Monograph Series, Rockland, MD.

Meeker, J. E. and Reynolds, P. C. (1990). Fetal and newborn death associated with maternal cocaine use. J Anal Toxicol, 14(6): 379–382.

Miller, S., Salo, A., Boggan, W. et al. (1994). Determination of plasma cocaine and ethylcocaine (cocaethylene) in mice using gas chromatography-mass spectrometry and deuterated internal standards. J Chromatography B, 656: 335–341.

Morishima, H., Khan, K., Hara, T. et al. (1990). Age-related cocaine uptake in rats. Anesthesiology, 73(3A): A929.

Morishima, H., Masoka, T., Tsuji, A. et al. (1993). Pregnancy decreases the threshold for cocaine induced convulsions in the rat. J Lab Clin Med, 122(6): 748–756.

Nahas, G., Latour, C., Sandouk, P., and Arnaoudov, P. (1995). Cardiovascular tolerance and plasma cocaine levels after chronic administration of the alkaloid. Presented at the College of Problems of Drug Dependency, 57th Annual Meeting, Scottsdale, AZ, June 11, 1995.

Om, A., Ellahham, S., Ornato, J. et al. (1993). Medical complications of cocaine: possible relationship to low plasma cholinesterase enzyme. Am Heart J, 125: 1114–1117.

Perez-Reyes, M., Jeffcoat, A., Meyers, M. et al. (1994). Comparison in humans of the potency and pharmacokinetics of intravenously injected cocaethylene and cocaine. Psychopharm, 116: 428–432.

Pettit, H. and Pettit, A. (1994). Disposition of cocaine in blood and brain after a single pretreatment. Brain Res, 651: 261–268.

Pirwitz, M., Willard, J., Landau, C., et al. (1995). Influence of cocaine, ethanol, or their combination on epicardial coronary arterial dimensions in humans. Arch Intern Med, 155(11): 1186–1191.

Qiu, Z. and Morgan, J. (1993). Differential effects of cocaine and cocaethylene on intracellular Ca^{2+} and myocardial contraction in cardiac myocytes. Br J Pharmacol, 109: 293–298.

Ramcharitar, V., Levine, B., and Smialek, J. (1995). Benzoylecgonine and ecgonine methyl ester concentrations in urine specimens. J Forensic Sci, 40(1): 99–101.

Robinson, S., Enters, E., Jackson, G. et al. (1994). Maternal and fetal brain and plasma levels of cocaine and benzoylecgonine after acute or chronic maternal intravenous administration of cocaine. J Pharm Exp Ther, 271(3): 1234–1239.

Roe, D., Little, B., Bawdon, R., and Gilstrap, L. (1990). Metabolism of cocaine by human placentas — implications for fetal exposure. Am J Obstet Gyneco, 163(3): 715–718.

Schenker, S., Yang, Y., Johnson, R. et al. (1993). The transfer of cocaine and its metabolites across the term human placenta. Clin Pharm Ther, 53: 329–339.

Schreiber, M., Madden, J., Covert, R. et al. (1994). Effects of cocaine, benzoylecgonine, and cocaine metabolites on cannulated pressurized fetal sheep cerebral arteries. J Appl Physiol, 77(2): 834–839.

Shuster, L., Casey, E., and Welankiwar, S. (1983). Metabolism of cocaine and norcocaine to N-hydroxynorcocaine. Biochem Pharmacol, 32: 3045–3051.

Smart, R. and Anglin, R. (1986). Do we know the lethal dose of cocaine? J Forensic Sci, 32(2): 303–312.

Stewart, D., Inaba, T., Tang, B., and Kalow, W. (1977). Hydrolysis of cocaine in human plasma by cholinesterase. Life Sci, 20: 1557–1564.

Stewart, D., Inaba, T., Lucassen, M., and Kaklow, W. (1979). Cocaine metabolism: cocaine and norcocaine hydrolysis by liver and serum esterases. Clin Pharm Ther, 25: 464–468.

Turner, C., Ma, C., and ElSohly, M. (1979). Constituents in erythroxylon coca I: gas chromatographic analysis of coca from three locations in Peru. Bull Narc, 31: 71–76.

Vasiliades, J. (1993). Long-term stability of ecgonine methyl ester in urine. J Analyt Toxicol, 17: 253.

Weiss, R. and Gawin, F. (1988). Protracted elimination of cocaine metabolites in long-term, high-dose cocaine abusers. Am J Med, 85: 879–880.

Woodward, J., Mansbach, R., Carroll, F., and Balster, R. (1991). Cocaethylene inhibits dopamine uptake and produces cocaine-like actions in drug discrimination studies. Eur J Pharm, 197(2–3): 235–236.

Xu, Y., Crumb, W., and Clarkson, C. (1994). Cocaethylene, a metabolite of cocaine and ethanol, is a potent blocker of cardiac sodium channels. J Pharm Exp Ther, 271: 319–325.

1.7   Interpreting cocaine blood levels

In cases of alcohol intoxication, relatively accurate correlations can be drawn between specific blood levels and corresponding physiological and psychological states. This is not the case with cocaine. Euphoria and mood elevation do correlate well with peak blood levels, but the situation is complicated by the fact that the same level can be associated with either a euphoric or a dysphoric reaction, depending on whether or not blood levels are rising or falling. Both cardiovascular effects and feelings of euphoria decline more rapidly than do cocaine blood levels (Javaid et al., 1978), but the rush experienced by cocaine users follows a different time course than the cardiovascular changes (Kumor, 1988).

It had been thought that blood levels over 5,000 ng/mL would predictably cause seizures, respiratory depression, and death (Wetli and Fishbain, 1985). In fact, that is the case only for novice and intermittent users. Tolerance on a massive scale can occur. One case report described a man who was shot while drinking in a bar. His behavior was normal in all respects. After minimal attempted resuscitation, he was pronounced dead. When he was autopsied several hours later, multiple specimens showed a plasma cocaine of 30 mg/L (Howell and Ezell, 1990). In another case, a young woman with a history of chronic cocaine abuse was found dead at home. Though there was no indication that the woman was a body packer attempting to smuggle drugs, or that she had attempted to overdose, she had a blood level of over 300 mg/L (Peretti et al., 1990). If there is no upper limit for lethal blood concentrations, neither is there a lower limit that is safe. Death and toxicity can occur after the ingestion of trivial amounts of drug and be associated with very low plasma levels (Smart and Anglin, 1986). In a recent autopsy study of 59 cocaine-associated deaths, postmortem blood cocaine levels ranged from 0 to 12.2 mg/L with a mean of 1.2 mg/L. Benzoylecgonine concentrations were from 0.09 to 30.6 mg/L (Goggins et al., 1990). A second study had similar results with levels ranging from 0 to 27.6 mg/dL for cocaine and 0.2 to 30.6 mg/dL for benzoylecgonine (Mckelway et al., 1990). There are several reasons why such a wide range of values has been reported. Tolerance is certainly a factor, since chronic users may consume massive amounts of cocaine without apparent ill effects. Another factor is the unreliability of postmortem blood levels. Changes in postmortem cocaine levels begin immediately after death, occur in an unpredictable fashion, and vary depending on which site the sample is collected from. Cocaine accumulates in some tissues and redistributes after death. One study showed that samples from the subclavian vein were generally lower at autopsy than immediately after death, while samples from the heart and femoral vein were higher. In some instances the increases were over 200% (Hearn et al., 1991). Apparently, the release of cocaine from tissue stores more than compensates for the breakdown due to hydrolysis. Unfortunately, the change is inconsistent. In Hearn's study, half the samples of heart blood had higher levels immediately after death and half the samples had lower levels.

Perhaps the most important reason why cocaine levels cannot be used to explain the cause of death is that cocaine-associated sudden death is not dose-related. Chronic cocaine users may have alterations in their hearts (Karch and Stephens, 1991) and possibly their brains (Murray, 1986) that make arrhythmias more likely (see Section 1.10.2 on cardiovascular effects). Given the presence of appropriate morphologic changes in the heart, in conjunction with a positive history of cocaine abuse, there is nothing unreasonable about declaring cocaine the cause of death even when no cocaine or metabolite is detectable in the bloodstream.

In clinical practice, the experience has generally been that patients with myocardial infarct and stroke have low cocaine blood levels at the time of admission. Infarction may occur hours after the drug was last used (Del Aguila and Rosman, 1990). Why that should be the case has never been made clear. In patients with stroke, the delay may be accounted for by the fact that benzoylecgonine can act as a potent vasoconstrictor, at least *in vitro* (Madden and Powers, 1990). It takes some time for the metabolites to accumulate, and that could account for the delayed onset of vasospasm. The recent discovery of cocaethylene may have solved the riddle. Cocaethylene possesses the same ability to prevent catecholamine reuptake as cocaine, and it has a much longer half-life.

The probability that agitated delirium will occur is not dose-related either. Affected individuals are initially psychotic and ultimately die of respiratory arrest. Victims are invariably found to have only modest plasma levels (Wetli and Fishbain, 1985). The observed low levels are probably explained by the fact that they are measured late in the course of the illness. Cocaine levels are never obtained when the patient is agitated and psychotic (see discussion of agitated delirium in Section 1.10.2.6.5, below).

Other than proving that cocaine has been used, the only useful information to be derived from plasma cocaine and benzoylecgonine levels concerns the time the drug was taken. The ratio of cocaine to benzoylecgonine (BEG) offers a very useful index. Given that cocaine is rapidly converted to benzoylecgonine, and that benzoylecgonine is relatively stable (half-life of 5–6 hours), if there is more cocaine than BEG in the plasma, then that is a very strong indication of very recent ingestion. This relationship can be expressed mathematically. Using the known half-life of cocaine, it is possible to estimate the time when the drug was taken. The utility of this approach is somewhat limited by the fact that the amount taken is almost never known. However, the half-life of BEG is so much longer than the half-life of cocaine that inferences about time of ingestion can be drawn. Even very high levels of cocaine will be below limits of detection after six or seven half-lives (certainly less than 8 hours), but if a significant amount of cocaine was taken, BEG will still be detectable in the plasma more than 24 hours later. At this point, measurements of cocaethylene are problematic. The factors governing its conversion from cocaine are unknown and its presence cannot be relied upon.

Very low cocaine levels are also difficult to interpret. Chronic cocaine users sequester cocaine in deep body stores. Small amounts of this sequestered cocaine can leach back into the bloodstream and saliva for days after the drug was last used (Cone and Weddington, 1989). Failing to take account of this situation can have important forensic consequences. The National Transportation Safety Board's analysis of the only commercial airline crash ever blamed on drug intoxication is a good example. In 1988, Continental Express Flight #2286 crashed on approach to the Durango, Colorado, airport; the crew and several of the passengers were killed. The Board ruled that the probable cause of the accident was error on the part of the first officer flying the approach, in conjunction with "ineffective monitoring" by the captain due to his use of cocaine before the accident. Published reports do not mention the time that elapsed between death and autopsy, but specimens obtained at autopsy, analyzed at two different laboratories, showed benzoylecgonine levels of 22 and 26 nanograms per milliliter, respectively (Anon, 1989). Assuming that at one time the captain had a plasma cocaine level of 1,000 ng/mL, most of which was converted to BEG (Griesemer, 1983), then more than 30 hours must have elapsed between initial ingestion and the time samples were taken at autopsy. Even if the initial level had been several thousand (consistent with intravenous use or "crack" smoking, which seems not to have been the case in this instance), at least 24 hours would have passed between the time he used the drug and the time of the accident. Since it is now known that cocaine blood levels can actually increase after death, the captain's levels may have been even lower (Hearn et al., 1991). The amount of cocaine actually detected was not enough to have produced measurable physiological effects.

On the basis of what is known about cocaine metabolism, particularly in light of animal studies that suggest cocaine is stored in deep compartments (Nahas et al., 1995), it could be argued that a much longer period between the time of cocaine use and death had elapsed. Since unmetabolized cocaine, in addition to BEG, can be detected in the blood, saliva, and urine of chronic users for days after the last dose, attributing significance to very low cocaine levels is not considered to be a good idea.

The National Institute on Drug Abuse has promulgated regulations for drug testing which include "cutoffs." For benzoylecgonine, the cutoff is 150 ng/mL (Anon, 1988); levels below that are reported as negative. Of course, these "cutoffs" were formulated with living patients in mind, but the reasoning is still valid. In the absence of any other information, cocaine or cocaine metabolite levels of less than 50 ng/mL are of only historic interest and should not be taken as proof of recent ingestion. Even when levels are higher than 50 ng/mL, postmortem blood cocaine measurements must be interpreted with great care. In more than half the cases, cocaine blood levels measured at autopsy are likely to be higher than they were at the time of death (Hearn et al., 1991). In the long run, measurements of cocaine and benzoylecgonine in the brain are likely to be of much more value than blood or urine determinations. Levels appear to be more stable after death, and measurement of brain cocaine and benzoylecgonine concentration can also yield valuable historical information about prior use of the drug.

References

Anon (1988). Mandatory guidelines for federal workplace drug testing programs. Issued by the Department of Health and Human Services. Federal Register, 11970–11989.

Anon (1989, July 17). Safety board cites captain's failure to monitor approach as key in crash. Aviation Week and Space Technology, 103–105.

Cone, E. and Weddington, W., Jr. (1989). Prolonged occurrence of cocaine in human saliva and urine after chronic use. J Analyt Toxicol, 13(2): 65–68.

Del Aguila, C. and Rosman, H. (1990). Myocardial infarction during cocaine withdrawal. Ann Intern Med, 112(9): 712.

Goggins, M., Roe, S., and Apple, F. (1990). Cocaine and benzoylecgonine concentrations in postmortem blood and liver. Clin Chem, 36(6): 1023.

Griesmer, E., Liu, Y., Budd, R. et al. (1983). The determination of cocaine and its major metabolite, benzoylecgonine, in postmortem fluids and tissues by computerized gas chromatography/mass spectrometry. J Forensic Sci, 28(4): 894–900.

Hearn, W., Keran, E., Wei, H., and Hime, G. (1991). Site-dependent postmortem changes in blood cocaine concentrations. J Forensic Sci, 36(3), 673–684.

Howell, S. and Ezell, A. (1990). An example of cocaine tolerance in a gunshot wound fatality. J Analyt Toxicol, 14: 60–61.

Javaid, J., Fischman, M., Schuster, C. et al. (1978). Cocaine plasma concentrations: relation to physiological and subjective effects in humans. Science, 202: 227–228.

Karch, S. and Stephens, B. (1991). When is cocaine the cause of death? Am J Forensic Med and Pathol, 12(1): 1–2.

Kumor, K., Sherer, M., Muntaner, C. et al. (1988). Pharmacologic aspects of cocaine rush. National Institute on Drug Abuse Monograph #90, L. S. Harris, (Ed.), 32.

Madden, J. and Powers, R. (1990). Effect of cocaine and cocaine metabolites on cerebral arteries *in vitro*. Life Sci, 47(13): 1109–1114.

Mckelway, R., Vieweg, V., and Westerman, P. (1990). Sudden death from acute cocaine intoxication in Virginia in 1988. Am J Psychiatr, 147(12): 1667–1669.

Murray, G. (1986). Cocaine kindling. JAMA, 256(22): 3094–3095.

Nahas, G., Latour, C., Sandouk, P., and Arnaoudov, P. (1995). Cardiovascular tolerance and plasma cocaine levels after chronic administration of the alkaloid. Presented at the College of Problems of Drug Dependency, 57th Annual Meeting, Scottsdale, AZ, June 11, 1995.

Peretti, F., Isenschmid, S., Levine, B. et al. (1990). Cocaine fatality: an unexplained blood concentration in a fatal overdose. Forensic Sci Int, 48: 135–138.

Smart, R. and Anglin, R. (1986). Do we know the lethal dose of cocaine? J Forensic Sci, 32(2): 303–312.

Wetli, C. and Fishbain, D. (1985). Cocaine-induced psychosis and sudden death in recreational cocaine users. J Forensic Sci, 30(3): 873–888.

1.8   Cocaine tissue disposition

Experimental studies have identified low-affinity cocaine receptors in the heart, lungs, gut and kidney (Calligaro and Elderfrawi, 1987), and testes (Yazigi and Polakoski, 1992). Distribution of (C^{11}) cocaine has been studied in humans using PET scanning (Volkow et al., 1992), and the results generally parallel the results seen in isotopic studies done in animals (Som et al., 1989; Som et al., 1994). Of course, the distribution of drug immediately after it has been taken may not necessarily be the same as its distribution some hours later at autopsy (Prouty and Anderson, 1990), and the utmost caution must be taken when interpreting postmortem tissue levels. Postmortem cocaine blood levels vary, depending on which blood vessel they are obtained from, and may be considerably higher or lower than they were at the time of death. If the collection site is not specified, drawing inferences about either the time of death, or the role of cocaine, becomes a very dubious undertaking. In such cases, all that can be legitimately concluded is whether or not cocaine was used prior to death.

1.8.1   Brain

Brain may be the best matrix for postmortem cocaine determinations. Cocaine blood concentrations change significantly, but unpredictably, after death, and levels measured at autopsy may bear little relationship to levels at the time of death (Spiehler and Reed, 1985). However, cocaine appears to be more stable in the brain's lipid-rich environment, and many toxicologists feel that cocaine brain levels are, indeed, representative of levels at the time of death (Hernandez et al., 1994).

Because cocaine is so lipophilic, it freely crosses the blood-brain barrier (Misra et al., 1975; Nayak et al., 1976; Mule et al., 1976), as does cocaethylene (Hearn et al., 1991b). Receptors with varying affinities for cocaine are found throughout the brain. The region with the highest density of cocaine receptors, which is also the region containing the receptors with the greatest affinity for cocaine, is the striatum. However, when cocaine is taken in behaviorally-active doses, uptake occurs in a number of other, lower affinity sites (Volkow et al., 1995). Lower levels of activity are found in the frontal and occipital cortices (Calligaro and Elderfrawi, 1987). In experimental animals, and in autopsied cases of cocaine-related death, the concentration of cocaine found in the brain is 4–10 times higher than in the plasma when measured from 0.5 to 2 hours after the drug was taken (Benuck et al., 1988; Spiehler and Reed, 1985). Cocaine's principal metabolite, BEG, crosses the blood-brain barrier only with great difficulty (Misra et al., 1975).

In animal studies, peak cocaine concentrations in the brain were also four times higher than in the blood (Nayak et al., 1976), and that is the case in humans as well. In an autopsy study of 37 patients dying of cocaine toxicity, the mean blood cocaine concentration was 4.6 mg/L (range 0.04–31 mg/L), while the mean BEG level was 0.88 mg/L (range 0–7.4 mg/L). The mean concentration of cocaine found in the brain was 13.3 mg/kg (range 0.17–31 mg/kg), and that of benzoylecgonine was 2.9 mg/kg (range 0.1–22 mg/kg). In most cases, the blood/brain ratio was close to 4. In a second study of 14 deaths, where cocaine was only an incidental finding (instances of murder, accidental death, etc.), the average blood/brain ratio was only 2.5 (Spiehler and Reed, 1985). Unmetabolized cocaine can be detected in the CSF for at least 24 hours after use (Rowbotham et al., 1990).

Because BEG does not cross the blood brain barrier, levels of benzoylecgonine in the brain are lower than in the blood for up to two hours

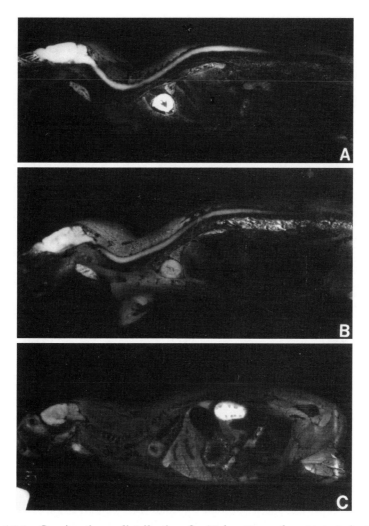

Figure 1.8.1 Cocaine tissue distribution. Sagittal sections of a rat injected with C[14]-labeled cocaine. Sections B and C are from animals pretreated with drugs blocking cocaine uptake. Section A shows intense uptake in the heart, brain, spinal cord, and salivary glands. From J Nuc Med, 30: 831, 1989, with permission.

after ingestion. Essentially all of the benzoylecgonine found in the brain is produced there. Not only does postmortem analysis of brain tissue give a good indication of levels at the time of death, brain levels can also be an indicator of chronic abuse, because extensive prior use is the only way to explain why a deceased person would have more BEG in the brain than in the blood. Testing brain tissue has other advantages as well, because cocaine is stable in frozen brain for months (Spiehler et al., 1985). There are now methods that allow for the simultaneous determination of cocaine, benzoylecgonine, and cocaethylene using solid phase extraction and gas chro-

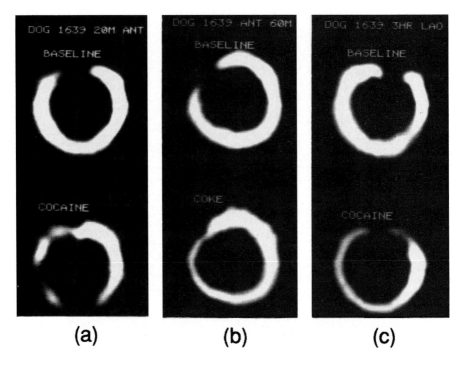

Figure 1.8.2   Decreased myocardial perfusion after treatment with cocaine. Scans are from three different dogs given cocaine intravenously, then injected with 2–4 mCi [201]Ti-chloride. Significant decreases in septal and apical perfusion were evident within five minutes and there was evidence for decreased cardiac output. From Oster et al., J Nuc Med, 32: 1569, 1991, with permission.

matography/ion trap spectrometry with electron impact and full scan analysis (Hernandez et al., 1994).

Brain concentrations in the fetus appear to be lower than in the mother. In the case reported by Mittleman the maternal to fetal brain cocaine ratio was 6.5:1 (Mittleman et al., 1989). A study of fetal demise, including 47 cocaine-related cases where both blood and brain cocaine levels were measured, found that mean blood concentrations of cocaine were 800 ng/mL, while the mean brain concentration of cocaine was 1,100 ng/mg (Morild and Stajic, 1990; Critchley et al., 1988). At present, there is too little data to be sure, but preliminary investigations suggest that cocaethylene levels in the brain are generally equal to cocaine levels (Hearn et al., 1991b).

1.8.2   Heart

PET scanning studies of humans show that there is high uptake in the heart. Within two to three minutes after injection, 2.5% of the administered dose appears in the heart and is then cleared rapidly over the next 10 minutes. When pharmacologic doses of cocaine are given to baboons, the pattern of uptake and washout is similar to that seen in humans. However, inhibition of the norepinephrine transporter persists for some time after the cocaine is gone (Fowler et al., 1994). Although the half-life of cocaine in the baboon heart is 2.5–9 minutes, 78 minutes after cocaine injection, reuptake of norepinephrine was only 48% of normal. This finding suggests that toxic levels of norepinephrine may persist in the heart for some time after the cocaine has been cleared. It may explain the typical patterns of catecholamine-induced necrosis seen in the hearts of some abusers.

In spite of the relatively high uptake by the heart, the rapid rate at which the cocaine is cleared makes it unlikely that high levels will be detected at autopsy. This is borne out by the few measurements that have been reported. In the case described by Poklis et al., where the person died after an intravenous dose of undetermined size, the concentration of cocaine was 6,000 ng/mg in the heart when the cocaine concentration in the blood was only 1,800 ng/mL. Unfortunately, the report does not state how many hours had lapsed between the time of death and the time of autopsy (Poklis et al., 1985).

How much cocaine actually gets to the heart is a matter of some importance. Large doses of cocaine are only lethal to experimental animals when they are given via a route that guarantees that high concentrations of cocaine actually reach the heart. If the cocaine passes through the liver first, only minimal effects are observed (Jones and Tackett, 1992).

1.8.3 Liver

Hepatic cocaine receptors are present in higher concentrations, and have greater affinity for cocaine, than those located in the brain (Calligaro and Elderfrawi, 1987). In Volkow's PET studies, hepatic accumulation of drug was very high, although the rate of uptake is much slower than for most of the other organs. Peak uptake occurs 10–15 minutes after intravenous injection. More than 20% of a given dose reaches the liver, and remains at stable levels for more than 40 minutes. The findings of these dynamic studies are generally in agreement with autopsy studies that have also shown high levels in the liver.

In Spiehler's autopsy study, the mean hepatic cocaine level in patients dying of cocaine toxicity was 6.7 mg/L, and the BEG concentration was 21.3 mg/L (Spiehler and Reed, 1985). An earlier retrospective study of fifteen cases gathered from several centers yielded slightly different results. More cocaine was detected in the blood than in the liver with a blood/liver ratio of 1.4 (Finkle and McCloskey, 1978). High concentrations of BEG are hardly surprising given that the major metabolic pathways of cocaine metabolism involve plasma and hepatic esterase activity. Cocaethylene is also synthesized in the liver, and hepatic cocaethylene levels are much higher than hepatic cocaine levels (Hearn et al., 1991b). Whether this concentration difference explains why cocaethylene appears to be more hepatotoxic than cocaine (Odeleye et al., 1993), or whether cocaethylene is actually more toxic, remains to be seen.

Hepatic oxidation of the nitrogen atom in the tropane ring also occurs. The resulting products are N-hydroxynorcocaine and the free radical norcocaine nitroxide. Norcocaine also can be found as a contaminant in illicit cocaine (Kumar, 1991). Norcocaine found in illicit samples is there as a byproduct of the refining process. When potassium permanganate is added to crude cocaine mixtures, norcocaine can be formed. Norcocaine is believed to be responsible for the hepatotoxicity observed when cocaine is given to experimental animals (Thompson et al., 1979). Mice pretreated with phenobarbital whose P-450 microsomal systems have been activated, develop a specific type of hepatic necrosis (Kloss, 1984).

Norcocaine can be detected in man, but only in very small amounts. In addition to the norcocaine that may contaminate a sample, norcocaine can also be formed in the human body, though hepatic oxidation is not a preferred route of metabolism. Human volunteers given both cocaine and alcohol will produce more norcocaine than controls given cocaine alone. An explanation for this phenomenon is still wanting. It has been suggested that, given enough alcohol, blood pH will drop slightly and plasma cholinesterases will become less efficient, leaving more cocaine to circulate through the liver (Camí et al., 1992). No matter how the norcocaine gets into the body, its relationship to hepatic injury in cocaine users is unclear (Inaba, 1978). Lesions in man, histologically similar to those seen in mice, have been described but are quite rare (Freeman and Harbison, 1981; Marks and Chapple, 1986; Perino et al., 1987; Powell et al., 1991).

1.8.4   Kidneys

In human radioactive uptake studies, renal uptake is higher than cardiac uptake, but still considerably less than hepatic uptake. Uptake occurs in the renal cortex only. As in the heart, peak uptake occurs at 2–3 minutes, and after 10 minutes, half of the dose has been cleared (Volkow et al., 1992). Few autopsy measurements of renal cocaine levels have been reported. The values that have been observed have ranged from 1–28 mg/kg (Poklis et al., 1985; Lundberg et al., 1977; DiMaio and Garriott, 1978; Price, 1974), but comparing the results is difficult because, in most cases, the time elapsed from death to autopsy is not mentioned.

1.8.5   Adrenals

Rapid, intense adrenal uptake is seen in the rat, presumably a result of binding to the norepinephrine transporter. Uptake by rat adrenal gland is second only to uptake within the brain and spinal cord (Som et al., 1994). In human tracer studies, the adrenal glands take up more of an intravenous tracer dose than the liver. In humans, peak uptake occurs 10 minutes after injection. Within the adrenal, the half-life of the labeled cocaine is 20 minutes (Volkow et al., 1992). There have been no reported autopsy measurements, but the relatively slow rate at which the cocaine is washed out makes it probable that significant amounts of cocaine could be found at autopsy.

1.8.6 Hair

Like most of the other abused drugs, cocaine can be detected in the hair of cocaine users although there are conflicting opinions about how it gets there (Valente et al., 1981; Baumgartner et al., 1982). It is even possible to calculate a half-life (Ferko, 1992). Some researchers maintain that hair follicles take up cocaine from the blood, while others insist that drugs get into hair when the hair shaft is bathed in drug-containing sweat (Baumgartner et al., Black, 1978; Blank and Kidwell, 1993; Blank and Kidwell, 1995). Whatever the explanation, cocaine does get deposited in hair. For reasons that are not clear, cocaine metabolites are not so readily taken up (Fritch et al., 1992; Nakahara and Kikura, 1994). Once the cocaine is present, it remains there. A study of hair samples from patients in a detoxification program found that cocaine and metabolites were still detectable 10 months after the last verified episode of drug use. Cocaine has been detected in the hair of ancient mummies (Balabanova et al., 1992), and provides an excellent matrix for analysis when cause of death is to be reconsidered and exhumation has been ordered.

While cocaine is the predominant analyte, substantial amounts of benzoylecgonine, cocaethylene, and norcocaine can also be detected (Ferko et al., 1992; Digregorio et al., 1993). Ecgonine methyl ester, one of the two principal cocaine metabolites, was present only in trace amounts (Cone et al., 1991). Given the fact that it is primarily cocaine, and not the metabolites, that accumulates in hair, antibody-based screening tests that use antibody directed against metabolites are very likely to give falsely low results. In various case reports, cocaine levels have ranged anywhere from 1 to 200 ng/mL, with the higher values having been observed in known regular users (Henderson and Harkey, 1993).

Dose-response curves have not been established, and the relationship between the amount of cocaine ingested and the amount subsequently appearing in the hair is unknown. Important methodologic issues remain to be resolved, particularly possible bias related to sex and gender. There is, for instance, preliminary evidence suggesting that hair color and sex may have a profound effect on the rate at which drugs are taken up by hair (Cone, 1994; Gygi, 1995). The results of other studies suggest that it may be impossible to tell the difference between cocaine deposited in hair from the blood of a user and hair contaminated with cocaine from the external environment (Blank and Kidwell, 1995). Findings in still other experiments suggest that hair care practices can affect test results. Because so many issues remain to be resolved, most toxicologists believe that hair analysis for employee drug testing is premature, although such testing may be useful in some forensic situations, provided it was supported by other types of evidence. There is also a general consensus that laboratories should be prohibited from reporting unconfirmed immunoassay hair test results.

Several different analytic techniques are available that can be used to quantitate cocaine in hair (Baumgartner et al., 1982; Cone et al., 1992), but specimen preparation appears to be a problem for all of them, since it is virtually impossible to wash off cocaine applied to hair through soaking in a cocaine solution (Cone et al., 1991).

Nor can positive results be validated by the detection of so-called "unique" metabolites. It has been suggested that the simultaneous detection of cocaine and cocaethylene should constitute absolute proof of cocaine abuse; since cocaethylene is produced only when alcohol and cocaine are consumed at the same time, there would be no circumstance where cocaethylene's presence could plausibly be explained by external contamination. The problem with that approach is that many laboratories, both clandestine and legal, use alcohol extraction to get cocaine out of the coca leaf, sometimes resulting in cocaethylene production. DEA chemists have found that samples of pharmaceutical grade cocaine, used to prepare standards, may contain anywhere from 0.2 to 1.16% cocaethylene (Casale and Moore, 1994; Janzen, 1992).

Depending on how the hair is treated, false negatives could also be a problem with this approach. Hair bleaching is done with highly alkaline solutions, and cocaine is rapidly degraded under such conditions, but the issue of environmental effects on hair testing has never been adequately evaluated.

1.8.7   Fat

The brown fat of experimental rats avidly takes up cocaine. Nuchal brown fat is richly supplied with sympathetic nerve terminals, which probably accounts for the high degree of uptake (Som et al., 1994). Human newborns rely on catecholamine mediated liberation of energy from fat stores. The children of cocaine-using mothers probably have detectable levels of cocaine in their fat stores, but measurements have not been reported.

1.8.8   Biofluids

1.8.8.1   Saliva

Saliva contains very little protein, so unbound drugs in the plasma appear in almost the same concentrations in both plasma and saliva. Because cocaine is weakly basic and saliva is normally more acidic than plasma, the concentration of ionized cocaine in saliva may be as much as five times higher than plasma cocaine concentrations. For the same reasons, concentrations of benzoylecgonine are two to three times higher in plasma than in saliva (Thompson, 1987; Ferko et al., 1990; Schramm et al., 1993). When human volunteers are given intravenous cocaine, saliva cocaine levels correlate well with plasma levels. Levels in both saliva and blood correlated equally well with behavioral and physiological effects. The half-life of cocaine in both fluids is the same, about 35 minutes in the case of saliva. Five hours after a 40-mg intravenous bolus of cocaine, levels in both saliva and blood are near the limits of detection (29 ng/mL for saliva and 8 ng/mL for plasma). Accordingly, if cocaine can be detected in saliva, it is a good sign of very recent use (Cone and Menchen, 1988; Ferko et al., 1990).

Cocaine is the predominant analyte in saliva but, because benzoylecgonine and ecgonine methyl ester both have much longer half-lives (2.3 to 6.5 hours) than cocaine, both of the metabolites will accumulate in saliva with repeated dosing. The relative proportions, and absolute concentrations of cocaine and its metabolites, are highly dependent on how the saliva is collected. Stimulated saliva (specimens collected after the donor has been given a piece of sour candy) tends to contain much less drug than nonstimulated samples (Kato et al., 1993). The results of animal studies suggest that cocaethylene also appears in saliva, and saliva cocaethylene levels correlate well with plasma cocaethylene levels, but studies in humans are lacking (Barbieri et al., 1994).

The same cautions apply to the interpretation of low cocaine levels in the saliva as in the blood. Chronic users may have persistent low levels even when they have abstained for several days or more. The presence of low levels in the saliva is certainly consistent with past cocaine use, but it is not necessarily diagnostic of recent ingestion. During cocaine withdrawal, lipophilic storage sites in the brain continue to release cocaine. Small amounts can appear in saliva and urine for weeks. Rats given 20 mg/kg twice a day for two weeks have measurable cocaine levels in their fat for as long as four weeks after the drug has been discontinued (Nayak et al., 1976). The same is true in man. Chronic users monitored during withdrawal continue to excrete unmetabolized cocaine, detectable by RIA, for 10 days or more after their last dose (Cone and Weddington, 1989).

1.8.8.2   Vitreous humor

Measurement of levels within the vitreous seems an obvious approach, but there have been only limited studies. Levels in blood, vitreous, and liver were measured in a 28-year old woman who died shortly after an intravenous injection. When the blood cocaine was 750 ng/mL, the concentration in the vitreous was 380 ng/mL and 130 ng/mL in the liver (Lundberg et al., 1977). Di Maio and Garriott described another case where the blood level was 370 ng/mL while the vitreous was 210 ng/mL (Di Maio and Garriott, 1978). Hearn et al. measured vitreous cocaine concentrations in one eye just after death and then measured concentrations in the other eye 18 hours later. The cocaine level, which was 1.0 mg/L just after death, rose to 3.5 mg/L after 18 hours. Benzoylecgonine levels also rose from 1.1 mg/L to 1.7 mg/L (Hearn et al., 1991a). An additional study has also demonstrated postmortem elevations of cocaine in the vitreous (Beno and Kriewall, 1989), suggesting that this is not a particularly good medium for postmortem investigations. Measurements have been made in one experimental model of massive overdose where the experimental animals were sacrificed five minutes after cocaine administration (McKinney et al., 1995). At the times of death, vitreous levels were lower than blood levels, but they equilibrated with femoral blood levels eight hours later. However, levels varied so widely from animal to animal that conclusions were hard to draw.

1.8.8.3   Spinal fluid

Measurements of spinal fluid may prove useful, especially since cocaine crosses the blood-brain barrier so readily. There have been no systematic studies, but one report suggests that unmetabolized cocaine can be detected in the CSF for at least 24 hours (Rowbotham et al., 1990).

1.8.8.4   Breast milk

Cocaine can be transferred to infants via mother's milk (Chasnoff et al., 1987), but the kinetics in humans have not been studied. Cocaine levels in the milk of lactating rats reach higher levels than in the mother's liver or brain. In one experimental study, cocaine levels in rat milk were eight times higher than blood levels. This may have to do with the high lipid content of the milk (Wiggins et al., 1989).

1.8.8.5   Urine

Cocaine is eliminated almost entirely by biotransformation with a renal clearance of less than 30 mL/minute (Chow et al., 1985). There is a general consensus that at least 80% of a given dose is converted to benzoylecgonine and ecgonine methyl ester (Fish and Wilson, 1969; Inaba et al., 1978; Ambre et al., 1988), but there is considerable variation from individual to individual. Smaller amounts of ecgonine, norcocaine, and various hydroxylated products all appear in the urine (Ambre et al., 1988; Zhang and Foltz, 1990). In a study of human volunteers, Ambre found an elimination half-life of 2.3–4.1 hours for EME and 2.8–6.5 hours for BEG. It is important to remember, however, that all of these determinations were made in drug-free individuals. Chronic abusers, who have not undergone detoxification, may well handle the drug differently. In cases of cocaine-related sudden death, urinary cocaine concentrations may well exceed concentrations of the metabolite (Ramcharitar et al., 1995).

Commercial screening tests are designed to detect cocaine metabolite, benzoylecgonine, not cocaine itself. There may be some cross-reactivity, but antibody-based screening tests generally do not detect cocaine, or other metabolites such as EME in the urine, even if they are present. Detection of cocaine chromatographically is a sign of recent ingestion, especially in occasional users. The absence of cocaine, on the other hand, is only evidence that the drug has not been taken within the last few hours (Jatlow, 1988). The window of detection for BEG in the urine can be altered by a number of factors, including chronicity of use, mode of administration, urine volume, and urine pH. In one study, the mean half-life for BEG in the urine was 6.8 ± 0.4 hours (Cone et al., 1989).

Compared to cocaine, the half-life of benzoylecgonine is a relatively long 6.5 hours, and metabolite may appear in the urine for days. Thus, the presence of benzoylecgonine is solid proof of past use, but the timing of the past use cannot be inferred from the urinalysis alone. Hospitalized patients undergoing detoxification continue to excrete metabolite for weeks after their last dose of cocaine (Weiss and Gawin, 1988; Burke et al., 1990; Cone and Weddington, 1989). The same caveats which apply to saliva and blood testing also apply to urine. It should also be apparent that no conclusions can be drawn about the degree of an individual's impairment, if any, at the time of urine testing. The presence of metabolite indicates only that the drug was used in the past.

1.8.8.6 Amniotic fluid

Amniotic fluid has not been systematically analyzed for cocaine or its metabolites, even though it is readily available at birth, and may provide a wider window of detectability than either urine or meconium testing. In one published report, cocaine and benzoylecgonine were quantitated in amniotic fluid, umbilical cord blood, and neonatal urine obtained at the time of delivery. Benzoylecgonine levels were 290 ng/mL and cocaine levels were 70 ng/mL. Levels of benzoylecgonine were much higher in the child's urine, although cocaine levels were roughly similar. Neither drug was detected in cord blood (Moore et al., 1993).

References

Ambre, J., Ruo, I. T., Nelson, J., and Belknap, S. (1988). Urinary excretion of cocaine, benzoylecgonine, and ecgonine methyl ester in humans. J Analyt Toxicol, 12: 301–306.

Balabanova, S., Parsche, F., and Pirsig, W. (1992). 1st Identification of drugs in egyptian mummies. Naturwissenschaften, 79(8): 358–358.

Barbieri, E., DiGregorio, J., Ferko, A. et al. (1994). Rat cocaethylene and benzoylecgonine concentrations in plasma and parotid saliva after the administration of cocaethylene. J Analyt Toxicol, 18: 60–61.

Baumgartner, W., Black, C., Jones, P., Bland, W. (1982). Radioimmunoassay of cocaine in hair: concise communication. J Nuc Med, 23(9): 790–792.

Beno, J. and Kriewall, S. (1989). Postmortem elevation of cocaine levels in vitreous humor. Cited in Hearn et al., Site-dependent postmortem changes in blood cocaine concentrations, J Forensic Sci, 36(3): 673–684.

Benuck, M., Reith, M. E., Sershen, H. et al. (1989). Oxidative metabolism of cocaine; comparison of brain and liver (42822). Proc Soc Exp Biol and Med, 190(1): 7–13.

Blank, D. and Kidwell, D. (1993). External contamination of hair by drugs of abuse. An issue in forensic interpretation. Forensic Sci Int, 63: 145–156.

Blank, D. and Kidwell, D. (1995). Decontamination procedures for drugs of abuse in hair: are they sufficient? Forensic Sci Intern, Jan 5, 70(1–3): 13–38.

Burke, W., Ravi, N., Dhopesh, V. et al. (1990). Prolonged presence of metabolite in urine after compulsive cocaine use. J Clin Psych, 51: 145–148.

Calligaro, D. and Eldefrawi, M. (1987). Central and peripheral cocaine receptors. J Pharm and Exp Ther, 243(1): 61–68.

Camí, J., de la Torre, R., Farré, M. et al. (1992). Cocaine-alcohol interaction in healthy volunteers: plasma metabolic profile including cocaethylene. In Problems of drug dependence 1991: Proceedings of the 53rd Annual Scientific Meeting of the Committee on Problems of Drug Dependence, Inc. National Institute on Drug Abuse Monograph Series, Rockland, MD.

Casale, J. and Moore, J. (1994). An in-depth analysis of pharmaceutical cocaine — cocaethylene and other impurities. J Phar Sci, 83(8): 1186–1186.

Chasnoff, I., Lewis, D., and Squires, L. (1987). Cocaine intoxication in a breast fed infant. Pediatrics, 80: 836–838.

Chow, M., Ambre, J., Ruo, T. et al. (1985). Kinetics of cocaine distribution, elimination, and chronotropic effects. Clin Pharmacol Ther, 38: 318–324.

Cone, E. and Menchen, S. (1988). Stability of cocaine in saliva. Clin Chem, 34(7): 1508.

Cone, E., Menchen, S., Paul, B. et al. (1989). Validity testing of commercial urine cocaine metabolite assays: 1. Assay detection times, individual excretion patterns, and kinetics after cocaine administration in humans. J Forensic Sci, 34: 15–31.

Cone, E. and Weddington, W., Jr. (1989). Prolonged occurrence of cocaine in human saliva and urine after chronic use. J Analyt Toxicol, 13(20): 65–68.

Cone, E., Yousenfnejad, D., Darwin, W., Maguire, T. et al. (1991). Testing human hair for drugs of abuse. II. Identification of unique cocaine metabolites in hair of drug abusers and evaluation of decontamination procedures. J Analyt Toxic, 15(5): 250–255.

Cone, E. (1992). Concerning norcocaine, ethylbenzoylecgonine, and the identification of cocaine use in human hair — reply. J Analyt Tox, 16(6): 402–402.

Cone, E., Hillsgrove, M., and Darwin, W. (1994). Simultaneous measurement of cocaine, cocaethylene, their metabolites, and crack pyrolysis products by gas chromatography mass spectrometry. Clin Chem, 40: 1299–1305.

Critchley, H., Woods, S., Barson, A. et al. (1988). Fetal death *in utero* and cocaine abuse. Case report. Br J Obst and Gynecol, 95(2): 195–196.

Digregorio, G., Barbieri, E., Ferko, A., and Ruch, E. (1993). Prevalence of cocaethylene in the hair of pregnant women. J Analyt Toxicol, 17: 445–446.

DiMaio, V. and Garriott, J. (1978). Four deaths due to intravenous injection of cocaine. Forensic Sci Int, 12: 119–125.

Ferko, A., Barabieri, E., Digregorio, G., and Ruch, E. (1990). The presence of cocaine and benzoylecgonine in rat parotid saliva, plasma, and urine after the intravenous administration of cocaine. Res Comm in Subst Abuse, 1–2.

Ferko, A., Barbieri, E., DiGregorio, G. et al. (1992). The accumulation and disappearance of cocaine and benzoylecgonine in rat hair following prolonged administration of cocaine. Life Sci, 51: 1823–1832.

Finkle, B. and McCloskey, K. (1978). The forensic toxicology of cocaine (1971–1976). J Forensic Sci, 22: 173–189.

Fish, F. and Wilson, W. (1969). Excretion of cocaine and its metabolites in man. J Pharm Pharmacol, 21, Suppl: 135S–138S.

Fowler, J., Ding, Y., Volkow, N. et al. (1994). PET studies of cocaine inhibition of myocardial norepinephrine. Synapes, 16: 312–317.

Freeman, R. and Harbison, R. (1981). Hepatic periportal necrosis induced by chronic administration of cocaine. Biochem Pharmacol, 30(7): 777–783.

Fritch, D., Groce, Y., and Rieders, F. (1992). Cocaine and some of its products in hair by RIA and GC/MS. J Analyt Toxicol, 16: 112–114.

Gygi, S., Wilkins, D., and Rollins, D. (1995). Distribution of codeine and morphine into rat hair after long-term daily dosing with codeine. J Analyt Toxicol, 19: 387–391.

Hearn, W., Keran, E., Wei, H., and Hime, G. (1991a). Site-dependent postmortem changes in blood cocaine concentrations. J Forensic Sci, 36(3): 673–684.

Hearn, W., Flynn, L., Hime, D. et al. (1991b). Cocaethylene — a unique cocaine metabolite displays high affinity for the dopamine transporter. J Neurochem, 56(2): 698–701.

Henderson, G. and Harkey, M. (1993). Hair analysis for drugs of abuse. Report prepared for NIJ and NIDA, September, 1993.

Hernandez, A., Andollo, W., and Hearn, W. (1994). Analysis of cocaine and metabolites in brain using solid phase extraction and full-scanning gas chromatography/ion trap mass spectrometry. Forensic Sci Int, 65: 149–156.

Inaba, T., Stewart, D., and Kalow, W. (1978). Metabolism of cocaine in man. Clin Pharmacol Ther, 23: 547–552.

Janzen, K. (1992). Concerning norcocaine, ethylbenzoylecgonine, and the identification of cocaine use in human hair. J Analyt Toxicol, 16: 402.

Jatlow, P. (1988). Cocaine: analysis, pharmacokinetics, and metabolic disposition. Yale J Biol and Med, 61(2): 105–113.

Jones, L. and Tackett, R. (1992). Differential routes of cocaine administration indicate a peripheral cardiotoxic action. Pharmacol Biochem Behav, 38: 601–603.

Kato, K., Hillsgrove, M., Weinhold, L. et al. (1993). Cocaine and metabolite excretion in saliva under stimulated and nonstimuated conditions. J Analyt Toxicol, 17: 338–341.

Kidwell, D. and Blank, D. (1995). Mechanisms of incorporation of drugs into hair and the interpretation of hair analysis data. Hair testing for drugs of abuse: international research on standards and technology. Washington, DC, National Institute on Drug Abuse, DHHS Publication.

Kloss, K., Rosen, G., and Rauckman, E. (1984). Cocaine-mediated hepatotoxicity: a critical review. Biochem Pharmacol, 33: 169–173.

Kumar, A. (1991). Identification and quantitation of norcocaine in illicit cocaine samples. Read at Annual Meeting of the American Academy of Forensic Sciences. Anaheim: AAFS, 73.

Lundberg, G., Garriott, J., Reynolds, P. et al. (1977). Cocaine-related death. J Forensic Sci, 22: 402–408.

Marks, V. and Chapple, P. (1967). Hepatic dysfunction in heroin and cocaine users. Br J Addict, 62: 189–195.

McKinney, P., Phillips, S., Gomez, H. et al. (1995). Vitreous humor cocaine and metabolite concentrations: do postmortem specimens reflect blood levels at the time of death? J Forensic Sci, 40: 102–107.

Misra, A., Nayak, P., Bloch, R., and Mule, S. (1975). Estimation and disposition of 3H-benzoylecgonine and pharmacological activity of some cocaine metabolites. J Pharm and Pharmacol, 27: 784–786.

Mittleman, R., Cofino, J., and Hearn, W. (1989). Tissue distribution of cocaine in a pregnant woman. J Forensic Sci, 34(2): 481–486.

Moore, C., Brown, S., Negrusz, A. et al. (1993). Determination of cocaine and its major metabolite, benzoylecgonine, in amniotic fluid, umbilical cord blood, umbilical cord tissue, and neonatal urine: a case study. J Analyt Toxicol, 17(1): 62–62.

Morlid, I. and Stajic, M. (1990). Cocaine and fetal death. Forensic Sci Int, 47: 181–189.

Mule, S., Casella, G., and Misra, A. (1976). Intracellular disposition of 3H-cocaine, 3H-norcocaine, 3H-benzoylecgonine, and 3H-benzoylnorecgonine in the brain of rats. Life Sci, 19: 1585–1596.

Nakahara, Y. and Kikura, R. (1994). Hair analysis for drugs of abuse. VII. The incorporation rates of cocaine, benzoylecgonine and ecgonine methyl ester into rat hair and hydrolysis of cocaine in rat hair. Arch Tox, 68: 54–59.

Nayak, P., Misra, A., and Mule, S. (1976). Physiological disposition and biotransformation of 3H-cocaine in acutely and chronically treated rats. J Pharm and Exp Ther, 196(3): 556–569.

Odeleye, O., Watson, R., Eskelson, C., and Earnest, D. (1993). Enhancement of cocaine-induced hepatotoxicity by ethanol. Drug Alcohol Depend, 31: 253–263.

Oster, Z., Som, P., Wang, G., and Weber, D. (1991). Imaging of cocaine-induced global and regional myocardial ischemia. J Nucl Med, 32: 1569–1572.

Perino, L., Warren, G., and Levine, J. (1987). Cocaine-induced hepatotoxicity in humans. Gastroenterology, 93: 176–180.

Poklis, A., MacKell, M., and Graham, M. (1985). Disposition of cocaine in fatal poisoning in man. J Analy Tox, 9: 227–229.

Powell, C. J., Connolly, A. K., and Charles, S. J. (1991). Shifting necrosis — butylated hydroxytoluene (BHT) and phenobarbital move cocaine-induced hepatic necrosis across the lobule. Toxicol Lett, 55(2): 171–178.

Price, K. (1974). Fatal cocaine poisoning. J Forensic Sci Soc, 14: 329–333.

Prouty, R. and Anderson, W. (1990). The forensic science implications of site and temporal influences on postmortem blood-drug concentrations. Am J Forensic Sci, 35(2): 243–270.

Ramcharitar, V., Levine, B., and Smialek, J. (1995). Benzoylecgonine and ecgonine methyl ester concentrations in urine specimens. J Forensic Sci, 1: 99–101.

Rowbotham, M., Kaku, D., Mueller, P. et al. (1990). Blood, urine, and CSF levels of cocaine and metabolites following seizures in cocaine abusers. Neurology, 40, Suppl 1: 133.

Schramm, W., Craig, P., Smith, R. et al. (1993). Cocaine and benzoylecgonine in saliva, serum, and urine. Clin Chem, 39(3): 481–487.

Som, P., Oster, Z., Volkow, N., and Sacker, D. (1989). Studies on whole-body distribution and kinetics of cocaine. J Nuc Med, 30: 831.

Som, P., Oster, Z., Wang, G. et al. (1994). Spatial and temporal distribution of cocaine and effects of pharmacological interventions: wholebody autoradiographic microimaging studies. Life Sci, 55(17): 1375–1382.

Spiehler, V. and Reed, D. (1985). Brain concentrations of cocaine and benzoylecgonine in fatal cases. J Forensic Sci, 30(4): 1003–1011.

Thompson, M., Shuster, L., and Shaw, K. (1979). Cocaine-induced hepatic necrosis in mice — the role of cocaine metabolism. Biochem Pharmacol, 28: 2389–2395.

Thompson, L., Yousenfnejad, D., Kumor, K. et al. (1987). Confirmation of cocaine in human saliva after intravenous use. J Analyt Toxicol, 11: 36–38.

Volkow, N., Fowler, J., Wolf, A. et al. (1992). Distribution and kinetics of carbon-11-cocaine in the human body measured with PET. J Nucl Med, 33: 521–525.

Volkow, N. N., Fowler, J., Logan, J. et al. (1995). Carbon-11-cocaine binding compared at subpharmacological and pharmacological doses: a PET study. J Nucl Med, 36: 1289–1297.

Weiss, R. and Gawin, F. (1988). Protracted elimination of cocaine metabolites in long-term, high-dose cocaine abusers. Am J Med, 85(6): 879–880.

Wiggins, R., Rolste, C., Ruiz, B., and Davis, C. (1989). Pharmacokinetics of cocaine: basic studies of route, dosage, pregnancy, and lactation. Neurotoxicology, 10: 367–382.

Yazigi, R. and Polakoski, K. (1992). Distribution of tritiated cocaine in selected genital and nongenital organs following administration to male mice. Arch Pathol Lab Med, 116: 1036–1039.

Zhang, J. and Foltz, R. (1990). Cocaine metabolism in man: identification of four previously unreported cocaine metabolites in human urine. J Analyt Toxicol, 14(4): 201–205.

1.9   Cocaine's effects on catecholamine metabolism

1.9.1   General considerations

Cocaine, and all of the other abused stimulants, disrupt catecholamine metabolism. Cocaine abusers have elevated circulating levels of catecholamines. This has been demonstrated both in experimental animals and in humans (Gunne and Jonsson, 1964; Chiueh and Kopin, 1978; Karch, 1987b; Schwartz et al., 1988; Dixon et al., 1988; Nahas et al., 1990; Kiritsy-Roy et al., 1990; Conlee et al., 1991; Trouve et al., 1991). Even the offspring of substance-abusing mothers have abnormal sympathetic function (Ward et al., 1991).

In opiate abuse, most of the medical complications are infectious or secondary to the presence of drug contaminants. Many, but not all, of the pathologic changes reported in conjunction with cocaine use appear to be catecholamine-mediated. Blood pressure elevations associated with cocaine use are centrally mediated, and the elevation is independent of any effect that cocaine exerts on peripheral catecholamine uptake (Schindler et al., 1992). Nonetheless, the mechanisms of catecholamine toxicity play a major role and require consideration in some detail.

Catecholamine's effects on the cardiovascular system are mediated by specific catecholamine receptors. A family of subtypes has been identified, but the receptors of principal concern are the α_1 adrenergic receptors which are mainly located on blood vessels, and β_1 receptors located in the heart. These receptors are coupled to phospholipase-C via a G-protein. When the receptor is activated, phosphoinositol is cleaved into inositol phosphate and diacylglycerol. Separation of the two fragments releases free calcium into the cytosol and causes the blood vessels to contract. The α_2 receptors are found on blood vessels and neurons. When receptors on vessels are stimulated, adenyl cyclase is inhibited, intracellular levels of cyclic AMP drop, and vasoconstriction results. Stimulation of the α_2 receptors located on nerves inhibits the release of norepinephrine from postganglionic nerve endings, thus decreasing sympathetic flow.

β_1 Receptors are found in the heart. When these receptors are stimulated, another G-protein is activated and adenyl cyclase activity is increased. The results include increases in heart rate, contractility, and conduction velocity. β_2 Receptors are found on bronchi and smooth muscle, and also exert their effects by activating a G-protein and adenyl cyclase. Stimulation of the β_2 receptors causes dilation of bronchi and blood vessels.

The principal catecholamine of the heart is norepinephrine. Within the heart's local circulation, norepinephrine functions as a neurotransmitter. Norepinephrine is released into the synaptic cleft each time an impulse is transmitted. Impulse transmission stops when norepinephrine is pumped back into the presynaptic nerve ending. In the heart, only 30% of norepinephrine is metabolized by catechol-o-methyl transferase (Goldstein et al., 1988); the rest is actively pumped back into the presynaptic terminal. Cocaine prevents the reuptake of norepinephrine, and unmetabolized norepinephrine overflows into the systemic circulation. The effects of cocaine on norepinephrine reuptake last much longer than would be expected, based on cocaine's half-life of 40 minutes. In studies on dogs using positron tomography, norepinephrine reuptake was still inhibited more than 2.5 hours after intravenous cocaine injection (Melon et al., 1994).

Once it enters the systemic circulation, norepinephrine acts as a circulating hormone ($\alpha 1,2$ and $\beta 1$), not as a neurotransmitter. Epinephrine and norepinephrine bind to both α and β receptors but differ in their relative affinities. Thus, both are full agonists for α and β_1 receptors, but epinephrine elicits a much greater response at β_2 receptors.

Cocaine is avidly taken up by, and has a direct effect on, the adrenals (Volkow et al., 1992). In rats, cocaine causes the increased release of both epinephrine and norepinephrine (Chiueh and Kopin, 1978; Gunne and Jonsson, 1964; Dixon, 1988). The same is true of squirrel monkeys (Trouve et al., 1990b). For unknown reasons, this increase in circulating catecholamines does not lead to CNS catecholamine depletion. Rats, given repeated doses of cocaine, show constant brain levels of catecholamines in the face of increased urinary excretion (Chiueh and Kopin, 1978). In a prospective study of "crack" users with chest pain, elevations in both epinephrine and norepinephrine levels were observed. In 10 such patients, norepinephrine levels ranged from 345 ng/L to 1,200 ng/L (normal range 0–90 ng/L) and epinephrine ranged from 135 to 300 ng/L (normal range 0–55 ng/L) (Karch, 1987b).

There is conflicting data on what happens to dopamine in the peripheral circulation. In the study of "crack" smokers cited above, no changes in dopamine levels were observed. However, when measurements were made in 15 chronic cocaine users admitted to a rehabilitation program, all of the patients were found to have dramatic increases in plasma dopamine sulfate levels ($89,626 \pm 121$ pg/mL vs. 2,356 pg/mL in controls). Even more interesting, a relationship was observed between elevation in plasma dopamine levels and the patients' estimate of the amount of cocaine being used (Faraj et al., 1993).

Catecholamine measurements in dogs given intravenous cocaine were comparable (Schwartz, 1988), as were elevations in exercising rats (Conlee et al., 1991). Elevated plasma norepinephrine levels have even been observed in infants born to cocaine-using mothers. When catecholamine levels were measured in the otherwise healthy children of cocaine-using mothers, venous norepinephrine levels were 1.8× those of controls, while there were no differences in epinephrine or dopamine levels (Ward et al., 1991).

Very limited data suggests that cocaine users respond abnormally to elevated catecholamine levels. Chronic catecholamine excess is usually associated with down-regulation of β receptors, but cocaine users do not down-regulate. Several groups have made lymphocyte receptor measurements, and found no change in binding sites or receptor affinity for either α- or β-adrenoreceptors, in spite of elevated circulating levels of catecholamines (Conlee et al., 1991; Costard-Jackle, 1989; Trouve et al., 1990a). This failure to down-regulate has also been observed in infants born to substance-abusing mothers, in spite of the fact that they, too, have increased circulating levels of norepinephrine.

Stimulation of both α and β receptors promotes elevation of intracellular calcium. When norepinephrine and epinephrine bind to β receptors, adenylate cyclase is activated, causing increased levels of 3'–5' cyclic AMP. The latter compound activates an AMP-dependent protein kinase capable of phosphorylating a family of regulatory proteins, including those that con-

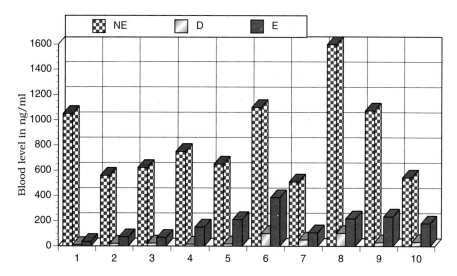

Figure 1.9.1   Elevated catecholamine levels in cocaine users with chest pain. Catecholamine levels measured in symptomatic crack smokers. Large checked column represents norepinepherine levels, which are markedly elevated. There were modest elevations in epinephrine (dotted columns), but not in dopamine. These levels are comparable to those seen in patients with pheochromocytoma. Unpublished data.

trol calcium movement, both on the cell surface and in the endoplasmic reticulum (Evans, 1986). As a direct consequence of catecholamine stimulation, calcium enters the cell and additional calcium is released from sequestered stores within the endoplasmic reticulum. Once intracytosolic calcium has risen to about 100 times resting concentrations, the myofilaments contract. The cycle terminates when the calcium is pumped back out of the cytosol. α Stimulation also elevates intracytosolic calcium. When α receptors are activated, phosphatidyl-inositol is hydrolyzed into diacylglycerol and inositol triphosphate. These two compounds are classified as "second messengers." Inositol triphosphate facilitates the release of calcium from the endoplasmic reticulum, and diacylglycerol enhances production of protein kinase-C which interacts with calcium channels and β receptors. This combination of activities further increases the amount of free calcium in the cytoplasm. If too much calcium accumulates within the cell, toxic effects can occur. These effects may be manifested as altered membrane potentials and abnormal impulse conduction, or even by the presence of visible lesions.

1.9.2   Mechanisms of catecholamine toxicity

Elevated levels of circulating catecholamines are associated with a number of undesirable effects. Increased α adrenergic stimulation of coronary vas-

Table 1.9.2   Conditions Associated With
Contraction Band Necrosis*

Reperfusion	Norepinephrine
Steroid therapy	Cobalt poisoning
Electrocution	Starvation
Defibrillation	Myocardial infarction
Drowning	Free-radical injuries
Cocaine	Brain death
Amphetamine	Phenylpropanolamine
Epinephrine	Intracerebral hemorrhage
Isoproteronol	

* From Karch and Billingham, Contraction bands
  revisited. Hum Pathol, 1987.

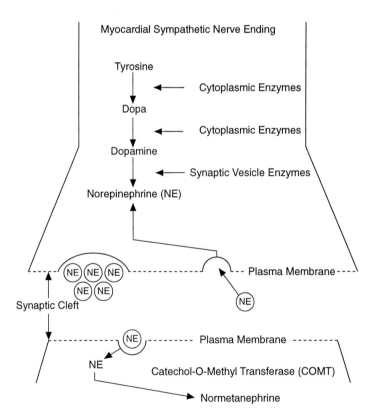

Figure 1.9.2.1   Synthesis and fate of norepinephrine. Norepinephrine is produced
within the sympathetic nerves that supply the heart. The heart handles norepinephrine differently than other parts of the body; instead of breaking norepinephrine
down, its actions in the heart are terminated mainly by reuptake.

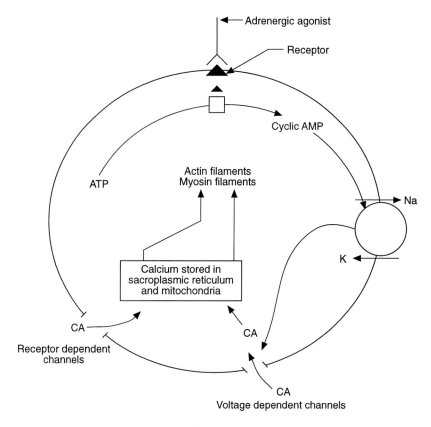

Figure 1.9.2.2 Sequence of events leading to cardiac myocyte contraction. Norepinephrine binds at both α and β receptor sites but has much greater affinity for the α receptor. Calcium enters via voltage dependent channels (known as "slow channels") and through other calcium channels that open when norepinephrine binds to an α receptor. Calcium is also released from storage sites within the myocyte. Once the level of calcium within the cell has risen 100-fold, myofilaments are able to contract. If cytosolic calcium levels become too high, irreversible damage occurs to the myofilaments; this is known as "contraction band necrosis."

cular smooth muscle causes vasoconstriction and ischemia (Mathias, 1986; Ascher et al., 1988). The combination of simultaneous α and β stimulation means that cocaine-induced vasoconstriction is accompanied by increased oxygen demand. In individuals with preexisting lesions, myocardial infarction can probably be explained by this combination of α and β effects.

At the cellular level, acutely elevated levels of epinephrine and norepinephrine can alter membrane potentials so that the occurrence of malignant ventricular arrhythmias is favored. This process was first suggested more than 50 years ago (Bozler, 1943). Chronic exposure to high levels of catecholamines, on the other hand, can induce morphologic changes which are also associated with arrhythmias and sudden death. The specific morphologic changes induced by catecholamine excess are essentially the same as those associated with cocaine toxicity (Karch and Billingham, 1988; Tazelaar et al., 1987). The changes associated with cocaine and catecholamine toxicity are, in turn, the same as the morphologic changes associated with intracellular calcium overload. And, depending on the experimental design, the morphologic changes induced by cocaine, like the changes associated with catecholamine toxicity, can be prevented by calcium channel blockade (Nahas et al., 1985; Trouve and Nahas, 1986; Trouve et al., 1990a). It is important to remember that calcium overload is not synonymous with catecholamine toxicity. Anything that disrupts membrane integrity, including ischemia, can result in calcium overload (Rona, 1985).

1.9.3 *Histopathology of catecholamine toxicity*

Catecholamines cause histologic changes within the myocardium (Szakacs et al., 1958). The morphologic changes seen in the hearts of cocaine and amphetamine users are similar. The best known, and the most important, morphologic alteration is the injury known as contraction band necrosis. This lesion has both pathologic and forensic significance. Contraction band necrosis (CBN), sometimes referred to as coagulative myocytolysis and sometimes as myofibrillar degeneration, is a nonspecific finding. It can be seen in a variety of conditions which are apparently unrelated. Often seen after reperfusion, CBN also occurs in the hearts of patients who have been subjected to multiple defibrillation attempts. Contraction bands are also prominent in the hearts of patients with intracerebral hemorrhage, drowning, pheochromocytoma, and other conditions associated with catecholamine excess. CBN is frequently observed in cases of sudden cardiac death. Meticulous studies have confirmed the presence of these lesions in over 80% of individuals with non-drug-related sudden death (Reichenbach and Moss, 1975; Cebelin and Hirsch, 1980). The incidence in drug-related deaths may be even higher (Rajis and Falconer, 1979; Tazelaar et al., 1987).

The term "Contraction Band Necrosis" was introduced by Caulfield and Kilonsky in 1959 (Caulfield and Klonsky, 1959), but the lesion had actually been described in the heart of a cocaine user in 1922 by Bravetta and Invernizzi (Maier, 1926)! Szakacs was the first to systematically characterize the effects of catecholamines on myocardial structure and was the first to note the unique distribution of these lesions. Areas of contraction band necrosis tend to occur "without any apparent preferential distribution" (Szakacs and Cannon, 1958; Szakacs, Dimmette, and Cowart, 1959). What Szakacs was referring to were the severely damaged cells often found nestled between totally normal cells. If the damage to the cell had been due to ischemia, then one would expect all the cells in a specific area to show signs of injury. Szakacs made a second important observation. He realized that the changes seen after chronic catecholamine administration were identical to those seen in patients with pheochromocytoma (Karch and Billingham, 1988; Karch and Billingham, 1986).

Calcium overload can be initiated by many different processes. Calcium enters the cells when calcium channels are opened by catecholamine stimulation. When there is myocardial ischemia, a loss of cell membrane integrity can lead to the same result and the cell floods with calcium. Whatever the cause, a continuum of morphologic alterations can be seen; these may range from hypereosinophilia to total disruption of the cell. As Szakacs discovered, the lesions are characterized as much by their location as by their appearance. They bear no apparent relationship to blood supply. Contraction bands may be found in myocytes adjacent to normal capillaries. They can, and do, occur in the absence of significant coronary artery disease. Unlike the picture seen in infarction, where the myofibrillar apparatus remains visible and in register, in CBN the sarcomers are hypercontracted and distorted. The contractile apparatus may not even be visible. Milder forms of the lesion consist of eosinophilic transverse bands separated by areas containing fine eosinophilic granules.

With electron microscopy, it is apparent that the myofilaments are completely out of register and the mitochondria translocated. The dense bands visible with light microscopy are seen as amorphous gray material. This material is all that remains of both the thick and thin filaments. This exact change has been observed in the hearts of rats chronically treated with cocaine (Nahas et al., 1991). Z-band remnants, the hallmark of dilated, congestive cardiomyopathy, are generally not seen; however, if the process were ongoing and particularly severe, then the presence of Z-band remnants would not be particularly surprising. In severe instances, as in open-heart defibrillation, the sarcomers look as if they have been torn apart, and dehiscence of the intercalated disks can occur (Karch and Billingham, 1986).

Initially, and probably not for at least 12 hours, there are no inflammatory cells in these lesions. Occasionally a mononuclear infiltrate may be seen. Eventually, the injured cells are resorbed and replaced with fibrous tissue. The pattern is classically seen in patients (and experimental animals) with pheochromocytoma. Illustrating the progression of lesions in humans is quite difficult, but lesions corresponding to each stage in the evolution of catecholamine injury have been reported. The resultant fibrosis, which is occasionally quite prominent in the hearts of cocaine users, may supply the substrate for lethal arrhythmias (Merx et al., 1977; Strain et al., 1983).

The catecholamine levels required to produce necrosis have been determined, largely as a result of research in the field of heart transplantation. Hearts from donors that have been maintained with pressor therapy frequently fail after surgery. In the course of research designed to explain the failure, experimenters found that a surge of catecholamines accompanies brain death, and that this surge is associated with the presence of contraction band necrosis. In the baboon model of brain death, catecholamine elevations comparable to those seen in some cocaine users are observed (Novitzky et al., 1987; Novitzky et al., 1988; Novitzky et al., 1984; Novitzky et al., 1986; Worstman et al., 1984). In the experimental model of brain death, the cardiac lesions can be prevented by denervation or β blockade. The occurrence of myocardial contraction bands must, in some way, be related to β receptor number, density, and regulation. These parameters, in turn, depend on how much drug has been used and for how long. Unfortunately, the impact of

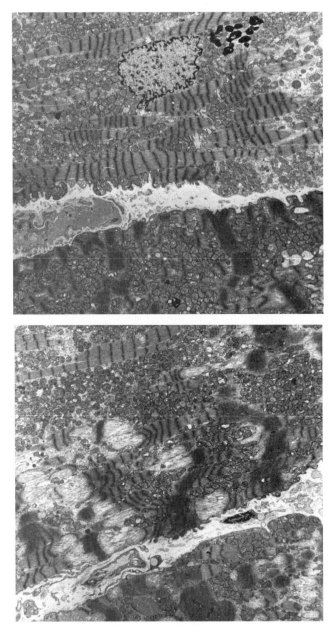

Figure 1.9.3   Effects of catecholamines on cardiac myocytes. The electron micrograph on top shows normal human myocardium. The myofilaments are in register; the mitochondria are of uniform size and are neatly packed between the filaments. The bottom micrograph illustrates the changes seen in contraction band necrosis. The dark electron-dense material is all that remains of the myofilaments; the mitochondria are swollen and translocated. Original magnification 4,320× (both top and bottom). Courtesy of Dr. Margaret Billingham and Marilyn Masek, Stanford University School of Medicine.

cocaine and chronic catecholamine excess on receptor physiology remains, for the most part, unstudied. The limited number of studies that have addressed this question have all reached the same conclusion. There is no indication of β receptor down-regulation either in lymphocytes or myocardium (Conlee et al., 1991; Costard-Jackle et al., 1989; Trouve et al., 1990a; Chiarasini et al., 1992). This failure of down-regulation distinguishes cocaine abuse from all other chronic hyperadrenergic states.

The fact that the general tendency for down-regulation to occur in hyperadrenergic states has not been confirmed in cocaine users is somewhat puzzling (Tsujimoto et al., 1984). Both the β and α receptors on lymphocytes and platelets down-regulate in the presence of catecholamine excess, and one would expect the same result whatever the reason, for the catecholamine elevation. It may well be that some alteration in signal transduction has occurred between the receptors and adenyl cyclase, although that possibility remains to be investigated. It has been shown that tyrosine hydroxylase activity is increased by cocaine administration (Taylor and Ho, 1977). That observation is consistent with the notion that increased catecholamine synthesis is occurring in an attempt to keep up with increased catecholamine turnover. Evidence from other fields suggests that when this happens, postsynaptic calcium channel receptors will down-regulate in an attempt to prevent calcium overload (Lefkowitz et al., 1984).

1.9.4   Contraction band necrosis and sudden death

Contraction band necrosis (CBN) is a marker for sudden death, whatever the cause. The incidence of CBN in various autopsy studies is over 80% (Baroldi and Mariano, 1979; Reichenbach and Moss, 1975; Cebelin and Hirsch, 1980). In drug-related deaths it may be even higher (Rajis and Falconer, 1979; Tazelaar et al., 1987). Contraction band necrosis heals by fibrosis, and postmortem studies of addicts in general, and stimulant users in particular, confirm the presence of reperative microfocal fibrosis (Rajs et al., 1984; Oehmichen et al., 1990).

The role of contraction band necrosis in cocaine-associated sudden death was established in a fairly large retrospective study (Karch, 1987a). Contraction band lesions were found to be significantly more common (P < 0.001) in cocaine users than in a group of controls dying of sedative-hypnotic overdose. Contraction band lesions were found in 93% of the cocaine group, but in less than 10% of the control. Over 25% of the cocaine users also had myocardial fibrosis, sometimes to quite striking degrees. The finding could represent previous episodes of ischemia, but the anatomic distribution of the fibrotic areas suggests that fibrosis is a result of the healing process that occurs after recurrent bouts of contraction band necrosis.

Contraction band necrosis and microfocal fibrosis have been observed in other autopsy studies of cocaine users (Simpson and Edwards, 1986; Roh and Hamele-Bena, 1990; Mckelway et al., 1990), and in experimental animals treated with cocaine (Knuepfer et al., 1993; Gardin et al., 1994; Keller and Todd, 1994). Contraction band necrosis has even been observed in tissue cultures of myocardium exposed to cocaine (Welder et al., 1993). Only one published study has failed to confirm an increased frequency of CBN in cocaine users, but since the frequency of CBN in that study's control group was so much lower than what is accepted as normal for the general population, the significance of this one study is difficult to assess (Virmani et al., 1988).

Contraction band necrosis never occurs as fixation artifact (Karch and Billingham, 1986). The presence of such lesions always indicates some underlying abnormality, usually catecholamine excess. By themselves, contraction bands constitute only presumptive indicators for cocaine use, especially if they are seen in biopsy specimens. Biopsy studies of symptomatic users have shown prominent contraction band necrosis (Peng, 1989), but some evidence of contraction bands is almost always seen in biopsy specimens (Adomian, 1978). Stronger inferences can be drawn if there are other supporting findings. For instance, if microfocal fibrosis is present, the differential diagnosis then becomes quite limited. Very few conditions produce contraction band necrosis with microfocal fibrosis. In fact, the only real alternative diagnosis is pheochromocytoma, which should not be all that difficult to rule out.

The underlying cause for contraction band necrosis is generally believed to be calcium overload (Karch, 1986), with excessively high calcium levels in the cytosol leading to hypercontraction and destruction of the myofilaments. The same mechanism is thought to account for the subendocardial hemorrhages that can be seen in the hearts of individuals dying of heat trauma and cocaine toxicity (Harrnuff, 1993). But, even short of cell destruction, the accumulation of calcium in cardiac myocytes is detrimental because it increases myocardial work by increasing the force of contraction and because it favors the occurrence of malignant arrhythmias (Opie et al., 1979; Billman, 1993a; Billman, 1993b).

References

Adomian, G., Laks, M., and Billingham, M. (1978). The incidence and significance of contraction bands in endomyocardial biopsies from normal human hearts. Am Heart J, 95(3): 348–351.

Ascher, E., Stauffer, J., and Gaash, W. (1988). Coronary artery spasm, cardiac arrest, transient electrocardiographic Q waves and stunned myocardium in cocaine-associated acute myocardial infarction. Am J Cardiol, 61(11): 938–941.

Baroldi, G. and Mariani, F. (1979). Sudden coronary death. A postmortem study in 208 selected cases compared to 97 "control" subjects. Am Heart J, 98: 20–31.

Billman, A. (1993a). Effect of calcium channel antagonists on cocaine-induced malignant arrhythmias: protection against ventricular fibrillation. J Pharm Exp Ther, 266(1): 407–416.

Billman, G. (1993b). Intracellular calcium chelator, BAPTA-AM prevents cocaine-induced ventricular fibrillation. Am J Physiol, 265: H1529–H1535.

Bozler, E. (1943). The initiation of impulses in cardiac muscle. Am J Physiol, 138: 273–282.

Caulfield, J. and Klonsky, B. (1959). Myocardial ischemia and early infarction: an electron microscopic study. Am J Pathol, 35(3): 489–501.

Cebelin, M. and Hirsch, C. (1980). Human stress cardiomyopathy: myocardial lesions in victims of homicidal assaults without internal injuries. Hum Pathol, 11: 123–132.

Chiarasini, D., Dingeon, P., Latour, C. et al. (1992). Cardiovascular tolerance to cocaine and its correlates. Read at the Annual Meeting of the British Pharmacological Society, London, September 9.

Chiueh, C. and Kopin, I. (1978). Centrally mediated release by cocaine of endogenous epinephrine and norepinephrine from the sympathoadrenal medullary system of unanesthetized rats. J Pharmacol Exp Ther, 205: 148–154.

Conlee, R., Barnett, D., Kelly, K., and Han, D. (1991). Effects of cocaine on plasma catecholamine and muscle glycogen concentrations during exercise in the rat. J Appl Physiol, 70(3): 1323–1327.

Costard-Jackle, A., Jackle, S., Kates, R., and Fowler, M. (1989). Electrophysiological and biochemical effect of chronic cocaine administration. Circulation, 80(4): II 15.

Dixon, W., Chang, A., Machado, J. et al. (1988). Effect of intravenous infusion and oral self-administration of cocaine on plasma and adrenal catecholamine levels and cardiovascular parameters in the conscious rat. In L. Harris (Ed.), Committee for Problems of Drug Dependency, Annual Scientific Conference; Published in National Institute on Drug Abuse Research Monograph #95. (1989), 335–336.

Evans, D. (1986). Modulation of cAMP: mechanism for positive inotropic action. J Cardiovasc Pharmacol, 8, Suppl 9: S22–S29.

Faraj, B., Camp, V., Davis, D. et al. (1993). Elevated concentrations of dopamine sulfate in plasma of cocaine abusers. Biochem Pharm, 46(8): 1453–1457.

Gardin, J., Wong, N., Alker, K. et al. (1994). Acute cocaine adminstration induces ventricular regional wall motion and ultrastructural abnormalities in an anesthetized rabbit model. Am Heart J, 128: 1117–1129.

Goldstein, D., Brush, J., Eisenhofer, G., Stull, R., and Esler, M. (1988). *In vivo* measurement of neuronal uptake of norepinephrine in the human heart. Circulation, 78: 41–48.

Gunne, L. and Jonsson, J. (1964). Effects of cocaine administration on brain, adrenal and urinary adrenaline and noradrenaline in rats. Psychopharmacologia, 6(2): 125–129.

Harrnuff, R. (1993). Subendocardial hemorrhages in forensic pathology autopsies. Am J Forensic Med and Pathol, 14(4): 284–288.

Karch, S. and Billingham M. (1986). Myocardial contraction bands revisited. Hum Pathol, 17: 9–13.

Karch, S. (1987a). Resuscitation-induced myocardial necrosis. Am J Forensic Med and Path, 8(1): 3–8.

Karch, S. (1987b). Serum catecholamines in cocaine-intoxicated patients with cardiac symptoms. Am J Emerg Med, 16(4): 481.

Karch, S. and Billingham, M. (1986). Myocardial contraction bands revisited. Hum Pathol, 17(11): 9–13.

Karch, S. and Billingham, M. (1988). The pathology and etiology of cocaine-induced heart disease. Arch Pathol Lab Med, 112: 225–230.

Keller, D. and Todd, G. (1994). Acute cardiotoxic effects of cocaine and a hyperadrenergic state in anesthetized dogs. Int J Cardiol, 24: 19-28.

Kiritsy-Roy, J., Halter, J., Gordon, B. et al. (1990). Role of the central nervous system in hemodynamic and sympathoadrenal responses to cocaine in rats. J Pharmacol Exp The, 255(1): 154–160.

Knuepfer, M., Branch, C., Gan, Q. et al. (1993). Cocaine-induced myocardial ultrastructural alterations and cardiac output responses in rats. Exp Mol Pathol, 59: 155–168.

Lefkowitz, R., Caron, M., and Stiles, G. (1984). Mechanisms of membrane-receptor regulation. N Engl J Med, 310: 1570–1579.

Maier, H. W. (1926). Der Kokainismus (O. J. Kalant from the German 1926 edition, Trans.). Toronto: Addiction Research Foundation.

Mathias, D. (1986). Cocaine-associated myocardial ischemia: review of clinical and angiographic findings. Am J Med, 81: 675–678.

Mckelway, R., Vieweg, V., and Westerman, P. (1990). Sudden death from acute cocaine intoxication in Virginia in 1988. Am J Psych, 147(12): 1667–1669.

Melon, P., Nguyen, N., DeGrado, T. et al. (1994). Imaging of cardiac neuronal function after cocaine exposure using carbon-11 hydroxyephedrine and positron emission tomography. J Am Coll Cardiol, 23(7): 693–699.

Merx, W., Yoon, M., and Han, J. (1977). The role of local disparity in conduction and recovery of ventricular vulnerability to fibrillation. Am Heart J, 94(5): 603–610.

Nahas, G., Maillet, M., Chiarasini, D., and Latour, C. (1995). Myocardial damage induced by cocaine administration of a week's duration in the rat. In L. Harris (Ed.), Committee for Problems of Drug Dependency, Annual Scientific Conference; National Institute on Drug Abuse Research Monograph Series.

Nahas, G., Trouve, R., Demus, J., and Sitbon, M. (1985). A calcium-channel blocker as antidote to the cardiac effects of cocaine intoxication. N Engl J Med, 313(8): 519–520.

Nahas, G., Trouve, R., and Manger, W. (1990). Cocaine, catecholamines and cardiac toxicity. Acta Anesthesiol Scand, 34(Suppl 94): 77–81.

Novitzky, D., Cooper, D., and Reichart, B. (1987). Haemodynamic and metabolic responses to hormonal therapy in brain dead potential organ donors. Transplantation, 43: 852–854.

Novitzky, D., Cooper, D., and Wicomb, W. (1988). Endocrine changes and metabolic responses. Transplantation Proc, 5(Suppl 7): 33–38.

Novitzky, D., Wicomb, W., Cooper, D. et al. (1984). Electrocardiographic, hemodynamic and endocrine changes occurring during experimental brain death in the Chacma baboon. J Heart Transplant, 4: 63–69.

Novitzky, D., Wicomb, W., Cooper, D. et al. (1986). Prevention of myocardial injury during brain death by total cardiac sympathectomy in the Chacma baboon. Ann Thorac Surg, 41: 520–524.

Oehmichen, M., Homann, P., and Pedal, I. (1990). Diagnostic significance of myofibrillar degeneration of cardiocytes in forensic pathology. Forensic Sci Int, 48: 163–173.

Opie, L., Nathan, D., and Lubbe, W. (1979). Biochemical aspects of arrhythmogeneis and ventricular fibrillation. Am J Cardiol, 48: 131–148.

Peng, S., French, W., Pelikan, P. (1989). Direct cocaine cardiotoxicity demonstrated by endomyocardial biopsy. Arch Pathol Lab Med, 113(8): 842–845.

Rajs, J. and Falconer, B. (1979). Cardiac lesions in intravenous drug addicts. Forensic Sci Int, 13, 193–209.

Rajs, J., Härm, T., and Ormstad, K. (1984). Postmortem findings of pulmonary lesions of older datum in intravenous drug addicts. Virchows Arch, 402: 405–414.

Reichenbach, D. and Moss, N. (1975). Box report with pathology of the heart in sudden cardiac death. Am J Cardiol, 39: 865–872.

Roh, L. and Hamele-Bena, D. (1990). Cocaine-induced ischemic myocardial disease. Am J Forensic Med and Pathol, 11(2): 130–135.

Rona, G. (1985). Catecholamine cardiotoxicity. J Mol Cell Cardiol, 17(4): 291–306.

Schindler, C., Tella, S., Katz, J., and Goldberg, S. (1992). Effects of cocaine and its quaternary derivative cocaine methiodide on cardiovascular function in squirrel monkeys. Euro J Pharmacol, 213: 99–105.

Schwartz, A., Boyle, W., Janzen, D., and Jones, R. (1988). Acute effects of cocaine on catecholamines and cardiac electrophysiology in the conscious dog. Can J Cardiol, 4(4): 188–192.

Simpson, R. and Edwards, W. (1986). Pathogenesis of cocaine-induced ischemic heart disease. Arch Patho Lab Med, 110: 479–484.

Strain, J., Grose, R., Factor, S., and Fisher, J. (1983). Results of endomyocardial biopsy in patients with spontaneous ventricular tachycardia but without apparent structural heart disease. Circulation, 68(6): 1171–1181.

Szakacs, J. and Cannon, A. (1958). l-Norepinephrine myocarditis. Am J Clin Pathol, 30: 425–434.

Szakacs, J., Dimmette, R., and Cowart, E. (1959). Pathologic implications of the catecholamines epinephrine and norepinephrine. U.S. Armed Forces Med J, 102: 908–925.

Taylor, D. and Ho, B. (1977). Neurochemical effects of cocaine following acute and repeated injection. J Neurosci Res, 32(2): 95–101.

Tazelaar, H., Karch, S., Billingham, M., and Stephens, B. (1987). Cocaine and the heart. Hum Pathol, 18: 195–199.

Trouve, R. and Nahas, G. (1986). Nitrendipine: an antidote to cardiac and lethal toxicity of cocaine. Proc Soc Exp Biol and Med, 183: 392–397.

Trouve, R., Nahas, G., Manger, W. et al. (1990b). Interactions of nimodipine and cocaine on endogenous catecholamines in the squirrel monkey. Proc Soc Exp Med, 193: 171–175.

Trouve, R., Nahas, G., and Manger, W. M. (1991). Catecholamines, cocaine toxicity, and their antidotes in the rat. Proc Soc Exp Biol Med, 196(2): 184–187.

Tsujimoto, G., Manger, W., and Hoffman, B. (1984). Desensitization of β-adrenergic receptors by pheochromocytoma. Endocrinology, 114: 1272–1278.

Virmani, R., Rabinowitz, M., Smialek, J., and Smyth, D. (1988). Cardiovascular effects of cocaine: an autopsy study of 40 patients. Am Heart J, 115(5): 1068–1076.

Volkow, N., Fowler, J., Wolf, A. et al. (1992). Distribution and kinetics of carbon-11-cocaine in the human body measured with PET. J Nuc Med, 33: 521–525.

Ward, S., Schuetz, S., Wachsman, L. et al. (1991). Elevated plasma norepinephrine levels in infants of substance-abusing mothers. Am J Dis Child, 145(1): 44–48.

Welder, A., Grammas, P., Fugate, R. et al. (1993). A primary culture system of rat heart-derived endothelial cells for evaluating cocaine-induced vascular injury. Tox Methods, 3(2): 109–118.

Worstman, J., Frank, S., and Cryer, P. (1984). Adrenomedullary response to maximal stress in humans. Am J Med, 77: 779–784.

1.10 Epidemiologic data

In 1994, the most recent year for which complete statistics are available, medical examiners reported 3,981 cocaine-related deaths, an increase of 18% from the 3,220 reported in 1992 (Substance Abuse and Mental Health Services Administration, 1995). Since the medical examiners participating in the DAWN survey perform only 60% of all autopsies done in the United States, the total of all cocaine-releated deaths in 1994 would be well over 6,500. Seventy-five percent of the deaths occurred in men, 56% in whites, 30% in blacks, and only 12% in Hispanics.

Fifty-four percent of these deaths were ruled accidental, 22.4% were suicides, but in the remaining 46%, the cause of death was unknown. In the 26–34-year age group, 53% of the deaths were due to cocaine. The percentage was only slightly lower among persons aged 35–44 years (49%). Cocaine is the most frequent cause of drug-related death in Atlanta, Birmingham, Detroit, Las Vegas, Miami, New Orleans, New York, Newark, Philadelphia, and San Antonio.

Useful information may be obtained by pooling data from across the country, but the process tends to obscure important local variations. Determining the cause of death in drug-related cases is often problematic; scene investigation and clinical history may prove to be more revealing than any findings at autopsy. The findings in any particular case must be compared to the known profile of drug deaths in that area. Significant deviation from the profile should raise suspicions.

Analysis of the roughly 100 cocaine-related deaths processed by the San Francisco Medical Examiner during 1992–1993 disclosed that 85% of the deceased were men, with an average age of 38 years. Cocaine or other drug paraphernalia were found at the scene 65% of the time. In contrast to the national averages, there were nearly equal numbers of whites and blacks but, in spite of the large Asian population, less than 5% were Asian. One-third of the deceased were found in hotels, and one-fifth in apartments. Unlike those dying of heroin abuse, hardly any were found on the street. Almost half of the deceased were also using heroin, but only one-fifth were using alcohol (unpublished data).

These percentages will obviously vary from location to location, and it is important for practitioners to be aware of the profile in their region. In Munich, for instance, heroin is the primary cause of drug-related deaths, usually in combination with alcohol, a much higher percentage are suicides, and the mean age is only 26.5 years (Penning et al., 1993).

References

Penning, R., Fromm, E., Betz, P. et al. (1993). Drug death autopsies at the Munich Institute of Forensic Medicine (1981–1992). Forensic Sci Int, 62: 135–139.
Substance Abuse and Mental Health Services Administration (1995). Annual Medical Examiner Data. Data from the Drug Abuse Warning Network. Statistical Series, Number 13-B. Rockville, MD: U.S. Department of Health and Human Services.

1.11 External markers of cocaine abuse

There are external markers for cocaine abuse that may be of clinical value. None of these changes are particularly common and they are only seen with intense and repeated use. The absence of these external signs has little, if any, significance. The presence of these changes, however, is a strong confirmatory sign that the individual has been a chronic user for some time.

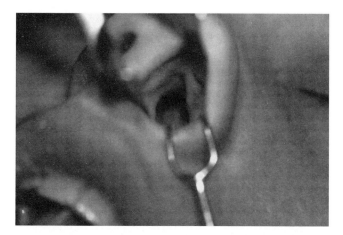

Figure 1.11.1   Perforated nasal septum. This lesion was first reported in conjunction with cocaine use in 1904. It is not absolutely diagnostic for cocaine abuse, since the same defect can be produced by the chronic use of vasoconstrictive nose drops. The first cases of cocaine-related septal perforation were reported just after the turn of the century. Courtesy of Dr. Russel Kridel, University of Texas, Health Sciences Center, Houston.

1.11.1   Perforated nasal septum

Septal perforation is the best known external manifestation of cocaine abuse. The first cases were described in the early 1900s, shortly after the practice of snorting cocaine became popular (Hautant, 1910; Maier, 1926). The presence of this lesion is, however, not pathognomic. Perforations of the nasal septum can also result from chronic abuse of nose drops containing vasoconstrictors (Vilensky, 1982) (see also Section 1.11.3.1).

1.11.2   Cocaine "tracks"

The adulterants most commonly found in cocaine are water soluble. Their repeated injection tends not to produce the chronic inflammatory reactions and granulomas associated with narcotic abuse. Recent injection sites appear as salmon colored bruises, sometimes with a clear central zone about the needle puncture site (Wetli, 1987a; Wetli, 1987b). As lesions become older, they turn blue and yellow, eventually disappearing without leaving any scar. Slowly healing cutaneous ulcers are also seen. The base of the ulcer may be red to gray, and the margins of the ulcers will have a pearly white appearance consistent with epidermal overgrowth (Yaffee, 1968). In experimental animals, healing of lesions is relatively rapid and complete (Bruckner, Beng, and Levy, 1982).

The histopathologic effects of subcutaneous cocaine injection have been studied on a limited scale (Bruckner et al., 1982). In one study, subcutaneous injections of 0.1–2.0% cocaine solutions were found to cause blanching and

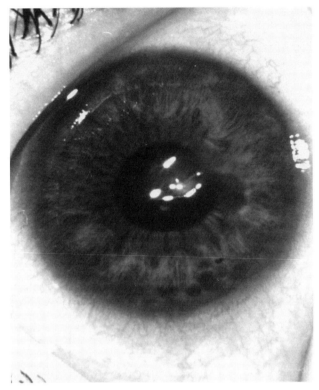

Figure 1.11.3   Crack keratitis. Volatilized cocaine anesthesizes the cornea so that abusers can't feel how hard they're rubbing their eyes. There is also evidence that crack smokers may be less able to resist corneal infection. Infected ulcers with corneal clouding may be the result. Courtesy of Dr. Peter S. Hersh, Chairman, Department of Ophthalmology, Bronx-Lebanon Hospital. Published with permission from the American Journal of Ophthalmology. Copyright 1991 by the Ophthalmic Publishing Co., Am J Opth, Vol. 111, No. 3, pp. 247–248.

hemorrhage. However, other workers have found no histologic damage, even after rats were repeatedly injected with substantial subcutaneous doses (32 mg/kg twice a day) of cocaine over a two week period (Durazzo et al., 1993). If changes do occur, it is not because of cocaine-induced vasoconstriction and ischemia. Epinephrine is a more powerful vasoconstrictor than cocaine, and it does not produce similar lesions.

1.11.3 "Crack keratitis"

Because "crack" smoke is a local anesthetic, the corneas of crack smokers may inadvertently be anesthetized. When the smoker rubs his eyes, too much pressure may be applied and a sizable piece of the cornea may be rubbed off. This type of corneal abrasion has been referred to as "crack eye" (Ravin and Ravin, 1979). The same mechanism may lead to keratitis with corneal ulcers and infections (Strominger, Sachs, and Hersh, 1990). Microbial and monilial keratitis have both been reported in crack smokers, suggesting that more than mechanical factors may be involved (Zagelbaum et al., 1991), and in one report of four patients, two were HIV-infected (Wakil et al., 1995). The results of some studies suggest that abnormalities of cell-mediated immunity develop in chronic cocaine users (Watzl and Watson, 1990). Chronic crack smokers may have a diminished ability to cope with normal bacterial flora.

1.11.4 Dental erosions

Chronic intranasal cocaine users may have erosions on the enamel of the upper front teeth. Erosions result when the teeth are bathed with acid cocaine hydrochloride that has trickled down from the sinuses and the posterior oropharynx (Krutchkoff et al., 1990).

1.11.5 "Crack thumb"

"Crack thumb" was first described in 1990, and is a "repetitive use" type of injury. Crack smokers often use disposable cigarette lighters to heat their pipes. They may do this many times a day, and a callus can result from repeated contact of the thumb with the serrated wheel that ignites the lighter. The callus is usually located on the ulnar aspect of the thumb (Larkin, 1990). Constant handling of a heated crack pipe can lead to superficial burns on the palmar aspect of the hands. The same type of injury happens in "ice" smokers.

1.11.6 "Crack hands"

This finding has much in common with "crack thumb." Examination of chronic "crack" smokers may disclose blackened, hyperkeratotic lesions on the palmar aspect of the hands. The pipes used to smoke cocaine can become quite hot, and chronic users are likely to sustain multiple small burns (Feeny and Briggs, 1992).

1.11.7 Evidence of terminal seizures

Another occasionally observed external marker is a bite mark on the lips and tongue. A minority of cocaine users may experience seizure activity as a terminal event (Wetli, 1987a; Wetli, 1987b). However, since seizures do not always occur, even in conjunction with massive overdose, and since many other agents can cause terminal seizure activity, the usefulness of this sign is somewhat limited.

References

Bruckner, J., Jiang, W., Beng, T., and Ho, T. (1982). Histopathological evaluation of cocaine induced skin lesions in the rat. J Cutaneous Pathol, 9: 83–95.

Durazzo, T., Gauvin, D., Goulden, K. et al. (1993). Technical report: subcutaneous administration of cocaine in the rat. Pharm Biochem Behav, 49: 1007–1010.

Feeny, C. and Briggs, S. (1992). Crack hands: a dermatologic effect of smoking crack cocaine. Cutis, 50: 193–194.

Hautant, A. (1910). Über den chronischen Kokainismus mit nasaler Anwendung. Int Zentralbl Laryngol Rhinol, 25: 138.

Krutchkoff, D., Eisenberg, E., O'Brien, J., and Ponzillo, J. (1990). Cocaine-induced dental erosions. N Engl J Med, 322(6): 408.

Larkin, R. (1990). The callus of crack cocaine. N Engl J Med, 323(10): 685.

Maier, H. (1926). Der Kokainismus (O. J. Kalant from the German 1926 edition, Trans.). Toronto: Addiction Research Foundation.

Ravin, J. and Ravin, L. (1979). Blindness due to illicit use of topical cocaine. Ann Opthalmol, 11(6): 863–864.

Strominger, M., Sachs, R., and Hersh, P. (1990). Microbial keratitis with crack cocaine. Arch Ophthalmol, 108(12): 1672.

Vilensky, W. (1982). Illicit and licit drugs causing perforation of the nasal septum: case report. J Forensic Sci, 27(4): 958–962.

Wakil, A., Hassman, E., and Lam, S. (1995). Infectious corneal ulcers associated with crack cocaine abuse. Ann Opth, 27: 96–100.

Watzl, B. and Watson, R. (1990). Immunomodulation by cocaine — a neuroendocrine mediated response. Life Sci, 46(19): 1319–1329.

Wetli, C. (1987a). Fatal reactions to cocaine. In A. Washington and M. Gold (Eds.), Cocaine: a clinician's handbook. New York, London: Guilford Press.

Wetli, C. (1987b). Fatal cocaine intoxication. Am J Forensic Med and Pathol, 8(1): 1–2.

Yaffee, H. (1968). Dermatologic manifestations of cocaine addiction. Cutis, 4: 286–287.

Zagelbaum, B., Tannenbaum, M., and Hersh, P. (1991). *Candida Albicans* corneal ulcer associated with crack cocaine. Am J Ophthalmol, 111(2): 248–249.

1.12 Toxicity by organ system

1.12.1 Skin

Subcutaneous drug injection (called "skin popping") is much more common among heroin than cocaine users, and cocaine users who elect this route generally experience fewer complications than heroin users. The adulterants found in cocaine are much more likely to be water soluble and, therefore, less likely to produce irritation. Occasionally the practice can lead to subcutaneous abcess formation, sometimes accompanied by cellulitis, lymphangitis, and lymphadenopathy. Infection is generally the result of oral flora sensitive to multiple antibiotics, but surgery is often required (Thomas et al., 1995).

Scleroderma is an uncommon disease. The estimated annual incidence is between four and twelve new cases per 1,000,000 per year. Scleroderma is three times more common in females, but when it occurs in young people, it is 15 times more common in women than men (Medsger and Masi, 1979). The median age of onset for scleroderma is between 40 and 50. Three cases of scleroderma have been reported in cocaine users, all males, two of whom were in their 20s, and a third in his 40s (Kerr, 1989; Trozak and Gould, 1984).

The principal abnormality in scleroderma is the deposition of pathologic amounts of normal collagen. In some instances, the process may be confined to the skin, but pathologic deposition may also be generalized. The etiology of scleroderma is not understood. Various theories have implicated alterations in cellular immunity, fibroblast function, and small vessel disease (Gay et al., 1980). The final common pathway by which the disease is manifested is believed to be a small vessel disorder that eventually produces fibrosis of the affected organ (Follansbee et al., 1984). Cocaine abuse and scleroderma share certain common features. Vascular abnormalities are common in both, particularly in the heart. In classic scleroderma, the heart becomes fibrotic and contraction band necrosis is frequently seen (Follansbee et al., 1984). The presence of myocardial fibrosis predisposes both groups to conduction defects and arrhythmias. Both groups are prone to heart failure and sudden death. The morphologic changes in the hearts of both groups are similar enough to raise the possibility that catecholamine toxicity is common to both.

There are other similarities. Both cocaine users and patients with scleroderma may develop isolated cerebral vasculitis. It is an uncommon complication of both disorders, but it has been observed in both, even in the absence of systemic vasculitis. In the two biopsy-proven cases of cocaine-associated vasculitis, the vessels were infiltrated with lymphocytes. In the one case of scleroderma-associated vasculitis, the biopsy was non-diagnostic (Pathak and Gabor, 1991).

References

Follansbee, W., Curtiss, E., Medsger, T. et al. (1984). Physiologic abnormalities of cardiac function in progressive systemic sclerosis with diffuse scleroderma. N Engl J Med, 310: 142–148.

Gay, R., Buckingham, R., Prince, R. et al. (1980). Collagen types synthesized in dermal fibroblast cultures from patients with early progressive systemic sclerosis. Arthritis Rheum, 23(2): 190–196.

Kerr, H. (1989). Cocaine and scleroderma. South Med J, 82(10): 275–276.

Medsger, T. and Masi, A. (1979). The epidemiology of systemic sclerosis. Clin Rheum Dis, 5: 15–25.

Pathak, R. and Gabor, A. (1991). Scleroderma and central nervous system vasculitis. Stroke, 22: 410–413.

Thomas, W., Almand, J., Stark, G. et al. (1995). Hand injuries secondary to subcutaneous illicit drug injection. Ann Plastic Surg, 34: 27–31.

Trozak, D. and Gould, W. (1984). Cocaine abuse and connective tissue disease. J Am Acad Dermatol, 10: 525.

1.12.2 Cardiovascular system

Cocaine causes vascular disease. Vessels throughout the body can be involved, but the brunt of the injury is borne by the heart. In general, there is little to distinguish cocaine-induced disease from naturally occurring disease, and no single abnormality is absolutely diagnostic for cocaine-associated disease. However, in some instances the pattern of histologic changes can be diagnostic. Specifically, the changes associated with catecholamine toxicity are distinctive and are common to stimulant abuse in general. In this section, the pathology of cocaine-associated vascular disease will be reviewed with special emphasis on the problem of catecholamine toxicity.

1.12.2.1 Coronary artery disease

Myocardial infarction is a relatively frequent complication of cocaine use, but several years into the second cocaine pandemic, there still is a paucity of autopsy data. Three separate mechanisms have been identified which could account for infarction in cocaine users. Most infarcts are due to the presence of fixed lesions. In various reported series, the incidence of fixed lesions, presumably atheromatous, but possibly thrombotic, has been anywhere from 0% (Virmani et al., 1987) to well over 50% (Mathias, 1986; Minor et al., 1991). Only a handful of published reports have included autopsy findings (Stenberg et al., 1989; Young and Glauber, 1947; Nanji and Filipenko, 1984; Kossowsky and Lyon, 1984; Isner et al., 1986; Simpson and Edwards, 1986), and occasionally angiographic findings (Kossowsky and Lyon, 1984; Pasternack et al., 1986; Cregler and Mark, 1985; Howard et al., 1985; Wilkins et al., 1985; Weiss, 1986; Ascher et al., 1988; Isner et al., 1986; Rollingher et al., 1986; Rod and Zucker, 1987; Smith et al., 1987; Zimmerman et al., 1987) have been described. Approximately half of the individual case reports describe lesions.

Failure to demonstrate lesions angiographically does not necessarily mean that they are not there. Certain types of cocaine-related coronary lesions are neither thrombotic nor atherosclerotic, and may involve long segments of vessels in a concentric fashion. The lesions may not be noticed on angiography unless earlier films are available for comparison (Karch and Billingham, 1988; Simpson and Edwards, 1986; Chow, Robertson, and Stein, 1990). An arteriogram which looks normal may actually be missing serious underlying disease. It may very well be that the frequency of these lesions is significantly underestimated.

Simpson and Edwards were the first to describe intimal hyperplasia as a cause of myocardial infarction in a cocaine user (Simpson and Edwards, 1986). The patient, a 21-year old construction worker, had multivessel obstruction due entirely to intimal hyperplasia. There was no sign of collagen or elastin deposition. This type of lesion is routinely seen in transplanted organs and also occurs in some connective tissue disorders (Dawkins et al., 1985). It is classified as a type of "chronic rejection" and presumably occurs secondary to an immunologic abnormality. Simpson and Edwards postulated that recurrent episodes of coronary spasm might lead to endothelial injury with platelet aggregation and release of smooth muscle growth factor producing obstructive intimal hyperplasia. Whether or not their explanation is correct, similar alterations have been observed in the hearts of other cocaine users (Roh and Hamele-Bena, 1990).

Lesions nearly identical to those described by Simpson and Edwards can be produced by catecholamine excess. Even though modern histologic studies of cocaine-induced changes are almost non-existent, the older liter-

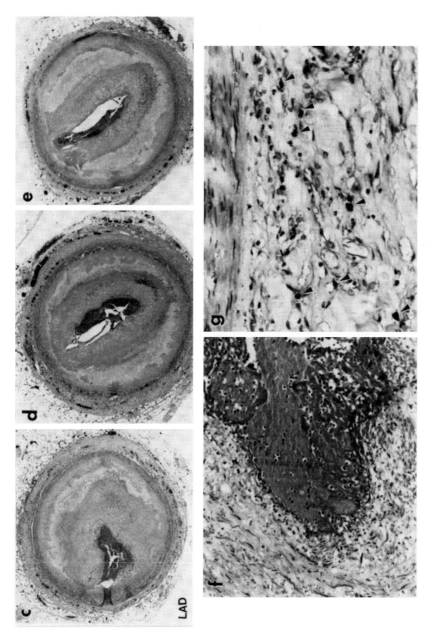

Figure 1.12.2.1 (1)   Adventitial mast cells in cocaine users. Compared to age and sex matched controls, more mast cells are present in the adventitia of cocaine users' coronary arteries, and the degree of luminal narrowing correlates well with the number of mast cells present. On the left are three cross-sections of severely diseased LAD from a chronic cocaine user. On the right are higher-power views of the adventitia in this vessel. Toluidine blue staining demonstrates the presence of numerous mast cells; orig. magnification 150×. Courtesy of Dr. Rene Virmani, Chairman, Dept. of Cardiovascular Pathology, Armed Forces Institute of Pathology.

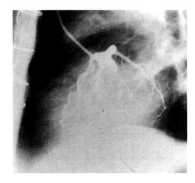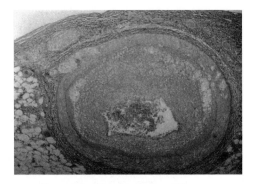

Figure 1.12.2.1 (2 and 3)   Coronary artery disease in cocaine users. The coronary arteries of cocaine users may undergo the same type of intimal hyperplasia as seen in transplant recipients. Because this sort of lesion concentrically involves the entire length of the involved vessel, obstructions may not be apparent unless earlier studies are available for comparison. The normal appearing study on the left was obtained just two weeks before the patient died of myocardial infarction. On the right is a cross section of the LAD from the same patient. Concentric intimal hyperplasia has almost entirely obstructed the lumen. H&E. Courtesy of Margaret Billingham, Stanford University School of Medicine.

ature contains many observations of what catecholamine treatment does to blood vessels. Thirty years ago, Szakacs found that dogs infused with norepinephrine at 1–1.5 µg/min/kg would consistently develop coronary artery lesions. The initial response was fibrinoid necrosis, followed by intimal hyperplasia. Szakacs also observed exactly the same types of lesions in humans who died after receiving prolonged infusions of vasopressors and in patients dying of pheochromocytoma. Similar lesions were also found in the gastrointestinal tract. Occasionally, these lesions completely obstructed the small arteries, resulting in bowel infarction and perforation (Szakacs et al., 1959). Bowel infarction and perforation have also been seen in cocaine users (Endress and King, 1990; Freudenberger et al., 1990; Nathan and Hernandez, 1990; Nalbandian et al., 1985; Mizrahi et al., 1988). Histologically, the picture is no different than the one described by Simpson and Edwards in the coronary arteries. A slight variation on this theme was seen in one patient with cocaine-related bowel infarction who had abnormalities of the submucosal arterioles with disruption of the internal elastic membrane that projected into and obstructed the lumen (Garfia et al., 1990). Endomyocardial biopsies from 11 cocaine users with symptoms of myocardial ischemia demonstrated marked medial thickening of small intramyocardial arteries (20–40 µM) in 7 of the 11 patients (Majid et al., 1990). In all 11 of these patients, arteriography, including ergonovine challenge, was unremarkable.

Thickening of the media and intimal hyperplasia has also been seen in the nasal submucosal vessels of chronic cocaine addicts (Chow et al., 1990), suggesting that the process occurs throughout the body. Further support for this notion is lent by the fact that similar changes are also seen in patients with pheochromocytoma (Szakacs et al., 1959). More modern studies on cocaine's effects, done with scanning electron microscopy, have tended to

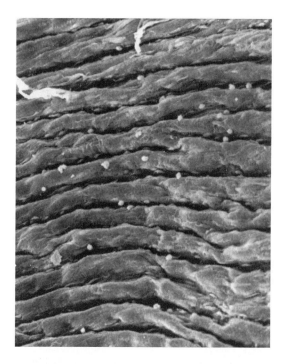

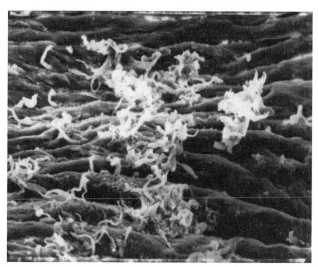

Figure 1.12.2.1 (4 and 5)   Effects of cocaine on endothelium. Both scanning micrographs are of a canine coronary artery. The photograph on top is from a control animal; orig. magnification 312×. The lower photograph is from a dog that received 1 mg/kg/day of cocaine for 4 weeks. Sloughing of endothelial cells is evident; orig. magnification 520×. Courtesy of Dr. Randall L. Tackett, Head, Dept. of Pharmacology and Toxicology, University of Georgia.

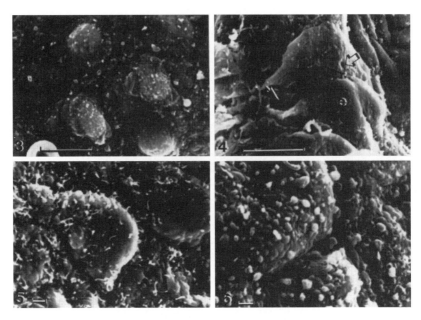

Figure 1.12.2.1 (6)   Transplacental cardiotoxicity. Whether or not cocaine exerts cardiotoxic effects in humans remains an open question. In animal models, toxicity is easily demonstrated. This pair of scanning micrographs shows endothelial slough-ing in hamster neonatal right atrium. The photograph on the left is a scanning micrograph of control right atria. The photograph on the right is from a neonate whose mother received cocaine on the 6th, 7th, and 9th day of gestation. The endo-thelium is abnormally flattened and no longer completely covers the underlying myocytes. Both scans are at the same magnification (scale bar = 10 μm). Courtesy of Dr. Jacques Gilloteaux, Department of Anatomy, College of Medicine, Northeastern Ohio Universities.

confirm Szakacs' earlier work with catecholamines. Coronary arteries from dogs chronically treated with cocaine show signs of endothelial cell slough-ing and occasional thrombus formation. Blood vessels from the same animals have also demonstrated increased responsiveness to norepinephrine and serotonin (Jones and Tackett, 1990).

Whatever the etiology of the underlying fixed lesions, cocaine use can make coronary artery lesions symptomatic. Intranasal cocaine (2 mg/kg body weight) causes increases in arterial pressure and rate-pressure product. At the same time the rate-pressure product is rising, coronary sinus blood flow significantly decreases (Lange et al., 1990). As a result, cocaine increases myocardial work and oxygen demand while, at the same time, decreasing blood flow. If asymptomatic lesions are already present, the extra work load imposed by the cocaine can lead to infarction, even without coronary spasm. Increased oxygen demand in the presence of preexisting lesions can be sufficient to cause infarction. The results of earlier studies suggest that cocaine induces platelet aggregation, thereby increasing the likelihood of thrombosis and infarction (Togna et al., 1985). More recent studies have found no evidence that cocaine mediates increases in platelet aggregation or dense granule release (Kugelmass and Ware, 1992), but many other cocaine-induced changes could lead to the same result. Increased thromboxane generation in the presence of underlying endothelial injuries can lead to thrombosis and infarction. (Stenberg et al., 1989; Kolodgie et al., 1990; Virmani et al., 1989). Clinical experience suggests that it is the combination of increased oxygen demand and decreased blood supply, with or without thrombosis, that has probably accounted for the majority of reported cases of infarction.

Autopsy studies and other epidemiologic data suggest that cocaine itself is atherogeneic (Escabedo et al., 1992). In one study, over 60% of patients with cocaine-associated sudden deaths had moderate to severe coronary atherosclerosis (the patients had a mean age of 47). In such a young age group, a much lower percentage of significant lesions would be expected (Dressler et al., 1990). Other autopsy studies have also noted the increased incidence of significant atherosclerotic lesions (Virmani et al., 1988; Kolodgie et al., 1990; Dressler et al., 1990; Karch et al., 1995). When the coronary arteries of cocaine abusers dying of thrombosis were compared to those of cocaine users without thrombosis, and to cases of sudden death unassociated with cocaine use, the average age for the cocaine-thrombosis group was only 29 years and the degree of luminal narrowing was much higher than would be expected in this age group. In the patients with thrombosis, there was moderate to severe coronary atherosclerosis and increased numbers of adventitial mast cells (Kolodgie et al., 1991). One feature that distinguished the cocaine group was the fact that, even though thrombi were present in vessels that had extensive atherosclerosis, there was no plaque rupture or hemorrhage as would normally be seen in atherosclerotic lesions not associated with cocaine use.

The role of histamine in atherosclerosis is controversial (Born, 1991), but there is good evidence that histamine-containing mast cells may be implicated in the pathogenesis of human coronary vasospasm (Ginsberg et al., 1981). The presence of increased numbers of histamine-rich mast cells has been noted in atherosclerotic coronary vessels, even in non-drug using populations. Histamine is not the only vasoactive compound contained in mast cells. Prostaglandin D_2, and leukotrienes C_4 and D_4 have also been demonstrated (Maseri et al., 1978). The potential exists for a large number of possibly harmful interactions between elevated circulating catecholamines, cytokines, and other tissue factors, and it would not be surprising if cocaine users did have accelerated atherosclerosis. Cocaine users have elevated circulating catecholamines, and it has been shown that LDL uptake by arterial walls is accelerated by both epinephrine and norepinephrine (Born, 1991). The difficulty in interpreting these studies is that the patients involved are frequently polydrug abusers and, more often than not, cigarette smokers. Singling out one causal agent on the basis of such limited retrospective is a formidable task.

1.12.2.2 Coronary artery spasm

Cocaine-induced spasm has been demonstrated angiographically, but the mechanism is not known. Human and animal studies have yielded conflicting results, and there is no assurance that the changes produced by cocaine *in vitro* occur *in vivo*. Nor is there reason to suppose that the same mechanism producing spasm in coronary arteries will produce spasm in cerebral vessels.

Experimental results can be influenced by the type of tissue being studied, by the age of the experimental animal being used, and by the type and amount of anesthetic given to the animal. Outcome is also determined by the functional state of the vascular endothelium, the presence or absence of other abused drugs, and the underlying level of sympathetic adrenergic activity. None of the published studies have included receptor measurements, and without knowing the receptor status of the animal (or the patients), there is no way to know if responses of the sympathetic nervous system are comparable. The rate at which cocaine is metabolized in different species is widely disparate. This could explain the confusing and conflicting responses that have been reported (Perreault et al., 1993; Busija, 1994; Tella et al., 1993). Since almost all of the reported studies on cocaine-related spasm were done before it was widely appreciated that the endothelium-derived relaxing factor was actually nitric oxide (Furchgott, 1988), the role of nitric oxide in cocaine-associated coronary spasm remains to be seen. However, preliminary data suggest that mice treated with agents which inhibit nitric oxide production do not develop cocaine sensitization, and do not manifest the typical lethal response seen with long-term high dose cocaine administration (Itzhak, 1993).

Isolated rat hearts perfused with cocaine (100 µg–500 µg/mL) display physiologic and morphologic evidence of spasm (Vitullo et al., 1989). In the smaller vessels (10 µm–65 µm) endothelial cells were seen bulging into the lumen of constricted vessels. Scalloping of the internal elastic lamina and separation of the vessels from surrounding tissues were also observed. Ultrastructural studies of these vessels showed vacuolization of the cytoplasm in both endothelial and smooth muscle cells. Microvascular constriction is also suggested by studies in swine, where cumulative intravenous doses of cocaine produce myocardial ischemia and cardiogenic shock, even though epicardial artery diameter is decreased by only 37–45% (Núñez et al., 1994).

Others researchers have shown different results. Bedotto et al., found no sign of spasm or decreased contractility, though he did note peripheral venous and arterial constriction (Bedotto et al., 1988). And, in one well designed study, intravenous cocaine produced rapid, dose-dependent coronary vasodilation in anesthetized beagles. One minute post injection, flow increased by up to 175% (Friedrichs et al., 1990).

Nonetheless, well designed clinical studies have also demonstrated cocaine-mediated coronary artery constriction in man. Two milligrams per kilogram of cocaine given intranasally to 45 patients undergoing cardiac catheterization caused no chest pain, but did reduce the diameter of the left coronary artery by at least 8–12% (Lange et al., 1989; Lange et al., 1989). In related studies, the same workers found that vasoconstriction is more intense in atherosclerotic vessels (Flores et al., 1990). Further, it was found that cocaine and cigarettes act synergistically in these diseased segments to produce even greater degrees of vasoconstriction (19% for cigarettes and cocaine combined vs. 9% after cocaine and 5% after smoking) (Moliterno et al., 1994). If the combination of cigarette smoking and cocaine leads to increased vasoconstriction, there is evidence that combining alcohol with cocaine has just the opposite effect. When patients being evaluated for chest pain were given alcohol and cocaine in combination, significant increases in myocardial oxygen demand occurred. However, there was also a concomitant increase in measured epicardial coronary artery diameter, suggesting that there was no net decrease in myocardial oxygen supply (Pirwitz et al., 1995).

These findings are consistent with generally held beliefs that coronary artery spasm occurs at the site of preexisting narrowing, and are particularly important given the high incidence of coronary artery disease in cocaine users (Karch et al., 1995). But, by themselves, these observations will not account for many episodes of infarction in cocaine users. In man, at least, anything less than a 75% cross-sectional coronary obstruction produces no symptoms. Epicardial vessel constriction of only 10–12%, as described in these studies, should be asymptomatic, unless severe atherosclerotic disease was already present. And, in fact, other studies have shown no electrocardiographic evidence of ischemia. After giving 1.2 mg/kg of cocaine intravenously to 20 human volunteers (resulting in mean cocaine levels of 709 ng/mL, vs. levels of only 120 ng/mL in Lange et al.'s studies cited above), only non-specific T and R wave changes occurred (Eisenberg et al., 1995), and there were no changes in the left ventricular ejection fraction or wall motion score index.

As more evidence accumulates, it is becoming increasingly apparent that central stimulation of the sympathetic axis plays an important role in the vascular adjustments to cocaine use, and that cocaine-related pressor effects (and therefore cocaine-related vasoconstriction) are mediated by norepinephrine released from neurons of the sympathetic nervous system, while other changes, such as heart rate, are mediated by centrally-mediated release of epinephrine from the adrenal medulla (Tella et al., 1993). In intact organisms, the net effects of cocaine are closely linked to the underlying level of sympathetic adrenergic activity (Perreault et al., 1993).

The first suggestion that there was a relationship between coronary vasospasm and alterations in adrenergic function came from studies of Prinzmetal's angina. In that disorder, repolarization abnormalities (QT prolongation) precede episodes of spasm (Roberts et al., 1982; Ricci et al., 1979). It is well known that QT interval prolongation may be secondary to increased sympathetic discharge. In animal studies, unilateral stellate ganglion stimulation causes selective coronary spasm, QT prolongation, and a marked increase in coronary artery resistance. These changes can all be prevented with α adrenergic blockade (Randall et al., 1972), and all of these changes can be produced by giving cocaine. Animals infused with cocaine develop PR and QT prolongation (Parker et al., 1989; Rosen et al., 1988; Beckman et al., 1991). Torsades-de pointes (reciprocating ventricular tachycardia associated with QT interval prolongation) has occurred in cocaine-intoxicated patients (Rosen et al., 1988). A second report describing cocaine-induced torsades in a patient with congenital idiopathic long QT syndrome lends further support to the notion that sympathetic function is altered in cocaine users (Schrem et al., 1990).

Finally, it has been argued that contraction band necrosis is an anatomic marker for coronary spasm. Factor and Cho believe they have identified what they feel are contraction bands in the media of coronary arteries (Factor and Cho, 1985), and other studies have confirmed the findings in cases of brain death (Novitzky et al., 1984). Lesions appear in the media as discrete zones of hypereosinophilia, usually in widened cells with rarefaction of the cytoplasm on either side of the eosinophilia area. It has been suggested that this morphologic finding is a marker both for coronary artery spasm and sudden death. Similar lesions have been produced in the coronary arteries of animals infused with catecholamines (Joris and Majno, 1981). When observed in humans, such lesions are frequently associated with the presence of nonocclusive microthrombi and, more often than not, are found adjacent to atherosclerotic plaque ruptures and mural plaque hemorrhages. Such lesions have yet to be identified in cocaine users.

1.12.2.3 Myocardial diseases

Chronic cocaine users have enlarged hearts. Compared with controls, rats chronically treated with cocaine have larger left ventricles (Besse et al., 1994; Tseng et al., 1994), increased collagen content, higher levels of atrial naturetic hormone (Besse et al., 1994; Hargrave and Castle, 1995), and increased expression of the low ATPase myosin isoform V3 (Morris et al., 1994; Besse et al., 1994). Echocardiographic studies of asyptomatic cocaine users have produced conflicting results. Several have found significant increases in left ventricular mass and posterior wall thickness (Brickner et al., 1991; Om et al., 1993), but others have not (Hoegerman et al., 1995; Eisenberg et al., 1995). The conflicting results are probably explained by the sensitivity of the techniques used. In most cocaine users, the increase in heart size is less than 10% (Karch et al., 1995). It is an open question whether echocardiography can reliably detect increases in heart size amounting to less than 50 grams.

Myocardial hypertrophy in cocaine users has also been confirmed in studies comparing electrocardiograms of age-sex matched controls to those of asymptomatic cocaine users in rehabilitation, and to symptomatic cocaine users with chest pain (Chakko et al., 1994; Nademanee et al., 1994). More importantly, increased heart size has also been confirmed by direct measurements made at autopsy (Escabedo et al., 1992; Karch et al., 1995; Wetli, 1995). Heart weights of asymptomatic cocaine-using trauma fatalities were found to be 10% heavier than those of controls, even though the heart weights of both groups fell within ranges generally considered to be normal. How cocaine use induces myocyte hypertrophy is not known. Many different chemical and mechanical signals can make myocytes enlarge. Most of the stimuli associated with myocardial hypertrophy cause activation of a G-protein and either adenyl cyclase or phospholipase-C. Activation of either leads to activation of the genes

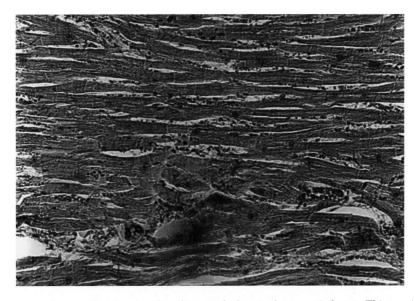

Figure 1.12.2.3.1 Contraction band necrosis in cocaine user's heart. This section of myocardium, stained with H&E, is from the heart of a cocaine user with sudden death syndrome. The dark bands traversing the cells are composed of clumped myofilaments that are no longer functional. Lesions are extremely focal, with damaged myocytes surrounded by apparently normal cells. San Francisco Medical Examiner Case # 92-0147.

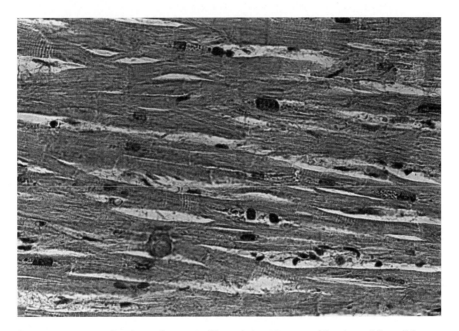

Figure 1.12.2.3.2 Section of myocardium from 32-year old man with sudden arrhythmic death. H&E stain. Widespread contraction band necrosis is evident throughout. San Francisco Medical Examiner Case # 95-0752.

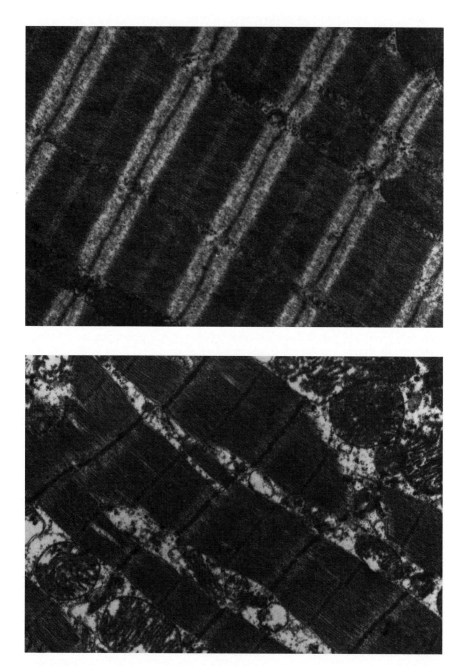

Figure 1.12.2.3.3 Mitochondria disruption and myofibrillar damage. The photograph on top is from a control rat, that below is from a rat infused with 40 mg/kg/day for 21 days. The mitochondria are swollen and translocated, and many of the myofilaments are degenerating. Original magnification 7,200×. Courtesy of Prof. M. Maillet, Hôpital Lariboisière, Paris.

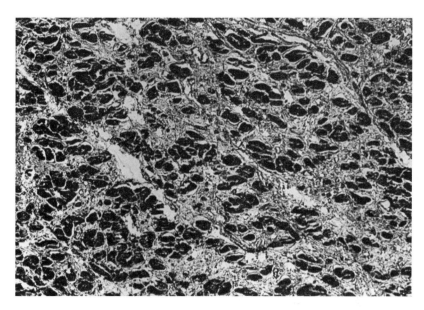

Figure 1.12.2.3.4 Myocardial fibrosis is frequently observed in the hearts of both opiate and stimulant abusers. The etiology for fibrosis in these individuals is not always clear, but much of the change may reflect healing bouts of contraction band necrosis. This section is from a 33-year-old woman with cocaine-associated sudden death. H&E stain. San Francisco Medical Examiner Case # 88-0708.

needed to make the proteins necessary for cell growth (Francis and Carlyle, 1993). The myocardial hypertrophy that occurs after infarction is accompanied by activation of early expression genes such as c-*fos*, c-*jun*, and c-*myc*. However, that is not the case in cocaine users, or at least not the case in rats with cocaine-associated myocardial hypertrophy (Besse et al., 1994), even though the expression of these early genes is well documented in experimental animal brains. Whatever the cause, heart size is an independent risk factor for sudden death (Kannel et al., 1969; Dunn and Pringle, 1993). Regardless of drug use, it would be difficult to overstate the importance of this observation.

Unfortunately, a 10% increase in heart weight is likely to go unrecognized at autopsy; in life, without serial studies, an increase in weight of only 40–50 grams will not be disclosed by ultrasonography, nor would such a modest weight increase cause wall thickness beyond generally accepted limits. Even if wall thicknesses were fastidiously measured at autopsy, which is not always the case, the increase would most likely go undetected. Weighing of the heart could disclose increased weight, but since there is no universally accepted way to determine heart weight, methadologic differences are likely to obscure the findings.

Several different systems for determining normal heart weight are in use. Some pathologists use arbitrary cutoffs; 380 or 400 grams for men and 350 grams for women. Others consider heart weight to be normal provided the heart weighs less than 0.4% of the body weight (0.45% for women) (Ludwig, 1979). However, the most reliable approach is to use the Mayo Clinic nomogram relating heart weight to body weight (see the Appendix

Table 1.12.2.3.1 Differences Between Ischemic and Catecholamine Necrosis

Ischemic Necrosis	Catecholamine Necrosis
Involves many cells in area supplied by a single vessel	Very focal, necrotic cell may be surrounded by normal cells
Myofilaments remain in register	Myofilaments destroyed, forming eosinophilic clumps
Mitochondria remain neatly packed and are of uniform size	Mitochondria are translocated with distorted shapes

for nomogram). This nomogram is based on measurements made in 890 autopsies of individuals found to be free of heart disease (Kitzman et al., 1988). Hearts weighing significantly more than predicted by the nomogram are abnormal, even if the heart weighs less than the 400 grams or 0.4% of body weight. In cases of sudden death, increased heart size may well have been a contributing factor, and should not be ignored. Hearts of cocaine users that significantly exceed the weight predicted by the nomogram are abnormal, and the weight increase may, in some cases, be the cause of death.

A handful of clinical reports have noted an association between dilated cardiomyopathy and long-term cocaine use. Most of these reports are not very informative, since they merely describe the occurrence of heart failure in polydrug abusers, although one pregnant abuser did have biopsy proven sarcoid (Seballos et al., 1994). Without angiography or biopsies, the diagnosis remains in question (Wiener et al., 1986; Chokshi et al., 1989b; Duell, 1987; Wolfson and Hoyga, 1990; Mendelson and Chandler, 1992). The limited number of morphologic observations that have been published suggest that cardiomyopathy, when it occurs in cocaine and amphetamine users, is catecholamine-mediated (Karch and Billingham, 1988; Peng et al., 1989; Henzlova et al., 1991). The myocardial response to chronic catecholamine toxicity has been well characterized and is the same in man and animals. Norepinephrine "myocarditis" was observed almost as soon as intravenous pressor agents were introduced (Szakacs and Cannon, 1958). Histologically, this type of necrosis is indistinguishable from what is seen in patients and animals with pheochromocytoma (Rosenbaum et al., 1987). Contraction band necrosis is the earliest recognizable lesion.

Catecholamine-induced necrosis and ischemic necrosis can be distinguished by their pattern of distribution. In cases of ischemic injury, all the cells supplied by a given vessel will be affected. When the injury is due to catecholamine excess, individual necrotic myocytes are found interspersed between normal cells. Distribution is, in fact, one of the principal diagnostic features of catecholamine injury. Another feature which separates the two is the arrangement of the myofilaments. When the insult is ischemic, the myofilaments remain in register. When the damage is due to catecholamine excess, the filaments are disrupted. There is no "zone" of injury with catecholamine necrosis, and there is no apparent relationship to blood supply. After 12 or more hours have elapsed, a mononuclear infiltrate, predominantly lymphocytic, may be seen. The necrotic myocytes are eventually reabsorbed and replaced by non-conduction fibrous tissue. The hallmark of both the acute and healed catecholamine lesions is that they are extremely focal. With repeat bouts of necrosis, the ventricle becomes increasingly fibrotic, leading to altered function and abnormal impulse propagation (Karch and Billingham, 1987; Weber et al., 1994).

One study describes the findings in three patients with histories of cocaine abuse and end-stage chronic heart failure who underwent cardiac transplantation. The morphologic changes in the native hearts were noted to be distinctly different from those seen in other patients with the same clinical diagnosis. There were fewer nuclear abnormalities and less myocyte hypertrophy. The fibrosis was much more focal in distribution and there were focal lymphocytic infiltrates (Karch and Billingham, 1988). Biopsy findings in a second group of seven patients, six with recent onset of congestion failure and one with chest pain, showed very similar changes. There was myocyte necrosis in five of the seven patients, and its distribution was identical to that seen when contraction band necrosis occurs as a result of catecholamine toxicity. Necrotic cells were found next to normal cells with no apparent relationship to blood supply. Focal interstitial fibrosis, of varying degrees of severity, was noted throughout. In two specimens, necrosis was associated with predominantly lymphocytic infiltrates. Nor was there eosinophilia (Peng et al., 1989) (see below). Similar changes have been described in chronic amphetamine abusers (Smith et al., 1976).

Contraction band necrosis is a prominent feature of all myocardial biopsies, regardless of the underlying cause. For that reason, contraction bands found in biopsy material are difficult to assess (Adomina et al., 1967; Karch and Billingham, 1986). Clinical experience suggests that the presence of nuclear pyknosis may be one way to distinguish preexisting contraction band lesions from those produced by the biopsy process itself; however, that has never been proven in a controlled study. In some of the biopsies, Z-band remnants can be seen with electron microscopy. This particular finding is classically associated with dilated congestion cardiomyopathy and is not generally associated with the type of necrosis resulting from catecholamine toxicity. While it has not been observed in other patients with cocaine-related heart disease, it has been seen in patients with amphetamine toxicity (Smith et al., 1976). Its presence probably signifies only that necrosis was very severe.

Bravetta and Invernezzi were the first researchers to report finding cellular infiltrates in the heart of a cocaine user, and that was more than 70 years ago (Bravetta and Invernizzi, 1922)! Since then, the observations have been repeated many times. However, 64 years elapsed between the publication of the Bravetta and Invernizzi paper and the appearance of a paper by Isner et al. that reported finding eosinophilic infiltrates in an endomyocardial biopsy specimen from a 29-year old man with cocaine-related cardiac symptoms (Isner et al., 1986). Others have observed both lymphocytic and eosinophilic interstitial infiltrates (Simpson and Edwards, 1986; Virmani et al., 1987; Virmani et al., 1988; Talebzadeh et al., 1990; Turnicky et al., 1992). In a San Francisco study, mononuclear infiltrates were frequently seen, but they were not associated with myocyte necrosis (Tazelaar et al., 1987).

Table 1.12.2.3.1.2   Types of Cocaine Adulterants*

A.	Sugars	D.	Inert Agents
	dextrose		inositol
	lactose		corn starch
	mannitol	E.	Others
	sucrose		acetaminophen
B.	Stimulants		aminopyrine
	caffeine		aspirin
	ephedrine		ascorbic acid
	phenylpropanolamine		boric acid
	phentermine		diphenhydramine
C.	Local Anesthetics		niacinamide
	lidocaine		phenactin
	benzocaine		quinine
	procaine		
	tetracaine		

* Based on information supplied by the Drug Enforcement Agency
and Shannon, 1988.

The presence of eosinophilic infiltrates suggests that what is being described is a hypersensitivity phenomenon. Hypersensitivity myocarditis is distinguished from toxic myocarditis by the fact that its occurrence is not dose-related. Lesions are all of the same age, hemorrhages are rare, and there is no myocyte necrosis. The list of drugs causing hypersensitivity myocarditis is increasing (Billingham, 1985). Eosinophilic myocarditis is a very rare disorder. Fewer than six instances were observed in 10,000 biopsies performed at Stanford. When eosinophilic myocarditis occurs, it is usually as the result of a hypersensitivity reaction. When eosinophils have been observed in the myocardium of cocaine users, it has often been as an incidental finding, either as a surprise finding at autopsy or in biopsy specimens obtained to evaluate chest pain, heart failure, or arrhythmia. Most of the time, the clinical manifestations of this disorder are so nonspecific that the diagnosis is rarely suspected during life (Taliercio et al., 1985).

None of the cocaine users with eosinophilic infiltrates have had signs of extracardiac involvement such as polyarteritis nodosa or eosinophilic leukemia. These patients do not match the picture classically associated with acute necrotizing myocarditis (Herzog et al., 1984), nor do they resemble patients with eosinophilic coronary arteritis (Churg-Strauss syndrome, also called allergic granulomatosis angiitis).

A heterogeneous group of agents can cause toxic myocarditis, and since cocaine can be adulterated with an even longer list of agents, implicating cocaine as the cause of eosinophilic myocarditis becomes very difficult. Further confounding the issue is the fact that most adult drug abusers are polydrug abusers. Virtually all the patients in the San Francisco study had other drugs present (Tazelaar et al., 1987). Benzodiazepines were found in over half of the San Francisco cases, and opiates were identified nearly as often. A review paper published in 1988 listed sugars (lactose, sucrose, and mannitol) as the most common cocaine adulterants, followed by stimulant drugs (caffeine, amphetamines) and local anesthetic agents (Shannon, 1988).

After an initial flurry of reports in 1986 and 1987, recent mention of eosinophilic infiltrates has become uncommon. One explanation may be that most cocaine users are now "crack" smokers. And "crack," while it may contain large amounts of bicarbonate, is otherwise largely free of contaminants. Finally, it must be emphasized that the mere presence of cells in the myocardium does not necessarily mean that there is active myocarditis. The lymphocytic infiltrates seen in cocaine users are generally not accompanied by myocyte necrosis and, according to the Dallas criteria, infiltrates without necrosis are not myocarditis (Aretz et al., 1986). What these infiltrates represent is not clear, but similar infiltrates are also seen in experimental animals with catecholamine toxicity, and the same process may be occurring in cocaine users. Another possibility that must be considered when infiltrates are encountered in the hearts of drug users is that they may have AIDS. A variety of opportunistic infections occur. In most areas of the country, the probability is that an obvious infiltrate in the heart of an HIV+ cocaine user represents an opportunistic infection and not a cocaine-related injury.

The first report describing AIDS-related myocardial disease was published in 1985. An assortment of opportunistic agents was found in 10 of the 41 hearts studied (Commarosano and Lewis, 1985). In a second series of 82 patients dying of AIDS, 17% were found to have infectious agents in their hearts. The usual pathogens associated with decreased immune function, including toxoplasmosis, mycobacteria, histoplasmosis, cryptococcus, cytomegalovirus, and pneumocystitis, have all been reported (Anderson et al., 1987). Several studies have noted histologic changes consistent with the diagnosis of myocarditis (inflammatory infiltrates with myocardial cell necrosis) in between one-third and one-half of autopsied cases (Anderson et al., 1988; Lafont et al., 1988). There is also evidence that the HIV virus itself invades the myocardium (Grody et al., 1990). Kaposi's sarcoma, most often involving the pericardium, has been reported (Anderson et al., 1987), as has lymphomatous infiltration of the heart.

The risk of HIV transmission makes intravenous cocaine users unlikely candidates for organ donation. However, the outcome in patients who receive hearts from non-intravenous cocaine users, and it appears that fairly large numbers of donors fall into that category, is comparable to that observed in those receiving hearts from non-drug users (Freimark et al., 1994). A positive history for non-intravenous cocaine abuse should not disqualify possible donors.

1.12.2.4 Valvular heart disease

Intravenous drug users get endocarditis and there is no reason to suppose that the subgroup of cocaine abusers is any different. Unfortunately, there are no autopsy data to review and no animal models. One clinical study reviewed the records of 115 intravenous drug abusers who were admitted to the hospital for evaluation of fever (Chambers et al., 1987). Endocarditis was proven in 20% of the drug abusers. When the subgroup was further analyzed, 80% of those with endocarditis were found to be intravenous cocaine users. Logistic regression analysis of the patients' histories demonstrated that cocaine use was the single variable most strongly predictive for endocarditis. History of cocaine use was, in fact, a better predictor than even the presence of a mitral or aortic murmur, the findings classically associated with endocarditis. These retrospective findings have never been confirmed by any other clinical observations, and valvular pathology in experimental animals has not been studied. If there is a relationship between intravenous cocaine use and endocarditis, it may have to do with the fact that injected cocaine has a very short half-life. Maintaining a "high" takes repeated injections — many more injections than will be required by an opiate addict — increasing the probability of sepsis.

1.12.2.5 Aorta and peripheral vessels

Fewer than a dozen cases of aortic dissection have been described. Most have been Type I dissections with the process extending from the ascending aorta to the iliacs (Barth et al., 1986; Gadaleta et al., 1989; Edwards and Rubin, 1987; Tardiff et al., 1989; Grannis et al., 1988; Om et al., 1992; Adkins et al., 1993; Cohle and Lie, 1992; Sherzoy et al., 1994). One of these individuals had the typical medial degeneration associated with Marfan's syndrome, but without any other stigmata of the disorder (Cohle and Lie, 1992). Two recognized factors contribute to aortic dissection: aortic medial disease and hypertension. Cocaine use is certainly associated with at least one, and possibly with both disorders. Transient hypertension occurs in virtually all users, and some preliminary studies have shown damage to the media and elastic layers in the aortas of rats chronically treated with cocaine (Langner and Bement, 1991).

Aortic dissection is initiated by transverse tears in the aortic wall. For dissection to occur, tears must extend through the intima and at least halfway through the media (Crawford, 1990). The case reported by Barth is interesting because the initiating tear was so extensive. A 45-year old crack smoker, with a blood cocaine level of 9 mg/L, suddenly collapsed and could not be resuscitated. The heart weighed 500 grams. A circumferential tear through the intima and media was found in the ascending aorta 2 cm above the sinotubular junction. There was no distal dissection but there was medial extension proximally to the level of the aortic valve cusps, and there was adventitial hemorrhage around the aortic root extending into the proximal portion of the right and left coronary arteries (without compression). Adventitial hemorrhage even extended down into the pulmonary arteries (Barth et al., 1986). The most plausible explanation for these changes is hypertension-induced shearing injury to an aortic media that had, in some way, been weakened by chronic cocaine exposure, although in one case (Bacharach et al., 1992), aneurysmal dilatation was seen in conjunction with nonspecific aortitis. A predominantly lymphoplasmacytic infiltrate in the media was interspersed with occasional scattered giant cells. Since this individual's serology was negative, and since there was nothing in the history to suggest

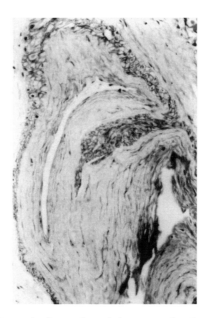

Figure 1.12.2.5   Accelerated atherosclerosis is not confined to the coronary arteries. This section of segmental artery, demonstrating severe intimal fibrosis and medial thickening, was obtained from a cocaine user with renal failure. PAS stain, reproduced with permission from Fogo et al., 1992. Am J Kidney Dis, with permission.

Takayasu's disease or giant cell arteritis, it seems likely that cocaine was responsible for the process.

Several postmortem studies have found evidence for accelerated atherosclerosis, involving both the coronary arteries and the aorta itself (Kolodgie et al., 1990; Kolodgie et al., 1993; Karch et al., 1995), but the mechanism is unknown, and the clinical consequences of the aortic changes, if any, are unclear.

There have been occasional reports of atherosclerotic changes in other vessels besides coronary arteries, several involving the renal arterio (Fogo, 1992). Whether or not peripheral vessels respond to cocaine in the same fashion as coronary arteries is not known.

Superficial and deep thrombophlebitis both occur as complications of cocaine abuse. Superficial venous involvement as a consequence of intravenous cocaine abuse is in no way different from the phlebitis that results from the abuse of any other drug. Much more interesting is the apparent increased risk of Paget-Schroetter syndrome, deep vein thrombosis of the upper extremity. In one retrospective study, 12 radiologically proven cases of upper extremity thrombosis were identified over a three-year period. Five of the cases were intravenous cocaine users. Compared to non-drug related cases, the cocaine users were much younger (mean age 35.8 years vs. 56.5 years) and all males, compared to 57% females in the non-drug-related group (Lisse et al., 1989). There is no experimental model for this condition and its mechanism remains obscure. Thrombosis might be the result of cocaine-enhanced platelet aggregation and thromboxane production (Tonga et al., 1985), or it may be due to some adulterant that was injected with the cocaine.

1.12.2.6 Sudden cardiac death

Sudden death is certainly the most dramatic consequence of cocaine abuse, and it is also the least understood. This syndrome poses major problems for medical examiners and clinicians alike. The probability of a lethal outcome is unrelated to the amount of cocaine ingested (Smart and Anglin, 1986; Karch and Stephens, 1991), but the explanation of why that should be the case has only recently become clear. Depending on whether or not the victim is a novice or chronic user, different mechanisms may come into play. One reason answers have been slow in coming is that most research has been done with rats. In the rat model the doses of cocaine required to produce cardiovascular death are much higher than the doses required to trigger fatal convulsions. On the basis of such experiments, it has been suggested that cocaine-associated sudden death in humans is primarily a neurologic event as well (Anon, 1992). While it is true that some neurologic events, particularly pontine hemorrhage (Kibayashi et al., 1995), can cause sudden death syndrome, neurologic lesions are rarely found in cases of cocaine-associated sudden death.

It is highly unlikely that any study of sudden death using small rodents will ever demonstrate heart disease as the cause. The rodent heart, like the heart of other small animals, is extremely resistant to the induction of lethal arrhythmias. A critical mass of myocardium is needed in order to sustain rhythms such as ventricular tachycardia, and in the absence of sufficient mass, abnormal rhythms terminate spontaneously (McWilliam, 1887; Porter, 1894; Zipes et al., 1975). In 1914, Garrey found that when pieces of fibrillating left ventricle with a surface area of less than 4 cm^2 were shaved from a heart, the smaller fragments stopped fibrillating, but the remaining ventricle continued to fibrillate until three-quarters of the muscle mass had been removed (Garrey, 1914). It is not very surprising that the results of the rodent experiments favor neurologic mechanisms.

According to the most recent DAWN survey, there were 3,981 cocaine-associated deaths in 1994 (Substance Abuse and Mental Health Services Administration, 1995); however, the real number is believed to be much higher (Brookoff et al., 1993). More often than not, the cause of these deaths remains obscure. After eliminating a small percentage of deaths due to stroke and subarachnoid hemorrhage (Brust, 1993), and a somewhat larger number of cases due to hyperthermia and agitated delirium, the remaining cases fall into two categories: those where death is clearly the result of myocardial infarction, and those where it is not. Most deaths fall into the second category.

Autopsies of patients with cocaine-related infarcts demonstrate fixed atherosclerotic lesions more than half the time (Virmani et al., 1988; Karch and Billingham, 1988), and cocaine's ability to cause coronary artery vasospasm is now well established (see Section 1.11.2.2). Even modest degrees of spasm can convert asymptomatic high grade obstructions into symptom-

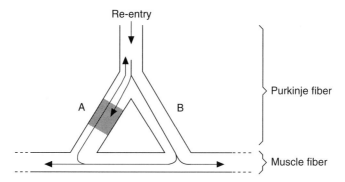

Figure 1.12.2.6 (1)   Unidirectional heart block. Zones of patchy myocardial fibrosis may provide the anatomic substrate for reentry arrythmia. This mechanism is thought to account for many cases of cardiac sudden death. Reprinted with permission. Textbook of Advanced Cardiac Life Support, 1987. Copyright American Heart Association.

atic ones, so sudden death in the subgroup of cocaine abusers with existing coronary artery disease is hardly surprising. Deaths in this same subgroup can also be explained by cocaine-induced elevations in pulse and blood pressure. Under such circumstances, the increased metabolic demands of the heart can convert previously asymptomatic obstructions into symptomatic ones. Ischemia, arrhythmia, and infarction are predictable results, just as

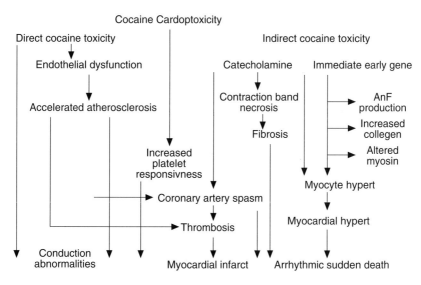

Figure 1.12.2.6 (2)   Mechanisms of cocaine cardiotoxicity. This flow chart has been constructed from both human and experimental data, and many of the mechanisms remain unclear. Toxicity may be the result of direct or indirect actions of cocaine on the heart. Direct effects included myocardial infarction and conduction abnormalities secondary to cocaine's local anesthetic effects; however, the latter are only seen when massive amounts of cocaine are consumed. From Kolodgie et al., Human Pathology, 1995. With permission.

they would be, for example, in a patient with asymptomatic coronary artery disease who takes up jogging and has a cardiac arrest.

Determining the cause of cardiac arrest in individuals who do not have coronary artery disease is much more difficult. Cocaine has two completely different, and unrelated, effects on the heart. Because it blocks the reuptake of norepinephrine, and also causes the release of epinephrine from the adrenals (Gunne and Jonsson, 1964), cocaine is, in effect, an adrenergic agonist. Independent of its adrenergic effects, cocaine is also a local anesthetic, with actions similar to those of quinidine or lidocaine. Cocaine and cocaethylene block sodium channels. In so doing, they decrease both resting membrane potential and action potential amplitude, while, at the same time, prolonging action potential duration (Wang and Carpentier, 1994). Preliminary studies suggest that cocaethylene, the cocaine metabolite formed when alcohol and cocaine are consumed together, is an even more potent sodium channel blocker than the parent compound (Xu et al., 1994).

In theory, cocaine-associated cardiac arrest could be the result of adrenergic or local anesthetic effects, or some combination of both. In the following sections the possible consequences of cocaine's anesthetic and adrenergic effects are discussed in detail. In practice, cocaine's local anesthetic actions seem rarely to be involved, mainly because cocaine's membrane stabilizing effects become prominent only at very high blood levels. Anesthetic effects are only likely to be a factor in the occasional massive overdose due to rupture of a cocaine-filled condom in a body packer's intestines, or in binge users with an unlimited supply of drug. In such cases, blood levels may exceed 50,000 ng/mL, and asystolic arrest may well occur. If the victim has been consuming alcohol, cocaethylene will be formed, and asystolic arrest is even more likely because of cocaethylene's greater affinity for the sodium channel.

Sudden death can also be a consequence of cocaine-related, long-term catecholamine toxicity. Chronic toxicity is manifested by changes in the molecular structure and weight of the left ventricle that favor the occurrence of lethal tachyarrhythmias. For a tachyarrhythmia to occur, some type of underlying anatomic substrate must be present. The biggest problem for pathologists, at least until recently, was identifying the anatomic substrate. Certain abnormalities, such as contraction band necrosis and microfocal fibrosis, are common findings in the hearts of cocaine and stimulant abusers (Rajs and Falconer, 1979; Karch and Billingham, 1988), but not in the hearts of all, or even most abusers. This has lead to considerable confusion in determining the cause of death (Karch and Stephens, 1991). Within the last few years it has become increasingly apparent that the substrate is increased ventricular mass.

A convincing array of laboratory (Tseng et al., 1994; Besse et al., 1994), clinical (Chakko et al., 1994; Nademanee et al., 1994), and autopsy findings (Escabedo et al., 1992; Karch et al., 1995) have confirmed the presence of myocardial hypertropy in cocaine users. It occurs because cocaine alters genetic expression within the myocardium. Four hours after rats are injected with 40 mg/kg of cocaine, measurable increases in mRNA levels for atrial naturetic factor (ANF) can be detected. Similar findings have been observed in the sheep fetus, with increased levels of ANF detected within minutes of administering cocaine to ewes (Hargrave and Castle, 1995).

When treated for 14 days, there are also increases in mRNA coding for collagen, and for α and β myosin. Chronic administration for 28 days shifts the normal ratios of α and β myosin, and also produces a 20% increase in left ventricular mass (Besse et al., 1994). Shifts in myosin production have been observed by other experimenters (Morris et al., 1994).

High levels of ANF are produced in response to hemodynamic overload (Lerman et al., 1993). In the face of chronic hemodynamic overload, ventricular remodelling occurs, ventricular collagen content increases, myocyte hypertrophy occurs, and left ventricular hypertrophy results. Left ventricular enlargement is an independent risk factor for sudden cardiac death (Shapiro et al., 1984; Dunn and Pringle, 1993; Messerli, 1993). The impact of these changes within the general population, particularly hypertensive patients, has been recognized for some time. The evidence is quite good that the hearts of cocaine users undergo similar changes as those seen in patients with poorly treated hypertension.

Researchers at the University of Miami and at the Miami-Dade Medical Examiner's office have accumulated a large data base containing autopsy and clinical findings in hundreds of cocaine-associated deaths. In a detailed study of several hundred asymptotic cocaine rehabilitation patients, they found electrocardiographic changes, diagnostic for left ventricular enlargement, in roughly one-third of the patients (Chakko et al., 1994). Similar changes have been observed by other researchers who used echocardiography to evaluate asymptomatic cocaine users (Om et al., 1993).

Cocaine-using cardiac arrest survivors have also been studied by electrophysiologists (Nademanee et al., 1994). Of 19 cocaine abusers with cardiac arrest, 11 cases were due to ventricular fibrillation, and in each one an anatomic substrate for the arrhythmia was present: two cases of myocardial infarction, three cases of Wolff-Parkinson-White syndrome, and six patients (54%) with left ventricular hypertrophy or cardiomyopathy. The remaining cardiac arrest patients had asystole. In five of the eight cases, cardiac arrest was due to massive overdose, while the other three had intracranial hemorrhages.

Cocaine-related cardiac hypertrophy has also been confirmed at autopsy. When the hearts of trauma victims incidentally found to be positive for cocaine at autopsy were compared with the hearts of other trauma victims who tested negative for stimulant drugs, there were very significant differences in heart weight (Karch et al., 1995). The median weight was 375 grams ($\pm$ 82) in 32 cocaine-positive men, less than the generally accepted value of 380 grams used by many pathologists as the cutoff for normal, but significantly more than the mean weight of 337 grams ($\pm$ 55) seen in the controls. Even though heart weights for both groups fell within generally accepted size limits, the hearts of the cocaine users were, in fact, 10% heavier than the hearts of the non-users. Such a small increase is unlikely to produce measurable increases in wall thickness and would almost certainly go unnoticed at autopsy.

In animal studies, increased left ventricular mass is associated with a decreased threshold for ventricular fibrillation, apparently because hypertrophic cells display abnormal, cell to cell, variations in effective refractory period and action potential duration (Kowey et al., 1991). Even in the absence of scarring, infiltrates, or abnormal conduction pathways, myocardial hypertrophy alone can cause enough local tissue variation to disrupt orderly conduction and favor the occurrence of arrhythmias. The increased collagen production detected in rats treated with cocaine can actually be seen in the hearts of cocaine users. Myocardial fibrosis occurs in cocaine users for at least two reasons: catecholamine-induced myocardial necrosis, and cocaine-associated myocardial hypertrophy. Ventricular re-entry is more likely in chronic cocaine users because a cocaine user's heart contains more collagen fibrils that can disrupt the normal orderly progression of the activation front (Shapiro et al., 1984; Karch and Billingham, 1988).

Whether the increased expression of genes for production of atrial naturetic factor, collagen, and contractile filaments in cocaine users' hearts is the result of some directed effect exerted by cocaine, or catecholamine excess, or whether it is an indirect consequence of the heart pumping against increased resistance, ventricular hypertrophy occurs, even though its presence may not always be obvious.

The only reliable way to detect the subtle increases in heart weight in cocaine users is by comparison with a standard nomogram, such as the one from Mayo Clinic. Even in the absence of apparent wall thickening or identifiable lesions, the heart of a cocaine user weighing significantly more than the weight predicted by the nomogram is abnormal. Until contrary evidence has been introduced, the increased weight of the heart can be presumed to have supplied the substrate for the individual's arrhythmic sudden death.

1.12.2.6.1 Acute anesthetic-related effects. Sudden death in novice users may have more to do with cocaine's anesthetic properties than with its adrenergic effects. In addition to its effects on catecholamine metabolism, which ultimately result in intracytosolic calcium elevations and cellular necrosis, cocaine also blocks the fast sodium channel, thereby inhibiting action potential generation (Weidmann, 1955). It also blocks potassium efflux channels (Przywara, 1989), further inhibiting generation of the action potential. In experimental models cocaine exerts variable effects on sodium and potassium currents, depending on the cocaine concentration (Grawe et al., 1994).

Conduction velocity in cardiac tissue depends on how fast depolarization occurs. If sodium influx and potassium efflux are blocked, impulse propagation is impaired and conduction is depressed. There is evidence that cocaethylene may impair depolarization more than cocaine, at least in some tissues (Wang and Carpentier, 1994), and different areas of the heart respond differently to local anesthetic agents. Thus the refractory period in each of the different locations will lengthen by variable amounts. Orderly transmission of impulses is interrupted by cocaine use and the result is temporal dispersion of the wavefronts. Occasionally, an impulse may arrive at a point where it cannot be conducted. Described as a unidirectional conduction block, such blocks can be caused by any amide local anesthetic (Kasten, 1986). The process has been demonstrated in animals but clinical studies are still lacking (Schwartz, 1989).

Another local anesthetic effect which may lead to sudden death is conduction block. Dogs given intravenous cocaine in quantities mimicking "recreational" doses (infusions starting at 3 mg/kg over 30 seconds) develop severe prolongation of conduction times through the His-Purkinje system into the ventricle. Slowing of conduction is dose-dependent. The more cocaine given, the slower conduction (Kabas et al., 1990). In other animal studies, high dose cocaine treatment has been noted to have potent negative inotropic and Type I electrophysiological effects. Blood pressure drops, while both coronary blood flow and cardiac output decrease. At the same time the PR, QRS, QT, and QT$_c$ intervals all increase (Beckman et al., 1991; Clarkson et al., 1993). Rats given cocaine by inhalation develop blood levels comparable to those seen in humans. In one rat experimental model, 70% of the animals demonstrated electrophysiological abnormalities, including atrial arrhythmias and incomplete heart block (Boni et al., 1991).

Electrophysiologic measurements in a dog model of acute intoxication showed that ectopic activity and ventricular tachycardia were easily induced and that cocaine had a proarrhythmic effect due to multiple mechanisms (Gantenberg and Hageman, 1992). These experimental models may or may not be relevant to humans. Not all the sodium/potassium changes are due to cocaine's channel blocking abilities. Many of the electrophysiologic effects observed in animals are actually the result of altered sympathetic tone, which is, in turn, a result of cocaine acting directly on the brain, and not the heart. In clinical practice, the net cardiac effects of cocaine are probably more dependent on the underlying level of sympathetic adrenergic activity than they are on sodium channel blockade or any pure anesthetic effects (Clarkson et al., 1993; Tella et al., 1993; Perreault et al., 1993).

Cocaine users will take ever increasing amounts to maintain their "high," and they will keep on taking the drug as long as it is available. Tolerance to the stimulant effects and some of the vascular effects may occur, but tolerance to the local anesthetic effects does not. If sufficient drug is taken, complete heart block can result. Cocaine-induced asystole and complete heart block have been described clinically and experimentally (Nanji and Filipenko, 1984; Watt and Pruitt, 1964), but since it takes 10 times as much cocaine to produce anesthetic effects as it does to block norepinephrine reuptake (Yasuda et al., 1984), anesthetic effects are unlikely to be much of a problem, except in cases of truly massive overdose (such as a body packer with a ruptured packet of drug or a binge user with an unlimited supply of drug).

1.12.2.6.2 Acute catecholamine-related effects. Electrophysiologic studies strongly suggest that acute changes occurring in the hearts of cocaine users are the result of both local anesthetic and adrenergic effects of cocaine (Temsey-Armos, 1992). Myocardial alterations are associated with chronic cocaine use, and these changes could well provide a substrate for arrhythmic sudden death. What happens acutely is less clear. Very large, non-physiologic doses of cocaine given to rats will produce focal hemorrhages, contraction band necrosis, and ultimately death from prolonged seizure activity (Nahas et al., 1985; Trouve and Nahas, 1986; Maillet, 1991; Chiarasini et al., 1992).

The most obvious explanation for cocaine-related sudden death is cate-cholamine-induced ischemia. Enhanced α adrenergic stimulation results in coronary artery contraction, decreased blood flow, and ischemia. Decreased epicardial artery diameters have been demonstrated in man, even at rela-tively low doses, making ischemic induction of arrhythmias a real possibility, especially in an individual who has preexisting disease (Flores et al., 1990; Lange et al., 1990). At the same time α stimulation is increasing, β adrenergic stimulation occurs and also leads to elevated intracytosolic calcium. Mod-erate elevations can cause the type of after-depolarizations that are associated with ventricular tachycardia (Bozler, 1943). If myocytes accumulate even more calcium, contraction band necrosis occurs and these lesions certainly can provide an adequate substrate for arrhythmic generation (Michelson et al., 1980). The association between contraction band necrosis and sudden death is well established (Reichenbach and Moss, 1975; Cebelin and Hirsch, 1980). Even if contraction band necrosis is not apparent at autopsy, catechola-mine-induced changes still may be responsible for sudden death. Calcium overload is not an all-or-nothing phenomenon. A spectrum of cellular alter-ations precede frank contraction band necrosis. Some of the alterations, such as mild eosinophilia, may be reversible. Similarly, changes in the cell mem-brane which allow the excessive entry of calcium may also be reversible. Athough there are no apparent abnormalities seen at autopsy, that does not necessarily mean that the changes are "functional." It may be that changes are present, but only detectable with electron microscopy. These studies are yet to be done.

1.12.2.6.3 Chronic cocaine effects.   Many different anatomic alterations have been reported in the hearts of cocaine users with sudden death. In the San Francisco study, nearly one-third had patchy myocardial fibrosis not present in controls. Most had prominent contraction band necrosis and many had mononuclear infiltrates (Tazelaar et al., 1987). Myocardial fibrosis is a multifactorial process, but in cases of cocaine and catecholamine toxicity, it is probably the result of healing contraction band necrosis. If fibrosis is extreme, cardiomyopathy may result (Karch and Billingham, 1986; Karch and Billingham, 1988). Cardiomyopathy is a major risk factor for malignant rhythm disorders and so is myocardial fibrosis. In the population of non-drug-using patients with spontaneous ventricular tachycardia or fibrillation and normal arteriograms (which is a somewhat small group), nearly all patients will be found to have abnormal endomyocardial biopsies. In Strain's series, over half the patients had interstitial and perivascular fibrosis associated with other cardiomyopathic changes, such as myocellular hypertrophy. Nearly 20% had histologic alterations consistent with the diagnosis of subacute myocarditis (Strain et al., 1983). If these changes are associated with serious ventricular arrhythmias in patients who are not drug users, there is every reason to suppose the same holds true in the drug-using population. Abnormal interstitial fibrosis is found in other types of drug abusers as well (Kringsholm and Christoffersen, 1987).

1.12.2.6.4 Relationship between seizures and sudden death. Cocaine-associated seizures have been recognized for over a century and can occur after relatively small doses of the drug. They are usually a benign phenomenon, and close questioning of users will often elicit a history of "small fits" that may temporarily interrupt a smoking session, but are not severe enough to warrant seeking medical attention. Except in the case of the occasional body packers, continuous seizure activity is rarely the cause of death in humans. That is not true in some experimental models. In dogs infused with massive amounts of cocaine, continuous seizure activity is the cause of death (Catravas and Waters, 1981; Catravas et al., 1978). That is not the case in mice and rats, where seizures and lethality appear to be mediated by different mechanisms (George, 1991).

The origin of cocaine-induced seizures is not known with certainty. Contrary to what may be expected, experiments have shown that cocaine seizures are not mediated by noradrenergic mechanisms (Jackson et al., 1990), but may be due to interference with the serotonin transporter (in contrast to the behavioral effects which appear to be secondary to cocaine's effects on the dopamine transporter) (George and Ritz, 1991). Repeated use of cocaine increases susceptibility to seizures, and it has been argued that this process is a result of cocaine's local anesthetic properties. Animal studies confirm the tendency to increased seizure susceptibility, but also suggest that some other property, besides cocaine's local anesthetic effects, is responsible (Marley et al., 1991). Whatever the cause, the important relationship in humans is that what begins as a cocaine-induced seizure discharge may end up as a cardiac arrhythmia. Epileptogenic foci can cause sudden cardiac death.

A relationship between cerebral epileptogenic foci and cardiac arrhythmias has been recognized for years. Electrocardiographic abnormalities, as a consequence of central nervous system disease, were first described almost 50 years ago (Byer et al., 1947). Patients with subarachnoid hemorrhage and other severe neurologic diseases exhibit a stereotyped pattern of EKG changes with peaked T waves and QT prolongation (Burch et al., 1954). Sometimes the T and QT changes are associated with ventricular ectopy (Novitzky et al., 1984; Samuels, 1987). Ectopy and T wave elevation are both seen in cases of brain death, and the pattern abruptly reverts to normal when brain herniation is complete. The rapidity with which the EKG tracing returns to normal suggests strongly that neural, rather than hormonal, events are involved.

Most epileptics who die suddenly do so as a result of trauma or status epilepticus. A small percentage of young patients with infrequent seizure activity, and subtherapeutic anticonvulsant levels, will have no cause of death identifiable at autopsy (Hirsch and Martin, 1971). An emerging consensus holds that arrhythmias may be the cause of death in this subgroup (Oppenheimer, 1990; Lip and Brodie, 1992). The reverse sequence also occurs. Investigation of patients with cardiac arrhythmia occasionally discloses the presence of a seizure focus, the treatment of which abolishes the arrhythmia (Gilchrist, 1985; Kiok et al., 1986).

The relationship between seizures and arrhythmia has been studied in animals. Chemical induction of seizures (pentylenetetrazol) in paralyzed, ventilated cats causes measurable increases in the discharge rate from the cardiac sympathetic nerve and the vagus. Electrocardiograms show ventricular ectopic beats, T wave changes, and QT prolongation, similar to the pattern seen in humans with subarachnoid hemorrhage. Larger doses of pentylenetetrazol result in more intense seizure activity as well as ventricular fibrillation and/or asystole supervena (Lathers and Schraeder, 1982). As seizure activity becomes more intense, the normal synchronization between the branches of the cardiac nerve is lost. It has been suggested that, because these branches supply different areas of the myocardium, unbalanced activity results in temporal dispersion of the depolarizing wavefront (Oppenheimer, 1990). The result would be much the same as with sodium channel blockade: malignant re-entry arrhythmia (Oppenheimer, 1990).

1.12.2.6.5   Agitated delirium and the neuroleptic malignant syndrome.   The first modern mention of cocaine-associated agitated delirium was in 1985 (Wetli and Fishbain, 1985). Reports of patients with similar symptoms had appeared in the early 1900s (Williams, 1914), but because these reports were deeply interwoven with elements of racist hysteria, they were never taken seriously. The syndrome is comprised of four components which appear in sequence: hyperthermia, delirium with agitation, respiratory arrest, and death. Individuals succumbing to this disorder uniformly have low-to-modest cocaine blood levels and do not behave like patients with massive overdose (continuous seizures, respiratory depression, and death). The incidence of this disorder is not known with any certainty, but there is little doubt that the number of cases has increased markedly since the late 1980s.

In the early stages of the disorder, victims are hyperthermic and grossly psychotic, with marked physical agitation. They often perform amazing feats of strength. What happens next is not entirely clear. After a relatively short interval, agitation ceases and the patient becomes quiet. Death occurs shortly afterward. Often these individuals have been restrained by police who fear injury to themselves, or innocent bystanders. Not uncommonly, victims are "hogtied." Their wrists and ankles are bound together behind their back while they lie prone (O'Halloran and Lewman, 1993). Victims who do not come to police attention are often found dead in their bathrooms. Because of their hyperthermia they will often be found surrounded

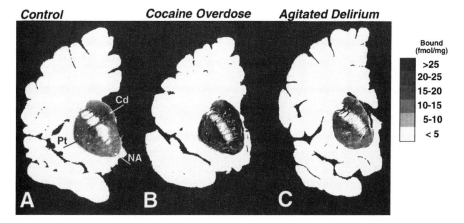

Figure 1.12.2.6.5 Agitated delirium. Adaptive increases in the number of dopamine transporters can be seen in the brains of cocaine users dying of overdose, but not in the brains of patients with agitated delirium. *In vitro* autoradiographic maps of [³H]WIN 35,428 labeling of the dopamine transporter in coronal sections of the human brain from a representative (A) age-matched and drug free subject, (B) cocaine overdose victim, and (C) cocaine-related agitated delirium victim. An adaptive increase is evident in dopamine transporter density over the striatum in the cocaine overdose victim, but not in the victim presenting with agitated delirium. The dopamine transporter regulates synaptic concentrations of neurotransmitter, so the lack of compensatory upregulation may result in a dopamine overflow following a cocaine "binge." Repeated exposures may kindle the mergence of agitated delirium syndrome. Gray scale codes are presented at the right and are matched for the range of density values across the groups. (Black = high densities; gray = intermediate; light gray to white = low to background densities. Abbreviations: Cd, caudate; NA, nucleus accumbens; Pt, putamen.) Courtesy of Professor Debra Mash, University of Miami School of Medicine.

by wet towels and clothing, sometimes even with empty ice trays scattered about.

In Wetli's first report, he described seven cases. All had fairly stereotyped histories. Typical was the case of a 33-year old man who started pounding on the door of a house he had moved out of some time previously: "He was shouting that he wanted to see his wife and daughter. The occupants informed him that nobody by that name resided there, yet he pursued his actions. Four bystanders finally restrained him and assisted police units upon their arrival. The subject was handcuffed and put into a police car, whereupon he began to kick out the windows of the vehicle. The police subsequently restrained his ankles and attached the ankle restraints and handcuffs together. He was then transported to a local hospital. While en route, the police officers noted he became tranquil (about 45 minutes after the onset of the disturbance). Upon arrival at the hospital a few minutes later, the subject was discovered to be in a respiratory arrest. Resuscitative attempts were futile. A postmortem examination was performed 1 hour and 45 minutes later (about 3 hours after the onset of the disturbance), and a rectal temperature of 41°C (106°F) was recorded. He had needle marks typical of intravenous drug abuse and pulmonary and cerebral edema. Abrasions and contusions of the ankles and wrists were also evident from his struggling against the restraints. Toxicologic analysis of postmortem blood disclosed 52.3 mg/L of lidocaine and 0.8 mg/L of cocaine. No lidocaine was administered to the victim during resuscitative attempts."

The clinical presentation of agitated psychotic cocaine abusers is quite different from that of non-psychotic cocaine abusers with sudden death or massive drug overdose. The psychotic cocaine users are almost always men. They are more likely to die in custody, and are more likely to live for 1 hour after onset of symptoms. In Miami, men with agitated delirium account for 10% of cocaine deaths. Their deaths tend to occur in summer, especially when the weather is warm and humid. Two-thirds of the victims die on the scene, or while being transported by paramedics to the hospital. The few who live long enough to be hospitalized succumb to disseminated intravascular coagulation, rhabdomyolyis, and renal failure. In the Miami patients, the average temperature at the time of first medical encounter is 104.8°F (Wetli, 1995, personal communication).

The mean cocaine concentration in 45 cases seen by the Dade County Medical Examiner was 1.32 mg/L (range .05–11.8; mg/L, n = 34), while the benzoylecgonine level was 3.78 mg/L (range .08–14.75 mg/L, n = 38). In these same patients, the mean brain cocaine concentration was 1.90 mg/kg (range .05–4 mg/kg, n = 10), while the mean benzoylecgonine concentration was 2.69 mg/kg (range .85–3.5 mg/kg, n = 6) (Wetli, 1995, personal communication). A consistent finding at autopsy was cardiomegally. The median heart weight in 44 men was over 420 grams.

The cellular and molecular changes associated with this disorder are starting to become clearer. Using ligand binding and autoradiographic methods, researchers have identified three different neurochemical abnormalities in the brains of cocaine abusers dying of agitated delirium (Staley et al., 1994). The abnormalities have to do with the number and type of dopamine receptor, and with the number of sites where cocaine can bind with brain tissue. Dopamine receptors were initially classified into two main groups. With advances in molecular biology, these main groups have been subdivided into five different recognizable types of receptors, but they are still considered as two groups: the "D1-like receptors" (dopamine receptors D1 and D5), and the "D2-like receptors" (dopamine receptors D2, D3, and D4) (Seeman and Van Tol, 1994).

The situation is somewhat confusing and difficult to understand, largely because of the nomenclature used to describe dopamine receptors. Most antipsychotic drugs block the D2 receptors in direct correlation to their clinical potency, except clozapine, which prefers the D4 receptor. D1 and D2 receptors can interact with each other and enhance each other's actions, possibly thorough subunits of G proteins. In schizophrenia, D2 and D3 receptor density is elevated by 10% while the D4 receptor is elevated by 600%. It has been suggested that cocaine craving may be the result of marked D3 receptor elevation over the limbic sectors of the striatum.

The occurrence of agitated delirium has something to do with the fact that the numbers of both D1 and D2 receptors are altered by cocaine use (Seeman and Van Tol, 1994). In comparison with drug-free controls, the brains of non-psychotic cocaine abusers contain an elevated number of cocaine recognition sites on the striatal dopamine transporter. No such increase is seen in the agitated delirium victims. The fact that the psychotic cocaine users fail to demonstrate this compensatory increase means that they cannot clear excess dopamine from their synapses. Pathologically high dopamine levels may occur after a "binge," and that, in turn, may lead to psychosis.

Psychotic and non-psychotic cocaine users can also be distinguished by the number of dopamine binding sites. In most people, chronic cocaine abuse leads to striking decreases in the density of the D1 receptor subtype through-out the striatal reward centers, probably as a result of receptor down-regu-lation. The fact that cocaine users quickly become tolerant to the drug's euphoriant effects is probably explained by the change in the number of dopamine binding sites. D2 receptors in non-psychotic cocaine abusers are unchanged. However, in the psychotic subgroup, marked reductions in the number of D2 receptors found in the hypothalamus have been observed. Since these receptors are known to mediate temperature control, decreased numbers of D2 receptors may explain the occurrence of malignant hyper-thermia in the psychotic patients. With fewer D2 receptors available, D1-mediated temperature increases would be unopposed.

Agitated delirium can be the result of other medical disorders, not just cocaine toxicity. It has been suggested that this constellation of symptoms is actually a variant of neuroleptic malignant syndrome (Kosten and Kleber, 1988; Kosten and Kleber, 1987). Neuroleptic malignant syndrome (NMS) is a highly lethal disorder seen in patients taking dopamine antagonists, and in individuals who have been withdrawn from dopaminergic agents such as bromocriptine and levodopa (Levinson, 1985; Friedman et al., 1985). NMS is usually associated with muscle rigidity, though variants of the syndrome without rigidity are also recognized (Kosten and Kleber, 1988).

Alterations in the number of dopamine receptors and cocaine binding sites may not be the sole explanation for the death of these individuals. There is mounting evidence that the stress of restraint makes fatal outcomes more likely. Rats injected daily with moderate doses of cocaine (30 mg/kg), and then restrained, are three times more likely to die from seizures than rats injected with the same amount of drug and allowed free access to their cages (Pudiak and Bozarth, 1994). Since so many of the agitated delirium patients die while restrained, it has been suggested that the mechanism of death may involve a surge of catecholamines released by the stress response, acting upon a myocardium already sensitized by cocaine (Mirchandani et al., 1994)

Whatever the cause, the syndrome is occurring with some regularity. And, because violent behavior is part of the syndrome, the police are almost inevitably involved, and the affected individual dies in police custody or on the way to the hospital (O'Halloran and Lewman, 1993; Mirchandani et al., 1994). In some jurisdictions, "Tasers" are used to subdue the violently agitated. This device produces an electrical charge sufficient to produce immobilization. Although it is claimed that the devices are quite safe, fatalities have occurred. Almost all of the fatalities associated with "Taser" use have been in agitated cocaine or phencyclidine users (Kornblum and Reddy, 1991; Mirchandani et al., 1994; O'Halloran and Lewman, 1993). It may be that the device activates a stress response similar to being "hogtied." On the other hand, death and the use of the "Taser" could have been purely coincidental. Similar considerations apply to the pepper sprays used by some police departments. Deaths have been associated with use of the sprays, usually only in cases where the pepper spray has been directed into the larynx, causing edema and airway obstruction.

Because cocaine blood levels are low at autopsy, and because there is a general misunderstanding about cocaine blood levels and the probability of death, police are often accused of brutality or inappropriate use of a choke hold (Luke and Reay, 1992). Unless the findings of strangulation are specifically ruled out at autopsy, considerable liability may result. Attributing death to a trivial head injury (minor cerebral contusions or subdural hematomas) (Mirchandani and Rorke et al., 1994) is an obvious temptation, best avoided. In some areas, medical examiners have taken the sensible approach of contacting the deceased family and asking them to retain their own pathologist to witness the autopsy. But until this disorder is better understood, even the presence of an independent observer may not be enough to prevent litigation.

References

Adkins, M., Gaines, W., Anderson, W. et al. (1993). Chronic type A aortic dissection: an unusual complication of cocaine inhalation. Ann Thorac Surg, 56: 977–979.

Adomian, G., Laks, M., and Billingham, M. (1978). The incidence and significance of contraction bands in endomyocardial biopsies from normal human hearts. Am Heart J, 95: 348–351.

Anderson, D., Virmani, R., Reilly, J. et al. (1988). Prevalence of myocarditis at necropsy in Acquired Immunodeficiency Syndrome. J Am Coll Cardiol, 11(4): 729–799.

Anderson, D., Virmani, R., and Macher, A. (1987). Cardiac pathology and cardiovascular cause of death in patients dying with the Acquired Immunodeficiency Syndrome (AIDS). In The Third International Conference on AIDS, Cited in Curr Probl in Cardiol, June 1991: 389.

Anon (1992). NIDA researchers investigate cocaine toxicity, seizures link. DAWN Briefings, September 1992. National Institute on Drug Abuse. Bethesda, MD.

Aretz, T. H., Billingham, M., Edwards, W. et al. (1986). Myocarditis: a histopathologic differentiation and classification. Am J Cardiovasc Path, 1(1): 3–14.

Ascher, E., Stauffer, J., and Gaasch, W. (1988). Coronary artery spasm, cardiac arrest, transient electrocardiographic Q waves and stunned myocardium in cocaine-associated acute myocardial infarction. Am J Cardiol, 61: 939–941.

Bacharach, J., Colville, D., and Lie, J. (1992). Accelerated atherosclerosis, aneurysmal disease, and aortitis: possible pathogenetic association with cocaine abuse. Int Angiol, 11: 83–86.

Barth, C., Bray, M., and Roberts, W. (1986). Rupture of the ascending aorta during cocaine intoxication. Am J Cardiol, 57: 496.

Bauman, J., Grawe, J., Winecoff, A. et al. (1994). Cocaine-related sudden cardiac death: a hypothesis correlating basic science and clinical observations. J Clin Pharmacol, 34: 902–911.

Beckman, K., Parker, R., Hariman, R. et al. (1991). Hemodynamic and electrophysiological actions of cocaine — effects of sodium bicarbonate as an antidote in dogs. Circulation, 83(5): 1799–1807.

Bedotto, J., Lee, R., Lancaster, L. et al. (1988). Cocaine and cardiovascular function in dogs: effects on heart and peripheral circulation. J Am Coll Cardiol, 11(6): 1337–1342.

Besse, S., Assayag, P., Latour, C. et al. (1994). Myocardial effects of acute and chronic cocaine treatment. Circulation, 90(4, Part 2): I–580.

Billingham, M. (1985). Pharmacotoxic myocardial disease: an endomyocardial study. Heart Vessels, 1(Suppl. 1): 386–394.

Boni, J., Barr, W., and Martin, B. (1991). Cocaine inhalation in the rat — pharmacokinetics, and cardiovascular response. J Pharmacol Exp Ther, 257(1): 307–315.

Born, G. (1991). Recent evidence for the involvement of catecholamines and macrophages in atherosclerotic process. Ann Med, 23: 569–572.

Bozler, E. (1943). The initiation of impulses in cardiac muscle. Am J Physiol, 138: 273–282.

Bravetta, E. and Invernizzi, G. (1922). Il Cocainismo. Osservazione cliniche. Ricerche sperimentali e anatomo-patoligiche. Note Riv Psichiatr, 10: 543.

Brickner, E., Willard, J., Eichhorn, E. et al. (1991). Left ventricular hypertrophy associated with chronic cocaine abuse. Circulation, 84(3): 1130–1135.

Brookoff, D., Campbell, E., and Shaw, L. (1993). The underreporting of cocaine-related trauma: Drug Abuse Warning Network reports vs. hospital toxicology tests. Am J Pub Health, 83(3): 369–371.

Brust, J. (1993). Clinical, radiological, pathological aspects of cerebrovascular disease associated with drug abuse. Stroke, 24(12): I-129–133.

Burch, G., Meyers, R., and Abildskov, J. (1954). A new electrocardiographic pattern observed in cerebrovascular accidents. Circulation, 9: 719–723.

Busija, D. (1994). Editorial comment. Stroke, 25: 631–638.

Byer, E., Ashman, R., and Toth, L. (1947). Electrocardiogram with large upright T waves and long QT intervals. Am Heart J, 33: 796–801.

Camí, J., de la Torre, R., Farré, M. et al. (1991). Cocaine-alcohol interaction in healthy volunteers: plasma metabolic profile including cocaethylene. In Committee on Problems of Drug Dependency Annual Scientific Meeting, in press. West Palm Beach: National Institute on Drug Abuse.

Cammarosano, C. and Lewis, C. (1985). Cardiac lesions in Acquired Immune Deficiency Syndrome (AIDS). J Am Coll Cardiol, 5: 703–706.

Catravas, J. and Waters, I. (1981). Acute cocaine intoxication in the conscious dog: studies on the mechanism of lethality. J Pharm Exp Ther, 217: 350–356.

Catravas, J., Waters, I., Walz, M. et al. (1978). Acute cocaine intoxication in the conscious dog: pathophysiologic profile of acute lethality. Arch Int Pharmacodyn Ther, 235: 328–340.

Cebelin, J. and Hirsch, C. (1980). Human stress cardiomyopathy: myocardial lesions in victims of homicidal assaults without internal injuries. Hum Pathol, 11: 123–132.

Chakko, S., Sepulveda, S., Kessler, K. et al. (1994). Frequency and type of electrocardiographic abnormalities in cocaine abusers (electrocardiogram in cocaine abuse). Am J Cardiol, 74: 710–713.

Chambers, H., Morris, D., Tauber, M. et al. (1987). Cocaine use and the risk for endocarditis in intravenous drug users. Ann Intern Med, 106: 833–836.

Chiarasini, D., Dingeon, P., Latour, C. et al. Cardiovascular tolerance to cocaine and its correlates. Read at annual meeting of The British Pharmacological Society, London, September 1992.

Chokshi, S., Moore, R., Pandian, N., and Isner, J. (1989b). Reversible cardiomyopathy associated with cocaine intoxication. Ann Intern Med, 111: 1039–1040.

Chow, J., Robertson, A., and Stein, R. (1990). Vascular changes in the nasal submucosa of chronic cocaine addicts. Am J Forensic Med and Pathol, 11(2): 136–143.

Clarkson, C., Chang, C., Stolfi, A. et al. (1993). Electrophysiological effects of high cocaine concentrations on intact canine heart. Circulation, 87: 950–962.

Cohle, S. and Lie, J. (1992). Dissection of the aorta and coronary arteries associated with acute cocaine intoxication. Arch Pathol Lab Med, 116: 1239–1241.

Crawford, E. (1990). The diagnosis and management of aortic dissection. JAMA, 264(19): 2537–2541.

Cregler, L. and Mark, H. (1985). Relation of acute myocardial infarction to cocaine abuse. Am J Cardiol, 56: 794.

Danielson, T., Coutts, R., Coutts, K. et al. (1985). Reserpine-induced hypothermia and its reversal by dopamine antagonists. Life Sci, 37: 31–38.

Dawkins, K., Jamieson, S., Hunt, S. et al. (1985). Long-term results, hemodynamic, and complications after combined heart and lung transplantation. Circulation, 71: 919–926.

Dohi, S., Jones, M., Hudak, M., and Traystman, R. (1990). Effects of cocaine on pial arterioles in cats. Stroke, 21(12): 1710–1714.

Dressler, F., Malekzadeh, S., and Roberts, W. (1990). Quantitative analysis of amounts of coronary arterial narrowing in cocaine addicts. Am J Cardiol, 65(5): 303–308.

Duell, P. (1987). Chronic cocaine abuse and dilated cardiomyopathy. Am J Med, 83: 601.

Dunn, F. and Pringle, S. (1993). Sudden cardiac death, ventricular arrhythmias and hypertensive left ventricular hypertrophy. J Hypertension, 11: 1003–1010.

Edwards, J. and Rubin, R. (1987). Aortic dissection and cocaine abuse. Ann Intern Med, 107(5): 779–780.

Eisenberg, M., Jue, J., Mendelson, J. et al. (1995). Left ventricular morphologic features and function in nonhospitalized cocaine users: a quantitative two-dimensional echocardiographic study. Am Heart J, 129: 941–946.

Endress, C. and King, G. (1990). Cocaine-induced small-bowel perforation. Am J Radiol, 154: 1346–1347.

Escobedo, L., Ruttenber, A., Anda, R. et al. (1992). Coronary artery disease, left ventricular hypertrophy, and the risk of cocaine overdose death. Coronary Artery Disease, 3: 853–857.

Factor, S. and Cho, S. (1985). Smooth-muscle contraction bands in the media of coronary arteries: postmortem marker of ante-mortem coronary spasm? J Am Coll Cardiol, 6: 1329–1337.

Flores, E., Lange, R., Cigarroa, R., and Hillis, L. (1990). Effect of cocaine on coronary artery dimensions in atherosclerotic coronary artery disease — enhanced vasoconstriction at sites of significant stenoses. J Am Coll Cardiol, 16(1): 74–79.

Fogo, A., Superdock, K., and Atkinson, J. (1992). Severe atherosclerosis in the kidneys of a cocaine addict. Am J Kidney Dis, 20: 513–515.

Francis, G. and Carlyle, W. (1993). Hypothetical pathways of cardiac myocyte hypertrophy: response to myocardial injury. Euro Heart J, 14(Suppl J): 49–56.

Freimark, D., Czer, L., Admon, D. et al. (1994). Donors with a history of cocaine use: effect on survival and rejection frequency after heart transplantation. J Heart Lung Transplant, 13(6): 1138–1144.

Freudenberger, R., Cappell, M., and Hutt, D. (1990). Intestinal infarction after intravenous cocaine administration. Ann Intern Med, 113(9): 715–716.

Friedman, J., Feinberg, S., and Feldman, R. (1985). A neuroleptic malignant-like syndrome due to levodopa therapy withdrawal. JAMA, 254: 2792–2795.

Friedrichs, G., Wei, H., and Merrill, G. (1990). Coronary vasodilation caused by intravenous cocaine in the anesthetized beagle. Can J Physiol Pharmacol, 68(7): 893–897.

Furchgott, R. (1988). Studies on relaxation of rabbit aorta by sodium nitrite: the basis for the proposal that the endothelium-derived relaxing factor is nitric oxide. In Mechanisms of vasodilation. In P. Vanhoatte (Ed.), New York: Raven Press, 401–409.

Gadaleta, D., Hall, M., and Nelson, T. (1989). Cocaine-induced acute aortic dissection. Chest, 96(5): 1203–1205.

Gantenberg, N. and Hageman, G. (1992). Cocaine-enhanced arrhythmogenesis: neural and nonneural mechanisms. Can J Physiol Pharmacol, 70: 240–246.

Garfia, A., Valverde, J., Borondo, J. et al. (1990). Vascular lesions in intestinal ischemia induced by cocaine-alcohol abuse: report of a fatal case due to overdose. J Forensic Sci, 35(3): 740–745.

Garrey, W. (1914). The nature of fibrillatory contraction of the heart — its relation to tissue mass and form. Am J Physiol, 33: 397–414.

George, F. and Ritz, M. (1993). Cocaine-induced seizures and lethality appear to be associated with distinct nervous system binding sites. J Pharm Exp Ther, 264: 1333–1343.

George, F. (1991). Cocaine toxicity: genetic evidence suggests different mechanisms for cocaine-induced seizures and lethality. Psychopharmacology, 104(3): 307–311.

Gilchrist, J. (1985). Arrhythmogenic seizures: diagnosis by simultaneous EEG/ECG recording. Neurology, 35: 1503–1506.

Ginsburg, R., Bristow, M., Kantrowitz, N. et al. (1981). Histamine provocation of clinical coronary artery spasm: implications concerning pathogenesis of variant angina pectoris. Am Heart J, 102: 819–822.

Grannis, F., Bryant, B., Caffaratti, C., and Turner, A. (1988). Acute aortic dissection associated with cocaine abuse. Clin Cardiol, 11(8): 572–574.

Grawe, J., Hariman, R., Winecoff, A. et al. (1994). Reversal of the electrocardiographic effects of cocaine by lidocaine. Part 2. Concentration-effect relatonships. Pharmacotherapy, 14(6): 704–711.

Grody, W., Cheng, L., and Lewis, W. (1990). Infection of the heart by the Human Immunodeficiency Virus. Am J Cardiol, 66: 203–206.

Gunne, L. and Jonsson, J. (1964). Effects of cocaine administrastion on brain, adrenal and urinary adrenaline and noradrenaline in rats. Psychopharmacologia, 6(2): 125–129.

Hargrave, B. and Castle, M. (1995). Intrauterine exposure to cocaine increased plasma ANP (atrial naturetic peptide) but did not alter hypoxanthine concentrations in the sheep fetus. Life Sci, 56: 1689–1697.

Hearn, W., Flynn, D., Hime, G. et al. (1991). Cocaethylene — a unique cocaine metabolite displays high affinity for the dopamine transporter. J Neurochem, 56(2): 698–701.

Henzlova, M., Smith, S., Prchal, V., and Helmcke, F. (1991). Apparent reversibility of cocaine-induced cardiomyopathy. Am Heart J, 122(2): 577–579.

Herzog, C., Snover, D., and Staley, N. (1984). Acute necrotising eosinophilic myocarditis. Br Heart J, 52: 343–348.

Hirsch, C. and Martin, D. (1971). Unexpected death in young epileptics. Neurology, 21: 682–690.

Hoegerman, G., Lewis, C., Flack, J. et al. (1995). Lack of association of recreational cocaine and alcohol use with left ventricular mass in young adults. J Am Coll Cardiol, 25: 895–900.

Howard, R., Hueter, D., and Davis, G. (1985). Acute myocardial infarction following cocaine abuse in a young woman with normal coronary arteries. JAMA, 254(1): 95–96.

Isner, J., Estes, N., Thompson, P. et al. (1986). Acute cardiac events temporally related to cocaine abuse. N Engl J Med, 315: 1438–1443.

Itzhak, Y. (1993). Nitric oxide (NO) synthatase inhibitors abolish cocaine-induced toxicity in mice. Neuropharm, 32(10): 1069–1070.

Jackson, H., Ball, D., and Nutt, D. (1990). Noradrenergic mechanisms appear not to be involved in cocaine-induced seizures and lethality. Life Sci, 47(4): 353–359.

Jones, L. and Tackett, R. (1990). Chronic cocaine treatment enhances the responsiveness of the left anterior descending coronary artery and the femoral artery to vasoactive substances. J Pharmacol Exp Ther, 255(3): 1366–1370.

Joris, I. and Majno, G. (1981). Medial changes in arterial spasm induced by L-norepinephrine. Am J Pathol, 105(3): 212–222.

Kabas, J., Blanchard, S., Matsuyama, Y. et al. (1990). Cocaine-mediated impairment of cardiac conduction in the dog: a potential mechanism for sudden death after cocaine. J Pharmacol Exp Ther, 252(1): 185–191.

Kannel, W., Gordon, T., and Offutt, D. (1969). Left ventricular hypertrophy by electrocardiogram. Prevalence, incidence and mortality in the Framingham Study. Ann Intern Med, 71: 89–105.

Karch, S. and Billingham, M. (1988). The pathology and etiology of cocaine-induced heart disease. Arch Pathol Lab Med, 112: 225–230.

Karch, S. and Billingham M. (1986). Myocardial contraction bands revisited. Hum Pathol, 17: 9–13.

Karch, S. and Stephens, B. (1991). When is cocaine the cause of death? Am J Forensic Med and Pathol, 12(1): 1–2.

Karch, S., Green, G., and Young, S. (1995). Myocardial hypertrophy and coronary artery disease in male cocaine users. J Forensic Sci, 40: 579–583.

Kasten, G. (1986). Amide local anesthetic alterations of effective refractory period temporal dispersion: relationship to ventricular arrhythmias. Anesthesiology, 65: 61–66.

Kibayashi, K., Mastri, A., and Hirsch, C. (1995). Cocaine-induced intracerebral hemorrhage — analysis of predisposing factors and mechanisms causing hemorrhagic strokes. Hum Pathol, 26: 659–663.

Kiok, M., Terrence, C., Fromm, G., and Lavine, S. (1986). Sinus arrest in epilepsy. Neurology, 36: 115–116.

Kitzman, D., Scholz, D. H. et al. (1988). Age-related changes in normal human hearts during the first 10 decades of life. Part II (Maturity): a quantitative anatomic study of 765 specimens from subjects 20 to 99 years old. Mayo Clin Proc, 63: 137–146.

Kolodgie, F., Virmani, R., Cornhill, J. et al. (1990). Cocaine: an independent risk factor of atherosclerosis. Circulation, 82, Supplement III(4): III–447.

Kolodgie, F., Virmani, R., Cornhill, J. et al. (1991) Increase in atherosclerosis and adventitial mast cells in cocaine abusers: an alternative mechanism of cocaine-associated coronary vasospasm and thrombosis. J Am Coll Cardiol, 17(7): 1553–1560.

Kolodgie, F., Wilson, P., Cornhill, J. et al. (1993). Increased prevalence of aortic fatty streaks in cholesterol-fed rabbits administered intravenous cocaine: the role of vascular endothelium. Tox Path, 21(5): 425–435.

Kolodgie, F., Farb, A., and Virmani, R. (1995). Pathobiological determinants of cocaine-associated cardiovascular syndromes. Hum Pathol. 26: 583–586.

Kornblum, R. and Reddy, S. (1991). Effects of the taser in fatalities involving police confrontation. J Forensic Sci, 36(2): 434–449.

Kossowsky, W. and Lyon, A. (1984). Cocaine and acute myocardial infarction: a probable connection. Chest, 86: 729–731.

Kosten, T. and Kleber, H. (1988). Rapid death during cocaine abuse: a variant of the neuroleptic malignant syndrome? Am J Drug Alcohol Abuse, 14(3): 335–346.

Kosten, T. and Kleber, H. (1987). Sudden death in cocaine abusers: relation to neuroleptic malignant syndrome (letter). Lancet, 1: 1198–1199.

Kowey, P., Friehling, T., Sewter, L. et al. (1991). Electrophysiological effects of left ventricular hypertrophy. Effect of calcium and potassium channel blockers. Circulation, 83: 2067–2075.

Kringsholm, B. and Christoffersen, P. (1987). Lung and heart pathology in fatal drug addiction. A consecutive autopsy study. Forensic Sci Int, 34: 39–51.

Kugelmass, A. and Ware, J. (1992). Cocaine and coronary artery thrombosis (letter). Ann Intern Med, 116(9): 776–777.

Lafont, A., Marche, C., Wolff, M. et al. (1988). Myocarditis in acquired immunodeficiency syndrome (AIDS) . Etiology and prognosis (abstract). J Am Coll Cardiol, 11: 196A.

Lange, R., Cigarroa, R., Yancy, C. et al. (1989). Cocaine-induced coronary-artery vasoconstriction. N Engl J Med, 321(23): 1557–1562.

Lange, R., Cigarroa, R., Flores, E. et al. (1990). Potentiation of cocaine-induced coronary vasoconstriction by β-adrenergic blockade. Ann Intern Med, 112(12): 897–903.

Lange, R., Cigarroa, R., and Hillis, L. (1989). Cocaine-induced reduction in cross-sectional area of coronary artery stenoses in man: a quantitative assessment. Circulation, 80(4): II–351.

Langner, R. and Bement, C. (1991). Cocaine-induced changes in the biochemistry and morphology of rabbit aorta. NIDA Research Monograph, 108: 154–166.

Lathers, C. and Schraeder, P. (1982). Autonomic dysfunction in epilepsy: characterization of autonomic cardiac neural discharge associated with pentylenetetrazol-induced epileptogenic activity. Epilepsia, 23(6): 633–647.

Lerman, A., Gibbons, R., Rodeheffer, R. et al. (1993). Circulating N-terminal atrial natriuretic peptide as a marker of symptomless left-ventricular dysfunction. Lancet, 341: 1105–1109.

Levinson, J. (1985). Neuroleptic malignant syndrome. Am J Psychiatry, 142: 1137–1145.

Lip, G. and Brodie, M. (1992). Sudden death in epilepsy: an avoidable outcome. J Royal Soc Med, 85: 609–613.

Lisse, J., Davis, C., and Thurmond-Anderle, M. (1989). Upper extremity deep venous thrombosis: increased prevalence due to cocaine abuse. Am J Med, 87(4): 457–458.

Lisse, J., Davis, C., and Thurmond-Anderle, M. (1989). Cocaine abuse and deep venous thrombosis. Ann Intern Med, 110(7): 571–572.

Ludwig, J. (1979). Current methods of autopsy practice. Philadelphia: WB Saunders Company.

Luke, J. and Reay, D. (1992). The perils of investigating and certifying death in police custody. Am J Forensic Med and Pathol, 13(2): 98–100.

Madden, J. and Powers, R. (1990). Effect of cocaine and cocaine metabolites on cerebral arteries *in vitro*. Life Sci, 47(13): 1109–1114.

Majid, P., Patel, B., Kim, H. et al. (1990). An angiographic and histologic study of cocaine-induced chest pain. Am J Cardiol, 65(11): 812–814.

Marley, R., Witkin, J., and Goldberg, S. (1991). A pharmacogenetic evaluation of the role of local anesthetic actions in the cocaine kindling process. Brain Res, 562: 251–257.

Maseri, A., L'Abbate, A., Baroldi, G. et al. (1978) Coronary vasospasm as a possible cause of myocardial infarction: a conclusion derived from the study of "preinfarction" angina. N Engl J Med, 299(23): 1271–1277.

Mathias, D. (1986). Cocaine-associated myocardial ischemia: review of clinical and angiographic findings. Am J Med, 81: 675–678.

McWilliam, J. (1887). Fibrillar contraction of the heart. J Physiol, 8: 296–310.

Mendelson, M. and Chandler, J. (1992). Postpartum cardiomyopathy associated with maternal cocaine abuse. Am J Cardiol, 70: 1092–1094.

Messerli, F. (1993). Hypertension, left ventricular hypertrophy, ventricular ectopy, and sudden death. Am J Hypertension, 6: 335–336.

Michelson, E., Spear, J., and Moore, E. (1980). Electrophysiologic and anatomic correlates of sustained ventricular tachyarrhythmias in a model of chronic myocardial infarction. Am J Cardiol, 45: 583–590.

Minor, R., Jr., Scott, B., Brown, D. et al. (1991). Cocaine-induced myocardial infarction in patients with normal coronary arteries. Ann Intern Med, 115(10): 797–806.

Mirchandani, H., Rorke, L., Sekula-Perlman, A., and Hood, I. (1994). Cocaine-induced agitated delirium, forceful struggle, and minor head injury. Am J Forensic Med Pathol, 15(2): 95–99.

Mizrahi, S., Laor, D., and Stamler, B. (1988). Intestinal ischemia induced by cocaine abuse. Arch Surg, 123: 394.

Moliterno, D., Willard, J., Lange, R. et al. (1994). Coronary-artery vasoconstriction induced by cocaine, cigarette smoking, or both. N Engl J Med, 330: 454–459.

Morris, G., Fiore, P., Hamlin, R. et al. (1994). Effects of long-term administration and exercise on cardiac metabolism and isomyosin expression. Can J Physiol Pharmacol, 72: 1–5.

Nademanee, K., Taylor, R., Bailey, W. et al. (1994). Mechanisms of cocaine-induced sudden death and cardiac arrhythmias. Circulation, 90(4, Pt 2): I–455.

Nahas, G., Trouve, R., Demus, J., and Sitbon, M. (1985). A calcium-channel blocker as antidote to the cardiac effects of cocaine intoxication. N Engl J Med, 313(8): 519–520.

Nahas, G., Trouve, R., Latour, C., and Maillet, M. (1991). Acute cardiovascular toxicity of cocaine and its antidote. Journal de Toxicologie Clinique et Experimentale, 11: 313–319.

Nahas, G., Maillet, M., Chiarasini, D., and Latour, C. (1992). Myocardial damage induced by cocaine administration of a week's duration in the rat. In L. Harris (Ed.), Committee for Problems of Drug Dependency, 1991 Annual Conference. NIDA Research Monograph 119, Washington, D.C.: U.S. Government Printing Office.

Nalbandian, H., Sheth, N., Dietrich, R., and Georgiou, J. (1985). Intestinal ischemia caused by cocaine ingestion: report of two cases. Surgery, 97(3): 374–376.

Nanji, A. and Filipenko, J. (1984). Asystole and ventricular fibrillation associated with cocaine intoxication. Chest, 85: 132–133.

Nathan, L. and Hernandez, E. (1990). Intravenous substance abuse and a presacral mass. JAMA, 263(11): 1496.

Novitzky, D., Wicomb, W., Cooper, D. et al. (1984). Electrocardiographic, hemodynamic and endocrine changes occurring during experimental brain death in the Chacma baboon. J Heart Transplant, 4: 63–69.

Núñez, B., Miao, L., Ross, J. et al. (1994). Effects of cocaine on carotid vascular reactivity in swine after balloon vascular injury. Stroke, 25: 631–638.

Núñez, B., Miao, L., Kuntz, R. et al. (1994). Cardiogenic shock induced by cocaine in swine with normal coronary arteries. Cardiovasc Res, 28: 105–111.

O'Halloran, R. and Lewman, L. (1993). Restraint asphyxiation in excited delirium. Am J Forensic Med Pathol, 14(4): 289–295.

Om, A., Porter, T., and Mohanty, P. (1992). Transeophageal echocardiographic diagnosis of acute aortic dissection complicating cocaine abuse. Am Heart J, 123(2): 532–534.

Om, A., Ellahham, S.,Vetrovec, G. et al. (1993). Left ventricular hypertrophy in normotensive cocaine users. Am Heart J, 5(1): 1441–1443.

Oppenheimer, S. (1990). Cardiac dysfunction during seizures and the sudden epileptic death syndrome. J Royal Soc Med, 83(3): 134–136.

Parker, R., Beckman, K., Baumann, J., and Hariman, R. (1989). Sodium bicarbonate reverses cocaine-induced conduction defects. Circulation, 80(4): II–15.

Pasternack, P., Colvin, S., and Bauman, F. (1986). Cocaine-induced angina pectoris and acute myocardial infarction in patients younger than 40 years. Am J Cardiol, 55: 847.

Peng, S., French, W., and Pelikan, P. (1989). Direct cocaine cardiotoxicity demonstrated by endomyocardial biopsy. Arch Pathol Lab Med, 113(8): 842–845.

Perreault, C., Hague, N., Mortgan, K. et al. (1993). Negative inotropic and relaxant effects of cocaine on myopathic human ventricular myocardium and epicardial coronary arteries *in vitro*. Cardiovascular Res, 27: 262–268.

Pirwitz, M., Willard, J., Landau, C. et al. (1995). Influence of cocaine, ethanol, or their combination on epicardial coronary arterial dimensions in humans. Arch Int Med, 155: 1186–1191.

Porter, W. (1894). On the results of ligation of the coronary arteries. J Physiol (London), 15: 121–138.

Przywara, D. and Dambacon, G. (1989). Direct actions of cocaine on cardiac cellular electrical activity. Circulation Res, 65: 185–192.

Pudiak, C. and Bozarth, M. (1994). Cocaine fatalities increased by restraint stress. Life Sci, 55(19): 379–382.

Rajs, J. and Falconer, B. (1979). Cardiac lesions in intravenous drug addicts. Forensic Sci Int, 13: 193–209.

Randall, W., Armour, J., Geis, W. et al. (1972). Regional cardiac distribution of the sympathetic nerves. Fed Proc, 21: 1199–1208.

Reichenbach, D. and Moss, N. (1975). Myocardial cell necrosis and sudden death in humans. Circulation, 51, 52(Suppl III), III: 60–62.

Ricci, D., Orlick, A., Cipriano, P. et al. (1979). Altered adrenergic activity in coronary arterial spasm: insight into mechanism based on study of coronary hemodynamics and the electrocardiogram. Am J Cardiol, 43: 1073–1079.

Roberts, W., Curry, R., Jr., Isner, J. et al. (1982). Sudden death in Prinzmetal's angina with coronary spasm documented by angiography. Am J Cardiol, 50: 203–210.

Rod, J. and Zucker, R. (1987). Acute myocardial infarction shortly after cocaine inhalation. Am J Cardiol, 59: 161.

Roh, L. and Hamele-Bena, D. (1990). Cocaine-induced ischemic myocardial disease. Am J Forensic Med and Pathol, 11(2): 130–135.

Rollingher, I., Belzberg, A., and Macdonald, I. (1986). Cocaine-induced myocardial infarction. Can Med Assoc J, 135: 45–46.

Rosen, T., Leopold, H., and Danilo, P. (1988). The effects of cocaine on the isolated fetal and adult guinea pig heart. Circulation, 78(4, Suppl. II): II–359.

Rosenbaum, J., Billingham, M., Ginsburg, R. et al. (1987). Cardiomyopathy in a rat model of pheochromocytoma: morphological and functional alterations. J Pharmacol Exp Ther, 241: 354–360.

Ruttenber, H., Sweeny, P., Mendelin, J., and Wetli, C. (1991). Preliminary findings of an epidemiologic study of cocaine-related deaths in Dade County, Florida, 1978–1985. In S. Schober and C. Schade (Eds.), Epidemiology of cocaine use and abuse, NIDA Research Monograph 110, Washington, DC: U.S. Government Printing Office, 95–112.

Samuels, M. (1987). Neurogenic heart disease: a unifying hypothesis. Am J Cardiol, 60: 15J–19J.

Schwartz, A., Janzen, D., Jones, R., and Boyle, W. (1989). Electrocardiographic and hemodynamic effects of intravenous cocaine in awake and anesthetized dogs. J Electrocardiol, 22(2): 159–166.

Schrem, S., Belsky, P., Schwartzman, D., and Slater, W. (1990). Cocaine-induced Torsades de Pointes in a patient with the idiopathic long QT syndrome. Am Heart J, 120(4): 980–984.

Seballos, R., Mendel, S., Mirmiran-Yazdy, A. et al. (1994). Sarcoid cardiomyopathy precipitated by pregnancy with cocaine complications. Chest, 105(1): 303–305.

Seeman, P. and Van Tol, H. (1994). Dopamine receptor pharmacology. Trends in Pharmacol Sci, 15: 264–270.

Shannon, M. (1988). Clinical toxicity of cocaine adulterants. Ann Emerg Med, 17(11): 1243–1247.

Shapiro, L., Moore, R., Logan-Sinclair, R. et al. (1984). Relation of regional echo amplitude to left ventricular function and the electrocardiogram in left ventricular hypertrophy. Br Heart J, 52: 99–105.

Sherzoy, A., Sadler, D., and Brown, J. (1994). Cocaine-related acute aortic dissection diagnosed by transesophageal echocardiography. Am Heart J, 128(4): 841–843.

Simpson, R. and Edwards, W. (1986). Pathogenesis of cocaine-induced ischemic heart disease. Arch Path Lab Med, 110: 479–484.

Smart, R. and Anglin, R. (1986). Do we know the lethal dose of cocaine? J Forensic Sci, 32(2): 303–312.

Smith, H., Liberman, H., Brody, S. et al. (1987). Acute myocardial infarction temporarily related to cocaine use. Ann Intern Med, 107: 13–18.

Smith, H., Roche, A., Jagusch, M., and Herdson, P. (1976). Cardiomyopathy associated with amphetamine administration. Am Heart J, 91: 792–797.

Staley, J., Hearn, L., Ruttenber, A. et al. (1994). High affinity cocaine recognition sites on the dopamine transporter are elevated in fatal cocaine overdose victims. J Pharm Exp Ther, 271: 1678–1685.

Stenberg, R., Winniford, M., Hillis, D. et al. (1989). Simultaneous acute thrombosis of two major coronary arteries following intravenous cocaine use. Arch Pathol Lab Med, 113: 521–524.

Strain, J., Grose, R., Factor, S., and Fisher, J. (1983). Results of endomyocardial biopsy in patients with spontaneous ventricular tachycardia but without apparent structural heart disease. Circulation, 68(6): 1171–1181.

Substance Abuse and Mental Health Services Administration. (1995). Annual Medical Examination Data, 1994, data from the drug abuse warning network (DAWN). Series I, November 13–14, Washington, D.C.

Szakacs, J. and Cannon, A. (1958). L-Norepinephrine myocarditis. Am J Clin Pathol, 30: 425–434.

Szakacs, J., Dimmette, R., and Cowart, E. (1959). Pathologic implications of the catecholamines epinephrine and norepinephrine. U.S. Armed Forces Med J, 10: 908–925.

Talebzadeh, V., Chevrolet, J., Chatelain, P. et al. (1990). Myocardite à éosinophiles et hypertension pulmonaire chez une toxicomane. Ann Pathol, 10(1): 40–46.

Taliercio, C., Olney, B., and Lie, J. (1985). Myocarditis related to drug hypersensitivity. Mayo Clin Proc, 60: 463–468.

Tardiff, K., Gross, E., Wu, J. et al. (1989). Analysis of cocaine-positive fatalities. J Forensic Sci, 34(1): 53–63.

Tazelaar, H., Karch, S., Billingham, M., and Stephens, B. (1987). Cocaine and the heart. Hum Pathol, 18: 195–199.

Tella, S., Korupolu, G., Schindler, C., and Goldberg, S. (1992). Pathophysiological and pharmacological mechanisms of acute cocaine toxicity in conscious rats. J Pharm Exp Ther, 262: 936–946.

Tella, S., Schindler, C., and Goldberg, S. (1993). Cocaine: cardiovascular effects in relation to inhibition of peripheral monomamine uptake and central stimulation of the sympathoadrenal system. J Pharm Exp Ther, 267(1): 153–167.

Temsey-Armos, P., Fraker, T., Brewster, P., and Wilkerson, D. (1992). The effects of cocaine on cardiac electrophysiology in conscious, unsedated dogs. J Cardiovasc Pharmacol, 19: 883–891.

Togna, G., Tempesta, E., Togna, A. et al. (1985). Platelet responsiveness and biosynthesis of thromboxane and prostacylin in response to *in vitro* cocaine treatment. Haemostasis, 15: 100–107.

Trouve, R. and Nahas, G. (1986). Nitrendipine: an antidote to cardiac and lethal toxicity of cocaine. Proc Soc Exp Biol Med, 183: 392–397.

Tseng, Y., Rockhold, R., Hoskins, B. et al. (1994). Cardiovascular toxicities of nandrolone and cocaine in spontaneously hypertensive rats. Fund Appl Toxicol, 22: 113–121.

Turnicky, R., Goodin, J., Smialek, J. et al. (1992). Incidental myocarditis with intravenous drug abuse. The pathology, immunopathology, and potential implications for human immunodeficiency virus-associated myocarditis. Hum Pathol, 23: 138–143.

Virmani, R., Kolodgie, F., Rabinowitz, M. et al. (1989). Cocaine-associated coronary thrombosis coexists with atherosclerosis and increased adventitial mast cells. Circulation, 80(4), II–647.

Virmani, R., Rabinowitz, M., and Smialek, J. (1987). Cocaine-associated deaths: absence of coronary thrombosis and a high incidence of myocarditis. Lab Invest, 56: 83.

Virmani, R., Rabinowitz, M., Smialek, J., and Smyth, D. (1988). Cardiovascular effects of cocaine: an autopsy study of 40 patients. Am Heart J, 115(5): 1068–1076.

Vitullo, J., Karam, R., Mekhail, N. et al. (1989). Cocaine-induced small vessel spasm in isolated rat hearts. Am J Pathol, 135(1): 85–91.

Wang, J. and Carpentier, R. (1994). Electrophysiologic *in vitro* effects of cocaine and its metabolites. Int J Cardiol, 46: 235–242.

Watt, T. and Pruitt, R. (1964). Cocaine-induced incomplete bundle branch block in dogs. Circ Res, 15: 234–239.

Weber, K., Sun, Y., Tyagi, S. et al. (1994). Collagen network of the myocardium: function, structural remodeling and regulatory mechanisms. J Mol Cell Cardiol, 26: 279–292.

Weidmann, S. (1955). Effects of calcium ions and local anaesthetics on electrical properties of Purkinje fibers. J Physiol, 129: 568–582.

Weiss, R. (1986). Recurrent myocardial infarction caused by cocaine abuse. Am Heart J, 111: 793.

Wetli, C. and Fishbain, D. (1985). Cocaine-induced psychosis and sudden death in recreational cocaine users. J Forensic Sci, 30(3): 873–880.

Wetli, C. (1995). Personal communication.

Wiener, R., Lockhart, J., and Schwartz, R. (1986). Dilated cardiomyopathy and cocaine abuse: report of two cases. Am J Med, 81: 699–701.

Wilkins, C., Mathur, V., Ty, R., and Hall, R. (1985). Myocardial infarction associated with cocaine abuse. Texas Heart Inst J, 12: 385–387.

Williams, E. (1914). Negro cocaine "fiends" are a new Southern menace. New York Times, p. 12, Section 5. February 8.

Wolfson, H., Hogya, P., and Wolfson, A. (1990). Chronic cocaine abuse associated with dilated cardiomyopathy. Am J Emerg Med, 8: 203–204.

Xu, Y., Crumb, W., and Clarkson, C. (1994). Cocaethylene, a metabolite of cocaine and ethanol, is a potent blocker of cardiac sodium channels. J Pharm Exp Ther, 271: 319–325.

Yasuda, R., Zahniser, N., and Dunwidde, T. (1984). Electrophysiological effects of cocaine in rats hippocampus *in vitro*. Neurosci Lett, 45: 199–204.

Young, D. and Glauber, J. (1947). Electrocardiographic changes resulting from acute cocaine intoxication. Am Heart J, 34: 272–279.

Zimmerman, F., Gustafson, G., and Kemp, H. (1987). Recurrent myocardial infarction associated with cocaine abuse in a young man with normal coronary arteries: evidence for coronary artery spasm culminating in thrombosis. J Am Coll Cardiol, 9: 964–968.

Zipes, D., Fischer, J., King, R. et al. (1975). Termination of ventricular fibrillation in dogs by depolarizing a critical amount of myocardium. Am J Cardiol, 36: 37–44.

1.12.3 Pulmonary disease

Cocaine-related pulmonary disorders can be grouped into four categories: local inflammatory and infectious processes, barotrauma, parenchymal disease, and vascular adaptations. Most of the changes in the upper airway are a result of local inflammatory processes, but all four types of alterations may be seen in the lower portions of the airway. Cocaine's effects on the upper airway are primarily local. The most common cocaine-induced disorder of the upper airway is perforation of the nasal septum. This disorder has been recognized for nearly 100 years (Maier, 1926). Much less common are chronic inflammatory processes involving the oropharynx. Occasionally, the inflammatory process may be so intense that it mimics limited Wegner's granulomatosis (Daggett et al., 1990). A heterogeneous group of disorders, ranging from decreased diffusing capacity (Itkonen et al., 1984) and pneumomediastinum (Hunter et al., 1986) to bronchiolitis obliterans (Patel et al., 1987), and pulmonary edema (Allred and Ewer, 1981) have all been attributed to cocaine use. It is not known with any certainty whether intravenous cocaine abuse carries with it the same increased risks for community-acquired pneumonia and septic pulmonary emboli as heroin use, and experimental studies of the effects of cocaine on the lung are almost non-existent. There is now a rat model for cocaine smoking (Boni et al., 1991), and also an ongoing clinical study in cohorts of cigarette, marijuana, and cocaine smokers (Tashkin et al., 1993). Preliminary results of the latter suggest that habitual cocaine smoking has no effect on nonspecific airway hyperresponsivness (thought to be a marker for airway injury).

Because intravenous cocaine abuse is less common than intravenous heroin abuse, and because the contaminants in illicit cocaine are water soluble while those in heroin are not, the complications of intravenous abuse are seen less frequently in cocaine users. Nonetheless, intravenous cocaine abuse can lead to infectious complications: pneumonia, vascular complications, such as foreign particle embolization, and mechanical complications, such as pneumothorax. Perhaps the most important difference between intravenous heroin and cocaine abuse is that cocaine users inject themselves much more frequently. As a consequence, they are at a greater risk of developing infectious complications, including HIV infection.

1.12.3.1 Local inflammation

Chronic coca leaf chewers may develop stomatitis, glossitis, and buccal mucosal leukoderma (Hammer and Villegas, 1969). The practice of "snorting" probably did not begin until shortly before 1903, the year when the first cases of septal perforation were reported (Maier, 1926). Septal perforation is now a well known complication of drug abuse (Pearman, 1979), but little is known about the histologic changes accompanying the process. One controlled autopsy study compared histological findings in septal mucosa from 20 individuals with proven histories of chronic nasal inhalation of cocaine and 15 controls. As might be expected, chronic inflammatory disease was seen in the cocaine users. The glandular elements were in total disarray and mononuclear cells, particularly lymphocytes, were seen surrounding arterioles and glands. An unexpected finding was the presence of thickened submucosal arterioles. Intimal hyperplasia and fibrosis of these vessels were seen in the majority of cases. There was also increased perivascular deposition of collagen (Chow et al., 1990). The arterial findings were similar to, but not nearly so marked, as those that have been observed in the coronary arteries of cocaine users (Simpson and Edwards, 1986; Roh and Hamele-Bena, 1990), or in cases of catecholamine toxicity (Szakacs et al., 1959). Sampling septal mucosa at autopsy might prove quite useful in confirming a suspected diagnosis of cocaine toxicity, since the finding would suggest a pattern of chronic prior use. At a minimum, the mucosa should be swabbed with saline, since cocaine may be recovered for some time, possibly days, after it was last used.

Besides the changes in the septum, upper respiratory tract necrosis, sometimes on a fairly massive scale, also occurs (Becker and Hill, 1988; Deutsch and Millard, 1989; Daggett et al., 1990). The etiology is thought to be ischemic, secondary to chronic cocaine-induced vasoconstriction, but could also be secondary to contaminants in the inhaled cocaine. Biopsies of a posterior oropharyngeal ulcer in one patient showed only necrosis and a mixed inflammatory cell infiltrate, and there is nothing diagnostic about the tissue changes. The causative role of cocaine is generally confirmed by the resolution of the lesions with cocaine abstinence.

In some cases, the lesions seem to be burns, caused by the inhalation of hot particulate matter from inadequately filtered crack pipes (Bezmalinovic et al., 1988; Loftus and Pearlman, 1989; Snyderman et al., 1991; Reino and Lawson, 1993). Some of these patients experience severe stridor, but others may have uvular edema without apparent respiratory distress. There is no predicatable pattern of symptoms suggesting that upper airway injury is a consequence of cocaine use (Reino and Lawson, 1993).

1.12.3.2 Barotrauma

The general classification of barotrauma includes disorders where increased intraalveolar pressure or decreased interstitial pressure leads to rupture of an alveolus with leakage of air. Whether pneumothorax or pneumomediastinum occurs depends on the location of the alveolus. Abnormalities have been recognized in cocaine users that could account for this pressure imbalance. Increased intraalveolar pressure is usually the result of coughing or performing the Valsalva maneuver, which crack smokers routinely do. There are, however, other possibilities. Pulmonary inflammation could weaken the alveolar wall and lead to leakage of air. Alternatively, vasoconstriction in the vessels adjacent to an alveoli could cause decreased interstitial pressure, leading to alveolar rupture without any great increase in intraalveolar pressure (Seaman, 1989; Macklin and Macklin, 1944). In cocaine users, all of these possibilities should be considered.

Another possible cause for pneumo- and hemothorax is injection into central veins, although this practice is much more common in heroin abusers. Heroin tends to be adulterated with material that is not water soluble. Repeated injections of adulterated heroin can lead to sclerosis of peripheral veins. When that happens, the user is forced to inject central veins. The two most popular central sites are the great vessels in the neck ("pocket shot") (Lewis et al., 1980) and the vessels of the femoral triangle ("groin shot") (Pace et al., 1984). Injections are made into the general area of the supraclavicular fossa, either by the addict himself or by a hired "street doc." Since the lung apex is directly contiguous with the area, pneumothorax commonly results (Kurtzman, 1970; Lewis, 1980; Merhar et al., 1981; Douglas and Levinson, 1986).

Cocaine-associated pneumomediastinum occurs with some frequency (Aroesty et al., 1986; Brody et al., 1988; Bush et al., 1984; Christou et al., 1990; Hunter et al., 1986; Leitman et al., 1988; Luque et al., 1987; Mir et al., 1986; Morris and Shuck, 1985; Ponn et al., 1987; Salzman et al., 1987; Schweitzer, 1986; Shesser et al., 1981; Savader et al., 1988). Since pneumomediastinum is a benign condition, and since no fatal cases of pneumothorax have been reported, there are no autopsy studies. Presumably, the mechanism has to do with the performance of a Valsalva maneuver by a deeply inhaling

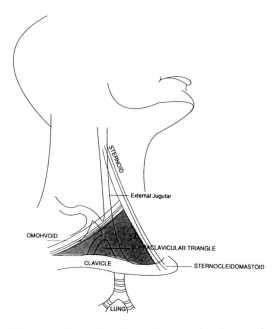

Figure 1.12.3.2 The supraclavicular fossa. As peripheral veins become sclerosed, chronic abusers resort to injecting themselves in the supraclavicular fossa and in the femoral triangle. The supraclavicular fossa overlies the great vessels and the apex of the lung. Pneumothorax and hemothrox are the predictable results.

smoker. No cases have been reported after intravenous or intranasal use. Surprisingly, barotrauma has not been proposed as the mechanism for the increasing number of cocaine-related strokes that have been reported (see Section 1.11.5), but it might offer just as good an explanation as cocaine-induced vasospasm. Air from ruptured alveoli may diffuse into pulmonary capillaries and veins, then pass through the left side of the heart and embolize, via the systemic arteries, to the brain. The diagnosis is particularly difficult to make. If the patient survives for more than a few hours, the air bubbles will have dissolved and typical morphologic changes (multiple small, well-circumscribed foci of cortical necrosis, sometimes associated with laminar necrosis) will not have had time to develop (Wolf et al., 1990).

1.12.3.3 Parenchymal disease

Pulmonary congestion and edema are common findings in drug-related deaths. Osler first wrote about morphine-induced pulmonary edema over 100 years ago (Osler, 1880), and turn-of-the-century pathologists also recognized a connection between pulmonary congestion and opiate-related deaths (Hamilton, 1905). Edema, secondary to heroin abuse, has been a common problem since the 1960s (Steinberg and Karliner, 1968; Duberstein and Kaufman, 1971). Pulmonary congestion in cocaine-related deaths was also recognized at the turn of the century (Hamiltron, 1984), but pulmonary edema in cocaine users also can occur in non-fatal cases (Allred and Ewer, 1981; Hoff-

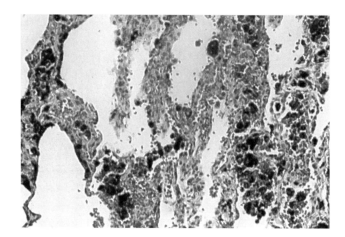

Figure 1.12.3.3   Pulmonary anthracosis. The lungs of crack smokers often are emphysematous and contain dense carbanecous deposits. The changes can be apparent to the naked eye. Hemosiderin laden macrophages are often present, probably reflecting recurrent bouts of focal hemorrhage. San Francisco Medical Examiner, Case # 95-701.

man and Goodman, 1989; Efferen, Palat, and Meisner, 1989; Cucco et al., 1987; Purdie, 1982; Kline and Hirasuana, 1990; Bakht et al., 1990; Battle and Wilcox, 1993; Raijmakers et al., 1994). The etiology of cocaine-associated pulmonary edema is obscure. It could be another manifestation of catecholamine toxicity (Kurachek and Rockoff, 1985; Karch, 1990), and it might share common mechanisms with "neurogenic" pulmonary edema (Robin et al., 1989). Cocaine-induced pulmonary edema could also be explained by the fact that both cocaine and catecholamine excess can lead to decreased contractility (Perreault et al., 1989; Strichartz, 1987; Szakacs et al., 1959). If contractility is depressed enough to lower cardiac output, heart failure and pulmonary edema could develop. Still, another possible mechanism might be a direct effect of cocaine on the lung. It has been suggested that cocaine's local anesthetic actions might impair the movement of sodium and fluid across the aveolar epithelium (Raijmakers et al., 1994), but none of these theories have been proven.

Hemosiderin-laden macrophages are a common finding in the lungs of drug abusers. This change was first recognized in narcotic abusers (Siegel, 1972; Rajs et al., 1984; Kringsholm and Christoffersen, 1987), but similar macrophages are commonly seen in the subgroup abusing cocaine. Hemosiderin-laden cells are not seen in any particular relationship to recent hemorrhage, and their etiology is obscure. Siegel thought that hypoxia was in some way responsible (Siegel, 1972). That theory has never been proven, but the possibility certainly exists that focal vasospasm in the pulmonary bed could result in localized ischemia changes. Whether the changes would be similar to those produced by generalized hypoxia, as seen in opiate abusers, is not clear. Direct toxicity is another, unproven, possibility.

Diffuse alveolar hemorrhage has been described (Murray et al., 1988), and clinical reports suggest that spontaneously resolving hemoptysis is not that uncommon among cocaine smokers (Forrester, 1990; Murray et al., 1988; Murray et al., 1989; Bouchi et al., 1992). Retrospective autopsy studies of cocaine users have disclosed hemorrhages and hemosiderin-laden macrophages in 27% to 58% of the patients (Murray et al., 1988; Bailey et al., 1994). Bailey et al. found evidence for acute or chronic hemorrhage in 71% of the cases, even in the absence of any clinical history suggesting massive hemoptysis, and concluded that relying on that particular clinical sign would lead to serious underestimation of how frequent alveolar hemorrhage actually was in crack smokers.

Interstitial fibrosis is a common occurrence in cocaine users, regardless of whether the cocaine is smoked or injected, and the areas of fibrosis and hemorrhage often coincide (Bailey et al., 1994). Clinical experience suggests that some degree of interstitial fibrosis can be detected in most chronic cocaine smokers, with a documented incidence in some series of nearly 40% (Bailey et al., 1994).

But by comparison, the incidence of this finding is much higher in narcotic abusers (>90%) (Kringsholm and Christoffersen, 1987). The results of other studies suggest that the change may simply be the result of alveolar deposition of particulate matter (Klinger et al., 1992). Accordingly, the presence of iron-containing macrophages has little diagnostic value and is, in fact, more consistent with a history of narcotic abuse than with cocaine.

The smoking habits of crack smokers can sometimes produce diagnostic changes in the appearance of their sputum. The sputum is often very dark in color due to intracellular pigment found within pulmonary alveolar macrophages, and extracellular carbonaceous pigment fragments found floating free. Some of the fragments may measure up to 1 mm across. Similar changes may be seen in the sputum of city dwellers living in regions with poor air quality, but the changes seen in crack smokers are of a different magnitude. It has been suggested that the black sputum is a consequence of the smoking habits of crack users. As crack is smoked, a dark tarry residue forms in the crack pipe. Some crack smokers believe that the residue contains concentrated cocaine, so they scrape it off and smoke it. Normally pulmonary macrophages would collect and remove the concentrated residue, but if the process is repeated enough times, it can overload the normal clearance mechanisms of the lungs and black sputum results (Greenbaum, 1993).

Prior to the advent of smokable cocaine, mentions of cocaine-related pulmonary disease were rare. As smoking cocaine became more popular, reports of patients with inflammatory infiltrates, sometimes associated with fever, hypoxia, hemoptysis, and even respiratory failure, began to appear (Forrester et al., 1990). Specimens from several of these patients have demonstrated diffuse alveolar damage with hyaline membrane formation and Type II cell hyperplasia as well as intraalveolar and interstitial inflammatory infiltrates with eosinophilia. Some cocaine users with x-ray-demonstrated inflammatory infiltrates have had peripheral eosinophilia (Murray et al.,

1988a; Murray et al., 1988b) while others did not (Forrester et al., 1990; Patel et al., 1987; Cucco et al., 1987; Talebzadeh et al., 1990; Oh and Balter, 1992; Nadeem et al., 1994). As with many of the other syndromes that have been attributed to cocaine use, there is virtually no experimental data that would suggest a mechanism for these changes. Nonetheless, a reasonable argument could be made that hypersensitivity is at least partially responsible. Several biopsy specimens have shown deposition of IgE in both lymphocytes and alveolar macrophages (Forrester et al., 1990), and eosinophilic infiltrates have been observed in the heart (see Section 1.11.2.3 for discussion of eosinophilic infiltrates in myocardium), and the pulmonary findings could be just another manifestation of the same underlying process. The difficulty with this theory is that at least half of the reported cases have been in polydrug abusers, and it is hard to know which drug is the culprit.

Finally, the high rate of HIV infection among intravenous drug users should not be forgotten. Most of the pathology encountered in cocaine users is non-infectious. But, like other patients with AIDS, any number of opportunistic and non-opportunistic infections can be encountered. In a recently published univariate analysis of HIV seropositive individuals with bacterial pneumonia, crack smoking was a more powerful predictor than the CD4 count (Caiaffa et al., 1994).

1.12.3.4 Vascular adaptations

Findings described in several case reports suggest that crack smokers may be subject to vasospasm, sometimes sufficiently intense to simulate the radiographic appearance of pulmonary embolism (Smith et al., 1995). Hypertrophy of the smooth muscle in the walls of pulmonary arteries, along with proliferation of the elastic fibers, is consistent with the diagnosis of pulmonary hypertension. This alteration is seen in the lungs of narcotics abusers and is the result of intravascular deposition of foreign materials that have been injected along with the narcotic. Granuloma formation results, and sets in train a series of events which eventually lead to pulmonary hypertension. The three agents most commonly responsible for granuloma formation are talc, cornstarch, and microcrystalline cellulose (Radow et al., 1983). All three materials are strongly birefringent. Starch granules are particularly simple to identify because they exhibit the "Maltese cross" pattern when viewed with polarized light. Particles can also be differentiated by their staining properties. Both starch and cellulose are PAS-positive, while microcrystalline cellulose stains black with GMS (Tomashefski et al., 1981).

In autopsy studies of narcotic and polydrug abusers, the incidence of medial hypertrophy has ranged from 8% (Hopkins, 1972) to as high as 40% (Rajs et al., 1984). The mechanism, however, remains controversial, and in at least two controlled studies, intravenous drug users with multiple talc-induced granulomas had no more medial hypertrophy than controls (Tomashefski and Hirsch, 1980; Kringsholm and Christoffersen, 1987). See Section 5.8.1.4 for a more complete discussion of talc granulomas and angiothrombosis.

Medial hypertrophy and talc granulomas can be seen in the lungs of cocaine users. Murray et al. examined the lungs of 20 individuals who had died of cocaine intoxication. Individuals with histories of polydrug abuse, or with toxicology screens that were positive for drugs besides cocaine, were specifically excluded from the study. Also excluded were cases in which birefringent material was found within the lungs. Four patients (20%) were found to have medial hypertrophy involving either the small or medium sized pulmonary arteries (Murray et al., 1989). The authors suggest that chronic exposure to cocaine-induced high levels of catecholamines may have resulted in pulmonary hypertension. Other authors have made the same suggestion (Itkonen et al., 1984). The variable rates of medial hypertrophy found in different autopsy studies may be explained by the drug-use practices of the local populations. Narcotic abuse is not associated with catecholamine excess, but stimulant abuse is. The problem with the catecholamine thesis is that patients with pheochromocytoma are not prone to pulmonary hypertension, except as a consequence of heart failure (Rose et al., 1988). The patients in Murray's study with medial hypertrophy had no other signs of heart disease. Without more data, the significance of medial hypertrophy in cocaine users is impossible to assess. Another inconsistency with the argument is the fact that granulomatous changes can also occur in the lungs of individuals who only sniff cocaine. Cellulose granulomas were identified in a patient who denied intravenous drug use and who had no occupational exposure to cellulose products (Cooper et al., 1983), and talc granulomas have been identified in two other patients (Buchanan et al., 1981; Oubeid et al., 1990).

Finally, the great vessels of the neck are subject to mechanical injury. "Pocket shooters" may lacerate the brachial, subclavian, or jugular veins. Hemothorax, hematoma, and pseudoaneurysm are all recognized complications of central venous injection. Since the material injected is far from sterile, local and distant complications may occur. Mycotic aneurysm formation, local cellulitis, and abscess formation have all been described, although the incidence is much higher in heroin than in cocaine users (McCarroll and Rozler, 1991).

References

Allred, R. and Ewer, S. (1981). Fatal pulmonary edema following intravenous "freebase" cocaine use. Ann Emerg Med, 10(8): 441–442.

Aroesty, D., Stanley, R., and Crockett, D. (1986). Pneumomediastinum and cervical emphysema from the inhalation of "freebased" cocaine: report of three cases. Otolaryngol Head Neck Surg, 3: 372–374.

Bailey, M., Fraire, A., Greenberg, S. et al. (1994). Pulmonary histopathology in cocaine abusers. Human Pathol, 25(2): 203–207.

Bakht, F., Kirshon, B., Baker, T., and Cotton, D. (1990). Postpartum cardiovascular complications after bromocriptine and cocaine use. Am J Obstet Gynecol, 162: 1065–1066.

Battle, M. and Wilcox, W. (1993). Pulmonary edema in an infant following passive inhalation of freebase ("crack") cocaine. Clin Peds, (February): 105–106.

Becker, G. and Hill, S. (1988). Midline granuloma due to illicit cocaine use. Arch Otolaryngol Head Neck Surg, 114: 90–91.

Bezmalinovic, Z., Gonzalez, M., and Farr, C. (1988). Cricopharyngeal injury possibly due to freebase cocaine. N Engl J Med, 319: 1420–1421.

Boni, J., Barr, W., and Martin, B. (1991). Cocaine inhalation in the rat: pharmacokinetics and cardiovascular response. J Pharmacol Exp Ther, 257(1): 307–315.

Bouchi, J., el Asmar, B., Covetil, J. et al. (1992). Alveolar hemorrhage after cocaine inhalation. Presse Medicale, 21(22): 1025–1026.

Brody, S., Anderson, C., and Gutman, J. (1988). Pneumomediastinum as a complication of "crack" smoking. Am J Emerg Med, 6: 241–243.

Buchanan, D., Lam, D., and Seaton, A. (1981). Punk rocker's lung: pulmonary fibrosis in a drug snorting fire-eater. Br Med J, 283(6307): 1661.

Bush, M., Rubenstein, R., Hoffman, I., and Bruno, M. (1984). Spontaneous pneumomediastinum as a consequence of cocaine use. NY State J Med, (December): 618–619.

Caiaffa, W., Vlahov, D., Graham, N. et al. (1994). Drug smoking, Pneumocystis carinii pneumonia, and immunosuppression increase risk of bacterial pneumonia in human immunodeficiency virus-seropositive injection drug users. Am J Resp Care Med, 150: 1493–1498.

Chow, J., Robertson, A., and Stein, R. (1990). Vascular changes in the nasal submucosa of chronic cocaine addicts. Am J Forensic Med and Pathol, 11(2): 136–143.

Christou, T., Turnbull, T., and Cline, D. (1990). Cardiopulmonary abnormalities after smoking cocaine. South Med J, 83(3): 335–338.

Cohen, H. and Cohen, S. (1984). Spontaneous bilateral pneumothorax in drug addicts. Chest, 86(4): 645–647.

Cooper, C., Bai, T., and Heyderman, E. (1983). Cellulose granulomas in the lungs of a cocaine sniffer. Br Med J, 286: 2021–2022.

Cucco, R., Yoo, O., Cregler, L., and Chang, J. (1987). Nonfatal pulmonary edema after "freebase" cocaine smoking. Am Rev Respir Dis, 136: 179–181.

Daggett, R. B., Haghighi, P., and Terkeltaub, R. (1990). Nasal cocaine abuse causing an aggressive midline intranasal and pharyngeal destructive process mimicking midline reticulosis and limited Wegener's granulomatosis. J Rheumatol, 17(6): 838–840.

Deutsch, H. and Millard, D. J. (1989). A new cocaine abuse complex. Arch Otolaryngol Head Neck Surg, 115: 235–237.

Douglas, R. and Levison, M. (1986). Pneumothorax in drug abusers. An urban epidemic? Chest, 4: 613–617.

Duberstein, J. and Kaufman, D. (1971). A clinical study of an epidemic of heroin intoxication and heroin-induced pulmonary edema. Am J Med, 51: 704–714.

Efferen, L., Palat, D., and Meisner, J. (1989). Nonfatal pulmonary edema following cocaine smoking. NY State J Med, (July): 415–416.

Forrester, J., Steele, A., Waldron, J., and Parsons, P. (1990). Crack lung: an acute pulmonary syndrome with a spectrum of clinical and histopathologic findings. Am Rev Respir Dis, 142(2): 462–467.

Greenbaum, E. (1993). Blackened bronchoalveolar lavage fluid in crack smokers, a preliminary study. Am J Clinc Path, 100: 481–487.

Hamilton, A. M. (1894). A system of legal medicine. New York: E. B. Treat and Company.

Hammer, J. and Villegas, O. (1969). The effect of coca leaf chewing on the buccal mucosa of Aymara and Quechua Indians in Bolivia. Oral Surg, 28: 287–295.

Hind, C. R. (1990). Pulmonary complications of intravenous drug misuse, part I. Thorax, 45: 891–898.

Hind, C. R. (1990). Pulmonary complications of intravenous drug misuse, part II. Thorax, 45: 957–961.

Hoffman, C. and Goodman, P. (1989). Pulmonary edema in cocaine smokers. Radiology, 172 (August): 463–465.

Hopkins, G. (1972). Pulmonary angiothrombotic granulomatosis in drug offenders. JAMA, 221(8): 909–911.

Hunter, J., Loy, H., Markovitz, L., and Kim, U. (1986). Spontaneous pneumomediastinum following inhalation of alkaloidal cocaine and emesis. Mt Sinai J Med, 53(6): 491–493.

Itkonen, J., Schnoll, S., and Glassroth, J. (1984). Pulmonary dysfunction in 'freebase' cocaine users. Arch Intern Med, 144: 2195–2197.

Karch, S. (1990). Problems with high-dose epinephrine therapy. Am J For Med and Path, 11(2): 178–179.

Kline, J. and Hirasuana, J. (1990). Pulmonary edema after freebase cocaine smoking — not due to an adulterant. Chest, 97(4): 1009–1010.

Klinger, J., Bensadoun, E., and Corrao, W. (1992). Pulmonary complications from alveolar accumulation of carbonaceous material in a cocaine smoker. Chest, 101: 1171–1173.

Kringsholm, B. and Christoffersen, P. (1987). Lung and heart pathology in fatal drug addiction. A consecutive autopsy study. Forensic Sci Int, 34: 39–51.

Kurachek, S. and Rockoff, M. (1985). Inadvertent intravenous administration of racemic epinephrine. JAMA, 253(10): 1441–1442.

Kurtzman, R. S. (1970). Complications of narcotic addiction. Radiology, 96: 23–30.

Leitman, B., Greengart, A., and Wasser, H. (1988). Pneumomediastinum and pneumopericardium after cocaine abuse. Am J Radiol, 151: 614.

Lewis, J., Groux, N., Elliot, J. et al. (1980). Complications of attempted central venous injections performed by drug abusers. Chest, 74: 613–617.

Loftus, B. and Perlman, S. (1989). Upper airway distress associated with crack abuse (abstr). Otolaryngol Head Neck Surg, 101: 228.

Luque, M., Cavallaro, D., Torres, M. et al. (1987). Pneumomediastinum, pneumothorax and subcutaneous emphysema after alternate cocaine inhalation and marijuana smoking. Ped Emerg Care, 3: 107–110.

Macklin, M. and Macklin, C. (1944). Malignant interstitial emphysema of the lungs and mediastinum as an important occult complication in many respiratory diseases and other conditions. Medicine, 23: 281–358.

Maier, H. W. (1926). Der Kokainismus (O. J. Kalant from the German 1926 edition, Trans.) Toronto: Addiction Research Foundation.

McCarroll, K. and Rozler, M. (1991). Lung disorders due to drug abuse. J Thorac Imaging, 6(1): 30–35.

Merhar, G., Colley, D., and Clark, R. (1981). Cervicothoracic complications of intravenous drug abuse. Comput Tomog, 5(12): 271–282.

Mir, J., Galvette, J., Plaza, M. et al. (1986). Spontaneous pneumomediastinum after cocaine inhalation. Respiration, 50: 230–232.

Morris, J. and Shuck, J. (1985). Pneumomediastinum in a young male cocaine user. Ann Emerg Med, 14: 164–166.

Murray, R., Albin, R., Megner, W., and Criner, G. (1988). Diffuse alveolar hemorrhage temporally related to cocaine smoking. Chest, 93(2): 427–429.

Murray, R., Simalek, J., Golle, M., and Albin, R. (1989). Pulmonary artery medial hypertrophy without foreign particle microembolization in cocaine users. Chest, 94S: 48.

Murray, R., Simalek, J., Golle, M., and Albin, R. (1988). Pulmonary vascular abnormalities in cocaine users. Am Rev Respir Dis, 137(Suppl 4, part 2): 459.

Nadeem, S., Nasir, N., and Israel, R. (1994). Löffler's syndrome secondary to crack cocaine. Chest, 105(5): 1599–1600.

Oh, P. and Balter, M. (1992). Cocaine-induced eosinophilic lung disease. Thorax, 47: 478–479.

Osler, W. (1880). Oedema of the left lung; morphia poisoning. Montreal Gen Hosp Rep, 1: 2291.

Oubeid, M., Bickel, J., Ingram, E., and Scott, G. (1990). Pulmonary talc granulomatosis in a cocaine sniffer. Chest, 98(1): 237–239.

Pace, B., Doscher, W., and Margolis, I. (1984). The femoral triangle: a potential death trap for the drug abuser. NY State J Med, 84: 596–598.

Patel, R., Dutta, D., and Schonfeld, S. (1987). Freebase cocaine use associated with bronchiolitis obliterans organizing pneumonia. Ann Int Med, 107(2): 186–187.

Pearman, K. (1979). Cocaine: a review. J Laryngol Otol, 93: 1191–1199.

Perreault, C., Allen, P., Hague, N. et al. (1989). Differential mechanisms of cocaine-induced depression of contractile function in cardiac vs. vascular smooth muscle. Circulation, 80(4): II–15.

Ponn, R., Ruiz, R., Toole, A., and Stern, H. (1987). Pneumomediastinum from cocaine inhalation. Conn Med, 51(6): 366–367.

Purdie, F. (1982). Therapy for pulmonary edema following IV "freebase" cocaine use. Ann Emerg Med, 11(4): 228–229.

Radow, S., Nachamkin, I., Morrow, C. et al. (1983). Foreign body granulomatosis: clinical and immunologic findings. Am Rev Respir Dis, 127(5): 575–580.

Raijmakers, P., Groenveveld, A., deGroot, C. et al. (1994). Delayed resolution of pulmonary oedema after cocaine/heroin abuse. Thorax, 49: 1038–1040.

Rajs, J., Härm, T., and Ormstad, K. (1984). Postmortem findings of pulmonary lesions of older datum in intravenous drug addicts. Virchows Arch, 402: 405–414.

Reino, A. and Lawson, W. (1993). Upper airway distress in crack-cocaine users. Otolaryngology Head Neck Surg, 109(5): 937–940.

Robin, E., Wong, R., and Ptashne, K. (1989). Increased lung water and ascites after massive cocaine overdosage in mice and improved survival related to β-adrenergic blockade. Ann Intern Med, 110(3): 202–207.

Roh, L. and Hamele-Bena, D. (1990). Cocaine-induced ischemic myocardial disease. Am J Forensic Med and Pathol, 11(2): 130–135.

Rose, A., Novitzky, D., and Cooper, D. (1988). Myocardial and pulmonary histopathologic changes. Transpl Proc, 20(5, Suppl 7): 29–32.

Salzman, G., Khan, F., and Emory, C. (1987). Pneumomediastinum after cocaine smoking. South Med J, 80(11): 1427–1429.

Savader, S., Omori, M., and Martinez, C. (1988). Pneumothorax, pneumomediastinum and pneumopericardium: complications of cocaine smoking. J Fla Med Assoc, 75: 151–152.

Schweitzer, V. (1986). Osteolytic sinusitis and pneumomediastinum: deceptive otolaryngologic complications of cocaine abuse. Laryngoscope, 96 (February): 206–210.

Seaman, M. E. (1989). Barotrauma related to inhalation drug abuse. J Emerg Med, 8: 141–149.

Shesser, R., Davis, C., and Edelstein, S. (1981). Pneumomediastinum and pneumothorax after inhaling alkaloidal cocaine. Ann Emerg Med, 10(4): 213–215.

Shetty, P., Krasicky, C., Sharma, G., and Berke, M. (1985). Mycotic aneurysms in intravenous drug abusers: the utility of intravenous digital subtraction angiography. Radiology, 155: 319–321.

Siegel, H. (1972). Human pulmonary pathology associated with narcotic and other addictive drugs. Hum Pathol, 3: 55–66.

Simpson, R. and Edwards, W. (1986). Pathogenesis of cocaine-induced ischemic heart disease. Arch Pathol Lab Med, 110: 479–484.

Smith, G., McClaughry, P., Purkey, J. et al. (1995). Crack cocaine mimicking pulmonary embolism on pulmonary ventilation/perfusion lung scan, a case report. Clin Nuclear Med, 20(1): 65–68.

Snyderman, C., Weissmann, J., Tabor, E. et al. (1991). Crack cocaine burns of the larynx. Arch Otolaryngol Head Neck Surg, 117: 792–795.

Steinberg, A. and Karliner, J. (1968). The clinical spectrum of heroin pulmonary edema. Arch Int Med, 122: 122–127.

Strichartz, G. (1987). Handbook of experimental pharmacology, Volume 81: Local anesthetics. New York: Springer-Verlag.

Szakacs, J., Dimmette, R., and Cowart, E. (1959). Pathologic implications of the catecholamines epinephrine and norepinephrine. U.S. Armed Forces Med J, 10: 908–925.

Talebzadeh, V., Chevrolet, J., Chatelain, P. et al. (1990). Myocardite à éosinophiles et hypertension pulmonaire chez une toxicomane. Ann Pathol, 10(1): 40–46.

Tashkin, D., Simmons, M., Chang, P. et al. (1993). Effects of smoked substance abuse on nonspecific airway hyperresponsiveness. Am Rev Respir Dis, 147: 97–103.

Tomashefski, J. and Hirsch, C. (1980). The pulmonary vascular lesions of intravenous drug abuse. Human Pathol, 11: 133–145.

Tomashefski, J., Hirsch, C., and Jolly, P. (1981). Microcrystalline cellulose pulmonary embolism and granulomatosis. Arch Pathol and Lab Med, 105: 89–93.

Wolf, H., Moon, R., Mitchell, P., and Burger, P. (1990). Barotrauma and air embolism in hyperbaric oxygen therapy. Am J Forensic Med and Pathol, 11(2): 149–153.

Zorc, T., O'Donnell, A., Holt, R. W. et al. (1988). Bilateral pyopneumothorax secondary to intravenous drug abuse. Chest, 93: 645–647.

1.12.4 Gastrointestinal disorders

Most of the gastrointestinal problems associated with cocaine use are due to catecholamine-mediated effects on blood vessels. However, cocaine metabolites, and possibly cocaine itself, may be directly toxic to the liver. Norcocaine is hepatotoxic in experimental animals as is cocaethylene, which is synthesized in the liver and which has overall toxicity similar to that of cocaine itself. Presently, there is no evidence that cocaine is hepatotoxic in humans.

1.12.4.1 Ischemic injuries

Ischemic colitis due to cocaine abuse was first described in 1985 (Fishel et al., 1985). There have been regular reports ever since (Mizrahi et al., 1988; Nalbandian et al., 1985; Garfia et al., 1990; Czyrko et al., 1991; Endress and King, 1990; Riggs and Weibley, 1991; Freudenberger et al., 1990; Nathan and

Hernandez, 1990; Yang et al., 1991; Mustard et al., 1992; Endress et al., 1992; Hall et al., 1992; Ottolini and Foster, 1994; Dehsa and Cebrián, 1995; Pugh et al., 1995). The case originally described by Fishel was that of a 37-year old with right lower quadrant pain and diarrhea. A right hemicolectomy was performed for removal of a mass that proved to be an inflamed cecum. Microscopic examination of the removed bowel disclosed "findings consistent with pseudomembranous colitis and some areas that were suggestive of ischemic colitis." In the case reported by Endress, the ilium had zones of hemorrhage and ulceration but no particularly distinctive features (Endress, and King, 1990).

A retrospective study of patients with gastroduodenal perforations suggests that "crack" cocaine smokers may constitute a specific subgroup of patients who develop their perforation on the basis of an acute ischemic event, rather than as a complication of chronic ulcer disease (Lee et al., 1990). In such patients perforation is more likely to be duodenal rather than gastric (Abramson et al., 1992; Fennell et al., 1995). It is yet to be established whether ulceration in cocaine users is a direct result of ischemia, or excess acid accumulation due to arteriolar vasoconstricion in the gastric mucosa allowing excess acid to accumulate (Marrone and Silen, 1984).

Evidence continues to accumulate implicating maternal cocaine use with necrotizing enterocolitis in the neonate. The etiology of this disorder is not known, and its occurrence has been reported in conjunction with a host of different risk factors (Amoury, 1993; Dowing et al., 1991; Santulli et al., 1975), cocaine being just the most recent addition to the list. The likelihood of a connection is strengthened by the fact that identical pathologic changes have been induced in a rat model (Büyükünal et al., 1994). Regardless of the etiology, the pathologic changes observed in the colon are the same. Air accumulates in the submucosal or subserosal layers of the bowel wall, sometimes coalescing into visible blebs, with fluid and blood accumulating in the lumen.

The ileum and proximal colon are the segments most commonly involved; however, the distribution of lesions may be quite spotty, with diseased and normal segments interspersed. The mucosa is inflamed, with fluid and blood extravisated into the bowel wall. Gangrenous changes are not uncommon, though differentiating hemorrhagic from gangrenous segments at the time of surgery may be difficult. Single or multiple perforations may be present and are usually found on the antimesenteric aspect of the bowel. Localized swelling in any portion of the bowel may allow it to act as a lead point for intussusception (Ottolini and Foster, 1994).

Mesenteric blood flow in swine injected with cocaine decreases enough to produce ischemic changes in the bowel wall (Hebra et al., 1993), although the mechanism for this decrease is not known. However, the role of catecholamine excess in cocaine-related bowel disease is strongly suggested by the fact that bowel obstruction and ischemia, with similar pathologic findings, occurs in patients with pheochromocytoma. Khafagi et al. described a patient with extremely high catecholamine levels who developed pseudo-bowel obstruction that rapidly resolved with intravenous phentolamine infusions (Khafagi et al., 1987). In fact, catecholamine-mediated gastrointestinal lesions have been recognized since the 1930s, when treatment of asthmatics with nebulized epinephrine came into fashion. Occasionally, treatment was complicated by tracheal hemorrhages and ulceration of the gastrointestinal mucosa (Galgaini et al., 1939).

Szakacs systematically studied the effects of chronic catecholamine administration in experimental animals and humans. He reported in the 1950s that fibrinoid degeneration and necrosis could be seen in the arteriolar walls of vessels both in the heart and in the gastrointestinal tract. Prolonged norepinephrine infusion induced endothelial proliferation, occasionally sufficient to cause "complete obstruction of small arteries of the gastrointestinal tract, leading to infarction and perforation of the bowel." Similar lesions were observed in experimental animals and in patients with pheochromocytoma (Szakacs et al., 1959). Nearly forty years later, precisely the same lesion has been identified in cocaine users (Garfia et al., 1990). Thrombotic lesions have also been described, presumably caused by the same sequence of events that lead to thrombosis in the heart and other blood vessels.

Bowel is not the only part of the gastrointestinal tract subject to ischemic injury. There is at least one report of spontaneous hepatic rupture in a pregnant cocaine user (Moen et al., 1993), presumably a result of the same mechanism responsible for ischemic gut injury.

1.12.4.2 Hepatic disease

Hepatocellular necrosis can be produced in animal models of cocaine toxicity. Clinical studies of chronic cocaine abusers are contradictory. One study found significant transaminase elevations in chronic cocaine users (Marks and Chapple, 1967), but other studies failed to demonstrate liver function abnormalities, or showed only minimal enzyme changes (Kothur et al., 1991). Normal liver function has been observed in both parenteral (Rippetoe et al., 1991) and non-parenteral users, provided the users were not hepatitis B carriers (Tabasco-Minguillan et al., 1990).

The relative absence of cocaine-related liver disease has to do with the fact that oxidative cocaine metabolism plays a very minor role in man. In animals, however, cytochrome P450 and flavin adenine dinucleotide containing monooxygenase metabolize significant amounts of cocaine to norcocaine. Further enzymatic breakdown yields N-hydroxynorcocaine and norcocaine nitroxide (Shuster et al., 1977; Shuster et al., 1983). Norcocaine nitroxide, once thought to be a highly reactive free radical, is now known to be stable. It reacts neither with proteins nor glutathione (Rauckman et al., 1982). However, further oxidation to the norcocaine nitrosodium ion produces a compound that is highly reactive with glutathione. If glutathione stores fall below a certain level, lipid peroxidation is unopposed and cocaine metabolites bind to hepatic proteins, eventually leading to cell death (Evans, 1983; Kloss et al., 1984). Necrosis is worse if animals are pretreated with agents that induce P450 synthesis and is less if they are treated with P450 inhibitors. In animals, one of two different patterns may be observed. Fatty infiltration and periportal inflammation occur in association with periportal

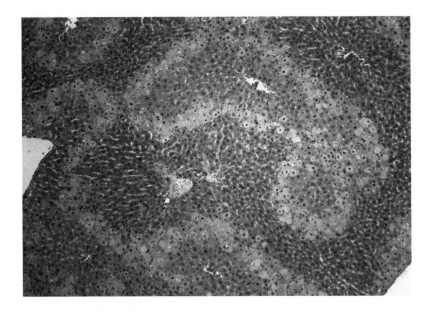

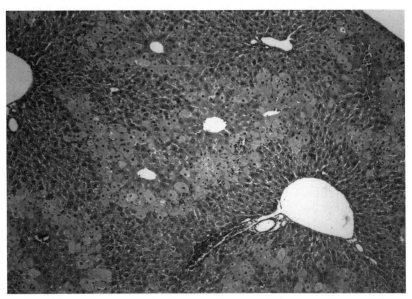

Figure 1.12.4.2   Effects of cocaine and cocaethylene on the rat liver. The micropho-
tograph on top is from a rat treated with cocaine. Photograph on bottom is from a
rat treated with cocaethylene; patterns of injury are the same. Courtesy of Stephen
M. Roberts, University of Florida, Center for Environmental and Human Toxicology.

(Evans and Harbison, 1978; Evans, 1983) or centrolobular necrosis (Shuster
et al., 1977). Both types of necrosis can be prevented if the animal is pretreated
with P450 inhibitors (Evans, 1983). In addition, cocaine given to mice causes
depression of hepatic mitochondrial function, sometimes to a marked degree

(León-Velarde et al., 1991), but whether this also occurs in humans is not known.

The situation is much more complex in humans. The first case of human hepatotoxicity to be reported was that of a polydrug abuser who had sustained a cardiac arrest. In addition to cocaine, his toxicology screen was positive for alcohol and barbiturates, but negative for acetaminophen. Examination of the liver disclosed a Zone-1 type injury, with periportal necrosis and sparing of the centrozonal hepatocytes (Perino et al., 1987). A 24-year old with fulminant liver failure was described in another report. His toxicology was negative for everything except cocaine. Morphologic features included coagulative-type perivenular and midzonal necrosis along with periportal microvesicular fatty change (Kanel et al., 1990). Another report described a group of four patients, two with well-demarcated Zone-3 necrosis identical to that seen in cases of acetaminophen poisoning (Wanless et al., 1990). In a controlled autopsy study of cocaine-related deaths, the livers of the cocaine users showed no more sign of hepatotoxicity than did the control group (Copeland, 1989).

Because most cytochrome P450 activity is located in Zone 3, it is not surprising to find that acetaminophen and cocaine cause similar lesions. The difficulty in predicting a pattern of injury in humans is that humans use multiple drugs. The first patient described had used both alcohol and barbiturates. Both of these agents are capable of inducing the P450 system. Until more cases of liver injury have been reported, it would be unwise to consider any pattern of hepatic injury as diagnostic for cocaine toxicity. Conceivably, a patient could develop hepatic failure secondary to acetaminophen ingestion and incidentally test positive for cocaine metabolism. The presence of Zone-3 lesions would not, then, be proof of cocaine toxicity. The likelihood of hepatic injury is increased by concurrent retroviral infection (Odeleye et al., 1992). If this alteration also occurs in humans, then the incidence of liver disorders in drug users should rise as HIV infection becomes more widespread.

An additional possibility to be considered is that hepatic injury could be secondary to cocaethylene production. This compound is produced in the liver, by transesterification, but only in the presence of ethanol (Hearn et al., 1991). In animal experiments, cocaethylene is nearly as toxic as cocaine itself, and when experimental animals are simultaneously treated with ethanol and cocaine, tissue necrosis, presumably secondary to lipid peroxidation, is much worse than when the animals are treated with cocaine alone (Odeleye et al., 1993). When cocaethylene is given to mice, it produces dose-dependent hepatic Zone 2 (midlobular) necrosis. Pretreatment with cytochrome P450 inducers makes the necrosis worse and shifts the zone of necrosis to Zone 1 in the periphery. Treatment with inhibitors, such as cemitidine, reduces toxicity. This is essentially the same pattern seen in mice given cocaine, suggesting that both cocaine and cocaethylene share common mechanisms of toxicity (Roberts et al., 1992; Roth et al., 1992; Boelsterli et al., 1993).

In vivo studies are lacking, but the cytotoxic effects of cocaine on isolated human hepatocytes have been evaluated (Ponsoda et al., 1992). In this system, even low levels of cocaine cause decreases in the ability to synthesize urea, and in hepatic glycogen and glutathione content. In the presence of alcohol, the cytotoxic effects become more pronounced.

There is one report of hepatic rupture in a pregnant cocaine user. The histopathologic changes were not described, but pregnant women are thought to be at increased risk for vasospasm, and cocaine could certainly facilitate that process (Bis and Waxman, 1976; Moen et al., 1993).

References

Abramson, D., Gertler, J., Lewis, T. et al. (1992). Crack and gastroduodenal perforation. Gastroenterology, 102: 1431–1438.

Amoury, R. (1993). Necrotizing enterocolitis: a continuing problem in the neonate. World J Surg, 17: 363–373.

Bis, K. and Waxman, B. (1976). Rupture of the liver associated with pregnancy: a review of the literature and report of two cases. Obstet Gynecol Surg, 31: 763–773.

Boelsterli, U., Wolf, A., and Gödlin, C. (1993). Oxygen free radical production mediated by cocaine and its ethanol-derived metabolite, cocaethylene, in rat hepatocytes. Hepatology, 18(5): 1154–1161.

Büyükünal, C., Kilic, N., Dervisogul, S. et al. (1994). Maternal cocaine abuse resulting in necrotizing enterocolitis — an experimental study in a rat model. Acta Paediatr, 396(Suppl): 91–93.

Copeland, A. (1989). The microscopic pathology of the liver in fatal cocaine intoxication. J Forensic Sci, 29: 185–189.

Dehesa, A. and Cebrián, J. (1995). Ischemic colitis induced by cocaine abuse. Br J Surg, 82: 134–139.

Downing, G., Horner, S., and Kibride, H. (1991). Characteristics of prenatal cocaine exposed infants with necrotizing enterocolitis. AJDC, 145: 26–27.

Endress, C. and King, G. (1990). Cocaine-induced small-bowel perforation. Am J Radiol, 154: 1346–1347.

Endress, C., Gray, D., and Wollschlaeger, G. (1992). Bowel ischemia and perforation after cocaine use. Am J Roent, 159: 73–75.

Evans, M. A. (1983). Role of protein binding in cocaine-induced hepatic necrosis. J Pharmacol Exp Ther, 224: 73–79.

Evans, M. and Harbison, R. (1978). Cocaine-induced hepatotoxicity in mice. Toxicol Appl Pharmacol, 45: 739–754.

Fennell, D., Gandhi, S., and Prichard, B. (1995). Gastrointestinal hemorrhage associated with freebase (crack) cocaine. Postgrad Med J, 71: 377–378.

Fishel, R., Hamamoto, G., Barbul, A. et al. (1985). Cocaine colitis: is this a new syndrome? Dis Colon Rectum, 28: 264–266.

Freudenberger, R., Cappell, S., and Hutt, D. (1990). Intestinal infarction after intravenous cocaine administration. Ann Intern Med, 113(9): 715–716.

Galgaini, J., Proescher, F., Dock, W., and Tainter, M. (1939). Local and systemic effects from inhalation of strong solutions of epinephrine. JAMA, 112: 1929–1933.

Garfia, A., Valverde, J., Borondo, J. et al. (1990). Vascular lesions in intestinal ischemia induced by cocaine-alcohol abuse: report of a fatal case due to overdose. J Forensic Sci, 35(3): 740–745.

Hall, T., Zaninovic, A., Lewis, D. et al. (1992). Neonatal intestinal ischemia with bowel perforation: an *in utero* complication of maternal cocaine abuse. Am J Roent, 150(6): 1303–1304.

Hearn, W., Flynn, D., Hime, D. et al. (1991). Cocaethylene — a unique cocaine metabolite displays high affinity for the dopamine transporter. J Neurochem, 56(2): 698–701.

Hebra, A., Brown, M., Mcgeehin, K. et al. (1993). Systemic and mesenteric vascular effects of platelet-activating factor and cocaine. Am Surgeon, 59(1): 50–54.

Kanel, G., Cassidy, W., Shuster, L., and Reynolds, B. (1990). Cocaine-induced liver cell injury: comparison of morphological features in man and experimental models. Hepatology, 11: 646–651.

Khafagi, F., Lloyd, H., and Gough, I. (1987). Intestinal pseudo-obstruction in pheochromocytoma. Aust N Z J Med, 17(2): 246–248.

Kloss, M., Rosen, G., and Rauckman, E. (1984). Cocaine-mediated hepatotoxicity: a critical review. Biochem Pharmacol, 33: 169–173.

Kothur, R., Marsh, F., and Posner, G. (1991). Liver function tests in nonparenteral cocaine users. Arch Intern Med, 151: 1126–1128.

Lee, H., LaMaute, H., Pizzi, W. et al. (1990). Acute gastroduodenal perforations associated with use of crack. Ann Surg, 211(1): 15–17.

León-Velarde, F., Huicho, L., and Monge, C. (1991). Effects of cocaine on oxygen consumption and mitochondrial respiration in normoxic and hypoxic mice. Life Sci, 50: 213–218.

Marks, V. and Chapple, P. (1967). Hepatic dysfunction in heroin and cocaine users. Br J Addict, 62: 189–195.

Marrone, G. and Silen, W. (1984). Pathogenesis, diagnosis and treatment of gastric mucosal lesions. Clin Gastroenterol, 13: 635–651.

Mizrahi, S., Laor, D., and Stamler, B. (1988). Intestinal ischemia induced by cocaine abuse. Arch Surg, 123: 394.

Moen, M., Caliendo., M., Marshall, W. et al. (1993). Hepatic rupture in pregnancy associated with cocaine use. Obstet Gynecol, 82(4): 687–689.

Mustard, R., Gray, R., Maziak, D. et al. (1992). Visceral infarction caused by cocaine abuse: a case report. Surgery, 112: 951–955.

Nalbandian, H., Sheth, N., Dietrich, R., and Georgiou, J. (1985). Intestinal ischemia caused by cocaine ingestion: report of two cases. Surgery, 97(3): 374–376.

Nathan, L. and Hernandez, E. (1990). Intravenous substance abuse and a presacral mass. JAMA, 263(11): 1496.

Odeyleye, O., Lopez, M., Smith, B. et al. (1992). Cocaine hepatotoxicity during protein undernutrition of retrovirally infected mice. Can J Physiol Pharmacol, 70: 338–343.

Odeyleye, O., Watson R., Eskelson, C., and Earnest, D. (1993). Enhancement of cocaine-induced hepatotoxicity by ethanol. Drug Alcohol Depend, 31: 253–263.

Ottolini, M. and Foster, K. (1994). Intussusception in association with childhood cocaine intoxication: a case report. Ped Emerg Care, 10(6): 342–343.

Perino, L., Warren, G., and Levine, J. (1987). Cocaine-induced hepatotoxicity in humans. Gastroenterology, 93: 176–180.

Ponsoda, X., Jover, R., Castell, J., and Gómez-Lechón, P. (1992). Potentiation of cocaine hepatotoxicity in human hepatocytes by ethanol. Toxic in vitro, 6(2): 155–158.

Pugh, C., Mezghebe, H., and Leffall, L. (1995). Spontaneous bowel perforation in drug abusers. Am J Emerg Med, 13(1): 113–114.

Radin, D. (1992). Cocaine-induced hepatic necrosis: CT demonstration. J Comp Assist Tomography, 16(1): 155–156.

Rauckman, E., Rosen, G., and Cavagnaro, J. (1982). Norcocaine nitroxide: a potential hepatotoxic metabolite of cocaine. Mol Pharmacol, 21: 458–463.

Riggs, D. and Weibley, R. (1991). Acute hemorrhagic diarrhea and cardiovascular collapse in a young child owing to environmentally-acquired cocaine. Ped Emerg Care, 7(3): 154–155.

Rippetoe, L., Phillips, R., and Lange, W. (1992). No association between IV cocaine use and liver toxicity. In L. Harris (ed.) Committee for Problems of Drug Dependency, 1991 Annual Conference. NIDA Research Monograph 119, Washington, D.C.: U.S. Government Printing Office.

Roberts, S., Roth, L., Harbison, R., and James, R. (1992). Cocaethylene hepatotoxicity in mice. Biochem Pharmacol, 43: 1989–1995.

Roth, L., Harbison, R., James R. et al. (1992). Cocaine hepatotoxicity: influence of hepatic enzyme inducing and inhibiting agents on the site of necrosis. Hepatology, 15: 934–940.

Santulli, T., Schullinger, J., Heird, W. et al. (1975). Acute necrotizing enterocolitis in infancy: a review of 64 cases. Pediatrics, 55: 376–381.

Shuster, L., Quimby, F., Bates, A., and Thompson, M. (1977). Liver damage from cocaine in mice. Life Sci, 20: 1035–1041.

Shuster, L., Casey, E., and Welankiwar, S. (1983). Metabolism of cocaine and norcocaine to N-hydroxynorcocaine. Biochem Pharmacol, 32: 3045–3051.

Szakacs, J., Dimmette, R., and Cowart, E. (1959). Pathologic implications of catecholamines epinephrine and norepinephrine. U.S. Armed Forces Med J, 10: 908–925.

Tabasco-Minguillan, J., Novick, D., and Kreek, M. (1990). Liver function tests in nonparenteral cocaine users. Drug Alcohol Depen, 26(2): 169–174.

Wanless, I., Goponath, D., Tan, J. et al. (1990). Histopathology of cocaine hepatotoxicity: report of four patients. Gastroenterology, 98(2): 497–501.

Yang, R. D., Han, M., and McCarthy, J. (1991). Ischemic colitis in a crack abuser. Dig Dis Sci, 36(2): 238–240.

1.12.5 Neurologic disorders

The first reports of neurologic complications were published almost as soon as purified cocaine became widely available. The first cocaine-related stroke was described in 1886 (Catlett, 1886), only two years after cocaine had come into widespread use as a local anesthetic. Today, neurologic complaints are the most common manifestation of cocaine toxicity, at least in patients going to the emergency room (Derlet and Albertson, 1989). During the late 1980s, cocaine-related stroke reemerged as a significant medical problem, and in patients less than 35 years of age, drug abuse is the most commonly identified predisposing condition for stroke (Kaku and Lowenstein, 1990; Feldmann, 1991).

While the incidence of stroke in younger age groups is increasing, very little is known about the pathology of cocaine-related stroke, or, for that matter, the pathology of any other cocaine-related neurologic disorders. However, experimental studies have provided some surprising insights into the effects of cocaine on the brain, and plausible explanations for some types of cocaine toxicity. For example, evidence is emerging that nitric oxide formation plays an important role in cocaine neurotoxicity. In mice, repeated cocaine administration produces sensitization. When the same dose of cocaine was given to mice on a daily basis, seizures became worse and worse;

initially well tolerated doses become lethal after less than a week. Pretreatment with agents that inhibit nitric oxide synthetase completely abolishes the sensitization process, and all of the test animals survived (Itzhak, 1993). Whether similar changes occur in humans remains to be determined.

The effects of cocaine on gene expression, both in the heart and brain, are slowly becoming clearer. Within minutes of cocaine administration, there is increased expression of a number of several different genes. In the brain, there is increased expression of *c-fos,* the transcriptional regulator (Graybiel et al., 1990). Chronic administrion of cocaine to rats results in increased production of mRNA coding for tyrosine hydroxylase and tryptophan hydroxylase (Vrana et al., 1993). These two enzymes catalyze the rate limiting steps in the production of both dopamine and serotonin, the neurotransmitters most obviously involved in cocaine's ability to cause both euphoria and seizures.

Postmortem studies have shown that, in humans, both the numbers of D1 and D2 dopamine receptors are altered by cocaine use (Seeman and Van Tol, 1994). The brains of cocaine abusers usually contain an elevated number of cocaine recognition sites on striatal dopamine transporters, although no such increase is seen in victims of agitated delirium. Chronic cocaine abuse also produces striking decreases in the density of the D1 receptor subtype throughout the striatal reward centers, probably as a result of receptor downregulation, which also probably explains why cocaine users quickly become tolerant to cocaine's euphoriant effects (Staley et al., 1994). Similar changes in D1 receptor sensitivity and gene expression are also seen in experimental animals (Laurier et al., 1994).

The clinical features of cocaine-associated psychiatric disorders, especially psychosis, appear to be different from those seen in true schizophrenia and different also from the pattern seen in amphetamine abusers. The neurotoxicity produced by some amphetamines, as evidenced by chemical measurements and morphologic observations, does not occur in conjunction with cocaine abuse (Yeh and De Souza, 1991). Rats chronically treated either with high dose cocaine or amphetamine show pronounced degeneration in fasciculus retroflexus, but cocaine, unlike amphetamine, does not cause significant damage in the striatum (Ellison and Switzer, 1993).

Cocaine-related impairment is frequently an issue in court proceedings, but there are few satisfactory answers to be had. Regular cocaine users rapidly become tolerant to cocaine's stimulant effects, but whether this tolerance extends to performance and impairment is not known. Even if some correlation could be established in life, at autopsy there is no way to tell whether, or to what degree, the deceased was tolerant. In living subjects, there is limited data suggesting that cocaine improves the performance of some tasks (Stillman et al., 1993).

1.12.5.1 Psychiatric syndromes

Cocaine-induced paranoid psychosis was recognized by the early workers in the field. Magnon (Saury, 1890), Maier (Maier, 1926), and Lewin (Lewin, 1931) all wrote on the topic and took pains to distinguish cocaine psychosis from symptoms induced by alcohol and other drugs. More recent studies (Siegel, 1978; Gawin and Kleber, 1986) have tended to confirm the earlier observations. Transient or "binge" paranoia is common among heavy users. In one study, the incidence was nearly 70% (Satel and Gawin, 1990). What distinguishes the cocaine-associated syndrome from the syndrome induced by amphetamines is that the paranoia occurs only for a very brief period. The development of paranoia in this group of abusers is unpredictable, and is not dose-related. Some individuals appear to be more vulnerable than others.

Cerebral glucose metabolism, as accessed by (18F)-fluorodeoxyglucose positron tomography (PET) of cocaine abusers in early withdrawal, increases. This increase in glucose metabolism involves all areas of the brain, but is particularly noticeable in the basal ganglia and orbitofrontal cortex. The increase in the latter two areas correlates with clinical measures of cocaine craving, and is consistent with the notion that the changes are due to changes in brain dopamine activity (Volkow et al., 1991). Cocaine-induced changes in cerebral perfusion and glucose utilization appear to be gender related. In at least one controlled study, the brain scans of cocaine-dependent women failed to disclose the scanning abnormalities seen in the men (Levin et al., 1994).

Longer lasting episodes of psychosis, due to chronic cocaine abuse, can occur. When they do, there is a good chance that the victim will be misdiagnosed as a schizophrenic. Since drug users, schizophrenic or not, often deny drug use, routine drug screening of such patients is prudent (Shaner et al., 1993). Another important diagnosis to consider in cocaine users with psychiatric symptoms is stroke. Cocaine-induced ischemic infarcts have occasionally been mistaken for acute onset psychosis (Reeves et al., 1995).

1.12.5.2 Cerebral infarction

In the non-drug-using population, strokes are most often secondary to cerebral infarction. The principal causes of infarction are arterial thrombus formation, embolism, spasm, and circulatory compromise with secondary cerebral hypoperfusion. In non-drug-related cases, hemorrhage is the etiology only 15 percent of the time (subarachnoid 10%, intracerebral 5%). An occasional case may involve a child or young adult, but stroke has always been thought of as a disease affecting the elderly. In the past, over 80% of cases occurred in individuals over 65 years old (Adams et al., 1984). As cocaine abuse has become more common, both the age distribution and the underlying etiology of stroke appear to have changed. Case reports now number in the hundreds, and individual cases are so common they are no longer considered reportable.

In cocaine users with stroke, the cause is as likely to be hemorrhage as infarction, and most of the affected individuals are in their mid 30s. In roughly half the reported cases, onset of neurologic deficit occurs within three hours of cocaine use. However, it is not uncommon that victims wake up with a neurologic deficit after having indulged in an all-night binge (Daras et al., 1991).

There was a 100-year hiatus between the first reports of stroke in the 1880s and Brust's report in 1977 (Brust and Richter, 1977), but now case reports appear with great frequency. Even the more exotic syndromes, such as mesencephalic infarcts (Rowley et al., 1990), lateral medullary syndrome (Mody et al., 1988), anterior spinal syndrome (Mody et al., 1988), embolization from a left atrial thrombus (Petty et al., 1990), central retinal infarction (Zeiter et al., 1992; Libman and Paola, 1993; Devenyi et al., 1988; Sleiman et al., 1994), and massive cerebellar infarcts (Aggarwal and Byrne, 1991) have all been described. There are multiple reports of simple infarction (Golbe and Merkin, 1986; Levine et al., 1987; Levine and Welch, 1988; Jacobs et al., 1989; Klonoff et al., 1989; Engstrand et al., 1989; Moore and Peterson, 1989; Chasnoff et al., 1986; Rowbotham, 1988; Seaman, 1990; Daras et al., 1991; Kelly et al., 1992; Konzen et al., 1995).

Except for four instances of biopsy-proven vasculitis (Krendel et al., 1990; Fredericks et al., 1991; Scully et al., 1993) and one case of apparent embolism (Petty et al., 1990), the etiology of most cocaine-associated strokes is obscure. Autopsy reports of infarction are rare (Klonoff et al., 1989; Konzen et al., 1995) and the results unrevealing. Angiography and CT scanning have been equally unrewarding (Tuchman et al., 1994). In one of the latest case reports, histologic changes were entirely lacking, in spite of angiographs showing multifocal areas of segmental stenosis and dilatation (Martin et al., 1995). However, a second study, also published in 1995, described striking infolding of a markedly irregular elastic lamina, consistent with the notion that cocaine-induced vasoconstriction could damage the media of large cerebral vessels, perhaps enough to lead to thrombus formation (Konzen et al., 1995).

This absence of hard data allows ample room for speculation. Pharmacologically-induced vasospasm, resulting either from some direct action exerted by cocaine on cerebral blood vessels, or secondary to catecholamine elevation, is frequently suggested (Levine et al., 1987; Brust, 1993; Schreiber et al., 1994); however, there is very little information to substantiate either contention, and a number of other mechanisms are possible.

Increased platelet responsiveness may be the etiology for cerebral infarction in some cocaine users, but the case is far from clear. *In vitro* studies have yielded conflicting results (Levine et al., 1987; Jennings et al., 1993). Whole blood from some cocaine users has been found to contain higher levels of activated platelets (Rinder et al., 1994), and even higher levels of tissue plasminogen activator inhibitor (Moliterno et al., 1994), but others have found variable changes in platelet aggregation after administration of cocaine to healthy volunteers (Rezkalla et al., 1993).

Another promising line of research involves the effects of cocaine metabolites on the cerebral vasculature. Cocaine directly applied to cat pial arterioles causes vasodilation, and this action can be prevented with β blockade (Dohi et al., 1990), but other experiments with cat cerebral arteries have shown up to 50% decreases in average cross-sectional area when arteries are perfused with benzoylecgonine (Madden and Powers, 1990; Schreiber et al., 1994). If benzoylecgonine also causes cerebral vasoconstriction in man, then it would explain why patients frequently present with symptoms some time after they have last used the drug. The elimination half-life of cocaine itself is less than two hours, but the half-life for benzoylecgonine is closer to seven hours, and benzoylecgonine can be detected in the brain for days after cocaine was last used. The same considerations would apply to coca-ethylene.

Even if benzoylecgonine is vasoactive, that would not explain why cocaine users have demonstrable reductions in cerebral flow for weeks after their last drug use (Volkow et al., 1988). Frontal lobe hypoperfusion is commonly observed in patients entering rehabilitation (Mena et al., 1990; Volkow et al., 1988), as are multiple small superficial cortical areas of hypoperfusion, and it appears that there is no correlation between the severity of these abnormalities and the amount of drug used (Weber et al., 1993). Other studies have shown that blood flow to the dorsolateral prefrontal cortex is still depressed seven to ten days after cocaine use has been discontinued, and may remain that way indefinitely (Bell et al., 1994; Strickland et al., 1993). Interestingly, these flow abnormalities are much more pronounced in male cocaine users than in female (Levine and Tebbet, 1994). The sex difference remains unexplained, but since cocaine is atherogenic (Kolodgie et al., 1991), and premenopausal women have fewer atherosclerotic changes than men, decreased flow in the males may just be a reflection of early atherosclerotic disease (Levine and Tebbet, 1994).

Thus, cocaine users may be subject to decreased cerebral flow, even in the face of a normal cardiac output. Putting aside the issue of CNS athero-sclerosis, there is no question that cocaine users are subject to accelerated atherogenesis (Dressler et al., 1990; Kolodgie et al., 1990; Kolodgie et al., 1991; Karch et al., 1995). If cardiac output is reduced, blood pressure fluctu-ations could also lead to infarction, especially in the face of preexisting CNS atherosclerotic lesions. Cocaine-associated cardiomyopathy (Duell, 1987; Wiener et al., 1986; Chokshi et al., 1989; Karch and Billingham, 1988) and arrhythmias (Young and Glauber, 1947; Boag and Havard, 1985; Crumb et al., 1989; Crumb et al., 1990; Duke, 1986; Neely et al., 1989; Ruben and Morris, 1952; Temesy-Armos et al., 1989; Williams, 1990; Lathers et al., 1988) are both recognized occurrences, and either of them could result in sudden blood pressure fluctuations. A sudden drop in blood pressure, combined with asymptomatic stenotic lesions, could lead to infarction. One recent report described a woman with cardiomyopathy (presumably, cocaine-related) who sustained a cerebral embolism (Petty et al., 1990). The situation is somewhat analogous to cocaine-associated myocardial infarction. The presence of pre-existing lesions may exacerbate transient flow decreases which would have otherwise been asymptomatic.

1.12.5.3 Cerebral vasculitis

The frequency with which cerebral vasculitis causes stroke in cocaine users is unclear. The process has been documented only in four patients. A biopsy from one patient showed small vessels within an area of infarction with

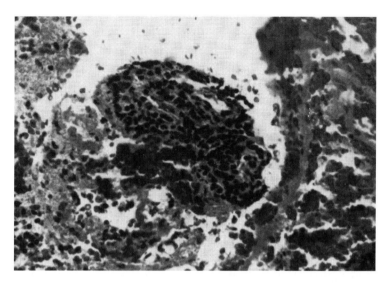

Figure 1.12.5.3 (1)   Cerebral vasculitis in a cocaine user. Biopsy specimen from patient surviving episode of vasculitis. Transmural infiltration of a small cortical vessel. Both acute and chronic inflammatory cells are present. Original magnification 800×. Courtesy of Dr. David A. Krendel, Section of Neurology, The Emory Clinic.

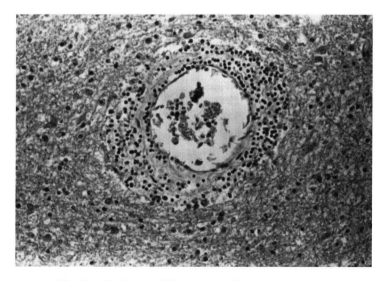

Figure 1.12.5.3 (2)   Cerebral vasculitis in a cocaine user. Autopsy specimen from another patient with cerebral vasculitis. Illustration shows a lymphocytic infiltrate around a small cerebral vessel. Original magnification 800×. Courtesy of Dr. David A. Krendel, Section of Neurology, The Emory Clinic.

transmural infiltration by both acute and chronic inflammatory cells. Occasional multinucleated giant cells were also present. In the other case, there was also lymphocytic infiltration of the small vessel walls with multiple cystic, necrotic, and gliotic areas in the cerebral white matter, especially in the frontal lobes. Multinucleated giant cells were seen in the gliotic areas. The process was most intense in the frontal lobes (Krendel et al., 1990). Fredericks et al. described a second case with marked endothelial swelling and small vessel lymphocytic infiltrates (Fredericks et al., 1991). The most recent report involved a 32-year old hypertensive man who became hemiplegic. Surgical specimens disclosed no evidence of fibrinoid necrosis or giant cells, but there was vasculitis involving venules and arterioles which were infiltrated with neutrophils, lymphocytes, and foamy macrophages. The endothelial cells were enlarged and, in addition, there was evidence of white-matter damage (Scully et al., 1993).

Data is limited, but if cocaine does cause vascular inflammation, then it probably does so by virtue of some direct toxic effect, unrelated to catecholamine toxicity. Patients with pheochromocytoma and animals treated with exogenous catecholamines have no signs of CNS inflammation. Small perivascular hemorrhages can be induced in animals by giving large amounts of epinephrine (Stief and Tokay, 1935), but cerebral vessel wall necrosis and infiltrates do not occur.

Necrotizing angiitis, a form of periarteritis nodosa associated with the abuse of amphetamine and other stimulant drugs (Citron et al., 1970; Kessler et al., 1978; Bostwick, 1981), has never been seen in cocaine users, except insofar as they used cocaine along with intravenous amphetamines and heroin. This disorder was first described in the early 1970s, but its incidence seems to have steadily declined over the last 20 years. The fact that this disorder has essentially disappeared, while intravenous amphetamine abuse has not, suggests that the disorder may have been due to a contaminant that had been introduced into the amphetamine during the course of manufacture and/or distribution. Quality control is nonexistent in illicit labs, and the potential for introducing agents with novel sorts of toxicity is quite real.

1.12.5.4 Subarachnoid and intraventricular hemorrhage

About half the strokes associated with cocaine abuse are due to either intracerebral (Lehman, 1987; Green et al., 1990; Mercado et al., 1989; Nolte and Gelman, 1989; Caplan et al., 1982; Lichtenfeld et al., 1984; Schwartz and Cohen, 1984; Wojak and Flamm, 1987; Lowenstein et al., 1987; Mody et al., 1988; Tardiff et al., 1989; Mittleman and Wetli, 1987; Jacobs et al., 1989; Rowley et al., 1990; Klonoff et al., 1989; Green et al., 1990; Oyesiku et al., 1993; Daras et al., 1994) or subarachnoid hemorrhage (Lundberg et al., 1977; Chynn, 1975; Levine and Welch, 1988; Lichtenfeld et al., 1984; Schwartz and Cohen, 1984; Rogers et al., 1986; Cregler and Mark, 1987; Wojak and Flamm, 1987; Lowenstein et al., 1987; Altes-Capella et al., 1987; Tardiff et al., 1989; Mittleman and Wetli, 1987; Jacobs et al., 1989; Klonoff et al., 1989; Oyesiku et al., 1993; Daras et al., 1994). Subarachnoid hemorrhage is more common than intracerebral hemorrhage by a ratio of 4:3. As is the case with cocaine-related infarction, individuals are in their early thirties. Most (80%) subarachnoid hemorrhages have been related to the presence of angiographically-proven saccular aneurysms. Of the cases reported to date, the majority involved the anterior communicating artery, with the posterior communi-

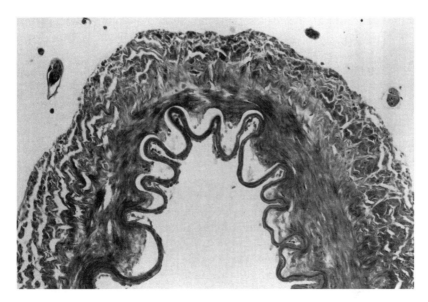

Figure 1.12.5.4   Markedly infolded, irregular internal elastic lamina in the anterior cerebral artery of cocaine with ischemia stroke. The irregularity of the elastic lamina may be a marker for cocaine induced vasospasm. Reprinted, with permission, from Konzen et al., Stroke, 26: 1114–1118, 1995.

cating system being the next most frequent site. The remainder of the lesions have been found scattered throughout the cerebral circulation.

Underlying lesions were found in only half of the reported intracerebral hemorrhages. Most often, the cause was an arteriovenous malformation. The other half of this group had no demonstrable underlying lesions and there was a propensity to bleed into the basal ganglia and thalamus (Green et al., 1990).

Bleeding at these sites is often from small saccular aneurysms. Saccular aneurysms involving the arteries at the base of the brain occur in 1–2% of the adult population, and are often found incidentally at autopsy. Usually they are located at arterial bifurcations. They form as a result of multiple factors, including atheroma and degenerative changes, and secondary flow abnormalities (Sekhar and Heros, 1980). The role of hypertension in the formation and rupture of saccular aneurysms is still unclear (Graham, 1989), but the role of hypertension in cocaine-associated subarachnoid bleeding is becoming increasingly clear (Kibayashi et al., 1995).

Intracerebral hemorrhage is usually due to hypertension, although in some series, the number of cases due to vascular malformation roughly equals the number due to hypertension (Gras et al., 1991). By far, the most common site for hypertensive hemorrhage is the basal ganglia, outnumbering the second most common site, the cerebral white matter, by a ratio of 7:1 (Adams et al., 1984). Hemorrhage in the white matter is usually the result of amyloid angiopathy, and probably has little to do with hypertension. Hemorrhage in the basal ganglia is classically associated with microaneurysm formation and atherosclerosis in the small basal perforating arteries. Microaneurysms have not been observed in cocaine users or experimental animals.

In the most recent study to address the problem, autopsy findings in 26 individuals with cocaine-induced intracerebral hemorrhage were compared with autopsy findings in 26 cases of cocaine-induced cerebral aneurysm rupture. Hypertensive cardiovascular disease was much more common in the former (mean heart weights of 497 vs. 380 grams), suggesting very strongly that hypertensive cardiovascular disease, which itself is a consequence of cocaine use, predisposes to cocaine-induced intracerebral hemorrhage (Kibayashi et al., 1995).

If long-term cocaine use can lead to hypertensive cardiovascular disease and intracerebral hemorrhage, even occasional use could lead to transient blood pressure elevations sufficient to the rupture of preexisting malformations, or bleeding into a tumor (Yapor and Guiterrez, 1992). There is experimental evidence that cocaine potentiates the increases in blood pressure and cerebral blood flow produced by the administration of norepinephrine (Muir and Ellis, 1993). Since cocaine users have elevated circulating levels of norepinephrine, potentiation of the normal response to catecholamines may account for much of the reported pathology. Hemorrhage in individuals without underlying lesions, as in a recently reported case of spinal epidural hematoma (Huff, 1994), remains unexplained.

1.12.5.5 Seizures

Seizures in cocaine users may be a consequence of stroke or intracerebral hemorrhage, or even of massive overdose. They may also be a manifestation of a preexisting seizure disorder that was exacerbated by cocaine use. Various series have placed the incidence of this complication at somewhere between 2% and 10% (Lowenstein et al., 1987; Derlet and Albertson, 1989). In one series of nearly 1,000 patients with acute medical complications of cocaine use, seizures were noted in nearly 10 percent. Only four of these patients had status epilepticus, and all of them were victims of massive overdose (Dhuna et al., 1991). Interestingly, seizures were three times as common in women as in men (18.4% vs. 6.2%). This finding is consistent with the results of other studies that suggest pregnancy and other hormonal alterations can exacerbate cocaine toxicity (Plessinger and Woods, 1990; Sharma et al., 1992).

"Kindling" is a term used to describe the development of generalized convulsions in response to repeated subconvulsive brain stimuli in animals. Cocaine-induced kindling has been demonstrated in animals. Whether this process also occurs in humans has been debated for some time, particularly in cases where cocaine is involved. It has been speculated, but without proof, that kindling, or some similar process, is the mechanism responsible for seizures in chronic cocaine abusers. The fact that kindling does occur in humans is suggested by one well-described case of a 37-year old woman who initially experienced generalized tonic-clonic seizures immediately after smoking crack. She then went on to develop generalized seizures even when she was not using the cocaine (Dhuna et al., 1991).

Although cocaine-related seizures are a frequent occurrence, and are often reported in patients with fatal "overdose," the results of convincing animal studies suggest that different mechanisms are responsible for seizures and lethality. Cocaine-induced seizures appear to result from cocaine's effect on the serotonin transporter, in concert with effects on muscarinic neurons and sigma receptors, while interactions with the dopamine transporter are important for lethality (Ritz and George, 1993).

1.12.5.6 Movement disorders

Movement disorders, including choreoathetosis, akathisia, and Parkinsonism with tremor, have all been described in cocaine users (Daras et al., 1994). Apparently this phenomenon has become common enough that it even has a street name — "crack dancing." Symptoms are generally self-limiting and do not bring the victims to medical attention. However, one recent controlled study using MRI scanning demonstrated an increased incidence of basal ganglia abnormalities that were not seen in controls (Bartzokis et al., 1995). Alterations in dopamenergic transmission are thought to be responsible for the movement disorder and may also be the reasons that cocaine users are also prone to multifocal tics and precipitate (Pascual-Leone and Dhuna, 1990) or exacerbate the clinical manifestations of Gilles de la Tourette syndrome.

References

Adams, J., Corsellis, J., and Duchen, L. (Eds.). (1984). Greenfield's neuropathology (4th ed.). London: Edward Arnold.

Aggarwal, S. and Byrne, B. (1991). Massive ischemic cerebellar infarction due to cocaine use. Neuroradiology, 33: 449–450.

Altes-Capella, J., Cabezudo-Artero, J., and Forteza-Rei, J. (1987). Complications of cocaine abuse. Ann Intern Med, 107: 940–941.

Bell, K., Milne, N., and Lyons, K. (1994). Regional cerebral blood flow and cocaine-abuse. Western J Med, 161(4): 412–413.

Boag, F. and Havard, C. (1985). Cardiac arrhythmia and myocardial ischaemia related to cocaine and alcohol consumption. Post Grad Med J, 61: 997–999.

Bostwick, D. (1981). Amphetamine-induced cerebral vasculitis. Hum Pathol, 12: 1031–1033.

Brust, J. and Richter, R. (1977). Stroke associated with cocaine abuse? NY State J Med, 77: 1473–1475.

Brust, J. (1993). Clinical, radiological, and pathological aspects of cerebrovascular disease associated with drug abuse. Stroke, 24(12): I-129–133.

Caplan, L., Hier, D., and Banks, G. (1982). Current concepts of cerebrovascular disease-stroke: stroke and drug abuse. Stroke, 13(6): 869–872.

Catlett, G. (1886). Cocaine: what was its influence in the following case? Medical Gazette, (February 6): 166–167.

Chasnoff, I., Bussey, M., Savich, R., and Stack, C. (1986). Perinatal cerebral infarction and maternal cocaine use. J Pediatrics, 108: 456–459.

Chokshi, S., Moore, R., Pandian, N., and Isner, J. (1989). Reversible cardiomyopathy associated with cocaine intoxication. Ann Intern Med, 111: 1039–1040.

Chynn, K. C. (1975). Acute subarachnoid hemorrhage. JAMA, 233: 55–56.

Citron, B., Halpern, M., McCarron, M. et al. (1970). Necrotizing angiitis associated with drug abuse. N Engl J Med, 283: 1003–1011.

Covert, R., Schreiber, M., Tebbett, I. et al. (1994). Hemodynamic and cerebral blood flow effects of cocaine, cocaethylene, and benzoylecgonine in conscious and anesthetized fetal lambs. J Pharm and Exp Ther, 270: 118–126.

Cregler, L. and Mark, H. (1987). Relation of stroke to cocaine abuse. NY State J Med, 87: 128–129.

Crumb, W., Clarkson, C., Xu, Y., and Kadowitz, P. (1989). Electrocardiographic evidence for cocaine cardiotoxicity in cats. Circulation, 80(4): II–132.

Crumb, W., Kadowitz, P., You-Qui, X., and Clarkson, C. (1990). Electrocardiographic evidence for cocaine cardiotoxicity in the cat. Canadian J Physiol and Pharmacol, 68(5): 622–625.

Daras, M., Tuchman, A., and Marks, S. (1991). Central nervous system infarction related to cocaine abuse. Stroke, 22(10): 1320–1325.

Daras, M., Koppel, B., and Atos-Radizon, E. (1994). Cocaine-induced choreoathetoid movements ('crack dancing'). Neurology, 44: 751–752.

Derlet, R. and Albertson, T. (1989). Emergency department presentation of cocaine intoxication. Ann Emerg Med, 18(2): 182–186.

Devenyi, P., Schneiderman, J., Devenyi, R., and Lawby, L. (1988). Cocaine-induced central retinal artery occlusion. Canad Med Assn J, 138: 129–130.

Dhuna, A., Pascual-Leone, A., and Langendorf, F. (1991). Chronic, habitual cocaine abuse and kindling-induced epilepsy: a case report. Epilepsia, 32: 890–894.

Dhuna, A., Pascual-Leone, A., Langendorf, F., and Anderson, C. (1991). Epileptogenic properties of cocaine in humans. Neurotoxicology, 12: 621–626.

Dohi, S., Jones, M. D., Hudak, M. L., and Traystman, R. J. (1990). Effects of cocaine on pial arterioles in cats. Stroke, 21(12): 1710–1714.

Dressler, F., Malekzadeh, S., and Roberts, W. (1990). Quantitative analysis of amounts of coronary arterial narrowing in cocaine addicts. Am J Cardiol, 65(5): 303–308.

Duell, P. (1987). Chronic cocaine abuse and dilated cardiomyopathy. Am J Med, 83: 601.

Duke, M. (1986). Cocaine, myocardial infarction, and arrhythmias — a review. Conn Med, 50: 440–442.

Ellison, G. and Switzer, R. I. (1993). Dissimilar patterns of degeneration in brain following four different addictive stimulants. NeuroReport, 5: 17–20.

Engstrand, B., Daras, M., Tuchman, A. et al. (1989). Cocaine-related ischemic strokes. Neurology, 39(Suppl 1): 186.

Feldmann, E. (1991). Intracerebral hemorrhage (Reprinted from Current Concepts of Cerebrovascular Disease and Stroke, 25: 31–35, 1990). Stroke, 22(5): 684–691.

Fredericks, R., Lefkowitz, D., Challa, V. et al. (1991). Cerebral vasculitis associated with cocaine abuse. Stroke, 22: 1437–1439.

Gawin, F. and Kleber, H. (1986). Abstinence symptomology and psychiatric diagnosis in cocaine abusers. Arch Gen Psychiatry, 43: 107–113.

Golbe, L. and Merkin, M. (1986). Cerebral infarction in a user of freebase cocaine ("crack"). Neurology, 36: 1602–1604.

Graham, F. (1989). Morphologic changes during hypertension. Am J Cardiol, 63: 6C–9C.

Gras, P., Arveux, P., Giroude, M. et al. (1991). Les Hémorrhagies intracérébrales spontanées du sujet jeune. Rev Neurol (Paris), 147(10): 653–657.

Graybiel, A., Mortalla, R., and Robertson, H. (1990). Amphetamine and cocaine induce drug-specific activation of the *c-fos* gene in striosome-matrix compartments and limbic subdivisions of the striatum. Proc Natl Acad Sci U.S., 87: 6912–6916.

Green, R., Kelly, K., Gabrielson, T. et al. (1990). Multiple intracerebral hemorrhages after smoking "crack" cocaine. Stroke, 21: 957–962.

Huff, J. (1994). Spinal epidural hematoma associated with cocaine abuse. Am J Emerg Med, 12: 350–352.

Itzhak, Y. (1993). Nitric oxide (NO) synthatase inhibitors abolish cocaine-induced toxicity in mice. Neuropharm, 32(10): 1069–1070.

Jacobs, I., Roszler, M., Kelly, S. et al. (1989). Cocaine abuse: neurovascular complications. Radiology, 170: 223–227.

Jennings, L., White, M., Sauer, C. et al. (1993). Cocaine-induced platelet defects. Stroke, 24(9): 1352–1359.

Kaku, D. A. and Lowenstein, D. H. (1990). Emergence of recreational drug abuse as a major risk factor for stroke in young adults. Ann Intern Med, 113(11): 821–827.

Karch, S. and Billingham, M. (1988). The pathology and etiology of cocaine-induced heart disease. Arch Pathol Lab Med, 112: 225–230.

Karch, S., Green, G., and Young, S. (1995). Myocardial hypertrophy and coronary artery disease in male cocaine users. J Forensic Sci, in press.

Kelly, M., Gorelick, P., and Mirza, D. (1992). The role of drugs in the etiology of stroke. Clin Neuropharmacol, 15: 249–275.

Kessler, J., Jortner, B., and Adapon, B. (1978). Cerebral vasculitis in a drug abuser. J Clin Psych, 39: 559–564.

Kibayashii, K., Mastri, A., and Hirsch, C. (1995). Cocaine-induced intracerebral hemorrhage: analysis of predisposing factors and mechanisms causing hemorrhagic strokes. Hum Pathol, 26(6): 559–663.

Klonoff, D., Andrews, B., and Obana, W. (1989). Stroke associated with cocaine use. Arch Neurol, 46: 989–993.

Kolodgie, F., Virmani, R., Cornhill, J. et al. (1990). Cocaine: an independent risk factor of atherosclerosis. Circulation, 82, Supplement III(4): III–447.

Kolodgie, F. D., Virmani, R., Cornhill, J. et al. (1991). Increase in atherosclerosis and adventitial mast cells in cocaine abusers — an alternative mechanism of cocaine-associated coronary vasospasm and thrombosis. J Am Coll Cardiol, 17(7): 1553–1560.

Konzen, J., Levine, S., and Garcia, J. (1995). Vasospasm and thrombus formation as possible mechanisms of stroke related to alkaloidal cocaine. Stroke, 26: 1114–1118.

Krendel, D. A., Ditter, S. M., Frankel, M. R., and Ross, W. K. (1990). Biopsy-proven cerebral vasculitis associated with cocaine abuse. Neurology, 40(7): 1092–1094.

Lathers, C., Tyau, L., Spino, M., and Agarwal, I. (1988). Cocaine-induced seizures, arrhythmias, and sudden death. J Clin Pharmacol, 28: 584–593.

Laurier, L., Corrigall, W., and George, S. (1994). Dopamine receptor density, sensitivity and mRNA levels are altered following self-administration of cocaine in the rat. Brain Research, 634: 31–40.

Lehman, L. (1987). Intracerebral hemorrhage after intranasal cocaine use. Postgrad Med, 81(8): 150–152.

Levin, J., Holman, B., Mendelson, J. et al. (1994). Gender differences in cerebral perfusion in cocaine abuse: technetium-99m-HMPAO SPECT study of drug-abusing women. J Nucl Med, 35: 1902–1909.

Levine, S., Washington, J., Jefferson, M. et al. (1987). "Crack" cocaine associated stroke. Neurology, 37: 1849–1853.

Levine, S. and Welch, K. (1988). Cocaine and stroke. Stroke, 19(6): 779–783.

Levine, B. and Tebbett, R. (1994). Cocaine pharmacokinetics in ethanol-pretreated rats. Drug Metab Disp, 22(3): 498–500.

Lewin, L. (1931). Phantastica: narcotic and stimulating drugs, their use and abuse (P. H. Wirth, Ph.C, B.Sc., Trans.). (Second English ed.). New York: E. P. Dutton and Company.

Libman, R., Masters, S., Paola, A., et al. (1993). Transient monocular blindness associated with cocaine abuse. Neurology, 43: 228–229.

Lichtenfeld, P., Rubin, D., and Feldman, R. (1984). Subarachnoid hemorrhage precipitated by cocaine snorting. Arch Neurol, 41: 223–224.

Lowenstein, D., Massa, S., Rowbotham, M. et al. (1987). Acute neurologic and psychiatric complications associated with cocaine abuse. Am J Med, 83: 841–846.

Lundberg, G., Garriott, J., Reynolds, P. et al. (1977). Cocaine-related death. J Forensic Sci, 22: 402–408.

Madden, J. and Powers, R. (1990). Effect of cocaine and cocaine metabolites on cerebral arteries *in vitro*. Life Sci, 47(13): 1109–1114.

Maier, H. W. (1926). Der Kokainismus (O. J. Kalant from the German 1926 edition, Trans.). Toronto: Addiction Research Foundation.

Martin, K., Rogers, T., and Kavanaugh, A. (1995). Central nervous system angiopathy associated with cocaine abuse. J Rheumatol, 22: 780–782.

Mena, I., Giombetti, R., Mody, C. et al. (1990). Acute cerebral blood flow changes with cocaine intoxication. Neurology, 40(Suppl 1): 179.

Mercado, A., Johnson, G., Calver, D., and Sokol, R. (1989). Cocaine, pregnancy and postpartum intracerebral hemorrhage. Obst and Gynecol, 73(3): 467–468.

Mittleman, R. and Wetli, C. (1987). Cocaine and sudden "natural" death. J Forensic Sci, 32(1): 11–19.

Mody, C., Miller, B., McIntyre, H. et al. (1988). Neurologic complications of cocaine abuse. Neurology, 38: 1189–1193.

Moliterno, D., Lange, R., Gerard, R. et al. (1994). Influence of intranasal cocaine on plasma constitutents associated with endogenous thrombosis and thrombolysis. Am Heart J, 96: 491–496.

Moore, P. and Peterson, P. (1989). Nonhemorrhagic cerebrovascular complications of cocaine abuse. Neurology, 39, Suppl 1: 302.

Muir, J. and Ellis, E. (1995). Acute cocaine administration alters posttraumatic blood pressure and cerebral blood flow in rats. Am J Physiol, 268(1 Pt 2): H68–73.

Neely, B., Urthaler, F., and Walker, A. (1989). Cocaine enhances spontaneous SR calcium release in length-clamped ferret papillary muscles. Circulation, 80(4): II–16.

Nolte, K. and Gelman, B. (1989). Intracerebral hemorrhage associated with cocaine abuse. Arch Pathol Lab Med, 113: 812–813.

Oyesiku, N., Colohan, A., Barrow, D. et al. (1993). Cocaine-induced aneurysmal rupture: an emergent negative factor in the natural history of intracranial aneurysms? Neurosurgery, 32(4): 519–526.

Pascual-Leone, A. and Dhuna, A. (1990). Cocaine-associated multifocal tics. Neurology, 40: 999–1001.

Petty, G. W., Brust, J. C. M., Tatemichi, T. K., and Barr, M. L. (1990). Embolic stroke after smoking 'crack' cocaine. Stroke, 21(11): 1632–1635.

Plessinger, M. and Woods, J. (1990). Progesterone increases cardiovascular toxicity to cocaine in nonpregnant ewes. Am J Obstet Gynecol, 163(5): 1659–1664.

Reeves, R., McWilliams, M., and Fitz-Gerald, M. (1995). Cocaine-induced ischemic cerebral infarction mistaken for a psychiatric syndrome. South Med J, 88(3): 352–354.

Rezkalla, S., Mazza, J., Kloner, R. et al. (1993). Effects of cocaine on human platelets in healthy subjects. Am J Cardiol, 72: 243–246.

Rinder, H., Ault, K., Jatlow, P. et al. (1994). Platelet α-granule release in cocaine users. Circulation, 90: 1162–1167.

Ritz, M. and George, F. (1993). Cocaine-induced seizures and lethality appear to be associated with distinct central nervous system binding sites. J Pharm Exp Ther, 264(3): 1333–1343.

Rogers, J., Henry, T., Jones, A. et al. (1986). Cocaine-related deaths in Pima County, Arizona, 1982–1984. J Forensic Sci, 31(2): 1404–1408.

Rowbotham, M., Root, R., Boushey, V. et al. (1988). Neurologic aspects of cocaine abuse. West J Med, 149: 442–448.

Rowley, H., Lowenstein, D., and Rowbotham, M. (1990). Thalmomesencephalic strokes after cocaine abuse. Neurology, 39: 428–430.

Ruben, H. and Morris, M. (1952). Effect of cocaine on cardiac automaticity in the dog. J Pharm Exp Ther, 55–64.

Satel, S. and Gawin, F. (1990). Seasonal cocaine abuse. Am J Psychiatry, 146(4): 534–535.

Saury, N. (1890). Du cocainisme. Contribution a l'étude du foli-toxique. Ann Méd-Psychol, 9: 439–440.

Schreiber, M., Madden, J., Covert, R. et al. (1994). Effects of cocaine, benzoylecgonine, and cocaine metabolites on cannulated pressurized fetal sheep cerebral arteries. J Appl Physiol, 77(2): 834–839.

Schwartz, K. and Cohen, J. (1984). Subarachnoid hemorrhage precipitated by cocaine snorting. Arch Neurol, 41: 705.

Scully, R., Mark, E., McNeely, W. et al. (1993). Case records of the Massachusetts General Hospital. Weekly clinicopathological exercises. Case 27-1993. A 32-year-old man with the sudden onset of a right-sided headache and left hemiplegia and hemianesthesia [clinical conference] [see comments]. N Engl J Med, 329(2): 117–124.

Seaman, M. (1990). Acute cocaine abuse associated with cerebral infarction. Ann Emerg Med, 19(1): 34–37.

Seeman, P. and Van Tol, H. (1994). Dopamine receptor pharmacology. Trends in Pharm Sci, 15(7): 264–270.

Sekhar, L. and Heros, R. (1980). Origin, growth and rupture of saccular aneurysms: a review. Neurosurgery, 8(2): 248–260.

Shaner, A., Khalsa, M., Roberts, L. et al. (1993). Unrecognized cocaine use among schizophrenic patients. Am J Psych, 150(5): 758–762.

Sharma, A., Plessinger, M., Sherer, D. et al. (1992). Pregnancy enhances cardiotoxicity of cocaine — role of progesterone. Toxicol Appl Pharmacol, 113(1): 30–35.

Siegel, R. (1978). Cocaine hallucinations. Am J Psychiatry, 135: 309–314.

Sleiman, I., Mangili, R., Semerao, F. et al. (1994). Cocaine-associated retinal vascular occlusion: report of two cases. Am J Med, 97: 198–199.

Staley, J., Hearn, L., Ruttenber, A. et al. (1994). High affinity cocaine recognition sites on the dopamine transporter are elevated in fatal cocaine overdose victims. J Pharm Exp Ther, 271(3): 1678–1685.

Stief, A. and Tokay, L. (1935). Further contributions to histopathology of experimental adrenalin intoxication. J Nerv and Ment Dis, 81: 633–648.

Stillman, R., Jones, R., Moore, D. et al. (1993). Improved performance 4 hours after cocaine. Psychopharm, 110: 415–420.

Strickland, T., Mena, I., Villanueva-Meyer, J. et al. (1993). Cerebral perfusion and neuropsychological consequence of chronic cocaine use. J Neuropsych, 5: 419–427.

Tardiff, K., Gross, E., Wu, J. et al. (1989). Analysis of cocaine-positive fatalities. J Forensic Sci, 34(1): 53–62.

Temesy-Armos, P., Fraker, T., and Wilkerson, R. (1989). Cocaine causes delayed cardiac arrhythmias in conscious dogs. Circulation, 80(4): II–132.

Volkow, N., Mullani, N., Gould, K. et al. (1988). Cerebral blood flow in chronic cocaine users: a study with positron emission tomography. Br J Psych, 152: 641–648.

Volkow, N., Fowler, J., Wolf, N. et al. (1991). Changes in brain glucose metabolism in cocaine dependence and withdrawal. Am J Psychiatry, 148(5): 621–626.

Vrana, S., Vrana, K., Koves, T. et al. (1993). Chronic cocaine administration increases CNS tyrosine hydroxylase enzyme activity and mRNA levels and tryptophan hydroxylase enzyme activity levels. J Neurochem, 61: 2262–2268.

Weber, D., Franceschi, D., Ivanovic, M. et al. (1993). SPECT and planar brain imaging in crack abuse: iodine-123-iodoamphetamine uptake and localization. J Nucl Med, 34: 899–907.

Wiener, R., Lockhart, J., and Schwartz, R. (1986). Dilated cardiomyopathy and cocaine abuse: report of two cases. Am J Med, 81: 699–701.

Williams, S. (1990). A FASEB sampler: cocaine's harmful effects. Science, 248: 166.

Wojak, J. and Flamm, E. (1987). Intracranial hemorrhage and cocaine use. Stroke, 18: 712–715.

Yapor, W. and Gutierrez, F. (1992). Cocaine-induced intratumoral hemorrhage: case report and review of the literature. Neurosurgery, 30(2): 288–291.

Yeh, S. and De Souza, E. (1991). Lack of neurochemical evidence for neurotoxic effects of repeated cocaine administration in rats on brain monoamine neurons. Drug Alcohol Depend, 27(1): 51–61.

Young, D. and Glauber, J. (1947). Electrocardiographic changes resulting from acute cocaine intoxication. Am Heart J, 34: 272–279.

Zeiter, J., Corder, D., Madion, M., McHenry, J. (1992). Sudden retinal manifestations of intranasal cocaine and methamphetamine abuse. Am J Opth, 113: 780–781.

1.12.6 Renal disease

It is not known whether cocaine is inherently nephrotoxic, but the results of animal studies have raised that possibility (Barroso-Moguel et al., 1995). But there is no question that cocaine users are subject to renal disease. Infarction (Sharff, 1984; Kramer and Turner, 1993; Goodman and Rennie, 1995), thrombosis (Wohlman, 1987), and even hemolytic-uremic syndrome (Tumlin et al., 1990) have been reported as complications of cocaine use; however, the most common renal problem in cocaine users is rhabdomyolysis and acute tubular necrosis. Rhabdomyolysis was recognized as a complication of both narcotic (Richter et al., 1971) and stimulant abuse (Kendrick et al., 1977) long before the current wave of cocaine popularity. The first case directly related to cocaine was described in 1987 (Merigian et al., 1987). The mechanism in cases of narcotic abuse is no better understood than the underlying process by which stimulant drugs produce rhabdomyolysis.

In some of the cocaine-related cases, the relationship to prolonged seizure activity is clear; however, seizures have been absent in most of the cocaine-associated cases. In a few instances, pressure-related injury seems to be the most likely explanation (Singhal and Faulkner, 1988). Cocaine-induced vasospasm leading to myocyte necrosis has been proposed as a

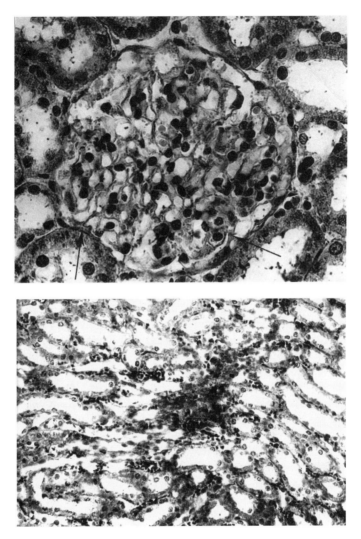

Figure 1.12.6 (1 and 2) In experimental models, long-term treatment with cocaine causes both glomerular and tubular lesions. These photographs are from rats sacrificed after 60 days of treatment. In the first illustration, the glomerular tufts are distended and have few mesangial cells remaining. Capillary lumens are reduced and there are numerous adhesions to Bowman's capsule. In the second photograph, foci of hemorrhage and necrosis are evident in the distal tubules. Courtesy of Professor Risarui Barroso-Moguel, Instituto Nacional de Neurologie y Neurologia y Neurocirguria. Reproduced with permission from Barroso-Moguel et al., 1995. Toxicology, 1995, by permission.

mechanism (Roth et al., 1988). Accelerated renal artery arteriosclerosis, with histologic changes reminiscent of those occasionally observed in cocaine users' coronary arteries, has also been reported (Fogo et al., 1992).

A common thread in many, but not all, cases is hyperthermia (Campbell, 1988; Loghmanee and Tobak, 1986; Lomax and Daniel, 1990; Menashe and Gottlieb, 1988; Rosenberg et al., 1986; Pogue and Nurse, 1989). There is also some evidence that cocaine can be directly toxic to skeletal muscle. In one *in vitro* study, exposure to moderate levels of cocaine resulted in increased leakage of creatinine kinase from slow twitch muscle, like soleus, but not from fast-twitch muscles, like extensor digitorum (Pagala et al., 1993).

The histologic changes accompanying the process are uncharacterized. In one study of two cases, the skeletal muscle was necrotic, but with no sign of vasculitis. There were no polarizable foreign bodies, and no specific lesions, though contraction band necrosis was very prominent in some fibers (Nolte, 1991). These findings tend to confirm the *in vitro* study described above, but even if a satisfactory explanation for the occurrence of rhabdomyolysis could be found, it would not necessarily explain why some individuals go on to develop renal failure while others do not. It seems likely that some other cofactor besides cocaine use is required before full-blown rhabdomyolysis develops (Enriquez et al., 1991).

The etiology for cocaine-associated tubular necrosis is multifactorial. Hypovolemia, renal arterial vasoconstriction, and myoglobinuria all combine to produce the syndrome. Except for one case report (Turbat-Herrera, 1994), morphologic alterations in cocaine users have not been described (Anand et al., 1989; Brody et al., 1990; Herzlich et al., 1988; Jandreski et al., 1989; Justiniani et al., 1990; Kokko, 1990; Krohn et al., 1988; Lombard et al., 1988; Menashe and Gottlieb, 1988; Merigian and Roberts, 1987; Parks et al., 1989; Reinhart and Stricker, 1988; Roth et al., 1988; Rubin and Neugarten, 1989; Schwartz and McAfee, 1987; Singhal et al., 1989; Singhal et al., 1990; Tabasco-Minguillan et al., 1990; Welch and Todd, 1990; Welch et al., 1991). In the one instance when a renal biopsy was done, there was no abnormal antibody deposition, myoglobin was identified in the tubules, and the picture was otherwise typical for acute tubular necrosis, with vacuolation, fragmentation and desquamation of the proximal lining tubular epithelial cells, with pigmented casts in some distal nephrons (Turbat-Herra, 1994).

Renal failure without rhabdomyolysis also occurs (Tumlin et al., 1990; Leblanc et al., 1994). In the first case, a 28-year old woman with nausea, vomiting, and severe abdominal pain developed anuria, hemolytic anemia, and thrombocytopenia (known as the HUS or Hemolytic-Uremic syndrome). Renal biopsy showed patchy areas of cortical necrosis, associated with the characteristic changes of thrombotic microangiopathy. Electron microscopy demonstrated extensive detachment of the endothelium from the basement membrane with the accumulation of electron lucent material and red cell debris in the subendothelial area. Catecholamine toxicity, thromboxane generation, and acute hypertensive reactions are well known sequelae of cocaine use, and any or all could lead to HUS syndrome. After the initial endothelial injury, intravascular coagulation and the other elements of the HUS syndrome could result. A second case involved a 16-year old girl who developed renal failure three days after snorting cocaine. A renal biopsy was unremarkable except for the rare dilatation of tubular lumens. Immunofluoresence staining was nonspecific (Leblanc et al., 1994). The findings in the second case are consistent with vasospasm.

The focal type of glomerulosclerosis associated with heroin-related nephrotic syndrome has not been reported in cocaine or stimulant abusers, but similar lesions have been produced in rats (Barroso-Moguel et al., 1995) and the results of several *in vitro* studies suggest that cocaine use may be a risk factor for this disorder (Mattana et al., 1994; Pan and Singhal, 1994). Mesangial cell expansion is generally considered to be a precursor for glomerulosclerosis and, at least *in vitro*, cocaine modulates mesangial cell proliferation via interaction with the secretory products (interleukin-6 and transforming growth factor-β) produced by macrophages after cocaine exposure. Substantial numbers of heroin users also inject themselves with cocaine (Diaz et al., 1994), so that when glomerulosclerois is seen in a cocaine abuser, causal relationships are difficult to establish.

The presence of such lesions in cocaine abusers should also raise the suspicion of HIV infection, since the most common renal lesion in AIDS patients is a similar sort of focal segmental glomerulosclerosis (Sanders and Marshall, 1989). Sometimes the picture becomes quite confusing because cocaine users, sometimes HIV positive, may present with refractory hypertension and renal failure, but only modest proteinura, and no renal shrinkage or cardiomegally (Dunea et al., 1995). Renal biopsies are no longer routinely performed in patients with end-stage renal disease and evidence of accelerated hypertension, so the etiology in such cases may never be determined.

Case reports describing congenital abnormalities of the genitourinary tract (Chavez et al., 1989) have never been substantiated by controlled surgical or autopsy studies. However, a prospective study using ultrasound to evaluate 100 consecutive infants exposed to cocaine *in utero* and failed to find any consistent teratogenic effect (Rosenstein et al., 1990).

Even though renal disorders are associated with cocaine abuse, organ donation is still a reasonable consideration. One-year survival rates for individuals receiving kidneys from cocaine abusers appear to be no different than rates for drug-free donors (Leikin et al., 1994). Donor hearts from cocaine abusers are similarly unaffected, with survival rates comparable to those for drug-free donors (Freimark et al., 1994).

References

Anand, V., Siami, G., and Stone, W. (1989). Cocaine-associated rhabdomyolysis and acute renal failure. South Med J, 82(1): 67–69.

Barroso-Moguel, R., Mendez-Armenta, M., and Villeda-Hernandez. (1995). Experimental nephropathy by chronic administration of cocaine in rats. Toxicology, 98: 41–46.

Brody, S., Wrenn, K., Wilber, M., and Slovis, C. (1990). Predicting the severity of cocaine-associated rhabdomyolysis. Ann Emerg Med, 19(10): 1137–1143.

Campbell, B. (1988). Cocaine abuse with hyperthermia, seizures and fatal complications. Med J Australia, 149(7): 387–389.

Chavez, G., Mulinare, J., and Cordero, J. (1989). Maternal cocaine use during early pregnancy as a risk factor for congenital urogenital anomalies. JAMA, 262(6): 795–798.

Diaz, T., Chu, S., Byers, R. et al. (1994). The types of drugs used by HIV-infected injection drug users in a multistate surveillance project: implications for intervention. Am J Pub Health, 84(12): 1971–1975.

Dunea, G., Arruda, J., Bakir, A. et al. (1995). Role of cocaine in end-stage renal disease in some hypertensive African Americans. Am J Nephrol, 15: 5–9.

Enriquez, R., Palacios, F., González, J. et al. (1991). Skin vasculitis, hypokalemia and acute renal failure in rhabdomyolysis associated with cocaine. Nephron, 59: 336–337.

Fogo, A., Superdock, K., and Atkinson, J. (1992). Severe arteriosclerosis in the kidney of a cocaine addict. Am J Kidney Dis, 20(5): 513–515.

Freimark, D., Czer, L., Admon, D. et al. (1995). Donors with a history of cocaine use: effect on survival and rejection frequency after heart transplantation. J Heart Lung Transplant, 13(6): 1138–1144.

Goodman, P. and Rennie, W. (1995). Renal infarction secondary to nasal insufflation of cocaine. Am J Emerg Med, 13: 421–423.

Herzlich, B., Arsura, E., Pagala, M., and Grob, D. (1988). Rhabdomyolysis related to cocaine abuse. Ann Intern Med, 109: 335–336.

Jandreski, M., Bermes, E., Leischner, R., and Kahn, S. (1989). Rhabdomyolysis in a case of freebase cocaine ("crack") overdose. Clin Chem, 35(7): 1547–1549.

Justiniani, F., Cabeza, C., and Miller, B. (1990). Cocaine-associated rhabdomyolysis and hemoptysis-mimicking pulmonary embolism. Am J Med, 88: 316–317.

Kendrick, W., Hull, A., and Knochel, J. (1977). Rhabdomyolysis and shock after intravenous amphetamine administration. Ann Int Med, 86: 381–387.

Kokko, J. (1990). Metabolic and social consequences of cocaine use. Am J Med Sci, 299(6): 361–365.

Kramer, R. and Turner, R. (1993). Renal infarction associated with cocaine use and latent protein C deficiency. South Med J, 86(12): 1436–1438.

Krohn, K., Slowman-Kovacs, S., and Leapman, S. (1988). Cocaine and rhabdomyolysis. Ann Int Med, 108: 639–640.

Leblanc, M., Hébert, M., and Mongeau, J. (1994). Cocaine-induced acute renal failure without rhabdomyolysis. Ann Int Med, 121(9): 721–722.

Leikin, J., Heyn-Lamb, R., Aks, S. et al. (1994). The toxic patient as a potential organ donor. Am J Emerg Med, 12: 151–154.

Loghmanee, F. and Tobak, M. (1986). Fatal malignant hyperthermia associated with recreational cocaine and ethanol use. Am J Forensic Med Pathol, 7: 246–248.

Lomax, P. and Daniel, K. (1990). Cocaine and body temperature in the rat — effect of exercise. Pharmacol Biochem Behav, 36(4): 889–892.

Lombard, J., Wong, B., and Young, J. (1988). Acute renal failure due to rhabdomyolysis associated with cocaine toxicity. Western J Med, 148(4): 466–468.

Mattana, J., Gibbons, N., and Singhal, P. (1994). Cocaine interacts with macrophages to modulate cell proliferation. J Pharm Exp Ther, 271: 311–318.

Menashe, P. and Gottlieb, J. (1988). Hyperthermia, rhabdomyolysis and myoglobinuric renal failure after recreational use of cocaine. South Med J, 81(3): 379–380.

Merigian, K. and Roberts, J. (1987). Cocaine intoxication: hyperpyrexia, rhabdomyolysis and acute renal failure. J Toxicol Clin Toxicol, 25: 135–148.

Nolte, K. (1991). Rhabdomyolysis associated with cocaine abuse. Hum Pathol, 22(11): 1141–1145.

Pagala, M., Amaladevi, B., Azad, D. et al. (1993). Effect of cocaine on leakage of creatine kinase from isolated fast and slow muscles of rat. Life Sci, 52: 751–756.

Pan, C. and Singhal, P. (1994). Coordinate and independent effects of cocaine, alcohol, and morphine on accumulation of IgG aggregates in the rat glomeruli. Proc Soc Exp Biol Med, 205: 29–34.

Parks, J., Reed, G., and Knochel, J. (1989). Case report: cocaine-associated rhabdomyolysis. Am J Med Sci, 297: 334–336.

Pogue, V. and Nurse, H. (1989). Cocaine-associated myoglobinuric renal failure. Am J Med, 86: 183–189.

Reinhart, W. and Stricker, H. (1988). Rhabdomyolysis after intravenous cocaine. Am J Med, 85: 579.

Richter, R., Challenor, Y., Pearson, J. et al. (1971). Acute myoglobinuria associated with heroin addiction. JAMA, 216: 1172–1176.

Rosenberg, J., Pentel, P., Pond, S. et al. (1986). Hyperthermia associated with drug intoxication. Crit Care Med, 14(11): 964–969.

Rosenstein, B., Wheeler, J., and Heid, P. (1990). Congenital renal abnormalities in infants with *in utero* cocaine exposure. J Urol, 144: 110–112.

Roth, D., Alarcon, F., Fernandez, J. et al. (1988). Acute rhabdomyolysis associated with cocaine intoxication. N Engl J Med, 319: 673–677.

Rubin, R. and Neugarten, J. (1989). Cocaine-induced rhabdomyolysis masquerading as myocardial ischemia. Am J Med, 86(5): 551–553.

Sanders, M. and Marshall, A. (1989). Acute and chronic toxic nephropathies. Ann Clin and Lab Sci, 19(3): 216–220.

Schwartz, J. and McAfee, R. (1987). Cocaine and rhabdomyolysis. J Fam Pract, 24 (2): 209.

Sharff, J. (1984). Renal infarction associated with intravenous cocaine use. Ann Emerg Med, 13(12): 1145–1147.

Singhal, P. and Faulkner, M. (1988). Myonecrosis and cocaine abuse. Ann Int Med, 109: 843.

Singhal, P., Horowitz, B., Quinones, M. et al. (1989). Acute renal failure following cocaine abuse. Nephron, 52: 76–79.

Singhal, P. C., Rubin, R., Peters, A. et al. (1990). Rhabdomyolysis and acute renal failure associated with cocaine abuse. J Toxicol-Clin Toxic, 28(3): 321–330.

Tabasco-Minguillan, J., Novick, D., and Kreek, M. (1990). Liver function tests in non-parenteral cocaine users. Drug Alcohol Depen, 26(2): 169–174.

Tumlin, J., Sands, J., and Someren, A. (1990). Special feature: hemolytic-uremic syndrome following crack cocaine inhalation. Am J Med Sciences, 229(6): 366–371.

Turbat-Herrera, E. (1994). Myoglobinuric acute renal failure associated with cocaine use. Ultrastructural Pathology, 18: 127–131.

Welch, R. and Todd, K. (1990). Cocaine-associated rhabdomyolysis. Ann Emerg Med, 19(4): 449.

Welch, R., Todd, K., and Krause, G. (1991). Incidence of cocaine-associated rhabdomyolysis. Ann Emerg Med, 20: 154–157.

Wohlman, R. (1987). Renal artery thrombosis and embolization associated with intravenous cocaine injection. South Med J, 80(7): 928–930.

1.12.7 Hematologic abnormalities

Thrombocytopenic purpura was recognized in heroin users more than a decade before the spread of HIV infection (Adams et al., 1978). What the etiology was then is not known, but now thrombotic thrombocytopenic purpura in heroin users is almost always linked to HIV infection (Karpatkin,

1990; Karpatkin and Nardi, 1988; Orser, 1991). For the moment, at least, that does not appear to be the case among cocaine users. One study described seven HIV-seronegative intravenous cocaine abusers with extensive cutaneous petechiae, ecchymoses, and heme-positive stools. All of the bone marrows of the patients had normal or increased numbers of megakaryocytes, and their platelet counts all improved promptly after steroid administration. No other etiology for their condition could be identified. As with many of the other cocaine-associated syndromes, possible etiologies include toxic contaminants or metabolites, as well as immune reactions to the cocaine itself. There are many other ways cocaine could affect platelet function. Circulating catecholamines are elevated in cocaine users and elevated catecholamine levels can alter α and β receptors located on circulating lymphocytes and platelets (Maki et al., 1990).

Studies have shown that cocaine can cause increased thromboxane generation *in vitro*; however, the clinical consequences of this fact have not been clinically confirmed (Tonga et al., 1985). Studies of platelet and clotting mechanisms in cocaine users have yielded conflicting results, and *in vitro* studies of platelet behavior cannot always be relied upon to give a valid picture of the situation in patients.

Volunteers given relatively modest doses of cocaine (2 mg/kg) were found to have higher plasminogen activator inhibitor (PAI-1) levels than controls (Moliterno et al., 1994), and increased PAI-1 activity favors thrombosis. Chronic cocaine users are also said to have higher circulating levels of activated platelets (e.g., platelets displaying the α-granule protein P-selectin on their membrane surface) (Rinder et al., 1994). However, other studies have produced conflicting results, finding no evidence that cocaine use favors platelet aggregation or granule release (Kugelmass and Ware, 1992), or that effects were unpredicatable (Rezkalla et al., 1993). One group of researchers even found evidence that cocaine disrupted several different elements of the clotting process and suggested that cocaine use prevents thrombosis formation (Jennings et al., 1993).

Of course the possibility exists that, depending on the clinical circumstances, cocaine may either promote or inhibit clotting. This observation may explain anecdotal reports that cocaine users are prone to postoperative bleeding (Johnson and Brown, 1993), and might also explain the incidence of hemorrhagic stroke on one hand and myocardial thrombosis on the other. In the absence of more substantial clinical research, conclusions are necessarily speculative.

Another hematologic abnormality associated with cocaine use, at least indirectly, is methemoglobinemia. Street-level cocaine is occasionally diluted with benzocaine or other related local anesthetics, and oxidation of ferrous (Fe^2) hemoglobin to the ferric (Fe^3) state is a well-recognized complication of benzocaine administration. One case report described a 27-year old man with a massive overdose who developed classic methemoglobinemia. Blood levels were not measured; however, urine cocaine levels were 106 mg/L, while benzocaine levels were 3.8 mg/L (McKinney et al., 1992). Cocaine itself has never been implicated as a cause of this disorder.

References

Adams, W., Rufo, R., Talarico, L. et al. (1978). Thrombocytopenia and intravenous heroin use. Ann Intern Med, 89: 207–211.

Jennings, L., White, M., Sauer, C. et al. (1993). Cocaine-induced platelet defects. Stroke, 24: 1352–1359.

Johnson, C. and Brown, R. (1993). How cocaine abuse affects post-extraction bleeding. J Am Dent Assn, 124: 60–62.

Karpatkin, S. and Nardi, M. (1988). Immunological thrombocytopenic purpura in human immunodeficiency virus-seropositive patients with hemophilia. J Lab Clin Med, 111(4): 441–448.

Karpatkin, S. (1990). HIV-1-related thrombocytopenia. Hematol Oncol Clin North Am, 4: 193–218.

Kugelmass, A. and Ware, J. (1992). Cocaine and coronary artery thrombosis (letter). Ann Intern Med, 116(9): 776–777.

Maki, T., Kontula, K., and Harkonen, M. (1990). The β-adrenergic system in man — physiological and pathophysiological response-regulation of receptor density and functioning. Scand J Clin Lab Invest, 50(S201): 25–43.

McKinney, C., Postiglione, K., and Herold, D. (1992). Benzocaine-adulterated street cocaine in association with methemoglobinemia. Clin Chem, 38(4): 596–597.

Moliterno, D., Lange, R., Gerard, R. et al. (1994). Influence of intranasal cocaine on plasma constitutents associated with endogenous thrombosis and thrombolysis. Am Heart J, 96: 491–496.

Orser, B. (1991). Thrombocytopenia and cocaine abuse. Anesthesiology, 74(1): 195–196.

Rezkalla, S., Mazza, J., Kloner, R. et al. (1993). Effects of cocaine on human platelets in healthy subjects. Am J Cardiol, 72: 243–246.

Rinder, H., Ault, K., Jatlow, P. et al. (1994). Platelet α-granule release in cocaine users. Circulation, 90: 1162–1167.

Tonga, G., Tempesta, E., Tonga, A. et al. (1985). Platelet responsiveness and biosynthesis of thromboxane and prostacyclin in response to *in vitro* cocaine treatment. Haemostasis, 15: 100–107.

1.12.8 Hormonal alterations

Over and above cocaine's local effects on catecholamine reuptake, cocaine also causes increased release of epinephrine and norepinephrine from the adrenal medulla (Gunne and Jonsson, 1964; Chiueh and Kopin, 1978; Trouve et al., 1990). Catecholamine metabolism in cocaine abusers is largely uncharacterized. On the other hand, cocaine-associated abnormalities of prolactin secretion have been demonstrated both in man and in experimental animals.

Initially it was thought that acute administration of cocaine causes an initial drop in prolactin levels, followed later by rebound hyperprolactinemia (Mello et al., 1990; Mendelson et al., 1988; Mendelson et al., 1989; Mendelson et al., 1991). However, more recent studies from other laboratories have yielded conflicting results suggesting that cocaine has no predictable effects on prolactin levels (Becketts et al., 1995).

Even if they occur, alterations in blood prolactin levels may not be of very great clinical significance. Under normal circumstances, the hormone's main function is the stimulation of lactation in the post-partum period. It

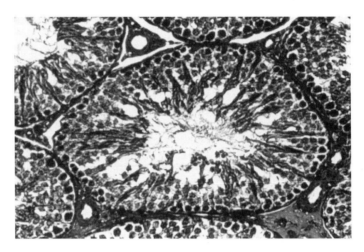

Figure 1.12.8 Testicular atrophy in chronic drug abusers is generally attributed to life-style and dietary deficiency. However, rats chronically exposed to moderate doses of cocaine undergo Lydig cell degeneration. Whether this also is true for humans is not known. Courtesy of Dr. Rosario Barroso-Moguel, Instituto Nacional de Neurologie y Neurocircuria, Mexico. Reprinted with permission, J Appl Tox, 14: 37–41, 1994.

does not appear to play a role in normal gonadal function, but its secretion can be altered in different physiologic states. Many drugs, especially dopamine antagonists, cause changes in prolactin secretion. Measuring changes in prolactin levels could be of some clinical value. Markedly depressed levels are a good confirmation of recent drug use. High levels, which have been noted in detoxification patients, are consistent with withdrawal. It has been suggested that very high levels may be a marker for those detoxification patients who subsequently fail treatment and resume drug use (Teoh et al., 1990). The usefulness of prolactin levels in monitoring the detoxification process is limited by the fact that cocaine's effects on anterior pituitary hormones is, in some way, mediated by gonadal function (Mello et al., 1995). Until these actions are better understood, prolactin levels are of little evidentiary value.

Chronic cocaine abusers have elevated concentrations of ACTH, cortisol, and β-endorphin without associated abnormalities in the normal secretory rhythm of these hormones (Vescovi et al., 1992). The results of animal studies suggest that increased ACTH secretion is the result of increased release of corticotropin-releasing factor (Rivier and Lee, 1994), but that increased corticotropin-releasing factor is not secreted until a critical threshold for cocaine plasma concentration is exceeded, and then only when cocaine levels are rapidly increasing (Torres and Rivier, 1992).

Testosterone levels in chronic cocaine abusers have not been characterized, and laboratory studies on gonadal uptake have yielded conflicting results. Mice testes avidly bind labeled cocaine (Yazigi and Polakoski, 1992), but rat testes do not show high levels of cocaine uptake (Som et al., 1994). Even so, chronic cocaine administration, at least in rats, produces testicular lesions (see Figure 1.12.8) which could result in decreased testosterone production and depressed spermatogenesis (Barroso-Moguel et al., 1994).

References

Barroso-Moguel, R., Méndez-Armenta, M., and Villeda-Hernández, J. (1994). Testicular lesions by chronic administration of cocaine in rats. J Appl Tox, 14(1): 37–41.

Chiueh, C. and Kopin, I. (1978). Centrally mediated release by cocaine of endogenous epinephrine and norepinephrine from the sympathoadrenal medullary system of unanesthetized rats. J Pharmacol Exp Ther, 205 (1): 148–154.

Gunne, L. and Jonsson, J. (1964). Effects of cocaine administration on brain, adrenal and urinary adrenaline and noradrenaline in rats. Psychopharmacologia, 6(2): 125–129.

Mello, N., Mendelson, J., Drieze, J., and Kelly, M. (1990). Acute effects of cocaine on prolactin and gonadotropins in female rhesus monkey during the follicular phase of the menstrual cycle. J Pharmacol Exp Ther, 254(3): 815–823.

Mello, N., Sarnyai, Z., Mendelson, J. et al. (1995) The acute effects of cocaine on anterior pituitary hormones in ovariectomized rhesus monkeys. J Pharm Exp Ther, 272: 1059–1066.

Mendelson, J., Mello, N., Teoh, S. et al. (1989). Cocaine effects on pulsatile secretion of anterior pituitary, gonadal and adrenal hormones. J Clin Endocrinol Metab, 69: 1256–1260.

Mendelson, J. H., Teoh, S., Lange, U. et al. (1988). Anterior pituitary, adrenal, and gonadal hormones during cocaine withdrawal. Am J Psychiatry, 145: 1094–1098.

Mendelson, J. H. (1991). Plasma prolactin levels and cocaine abuse. Am J Psychiatry, 148(3): 397.

Rivier, C. and Lee, S. (1994). Stimulatory effect of cocaine on ACTH secretion: role of the hypothalamus. Molecular and Cell Neurosci, 5: 189–195.

Som, P., Oster, H., Wang, G. et al. (1994). Spatial and temporal distribution of cocaine and effects of pharmacological interventions: wholebody autoradiographic microimaging studies. Life Sci, 55: 1375–1382.

Teoh, S. K., Mendelson, J. H., Mello, N. K. et al. (1990). Hyperprolactinemia and risk for relapse of cocaine abuse. Biol Psychiatry, 28(9): 824–828.

Torres, G. and Rivier, C. (1992). Cocaine-induced ACTH secretion: dependence of plasma levels of the drug and mode of exposure. Brain Res Bul, 29: 51–56.

Trouve, R., Nahas, G., and Manger, W. (1990). Cocaine, catecholamines, and cardiac toxicity. Acta-Anesthesiol Scand, 94(suppl): 77–81.

Vescovi, P., Coiro, V., Volpi, R. et al. (1992). Diurnal variations in plasma ACTH, cortisol and β-endorphin levels in cocaine addicts. Horm Res, 37: 221–224.

Yazigi R. and Polakoski K. (1992). Distribution of tritiated cocaine in selected genital and nongenital organs following administration to male mice. Arch Pathol Lab Med, 116(10): 1036–1039.

1.12.9 Immune system abnormalities

Chronic use of cocaine alters the immune response. Current thinking favors the notion that cocaine's effects are probably mediated via the central nervous system and catecholamine release. *In vitro* studies have shown that lidocaine has no effect on lymphocyte proliferation, but that all monoamine uptake inhibitors do (Berkeley et al., 1994). Since both serotonin and nor-epinephrine both inhibit lymphocyte proliferation, a connection seems likely (Walker and Codd, 1985).

Drawing conclusions from animal studies is difficult because not all animals respond to cocaine in the same way. In mice, for example, chronic cocaine administration results in the suppression of all immunological parameters except for lymphocyte transformation. Since lymphocyte trans-formation is the test most widely used to screen for drug-induced immun-osuppression, it would appear that the mouse may not be a good model for studying cocaine immunotoxicity (Shen et al., 1994), at least for screening purposes. Rats chronically treated with cocaine have altered T cell subsets with decreased numbers of CD8+ cells (suppressor) and a normal population of CD4+ (helper) cells (Bagasra and Forman, 1989).

Of major concern is the close link between cocaine use and HIV infection. In spite of the limitations inherent in the animal models, there is increasing evidence that cocaine use facilitates HIV infection. Mice chronically treated with cocaine are less able to resist some types of viral infection than are controls (Starec et al., 1991), and also manifest increased natural killer-cell activity, which is further increased in the presence of retroviral infection (Poet et al., 1991). Other studies have shown that cocaine treatment can suppress the secretion of gamma interferon from mice leukocytes (Watzl et al., 1992). The fact that cocaine modulates natural killer activity and inter-feron secretion may well have a bearing on the high rate of HIV seropositivity seen in HIV infected patients (Anthony et al., 1991).

In vitro studies of human cell lines tend to support the animal findings. Unstimulated peripheral blood mononuclear cells exposed to cocaine sup-port increased levels of HIV-1 replication when compared with unexposed monocytes, although this effect is not seen in cells that are already infected (Bagasra and Pomerantz, 1993). Other have demonstrated that both phago-cytic activity and T suppressor cell activity are suppressed (Ou et al., 1989; Bagasra and Forman, 1989). Inhibition of delayed type hypersensitivity has also been demonstrated (Watson et al., 1983).

Cocaine use also leads to abnormal cytokine production. Peripheral blood lymphocytes from cocaine users have higher levels of interleukin-2, and there is a positive correlation between cocaine concentrations and inter-leukin-2 levels (Chen et al., 1991). Cultured human peripheral mononuclear cells lose much of their ability to produce superoxide anion (which is how they attack intracellular pathogens), and the effects seem to be dose-related (Chao et al., 1991).

Many intravenous opiate abusers have antiplatelet antibodies (7S immu-noglobulin G) and signs of increased platelet destruction by the reticuloen-dothelial system, but this process has not been demonstrated in cocaine users (Karpatkin and Nardi, 1988). The findings in the cocaine-related cases of thrombocytopenia have suggested that an immune mechanism is also oper-ative (Orser, 1991).

The clinical relevance of all these abnormalities has not been demon-strated. Any correlation between cocaine use and HIV infection is likely to have had as much to do with the sexual practices of the infected individuals as with an underlying immune abnormality. And, in spite of the occasional case report (Lavoie, Espinel-Ingroff, and Kerkering, 1993), there is no convincing evidence that chronic cocaine users are more vulnerable to bacterial or fungal infections than members of the population at large.

References

Anthony, J., Vlahov, D., Nelson, K. et al. (1991). New evidence on intravenous cocaine use and the risk of infection with human immunodeficiency virus Type 1. Am J Epidemol, 134(10): 1175–1189.

Bagasra, O. and Forman, L. (1989). Functional analysis of lymphocyte subpopulations in experimental cocaine abuse. I. Dose-dependent activation of lymphocyte subsets. Clin Exp Immunol, 77: 289–293.

Bagasra, O. and Pomerantz, R. (1993). Human immunodeficiency virus type 1 replication in peripheral blood mononuclear cells in the presence of cocaine. J Infect Dis, 168: 1157–1164.

Berkeley, M., Daussin, S., Hernandez, M. et al. (1994). *In vitro* effects of cocaine, lidocaine and monoamine uptake inhibitors on lymphocyte proliferative responses. Immunopharm and Immunotox, 16(2): 165–178.

Chao, C. C., Molitor, T. W., Gekker, G. et al. (1991). Cocaine-mediated suppression of superoxide production by human peripheral blood mononuclear cells. J Pharmacol Exp Ther, 256(1): 255–258.

Chen, G.-J., Pillai, R., Erickson, J. et al. (1991). Cocaine immunotoxicity: abnormal cytokine production in Hispanic drug users. Toxicology Letters, 59: 81–88.

Karpatkin, S. and Nardi, M. (1988). Immunological thrombocytopenic purpura in human immunodeficiency virus-seropositive patients with hemophilia. J Lab Clin Med, 111(4): 441–448.

Lavoie, S., Espinel-Ingroff, A., and Kerkering, T. (1993). Mixed cutaneous phaehyphomyocosis in a cocaine user. Clin Infect Dis, 17: 114–116.

Maki, T., Kontula, K., and Harkonen, M. (1990). The β-adrenergic system in man — physiological and pathophysiological response-regulation of receptor density and functioning. Scand J Clin Lab Invest, 50(S201): 25–43.

Orser, B. (1991). Thrombocytopenia and cocaine abuse. Anesthesiology, 74(1): 195–196.

Ou, D., Shen, M., and Luo, Y. (1989). Effects of cocaine on the immune system of Balb/c mice. Clin Immunol Immunopathol, 52: 305–312.

Poet, T., Pillai, R., Wood, S., and Watson, R. (1991). Stimulation of natural killer cell activity by murine retroviral infection and cocaine. Toxicol Let, 59: 147–152.

Shen, M., Luo, Y., Hagen, K. et al. (1994). Immunomodulating activities of cocaine-evaluation of lymphocyte transformation related to other immune functions. Int J Immunopharmac, 16(4): 311–319.

Starec, M., Rouveix, B., Sinet, M. et al. (1991). Immune status and survival of opiate- and cocaine-treated mice infected with Friend virus. J Pharmacol Exp Ther, 259(2): 745–750.

Walker, R. and Codd, E. (1985). Neuroimmunomodulatory interactions of norepinephrine and serotonin. J Neuroimmunol, 10: 41–48.

Watson, E., Murphy, J., ElSohly, H. et al. (1983). Effects of the administration of coca alkaloids on the primary immune responses of mice: interaction with 9-tetrahydrocannabinol and ethanol. Toxicol Appl Pharmacol, 71: 1–13.

Watzl, B., Chen, G., Scuderi, P. et al. (1992). Cocaine-induced suppression of interferon-gamma secretion in leukocytes from young and old C57BL/6 mice. Int J Immunopharmac, 14: 1125–1131.

1.12.10 Pregnancy interactions

Neither the prevalence nor the long-term effects of prenatal cocaine exposure are known with any degree of certainty. Early surveys, based on the results of urine testing programs, probably understated the problem. More recent studies, utilizing meconium and hair testing, are much more sensitive, and suggest that 12% to 20% or more of the children born at inner city hospitals have been exposed to cocaine (Forman et al., 1994).

Most of the abnormalities that have been identified in the offspring of pregnant cocaine users, including low birth weight, are more directly related to the life-style of the drug user than to any pharmacologic effect of cocaine. Women who use cocaine during pregnancy are likely to be older (Richardson and Day, 1994), less likely to seek prenatal care (Cherukuri et al., 1988), more likely to be malnourished (Knight et al., 1994), and more likely to suffer from HIV infection, syphilis, and hepatitis (Ellis et al., 1993). They are also more likely to be cigarette smokers, and cigarette smoking is the apparent explanation for the lower birth weight of children born to cocaine-using mothers (Miller et al., 1995; Shiono et al., 1995).

Myometrial contractions are increased in gravid baboons given intravenous cocaine (Morgan et al., 1994). Cocaine also stimulates human myometrial contraction, both *in vitro* and *in vivo*. Strips of uterus obtained at the time of caesarean section contract much more forcefully when they are exposed to modest concentrations of cocaine (Monga et al., 1993). This may explain why the duration of labor in cocaine using women is decreased. In one study the mean duration of labor in 16 cocaine users was 7.9 hours vs. 14.7 hours in 14 cocaine-free women (Dempsey and Vittinghoff, 1994). There is evidence that the underlying mechanism for increased uterine contraction is the prevention of myometrial catecholamine reuptake (Saraf et al., 1995).

It has also been suggested that cocaine users are at increased risk for placenta praevia (Handler et al., 1991), but the increased risk, if real, is trivial compared to the greater than 2.3-fold increased risk of placenta praevia seen in cigarette smokers (Handler et al., 1991). Still, there is no question that cocaine interacts with the placenta. Cocaine binds to serotonin and norepinephrine transporters located in the brush border membrane of human term placenta (Ganapathy and Leibach, 1994). Elevated levels of either catecholamine could lead to constriction of uterine blood vessels, decreasing uteroplacental blood flow. In addition, human placenta exposed to cocaine produces more thromboxane and less prostacyclin than controls (Monga et al., 1994). That could also lead to decreased uteroplacental blood flow.

Hypertension and other clinical symptoms typical of preeclampsia have been observed in conjunction with cocaine use (Towers et al., 1993), and elevated levels of endothelin-1 have been detected in pregnant cocaine users (Samuels et al., 1993). Conflicting findings regarding seizure thresholds have been reported by different researchers (Morishima et al., 1993; Glantz and Woods, 1994), probably because of intraspecies variation.

Infants exposed *in utero* are more likely to have a lower birth weight (Bateman et al., 1993) and smaller head circumference than controls (Nulman et al., 1994). Controlled studies have also shown that maternal cocaine blood levels during the third trimester correlate inversely with birth weight and head circumference (Knight et al., 1994). But the numerous anectodal case reports describing cocaine-associated malformations (Chasnoff et al., 1985; Chasnoff et al., 1988; Hanning and Philips, 1991; Hoyme et al., 1990; Hume et al., 1994; Ho et al., 1994) have never been confirmed in subsequent controlled studies (Kalter and Warkany, 1994; Snodgrass, 1994; Robins et al., 1993; Hutchings, 1993), nor has an alleged increased risk for Sudden Infant Death Syndrome (SIDS) been substantiated in well designed, controlled studies (Bauchner et al., 1988; Kain et al., 1992).

Interestingly, there appear to be links between *in utero* cocaine exposure and gastrointestinal abnormalities. Human fetal exposure to cocaine induces bilirubin metabolizing pathways, making neonatal jaundice less likely (Wennberg et al., 1994). Evidence is accumulating that implicates fetal cocaine exposure in the development of necrotizing enterocolitis (Downing et al., 1991; Czyrko et al., 1991). Necrotizing enterocolitis is a poorly defined syndrome with a significant mortality rate, and a host of predisposing risk factors (asphyxia, hypoxia, apnea, jaundice, etc.) (Czyrko et al., 1991; Levy, 1993; Porat and Brodsky, 1991; Amoury, 1993; Downing et al., 1991), and an association with maternal cocaine use has become increasingly evident (see Section 1.12.4 for clinical and pathologic findings).

Histopathologic studies are sadly lacking, but other vascular changes have also been observed in the human fetus, at least by indirect means. Doppler studies have shown renal artery vasoconstriction and simultaneous decreased urine output (Mitra et al., 1994). Neonatal myocardial infarction and reversible myocardial calcification have both been described (Bulbul et al., 1994; Yap et al., 1994) and there seems to be an increased incidence of arrhythmia in the neonatal period (Frassica et al., 1994). All of these abnormalities could be explained by exposure of the fetal heart to high circulating levels of catecholamines *in utero*, but it is difficult to draw any firm conclusion based solely on isolated clinical reports, especially in the virtual absence of histopathologic studies.

References

Amoury, R. (1993). Necrotizing enterocolitis: a continuing problem in the neonate. World J Surg, 17: 363–373.

Bateman, D., Ng, S., and Hansen, C. et al. (1993). The effects of intrauterine cocaine exposure in newborns. Am J Pub Health, 83(2): 190–193.

Bauchner, H., Zuckerman, B., McClain, M. et al. (1988). Risk of sudden infant death syndrome among infants with *in utero* exposure to cocaine. J Pediatr, 112: 831–834.

Bulbul, Z., Rosentahl, D., and Kleinman, C. (1994). Myocardial infarction in the perinatal period secondary to maternal cocaine use. Arch Pediatr Adolesc Med, 148: 1092–1096.

Chasnoff, I., Burns, W., Schnoll, S. et al. (1985). Cocaine use in pregnancy. N Engl J Med, 313: 666–669.

Chasnoff, I., Chisum, G., and Kaplan, W. (1988). Maternal cocaine use and genitourinary tract malformations. Teratology, 37: 201–204.

Cherukuri, R., Minkoff, H., Feldman, J. et al. (1988). A short study of alkoloidal cocaine ("crack") in pregnancy. Obstet Gynecol, 72: 147–151.

Czyrko, C., Del Pin, C., O'Neill, J. et al. (1991). Maternal cocaine abuse and necrotizing enterocolitis. Outcome and survival. J Pediatr Surg, 26: 414–421.

Dempsey, D. and Vittinghoff, E. (1994). Cocaine associated with shorter labor. Clin Pharm Ther, February 94: 178.

Downing, G., Horner, S., and Kibride, H. (1991). Characteristics of prenatal cocaine exposed infants with necrotizing enterocolitis. AJDC, 145: 26–27.

Ellis, J., Byrd, L., Sexson, W. et al. (1993). *In utero* exposure to cocaine: a review. South Med J, 86(7): 725–731.

Forman, R., Klein, J., Barks, J. et al. (1994). Prevalence of fetal exposure to cocaine in Toronto, 1990–1991. Clin Invest Med, 17(3): 206–211.

Frassica, J., Orav, J., Walsh, E. et al. (1994). Arrhythmias in children prenatally exposed to cocaine. Arch Ped Adolesc Med, 148: 1163–1169.

Ganapathy, V. and Leibach, F. (1994). Current Topic: Human placenta: a direct target for cocaine action. Placenta, 15: 785–795.

Glantz, J. and Woods, J. (1994). Cocaine LD50 in Long-Evans rats is not altered by pregnancy or progesterone. Neurotox and Teretol, 16(3): 297–301.

Handler, A., Kistin, N., Davis, F. et al. (1991). Cocaine use during pregnancy: perinatal outcomes. Am J Epidemol, 2: 221–223.

Hanning, V. and Philips, J. (1991). Maternal cocaine abuse and fetal anomalies; evidence for teratogenic effects of cocaine. South Med J, 84: 498–499.

Ho, J., Afshani, E., and Stapleton, F. (1994). Renal vascular abnormalities associated with prenatal cocaine exposure. Clin Peds, 33: 155–156.

Hoyme, H., Jones, K., Dixon, S. et al. (1990). Prenatal cocaine exposure and fetal vascular disruption. Pediatrics, 85: 743–747.

Hume, R., Gringras, J., Martin, L. et al. (1994). Ultrasound diagnosis of fetal anomalies associated with *in utero* cocaine exposure: further support for cocaine-induced vascular disruption teratogenesis. Fetal Diagn Ther, 9: 239–245.

Hutchings, D. (1993). The puzzle of cocaine's effects following maternal use during pregnancy: are there reconcilable differences. Neurotox and Teratology, 15: 281–286.

Kain, Z., Kain, T., and Scarpelli, E. (1992). Cocaine exposure *in utero*: perinatal development and neonatal manifestations. J Tox Clin Tox, 30: 607–636.

Kalter, H. and Warkany, J. (1994). Congenital malformations. N Engl J Med, 308(9): 491–497.

Knight, E., Hutchinson, J., Edwards, C. et al. (1994). Relationships of serum illicit drug concentrations during pregnancy to maternal nutritional status. J Nutr, 124: 973S–980S.

Levy, M. (1993). Is cocaine a risk factor to necrotizing enterocolitis? Clin Peds, 32(11): 700–701.

Miller, J., Boudreaux, M., and Regan, F. (1995). A case-control study of cocaine use in pregnancy. Am J Obstet Gynecol, 172: 180–185.

Mitra, S., Ganesh, V., and Apuzzio, J. (1994). Effect of maternal cocaine abuse on renal arterial flow and urine output of the fetus. Am J Obstet Gynecol, 171: 1556–1559.

Monga, M., Chmielowiec, S., Andres, R. et al. (1994). Cocaine alters placental production of thromboxane and prostacyclin. Am J Obstet Gynecol, 171: 965–969.

Monga, M., Weisbrodt, N., Andres, R. et al. (1993). The acute effect of cocaine exposure on pregnant human myometrial contractile activity. Am J Obstet Gynecol, 169: 782–785.

Morgan, M., Wentworth, R., Silavin, S. et al. (1994). Intravenous administration of cocaine stimulates gravid baboon myometrium in the last third of gestation. Am J Obstet Gynecol, 170: 1416–1420.

Morishima, H., Masoka, T., Tsuji, A. et al. (1993). Pregnancy decreases the threshold for cocaine-induced convulsions in the rat. J Lab Clin Med, 122(6): 748–756.

Nulman, I., Rovet, J., Altmann, D. et al. (1994). Neurodevelopment of adopted children exposed *in utero* to cocaine. Can Med Assoc J, 151(11): 1591–1597.

Porat, R. and Brodsky, D. (1991). Cocaine: a risk factor for necrotizing enterocolitis. J Perinat, 11(1): 30–32.

Richardson, G. and Day, N. (1994). Detrimental effects of prenatal cocaine exposure: illusion or reality? J Am Acad Child Adolesc Psych, 33(1): 28–34.

Robins, L., Mills, J., Krulewitch, C. et al. (1993). Effects of *in utero* exposure to street drugs. Am J Pub Health, 83(Supplement).

Samuels, P., Steinfeld, J., Braitman, L. et al. (1993). Plasma concentration of endothelin-1 in women with cocaine-associated pregnancy complications. Am J Obstet Gynecol, 168: 528–533.

Saraf, H., Dombrowski, M., Leach, K. et al. (1995). Characterization of the effect of cocaine on catecholamine uptake by pregnant myometrium. Obstet Gynecol, 85(1): 93–95.

Shiono, P., Klebanoff, M., Nugent, R. et al. (1995). The impact of cocaine and marijuana use on low birth weight and preterm birth: a multicenter study. Am J Obstet Gynecol, 172: 19–27.

Snodgrass, S. (1994). Cocaine babies: a result of multiple teratognic influences. J Child Neurol, 9: 227–233.

Towers, C., Pircon, R., Nageotte, M. et al. (1993). Cocaine intoxication presenting as preeclampsia and eclampsia. Obstet Gynecol, 81: 545–547.

Wennberg, R., Miller, M., and Maynard, A. (1994). Fetal cocaine exposure and neonatal bilirubinemia. J Pediatr, 125: 613–616.

Yap, T., Diana, D., Herson, V. et al. (1994). Fetal myocardial calcification associated with maternal cocaine use. Am J Perinatology, 11(3): 179–183.

1.13 When is cocaine the cause of death?

Cocaine-related deaths pose a forensic problem of considerable and increasing importance. If cocaine is listed as the cause of death, that means the death is accidental. While many insurance policies exclude death by the self-administration of drugs, double indemnity claims can occur if death is deemed accidental, a decision most insurance companies will not willingly accept. The role of cocaine can be equally important in criminal cases. The social stigma associated with the diagnosis of drug-related death cannot be ignored, if for no other reason than the lawsuits sometimes brought by the family members who claim that the deceased never used drugs. Given the importance of the subject, it is disappointing to see how often deaths caused

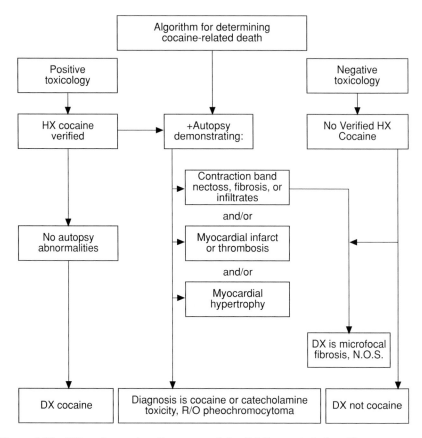

Figure 1.13   When is cocaine the cause of death? Suggested algorithm.

by cocaine are misclassified. Many misconceptions about cocaine-related deaths persist, and death certification practices are not standardized. In some cases, use of the ICD-9 classification system may even obscure important aspects of cocaine-related deaths, leading to both misdiagnosis and inaccurate mortality statistics (Young and Pollock, 1993).

The mere fact that cocaine is present does not prove that it was the cause of death, or even of toxicity. Drug use is pervasive in the United States, and postmortem testing frequently reveals the presence of minute amounts of cocaine (in the 5–15 ng range). That does not mean that cocaine was the cause of death. The presence of such low levels only proves environmental exposure. Cocaine levels of less than 50 ng/mL do not produce measurable physiologic effects, let alone toxicity. In the absence of any confirmatory histopathologic changes, cocaine levels of less than 50 ng/mL are not the cause of death. On the other hand, if the appropriate histologic changes are present, cocaine may be the cause of death, even when blood levels are zero.

The cause of death is easy to determine when cocaine blood levels exceed 1,000 ng/mL, benzoylecgonine levels are even higher, and there is florid pulmonary edema. But neither the absence of gross anatomic findings, nor the presence of confusing toxicology results, preclude the making of an accurate diagnosis. To ensure the correct diagnosis, physical and laboratory findings must be integrated with information from detailed case histories and meticulous scene investigations. Measurement of cocaine and ben-zoylecgonine levels only permits the estimation of when and perhaps how much drug was taken. Blood levels alone cannot be used to determine whether cocaine is the cause of death.

Cocaine-related deaths are generally not dose-related (Smart and Anglin, 1986). Blood levels of over 5,000 ng/mL may merely be incidental findings, and there is no upper limit that can be guaranteed fatal. Indeed, the anatomic alterations resulting from chronic cocaine use may be the cause of death, even when no cocaine or metabolite is detectable at the time of death. Partially, for that reason, many states (California is an exception) simply list the cause of death as "drug-related." Such a designation covers all deaths which are considered not to be suicide, but rather unexpected complications of chronic drug usage. There need be no attempt to make the artificial separation between toxicity and poisoning.

Even though cocaine-related deaths are not dose-related, such deaths can reasonably be divided into those resulting from acute vs. chronic toxicity. The very first dose of cocaine may lead to myocardial infarction from coronary spasm, even in individuals with otherwise normal arteries. If the infarction causes death, and is associated with positive toxicology testing, then the cause of death is cocaine toxicity. The same would apply to myocardial infarction in patients with existing coronary artery lesions; the increased workload (blood pressure × heart rate) imposed by cocaine on the myocardium may be sufficient to produce ischemia and arrhythmias, even in the absence of spasm or identifiable thrombosis (Kolodgie et al., 1991).

Cardiac standstill can be another manifestation of acute toxicity, but usually only at the very high blood levels (>20 mg/L) seen in "body packers." All local anesthetics have toxic effects on the myocardium and can cause marked depression of cardiac output (Rhee et al., 1990; Strichartz, 1987) leading to infarction, or asystolic arrest secondary to ion channel blockade (Nademanee et al., 1994; Xu et al., 1994).

Another manifestation of acute toxicity is contraction band necrosis. Cocaine users have elevated circulating levels of epinephrine, norepineph-rine, and atrial naturetic hormone. Acutely elevated levels of catecholamines may cause contraction band necrosis, and the presence of necrotic myocytes may disrupt the orderly progression of depolarization fronts. Fatal reentrant arrhythmia may result. In such cases, cocaine is likely to be detectable, but levels need not be particularly high.

Cases of chronic toxicity are more difficult to explain, because they, not infrequently, occur in individuals with low, or even absent, cocaine blood levels. Such cases are explained by the fact that chronic cocaine abuse causes changes in the structure of the heart, and all of these changes favor the occurrence of arrhythmias. Myocytes destroyed by contraction band necrosis heal by fibrosis. The process leads to permanant scarring of the myocardium, and the scars may disrupt conduction long after cocaine use has been discontinued.

In experimental animals, evidence for increased collagen production can be detected within a few hours of cocaine use (Besse et al., 1994). The presence of patchy microfocal fibrosis suggests earlier healed bouts of contraction band necrosis and earlier episodes of cocaine abuse. In isolation, microfocal fibrosis is an entirely non-specific finding (Karch and Billingham, 1986); it could just as well signify healed myocarditis as cocaine abuse, and without additional historical information, or a positive toxicology test, it may be impossible to tell the cause. Eosinophilic and lymphocytic infiltrates, which have been reported in cocaine users, are consistent with subacute injury (Isner et al., 1986; Virmani et al., 1987). None of these tissue responses is unique. If the deceased is a known cocaine user with typical changes of healing contraction band necrosis, then the cause of death is cocaine toxicity, even if the individual did not have detectable cocaine blood levels (or even metabolites) at the time of death.

Chronic cocaine users also develop myocardial hypertrophy. Evidence suggests that cardiac enlargement in cocaine users may be much more prevalent than has previously been appreciated (Brickner et al., 1991; Escabedo et al., 1992; Om et al., 1993; Karch et al., 1995; Karch, 1995). Since increased heart size is an accepted risk factor for sudden death (Kannel et al., 1969; Dunn and Pringle, 1993), the importance of this finding cannot be exaggerated. It could account for a number of deaths, even in the absence of contraction band necrosis, microfocal fibrosis, or even detectable levels of cocaine. The degree of myocardial hypertrophy seen in cocaine users, while highly significant, is modest (less than 10% above predicted weight). Because the increase is small, it is likely to go unrecognized. The only way to make the diagnosis is by comparing the heart weight of the deceased to a standard nomogram (Kitzman et al., 1988) (see Section 1.12.2.6 and the Appendix). Some confusion may arise in the case of competitive athletes; however, the pattern of hypertrophy generally seen in athletes (concentric hypertrophy) is different from that seen in hypertensives (eccentric hypertrophy), and close examination of the heart at the time of autopsy should allow the pattern to be identified.

In summary, in cases where there is a strong history of cocaine abuse with typical myocardial pathology present, cocaine is the cause of death, even in the face of negative toxicology testing. On the other hand, if typical pathologic findings are present, but toxicology and history are both negative, the diagnosis must be microfocal fibrosis, etiology "not otherwise specified." In the event that additional information becomes available at a later date (for example, exhumation with hair testing), the diagnosis can be revised, but the presence of isolated myocardial alterations is not sufficient for diagnosis. It may not always be possible to reach a firm diagnosis, but in today's society, the evaluation of sudden death in young people should begin with a consideration of the possible role of cocaine or other stimulant abuse.

References

Besse, S., Assayag, P., Latour, C. et al. (1994). Myocardial effects of acute and chronic cocaine treatment. Circulation, 90(4, Part 2): I–580.

Brickner, E., Willard, J., Eichorn, E. et al. (1991). Left ventricular hypertrophy associated with chronic cocaine abuse. Circulation, 84(3): 1130–1135.

Dunn, F. and Pringle, S. (1993). Sudden cardiac death, ventricular arrhythmias and hypertensive left ventricular hypertrophy [editorial]. J Hypert, 11(10): 1003–1010.

Dressler, F., Malekzadeh, S., and Roberts, W. (1990). Quantitative analysis of amounts of coronary arterial narrowing in cocaine addicts. Am J Cardiol, 65(5): 303–308.

Escabedo, L., Ruttenbur, A., Anda, R. et al. (1992). Coronary artery disease, left ventricular hypertrophy, and the risk of cocaine overdose death. Coronary Art Dis, 3: 853–857.

Isner, J., Estes, N., Thompson, P. et al. (1986). Acute cardiac events temporarily related to cocaine abuse. N Engl J Med, 315: 1438–1443.

Kannel, W., Gordon, T., and Offutt, D. (1969). Left ventricular hypertrophy by electrocardiogram. Prevalence, incidence and mortality in the Framingham Study. Ann Intern Med, 71: 89–105.

Karch, S. and Billingham, M. (1986). Myocardial contraction bands revisited. Hum Pathol, 17: 9–13.

Karch, S. (1995). Cardiac arrest in cocaine users. Am J Emerg Med, in press.

Karch, S., Green, G., and Young, S. (1995). Myocardial hypertrophy and coronary artery disease in male cocaine users. J Forensic Sci, in press.

Kitzman, D., Scholz, D. et al. (1988). Age-related changes in normal human hearts during the first 10 decades of life. Part II (Maturity): a quantitative anatomic study of 765 specimens from subjects 20 to 99 years old. Mayo Clin Proc, 63: 137–146.

Kolodgie, F., Virmani, R., Cornhill, J. et al. (1991). Increase in atherosclerosis and adventitial mast cells in cocaine abusers: an alternative mechanism of cocaine-associated coronary vasospasm and thrombosis. J Am Coll Cardiol, 17(7): 1553–1560.

Nademanee, K., Taylor, R., Bailey, W. et al. (1994). Mechanisms of cocaine-induced sudden death and cardiac arrhythmias. Circulation, 90(4, Pt 2): I–455.

Om, A., Ellahham, S., Vetrovec, G. et al. (1993). Left ventricular hypertrophy in normotensive cocaine users. Am Heart J, 5(1): 1441–1443.

Rhee, H., Valentine, J., and Lee, S., (1990). Toxic effects of cocaine to the cardiovascular system in conscious and anesthetized rats and rabbits — evidence for a direct effect on the myocardium. Neurotoxicology, 11(2): 361–366.

Smart, R. and Anglin, R. (1986). Do we know the lethal dose of cocaine? J Forensic Sci, 32(2): 303–312.

Strichartz, G. (1987). Handbook of experimental pharmacology, Volume 81: Local anesthetics. New York: Springer-Verlag.

Virmani, R., Rabinowitz, M., and Smialek, J. (1987). Cocaine-associated deaths: absence of coronary thrombosis and a high incidence of myocarditis. Lab Invest, 56: 83.

Xu, Y., Crumb, W., and Clarkson, C. (1994). Cocaethylene, a metabolite of cocaine and ethanol, is a potent blocker of cardiac sodium channels. J Pharm Exp Ther, 271: 319–325.

Young, T. and Pollock, D. (1993). Misclassification of deaths caused by cocaine, an assessment by survey. Am J Forensic Med and Pathol, 14(1): 43–47.

chapter two

Other naturally occurring stimulants

Cocaine is not the only plant that contains psychoactive alkaloids; at least four other species contain alkaloids capable of producing amphetamine-like effects. Absinthe abuse ceased being a problem at the turn of the century, but khat abuse, which had been confined to the sub-Sahara, is enjoying a renaissance and khat leaves are regularly smuggled into the United States and Europe. Xanthine derivatives, especially caffeine, are the world's most widely abused drugs. The other important alkaloid is ephedrine. Ephedrine is capable of abuse in its own right. When smoked or injected intravenously, it is a potent stimulant. Ephedrine was widely abused and considered a major threat to public health in Japan during the 1950s, but ephedrine's principal importance today lies in its role as a precursor in the illicit production of amphetamines and related compounds such as ephedrone (also known as "CAT"). Little is known about the actions of these compounds in man, and still less about the pathologic changes associated with their abuse.

2.1   Absinthe

2.1.1   History

Absinthe is a French word for wormwood (*Artemisia absinthium* and *Artemisia pontica*). A perennial herb related to sage *(Salvia officinalis)*, wormwood grows to a height of two to three feet. Plants have leafy stems and tiny, greenish yellow flowers. The Egyptians used wormwood for medical purposes. Pliny, in the first century A.D., recommended it as a vermifuge, and wormwood was mentioned in several of Shakespeare's plays. Late in the 1700s, techniques for the mass production of grain alcohol were introduced, and shortly afterward, herb-based liqueurs appeared on the market. In the early 1800s, Henri-Louis Pernod ushered in the era of absinthe abuse when he opened his factory in Pontarlier. Pernod's liquor, which was immensely popular in France and throughout Europe, was a distillate of herbs. The recipe included wormwood, anise, fennel (which was responsible for its green color), hyssop, and lemon balm (Arnold, 1989).

Figure 2.1 Absinthe drinkers. These gentlemen were obviously intoxicated, but whether from the terpenes or the alcohol in their drinks is not entirely clear. Some evidence suggests that the active ingredients in this drink may have been very similar to those in marijuana. From Harper's Magazine, April 1889.

Absinthe drinking became very popular just a few years before Mariani started selling his coca-fortified wines, and the popularity of both coca and absinthe seemed to rise almost in parallel. During the 1860s and 70s, Degas and Manet immortalized images of absinthe drinking. Toulouse-Lautrec painted van Gogh with a glass of absinthe just three years after Freud published "Über Coca." Baudelaire used both cocaine and absinthe, but wrote about only the latter. Valentine Magnan studied the medical complications of both drugs (Magnan, 1874; Magnan and Saury, 1889), and sounded warnings about the potential toxicity of each.

Just as the manufacturers of cocaine-containing patent medicines minimized the medical problems associated with cocaine use, so did the manufacturers of absinthe cordials. At first, the manufacturers were successful. During the period from 1875 to 1913, annual consumption of absinthe per French citizen increased by 1,500%. In 1912, just two years before the Harrison Narcotic Act banned cocaine from patent medications in the United States, the French government passed legislation limiting the alcohol and absinthe content of commercial products. In 1915 the sale and manufacture of absinthe was banned entirely. There was some resistance at first, but the prohibition stood, and absinthe abuse is now only an historical curiosity, while cocaine is enjoying a renaissance. Why one drug, but not the other, should have entirely disappeared, is probably explained by simple logistics. A few million dollars' worth of cocaine can be smuggled in a suitcase, while a few million dollars' worth of absinthe would fill several large tankers!

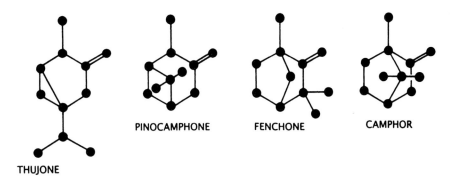

PINOCAMPHONE   FENCHONE   CAMPHOR

THUJONE

Figure 2.1.2   Terpenes. Absinthe contained many different compounds; thujone was the principal agent.

2.1.2   *Clinical and autopsy studies*

The compounds found in absinthe are terpenes, structural isomers of camphor. The structure of thujone, the principle terpene extracted from wormwood, was published in 1900. Modern clinical studies of thujone are all but nonexistent. Studies from the 1920s and 1930s suggest that its effects are indistinguishable from those of camphor. Camphor is a potent CNS stimulant and, before the introduction of electroconvulsant therapy, camphor was

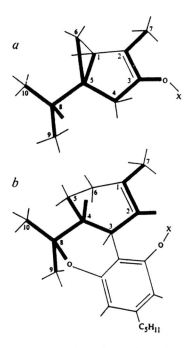

Figure 2.1.3   Similarities between absinthe and marijuana? The backbone of the terpene molecule bears a striking resemblance to the backbone of the THC molecule. Adapted from del Castillo et al., Nature, January 31, 1975.

used to treat depression. It has been suggested that, because the structure of thujone is very similar to that of tetrahydrocannabinol, both produce similar psychological effects (del Castillo et al., 1975), and that absinthe drinkers were not getting much more than a marijuana "high."

Small doses of camphor cause stimulation and euphoria, but ingestion of larger amounts (>30 mg/kg) can result in convulsions, coma, and death. Without knowing the thujone content of the absinthe being consumed at the turn of the century, it is hard to say how much thujone absinthe drinkers were actually getting, let alone whether that amount was sufficient to cause toxicity, but it seems likely that it was far less than 30 mg/kg. Blood and tissue levels in camphor-associated deaths have never been reported, and autopsy information is limited to observations in the older literature (Amory, 1868) and one slightly more recent case (Smith and Margolis, 1954). Absinthe abuse is now nonexistent, but camphor is still a common ingredient in many over-the-counter medications (Camphophenique®, Mentholatum®, Vicks Vaporub®, Sloan's Liniment®, etc.) and is responsible for occasional episodes of toxicity (Gibson, Moore, and Pfaff, 1989). Treatment is said to consist of airway maintenance and seizure control (Liebelt and Shannon, 1993), although so few cases have been reported that the appropriate treatment is not really known.

References

Amory, R. (1868). Absinthe. Boston Medical and Surgical Journal: 68.

Arnold, W. (1989). Absinthe. Scientific American, 6: 112–117.

Gibson, D., Moore, G., and Pfaff, J. (1989). Camphor Ingestion, Am J Emerg Med, 7: 41–43.

Liebelt, E. and Shannon, M. (1993). Small doses, big problems: a selected review of highly toxic common medications. Ped Emerg Care, 9: 292–297.

Magnan, V. (1874). On the comparative action of alcohol and absinthe. Lancet, 2: 2664(September 19): 410–412.

Magnan, V. and Saury, R. (1889). Trois cas de cocainisme chronique. Compt Rend Soc Biol, (Paris) 1: 60.

Smith, A. and Margolis, G. (1954). Camphor poisoning: anatomical and pharmaco-logic study; report of a fatal case; experimental investigation of protective action of barbiturate. Am J Pathol, 30: 857–868.

2.2 Caffeine

2.2.1 History

Caffeine is the world's most widely used stimulant drug. It shares with amphetamine and cocaine the same features usually associated with drugs of abuse (reinforcement), and chronic use results in tolerance to many of its effects (Holtzman, 1990). Annual consumption of caffeine is thought to be well over 100,000 tons. It is estimated that over 80% of the U.S. population drinks coffee or tea. In addition, formidable amounts are also consumed in soft drinks, cold medications, and pain relief formulas. Table 2.2.3 shows the

Table 2.2.3 Caffeine Content in Milligrams of Some Common Beverages and Medications*

Carbonated beverages (12 oz can)	
Coca Cola®	64.7
Dr. Pepper®	60.9
Mountain Dew®	54.7
Diet Dr. Pepper®	54.2
Pepsi-Cola®	43.1
RC Cola®	33.7
Tea bags (average per cup)	
Black teas	21 to 33
Green teas	9 to 19
Coffee (average per cup)	
Instant	62
Electric percolator	100
Stove percolator	105
Drip	140
Coca	10–17
Medications	
Norgesic Tablets®	30.0
Darvon Compound 65®	32.4
Fiorinal Capsules®	40.0
Excedrin Extra Strength®	65.0
Caffergot Tablet®	100.0
No Doz Tablets®	100.0
No Doz Maximum Strength®	200.0

* Data for caffeine-containing beverages taken from Bunker, M. and McWilliams, M. Caffeine content of common beverages, *J. Am. Dietetic Assn.*, 74: 28–32, 1979. Current labeling requirements do not require manufacturers to list caffeine content. Values may have changed since the Bunker and McWilliam paper was published. Data for medications taken from current PDR.

caffeine content of some commonly consumed beverages and medications. Average American caffeine consumption is estimated to be 2.4 mg/kg/day for adults and half that amount for children between the ages of 5 and 18. European consumption is thought to be even higher: 3.5 mg/kg/day (Commission of the European Communities, 1983). An average cup of coffee contains 40–100 mg of caffeine. The content of cola drinks is lower, ranging from 30 to 65 mg. Dedicated coffee drinkers can easily ingest more than a gram of caffeine per day, and per capita consumption appears to be increasing.

Caffeine can improve performance during athletic competitions. In a controlled study, elite marathon runners given 9 mg/kg of caffeine before testing were able to increase their time on a treadmill by an average of 70% (Graham and Spriet, 1991)! This improvement was achieved without evidence of toxicity and without exceeding the International Olympic Committee's requirement that testing reveal no more than 12 µg/mL of caffeine, or the National Collegiate Athletic Association's even more generous 15 μg/mL. It has been suggested that performance improvement, at least at doses of 5 mg/kg or less, is the result of increased lipolysis and glycogen sparing. Athletes who can metabolize lipids will have glycogen available for a longer period of time, and that should increase endurance (Essig et al., 1980; Smith and Perry, 1992). Other explanations may apply at higher dosage ranges (Van Soeren et al., 1993). Performance improvement seems to be more impressive with large doses, so further clandestine experimentation with doses high enough to produce toxicity seems likely.

The origins of coffee drinking are a mystery. According to legend, the prior of a Muslim convent observed that goats eating berries from certain trees tended to stay up all night. He thought that using the beans might help him and his followers stay awake during their prayer vigils in the mosque, so he brewed a beverage called "kahweh" and was said to have been quite pleased with the results. The first substantial evidence of widespread popularity is from the sixteenth century. In 1511, when a new Egyptian governor arrived in Mecca, he noticed people sitting around the mosques drinking coffee. He asked what they were doing and he was told that they were drinking coffee in order to get the energy they needed to pray all night. The governor had his doubts, and so he convened a meeting of clerics and elders to discuss whether or not coffee might not be some sort of intoxicating agent, and therefore prohibited by the Koran. The assembly concluded that coffee was indeed an intoxicant, and therefore should be banned. Sales of coffee were prohibited and stocks were burned. Had the new governor bothered to check with his superiors, he would have found that the Sultan of Cairo was an avid coffee drinker; the Sultan promptly overruled the governor's decision, and coffee drinking in Mecca has been legal ever since.

Venetian traders introduced coffee to Europe. The first coffee house in London was opened in 1652; it was located in St. Michael's Alley, Cornhill. Its owner, Pasqua Rosee, advertised extensively, making mostly medicinal claims for the drink. According to Rosee, coffee was "a very good help to the digestion…and makes you fit for business" (Thompson, 1928). In spite of Rosee's claims, coffee drinking was at first suspect. Coffee drinkers were said to have a haggard appearance and to be "subject to fits of agitation and depression." Coffee drinking had been introduced into France nine years earlier, and by 1690 there were 250 registered coffee houses; by 1782, that number had risen to 1,800. Some of the coffee houses were quite opulent, with marble tables and crystal chandeliers. Like the English, the French also had some doubts about the habit. Medical literature from that period contains reports both praising and condemning coffee's effects. It was alleged that coffee caused inflammation of the liver and spleen, and even that it caused renal colic.

Suspicions that coffee drinking is unhealthy have never entirely disappeared. Even Virchow classified caffeine, along with alcohol, as an addictive substance. Lewin, who generally thought that coffee drinking was a good thing, accepted reports of "delirium, vertigo, trembling, and even convulsions" as an occupational disease in coffee roasters (Lewin, 1931). In modern times epidemiologic investigations have focused on possible links between caffeine intake and myocardial infarction, sudden death, and fibrocystic disease. Alleged links to cancer have never been proven (Stavric, 1992). The histopathologic changes associated with caffeine abuse have been studied only in animals (Strubelt et al., 1976).

2.2.2   Chemical constants and tissue disposition

Caffeine is 3,7-Dihydro-1,3,7-trimethyl-1H-purine-2,6-dione or 1,3,7-trimethylxanthine. Other older names were methyltheobromine and thein. Its formula is $C_8H_{10}N_4O_2$, and it has a molecular weight of 194.19. It is composed of 49.5% carbon, 5.2% hydrogen, 28.9% nitrogen, and 16.5% oxygen. Purified caffeine crystallizes into hexagonal prisms with a melting point of 238°C. It is a basic alkaloid with a pK_a of 0.8.

Caffeine is a methylated purine derivative, and like cocaine, is classified as an alkaloid. The term was originally introduced to described compounds which could be extracted from plants and whose salts were crystallizable. Caffeine is found in naturally occurring plants, including kola nuts, cocoa beans, and tea. Chemical extraction of roasted coffee beans yields from 8 to 20 mg of caffeine per gram of coffee (Zuskin et al., 1983). Measurements made one hour after drinking two cups of coffee showed a peak caffeine value of 5.3 µgm/mL (Marks and Kelly, 1973), but in general, peak levels can be expected anywhere from 15–45 minutes after ingestion. The half-life is extremely variable. In healthy adults, reported half-lives have been anywhere between 3–7 hours (Levy and Zylber-Katz, 1982).

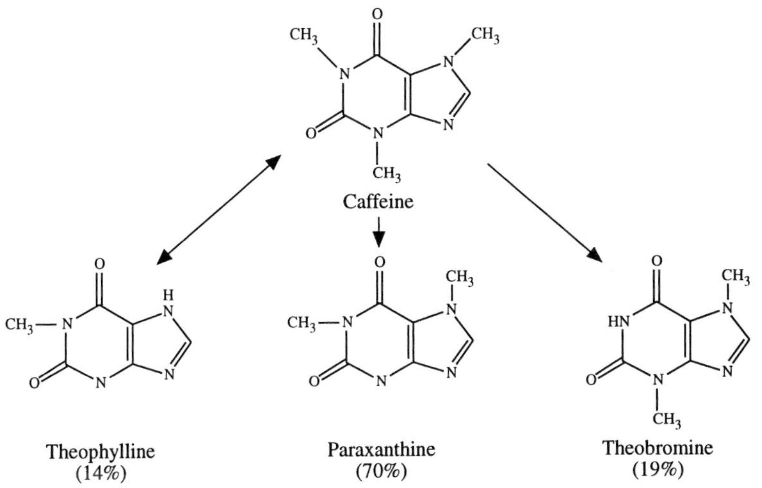

Figure 2.2.2   Caffeine metabolism. Assuming an average caffeine intake of roughly 500 mg per day, 70% will be excreted as paraxanthine, 20% as theobromine, and 14% as theophylline. The results may be quite different in smokers and patients with cirrhosis.

Caffeine is almost entirely metabolized by the liver to other xanthines, including theophylline, which is then excreted in the urine. Caffeine levels in saliva are easily measured and accurately reflect arterial blood levels (Cone, 1994). Using reversed-phase high-performance liquid chromatography and capillary electrophoresis, 14 different metabolites can be identified in human urine (Rodopoulos and Norman, 1994). On average, 14% of ingested caffeine is excreted as theophylline and 70% as paraxanthine. The latter is not found in nature, but is found as a metabolite in many different species (Ullrich et al., 1992). A healthy adult drinking two cups of very strong coffee would be expected to have urine caffeine levels no greater than 3–6 μg/mL.

2.2.3 Clinical studies of caffeine

For a drug that is so widely taken, surprisingly little is known about caffeine's chemistry or toxicology. Individual reactions to caffeine, at least at low doses, vary widely. It has been suggested that a caffeine dependence syndrome exists, and that it meets all the generic criteria for substance dependence, with affected individuals persisting in caffeine use, in spite of persistent problems related to its use. In one controlled study, dependence was diagnosed in 16 of 99 individuals evaluated; median daily caffeine consumption in this group was only 357 mg per day (Strain et al., 1994).

Caffeine is very similar in structure to theophylline and shares a common mechanism of toxicity, but on a weight-for-weight basis, theophylline is a good deal more toxic than caffeine. Since theophylline, paraxanthine, and caffeine are all present after caffeine ingestion, assessing caffeine's toxic potential is a difficult undertaking. Theophylline and caffeine are interconvertable in humans. The ratio of plasma theophylline to caffeine after caffeine administration is 8:6. After theophylline administration, the ratio of theophylline to caffeine is nearly the same (Stavric, 1988).

Little data about tissue disposition is available, and kinetics have been studied only at low doses in healthy volunteers. Furthermore, the pattern of caffeine metabolism is altered by chronic consumption. The clearance rates for both theophylline and paraxanthine decrease in chronic users (Denaro et al., 1990). Tissue measurements in rats have shown that, after dosing with caffeine, concentrations of caffeine and theophylline are equal in most tissues except the brain, where caffeine levels are 25% higher than theophylline levels (Ståhle et al., 1992). If this is also the case in man, then the difference may, at least partly, explain differences in the clinical profiles of theophylline and caffeine.

Newborns, like adults, can convert caffeine to theophylline and theophylline to caffeine, but the direction and degree of conversion are not always predictable. Measurements of cord blood caffeine levels in children born to cocaine-abusing mothers have shown that these women are likely to be abusing caffeine and nicotine as well; caffeine may be present in substantial concentrations (up to 10 mg/L) (Dempsy et al., 1993). In three newborns treated with therapeutic doses of intravenous aminophylline, the highest levels were observed in the blood and then the brain. Decreasing levels were found in the heart, liver, lung, and kidney. Brain theophylline levels ranged from 6–30 µg/gram, while caffeine levels ranged from 2.1–3.7 µg/gram. Caffeine can be detected in most biofluids, including saliva, semen, and breast milk (Bonati et al., 1982), but levels have not been systematically studied. Ingestion of even modest amounts of caffeine by naive mothers can produce significant effects on maternal and fetal circulation (Miller et al., 1994). Infants born to heavy coffee drinkers have elevated caffeine levels at birth (Khanna and Somani, 1984), but there is no evidence that the elevation results in toxicity in these children.

Two special situations are of clinical and forensic interest. In infants the plasma half-life of caffeine is 17 times longer than in healthy adults (Labow, 1983). Accordingly, infants being treated with aminophylline run a real risk of toxicity from caffeine, which continues to accumulate in their blood as aminophylline is converted to caffeine. Similar results can occur in patients with hepatic insufficiency or decreased cardiac output (Lacroix et al., 1985). Treatment with aminophylline under these circumstances runs a risk of caffeine toxicity. Measurement of both theophylline and caffeine levels in individuals at risk would be prudent.

Altered caffeine metabolism is also observed in children with cystic fibrosis, but the alterations remain poorly characterized. Some evidence suggests that xanthine oxidase activity is increased in these children (Hamelin et al., 1994). These children may be especially vulnerable to theophylline/caffeine toxicity because they frequently require antibiotic therapy. Some of the more popular antibiotics, such as ciprofloxacin, may inhibit caffeine metabolism (3-N-demethylation), resulting in dangerously high caffeine blood levels (Parker et al., 1994).

Table 2.2.3.1   Half-Life of Caffeine vs. Age

Age	Half-life of caffeine
Premature, at birth	65–102 hours
Term, at birth	82 hours
3–4.5 months old	14.4 hours
5–6 months old	2.6 hours
Adult	3–7.5 hours

All methylxanthines, including caffeine, are phosphodiesterase inhibitors. Excessive use causes typical symptoms of sympathetic stimulation. Coffee ingestion increases plasma catecholamine levels, but only to a very modest degree, and not in any predictable fashion. Early studies demonstrated that caffeine stimulates the release of catecholamines from the adrenal medulla, and there have been clinical reports suggesting fairly substantial catecholamine elevations (Benowitiz et al., 1982; Robertson et al., 1978). But in one study, human volunteers given a mean dose of 250 mg had statistically insignificant increases in catecholamines (Cameron et al., 1990). This limited rise in catecholamines is in contrast with the other naturally occurring psychostimulants and may explain why, even though enormous quantities of caffeine are consumed, few histologic abnormalities have been reported.

Over and above caffeine's ability to inhibit phosphodiesterase, caffeine and all the other methylxanthines have additional effects on cardiac myocytes; they cause the release of calcium ions from the sarcoplasmic reticulum, and they lower the effective concentration of calcium required for myofilament contraction (O'Neill et al., 1990). Some methylxanthines exert more potent effects than others. The differences in potency appear to be a function of differences in membrane permeability to the different drugs (Donoso et al., 1994).

There is one case report describing a patient with stroke following combined caffeine and amphetamine snorting (Lambrecht et al., 1993). Caffeine administration decreases cerebral blood flow. It also causes transient increases in systolic blood pressure (Cameron et al., 1990; Mathew and Wilson, 1991). A dose of 250 mg (approximately 2.5 cups of coffee) is enough to reduce cerebral blood flow for 90 minutes. The decrease in cerebral flow is unexplained. It is not due to changes in the general circulation or in CO_2 levels, but it might be the result of caffeine's ability to block adenosine receptors. Adenosine is a powerful cerebral vasodilator and it may be that adenosine receptor blockade results in decreased cerebral flow. Interactions with the adenosine receptor have also been suggested as a possible mechanism in caffeine-related seizures, though this suggestion remains unproven (Morgan and Durcan, 1990). Caffeine increases myocardial contractility by increasing the release of Ca^{2+} from the sarcoplasmic reticulum and elevating intracytosolic calcium concentration (Petersen, 1991). A relationship between caffeine intake and ventricular ectopy has always been presumed, but electrophysiologic studies of patients with recurrent ventricular tachycardia have failed to confirm any such action. In fact, some patients with ventricular ectopy have fewer extra beats after they are given coffee (Chelsky, 1990). There is also evidence that caffeine can inhibit plasma cholinesterase. Since few, if any, of the symptoms associated with caffeine toxicity are similar to those seen with cholinesterase deficiency, the significance of this observation also remains to be seen (Karadsheh et al., 1991).

2.2.4 Blood levels

There is one report of a 22-year old woman who committed suicide by taking an unknown number of caffeine tablets. She died of an apparent cardiac arrhythmia. Blood obtained during attempted resuscitation had 1,560 mg of caffeine per liter. Autopsy findings consisted mainly of pulmonary edema and visceral congestion (Mrvos et al., 1989). A second woman, age 19, also died of a ventricular arrhythmia. At autopsy, her caffeine blood level was 181 mg/L. No histopathologic alterations were identified. In 1985 Garriott reported on five fatalities, three of combined caffeine/ephedrine, and two cases of caffeine only. In these cases blood levels ranged from 130–344 mg/L. The report did not comment on histologic findings, if any. Fatalities have also been associated with much lower caffeine levels. A 1980 case report described two patients who expired after using repeated coffee enemas. Both had underlying diseases and both appeared to have succumbed to fluid and electrolyte abnormalities. Both of these women had negligible caffeine levels at the time of death (Eisele and Reay, 1980). Blood levels in cases of fatal intoxication have ranged from 79 mg/L to 1,560 mg/L (McGee, 1980; Mrvos et al., 1989). Aside from blood levels, data on the tissue distribution of caffeine is so sparse as to prohibit any generalization.

Equally high levels have been recorded in patients who survived caffeine overdoses. Blood levels of 200 mg/L were recorded in a woman who took 24 grams of caffeine in an unsuccessful suicide attempt. Her theophylline level was 17.2 mg/L (Benowitiz et al., 1982). Another report described the case of a 27-year old man who regularly ingested ground coffee in order to get "high." On one occasion he doubled his usual dose and swallowed half a kilogram of ground coffee. He arrived at the hospital comatose, febrile, hypertensive, tachycardic, and seizing. He survived, but required intense treatment with β blockers, and anticonvulsants. His caffeine blood level was 29 mg/L (Wurl, 1994).

2.2.5   Autopsy findings

Based on the very limited data available, it appears that caffeine-related deaths in humans are usually arrhythmic and are not accompanied by any distinct histologic changes. In studies designed to access caffeine cardiotoxicity, caffeine infusions of 0.5 mg/kg in miniswine produced neither EKG changes nor myocardial lesions (Vick et al., 1989). However, when the same amount of caffeine was infused along with low doses of isoproterenol (1 µg/kg/min, a dose that is too low to produce EKG changes or necrosis in this model), myocardial necrosis and arrhythmias were easily demonstrated. Contraction band necrosis and mitochondrial injuries occur when Langendorf preparations are perfused with caffeine. The observed pattern of injury suggests that calcium overload is the responsible mechanism (Daniels and Duncan, 1993). The findings in other experimental studies suggest similar conclusions (Whitehurst et al., 1994).

In spite of the cardiac lesions produced in animals, alterations have not been mentioned in the few published human autopsies. In a case of overdose with a postmortem caffeine level of 113.5 mg/L, and clinical evidence of acute heart failure, right atrial dilation, acute pulmonary edema, and passive congestion of the liver, no specific cardiac lesions could be identified (Bryant, 1981). Nor could an anatomic basis for death be found in a second case with even higher caffeine levels (181 mg/L) (McGee, 1980). Pulmonary edema and passive congestion of the liver were observed and seemed to be consistent findings (Alstott, 1973).

The failure to demonstrate myocardial lesions is consistent with the fact that caffeine toxicity is not associated with marked elevations in circulating catecholamines. It may be that caffeine's modest sympathomimetic activities are sufficient to produce toxicity only in the presence of some other β agonist (Strubelt et al., 1976).

References

Alstott, R., Miller, A., and Forney, R. (1973). Report of a human fatality due to caffeine. J Forensic Sci, 18(2): 135–137.

Benowitiz, N., Osterloh, J., Goldschlager, N. et al. (1982). Massive catecholamine release from caffeine poisoning. JAMA, 248(9): 1097–1098.

Bonati, M., Latini, R., Galletti, F. et al. (1982). Caffeine disposition after oral doses. Clin Pharm Ther, 32: 98–106.

Bryant, J. (1981). Suicide by ingestion of caffeine. Arch Pathol Lab Med, 105: 685–686.

Cameron, O., Modell, J., and Hariharan, M. (1990). Caffeine and human cerebral blood flow: a positron emission tomography study. Life Sci, 47(13): 1141–1146.

Caughlin, L. and O'Halloran, R. (1993). An accidental death related to cocaine, coca-ethylene, and caffeine. J Forensic Sci, 38(6): 1513–1515.

Chelsky, L., Cutler, J., Griffith, K. et al. (1990). Caffeine and ventricular arrhythmias: an electrophysiologic approach. JAMA, 17: 2236–2240.

Commission of the European Communities (1983). Report of the Scientific Committee for Food on Caffeine. Office for Official Publications of the European Communities.

Cone, E. (1994). Saliva testing for drugs of abuse. Ann NY Acad Sci, 694: 91–127.

Daniels, S. and Duncan, C. (1993). Cellular damage in the rat heart caused by caffeine or dinitrophenol. Biochemi Physiol. C: Comparative Pharmacology, 105(2): 225–229.

Dempsy, D., Rowbotham, M., Dattell, B. et al. (1993). Neonatal blood cocaine concentrations. Clin Pharm Ther, 150: Abstract PI–62.

Denaro, C., Brown, C., Wilson, M. et al. (1990). Dose-dependency of caffeine metabolism with repeated dosing. Clin Pharm Ther, 48: 277–285.

Eisele, J. and Reay, D. (1980). Deaths related to coffee enemas. JAMA, 244(14): 1608–1609.

Essig, D., Costill, D., and Van Handel, P. (1980). Effects of caffeine ingestion on utilization of muscle glycogen and lipid during leg ergometer cycling. Int J Sports Med, 1: 89–90.

Graham, T. and Spriet, L. (1991). Performance and metabolic responses to a high caffeine dose during prolonged exercise. J Appl Physiol, 71(6): 2292–2298.

Hamelin, B., Xu, K., Vallé, F. et al. (1994). Caffeine metabolism in cystic fibrosis: enhanced xanthine oxidase activity. Clin Pharm Ther, 56: 521–529.

Holloway, F., Michaelis, R., and Huerta, R. (1985). Caffeine-phenylethylamine combinations mimic the amphetamine discrimination cue. Life Sci, 36: 723–730.

Holtzman, S. (1990). Caffeine as a model drug of abuse. Trends in Pharm Sci, 11: 335–336.

Iversen, S., Murphy, P., Leakey, T. et al. (1984). Unsuspected caffeine toxicity complicating theophylline therapy. Hum Toxicol, 3(6): 509–512.

Karadsheh, N., Kussie, P., and Linthicum, D. (1991). Inhibition of acetylcholinesterase by caffeine, anabasine, methyl pyrolidine and their derivatives. Toxicology Letters, 55(3): 335–342.

Khanna, N. and Somani, S. (1984). Maternal coffee drinking and unusually high concentration of caffeine in newborn. J Clin Toxicol, 22(5): 473–483.

Labow, R. (1983). Effects of caffeine being studied for treatment of apnea in newborns. Can Med Ass J, 129: 230–231.

Lacroix, C., Nouveau, J., Laine, G. et al. (1985). Interaction théophylline — caféine chez des brochopathes atteints d'insuffisance cardiaque et hépatique. Press Méd, 14: 1340.

Lambrecht, G., Malbrain, M., Chew, S. et al. (1993). Intranasal caffeine and amphetamine causing stroke. Acta Neurologica Belgica, 93(3): 146–149.

Levy, M. and Zylber-Katz, E. (1982). Caffeine metabolism and coffee attributed sleep disturbances. Clin Pharm Ther, 33: 770–775.

Lewin, L. (1931). *Phantastica: narcotic and stimulating drugs, their use and abuse.* Second English edition, translated by P. H. Wirth, Ph.D., B.Sc. New York: E.P. Dutton and Company.

Marks, V. and Kelly, J. (1973). Absorption of caffeine from tea, coffee, and coca cola. Lancet, 1: 827.

Mathew, R. and Wilson, W. (1991). Substance abuse and cerebral blood flow. Am J Psychiatry, 148(3): 292–305.

McGee, M. (1980). Caffeine poisoning in a 19-year old female. J Forensic Sci, 25(1): 29–32.

Miller, R., Watson, W., Hackney, A. et al. (1994). Acute maternal and fetal cardiovascular effects of caffeine ingestion. Am J Perinatology, 11(2): 132–136.

Morgan, P. and Durcan, M. (1990). Caffeine-induced seizures: apparent proconvulsant activity of n-ethyl carboxamidoadenosine (NECA). Life Sci, 47(1): 1–8.

Mrvos, R., Reilly, P., Dean, B. et al. (1989). Massive caffeine ingestion resulting in death. Vet Hum Toxicol, 31(6): 571–572.

Parker, A., Preston, T., Heaf, D. et al. (1994). Inhibition of caffeine metabolism by ciprofloxacin in children with cystic fibrosis as measured by the caffeine breath test. Br J Clin Pharmac, 38: 577–580.

Petersen, O. (1991). Actions of caffeine. News Physiol Sci, 6(APR): 98–99.

Robertson, D., Frölich, J., Carr, R. et al. (1978). Effects of caffeine on plasma renin activity, catecholamines and blood pressure. N Engl J Med, 298(4): 181–186.

Rodopoulos, N. and Norman, A. (1994). Determination of caffeine and its metabolites in urine by high-performance liquid chromatography and capillary electrophoresis. Scan J Clin Lab Inv, 54(4): 305–315.

Smith, D. and Perry, P. The efficacy of ergogenic agents in athletic competition. Part II: other performance-enhancing agents. Ann of Pharmacotherapy, 26(5): 653–659.

Ståhle, L., Segersvärd, S., and Ungersted, U. (1992). Drug distribution studies with microdialysis III: caffeine and theophylline in blood, brain and other tissues in rats. Life Sci, 49: 1843–1852.

Stavric, B. (1988). Methylxanthines: toxicity to humans. 2. Caffeine. Fd Chem Toxic, 26(7): 645–662.

Stavric, B. (1992). An update on research with coffee/caffeine (1989–1990). Fd Chem Tox, 30: 533–555.

Strain, E., Mumford, G., Silverman, K. et al. (1994). Caffeine dependence syndrome. Evidence from case histories and experimental evaluations. JAMA, 272(13): 1043–1048.

Strubelt, O., Hoffman, A., Siegers, C., and Sierra-Callejas, J. (1976). On the pathogenesis of cardiac necrosis induced by theophylline and caffeine. Acta Pharmacol Toxicol, 39: 383–392.

Thompson, C. (1928). *The quacks of old London.* New York, London, Paris: Brentano's Ltd.

Ullrich, D., Compagnone, D., Münch, B. et al. (1992). Urinary caffeine metabolites in man. Age-dependent changes and pattern in various clinical situations. Euro J Clin Pharmacol, 43: 167–172.

Van Soeren, M., Sathasivam, P., Spriet, L. et al. (1993). Caffeine metabolism and epinephrine responses during exercise in users and nonusers. J Appl Physiol, 75(2): 805–812.

Vick, J., Whitehurst, V., Herman, E., and Balazs, T. (1989). Cardiotoxic effects of the combined use of caffeine and isoproterenol in the minipig. J Toxicol and Environ Health, 26: 425–435.

Whitehurst, V., Joseph, X., Alleva, F. et al. (1994). Enhancement of acute myocardial lesions by asthma drugs in rats. Toxicologic Pathology, 22(1): 72–76.

Wurl, P. (1994). Life-threatening caffeine poisoning by using coffee as a psychoactive drug. Wiener Klinische Wochenschrift, 106(11): 359–361.

Zuskin, E., Duncan, P., and Douglas, J. (1983). Pharmacological characterization of extracts of coffee dusts. Br J Ind Med, 40: 193–198.

2.3 Khat

2.3.1 History

Khat is an evergreen that grows at high altitudes in East Africa and on the Arabian peninsula. Its leaves contain a naturally occurring psychostimulant, closely related in structure to both ephedrine and amphetamine. Khat first came to the notice of Europeans in 1762, when the botanist Peter Forskal found it growing on the mountain slopes in Yemen (Pantelis et al., 1989). The habit of chewing khat leaves is, however, much older. There are historical references as far back as the thirteenth century, when the Arab physician Naguib Ad-Din gave khat leaves to soldiers to relieve fatigue (Giannini et al., 1986). Ad-Din might not have been the first ever to give soldiers psycho-stimulants, but he was certainly one of the earliest to experiment with performance-enhancing drugs. Since Ad-Din's pioneering experiments, the practice has been repeated many times. Aschenbrant gave cocaine to Prussian recruits during the Franco-Prussian war; Japan and the Allies issued amphetamines to their troops during World War II.

In 1852 James Vaughn, an English surgeon, published illustrations along with an account of khat chewing in the *Pharmaceutical Gazette* (Vaughn, 1852). Figure 2.3.1 is from Vaughn's paper. Vaughn speculated that the principal reason for khat's popularity was the fact that, unlike alcohol, its use was not forbidden by the Koran. Khat chewing is usually a social event, sessions often lasting for hours. In some areas of Africa where khat chewing is still popular (the WHO estimates that there are still millions of khat users), houses often have a special room, called a *muffraj*, just for khat chewing. The normal dose consumed at any one time is 100–200 grams of leaves and stems chewed over a 3–4 hour period (Max, 1991). An occasional solitary individual will chew to increase his work capacity. Users describe increased feelings of alertness and an improved ability to concentrate. Use is also said to make people friendlier and improve the flow of ideas (Kennedy et al., 1980). Nonetheless, use of this material conforms to most definitions of addiction. Chewers attempting to secure their daily supply of leaves will do so to the exclusion of all other activities. In Yemen 4% of all arable land is used to grow khat, and in Djibouti, 10% of the country's revenues is derived from

Bundle of *Subbare Kât*   Bundle of *Muktaree Kât*

Figure 2.3.1   Khat leaves. This drawing from 1852 was the first illustration of khat to appear in the English literature. Khat abuse is still a problem in some parts of Africa, where some of the gratuitous violence in areas such as Somalia is attributed to khat abuse. It appeared in the Pharmaceutical Journal (London).

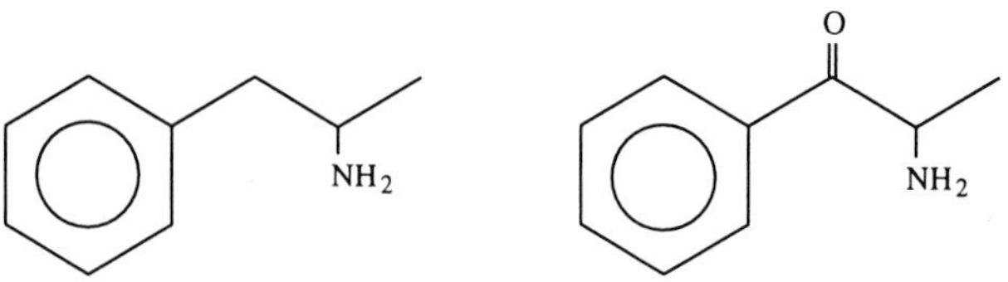

Figure 2.3.2 Cathinone molecule. Many of khat's effects are similar to those produced by amphetamine. The structures of both molecules bear strong resemblances to each other.

taxes on khat (Max, 1991). Anecdotal reports from Somalia suggest that soldiers from warring clans dose themselves liberally with khat before going into combat.

2.3.2 *Chemistry and clinical studies*

Cathinone is (s)-2-Amino-1-phenyl-1-propanone. Its formula is $C_9H_{11}NO$, with a molecular weight of 165.23. It is composed of 72.5% carbon, 7.4% hydrogen, 9.4% nitrogen, and 10.7% oxygen. The hydrochloride crystals ($C_9H_{11}ClNO$) have a melting point of 189–190°C.

If many of the mood alterations induced by khat resemble those produced by amphetamine, it is not by chance. The active ingredient, cathinone, has the same basic configuration as amphetamine. A second active component, cathine, is much less active because its lipid solubility is much lower than cathinone's. With the passage of time, cathinone is rapidly converted to cathine, and the result is a considerable loss of potency. Only fresh leaves have any commercial value, and the fragile nature of the product probably explains why it is not more widely distributed (Giannini, 1986; Critchlow and Siefert, 1987).

Analysis of khat leaves seized in Switzerland showed they contained, on average, 1 mg of cathinone, 0.86 mg of norpseudoephedrine, and 0.47 mg of norephedrine per gram of leaf (Widler et al., 1994). Absorption of cathinone from the leaves is a slow process. When volunteers were given leaf containing a total of 0.8 mg cathinone per kilogram body weight, maximal plasma concentrations (127 ng ± 53 ng/mL) were not reached until more than two hours after the subjects started to chew the leaves (127 minutes). The elimination half-life was on the order of 4.5 hours (206 ± 102 minutes). Peak norephedrine levels were 110 ± 51 ng/mL and 89 ± 49 ng/mL for norpseudoephedrine (Widler et al., 1994).

Urine levels were measured in six volunteers, 2, 4, 6, and 8 hours after taking 0.5 mg/kg of optically pure (S)-(–)cathinone. Resultant levels were from 0.2–3.8 μg/mL for the parent compound, 7.2–46 μg/mL for (R,S)-(–)norephedrine, and 0.5–2.5 μg/L for (R,R)-(–) norpseudoephedrine (Mathys and Brenneisen, 1992). It is not known if the normal antibody-based screening tests for amphetamine would be sufficiently cross-reactive to detect this compound, but it seems unlikely.

Khat chewing produces symptoms consistent with sympathetic activation. There are both positive inotropic and chronotropic effects. Chewing khat causes elevations in blood pressure, temperature, and respiratory rate, with inconsistent effects on heart rate. In isolated heart preparations, cathinone causes increased release of norepinephrine (Wagner, 1982). Khat also causes chronic constipation and reduced milk production in nursing mothers. Most of these effects are transient. There have been reports that in some parts of Saudi Arabia, the only patients seen with oral cancers are those with long histories of khat chewing (Soufi et al., 1991).

Papers in the older literature described cerebral hemorrhage, myocardial ischemia, and pulmonary edema (Halbach, 1972). Animal studies have shown that cathinone releases dopamine and, at very high concentrations, blocks dopamine uptake (Wagner et al., 1982). Rabbits treated daily with 6–10 mg oral doses of khat showed evidence for adrenocortical stimulation, with increased urinary 17-hydroxycorticosteroids and increased plasma free fatty acids (Ahmed and El-Qirbi, 1993). Cathinone has never been evaluated for neurotoxicity in animals and, lacking autopsy information, the situation in humans remains unclear.

Khat's cardiovascular effects appear to be catecholamine-related, but plasma catecholamines have not been measured. Urinary catecholamine excretion is increased after khat chewing. Unlike acute cocaine abuse, where prolactin levels are depressed (see Section 1.10.8 on cocaine's hormonal effects), and in spite of reports of decreased lactation, khat chewing seems not to affect prolactin levels (Nencini et al., 1983). Because the absorption of cathinone from chewed leaves is relatively slow, and because the breakdown of cathinone to cathine is relatively rapid, blood levels tend to plateau, which may explain why episodes of florid toxicity seem to be uncommon (Max, 1991). Like watercress, khat is a member of the celastraceae family, which means that the metacercaiae of *F. hepatica* may grow on the leaves; a recent case report described a woman from London who contracted fascioliasis after chewing imported leaves (Doherty et al., 1995).

Khat rapidly loses its potency, so its use is not widespread, however, air transport is possible and home cultivation is not very difficult. Possession of khat leaves is legal in the United Kingdom, which no doubt explains sporadic reports of khat-associated psychosis in that country. Samples have been confiscated on both coasts of the United States, and importation seems to be increasingly common. Khat's popularity is somewhat surprising, since for all physiologic and pathologic purposes, khat's effects are basically those of amphetamine. Since amphetamine is abundant and inexpensive in the United States, khat is unlikely to become an important drug of abuse any time soon.

References

Ahmed, M. and El-Qirbi, A. (1993). Biochemical effects of *Catha edulis*, cathine and cathinone on adrenocortical functions. J Ethnopharm, 39: 213–216.

Critchlow, S. and Siefert, R. (1987). Khat-induced paranoid psychosis. Br J Psychiat, 150: 247–249.

Giannini, A., Burge, H., Shaheen, J., and Price, W. (1986). Khat: another drug of abuse. J Psychoactive Drugs, 18(2): 155–158.

Group, WHO Advisory (1980). Review of the pharmacology of khat. Bulletin on Narcotics, 31: 83–99.

Halbach, H. (1972). Medical aspects of the chewing of khat leaves. Bull Wld Hlth Org, 47: 21–29.

Kalix, P. and Braenden, O. (1985). Pharmacological aspects of the chewing of khat leaves. Pharm Rev, 37: 149–164.

Kennedy, J., Teague , J., and Fairbanks, L. (1980). Qat use in North Yemen and the problem of addiction: a study in medical anthropology. Culture Med and Psych, 4: 311–344.

Mathys, K. and Brenneisen, R. (1992). Determination of (S)-(–)cathinone and its metabolites (R,S)-K(–)norephedrine and (R,R)-(–)norpseudoephedrine in urine by high-performance liquid chromatography with photodiode-array detection. J Chromatogr, 593: 1–2.

Max, B. (1991). This and that: the ethnopharmacology of simple phenethylamines, and the question of cocaine and the human heart. Trends Pharm Sci, 12: 320–333.

Nencini, P., Anania, A., Ahmed, M. et al. (1983). Physiological and neuroendocrine effects of khat in man. In Proceedings of First International Conference on Khat: Health and socio-economic aspects of khat use. Edited by B. Shahander, R. Geadah, A. Tounge, and J. Rolli. 148–152. Lausanne: International Council on Alcohol and Addictions.

Pantelis, C., Hindler, C., and Taylor, J. (1989). Use and abuse of khat (*Catha edulis*): a review of the distribution, pharmacology, side effects and a description of psychosis attributed to khat chewing. Psychological Med, 19: 657–668.

Soufi, H., Kameswaran, M., and Malatani, T. (1991). Khat and oral cancer. J Laryngol and Otology, 105(8): 643–645.

Vaughn, J. (1852). Notes upon the drugs observed at Aden, Arabia. Pharm J, 268–271.

Wagner, G., Preston, K., Ricaurte, G. et al. (1982). Neurochemical similarities between *d,l.*-cathinone and *d*-amphetamine. Drug Alcohol Depend, 9: 279–284.

Widler, P., Mathys, K., Brenneisehn, R. et al. Pharmacodynamics and pharmacokinetics of khat: a controlled study. Clin Pharm Ther, 55(5):556–562.

2.4   Ephedrine

2.4.1   History

Ephedrine is a naturally occurring stimulant with medically useful properties. Pliny accurately described both the plant and its medical value, but its modern rediscovery is generally attributed to Nagayoshi Nagi, a German-trained, Japanese-born chemist, who first isolated and synthesized ephedrine in 1885 (Holmstedt, 1991). Nagi's original observations were confirmed by Merck chemists who thought that the compound might have some commercial value. After some initial enthusiasm, they lost interest and ephedrine was forgotten for many decades. It was rediscovered in 1930 when Chen and Schmidt published a comprehensive paper recommending ephedrine in the treatment of asthma (Chen and Schmidt, 1930). Ephedrine was soon very much in demand.

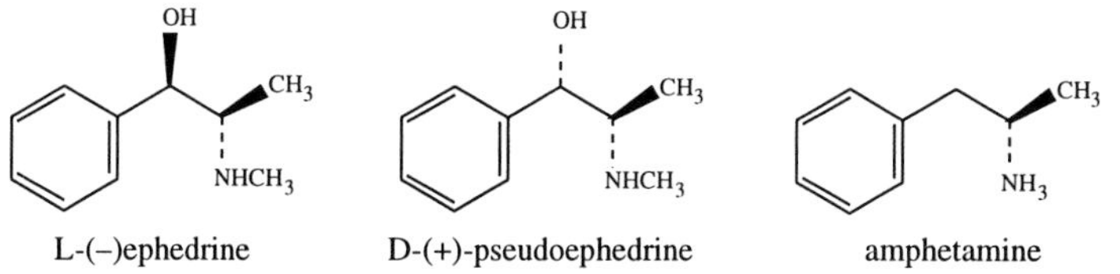

L-(−)ephedrine   D-(+)-pseudoephedrine   amphetamine

Figure 2.4   Ephedrine and pseudoephedrine. Ephedrine's principal importance is as a precursor in the illicit production of methamphetamine; however, ephedrine is a potent stimulant in its own right and has significant abuse potential.

Ephedrine quickly replaced epinephrine, which was the only effective agent available at the time, and it rapidly became the first-line drug against asthma. As it became more popular, concerns arose about its availability. The possibility of an ephedrine shortage fostered research on ways to synthesize it. Amphetamines were created largely as a by-product of those efforts. The anticipated ephedrine shortage never emerged, but ephedrine is still in use today as a component of some asthma and headache medications. Its most important use, however, is not medicinal. Clandestine laboratories use ephedrine as a precursor in the manufacture of methamphetamine, and many states now restrict ephedrine distribution.

Naturally occurring ephedrine is obtained from Ma Huang (*Ephedra vulgaris*), an herb that has been used by Chinese physicians for at least 5,000 years. Fifteenth-century Chinese texts recommend it as an antipyretic and antitussive, and it was used in Russia to treat arthritic symptoms. Indians and Spaniards in the Southwest used it to treat venereal diseases (Grinspoon and Hedblom, 1975). *Ephedra* species are found around the world, but the ephedrine content may vary quite considerably. Herbal teas are still brewed from it and have been referred to by a variety of names including teamsters' tea, Mormon tea, and chaparral tea (Max, 1991).

When compared to other stimulants, ephedrine has relatively greater peripheral effects and, in theory, less ability to produce central stimulation. In therapeutic doses, it and its optical isomer, pseudoephedrine, are used as nasal decongestants and bronchodilators chiefly because they are thought to be free of CNS side effects. Ephedrine's CNS-stimulating properties are, nonetheless, quite considerable and it is somewhat surprising that it is not more widely abused (Martin et al., 1971). Ephedrine injections, called *Philopon* (which means love of work) were given to Japanese *Kamikaze* pilots during World War II. A major epidemic of ephedrine abuse occured in postwar Japan. Abusers injected themselves with ephedrine, then called *hirapon*, in much the same way that methamphetamine is injected today (Deverall, 1954). Filipinos have, for many years, smoked a mixture of ephedrine and caffeine called "Shabu." In the late 1980s, Shabu smoking gave way to the practice of smoking methamphetamine ("ice"). In what is perhaps a tribute to the past, some "ice" is sold under the *hiropon* brand name. Today ephedrine is widely used for the prophylaxis and treatment of hypotension caused by spinal anesthesia (Flordal and Svensson, 1992).

2.4.2   Chemistry and metabolism

Ephedrine is α-[1-(Methylamino)ethyl]benzene-methanol. Its formula is $C_{10}H_{15}NO$, with a molecular weight of 165.23. It is composed of 72.7% carbon, 9.2% hydrogen, 8.5% nitrogen, and 9.7% oxygen. Isomeric forms include (±)ephedrine and (±)pseudoephedrine. The two naturally occurring isomers are (–)ephedrine and (+)pseudoephedrine. Racemic (±) ephedrine forms whitish crystals with a melting point of 79°C. Both ephedrine and pseudoephedrine are weak bases, with pK_a's of 9.6 and 9.4, respectively. Both agents share properties with cocaine and with the amphetamines because they: (1) stimulate β receptors directly, and (2) also cause the increased release of norepinephrine. As a result, both drugs have β1 and β2 activity. The number of β receptors on human lymphocytes decreases rapidly after the administration of ephedrine. The density of binding sites drops to 50% of normal after 8 days of treatment, which may explain why there is a gradual loss of bronchodilator efficacy when ephedrine is taken chronically. Receptor density returns to normal five to seven days after the drug has been withdrawn (Neve and Molinoff, 1986). The down-regulation of receptors that occurs with ephedrine use is in marked contrast to cocaine, where chronic exposure appears not to affect receptor density at all (Costard-Jackle et al., 1989). Blood and tissue levels of ephedrine are poorly characterized. Most of a given dose is excreted unchanged in the urine, where it can be detected by a number of tests.

The International Olympic Committee, while not entirely banning ephedrine consumption, has ruled that urine levels of over 500 ng/mL indicate abuse and are grounds for disqualification. Unlike amphetamines, acidification of the urine has no effect on ephedrine excretion (Beckett and Wilkinson, 1965). Ephedrine's elimination half-life is nearly 6 hours (Welling et al., 1971). The 500 ng/mL level set by the IOC is probably unrealistically low. In a recent study healthy volunteers, given realistic doses of ephedrine-containing nasal spray (roughly 14 mg), were found to have urine levels ranging from 0.09 to 1.65 µg/mL (Lefebvre et al., 1992).

2.4.3   Clinical studies

Studies of absorption and distribution are somewhat limited, especially considering the frequency with which this drug is prescribed. In one study, 50 mg of ephedrine given orally to six healthy, 21-year old women, produced mean peak plasma concentrations of 168 ng/ml, 127 minutes after ingestion, with a half-life of slightly more than 9 hours (Vanakoski et al., 1993). The results are comparable to those obtained in studies done nearly 30 years earlier (Wilkinson and Beckett, 1968). The degree of performance improvement associated with ephedrine ingestion has never been established, but its use has been prohibited by the IOC, and a host of analytic methods have been developed for detecting ephedrine, and its principal metabolite norephedrine, in the urine (Chicharro et al., 1993).

Ephedrine is frequently used in obstetric and urologic surgery, chiefly to combat the transient hypotension associated with epidural and spinal anesthetics. Complications from ephedrine use are decidedly rare, although there is some evidence that, in clinically relevant dosages, ephedrine impairs primary hemostasis, probably because of its interactions with platelet $\alpha2$ receptor, ephedrine may substantially prolong bleeding times (Flordal and Svensson, 1992).

The most frequently reported complications of ephedrine abuse are behavioral. Episodes of ephedrine-induced psychosis have been observed with some regularity (Herridge and Brook, 1968; Roxanas and Spalding, 1977; Otto and Nause, 1980) but other sorts of medical complications are rare. There have been scattered reports of pseudoephedrine-associated hypertension (Mariani, 1986), coronary artery spasm (Weiner et al., 1990), cardiomyopathy (To et al., 1980), and intracranial hemorrhage in association with ephedrine and pseudoephedrine overdose (Rutstein, 1963; Loizou et al., 1982; Wooten et al., 1983; Nadeau, 1984; Stoessl et al., 1985; Bruno et al., 1993), but the incidence seems to be much lower than with other agents such as phenylpropanolamine. There are no reported autopsy studies. Baselt and Cravey mention the case of a young woman who died several hours after ingesting 2.1 grams of ephedrine combined with 7.0 grams of caffeine, but tissue findings were not described. Her blood ephedrine level was 5 mg/L, while the concentration in the liver was 15 mg/kg (Baselt and Cravey, 1989).

References

Baselt, R. and Cravey, B. *Disposition of toxic drugs and chemicals in man.* 3rd ed. Chicago, London: Year Book Medical Publishers, 1989.

Beckett, A. and Wilkinson, G. (1965). Urinary excretion of (–)-methylephedrine, (–)-ephedrine, and (–)-norephedrine in man. J Pharm Pharmac, 17(Suppl): 107S–108S.

Bruno, A., Nolte, K., and Chapin, J. (1993). Stroke associated with ephedrine use. Neurology, 43(7): 1313–1316.

Chicharro, M., Zapardiel, A., Bermejo, E. et al. (1993). Direct determination of ephedrine and norephedrine in human urine by capillary zone electrophoresis. J Chromato Biomed Appl, 622: 103–108.

Costard-Jäckle, A., Jackle, S., Kates, R., and Fowler, M. (1989). Electrophysiological and biochemical effect of chronic cocaine administration. Circulation, 80(4): II–15.

Deverall, R. (1954). *Red China's dirty drug war. The story of opium, heroin, morphine, and philopon traffic.* 3rd ed. New York: American Federation of Labor.

Flordal, P. and Svensson, J. (1992). Hemostatic effects of ephedrine. Thrombosis Res, 68: 295–302.

Grinspoon, L. and Hedblom, P. (1975). *The speed culture: Amphetamine use and abuse in America.* Cambridge, MA, and London, England: Harvard University Press.

Herridge, C. and Brook, M. (1968). Ephedrine psychosis. Br Med J, 2: 160.

Holmstedt, B. (1991). Historical perspective and future of ethnopharmacology. J Ethnopharm, 32: 7–24.

Lefebvre, R., Surmont, F., Bouckaert, J., and Moerman, E. (1992). Urinary excretion of ephedrine after nasal application in healthy volunteers. J Pharm Pharmacol, 44: 672–675.

Loizou, L., Hamilton, J., and Tsementzis, S. (1982). Intracranial hemorrhage in association with pseudoephedrine overdose. J Neurol Neurosurg and Psychiat, 45: 471–472.

Mariani, P. (1986). Pseudoephedrine-induced hypertensive emergency treatment with labetalol. Am J Emerg Med, 4: 141–142.

Martin, W., Sloan, J., Sapira, J., and Jasinski, D. (1971). Physiologic, subjective and behavioral effects of amphetamine, methamphetamine, ephedrine, phenmetrazine and methylphenidate in man. Clin Pharmacol and Ther, 12: 245–248.

Max, B. (1991). This and that: the ethnopharmacology of simple phenethylamines, and the question of cocaine and the human heart. Trends Pharm Sci, 12: 329–333.

Nadeau, S. (1984). Intracerebral hemorrhage and vasculitis related to ephedrine abuse. Ann Neurol, 15(1): 114–115.

Neve, K. and Molinoff, P. (1986). Effects of chronic administration of agonists and antagonists on the density of β-adrenergic receptors. Am J Cardiol, 57: 17F–22F.

Otto, K. and Nause, R. (1980). Paranoid hallucinatory psychosis following chronic asthmolytan abuse. Psychiatrie, Neurologie Medizinische Psychologie, 32(8): 492–495.

Roxanas, M. and Spalding, J. (1977). Ephedrine abuse psychosis. Med J Aust, 2: 639–640.

Rutstein, H. (1963). Ingestion of pseudoephedrine. Hypertension and unconsciousness following: report of a case. Arch Otolaryngol, 77: 145–147.

Stoessl, A., Young, G., and Feasby, T. (1985). Intracerebral hemorrhage and angiographic beading following ingestion of catecholaminergics. Stroke, 16: 734–736.

To, L., Sangste, R. J., Rampling, D. et al. (1980). Ephedrine-induced cardiomyopathy. Med J Aust, 2: 35–36.

Vanakoski, J., Strömberg, C., and Sepppälä, T. (1993). Effects of a sauna on the pharmacokinetics and pharmacodynamics of midazolam and ephedrine on healthy young women. Eur J Clin Pharmacol, 45: 377–381.

Weiner, I., Tilkian, A., and Palazzolo, M. (1990). Coronary artery spasm and myocardial infarction in a patient with normal coronary arteries: temporal relationship to pseudoephedrine ingestion. Cath and Cardiovas Diag, 20: 51–53.

Welling, P., Lee, K., Patel, J. et al. (1971). Urinary excretion of ephedrine in man without pH control following oral administration of three commercial ephedrine sulfate preparations. J Pharm Sci, 60: 1629–1634.

Wilkinson, G. and Beckett, A. (1968). Absorption, metabolism and excretion of the ephedrine in man. II. J Pharm Sci, 57: 1933–1938.

Wooten, M., Khangure, M., and Murphy, M. (1983). Intracerebral hemorrhage and vasculitis related to ephedrine abuse. Ann Neurol, 13: 337–340.

chapter three

Synthetic stimulants

3.1 Amphetamine and methamphetamine

3.1.1 History

During the 1930s, there were concerns that the supply of naturally occurring ephedrine might not be sufficient to meet the needs of asthma sufferers. Several laboratories set out to synthesize ephedrine. A graduate student at UCLA, Gordon Alles, was assigned the task of synthesizing ephedrine as his thesis project. Alles reviewed the older literature and discovered research by Edeleano, who had synthesized and characterized the basic properties of the phenylisopropylamine molecule in 1887. Alles took the phenylisopropylamine molecule as a starting point, and from it tried to synthesize ephedrine. Alles was not able to synthesize ephedrine, but he did discover that phenylisopropylamine, later called dextroamphetamine, had novel stimulant properties. He gave samples to laboratory animals, and when he saw little evidence of toxicity, he tried it on himself. Amphetamine's mood-altering properties quickly became apparent. At an even earlier date, a Japanese chemist named Ogata had also started working on the same problem. Ogata synthesized a different amphetamine. He called the result d-phenyl-isopropylmethylamine hydrochloride, later known as methamphetamine. Ephedrine was finally synthesized by Emde in 1929, but the anticipated ephedrine shortage never occurred.

Ogata licensed his method of producing methamphetamine to the Burroughs Wellcome Company, which sold methamphetamine in the United States under the brand name Methedrine®, until it was taken off the market in 1968. In 1932, Smith, Kline and French marketed a nasal inhaler containing Benzedrine®, their patent name for racemic β-phenylisopropylamine (dl-amphetamine). The inhaler effectively relieved nasal congestion, but shortly after its introduction it became apparent that Benzedrine® also relieved drowsiness and fatigue. Exaggerated claims by both drug manufacturers and the popular press led to widespread interest and rampant amphetamine abuse.

The medical community responded to the introduction of amphetamine in almost exactly the same way it had responded to the introduction of

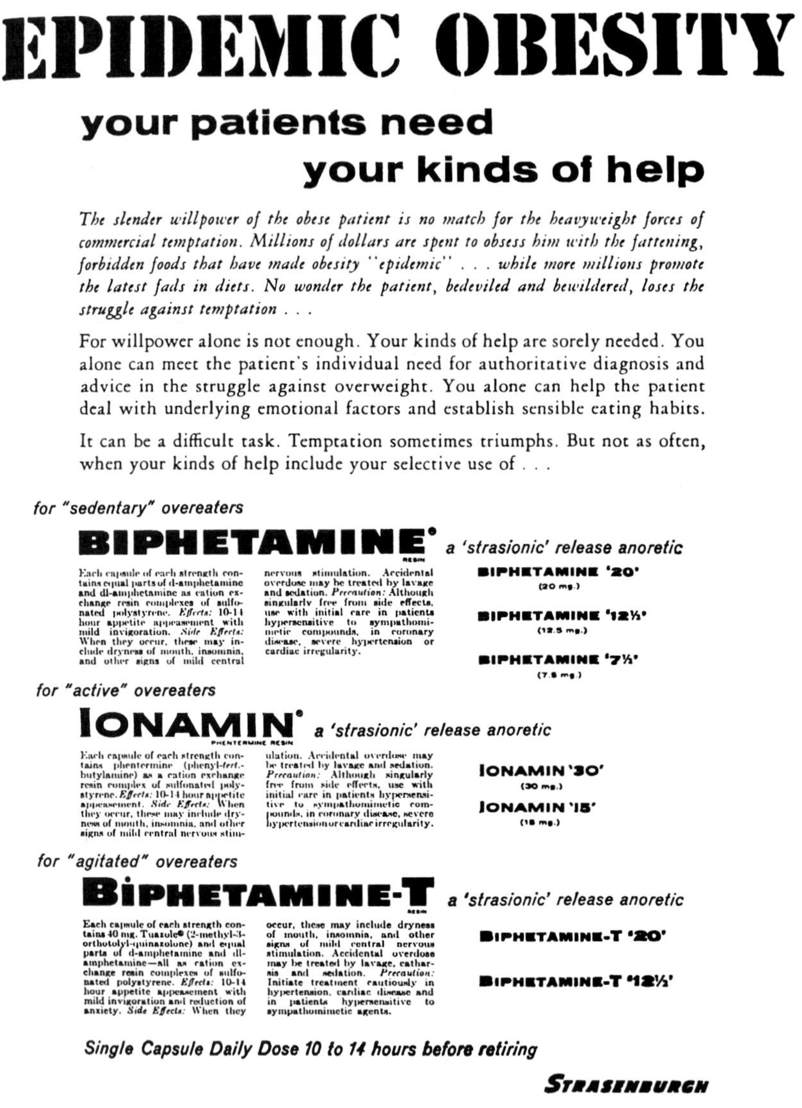

Figure 3.1　Medical use of amphetamine. For many years amphetamine was promoted as a treatment for obesity. When first introduced to the market, amphetamine was claimed to be something of a wonder drug. The same claims were made for amphetamine as were made for cocaine when it was first introduced. This advertisement was published in a 1961 issue of JAMA.

cocaine 50 years earlier. Amphetamines were recommended for the same assortment of unrelated conditions that had been treated with cocaine at the turn of the century. Given what is known today, some of the earlier recommended uses for the amphetamines appear bizarre. At one point, amphetamine was recommended as a "valuable adjunct" in the treatment of seizures and schizophrenia. Bearing in mind that amphetamine-induced psychosis is thought, by some, to be a useful model for the study of schizophrenia, it is difficult to imagine the reactions clinicians of the time were observing! Amphetamines were also said to be useful in treating barbiturate overdose, "caffeine mania," smoking, multiple sclerosis, myasthenia, head injuries, cerebral palsy, migraine, urticaria, seasickness, dysmenorrhea, ureteral colic, obesity, irritable colon, radiation sickness, Ekbom's syndrome, and other seemingly unrelated conditions, including loss of libido (Bett, 1946).

It should not be a surprise then, that amphetamine was also recommended for the treatment of morphine addiction. Freud's disastrous experiments of 1885 apparently had been forgotten by the mid 1940s. Troops of both the Allied and Axis forces during World War II were supplied with amphetamines, which may explain, perhaps, the demand for amphetamine when the war was over. Laws limiting the distribution of amphetamine were enacted during the 1940s, but a regulatory lapse allowed the continued sale of Smith, Kline and French's inhaler. Inside each inhaler were eight folded paper sections impregnated with 250 mg of amphetamine. Abusers opened the inhaler and chewed the papers. Friends mailed the strips to prison inmates, and abuse within the prison system became a problem (Monroe and Drell, 1947). In an escalating battle with would-be abusers, amphetamine manufacturers tried adding denaturants, such as emetine and picric acid to the strips, but abusers found ways to extract the amphetamine, or simply put up with the transient side effects.

Because of all the difficulties associated with their product, Smith, Kline and French reformulated it in 1949 and changed its name to Benzedrex®. The new formulation contained propylhexedrine, also a potent vasoconstrictor, but with only 1/12 the CNS stimulant potency of amphetamine. Smith, Kline and French's patents expired in 1953, and almost immediately Wyeth, Rexall, Squibb, Eli Lilly, and W. S. Merrell entered the market with competing products. Inhaler abuse continued, and in 1959 the amphetamine inhaler was finally classified a prescription item.

The first amphetamine-related deaths were reported within a few years of amphetamine's introduction. The serious complications associated with amphetamine abuse are essentially the same as for cocaine: arrhythmic sudden death, stroke, psychosis, and rhabdomyolysis. There are no controlled studies to confirm the fact, but it appears that psychotic behavior is more common among amphetamine users than among cocaine users. Based on the number of case reports, cardiomyopathy also seems to be more common than in cocaine users, while myocardial infarction is a less common event.

Most of these case reports are in the older literature, and mentions of toxicity were uncommon during the 1980s. Today, amphetamine abuse is a relatively minor problem compared to cocaine. Amphetamines accounted for less than 1% of drug-related emergency room visits, and less than 2% of drug-related deaths reported in the DAWN survey for 1990. Cocaine, on the other hand, accounted for 22% of emergency room visits and 43% of the deaths (National Institute on Drug Abuse, 1992).

With the appearance of smokable "ice," a pure form of (+)methamphet-amine hydrochloride, case reports of toxicity began reappearing. Metham-phetamine becomes "ice" when it crystallizes out of a saturated solution. Depending on how methamphetamine is prepared (there are a number of possible ways), solvent is captured within the structure of the crystals. The type of solvent is a clue to which processes were used in the manufacture, and may also suggest where the illicit drug was made. The volatility of the solvent in which the methamphetamine is dissolved determines how large the resultant crystals will be. With very volatile solvents, like freon, crystal-lization is rapid and only very small crystals form. With less volatile solvents, such as methanol, larger crystals are produced. No matter the size of the crystals, they are all equally smokable.

The first illicit "ice" labs were in Japan. The Japanese have referred to this particular form of methamphetamine by a number of different names, including Kaksonjae, Hanyak, Batu, and Hiropon. There is some irony in the use of the name Hiropon, since that was the name used for ephedrine during the epidemic of ephedrine abuse that swept Japan during the early 1950s. Large scale "ice" production began in the early 1980s. Enforcement efforts by police convinced the illegal chemists to transfer their operations out of Japan to Korea. To this day, Korea remains the principal manufacturer of "ice." At first, the market for this form of amphetamine was confined to Taiwan, Japan, and the Philippine Islands. Japanese and Korean abusers took it intravenously, but the Filipinos began smoking it. The Filipinos were already used to smoking stimulants, having smoked Shabu (a mixture of ephedrine and caffeine) for years; thus, "ice" became immensely popular.

Demand within the Filipino community was responsible for the intro-duction of "ice" into Hawaii. In the late 1980s, Korean chemists emigrated and established illicit laboratories in Portland, Oregon, and Los Angeles, California. Most of their production was shipped back to the Philippines. In 1988, there were sporadic seizures of "ice" across the U.S. No labs were seized in 1989. But in 1990, the DEA seized seven in California alone. Impres-sive amounts of "ice" continue to be seized in China and Korea, but not in the United States. No laboratories have been raided in the U.S. for several years.

Anecdotal reports suggest that cocaine users (crack smokers) do not particularly like "ice" because the high isn't as intense as cocaine, and the high lasts too long. Initially there was very little cross-over between cocaine and amphetamine abusers, and no real "ice" epidemic ever occurred; how-ever, methamphetamine, as evidenced by medical examiner experience in a number of cities, began to dramatically increase in mid-1994, and an "ice," or at least a methamphetamine, epidemic may yet materialize.

In addition to "ice," there are other structurally-related compounds such as fenfluramine and phenylpropanolamine which share some common mechanisms of action and toxicity with methamphetamine. A few of these synthetic agents also have a potential for neurotoxicity that does not appear to be associated with methamphetamine use, at least in humans.

Considering the amount of illicit amphetamine produced and consumed in the United States, episodes of toxicity are surprisingly uncommon, with only one methamphetamine-related death for every 10 attributed to cocaine. There is evidence that, among pregnant women, methamphetamine abuse is more common than cocaine, especially in cigarette smokers and in white women (Vega et al., 1993), but reports of pregnancy complications, in mother or child, are uncommon (Catanzarite and Stein, 1995). In 1993, amphetamines, as a group, accounted for 7.7 % of all drug-related deaths reported in the DAWN survey (Substance Abuse and Mental Health Administration, 1995). Of the deaths, 341 were the result of methamphetamine abuse, compared to the 3,566 deaths reported in cocaine abusers.

3.1.2   Illicit manufacture

In 1958, the annual legal production of amphetamine was 75,000 pounds. By 1970, it had risen to over 200,000 pounds, enough to make 10 billion 5-mg tablets (Kaplan, 1985). Consumption today is difficult to gauge. As the indications for amphetamine use became fewer and fewer, and more complications were recognized, legal production fell off. As legal manufacturers pulled out of the market, illegal labs began to fill the void. In 1980, 150 illicit methamphetamine (as opposed to "ice") labs were seized in the United States; by 1989, that number had risen to 650. Since then, the number of clandestine laboratory seizures has dropped steadily, to only 218 in 1993 (National Narcotics Intelligence Consumers Committee, 1994).

During the 1970s the preferred method among "meth cooks" began with phenyl-2-propanone (P2P) as the precursor. When P2P itself became a controlled substance, clandestine chemists were also forced to synthesize it. P2P can be synthesized in a number of ways: the most frequently used approach starts with phenylacetic acid, acetic anhydride, and sodium acetate. P2P is then converted to methamphetamine by reductive amination. Methylamine, aluminum foil, mercuric chloride, diethyl ether, and isopropanol are required. Fairly high yields can be obtained via this synthetic route.

The reaction product is a racemic mixture. Since the (+) form of methamphetamine is five times as potent as the (–) isomer, the potency and yield of the final product can be quite variable. Not only may the potency vary, but an assortment of contaminants may be introduced. Some of the contaminants have strong stimulant properties themselves (Soine, 1986), while others may be quite toxic, possibly more toxic than amphetamine. The declining popularity of this synthetic route, however, has diminished their importance (Van der Ark et al., 1978). Lead poisoning occurs in illicit amphetamine users (Allcott et al., 1987).

Mercury in trace amounts can also be found (Soine, 1989). Some samples containing over 1,300 ppm of mercury have been analyzed, but unlike the cases of lead contamination, mercury-related illnesses have not been reported in amphetamine users. Although some operators continue to use the P2P method, this approach has largely been replaced by the ephedrine reduction process.

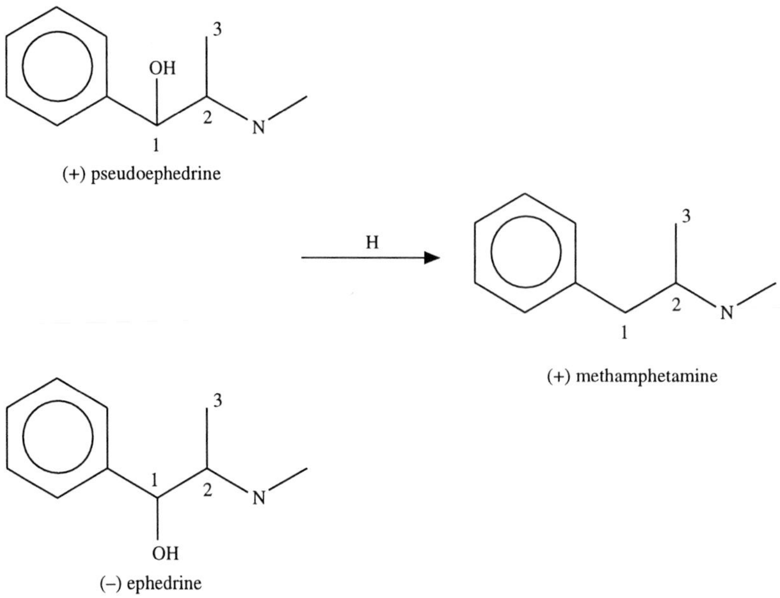

Figure 3.1.2 Making methamphetamine. The most popular formula for making methamphetamine starts with ephedrine and uses red phosphorus as a catalyst. Ephedrine used to be cheap and easily available, but now its sales are controlled.

Either (–)-ephedrine or (+)-pseudoephedrine can be converted to methamphetamine by reductive dehalogenation using red phosphorus as a catalyst. If (–)ephedrine is used as the starting point, the process generates (+)-methamphetamine. Pseudoephedrine also yields dextromethamphetamine. Regardless of the isomer produced, contaminants will be present. As is true with the P2P route, some of these contaminants, particularly 2-(phenylmethyl)phenethylamine, may also be toxic in their own right. Unfortunately, the subject has not been studied in any detail (Soine, 1989).

The increasing popularity of the red phosphorus route has created an increased demand for the necessary chemicals, especially ephedrine. Until the red phosphorus route became popular, ephedrine was a non-prescription item, easily obtained from vitamin and organic food vendors. However, demand is now so great that many states are moving to restrict sales of ephedrine. Ephedrine is now being moved in large quantitites from Mexico. Authorities in California report that, in 1993, they seized over 2.6 metric tons of ephedrine. Strict controls in California now make the purchase of hydroiodic acid difficult. Although it can still be obtained in other states, the price of hydroiodic acid has risen to nearly $600 per gallon. At the same time, sales of iodine crystals have soared. One chemical supplier reported that sales of iodine crystals rose from 161 pounds in 1992 to almost six tons during the first nine months of 1993 (National Narcotics Intelligence Consumers Committee, 1994)!

3.1.3   Chemistry

Possible chemical designations for methamphetamine include N-α-dimethyl benzenethanamine, *d*-N, α-dimethylphen ethylamine, and *d*-deoxyephedrine. The drug has been sold under many proprietary names (Desoxyn, Hiropon, Isophen, Methedrine, to name a few). Its formula is $C_{10}H_{15}N$, and its molecular weight is 149.2. It is 18.48% carbon, 10.13% hydrogen, and 9.39% nitrogen, with a melting point of 170–175°C. The low melting point permits it to be smoked, regardless of the crystal size (Sekine and Nakahara, 1987). Crystals have a bitter taste and are soluble in water, alcohol, chloroform, and freon. Methamphetamine is not soluble in ether. Manipulation of the amphetamine's phenyl ring yields fenfluramine, a widely prescribed anorectic. Manipulation of the side chain has led to the synthesis of a series of compounds with varying degrees of sympathomimetic activity.

3.1.4   Routes of administration

Methamphetamine can be swallowed, injected, smoked, or "snorted." In spite of the publicity accorded to "ice" smoking, most users still prefer to inject it intravenously or take it orally. Preference for the intravenous route seems to be increasing (Hall and Hando, 1993). In one study, 10 mg orally produced 30 ng/mL levels one hour later (Lebish et al., 1970), while in a second study, 10 subjects given 12.5 mg found peak levels of 20 ng/mL at two hours, decreasing to 10 ng/mL at 24 hours (Driscol et al., 1971). Similar studies on amphetamine produced comparable results, at least in terms of resultant blood levels.

The pharmacokinetics of smoked and intravenously injected methamphetamine have been compared in male volunteers who acted as their own controls. The average dose smoked was 21.8 mg (bioavailability was >90%). The dose injected intravenously was 15.5 mg. The mean plasma half-life was 11.1 hours for the smoked methamphetamine and 12.2 hours when the drug was injected. Peak methamphetamine blood levels after smoking and injecting were comparable, ranging from 50–100 ng/mL. Amphetamine concentrations were much lower, reaching peak values of only 4 ng/mL after 3.3 hours. Methamphetmine levels in saliva were very high after smoking, but saliva amphetamine levels were negligible (Cook et al., 1993). In other studies, larger doses of amphetamine have been given intravenously, but with comparable results. Volunteers given 160–200 mg of amphetamine intravenously had one-hour plasma concentration of 269 ± ng/mL (Änggård et al., 1970). In seven patients with evidence of amphetamine toxicity, blood levels ranged from 105 ng/mL–560 ng/mL (Lebish et al., 1970).

3.1.5   Metabolism

Methamphetamine has a long half-life, between 11 and 12 hours. It is cleared from the blood by multiple routes. Roughly 20% is N-demethylated to form amphetamine and ephedrine derivatives which are also psychoactive (Cald-well et al., 1972; Cho and Wright, 1978). These compounds are further metab-olized by a combination of deamination, hydroxylation, and conjugation. Demethylation to amphetamine has evidentiary significance. Only minute amounts of (–)-methamphetamine are converted in this fashion, and other related compounds such as ephedrine are not converted at all. Accordingly, the presence of amphetamine in methamphetamine-containing specimens is confirmatory evidence that the restricted, psychoactive drug, methamphet-amine is being detected, and not some harmless analog. Current National Institute on Drug Abuse regulations (NIDA) prohibit the reporting of meth-amphetamine in a urine specimen unless: (1) the methamphetamine level is over 500 ng/mL, and (2) there is more than 200 ng/mL of amphetamine present.

Over a period of several days, 35–45% of a given dose of methamphet-amine will appear unchanged in the urine (Cook et al., 1993). If the urine is acidic, that amount may increase to over 75%. On the other hand, when the urine is extremely alkaline the amount excreted unchanged may drop to as low as 2% (Beckett and Rowland, 1965). C14 tracer studies done on two volunteers disclosed that 23% of a given dose appeared in the urine within the first 24 hours. Other metabolites also appear in substantial quantities, including 4-hydroxymethamphetamine norephedrine, and 4-hydrox-ynorephedrine (Caldwell et al., 1972). The (+) isomer of amphetamine is metabolized more rapidly than the (–) isomer. If the urine is acidic, the difference is not of much consequence because the major route of elimination is renal excretion.

Daily oral dosing with methamphetamine appears to have little effect on either metabolism or peak blood levels. When a group of six volunteers was given 10 mg of methamphetamine/day for two weeks, there was no evidence for any change in the rate of metabolism, or in peak blood levels, which remained between 25–50 ng/mL. Interestingly, saliva concentrations were much higher than concentrations measured in plasma, with an average saliva to plasma ratio of 7:8 (Cook et al., 1992). Other studies have shown that both the *d* and *l* forms of amphetamine appear in the saliva in concen-trations that are 2–3 times higher than those measured in plasma. Detectable levels remain present for at least 48 hours (Wan et al., 1978). Although methamphetamine appears in saliva, its presence is unpredictable. In a dif-ferent study of 25 methamphetamine abusers, methamphetamine was found in the hair of 73%, in the nails of 65%, in the sweat of 50%, but in the saliva of only 16% of the participants (Suzuki et al., 1989).

Evidently, the general public is quite unaware of the fact that acidifica-tion of the urine hastens methamphetamine excretion. The underground press recommends drinking vinegar as a way to foil urine drug testing. Obviously, acidifying the urine will increase the probability of being caught. If the urine is alkaline, the difference in metabolic rate between the two assumes significance, because the (+) form is cleared about five hours more rapidly than the (–) isomer (17 hours vs. 12.7 hours) (Wan et al., 1978). Concomitant alcohol consumption appears to have relatively minor effects

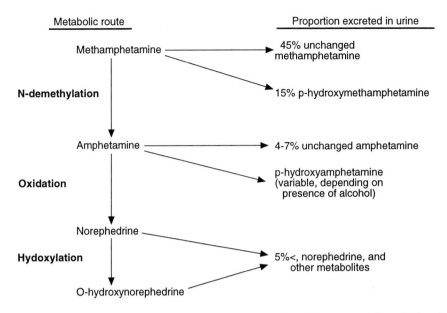

| Metabolic route | Proportion excreted in urine |

Methamphetamine → 45% unchanged methamphetamine

N-demethylation → 15% p-hydroxymethamphetamine

Amphetamine → 4-7% unchanged amphetamine

Oxidation → p-hydroxyamphetamine (variable, depending on presence of alcohol)

Norephedrine

Hydoxylation → 5%<, norephedrine, and other metabolites

O-hydroxynorephedrine

Figure 3.1.5.1 Methamphetamine metabolism. Methamphetamine is demethylated to produce amphetamine. Ephedrine and other analogs are not converted to amphetamine. Thus the presence of amphetamine in a sample containing methamphetamine is proof that methamphetamine, and not some harmlesss analog, was taken.

on methamphetamine pharmacokinetics, although simultaneous consumption of both drugs seems to produce a more intense high than either drug alone (Mendelson et al., 1995).

The metabolism of the amphetamine analogs varies considerably. After methamphetamine and amphetamine, the analog most likely to be encoun-

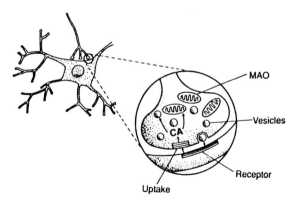

Figure 3.1.5.2 Effects of amphetamine on nerve endings. The effects of amphetamine on catecholamine metabolism are more complex than those of cocaine. In addition to blocking reuptake, amphetamine also causes increased release of neurotransmitters. Courtesy of Dr. Arthur K. Cho, Department of Pharmacology, UCLA School of Medicine.

tered is methylphenidate (Ritalin®). Like the other amphetamines, it is rapidly absorbed after oral administration, reaching peak levels between one and three hours after ingestion (Dayton et al., 1970; Wargin et al., 1983; Volkow et al., 1995). In therapeutic settings, peak levels may be as high as 0.07 mg/L (Gualtieri et al., 1984). Unlike methamphetamine, methylphenidate has a short half-life of only two to four hours. First-pass hydrolysis to ritalinic acid occurs in the intestine, and about 80% of a given dose will appear in the urine as ritalinic acid. The peak plasma levels of both ritalin and ritalinic acid occur at the same time. Methylphenidate competes with cocaine for the same binding sites on the dopamine transporters of the striatum. Unlike cocaine, which is washed out in a matter of minutes, methylphenidate remains localized in the striatum for several hours. This difference is thought by some to explain methylpheniate's lower abuse potential (Volkow et al., 1995).

3.1.6   Tissue disposition

When rabbits were sacrificed one hour after intravenous methamphetamine injection, levels of methamphetamine in the liver were twice as high as levels in the blood. Levels of amphetamine measured at the same time were eight times higher in the liver than in the blood. In the rabbit model, concentrations of both methamphetamine and amphetamine in skeletal muscle were equal to the concentration in the liver (Nagata, 1990).

The results of other animal studies suggest that the disposition kinetics of amphetamine may be stereoselective, with significant differences in pharmacokinetic parameters for *d*- and *l*-forms (Hutchaleelaha et al., 1994). Whether or not the different isomers possess different toxicity in humans is not known. In a Japanese study of methamphetamine-related deaths, some cases were associated with the *l*-form, and others with racemic mixtures (Mori et al., 1992). The metabolic conversion of methamphetamine to amphetamine is stereospecific; *d*- and *l*-methamphetamine are converted to *d*- and *l*-amphetamine, so the mixture of amphetamine forms detected in the urine will simply reflect the mixture of the methamphetamine that was ingested. If *l*-amphetamine is detected in the urine, then *l*-methamphetamine had to have been the compound originally ingested (e.g., the donor was taking Vicks®). The presence of both isomers in the urine proves that the psychoactive *d*-form methamphetamine was taken (Hornbeck and Czarny, 1993; Cooke, 1994).

Methamphetamine concentrates in breast milk. Measurements made in a mother at 10 and 42 days after delivery demonstrated that amphetamine concentrations were much higher in the woman's breast milk than in her plasma (Steiner et al., 1984). There is very little evidence that amphetamine found in mother's milk harms the fetus. One study found evidence for prematurity and lower birth weight (Oro and Dixon, 1987). A number of case reports however, have described women who took methamphetamine, either for narcolepsy, or as abusers, throughout pregnancy and while nursing, but with no apparent ill effects detectable in their children (Briggs et al.,

1975; Milkovich and van denBerg, 1977; Eriksson et al., 1978; Little et al., 1988; Ramin et al., 1992; Joffe and Kasnic, 1994). Nonetheless, at least one methamphetamine-using mother has been convicted of abuse, after being unsuccessfully tried for murder, for administering drugs by breast feeding (Ariango, 1995).

Very little data on the disposition of amphetamines in the fetus is available, though there is now a good experimental model. In pregnant ewes (125 days' gestation is the equivalent of a 34-week human pregnancy), methamphetamine has been shown to quickly cross the placenta, appearing in fetal tissues 2.5 minutes after intravenous injection into the mother. Methamphetamine's half-life in ewes given 1.2 mg/kg is 39 minutes. The peak level in the ewe was 10.2 mg/L and 7.2 mg/L in the fetus. Fetal half-life for methamphetamine was considerably longer than for the mother. Two hours after injection, levels were actually higher in the fetus than in the ewe. In this same study, tissue levels measured at two hours were, in every instance, higher than blood levels. The highest concentrations, both in ewe and fetus, were found in the intestine and lung, while the lowest concentrations were found in the brain and heart (Burchfield et al., 1991). This is exactly the opposite of the pattern observed with cocaine. Other studies using this same model have demonstrated short term increases in catecholamines, with secondary increases in pulse, blood pressure, blood sugar, and insulin levels (Dickinson et al., 1994; Stek et al., 1993). The long-term effects of these changes, if any, have not been studied.

The results of two human studies are consistent with the experimental model. In one case a 24-year old chronic amphetamine abuser delivered a premature, low Apgar score, 2-pound, 7.5-ounce child that expired at four hours. Autopsy findings were consistent with intrauterine anoxia. Both methamphetamine and amphetamine levels were quite low (0.246 μg/g to 0.857 μg/g and 0.030 μg/g to 0.120 μg/g). Methamphetamine concentration was highest in the lungs and lowest in the liver. The concentration in the lungs was nearly three times that in the blood (Garriott and Spruill, 1973). In another case, an amphetamine-abusing mother, who had been using intravenous amphetamine a few hours prior to delivery, gave birth to twins that died one to two hours after birth. The highest levels were in the kidney and liver and the lowest levels were in the blood and brain. Methamphetamine levels ranged from 4.53 mg/kg to 11.0 mg/kg. Amphetamine levels were less than 15% of the methamphetamine levels, ranging from 0.18 mg/kg to 1.40 mg/kg (Bost et al., 1989).

Environmental exposure to abused drugs is an increasing reality, especially in the inner city. Studies have repeatedly shown that, at inner city hospitals, 10%, or more, of children presenting for treatment at hospital emergency rooms are positive for one or more abused drugs (Schutzman et al., 1991). As the ability to detect nanogram quantities of drugs improves, drugs are being detected in more sick children. The mere fact that these drugs are present, however, is not sufficient reason to implicate them as a cause of illness or death in adults or in children. In order to establish death as a result of drug toxicity, there should be some evidence of toxicity! In the case of stimulants, such as methamphetamine and cocaine, evidence may be provided by the presence of infarction, cardiac enlargement, myocardial fibrosis, or contraction band necrosis. Absent all anatomic lesions, it is unreasonable, and certainly misleading, to attribute death to the presence of an abused drug that is present in quantities of only a few nanograms per milliliter.

Tissue level measurements in adult deaths are extremely limited. And, as is the case with almost all of the abused drugs, the phenomenon of tolerance makes tissue and blood levels all but impossible to interpret. Methamphetamine levels in fatal cases have ranged from less than 1 mg/L to over 14 mg/L with associated amphetamine levels that are usually less than one tenth as high (Cravey and Reed, 1970; Kojima et al., 1983; Matoba et al., 1985; Baselt and Cravey, 1989; Yamamoto et al., 1992). In one report describing three methamphetamine-associated deaths with classic anatomic findings (pulmonary edema and severe contraction band necrosis), blood methamphetamine levels were 27,200 ng/mL in one case, 6,430 ng/mL in a second, and 600 ng/mL in a third (Mori et al., 1992).

Detection of methamphetamine in the blood, urine, or liver is not, however, always proof of drug abuse. Selegiline (Eldepryl®, Deprenyl®) is a MAO inhibitor used in the treatment of Parkinsonism. It is a derivative of phenethylamine, and two of its principal metabolites are amphetamine and methamphetamine. Both may accumulate in substantial amounts in patients receiving anti-Parkinson therapy. In such cases, the clinical history will be necessary to make the correct diagnosis. Data on the tissue disposition of the amphetamine analogs is also sparse. A woman who died after injecting 40 mg of methylphenidate intravenously had a blood concentration of 2.8 mg/L (Levine et al., 1986). In that same case the concentration in the liver was 2.1 mg/kg, while the bile contained 5.7 mg/L and the kidneys 3.0 mg/kg. There is little accumulation of methylphenidate in the body. The blood level of a woman who died during a caesarean section, and who had presumably not had any drug for a number of hours, was only 9ng/mL (Lundquest et al., 1987).

3.1.7 Interpreting amphetamine levels

Methamphetamine levels are difficult, if not impossible, to interpret, and therefore of little clinical value. Long-term methamphetamine use sets in train a complicated series of interactions affecting both blood levels and behavioral responses. As is true in cases of cocaine abuse, death may be associated with very low or very high levels. Unlike alcohol, but like cocaine, blood levels do not correlate well with impairment. Since tolerance occurs, very high levels (>5000 ng/mL) should not be surprising (Von Hoof et al., 1974; Kojima et al., 1983; Kojima et al., 1984; Zalis and Parmley, 1963; Cravey and Reed, 1970; Orrenius and Maehly, 1970). Were it not for the problems associated with tolerance, it seems likely that blood levels would parallel those associated with cocaine toxicity. In the past it was thought that cocaine levels in the range of 5 mg/L were uniformly fatal.

With more experience, it has become clear that levels many times higher may be observed as incidental findings at autopsy. Since the degree of tolerance for any drug is impossible to determine at autopsy, attributing any significance to isolated levels is unwise. Low levels, sometimes thought to be incidental findings in association with traumatic deaths, are also hard to interpret. In most methamphetamine-related deaths, blood levels are 5000–10,000 ng/mL, or even higher. Nonetheless, levels of less than 1000 ng/mL have been observed in patients dying from what could only be described as classic stimulant toxicity, with agitation, hypertension, tachycardia, and hyperthermia (Fukunaga et al., 1987b).

The results of animal studies suggest that, over the long term, methamphetamine and amphetamine are stable in most tissues, no matter the degree of environmental exposure. Nagata found that the concentrations of both drugs in whole blood, liver, and skeletal muscle were nearly unchanged after two years of storage in sealed tubes, and only decreased by half in samples of bone exposed to the air over a two year period. The amphetamine content of marrow submerged in tap water for two years hardly decreased from baseline. Levels in blood and urine stains did decrease significantly with storage, but not to below detectable levels (Nagata, 1990).

In the short term, however, the situation is much different. At autopsy, levels measured in left heart blood are 1.9–2.6 times higher than levels measured in right heart blood, and levels in samples collected from other sites may differ by even more. Diffusion of methamphetamine out of lung tissue into the pulmonary circulation occurs more rapidly than diffusion from the liver into the vena cava. As a consequence, methamphetamine concentration in blood from the pulmonary artery may be many times higher than blood collected from either side of the heart. On the other hand, the ratio of methamphetamine to amphetamine appears to be the same regardless of where the specimen is obtained (Miyazaki et al., 1993).

In NIDA regulated testing programs, a urine screening test is not considered to be positive for amphetamine unless immunologic screening tests demonstrate that the specimen contains amphetamine or methamphetamine in concentrations of 1,000 ng/mL or more, and subsequent GC/MS analysis shows a concentration of at least 500 ng/mL. First-generation amphetamine screening tests often cross-reacted with compounds such as ephedrine, phenylpropanolamine (Olsen et al., 1992; Merrigan et al., 1993), and diet pills such as phenteramine (Wayamine®), phenmetrazine (Preludin®), and fenfluramine (Pondimin®). The Vicks® decongestant inhaler (Poklis et al., 1993) contains the levo-rotatory isomer of methamphetamine. This isomer has minimal CNS activity, but on both screening and confirmatory tests it may be confused with methamphetamine, unless special steps are taken. Newer generation screening tests, such as the EMIT® d.a.u. monoclonal immunoassay, seemed to have solved this particular problem, but not all laboratories use this methodology, and false positive screening tests still can occur.

Agents structurally dissimilar to the amphetamines, such as chlorpromazine and brompheniramine, and agents not so dissimilar, such as doxepin, famprofazone, clobenzorex, and trimethobenzamide, have been noted to cause positive reactions (Colbert, 1994; Tarver, 1994; Yoo et al., 1994). Even though manufacturers do extensive premarketing tests to rule out cross-reactivity of their reagents with other compounds, they are unable to test all of the possible metabolites. For that reason, among others, the results of screening tests can never be accepted without a confirmatory test that utilizes a different technology.

False positives due to the presence of ephedrine have been a perpetual problem. In more than a few NIDA-certified laboratories, specimens containing high levels of ephedrine were incorrectly analyzed as containing methamphetamine (Anon, 1990). As a result, NIDA issued a regulation requiring that, even if GC/MS showed > 500ng/mL of methamphetamine, specimens did not qualify as positive unless amphetamine was also detected in the sample. The reasons for the confusion relate to the analytic process itself. In some instances, contaminants in a derivitizing agent (heptaflurobutyric anhydride, also referred to as HFBA) were responsible for the confusion, while in other cases, the temperature at which samples were injected played a role (Wu et al., 1992; Hornbeck et al., 1993). Whatever the cause for the error, humans do not metabolize ephedrine to amphetamine, so the presence of amphetamine in a specimen is additional proof that methamphetamine, and not ephedrine, was responsible for the positive test result (DHHS, 1990). Considerable care must still be exercised during specimen preparation, because periodate degradation, the process used to rid urine samples of innocent compounds, such as ephedrine and phenylpropanolamine, can generate small amounts of amphetamine. This could be falsely interpreted as confirmatory evidence that the specimen actually came from a methamphetamine abuser (Paul et al., 1994).

False negatives can also occur, usually because the donor of the specimen added an adulterant. In most cases, the presence of an adulterant can be inferred from changes in the specimen (i.e., pH, odor, specific gravity). Metabolites of some legally used drugs can also interfere with the testing process. Aspirin metabolites, for example, can cause falsely low readings with the EMIT® d.a.u. assay (Wagener et al., 1994).

3.1.8   Toxicity by organ system

An important feature of methamphetamine intoxication, fatal or not, is hyperpyrexia. In a 1994 report, half the methamphetamine abusers who required ICU admission were hyperthermic (Chan et al., 1994; Derlet et al., 1989; Katsumata et al., 1993). Hyperthermia in these individuals was usually associated with rhabdomyolysis and renal failure severe enough to produce a fatal outcome. Whether the temperature rise is catecholamine-related, or secondary to some direct effect on brain stem temperature centers, is not entirely clear. Some of these cases had all the same features as those seen in cocaine-associated agitated delirium syndrome, which suggests that the same mechanism is involved in both situations.

3.1.8.1 Cardiovascular

Amphetamine's adverse effects on the heart are well established. For the most part, amphetamine toxicity shares common mechanisms with cocaine toxicity. In both instances, the underlying mechanism seems to be catecholamine excess. There are, however, some differences. Considering the vast numbers of individuals who have taken amphetamines, especially in the past, the reported incidence of cardiac events is lower than with cocaine. More than 50 years have passed since amphetamine became commercially available. There are still fewer cases of amphetamine-associated infarction in the literature than reports of cocaine-related myocardial infarction. On the other hand, cardiomyopathy seems to be a complication of amphetamine abuse more often than cocaine abuse.

Recent advances in molecular biology suggest a possible explanation for the apparent lack of cardiovascular toxicity. The rise in body temperature associated with amphetamine use leads to the increased production of myocardial heat shock proteins (Maulik et al., 1994). It is generally believed that cells produce these proteins in response to stressors such as ischemia and cellular injury (Lindquist, 1986). Animals pretreated with amphetamine are resistant to ischemia (Maulik et al., 1994). If the same set of responses occur in humans, that may well explain why methamphetamine appears to be less cardiotoxic than amphetamine.

Amphetamines, and other phenylisopropylamines, such as pseudoephedrine (Sudafed®), phenylpropanolamine (multiple cold and diet pills) and propylhexedrine (Benzedrex®), have a more complicated mechanism of action than cocaine. Cocaine and the amphetamines both cause norepinephrine to accumulate in the synaptic cleft, secondarily producing elevated levels of norepinephrine in the bloodstream. But, amphetamines exert multiple other effects. Amphetamine is also transported into the presynaptic terminal, where it inhibits monoamine oxidase and prevents further storage of catecholamines within the nerve ending (Cho, 1990). These actions, taken together, lead to increased sympathetic stimulation and increased circulating levels of catecholamines in the periphery (Fukunaga et al., 1987a).

High circulating catecholamine levels are cardiotoxic, regardless of the underlying cause. The very same morphologic alterations produced by amphetamine abuse have been seen in patients with pheochromocytoma (Szakacs and Cannon, 1958) and cocaine abuse (Tazelaar et al., 1987). They can be produced in experimental animals with catecholamine infusions (Rona, 1985). They have also been observed in methamphetamine-related fatalities (Mori et al., 1992). The clinical history in most of these cases is consistent with arrhythmic sudden death. Reports of amphetamine-related sudden death were first published shortly after amphetamine became commercially available. In 1939, the *Journal of the American Medical Association* carried a report describing a student who had collapsed during an examination and could not be resuscitated. He had taken a 10-mg tablet of dextroamphetamine shortly before the examination had begun. The only finding at autopsy was said to be visceral congestion; however, the appearance of the myocardium was not described and postmortem toxicologic determinations were not made (Smith, 1939). Presuming that the individual did die of amphetamine toxicity (and there really is no way to be sure), then the most likely explanation would have been arrhythmia secondary to myocardial fibrosis and scarring.

In Japan, where amphetamine abuse has been a problem since it was first invented, methamphetamine-induced arrhythmic sudden death is a recognized entity. Autopsy studies have shown typical catecholamine injuries in a pattern that is impossible to distinguish from that seen in cocaine abusers with sudden death. Myocardial alterations have included focal subendocardial hemorrhage, usually surrounding areas of myocyte disruption, sometimes with lymphocytic infiltrates (Fukunaga et al., 1987b). Just as in cocaine abusers, interstitial fibrosis can be a prominent finding. Granularity of myocyte fibers and occasional myocyte hypertrophy with disarray have also been seen. Additionally, medial hypertrophy of the arterioles has also been described (Matoba et al., 1985; Fukunaga et al., 1987b). Other proven cases have been associated only with pulmonary and visceral congestion (Cravey and Reed, 1970). The changes were not necessarily associated with very high blood levels.

There is evidence that just about all phenylisopropylamines can cause catecholamine-mediated cardiotoxicity. Phenylpropanolamine given to rats produces a typical pattern of injury indistinguishable from the pattern seen after infusions of isoproterenol or norepinephrine (Pentel et al., 1987). Clinical studies have demonstrated increased creatine kinase MB isoenzyme levels, along with ventricular arrhythmias and repolarization abnormalities in patients taking phenylpropanolamine-containing decongestant and appetite suppressant formulations (Pentel et al., 1982). Propylhexedrine (Benzedrex®) associated sudden deaths, which in the past were fairly common, are frequently accompanied by myocardial fibrosis (Anderson et al., 1979). The histologic changes in propylhexedrine-related deaths are more difficult to interpret than with the other amphetamines. Most of the reported deaths were in intravenous drug abusers with pulmonary granulomas and pulmonary hypertension. Myocardial fibrosis is common in that subpopulation, making the role of stimulant abuse more difficult to access (Kringsholm and Christoffersen, 1987).

Morphologic alterations, similar to those observed in cases of methamphetamine-related sudden death, are reproducible in animal models of amphetamine poisoning. Unanesthetized dogs, given 10 mg/kg of amphetamine, and autopsied 1.5–22 hours later, had subendocardial hemorrhages. In some cases, the hemorrhages were extensive enough to disrupt the conduction system. There was also myocardial fiber necrosis scattered throughout both ventricles, and many of the myocytes appeared eosinophilic and granular. In short, all the features associated with catecholamine toxicity were reproduced. In more extreme cases, hemorrhage into the mitral valve leaflets and in the papillary muscles occurs (Zalis et al., 1967). This pattern of bleeding into the leaflets and papillary muscles can be produced by infusing large amounts of norepinephrine. The connection was first recognized over 30 years ago (Szakacs and Cannon, 1958; Szakacs et al., 1959).

In spite of convincing laboratory evidence of amphetamine induced cardiotoxicity, and the fact that chest pain related to amphetamine ingestion was noted as early as 1936 (Anderson and Scott, 1936), myocardial infarction has only rarely been observed. Infarcts have been reported after "snorting" methamphetamine (Furst et al., 1990; Huang et al., 1993), after intravenous injection (Packe et al., 1990; Lam and Goldschlager, 1988; Carson et al., 1987; Packe, 1990), and after the oral use of various amphetamine analogs, including propylhexedrine (Marsden and Sheldon, 1972), dextrofenfluramine (Evrard et al., 1990), and pseudoephedrine (Wiener, 1990). None of these reports have been accompanied by autopsy studies, but in several cases angiography was performed and was found normal. The absence of fixed lesions in these patients suggests that the infarcts were due to coronary spasm, but the underlying mechanism is not known. Any, or all, of the same factors cited in the case of cocaine-related spasm could also be involved in amphetamine-related spasm.

Stimulant-related cardiomyopathy has occurred in association with amphetamine (Smith et al., 1976; Call et al., 1982; Jacobs, 1989), (+)-methamphetamine (Matoba et al., 1985; Hong et al., 1991), propyl-hexedrine (Croft et al., 1982), and methylphenidate (Stecyk et al., 1985) use. In one case endomyocardial biopsy showed patchy interstitial fibrosis with scattered mononuclear cells (Jacobs, 1989). Another report described a 45-year old female oral amphetamine abuser who died of heart failure. Her heart was enlarged (530 grams) and the coronary arteries were widely patent. Histologic examination revealed widespread interstitial edema with scattered lymphocytic and histocytic infiltrates. There was degeneration of individual fibers and patchy myocardial fibrosis. Electron microscopic studies showed myofilaments with rupture and disarray. The mitochondria contained many large electron-dense granules (Smith et al., 1976). This particular finding is associated with mitochondrial calcium overload, which is the myocytes response to both ischemia and to excessive catecholamine stimulation.

In another case, patchy myocardial fibrosis, without infiltrates, was observed in the heart of a young "ice" smoker who died of an acute posterior wall infarct (Hong et al., 1991). "Reversible" cardiomyopathy has been reported as a complication of both amphetamine and cocaine use (Call et al., 1982; Chokshi et al., 1989; Henzlova et al., 1991; Jacobs, 1989). In all cases, there was acute onset of heart failure associated with decreased cardiac output and increased wedge pressure that eventually resolved with medical therapy. Since the patients survived, the underlying morphologic changes, if any, remain uncharacterized. It should be emphasized that the term "cardiomyopathy" is often misused. The diagnosis should be reserved only for those patients with normal coronary arteries and specific myocyte changes demonstrable on biopsy or autopsy. In practice, the hearts of methamphetamine abusers are generally found to be slightly enlarged, containing areas of fibrosis that may be widespread. The pattern of fibrosis resembles that seen in cocaine users, is perimyocytic in distribution, and usually accompanied by hypertropy in adjacent myocytes.

3.1.8.2   Pulmonary toxicity

Pulmonary congestion may or may not be seen in acute fatalities (Von Hoof et al., 1974; Richards and Stephens, 1973), but the pattern seen in classic narcotic-related deaths has not been reported. The most commonly reported finding in the lung of stimulant abusers is thromboembolic arteriopathy. When drug tablets are crushed and injected intravenously, the insoluble fillers (microcrystalline cellulose, corn starch, or cotton fibers) contained in the tablet become trapped in the pulmonary microvasculature. Small vessels thrombose, and foreign body granulomas form. Eventually, some of the foreign material will work its way into the perivascular spaces, leading to further granuloma formation and more fibrosis (Tomashefski and Hirsch, 1980; Tomashefski et al., 1981). If injections are repeated often enough, there is a net reduction in the size of the pulmonary vascular bed and an increase in pulmonary vascular resistance. At autopsy, organizing and recanalizing thrombi will be seen, along with easily identifiable birefringent material (Rajs et al., 1984). Histologically, this sort of pulmonary hypertension can be distinguished from the much rarer primary variety by the presence of plexiform lesions at branching points of the obstructed small arteries (Pietra and Rütt-ner, 1987; Pietra et al., 1989). This complication seems to be associated more with some abused drugs than with others. In general, heroin abusers are much more prone to thromboembolic arteriopathy than stimulant abusers. Of the commonly abused stimulants, methylphenidate (Ritalin®) is the agent most often associated with pulmonary complications.

Granuloma formation and pulmonary fibrosis have been recognized as complications of methylphenidate abuse for many years (Hahn et al., 1969; Lewman, 1972; Arnett et al., 1976; Waller et al., 1980; Levine et al., 1986). Clinical reports suggest that a newer dosage form of methylphenidate (Ritalin-SA®) is particularly likely to be associated with pulmonary symptoms in intravenous abusers. In one study more than 90% of the patients were found to have abnormalities of pulmonary function (obstructive and restrictive) (Parran and Jasinski, 1991). However, if there is anything unique about the histopathology of methylphenidate abuse, it remains to be identified. Presumably, the deposition of birefringent material contained in the methylphenidate preparations is followed by a granulomatous inflammatory reaction and focal thrombosis (Byers et al., 1975). The situation has never been studied experimentally, and there is nothing to distinguish this finding in an amphetamine abuser from the same alterations seen in opiate addicts.

Intravenously injected methylphenidate, but not other stimulants, can produce obstructive lung disease. Panacinar emphysema, more pronounced in the lower lung fields, has been described in a group of young intravenous methylphenidate Ritalin® abusers who died of severe obstructive lung disease (Sherman et al., 1987; Schmidt et al., 1991). Autopsy findings included variable degrees of vascular involvement by talc granulomas, but no interstitial fibrosis. X-rays of these individuals show a distinctive picture with prominent, or even massive, fibrosis in the upper lobes and with translucence and bullae formation in the lower lobes (Paré et al., 1989). In most respects, the clinical and pathologic findings are the same as those associated with α-1-antitrypsin deficiency, though tests for that disorder are negative. Obstructive lung disease is an uncommon complication of intravenous drug abuse, regardless of the type, and its mechanism remains to be evaluated (Groth et al., 1972; Vevaina et al., 1974; Paré et al., 1989). It is unclear whether the apparent connection with methylphenidate has to do with the drug itself, or with the way it is compounded.

Some of the amphetamine analogs, especially fenfluramine, can cause acute and chronic respiratory failure (Simpson and McKinaly, 1975). In the rat model, respiratory arrest, probably mediated by some central mechanism, precedes terminal cardiac arrhythmias. If fenfluramine's effects are partially blocked with a serotonin antagonist, the animals develop extensive intraalveolar hemorrhages and edema, consistent with the diagnosis of acute pulmonary hypertension (Hunsinger and Wright, 1990). More difficult to explain is the occurrence of pulmonary hypertension in some individuals using therapeutic doses of amphetamine analogs, especially fenfluramine (Douglas et al., 1981; McMurray et al., 1986; Gaul et al., 1982; Pouwels et al., 1990; Bernot et al., 1993), dexfenfluramine (Atanassoff et al., 1992; Roche et al., 1992) and also propylhexedrine, phenformin (Fahlen et al., 1973; Schaiberger et al., 1993), phenmetrazine and methylene-dioxyamphetamine (Simpson and Rumak, 1981; Kendrick et al., 1977). One agent, aminorex fumarate, was removed from the European market in the early 1970s after it was implicated in an outbreak involving 32 cases of progressive pulmonary hypertension. The incidence of the disease so closely followed the sales of the drug that the likelihood of a causal relationship could not be ignored (Follath et al., 1971).

Although the histolgic changes are well characterized, the underlying mechanism is not. All of the drugs suspected of causing primary pulmonary hypertension block the reuptake and/or the metabolism of serotonin, while, at the the same time, causing increased release of serotonin from nerve endings and from platelets. High levels of serotonin cause pulmonary artery contraction in humans (Boe et al., 1980) and also favor proliferation of vascular smooth muscle (Nemecek et al., 1986). Humans with primary pulmonary hypertension have abnormally high circulating levels of serotonin (Hervé et al., 1995), which suggests that pulmonary hypertension in these individuals is a consequence of serotonin toxicity (Bernot et al., 1993).

The principal lesion seen in the aminorex fumarate-related cases, either at autopsy or biopsy, was medial hypertrophy with widening of the arterial media to occupy more than 10% of the vessel's cross sections. In one-third of the cases there was also evidence of eccentric intimal fibrosis with cushion-like thickening of the arterial intima (Pietra and Rüttne, 1987). Such lesions are reminiscent of those produced by Szakacs in his experimental studies of catecholamine toxicity (Szakacs et al., 1959). Similar medial hypertrophy has also been noted in the small coronary arteries of cocaine users, although the pulmonary vessels have not been studied (Majid et al., 1990).

3.1.8.3   *Central nervous system*

Other than the treatment of attention deficit disorder, the only other legitimate use for drugs in this group is appetite suppression. Amphetamine and phentermine are anorectic drugs by virtue of their ability to cause the release and/or prevent the reuptake of noradrenaline and dopamine. Phenylproplanolamine, and its isomer, dexfenfluramine, are active by virtue of their ability to directly stimulate a variety of serotonin receptors (Samanin and Garattini, 1993). Some, if not all, of the "designer" amphetamines are toxic to serotonergic neurons (Ricaurte et al., 1985), at least in animals.

In humans, the most obvious manifestations of toxicity are psychosis and stroke, but when large doses of methamphetamine (10–15 mg/kg) are given to experimental animals, the brain's serotonergic and dopaminergic systems are quickly altered. Tyrosine hydroxylase activity, the rate-limiting enzyme in the synthesis of dopamine and norepinephrine, decreases in a dose-related fashion and so does the brain's content of dopamine and homovanillic acid (Koda and Gibb, 1973; Gibb et al., 1990). These decreases are not uniform. For instance, some studies have shown that while dopamine levels in the caudate nucleus are decreased, levels in the nucleus accumbens actually go up at the same time (Swerdlow et al., 1991). The pattern of injury associated with chronic amphetamine treatment is similar to that seen with methamphetamine, though less severe, and quite different from that associated with phencyclidine (Ellison and Switzer, 1993).

These alterations persist for months after the initial treatment but, in the case of methamphetamine, have never been linked with any demonstrable CNS lesions, either in humans or experimental animals. In 1986, all of the same chemical alterations, except for decreased levels of tyrosine hydroxylase, were demonstrated in animals treated both with MDA (3,4-methylenedioxyamphetamine) and MDMA (3,4 methylenedioxymethylamphetamine) (Stone et al., 1986). More importantly, both MDA and MDMA were shown to cause CNS lesions in experimental animals. Similar lesions have not been demonstrated in humans (Yeh and Desouza, 1991).

In spite of the absence of demonstrable lesions in humans, the results of animal studies suggest that the dopamine depletion resulting from striatal damage may be a factor in some cases of lethal methamphetamine-related hyperthermia (Bowyer et al., 1994). The possibility that methamphetimerelated CNS injuries occur in humans is reinforced by the observation that patients with methamphetamine-related psychosis may remain in that state for months after the drug has been discontinued (Iwanami et al., 1994). Serotonin depletion after treatment with MDMA, or with the synthetic agents such as fenfluramine and dexfenfluramine, is easily demonstrated when experimental animals are given large doses of the drugs (Voelker, 1994), but the effects on humans are still being debated. Millions of overweight people have taken fenfluramine, in both the United States and Europe, with no apparent ill effects.

Amphetamine-related psychotic reactions were recognized very early. The first paper on the subject appeared in 1938 (Young and Scoville, 1938).

A paper published in 1958 reviewed 36 cases from the world's literature and commented on the similarities between the symptoms of amphetamine-induced psychosis and schizophrenia (Connell, 1958). It transpired that large numbers of amphetamine abusers were being admitted to mental hospitals with the mistaken diagnosis of schizophrenia. That amphetamine-related psychosis seems to be more common than psychosis in cocaine abusers may be explained by methamphetamines' affinity for sigma receptors. There is considerable evidence linking the ability to bind sigma receptors and the occurrence of psychosis (Itzhak and Stein, 1990). In animal studies, chronic methamphetamine administration leads to up-regulation of sigma receptors in the substantia nigra, frontal cortex, and cerebellum (Itzhak, 1993). Cultural determinants may have some bearing on the psychiatric manifestations of amphetamine abuse. Methamphetamine psychosis has been responsible for large numbers of psychiatric hospitalizations in Japan (Iwanami, 1994), but disease on a similar scale has never been seen in the United States.

Even without developing psychosis, amphetamine users may be restless, tense, and fearful. Some develop delusions of persecution and ideas of reference. They may have auditory, tactile, and visual hallucinations. Strangely, most are not disoriented and will act appropriately, given their paranoid state. The frequency with which hallucinations are visual, and the relative preservation of orientation in amphetamine users, is believed by some researchers to differentiate amphetamine psychosis from true schizophrenia (Kalant, 1966). Amphetamine toxicity in animals is associated with stereotyped, compulsive behavior such as grooming and pacing. Similar stereotypical behavior may be apparent in intoxicated humans. Generally, all of these symptoms disappear within a day or two of stopping the drug, though depression can be marked for some time afterwards. The syndrome of agitated delirium, known to occur in conjunction with cocaine use, has not been reported in amphetamine abusers but almost certainly occurs. In animals, at least, the behavioral abnormalities can be prevented by prior treatments which deplete dopamine.

Hemorrhagic and ischemic stroke occur in association with smoking (Rothrock et al., 1988), oral ingestion (Poteliakhoff and Roughton, 1956; Delaney and Estes, 1980; Yu et al., 1983), and intravenous injection of methamphetamine (Lukes, 1983; Bostwick, 1981; Caplan et al., 1982; Imanse and Vanneste, 1990; Delaney and Estes, 1980; D'Sousa and Shraberg, 1981; Lessing and Hyman, 1989; Yen et al., 1994; Goplen et al., 1995) although there are still fewer than 50 cases in the world literature. In some of these cases, vasculitis has been present (Yu et al., 1983; Shibata, 1991), while in others there was bleeding from a preexisting arteriovenous malformation (Lukes, 1983). Most of the time, no underlying CNS abnormalities are evident.

There are nearly as many reports of phenylpropanolamine-related stroke as there are cases related to methamphetamine use (Glick et al., 1987; Forman et al., 1989). Propylhexedrine (Benzedrex®) causes brain stem dysfunction when used intravenously (Fornazzai et al., 1986), and intracranial hemorrhage has been described in conjunction with pseudoephedrine overdose (Loizou et al., 1982). Stroke in young women has also been reported in conjunction with long-term use of phentermine (Kokkinos and Levine, 1993).

The mechanism for stroke in these patients is not always clear. There have been no experimental histologic studies and only a handful of reported autopsies (Bostwick, 1981). Amphetamine-related bleeds are more often intracerebral or simultaneously intracerebral and subarachnoid, than pure subarachnoid. Hemorrhage is most often confined to the frontal lobes, though it occasionally involves the basal ganglia. This distribution is in contrast with the pattern seen in hypertensive hemorrhages, which usually involve the basal ganglia and hypothalamus. The pattern is, however, almost exactly the same as that seen in cocaine abuse where the frontal lobes are most often involved.

About one quarter of the patients with intracranial hemorrhage secondary to amphetamine or methamphetamine had subarachnoid hemorrhage, and the appearance of "beading," considered to be angiographic evidence for arterial spasm. Beading has also been observed in association with phenylpropanolamine and norepinephrine-related strokes. This finding has been interpreted as evidence for arterial spasm, but caution is warranted, since beading is a relatively nonspecific finding and can result from subarachnoid hemorrhage itself (Weingarten, 1988).

Necrotizing vasculitis, as a consequence of amphetamine and polydrug abuse, was first described by Citron in 1970 (Citron et al., 1970). The histological appearance in the cases described was identical to that seen in polyarteritis nodosa. Lesions included fibrinoid necrosis of the intima and media with mixed cellular infiltrates. With longer periods of survival, there was intimal proliferation and marked luminal narrowing, especially at the bifurcation of vessels. Characteristically, giant cells were absent and the veins spared. Other reports described involvement of smaller (Stafford et al., 1975), and larger (Bostwick, 1981; Shibata, 1991), vessels. In the case described by Shibata, the smaller vessels were spared, but virtually all of the major vessels were necrotic with destruction of the smooth muscle layer, but with scarring of the elastic layer. No leukocytic infiltration of the vessels was seen. During the last ten years similar reports have been uncommon. A possible explanation for the apparent decline in the number of cases is that the process may have been the result of some contaminants or adulterants introduced during the manufacture of methamphetamine.

The underlying etiology of methamphetamine-related stroke has yet to be elucidated; treatment remains problematic. β blockers and calcium channel blockers appear to ameliorate cocaine toxicity, and there seems to be a general perception that such "anti-adrenergic" measures may be useful in the treatment of methamphetamine toxicity. While that may eventually prove to be the case, the results of some recent studies suggest that treatment with nimodipine raises blood and brain levels of both amphetamine and methamphetamine, and may enhance neuronal damage (Elkins et al., 1993).

3.1.8.4   Renal disease

The first report linking amphetamine ingestion and reversible renal failure was published in 1970 (Ginsberg et al., 1970). Even though cocaine abuse leads to rhabdomyolysis with some frequency, amphetamine-induced myoglobinuric renal failure is rare, with only a dozen cases in the world literature. A host of unrelated insults can lead to rhabdomyolysis, including heat, alcoholism, drug toxicity, hypokalemia, and muscle ischemia. When rhabdomyolysis occurs, myoglobin, potassium, and phosphorus are released into the plasma. The presence of these substances in the plasma sets in train a series of metabolic derangements and fluid shifts. The resultant damage to the kidneys can be indirect, resulting from hypotension and renal ischemia, or direct, as when myoglobin or its decomposition products cause tubular obstruction. Much of the damage may be mediated by free radical formation (Odeh, 1991).

What is not known about amphetamines is just which amphetamine-mediated effect causes the syndrome to occur. The first patient described had a consumptive coagulopathy and hyperpyrexia. Several other patients had been hypotensive and comatose, suggesting that prolonged immobilization played a role (Terada et al., 1988; Scandling and Spital, 1982). Other intravenous users had septic shock and disseminated intravascular coagulation (Kendrick et al., 1977). Even without presuming any direct drug toxicity, hyperthermia could account for a number of the cases. Hyperthermia in amphetamine users has multiple causes. Increased motor activity, even without seizures, can raise body temperature, especially when heat loss from the skin is inhibited because of catecholamine induced vasoconstriction. Altered thermoregulation may also be the result of amphetamines direct actions on the hypothalamic temperature center. The interesting question is: why is the syndrome so much more common in cocaine users than amphetamine abusers? There is no ready answer.

3.1.8.5 *Hepatic disease*

Two of the synthetic analogs, Pemoline® (2-1-amino-5-phenyl-4-oxazolidinone) and Ritalin® (methylphenidate) can cause hepatic damage (Tolman et al., 1973; Patterson, 1984; Goodman, 1972), but this complication is rare. Most reported cases have occurred as a result of legitimate drug treatment. In one review of 100 alleged cases of Pemoline-associated hepatotoxicity, there was sufficient data to analyze in only 43. Based on the results of enzyme measurements, and the findings in one autopsy, the injury pattern is said to be hepatocellular in nature, probably due to an idiosyncratic metabolic reaction (Nehra et al., 1990). In another case, an 11-year old, taking the medication for an attention deficit disorder, developed frank liver failure. Open-liver biopsy demonstrated submassive hepatic necrosis with extensive fibrovascular replacement (Pratt and Dubois, 1990).

Ritalin-associated hepatocellular injuries, unlike those that have been described in Pemoline users, have occurred in intravenous abusers (Mehta et al., 1984; Lundquest et al., 1987). In one instance, liver biopsy demonstrated portal inflammation and hepatocellular disarray in an intravenous abuser who survived a bout of liver failure (Mehta et al., 1984). In a second case, the autopsy findings in a polydrug user who died of amniotic fluid embolus included biventricular hypertrophy and multiple granulomas in the liver and lungs (Lundquest et al., 1987). The autopsy findings in a third polydrug abuser, who injected Ritalin® and Dilaudid®, are consistent with the sequence of events occurring when tablets meant for oral ingestion are repeatedly injected. Pulmonary hypertension is the ultimate outcome, but, because this particular individual had a patent foramen ovale, the elevated pulmonary pressure caused a right-to-left shunt. Talc granulomas were found throughout the body, including the brain and kidneys (Riddick, 1987).

Finally, methamphetamine may enhance the toxicity of other hepatotoxic agents. In experimental models, methamphetamine enhances the toxicity of carbon tetrachloride. The mechanism is thought to involve some, as yet uncharacterized, adrenoreceptor-related mechanism (Roberts et al., 1994).

References

Allcott, J., Barnhart, R., and Mooney, L. (1987). Acute lead poisoning in two users of illicit methamphetamine. JAMA, 258(4): 510–511.

Anderson, E. and Scott, W. (1936). Cardiovascular effects of benzedrine. Lancet, 2: 1461–1462.

Anderson, R., Garza, H., Garriott, J., and DiMaio, V. (1979). Intravenous propyl-hexedrine (Benzedrex®) abuse and sudden death. Am J Med, 67: 15–20.

Änggård, E., Gunne, L., Jönsson, L., and Niklasson, F. (1970). Pharmacokinetic and clinical studies on amphetamine-dependent subjects. Eur J Clin Pharmacol, 3: 3–11.

Anon. (1990). Method disputed as NIDA lab incurs false positives. Clin Chem News, 16: 1.

Ariango, R., Karch, S., Middleberg, R. et al. (1995). Methamphetamine ingestion by a breast-feeding mother and her infant's death: People vs. Henderson. JAMA, 274(3): 215.

Arnett, E., Battle, W., Russo, J. et al. (1976). Intravenous injection of talc-containing drugs intended for oral use — a cause of pulmonary granulomatosis and pulmonary hypertension. Am J Med, 60: 711–718.

Baselt, R. and Cravey, B. (1989). *The disposition of toxic drugs and chemicals in man.* Chicago, London: Year Book Medical Publishers.

Beckett, A. and Rowland, M. (1965). Urinary excretion kinetics of methamphetamine in man. J Pharm Pharmac, 17: 109S–114S.

Bett, W. (1946). Benzedrine sulphate in clinical medicine: a survey of the literature. Postgrad Med J, 22: 205.

Boe, J. (1981). Drug-induced changes of vasomotor tone in isolated human segmental pulmonary arteries. Eur J Resp Dis Suppl, 112: 1–45.

Bost, R., Kemp, P., and Hinlica, V. (1989). Tissue distribution of methamphetamine and amphetamine in premature infants. J Analyt Toxicol, 13: 300–302.

Bostwick, D. (1981). Amphetamine-induced cerebral vasculitis. Hum Pathol, 12: 1031–1033.

Bowyer, J., Davies, D., Schmued, L. et al. (1994). Further studies of the role of hyperthermia in methamphetamine neurotoxicity. J Pharm Exp Ther, 268(3): 1571–1580.

Briggs, G., Samson, J., and Crawford, D. (1975). Lack of abnormalties in a newborn exposed to amphetamine during gestation. Am J Dis Child, 129: 249–250.

Burchfield, D., Lucas, V., Abrams, R. et al. (1991). Disposition and pharmacodynamics of methamphetamine in pregnant sheep. JAMA, 265: 1968–1973.

Byers, J., Soine, J., Fisher, R., and Hutchins, G. (1975). Acute pulmonary alveolitis in narcotics abuse. Arch Pathol, 99: 273–277.

Caldwell, J., Dring, L., and Williams, R. (1972). Metabolism of (C-14) methamphetamine in man, the guinea pig, and the rat. Biochem J, 120: 11–22.

Call, T., Hartneck, J., Dickinson, W. et al. (1982). Acute cardiomyopathy secondary to intravenous amphetamine abuse. Ann Intern Med, 97: 559–560.

Caplan, L., Hier, D., and Banks, G. (1982). Current concepts of cerebrovascular disease-stroke: stroke and drug abuse. Stroke, 13: 869–872.

Carson, P., Oldroyd, K., and Phadke, K. (1987). Myocardial infarction due to amphetamine. Br Med J, 294: 1525–1526.

Catanzarite, V. and Stein, D. (1995). "Crystal" and pregnancy: methamphetamine-associated maternal deaths. West J Med, 162: 454-457.

Chan, P., Chen, J., Lee, M. et al. (1994). Fatal and nonfatal methamphetamine intoxication in the intensive-care unit. Clin Tox, 32(2): 147–155.

Cho, A. and Wright, J. (1978). Minireview: pathways of metabolism of amphetamine and related compounds. Life Sci, 22: 363–372.

Cho, A. (1990). Ice: a new dosage form of an old drug. Science, 249(4969): 631–634.

Chokshi, S., Moore, R., Pandian, N., and Isner, J. (1989). Reversible cardiomyopathy associated with cocaine intoxication. Ann Intern Med, 111: 1039–1040.

Citron, B., Halpern, M., McCarron, M. et al. (1970). Necrotizing angiitis associated with drug abuse. N Engl J Med, 283: 1003–1011.

Colbert, D. (1994). Possible explanation for trimethobenzamide cross-reaction in immunoassays of amphetamine/methamphetamine. Clin Chem, 40(6): 948–949.

Connell, P. (1958). *Amphetamine psychosis.* 1st ed. London: Chapman and Hall.

Cook, C., Jeffcoat, A., Hill, J. et al. (1993). Pharmacokinetics of methamphetamine self-administered to human subjects by smoking S-(+)-methamphetamine hydrochloride. Drug Metab Disp, 21(4): 717–723.

Cook, C., Jeffcoat, R., Sadler, B. et al. (1992). Pharmacokinetics of oral methamphetamine and effects of repeated dosing in humans. Drug Metab Disp, 20(6): 856–861.

Cooke, B. (1994). Chirality of methamphetamine and amphetamine from workplace urine samples. J Analyt Toxicol, 18: 49–51.

Cravey, R. and Reed, D. (1970). Intravenous amphetamine poisoning. Report of three cases. J Forensic Sci Soc, 10: 109–112.

Croft, C., Firth, B., and Hillia, L. (1982). Propylhexedrine-induced left ventricular dysfunction. Ann Intern Med, 97: 560–561.

D'Sousa, T. and Shraberg, D. (1981). Intracranial hemorrhage with amphetamine use. Neurology, 31: 922–923.

Dayton, P., Read, J., and Ong, V. (1970). Physiological disposition of methylphenidate-C-14 in man. Fed Proc, 29: 345.

Delaney, P. and Estes, M. (1980). Intracranial hemorrhage with amphetamine abuse. Neurology, 30: 1125–1128.

Derlet, R., Rice, P., Horowitz, B. et al. (1989). Amphetamine toxicity: experience with 127 cases. J Emerg Med, 7: 157–161.

DHHS/NIDA. (1990) Notice to DHHS/NIDA certified laboratories. December 19. Department of Health and Human Services.

Dickinson, J., Andres, R., and Parisi, V. (1994). The ovine fetal sympathoadrenal response to the maternal administration of methamphetamine. Am J Obstet Gynecol, 170: 1452–1457.

Douglas, J., Munro, J., Kitchin, A. et al. (1981). Pulmonary hypertension and fenfluramine. Br Med J, 283: 881–883.

Driscoll, R., Barr, F., Gragg, B., and Moore, G. (1971). Determination of therapeutic blood levels of methamphetamine and pentobarbital by GC. J Pharm Sci, 60: 1492–1495.

Elkins, K., Gibb, J., Hanson, G. et al. (1993). Effects of nimodopine on the amphetamine- and methamphetamine-induced decrease in tryptophan hydroxylase activity. Euro J Pharm, 250: 395–402.

Ellison, G. and Switzer, R. (1993). Dissimilar patterns of degeneration in brain following four different addictive stimulants. NeuroReport, 5: 17–20.

Eriksson, M., Larson, G., Winbladh, B. et al. (1978). The influence of amphetamine addiction on pregnancy and the newborn infant. Acta Paediatr Scan, 67: 95–99.

Evrard, P., Allaz, A., and Urban, P. (1990). Myocardial infarction associated with the use of dextrofenfluramine. Br Med J, 301(6747): 345.

Fahlen, M., Bergman, H., Helder, G. et al. (1973). Phenformin and pulmonary hypertension. Br Heart J, 35: 824–828.

Follath, F., Burkart, F., and Schweitzer, W. (1971). Drug-induced pulmonary hypertension? Br Med J, 1: 265–266.

Forman, H., Levin, S., Stewart, B. et al. (1989). Cerebral vasculitis and hemorrhage in an adolescent taking diet pills containing phenylpropanolamine: case report and review of literature. Pediatrics, 83(5): 737–741.

Fornazzari, L., Carlen, P., and Kapur, B. (1986). Intravenous abuse of propylhexedrine (Benzedrex®) and the risk of brainstem dysfunction in young adults. Can J Neurol Sci, 13: 337–339.

Fukunaga, T., Mizoi, Y., and Adachi, J. (1987a). Methamphetamine-induced changes of peripheral catecholamineamines: an animal experiment to elucidate the cause of sudden death after methamphetamine abuse. Jpn J Legal Med, 41(4a): 335–341.

Fukunaga, T., Mizoi, Y., Adachi, J., and Tatsuno, Y. (1987b). Methamphetamine concentrations in blood, urine and organs of fatal cases after abuse. Jpn J Legal Med, 41(4b): 328–334.

Furst, S., Fallon, S., Reznik, G., and Shah, P. (1990). Myocardial infarction after inhalation of methamphetamine. N Engl J Med, 323(16): 1147.

Garriott, J. and Spruill, F. (1973). Detection of methamphetamine in a newborn infant. J Forensic Sci, 18: 434–436.

Gaul, G., Blazek, G., Deutsch, E., and Heeger, H. (1982). Ein Fall von chronischer pulmonaler Hypertonie nach Fenfluramineinnahme. Wein Klin Wochenschr, 94: 618–622. (English abstract)

Gibb, J., Johnson, M., and Hanson, G. (1990). Neurochemical basis of neurotoxicity. Neurotoxicology, 11(2): 317–322.

Ginsberg, M., Hertzman, M., and Schmidt-Nowara, W. (1970). Amphetamine intoxication with coagulopathy, hyperthermia, and reversible renal failure. A syndrome resembling heat stroke. Ann Intern Med, 73: 81–85.

Glick, R., Hoying, J., Cerullo, L., and Perlman, S. (1987). Phenylpropanolamine: an over-the-counter drug causing central nervous system vasculitis and intracerebral hemorrhage. Neurosurgery, 20(6): 969–974.

Goodman, C. (1972). Hepatotoxicity due to methylphenidate hydrochloride. NY State J Med, 72: 2339–2340.

Goplen, A., Berg-Johnsen, J., and Dullerud, R. (1995). Fatal cerebral hemorrhage in young amphetamine addicts. Tidsskrift for den Norske Laegeforening, 115(7): 832–834.

Groth, D., Mackay, G., Crable, J., and Cochran, T. (1972). Intravenous injection of talc in a narcotics addict. Arch Pathol, 94: 171–178.

Gualtieri, C., Hicks, R., Patrick, K. et al. (1984). Clinical correlates of methylphenidate blood levels. Ther Drug Monit, 6(4): 379–392.

Hahn, H., Schweid, A., and Beaty, H. (1969). Complications of injecting dissolved methylphenidate tablets. Arch Intern Med 123: 656–659.

Hall, W. and Hando, J. (1993). Illicit amphetamine use as a public health problem in Australia. Med J Aust, 159: 643–644.

Henzlova, M., Smith, S., Prchal, V., and Helmcke, F. (1991). Apparent reversibility of cocaine-induced congestive cardiomyopathy. Am Heart J, 122(2): 577–579.

Herve, P., Launay, J., Scrobohaci, M. et al. (1995). Increased plasma serotonin in primary pulmonary hypertension. Am J Med, 99(3): 249–254.

Hong, R., Matsuyama, E., and Nur, K. (1991). Cardiomyopathy associated with the smoking of crystal methamphetamine. JAMA, 265(9): 1152–1154.

Hornbeck, C., Carrig, J., and Czarny, R. (1993). Detection of a CG/MS artifact peak as methamphetamine. J Analyt Toxicol, 17: 257–263.

Hornbeck, C. and Czarny, R. (1993). Retrospective analysis of some l-methamphetamine/l-amphetamine urine data. J Analyt Toxicol, 17: 23–33.

Hotchkiss, A. and Gibb, J. (1980). Long-term effects of multiple doses of methamphetamine on tryptophan hydroxylase activity in rat brain. J Pharmacol Exp Ther, 214: 257–262.

Huang, C., Wu, D., and Chen, K. (1993). Acute myocardial infarction caused by transnasal inhalation of amphetamine. Jpn Heart J, 34: 815–818.

Hunsinger, R. and Wright, D. (1990). A characterization of the acute cardiopulmonary toxicity of fenfluramine in the rat. Pharm Res, 22(3): 371–378.

Hutchaleelaha, A., Subunktherng, J., Chow, H. et al. (1994). Disposition kinetics of d- and l-amphetamine following intravenous administration of racemic amphetamine to rats. Drug Metab Disp, 22(3): 406–411.

Imanse, J. and Vanneste, J. (1990). Intraventricular hemorrhage following amphetamine abuse. Neurology, 40: 1318–1319.

Itzhak, Y. (1993). Repeated methamphetamine-treatment alters brain gamma receptors. Euro J Pharm, 230: 243–244.

Itzhak, Y. and Stein, I. (1990). Sigma binding sites in the brain: an emerging concept for multiple sites and their relevance for psychiatric disorders. Life Sci, 47: 1073–1073.

Iwanami, A., Sugiyama, A., Kuroki, N. et al. (1994). Patients with methamphetamine psychosis admitted to a psychiatric hospital in Japan. Acta Psychiatr Scand, 89: 428–432.

Jacobs, L. (1989). Reversible dilated cardiomyopathy induced by methamphetamine. Clin Cardiol, 12: 725–727.

Joffe, G. and Kasnic, R. (1994). Medical prescription of dextroamphetamine during pregnancy. J Perinatol, XIV: 301–303.

Kalant, O. J. (1966). *The amphetamines: toxicity and addiction.* Vol. 5. Brookside Monographs, P. Griffen and R. Popham (Eds.). Toronto: Charles C. Thomas.

Katsumata, S., Sato, K., Kashiwade, S. et al. (1993). Sudden death due presumably to internal use of methamphetamine. Forensic Sci Int, 62: 209–215.

Kendrick, W., Hull, A., and Knopchel, J. (1977). Rhabdomyolysis and shock after intravenous amphetamine administration. Ann Int Med, 86: 381–387.

Koda, L. and Gibb, J. (1973). Adrenal and striatal tyrosine hydroxylase activity after methamphetamine. J Pharmacol Exp Ther, 185: 42–48.

Kojima, T., Une, I., and Yashiki, M. (1984). CI-mass fragmentographic analysis of methamphetamine and amphetamine in human autopsy tissues after acute amphetamine poisoning. Forensic Sci Int, 21: 253–258.

Kojima, T., Une, I., Yashiki, M. et al. (1984). A fatal methamphetamine poisoning associated with hyperpyrexia. Forensic Sci Int, 24: 87–93.

Kokkinos, J. and Levine, S. (1993). Possible association of ischemic stroke with phentermine. Stroke, 24: 310–313.

Kringsholm, B. and Christoffersen, P. (1987). Lung and heart pathology in fatal drug addiction. A consecutive autopsy study. Forensic Sci Int, 34: 39–51.

Lam, D. and Goldschlager, N. (1988). Myocardial injury associated with polysubstance abuse. Am Heart J, 115(3): 675–680.

Lebish, P., Finkle, B., and Brackett, J. (1970). Determination of amphetamine, methamphetamine, and related amines in blood and urine by gas chromatography with hydrogen-flame ionization detector. Clin Chem, 16: 195–200.

Lessing, M. and Hyman, N. (1989). Intracranial hemorrhage caused by amphetamine abuse. J Roy Soc Med, 82(12): 766–767.

Levine, B., Caplan, Y., and Kauffman, G. (1986). Fatality resulting from methylphenidate overdose. J Analyt Toxicol, 10(5): 209–210.

Lewman, L. (1972). Fatal pulmonary hypertension from intravenous injection of methylphenidate (Ritalin®) tablets. Hum Pathol, 3: 67–70.

Lindquist, S. (1986). The heat shock response. Annu Rev Biochem, 55: 1151–1191.

Little, B., Snell, L., and Gilstrap, L. (1988). Methamphetamine abuse during pregnancy: outcome and fetal effects. Obstet Gynecol, 72(4): 541–544.

Loizou, L., Hamilton, J., and Tsementzis, S. (1982). Intracranial hemorrhage in association with pseudoephedrine overdose. J Neurol Neurosurg and Psychiat, 45: 471–472.

Lukes, S. (1983). Intracerebral hemorrhage from an arteriovenous malformation after amphetamine injection. Arch Neurol, 40: 60–61.

Lundquest, D., Young, W., and Edland, J. (1987). Maternal death associated with intravenous methylphenidate (Ritalin®) and pentazocine (Talwin®) abuse. J Forensic Sci, 32(3): 798–801.

Majid, P., Patel, B., Kim, H. et al. (1990). An angiographic and histologic study of cocaine-induced chest pain. Am J Cardiol, 65(11): 812–814.

Marsden, P. and Sheldon, J. (1972). Acute poisoning by propylhexedrine. Br Med J, i: 730.

Matoba, R., Onishi, S., and Shikata, I. Cardiac lesions in cases of sudden death in methamphetamine abusers. Heart and Vessels, 1(Suppl. 1, 1985): 298–300.

Maulik, N., Wei, Z., Liu, X. et al. (1994). Improved postischemic ventricular functional recovery by amphetamine is linked with its ability to induce heat shock. Mol Cel Biochem, 137(1): 17–24.

McMurray, J., Bloomfield, P., and Miller, H. (1986). Irreversible pulmonary hypertension after treatment with fenfluramine. Br Med J, 292: 239–240.

Mehta, H., Murray, B., and Loludice, T. (1984). Hepatic dysfunction due to intravenous abuse of methylphenidate hydrochloride. J Clin Gastroenterol, 6: 149–151.

Mendelson, J., Jones, R., Upton, R., and Jacob, P. (1995). Methamphetamine and ethanol interactions in humans. Clin Pharm Ther, 57: 559–568.

Merigan, K., Browning, R., and Kelerman, A. (1993). Doxepin causing false-positive urine test for amphetamine. Ann Emerg Med, 22(8): 1370.

Milkovich, L. and Van Den Berg, B. (1977). Effects of antenatal exposure to anorectic drugs. Am J Obstet Gynecol, 129: 637–642.

Miyazaki, T., Kojima, T., Yashiki, M. et al. (1993). Site dependence of methamphetamine concentrations in blood samples collected from cadavers of people who had been methamphetamine abusers. Am J Forensic Med Pathol, 14(2): 121–124.

Monroe, R. and Drell, H. (1947). Oral use of stimulants obtained from inhalers. JAMA, 135(14): 909–915.

Mori, A., Suzuki, H., and Ishiyama, I. (1992). Three cases of acute methamphetamine intoxication — analysis of optically active methamphetamine. Jpn J Leg Med, 46(4): 266–270.

Nagata, T., Kimura, K., Hara, K., and Kudo, K. (1990). Methamphetamine and amphetamine concentrations in postmortem rabbit tissues. Forensic Sci Int, 48: 39–47.

National Narcotics Intelligence Consumers Committee. (1994). The NICC report 1993: The supply of illicit drugs to the United States.

Nehra, A., Mullick, F., Ishak, K., and Zimmerman, H. (1990). Pemoline-associated hepatic injury. Gastroenterology, 99: 1517–1519.

Odeh, M. (1991). The role of reperfusion-induced injury in the pathogenesis of the crush syndrome. N Engl J Med, 324(20): 1417–1422.

Olsen, K., Gulliksen, M., and Christophersen, A. (1992). Metabolites of chloropromazine and brompheniramine may cause false-positive urine amphetamine results with monoclonal EMIT dau immunoassay. Clin Chem, 38: 611–612.

Oro, A. and Dixon, S. (1987). Perinatal cocaine and methamphetamine exposure; maternal and neonatal correlates. J Pediatr, 111: 571–578.

Orrenius, S. and Maehly, A. (1970). Lethal amphetamine intoxication — a report of three cases. Z Rechtsmed, 67: 184–189.

Packe, G., Garton, M., and Jennings, K. (1990). Acute myocardial infarction caused by intravenous amphetamine abuse. Br Heart J, 64(1): 23–24.

Paré, J., Cote, G., and Fraser, R. (1989). Long-term follow-up of drug abusers with intravenous talcosis. Am Rev Resp Dis, 139(1): 233–241.

Parran, T. and Jasinski, D. (1991). Intravenous methylphenidate abuse — prototype for prescription drug abuse. Arch Intern Med, 151(4): 781–783.

Patterson, J. (1984). Hepatitis associated with pemoline. South Med J, 77(7): 938.

Paul, B., Past, M., McKinley, R. et al. (1994). Amphetamine as an artifact of methamphetamine during periodate degradation of interfering ephedrine, pseudoephedrine, phenylpropanolamine: an improved procedure for accurate quantitation of amphetamines in urine. J Analyt Toxicol, 18: 331–336.

Pentel, P., Jentzen, J., and Sievert, J. (1987). Myocardial necrosis due to intraperitoneal administration of phenylpropanolamine in rats. Fundam Appl Toxicol, 9: 167–172.

Pentel, P., Mikell, F., and Zavoral, S. (1982). Myocardial injury after phenylpropanolamine ingestion. Br Heart J, 47: 51–54.

Pietra, G., Edwards, W., Kay, J. et al. (1989). Histopathology of primary pulmonary hypertension. A qualitative and quantitative study of pulmonary blood vessels from 58 patients in the National Heart, Lung, and Blood Institute, Primary Pulmonary Hypertension Registry. Circulation, 80: 1198–1206.

Pietra, G. and Rüttner, J. (1987). Specificity of pulmonary vascular lesions in primary pulmonary hypertension. Respiration, 52: 81–85.

Poklis, A., Jortani, S., Brown, C. et al. (1993). Response of the Emit II amphetamine/methamphetamine assay to specimens collected following use of Vicks® inhalers. J Analyt Toxicol, 17: 284–292.

Poteliakhoff, A. and Rougton, B. (1956). Two cases of amphetamine poisoning. Br Med J, 7: 26–27.

Pouwels, H., Smeets, J., Cheriex, E., and Wouters, E. (1990) Pulmonary hypertension and fenfluramine. Eur Respir J, 3(5): 606–607.

Pratt, D. and Dubois, R. (1990). Hepatotoxicity due to pemoline (Cylert): a report of two cases. J Ped Gastro and Nutr, 10: 239–242.

Rajs, J., Härm, T., and Ormstad, K. (1984). Postmortem findings of pulmonary lesions of older datum in intravenous drug addicts. Virchows Arch, 402: 405–414.

Ramin, S., Little, B., Trimmer, J. et al. (1992). Methamphetamine use during pregnancy. J Perinat, 14: 307.

Ricaurte, G., Bryan, G., Strauss, L. et al. (1985). Hallucinogenic amphetamines selectively destroy brain serotonin nerve terminals. Science, 229: 986–988.

Richards, H. and Stephens, A. (1973). Sudden death associated with the taking of amphetamines by an asthmatic. Med Sci Law, 13(1): 35–38.

Riddick, L. (1987). Disseminated granulomatosis through a patent foramen ovale in an intravenous drug user with pulmonary hypertension. Am J Forensic Med and Pathol, 8(4): 326–333.

Roberts, S., Harbison, R., and James, R. (1994). Methamphetamine potentiation of carbon tetrachloride hepatotoxicity in mice. J Pharm Exp Ther, 271(2): 1951–1957.

Rona, G. (1985). Catecholamineamine cardiotoxicity. J Mol Cell Cardiol, 17: 291–306.

Rothrock, J., Rubenstein, R., and Lyden, P. (1988). Ischemic stroke associated with methamphetamine inhalation. Neurology, 38: 589–592.

Samanin, R. and Garattini, S. (1993). Neurochemical mechanism of action of anorectic drugs. Pharm Tox, 73(2): 63–68.

Scandling, J. and Spital, A. (1982). Amphetamine-associated myoglobinuric renal failure. South Med J, 75(2): 237–240.

Schaiberger, P., Kennedy, T., Miller, F. et al. (1993). Pulmonary hypertension associated with long-term inhalation of "crank methamphetamine." Chest, 104: 614–616.

Schmidt, R., Glenny, R., Godwin, J. et al. (1991). Panlobular emphysema in young intravenous Ritalin® abusers. Am Rev Respir Dis, 143: 649–656.

Schutzman, D., Frankenfield-Chernicoff, M. et al. (1991). Incidence of intrauterine cocaine exposure in a suburban setting. Pediatrics, 88(4): 825–827.

Sekine, H. and Nakahara, Y. (1987). Abuse of smoking methamphetamine mixed with tobacco: I. Inhalation efficiency and pyrolysis products of methamphetamine. J Forens Sci, 32(5): 1271–1280.

Sherman, C., Hudson, L., and Pierson, D. (1987). Severe precocious emphysema in intravenous methylphenidate (Ritalin) abusers. Chest, 92(6): 1085–1087.

Shibata, S., Mori, K., Sekine, I., and Suyama, H. (1991). Subarachnoid and intracerebral hemorrhage associated with necrotizing angiitis due to methamphetamine abuse, an autopsy case. Neurol Med Chir, 31(Tokyo): 49–52.

Simpson, D. and Rumak, B. (1981). Methylenedioxyamphetamine: clinical description of overdose, death and review of pharmacology. Arch Intern Med, 41: 1507–1509.

Simpson, H. and McKinaly, I. (1975). Poisoning with slow-release fenfluramine. Br Med J, 4: 462–463.

Smith, H., Roche, A., Jagusch, M., and Herdson, P. (1976). Cardiomyopathy associated with amphetamine administration. Am Heart J, 91: 792–797.

Smith, L. (1939). Collapse with death following the use of amphetamine sulfate. JAMA, 113: 1022–1023.

Soine, W. (1986). Clandestine drug synthesis. Med Res Rev, 6: 41–74.

Soine, W. (1989) Contamination of clandestinely prepared drugs with synthetic by-products. In Proceedings of the 50th Annual Scientific Meeting, The Committee on Problems of Drug Dependence, in NIDA Research Monograph 95, L. S. Harris (Ed.). National Institute on Drug Abuse, 44–50.

Stafford, C., Bogdanoff, B., Green, L., and Spector, H. (1975). Mononeuropathy multiplex as a complication of amphetamine angiitis. Neurology, 25: 570–572.

Stecyk, O., Loludice, T., Demeter, S., and Jacobs, J. (1985). Multiple organ failure resulting from intravenous abuse of methylphenidate hydrochloride. Ann Emerg Med, 14(6): 597–599.

Steiner, E., Envill, T., Hallberg, M., and Rane, A. (1984). Amphetamine secretion in breast milk. Euro J Clin Pharm, 27: 123–124.

Stek, A., Fisher, B., Baker, R. et al. (1993). Maternal and fetal cardiovascular responses to methamphetamine in pregnant sheep. Am J Obstet Gynecol, 169(4): 888–896.

Stone, D., Stahl, D., Hanson, G., and Gibb, J. (1986). The effects of 3,4-methylene-dioxymethamphetam (MDMA) and 3,4methylenedioxyamphetamine (MDA) on monoaminergic systems in the rat brain. Eur J Pharmacol, 128: 41–48.

Suzuki, S., Inoue, T., Hori, V. et al. (1989). Analysis of methamphetamine in hair, nail, sweat, and saliva by mass fragmentography. J Analyt Toxicol, 13: 176–178.

Swerdlow, N., Hauger, R., Irwin, M. et al. (1991). Endocrine, immune, and neuro-chemical changes in rats during withdrawal from chronic amphetamine intoxication. Neuropsychopharmacology, 5(1): 23–31.

Szakacs, J. and Cannon, A. (1958). l-Norepinephrine myocarditis. Am J Clin Pathol, 30: 425–434.

Szakacs, J., Dimmette, R., and Cowart, E. (1959). Pathologic implications of the catecholamineamines: epinephrine and norepinephrine. U.S. Armed Forces Med J, 10: 908–925.

Tarver, J. (1994). Amphetamine-positive drug screens from use of Clobenzorex hydrochlorate. J Analyt Toxicol, 18: 183.

Tazelaar, H., Karch, S., Billingham, M., and Stephens, B. (1987). Cocaine and the heart. Hum Pathol, 18: 195–199.

Terada, Y., Shinohara, S., Matui, N., and Ida, T. (1988). Amphetamine-induced myo-globinuric acute renal failure. Jpn J Med, 27: 305–308.

Tolman, K., Freston, J., Berenson, M., and Sannella, J. (1973). Hepatotoxicity due to pemoline: report of two cases. Digestion, 9: 532–539.

Tomashefski, J. and Hirsch, C. (1980). The pulmonary vascular lesions of intravenous drug abuse. Human Pathol, 11: 133–145.

Tomashefski, J., Hirsch, C., and Jolly, P. (1981). Microcrystalline cellulose pulmonary embolism and granulomatosis. Arch Pathol and Lab Med, 105: 89–93.

Van der Ark, A., Verweij, A., and Sinnema, A. (1978). Weakly basic impurities in illicit amphetamine. J Forensic Sci, 23: 693–700.

Vega, W., Kolody, B., Hwang, J., Nobel, A. (1993). Prevalence and magnitude of perinatal substance exposures in California. N Engl J Med, 329: 850–854.

Vevaina, J., Civantos, F., Viamonte, M., and Avery, W. (1974). Emphysema associated with talcum granulomatosis in a drug addict. South Med J, 67: 113–116.

Voelker, R. (1994). Obesity drug renews toxicity debate. JAMA, 272(14): 1087–1088.

Volkow, N., Ding, Y., Fowler, J. et al. (1995). Is methylphenidate like cocaine? Arch Gen Psychiatry, 52: 456–681.

Von Hoof, F., Heyndrickx, A., and Timperman, J. (1974). Report of a human fatality due to amphetamine. Arch Toxicol, 32: 307–312.

Wagener, R., Linder, M., and Valdes, J. (1994). Decreased signal in EMIT assays of drugs of abuse in urine after ingestion of aspirin: potential for false negative results. Clin Chem, 40(4): 608–612.

Waller, B., Brownlee, W., and Roberts, R. (1980). Self-induced pulmonary granulo-matosis. Chest, 78: 90–94.

Wan, S., Matin, S., and Azarnoff, D. (1978). Kinetics, salivary excretion of amphet-amine isomers, and effect of urinary pH. Clin Pharmacol Ther, 23: 585–590.

Wargin, W., Patrick, K., Kilts, C. et al. (1983). Pharmacokinetics of methylphenidate in man, rat, and monkey. J Pharmacol Exp Ther, 226(2): 382–386.

Weingarten, K. (1988). Cerebral vasculitis associated with cocaine abuse or subarachnoid hemorrhage? JAMA, 259: 1648–1649.

Wu, A., Wong, S., Johnson, K. et al. (1992). The conversion of ephedrine to methamphetamine-like compounds during and prior to gas chromatographic/mass spectrometric analysis of CB and HFB derivatives. Biol Mass Spect, 21: 278–284.

Yamamoto, K., Watanabe, H., Ukita, K. et al. (1992). 3 Tödesfalle nach gemeinschaftlichem Konsum von Methaphetamin. Archive Kriminologie, 188: 72–76.

Yeh, S. and De Souza, E. (1991). Lack of neurochemical evidence for neurotoxic effects of repeated cocaine administration in rats on brain monoamine neurons. Drug Alcohol Depend, 27(1): 51–61.

Yen, D., Wang, S., Ju, T. et al. (1994). Stroke associated with methamphetamine inhalation. Eur Neurolo, 34: 16–22.

Yoo, Y., Chung, H., and Choi, H. (1994). Urinary methamphetamine concentration following famprofazone administration. J Analyt Toxicol, 18: 265–268.

Young, D. and Scoville, W. (1938). Paranoid psychosis in narcolepsy and the possible danger of Benzedrine® treatment. Med Clin N Amer, 22(3): 637.

Yu, Y., Cooper, D., Wellenstein, D. et al. (1983). Cerebral angiitis and intracerebral hemorrhage associated with methamphetamine abuse. J Neurosurg, 58: 109–111.

Zalis, E., Lundberg, C., and Knutson, R. (1967). The pathophysiology of acute amphetamine poisoning with pathologic correlation. J Pharmacol Exp Ther, 158(1): 115–127.

Zalis, E. and Parmley, L. (1963). Fatal amphetamine poisoning. Arch Intern Med, 112: 822–826.

3.2   Phenylpropanolamine

3.2.1   Historical aspects

Structurally and functionally, phenylpropanolamine (PPA) is similar to ephedrine and amphetamine. Like the amphetamines, PPA causes the increased release of norepinephrine from nerve terminals. Like ephedrine, it is also a directly acting α and, to a lesser degree, β agonist (Pentel, 1984; Schmidt and Fleming, 1962). Its ability to induce a modest degree of weight loss is a consequence of its ability to directly stimulate α_1 adrenoreceptors (Samanin and Garattini, 1993). Given the large amount of PPA consumed in the United States, PPA abuse and toxicity are surprisingly rare occurrences, accounting for less than one-third of one percent of the drug-related deaths reported in the DAWN survey. The DAWN report for 1994 (Substance Abuse and Mental Health Sources Agency, 1995) makes no mention of any deaths related to phenylpropanolamine or any over-the-counter diet pill.

PPA is the fifth most consumed medicinal chemical used in the United States. It is the major ingredient in numerous over-the-counter preparations. According to industry surveys, more than six billion doses are consumed annually at a cost of well over $200 million (Morgan, 1990). PPA is a component in over 100 different products sold in the United States. Most of the drug is used to make cough and cold products, but since 1979, when the

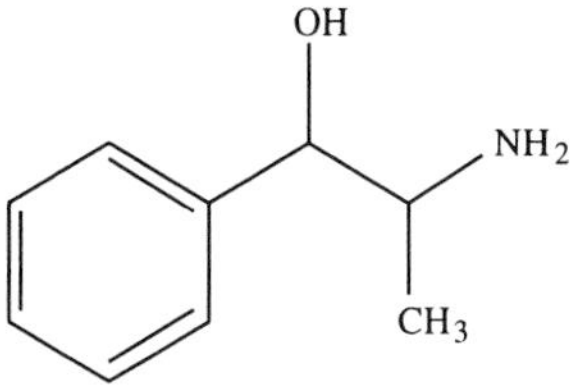

Figure 3.2   The phenylpropanolamine molecule.

FDA published a monograph declaring that PPA was safe and effective when used as an anorectic, increasing amounts have been used to produce over-the-counter diet pills. During the early 1980s, additional amounts were funneled into the making of "look-alike" stimulants. In 1981 and 1982, nearly half of the confiscated samples of amphetamine contained PPA, along with caffeine and ephedrine (Morgan et al., 1987).

During the mid-1970s an enterprising truck driver named Edward Seay began merchandising caffeine tablets that had been designed to look exactly like prescription amphetamine (Morgan et al., 1987). Sales through truck stops and mail-order catalogs amounted to millions of tablets per month. The Seay Drug Company of Union City, Georgia sold imitations of virtually all the Schedule III and IV amphetamines and stimulants. In 1977, Seay began advertising in magazines such as *Penthouse, Hustler,* and *High Times,* as well as in women's beauty magazines. At about that same time, Seay and other similar manufacturers began adding caffeine and ephedrine to their pills. Almost immediately, reports of toxicity began to appear. There is some debate as to whether these products really have stimulant or euphorogenic properties when used at recommended levels (Lake et al., 1990), but there is no question that phenylpropanolamine use can be associated with stroke, infarction, and myocardial necrosis. The fact that fewer cases are being reported may have to do with a decrease in the popularity of the "look-alike" drugs.

Even though the apparent toxicity of PPA is low, there have been a sizable number of case reports documenting exactly the same types of disorders as are seen in association with amphetamine abuse (Winick, 1990; Miller, 1990). And, in controlled studies, using non-invasive methods to measure blood pressure, stroke volume, and peripheral resistance, standard therepeutic doses of phenylporpanolamine were found to increase both blood pressure and peripheral resistance (Thomas et al., 1991).

3.2.2   Chemistry

Phenylpropanolamine is α-(1-aminoethyl)benzene methanol hydrochloride. Its formula is $C_9H_{14}ClNO$, with a molecular weight of 187.67. It is composed of 57.6% carbon, 7.5% hydrogen, 18.9% chloride, 7.5% nitrogen, and 8.5% oxygen. Crystals composed of racemic forms have a melting point of 194°–199°C.

3.2.3   *Metabolism*

Phenylpropanolamine, also called norephedrine, has very nearly the same half-life as ephedrine, attains nearly the same blood levels, and produces similar effects as ephedrine. Peak levels occur between 0.67 and 2.5 hours after oral dosing. Regardless of the dose taken, the half-life is on the order of 1.5 hours, though in some individuals it may be much shorter. Almost all of a given dose is excreted unchanged in the urine (Heimlich et al., 1961). Table 3.2.1 shows the peak concentrations produced after different dosing regimens (Dowse et al., 1990).

Toxic blood and tissue levels are poorly characterized (Pentel et al., 1987). Postmortem blood from a woman who expired from an apparent cardiac arrest after taking an unspecified number of cold pills had a concentration of 2 mg/L (Baselt and Cravey, 1989). A 20-year old suicide victim described as taking a "large overdose" had a postmortem blood level of 48 mg/L and hepatic levels that were 10 times higher than the blood level. The concentration in the brain was twice that in the blood (Baselt and Cravey, 1989). Because this level is hundreds of times higher than therapeutic levels, or even previously reported toxic levels, its relevance is open to some question. Blood levels in 12 pediatric deaths reported to the National Association of Medical Examiners Pediatric Toxicology Registry ranged from as low as 0.04 mg/L to as high as 0.84 mg/L (Hanzlick and Davis, 1992).

PPA is mainly an α adrenergic agonist, but it also possesses some β activity, and as a result, toxic (as opposed to fatal) reactions appear to be not uncommon. The standard PPA dose of 50–75 mg is not associated with significant increases in levels of circulating catecholamines (Lake et al., 1990), but doses of 85–100 mg have been implicated as the cause of severe hypertensive reactions (Pentel, 1984).

PPA increases plasma caffeine levels, and when the two agents are taken at the same time, the resultant blood pressure increases are greater than those observed when either drug is taken alone. When test subjects were given 400 mg of caffeine and 75 mg of PPA at the same time, the peak plasma

Table 3.2.1 Peak PPA Blood
Levels in Five Volunteers after
Different Oral Doses

Dosage	Range of peak blood levels
25 mg	67–185.3 ng/mL
50 mg	147.7–190.1 ng/mL
100 mg	290.6–480.6 ng/mL

Note: Except for modest increases in systolic blood pressure with 50 and 100 mg doses, these individuals were otherwise asymptomatic (from Dowse et al., 1991).

caffeine concentration was 8.0 ± 2.2 µg/mL, almost four times higher than the result when the same amount of caffeine is given alone (Lake et al., 1990). This interaction may explain why there is an increased incidence of adverse reactions when PPA is taken together with caffeine and/or ephedrine.

Case reports have described patients with arrhythmias, chest pain, and even electrocardiographic changes (Pentel et al., 1982). Arrhythmic sudden death also occurs (Bernstein, 1973; Dietz, 1981; Pentel, 1984), but no autopsy findings have been reported. In experimental animals, PPA produces exactly the same constellation of lesions that are associated with classic catecholamineamine toxicity. Rats given varying doses of intraperitoneal PPA displayed dose-related myocardial necrosis with contraction bands, eosinophilia, and occasional infiltrates (Pentel et al., 1987). Myocardial fibrosis was not observed in this model because the animals were sacrificed before it could develop (Karch and Billingham, 1986). However, the lesions which were observed are known to heal by fibrosis and the presence of microfocal fibrosis could well account for the arrhythmias which have been described in PPA users. Based on the number of published case reports, PPA seems to be more toxic to the cerebral than the coronary vasculature. The difference is unexplained, but it likely has to do with receptor distribution and regulation.

3.2.4   Toxicity by organ system

3.2.4.1   Neurologic disease

The most commonly encountered complications of PPA use are neurologic. Frank psychotic episodes have occurred after using therapeutic doses of PPA-containing decongestants (Traynealis and Brick, 1986; Kane and Green, 1966; Wharton, 1970; Norvenious et al., 1979; Lake, 1991). Seizures also have been described (Cornelius et al., 1984; Muller, 1983). Stroke has been reported with some frequency (Johnson et al., 1983; Kizer, 1984; Mesnard and Ginn, 1984; Fallis and Fisher, 1985; Traynealis and Brick, 1986; Maher, 1987; Maertens et al., 1987; Le Coz et al., 1988; King, 1979; Bernstein and Diskant, 1982; Kase et al., 1987; Kita et al., 1985; Forman et al., 1989; McDowell and LeBlanc, 1985; Bale et al., 1984; Stoessl et al., 1985; Glick et al., 1987; Lake, 1991). When angiograms were done, these patients usually, but not always, were found to have changes consistent with vasospasm or angiitis. Many of these patients are normotensive when they are first seen, and almost all are women. In other cases, hypertension has been a factor. Doses much over 50 mg are associated with significant blood pressure increases (Lake, 1991). As is the case with cocaine and amphetamine, most of the PPA-associated stroke patients are quite young, usually in their late 20s or early 30s.

The mechanism for stroke in PPA users has not been explained. Animal studies have shown that very high doses of PPA (200 mg/kg) produce a slight decrease in formal cortex dopamine levels but no other effects on the monoamine systems (Woolverton, 1986). Biopsy findings are available from only one case, and there have been no autopsy studies. The biopsy was from a 35-year old woman with an intracerebral hemorrhage (Glick et al., 1987). Arteriography showed diffuse segmental narrowing. When the hemorrhage was evacuated, multiple specimens of tissue were obtained. There was necrotizing vasculitis of the small arteries and veins which were infiltrated with polymorphonuclear leukocytes. There was lumenal narrowing and even vessel occlusion. As in intravenous methamphetamine abuse, there was fragmentation of the elastic lamina and occasional microaneurysm formation, but no granulomas and no giant cells. In general, the findings are consistent with a drug-induced vasculitis and contrast markedly with the findings in primary or idiopathic cerebral vasculitis where granulomas and giant cells are always seen.

3.2.4.2   Cardiac disease

EKG changes, arrhythmias, and chest pain have all been described (Pentel et al., 1982; Chouinard et al., 1978; Conway, 1989). Typical catecholamine lesions can easily be produced in rats treated with PPA, but only at dosages that produce blood levels 4–6 times as high as seen with normal clinical regimens (Pentel et al., 1987). Therapeutic doses given to healthy volunteers increase pulse rate, blood pressure, and peripheral resistance (Thomas et al., 1991). Individuals with preexisting, but asymptomatic, coronary artery lesions might well become symptomatic.

3.2.4.3   Pulmonary disease

Autopsy information is sparse. In one case, a 15-year old who died 32 hours after taking 400 mg of PPA was found to have changes consistent with the diagnosis of Acute Respiratory Distress Syndrome (ARDS) (Logie and Scott, 1984). In a second case, death resulted from a 600-mg overdose. Multiple pulmonary emboli were found in addition to changes consistent with ARDS (Patterson, 1980). Blood and tissue levels were not reported for either case.

3.2.4.4   Renal disease

Like the amphetamines, PPA can cause acute myoglobinuria renal failure (Swenson et al., 1982). There is one report of biopsy-proven interstitial nephritis (Bennett, 1979). The incidence of both complications seems to be quite low.

3.2.4.5   Gastrointestinal disorders

Phenylpropanolamine is not known to cause liver disorders, but like methamphetamine (Roberts et al., 1994) and like other symphathomimetic agents active at the α-2 receptor, phenylpropanolamine enhances the amount of necrosis produced when carbon tetrachloride is given to mice. The mechanism for this change has yet to be identified (Roberts et al., 1991).

References

Atanassoff, P., Weiss, B., Schmid, E. et al. (1992). Pulmonary hypertension and dexfenfluramine. Lancet, 339: 436.

Bale, J., Fountain, M. M., and Shaddy, R. (1984). Phenylpropanolamine associated CNS complications in children and adolescents. Am J Dis Child, 138: 683–685.

Baselt, R. and Cravey, R. (1989). *Disposition of toxic drugs and chemicals in man.* 3rd ed. Chicago, London: Year Book Medical Publishers, 687–689.

Bennett, W. (1979). Hazards of appetite suppressant phenylpropanolamine. Lancet, 2: 42–43.

Bernstein, E. and Diskant, B. (1982). Phenylpropanolamine: a potentially hazardous drug. Ann Emerg Med, 11: 311–315.

Chouinard, G., Ghadirian, A., and Jones, B. (1978). Death attributed to ventricular arrhythmia induced by thiordiazine in combination with a single Contac-C® capsule. Can Med Assoc J, 119: 729–731.

Conway, Jr., E., Walsh, C., and Palomba, A. (1989). Supraventricular tachycardia following the administration of phenylpropanolamine in an infant. Pediatr Emerg Care, 5(3): 173–174.

Cornelius, J., Soloff, P., and Reynolds, C. (1984). Paranoia, homicidal behavior, and seizures associated with phenylpropanolamine. Am J Psychiat, 141: 120–121.

Dietz, A. (1981). Amphetamine-like reactions to phenylpropanolamine. JAMA, 245: 601–602.

Dowse, R., Scherzinger, S., and Kanfer, I. (1990). Serum concentrations of phenylpropanolamine and associated effects on blood pressure in normotensive subjects: a pilot study. Int J Clin Pharmacol Ther Toxicol, 28(5): 205–210.

Fallis, R. and Fisher, M. (1985). Cerebral vasculitis and hemorrhage associated with phenylpropanolamine. Neurology, 35: 405–407.

Forman, H., Levin, S., Stewart, B. et al. (1989). Cerebral vasculitis and hemorrhage in an adolescent taking diet pills containing phenylpropanolamine: case report and review of literature. Pediatrics, 83(5): 737–741.

Glick, R., Hoying, J., Cerullo, L., and Perlman, S. (1987). Phenylpropanolamine: an over-the-counter drug causing central nervous system vasculitis and intracerebral hemorrhage. Neurosurgery, 20(6): 969–974.

Hanzlick, R. and Davis G. (1992). National Association of Medical Examiners Pediatric Toxicology Registry. Report 1: phenylpropanolamine. Am J Forensic Med and Pathol 13 (1):37–41.

Heimlich, K., MacDonnell, D., Flanagan, T., and O'Brien, P. (1961). Evaluation of a sustained release form of phenylpropanolamine hydrochloride by urinary excretion studies. J Pharm Sci, 50: 232–237.

Hervé, P., Drouey, L., Bosquet, C. et al. (1990). Primary pulmonary hypertension in a patient with a familial platelet storage pool disease. Am J Med, 89: 117–120.

Johnson, D., Etter, H., and Reeves, D. (1983). Stroke and phenylpropanolamine use. Lancet, 2: 970.

Kane, F. and Green, B. (1966). Psychotic episodes associated with the use of common proprietary decongestants. Am J Psychiat, 123(4): 484–487.

Karch, S. and Billingham M. (1986). Myocardial contraction bands revisited. Hum Pathol, 17: 9–13.

Kase, C., Foster, T., Reed, J. et al. (1987). Intracerebral hemorrhage and phenylpropanolamine use. Neurology, 37: 399–404.

Kikta, D., Devereaux, M., and Chandar, K. (1985). Intracranial hemorrhages due to phenylpropanolamine. Stroke, 16: 510–512.

King, J. (1979). Hypertension and cerebral hemorrhage after timolets ingestion. Med J Aust, 2(5): 258.

Kizer, K. (1984). Intracranial hemorrhage associated with overdose of decongestant containing phenylpropanolamine. Am J Emerg Med, 2: 180–181.

Kokkinos, J. and Levine, S. (1993). Possible association of ischemic stroke with phentermine. Stroke, 24(2): 310–313.

Lake, C., Rosenberg, D., and Quirk, R. (1990). Phenylpropanolamine use among diet patients. Int J Obesity, 14: 575–582.

Lake, C., Rosenberg, D., Gallant, S. et al. (1990). Phenylpropanolamine increases plasma caffeine levels. Clin Pharmacol Ther, 47: 675–685.

Lake, C., Gallant, S., Masson, E., and Miller, P. (1990). Adverse drug effects attributed to phenylpropanolamine: a review of 142 case reports. Am J Med, 89: 195–208.

Lake, C. (1991). Manic psychosis after coffee and phenylpropanolamine. Biol Psychiatry, 30: 401–404.

Le Coz, P., Woimant, F., Rougemont, D. et al. (1988). Angiopathies cerebrales benignes et phenylpropanolamine. Rev Neurol (Paris), 144: 295–300.

Logie, A. and Scott C. (1984). Fatal overdosage of phenylpropanolamine. Br Med J, 289: 591.

Maertens, P., Lum, G., Williams, J. et al. (1987). Intracranial hemorrhage and cerebral angiopathic changes in a suicidal phenylpropanolamine poisoning. South Med J, 80: 1584–1586.

Maher, L. (1987). Post-partum intracranial hemorrhage and phenylpropanolamine use. Neurology, 37: 1686.

McDowell, J. and LeBlanc, H. (1985). Phenylpropanolamine and cerebral hemorrhage. West J Med, 142: 688–691.

Mesnard, B. and Ginn, D. (1984). Excessive phenylpropanolamine ingestion followed by subarachnoid hemorrhage. South Med J, 77: 939.

Miller, L. (1991). Phenylpropanolamine: the saga continues. J Clin Psychopharm, 11: 82–83.

Morgan, J. (1990). Cardiovascular toxicity of cocaine. J Appl Cardiol, 5: 321–322.

Morgan, J., Wesson, D., Puder, K., and Smith, D. (1987). Duplicitous drugs: the history and recent status of look-alike drugs. J Psychoactive Drugs, 19: 21–23.

Muller, S. (1983). Phenylpropanolamine, a nonprescription drug with potentially fatal side effects. N Engl J Med, 308: 653.

Nagata, T., Kimura, K., Hara, K., and Kudo, K. (1990). Methamphetamine and amphetamine concentrations in postmortem rabbit tissues. Forensic Sci Int, 48: 39–47.

National Institute on Drug Abuse. (1990a). Annual Emergency Room Data. Data from the Drug Abuse Warning Network. Statistical Series, Number 10-A. Rockville, MD, U.S. Department of Health and Human Services.

National Institute on Drug Abuse. (1990b). Annual Medical Examiner Data. Data from the Drug Abuse Warning Network. Statistical Series, Number 10-B. Rockville, MD, U.S. Department of Health and Human Services.

Neelakantan, L. and Kostenbauder, H. (1976). Electron-capture GLC determination of phenylpropanolamine as a pentafluorophenyloxazolidine derivative. J Pharm Sci, 65: 740–742.

Nemecek, G., Coughlin, S., Handley, D. et al. (1986). Stimulation of aortic smooth muscle cell mitogenesis by serotonin. Proc Nat Acad Sci, 83: 674-678.

Norvenious, G., Widerlov, E., and Lonnerhom, G. (1979). Phenylpropanolamine and mental disturbances. Lancet, 2: 1367–1368.

Patterson, F. (1980). Delayed fatal outcome after possible Rutuss overdose. J Forensic Sci, 25: 349–352.

Pentel, P. (1984). Toxicity of over-the-counter stimulants. JAMA, 252: 1898–1903.

Pentel, P., Jentzen, J., and Sievert, J. (1987). Myocardial necrosis due to intraperitoneal administration of phenylpropanolamine in rats. Fundam Appl Toxicol, 9(1): 167–172.

Pentel, P., Mikell, F., and Zavoral, S. (1982). Myocardial injury after phenylpropanolamine ingestion. Br Heart J, 47: 51–54.

Roberts, S., Harbison, R., Seng, J. et al. (1991). Potentiation of carbon tetrachloride hepatotoxicity by phenylpropanolamine. Tox Appl Pharm, 111: 175–188.

Roberts, S., Harbison, R., and James, R. (1994). Methamphetamine potentiation of carbon tetrachloride hepatotoxicity in mice. J Pharm Exp Ther, 271(2): 1951–1957.

Samanin, R. and Garattini, S. (1993). Neurochemical mechanism of action of anorectic drugs. Clin Pharm Tox, 73: 63–68.

Stoessl, A., Young, G., and Feasby, T. (1985). Intracerebral hemorrhage and angiographic beading following ingestion of catecholamineaminergics. Stroke, 16: 734–736.

Swenson, R., Golper, T. and Bennet, W. (1982). Acute renal failure and rhabdomyolysis after ingestion of phenylpropanolamine-containing diet pills. JAMA, 248: 1216.

Thomas, S., Clark, K., Allen, R. et al. (1991). A comparison of the cardiovascular effects of phenylpropanolamine and phenylephrine-containing proprietary cold remedies. Br J Clin Pharm, 32: 705–711.

Traynealis, V. and Brick, J. (1986). Phenylpropanolamine and vasospasm. Neurology, 36: 593.

Voelker, R. (1994). Obesity drug renews toxicity debate. JAMA, 272: 1067–1068.

Wharton, B. (1970). Nasal decongestants and paranoid psychosis. Br J Psych, 117: 429–440.

Winick, C. (1991). Phenylpropanolamine: toward resolution of a controversy. J Clin Psychopharm, 11: 79–81.

Woolverton, W., Johanson, C., de la Garza, R. et al. (1986). Behavioral and neurochemical evaluation of phenylpropanolamine. J Pharmacol Exp Ther, 237(3): 926–930.

3.3   Fenfluramine

3.3.1   Historical aspects

Fenfluramine (Ponderax®, Pondimin®) was first synthesized in 1963 for use as an anorectic. Fenfluramine is still primarily used as an appetite suppressant (Pondimin®, Wyeth-Ayerst Laboratories), though it has been suggested as a treatment for autism. The dextro isomer, dexfenfluramine, is widely used in Europe. Applications for its release in the United States are pending. Fenfluramine causes anorexia by stimulating satiety centers located in the ventromedial hypothalamic nuclei (Teitelbaum, 1970). This action seems to be a result of fenfluramine's ability to cause the release of serotonin (5-HT) and its added ability to interfere with the 5-HT uptake carrier (Fuller et al., 1988). In the rat, fenfluramine's effects are specifically mediated by the 5-HT1B-receptor. However, the behavior of the human HT1B receptor differs so radically from the rat version, it is not clear whether any of the animal findings can legitimately be extrapolated to humans (Samanin amd Garattini, 1993).

In experimental animals, fenfluramine treatment causes large, rapid decreases in brain serotonin and 5-hydroxyindoleacetic acid (5-HIAA) (Garattini, 1980). Tryptophan hydroxylase activity is decreased as well (Steranka and Sanders-Bush, 1979). Rats given one dose of fenfluramine still have decreased serotonin levels as long as 30 days afterward (Harvey and McMaster, 1975). Fenfluramine hydrochloride is not truly a drug of abuse, but it is

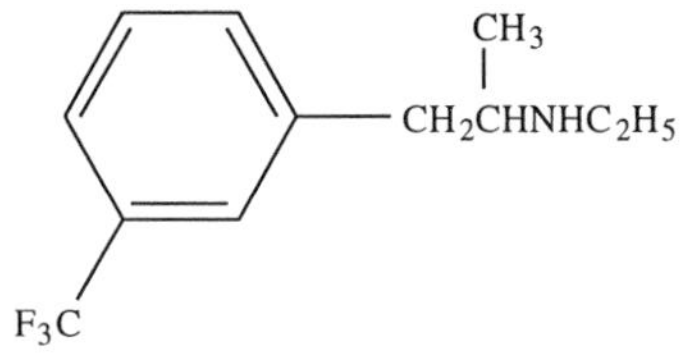

Figure 3.3   The fenfluramine molecule.

an amphetamine derivative with significant pulmonary and neurologic toxicity. A closely related compound, aminorex fumarate, widely prescribed
during the early 1960s as an appetite suppressant, was withdrawn from the
market when it became apparent that users were developing pulmonary
hypertension (Follath et al., 1971).

3.3.2   Drug constants

Fenfluramine is N-ethyl-α-methyl-3(trifluromethyl) benzenethanamine. Its
formula is $C_{12}H_{16}F_3N$, with a molecular weight of 231.27. It is composed of
62.3% carbon, 7% hydrogen, 24.7% fluorine, and 6.1% nitrogen. Crystals of
the racemic mixture have a melting point of 108–112°C. Commercial fenfluramine is supplied as a racemic mixture.

3.3.3   Metabolism

Following a single oral dose of 60 mg of fenfluramine, peak plasma concentrations are 0.05 to 0.07 mg/L at three hours. This drug has a very long half-
life (13–30 hours), and patients tend to maintain consistent steady-state
concentrations (average of 0.16 mg/L) when therapeutic doses are regularly
taken (Campbell, 1970). In stabilized patients, levels of its principal metabolite, norfenfluramine, are about half as high (Innes et al., 1977). Like the
other amphetamines, fenfluramine's excretion depends on the urinary pH.
About 20% is excreted unchanged in the urine, and another 20% as the N-
dealkylation product norfenfluramine (Beckett and Brookes, 1967).

3.3.4   Blood and tissue levels

One adult surviving a 1,600-mg overdose of fenfluramine had peak concentrations of 0.85 mg/L in the plasma (Richards, 1969) and a 2-year old who
ingested 440 mg had a peak level of 0.78 mg/L with 0.17 mg/L of norfenfluramine (Campbell and Moore, 1969). Overdose-related deaths have been
reported, though not very frequently. Fenfluramine blood levels in three
different children who died after ingesting up to 1,200 mg ranged from 6.5
to 16 mg/L. Hepatic concentrations in these same children were four to nine
times higher (24–136 mg/Kg) (Gold et al., 1969; Simpson and McKinaly,
1975). Similar levels were seen in a teenager who died 3.5 hours after taking
2 grams of fenfluramine. Both liver and brain had fenfluramine concentrations nine times as much as that found in the blood (6.5 mg/L) (Fleisher and

Campbell, 1969). Low CNS concentrations were seen in the patient reported by Kintz and Mangin. They described the case of a 36-year old woman who died after ingesting an unknown amount of fenfluramine. The blood level was 7.46 mg/L but the brain level was only 0.48 mg/L, and the concentration in the liver was over 155 mg/L. Fenfluramine levels in the hair were 14.1 ng/mg (Kintz and Mangin, 1992).

3.3.5 Toxicity by organ system

3.3.5.1 Cardiopulmonary

Two patients with fenfluramine-associated pulmonary hypertension came to notice in 1981. Both patients were women who had been taking the medication for over eight months. In both cases, thorough evaluation disclosed that pulmonary hypertension was due to greatly increased vascular resistance that cleared when the drug was discontinued (Douglas et al., 1981). Since then, a number of additional reports have appeared (Atanassoff et al., 1992; Roche et al., 1992). In one report from a European referral center specalizing in the treatment of primary pulmonary hypertension, 15 out of 73 patients referred for treatment had histories of fenfluramine use (Brenot et al., 1993). Autopsies have been done in several cases and have demonstrated the classic findings of plexogenic arteriopathy.

Fenfluramine-associated pulmonary toxicity has been simulated in an animal model. Dogs infused with fenfluramine have increased pulmonary diastolic pressure. In the rat, massive overdose (130 mg/kg) causes respiratory depression and cardiac ischemia. Electrocardiographic changes in this model include ischemia and conduction delays with widening of the QRS and PR prolongation. Animals given smaller doses still develop respiratory distress and extensive alveolar and interstitial pulmonary hemorrhages after 24 hours. The changes are worse when animals are pretreated with a serotonin antagonist (Hunsinger and Wright, 1990).

3.3.5.2 Neurological

Neurotoxicity has been demonstrated in several animal models. In the rat, structural damage to the serotonergic (5-HT) neurons is evident 36 hours after injecting a single 10 mg/kg dose. Immunochemical studies showed 5-HT axons that were markedly swollen while the cell body remained intact (Molliver and Molliver, 1990). Other studies have demonstrated the presence of intralysosomal lamellar bodies in the endothelial cells, pericytes, and perivascular astrocytic process of rats given 5 mg/kg doses of fenfluramine. These findings suggest that the rats were unable to metabolize a yet-to-be identified fenfluramine-phospholipid reaction product. Human studies are nonexistent (Thakkar et al., 1990).

References

Atanassoff, P., Weiss, B., Schmid, E. et al. (1992). Pulmonary hypertension and dexfenfluramine. Lancet, 339: 436.

Beckett, A. and Brookes, L. (1967). The absorption and urinary excretion in man of fenfluramine and its main metabolite. J Pharm Pharmac, 19: 42S–52S.

Brenot, F., Herve, P., Petipretz, P. et al. (1993). Primary pulmonary hypertension and fenfluramine use. Br Heart J, 70: 537–541.

Campbell, D. (1970). Gas chromatographic measurement of levels of fenfluramine and norfenfluramine in human plasma, red cells and urine following therapeutic doses. J Chrom, 49: 442–447.

Campbell, D. and Moore, B. (1969). Fenfluramine overdosage. Lancet, 2: 1306.

Douglas, J., Munro, J., Kitchin, A. et al. (1981). Pulmonary hypertension and fenfluramine. Br Med J, 283: 881–883.

Fleisher, M. and Campbell, D. (1969). Fenfluramine overdosage. Lancet, 2: 1306.

Follath, F., Buckart, F., and Schweitzer, W. (1971). Drug-induced pulmonary hypertension? Br Med J, i: 265–266.

Fuller, R., Snoddy, H., and Robertson, D. (1988). Mechanisms of effects of d-fenfluramine on brain serotonin metabolism in rats: uptake inhibition versus release. Pharmacol Biochem Behav, 30: 715–721.

Garattini, S. (1980). Recent studies on anorectic agents. Trends Pharmaceut Sci, 1: 354–356.

Gold, R., Gordon, H., DaCoasta, R. et al. (1969). Fenfluramine overdosage. Lancet, 2: 1306.

Harvey, J. and McMaster, S. (1975). Fenfluramine: evidence for a neurotoxic action on mid-brain and a long-term depletion of serotonin. Psychopharmacol Commun, 1: 217–228.

Hunsinger, R. and Wright, D. (1990). A characterization of the acute cardiopulmonary toxicity of fenfluramine in the rat. Pharm Res, 22(3): 371–378.

Innes, J., Watson, M., Ford, M. et al. (1977). Plasma fenfluramine levels, weight loss, and side effects. Br Med J, 2: 1322–1325.

Kintz, P. and Mangin, P. (1992). Toxicological findings after fatal fenfluramine self-poisoning. Hum and Exp Tox, 11: 51–52.

Molliver, D. and Molliver, M. (1990). Anatomic evidence for a neurotoxic effect of (+/–)-fenfluramine upon serotonergic projections in the rat. Brain Res, 511: 165–168.

Richards, A. (1969). Fenfluramine overdosage. Lancet, 2: 1367.

Roche, N., Labrune, S., Braun, J. et al. (1992). Pulmonary hypertension and dexfenfluramine. Lancet, 339: 436–437.

Samanin, R. and Garattini, S. (1993). Neurochemical mechanism of action of anorectic drugs. Pharm Tox, 73(2): 63–68.

Schmidt, J. and Fleming, W. (1962). The structure of sympathomimetics as related to reserpine induced sensitivity changes in the rabbit ileum. J Pharmacol Exp Ther, 139: 230–237.

Simpson, H. and McKinaly, I. (1975). Poisoning with slow-release fenfluramine. Br Med J, 4: 462–463.

Steranka, L. and Sanders-Bush, E. (1979). Long-term effects of fenfluramine on central serotonergic mechanisms. Neuropharmacology, 18: 895–903.

Teitelbaum, P. (1970). The biology of drive. In *The neurosciences*, G. C. Guarton, T. Melnechuck, and F. Schmitt (Eds.). New York: The Rockefeller University Press, 557.

Thakkar, B., Dastur, D., and Manghani, D. (1990). Neuropathology and pathogenesis of experimental fenfluramine toxicity in young rodents. Ind J Med Res, B92: 54–65.

chapter four

Hallucinogens

Criteria for membership in this group are difficult to define, partially because the hallucinogens themselves are hard to define. According to the most widely accepted definition, hallucinogens share five common features: (1) in proportion to any other effects such drugs might exert, changes in mood and perception dominate; (2) there is mimimal memory or intellectual impairment; (3) use is not associated with either stupor or excessive agitation; (4) there are minimal side effects from autonomic nervous system stimulation; (5) craving and addiction do not occur (Hollister, 1968). Traditionally, hallucinogens have been divided into two groups: phenylalkylamines (drugs like mescaline, DOM, DOB), and the indoylalkylamines (psilocybin, bufoteine, LSD, harmaline). If Hollister's criteria are strictly applied, disassociative anesthetics (phencyclidine) would not qualify for membership in this group. However, the toxicologic effects are similar enough to warrant their inclusion in this group.

4.1 Phenylethylamine derivatives

According to the most recent DAWN report, hallucinogen-related deaths increased by 38% in 1993. Compared to heroin and the stimulant-related deaths, the absolute numbers are quite low, with fewer than 200 reported deaths (Substance Abuse and Mental Health Administration, 1995). Virtually all of the deaths were the result of PCP (196 cases), with only four of the deaths being attributed to LSD use. Most of the popular hallucinogens are mescaline derivatives. Dozens of mescaline analogs have been produced, but their pharmacologic and toxicologic properties are largely unknown, and not that much more is known about the parent compound, mescaline. Experience in Europe suggests that some of these drugs, particularly MDMA, may be more toxic than had previously been appreciated. As MDMA has become increasingly popular, so have the reported cases of toxicity.

4.1.1 Mescaline

4.1.1.1 Historical aspects

Mescaline comes from the cactus referred to as either *Lophora williamsii* or *Anhalonium Lewinii*. Lewin was one of the first to systematically study this

Figure 4.1.1 Peyote cactus. Even though it grows wild throughout the American Southwest, it can be very hard to find. Except when it is in bloom, it tends to resemble a small rock.

group of plants and their active principle, mescaline. This small cactus can be found growing in dry places and rocky slopes throughout the southwestern United States. It grows singly or in clusters. It is an inconspicuous plant that can be hard to find. Unless it is in flower, it tends to look like a small rock. The dried tops of the plants, known as peyote buttons, have been used by Indian shamans for centuries. During the early 1800s, the Apaches, Kiowas, and Commanches of the Great Plains began to chew the buttons and incorporated them into their religious rites. The practice quickly spread among the Plains Indians who combined its use with elements of Christianity. Today their ceremonies still begin with the chewing of peyote buttons, followed by nights of prayers and singing. The sect is now known as the Native American Church and has more than 200,000 members (Barron et al., 1964). Mescaline, or 3,4,5-trimethoxy-β-phenethylamine, is the active principle found in peyote cactus. The average mescaline content is 6%. No mescaline-related deaths or emergency room visits were reported in the 1990 DAWN survey (National Institute on Drug Abuse, 1993).

The first systematic chemical and pharmacologic studies were reported by Lewin and Henning in 1888 (Lewin and Henning, 1888). Lewin's work attracted the attention of the famous American neurologist, S. Weir Mitchell (Prentiss and Morgan, 1893). Mitchell, who was a prolific writer and a pioneer in the study of peripheral nerve injuries, was also interested in toxicology and psychiatry (Metzer, 1989). He obtained some peyote buttons and used them himself. Mitchell then published an account of his experiences in the *British Medical Journal* (Mitchell, 1896). He believed that the plant might be of great value in the study of psychological disorders, but he also warned of the abuse potential. The famous sexologist, Havelock Ellis, also dabbled with mescaline, and described the many benefits to be derived from its use (Anon, 1898). Neither the benefits nor the epidemic of abuse ever really materialized. The active principal alkaloid was isolated in 1896, but its structure was not elucidated until 1919. Since that time, structural modifications of the mescaline molecule have been used to create a host of other psychoactive compounds, most of which have been laboratory curiosities. Others, such as MDMA, are widely used today.

4.1.1.2 Drug constants and drug preparation

Mescaline is 3,4,5-trimethoxybenzeneethanamine or 3,4,5, trimethoxyphenethylamine. Its formula is $C_{11}H_{17}NO_3$, with a molecular weight of 211.23. It is composed of 62.5% carbon, 8.1% hydrogen, 6.6% nitrogen, and 22.7% oxygen. Mescaline crystals have a melting point of 35–36°C. Pure mescaline will combine with carbon dioxide in the air to form crystalline carbonates. The hydrochloride form of mescaline, $C_{11}H_{18}CLNO_3$, forms colorless, needle-like crystals, with a melting point of 181°C.

Mescaline is extracted from the cactus by first drying and then grinding the tops of the plants. The ground material is then soaked in methanol for a day, filtered, and acidified. After the alcohol has been evaporated off, the solution is neutralized and the mescaline extracted with chloroform. Less sophisticated chemists cook the cactus in a pressure cooker until they end up with a tarry material that can be formed into small pills. Some clandestine producers apply an enteric coating, or place the tarry material in gelatin

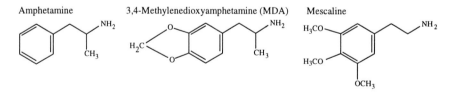

Figure 4.1.1.2   Mescaline and the "designer" amphetamines. Whether small recreational doses of these drugs are hallucinogenic is hard to say, but all of these agents can impair judgment and their use occasionally leads to fatal accidents.

capsules; the objective is to reduce the nausea that often accompanies mescaline use.

4.1.1.3 *Metabolism and tissue levels*

In one case report, where accidental death was a consequence of a mescaline-induced confusional state (Reynolds and Jindrich, 1985), the mescaline blood level was 9.7 mg/L with a urine concentration of 1163 mg/L. Most of the published metabolic studies were published nearly 30 years ago and were done with techniques that are now considered antiquated. The hallucinogenic dose is estimated to be on the order of 200–500 mg. Tracer studies in healthy volunteers showed levels of 3.88 mg/L two hours after a 500-mg dose. A 350-mg dose given intravenously produced a peak blood level of 14.8 mg/L at 15 minutes, declining to 2.1 mg/L at two hours. The half-life of mescaline is on the order of six hours. Most of a given dose is excreted in the urine. About 60% will be excreted unchanged, and about 30% as 3,4,5-trimethoxyphenylacetic acid. Smaller amounts of other inactive metabolites also appear (Charalampous et al., 1966; Charalampous et al., 1964; Mokrasch and Stevenson, 1959). Generalizing from animal studies is difficult because mescaline is metabolized differently by different species.

When dogs are injected subcutaneously with mescaline, the highest concentrations are found in the liver and kidneys. Concentrations in the liver, spleen, and kidneys are three to six times the concentration found in the bloodstream. Brain levels tend to parallel the blood levels (Kapadia and Fayez, 1970). Tissue levels have been measured at autopsy in only one case. A mescaline user who died of a head injury had a blood level of 9.7 mg/L with a concentration eight times as high in the liver (Reynolds and Jindrich, 1985).

4.1.1.4 *Clinical syndromes*

Half a milligram of mescaline given to healthy volunteers produces an artificial psychosis that is indistinguishable from acute schizophrenia. Neuropsychologic measurements made during mescaline intoxication suggest that the behavioral changes are due to right hemispheric striato-limbic hyperactivity, with associated left hemispheric dysfunction (Oepen et al., 1989). SPECT imaging of human volunteers during mescaline-induced psychosis shows increased regional flow in the frontal lobes bilaterally with a pronounced increase of the metabolic rate on the right, referred to as a "hyperfrontal pattern" (Hermle et al., 1992). Otherwise, the symptoms associated with mescaline abuse are mostly those of sympathetic stimulation. Transient rises in pulse, blood pressure, and temperature all occur (Kapadia, 1970). Laboratory studies on mescaline's cardiovascular effects have yielded inconsistent results.

4.1.1.5 *Pathologic findings*

Lethal overdoses of mescaline have never been reported, nor have there been any reports of medical complications associated with its use. The deaths that have been reported have been accidental, usually as a result of drug-induced confusion (Reynolds and Jindrich, 1985).

4.1.2 Other 2-carbon phenethylamine derivatives

Many of the drugs in this class are mescaline analogs that have been substituted at the 4-position. On a weight for weight basis, many of these compounds (e.g., escaline, proscaline, buscaline) are much more potent than mescaline. Alkoxylated mescaline homologs (e.g., metaescaline, metaproscaline) are less potent. A series of thiomescaline analogs have also been synthesized, with substitution both at the 3 and 4 position. The clinical effects of these agents have never been systematically studied, and virtually nothing is known about their pharmacology, either in man or animal.

4.2 Substituted amphetamines (phenylisopropylamines)

Since 1947, when researchers produced the first psychoactive mescaline analog (TMA), structural modifications of the mescaline molecule have been used to produce a succession of psychoactive derivatives. Except for MDMA, very little information is available about these drugs. MDMA toxicity is poorly characterized, but during the last several years, as it has come into wider use, the number of reported medical complications has been steadily rising. The toxicity of other drugs in this group is poorly characterized and, in most cases, even meaningful animal experiments are lacking. Anecdotal reports suggest that methcathinone, which is extremely simple to make and increasingly popular, may be more toxic than other members of the group.

4.2.1 TMA (2,4,5-trimethoxyamphetamine)

TMA has twice the psychoactive potency of mescaline (Shulgin et al., 1973). It was first synthesized in 1933, but was never used as a psychedelic until 1962. It produces all the same effects as mescaline, but is said to have a lower therapeutic index. The amount required to cause hallucinatory or psychedelic experiences is not very different from the amount needed to produce toxicity (Chesher, 1990).

4.2.2 DOM (methyl-2,5-dimethoxyamphetamine)

DOM was first synthesized in 1963, shortly after TMA (Shulgin et al., 1977). The first reports of abuse appeared in 1967. DOM was also referred to as "STP" ("serenity, tranquility, and peace"). It is a white solid, soluble in most organic solvents and has a melting point of 60–61°C. The melting point for the hydrochloride salt is 190–191°C. In doses of less than 3 mg, DOM's effects are said to be similar to mescaline. Higher doses cause hallucinations and unpleasant side effects that may last for as long as eight hours (Snyder et al., 1967).

DOM rapidly developed a bad reputation on the streets, probably because it was being used in excessively high doses (Snyder et al., 1967; Shulgin, 1977). Regardless of the dose, about 20% will appear unchanged in the urine with peak excretion occurring at between three and six hours, the period when intoxication is most intense. Hallucinations produced by higher doses are associated with nausea, diaphoresis, and tremor. Moderate elevations in pulse and systolic, but not diastolic, pressure occur. Blood and tissue levels have never been determined and the pathologic changes associated with its use, if any, are unknown.

4.2.3 PMA (paramethoxyamphetamine)

PMA, an interesting compound, is a potent hallucinogen that also has sympathomimetic effects. Animal studies done in the early 1960s suggested that PMA's hallucinogenic potency was nearly as great as LSD's (Smythies et al., 1967), although the effects were not quite so marked in man. In limited human studies, occasional instances of marked hypertension were observed. The first PMA fatalities were reported in 1974 (Cimbura, 1974). All of the dead persons were male, aged 17–30 years. Clinical observations on those who died are rather sparse, but they all suffered from the same constellation of symptoms: agitation, seizures, and hyperthermia. Autopsy findings were not described. PMA was rapidly classified as a restricted drug, and there have been no further reports of abuse or fatalities.

4.2.4 DOB (4-bromo-2,5-dimethoxyamphetamine, also called bromo-DMA)

DOB is also an agent with potent hallucinogenic and sympathomimetic properties. It is fairly long acting. Symptoms begin three to four hours after ingestion and may take 24 hours to resolve. Because of its high potency, DOB can be sold impregnated in blotter paper, and sometimes has been passed off for LSD (Shulgin, 1981). DOB was especially popular in Australia where it was often falsely represented as LSD. After synthesis, DOB is impregnated onto sheets of colored paper, usually embossed with some type of logo or animal sketch. The impregnated sheets were then cut up and sold as 1-cm squares. The problem with this method of distribution is that during preparation the drug may migrate to the corners or bottom of the sheet. Users who bought squares from the center often received less DOB than they paid for, while those who bought squares from the margins of the sheet often got more than they bargained for. This may explain why so many bad experiences were associated with use of the drug (Delliou, 1980).

DOB produces amphetamine-like effects in dogs, with pupillary dilitation, and increased pulse, blood pressure, and temperature. Human pharmacokinetics have not been studied, but the effective dose is said to be between 2–3 mg. This agent is associated with more morbidity than the others (Bohn, 1981; Buhrich et al., 1983; Wineck et al., 1981). Diffuse vascular spasm, identical to the classic picture of ergotism, has been reported after DOB use (Bowen et al., 1983), and grand mal seizures have also been reported (Delliou, 1983). This syndrome has not been reported in conjunction with other "designer" amphetamines, but it is a well-known complication of LSD use. Scant autopsy information about DOB is available. In one reported case

(Wineck et al., 1981), a 21-year old woman was found dead at the wheel of her parked car. Gross autopsy findings included cerebral edema with uncal herniation. The lungs were minimally congested. Microscopic findings were not reported. Blood and tissue concentrations were as below:

Table 4.2.4 Blood Levels in a
Case of Fatal DOB Intoxication

Tissue	Blood Level, mg/L
Blood	0.90
Bile	0.64
Vitreous	0.51
Brain	0.25
Liver	9.00
Kidney	1.10

4.2.5 Nexus (4-bromo-2,5-dimethoxyphenethylamine, 2-C-B, bromo, toonies)

The agent Nexus was first detected in 1994. It was found in confiscated samples of LSD and MDMA that had been obtained in the western and southeastern United States. Nexus is generally sold under its own name, but occasionally it is falsely represented as a synthetic form of khat. Along with MDMA and gamma hydroxy butyrate (GHB), Nexus has become a standard "club drug," sold at "raves" and discos (Anon, 1994a).

Nexus shares structural and behavioral characteristics with older, more familiar designer amphetamines such as STP and DOM. It is said to produce euphoria and sensory enhancement with effects lasting six to eight hours, but otherwise, little is known about Nexus. A typical dose is said to be 10–20 mg of the hydrochloride salt taken orally, however Nexus can also be snorted. The recreational dose is thought to be 0.1–0.2 mg/kg, and the effects are said to last for six to eight hours. Frightening hallucinations can occur at higher dosage levels. Because Nexus is effective at relatively low doses, it can also be impregnated in sugar cubes or even sold as blotter tabs. There are no published animal studies, the human pharmacokinetics are unknown, and there have been no reported fatalities (Anon, 1994b). According to DEA reports, Nexus displays a high affinity for serotonin receptors. It can be substituted for either DOM or DOB in rat drug discrimination studies.

4.2.6 MDA (3,4-methylenedioxyamphetamine, "the love drug")

MDA was first synthesized in 1910 by two Merck chemists, Mannich and Jacobsohn (Mannich and Jacobsohn, 1910). Its marked sympathomimetic effects were immediately apparent, since in even moderate doses MDA can produce both tachycardia and hypertension (Gunn et al., 1939). Gordon Alles tried it on himself in a series of experiments which were described in Hoffer and Osmond's text on the hallucinogenic drugs (Hoffer and Osmond, 1967). MDA was patented as an anorectic agent and as an antitussive (Lukaszewski, 1979), but it never saw commercial distribution.

Like the other members of this group, MDA exhibits both amphetamine and hallucinogenic properties. The amphetamine-like actions are more pronounced with the (*l*)-isomer and the hallucinogenic effects with the (*d*)-isomer. The (*d*)-isomer, at least in rats, is extremely arrhythmogenic and even moderate doses can provoke ventricular tachycardia. This may explain some reported cases of MDA-associated sudden death. Illicitly manufactured MDA is always a racemic mixture (Marquardt et al., 1978), but the proportions of each isomer present may vary. Some batches may be more toxic than others, even if they contain pure MDA. Amphetamine-associated effects include vasoconstriction, tachycardia, and pupillary dilatation. There may also be convulsions and hyperthermia. MDA first appeared on the illicit market in the early 1960s and was responsible for a number of deaths. Its share of the illicit market rapidly faded when MDMA was introduced, but it still remains available on the black market. The last death to be reported was in 1990 (Nichols et al., 1990). Other than that one case, there were no mentions in the 1993 DAWN survey.

The simplest way to make MDA (and MDMA) is with the commercially available ketone MDP-2-P. However, the sale of MDP-2-P has been regulated since 1989, forcing clandestine chemists to utilize other routes. One involves the principal oil found in nutmeg and safrole. Treatment of safrole with hydrogen bromide yields an intermediate 2-bromo compound that can be converted to MDMA (Dal Cason, 1990; Clark et al., 1994).

Illicitly produced MDA is sold in powder or liquid form, almost always as hydrochloride salt (Ratcliffe, 1974). It is generally taken orally, but can be snorted or injected. Fatalities have been associated with each route. Clinical studies with MDA are limited. The effects of a 150-mg dose will peak at 1.5 hours, but can last for as long as eight hours. MDA is said to produce feelings of well-being and heightened tactile sensations. Detection of this drug is likely to be serendipitous. Both MDA and MDMA cross-react with the screening agents used to detect amphetamine and methamphetamine (Ramos et al., 1988). Blood and tissue levels have been reported in several fatal cases; reported levels have been remarkably similar in all cases.

Dogs treated with large doses of MDA die from hyperthermia and acidosis (Davis et al., 1987). Human autopsy findings in one case included visceral congestion, and epicardial, subendocardial, gastric, and subpleural petechiae (Poklis et al., 1979). Five cases were described in a second report where symptoms included agitation, hallucinations, and delirium. Autopsy findings were, unfortunately, not mentioned. Compared to other amphetamines, blood levels in these five individuals were quite high, ranging from 6–26 mg/L. In two of the cases, hepatic concentrations were lower than blood levels; in one case, they were higher (Cimbura, 1972). Another case report described visceral congestion with pulmonary edema and petichae on the surface of the heart (Reed et al., 1972). The latter is probably not of great significance since the patient had undergone resuscitative measures which can cause such petichae (Karch, 1987). The last reported case was that of a 26-year-old individual whose clinical history suggested arrhythmia. At autopsy, fresh thrombosis was found in a severely obstructed (75%) left main coronary artery. Microscopic features were not described (Nichols et al., 1990).

4.2.7 MDMA (3,4-methylenedioxymethamphetamine; other names include XTC, Adam, MDM)

The freebase MDMA is white and musty smelling. Salts are readily soluble in water. The empiric formula is $C_{11}H_{15}NO_2$. Such a wide range of melting points has been reported for the different salts as to make them of little value. Merck was issued a patent for MDMA in 1914, but the toxicology of this compound was not systematically studied until the early 1950s when the U.S. Army contracted with a group at the University of Michigan to study MDMA's toxicity.

The results of the Michigan studies, which were finally declassified and published in 1973, showed that MDMA was somewhat less toxic than MDA, but more toxic than mescaline (Hardman et al., 1973). Prior to its classification as a Schedule I drug in 1985, MDMA enjoyed some popularity in the psychiatric community. Arguments were, and continue to be, made for its therapeutic value (Shulgin, 1986; Grob et al., 1992). It has been suggested that the use of MDMA, in a controlled, therapeutic setting, promotes trust and confidence between patients and therapists. MDMA's reputation is generally touted as an empathy-enhancing compound (Eisner, 1989), or "empathogen" or "entactogen," from the Greek, "en" meaning "inside,"

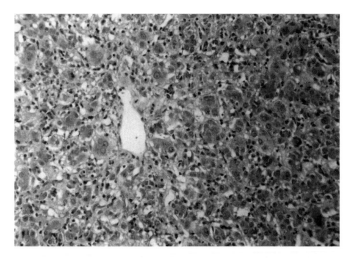

Figure 4.2.7 MDMA hepatitis. Florid hepatitis with inflammatory cell infiltrates and lobular disarray. The infiltrate is predominantly mononuclear, but a number of eosinophils and neutrophils are present in the portal tracts. It is not clear whether these changes represent a reaction to MDMA or to some contaminant in the drug. Courtesy of Dr. N. G. Ryley, John Radclyffe Hospital, Oxford.

"gen" meaning "to produce," and "tactus" from the Latin for touch (Nichols et al., 1986).

Illicit production of this drug is relatively simple. Safrole, the active ingredient in nutmeg, can be used to prepare the starting ketone (3,4-(methylenedioxy)phenylpropanone) by oxidizing it with hydrogen peroxide in an acid medium. The resulting compound is then combined with methylamine in alcohol. Aluminum powder, freshly treated with mercuric chloride in ethanol, is added to the mixture which is then boiled for several hours. MDMA is then distilled off under pressure (Verweij, 1990).

MDA is a known breakdown product of MDMA, but how much is metabolized via this pathway is hard to say, because illicitly manufactured MDMA usually also contains small amounts of MDA. Very little is known about the pharmacology of MDMA in humans. Its half-life is on the order of eight hours, but levels in intoxicated patients are poorly characterized. The clinical pharmacology has been studied in only one patient. In Army experiments, the LD_{50} in dogs was found to be 8–23 mg/kg when the drug was injected intravenously. In Rhesus monkeys, the range was 17–28 mg/kg.

After ingesting 50 mg orally, a 74-kg man had a peak level of 105 ng/mL at two hours. Blood levels declined to 5.1 ng/mL at 24 hours. Over the course of three days, 72% of the dose was excreted unchanged in the urine (Verebey et al., 1988). Simultaneous measurements made in volunteers given a 1.7 mg/kg dose of MDMA disclosed urine MDMA concentrations ranging from 1.48–5.05 µg/mL and urine MDA levels of 0.07–0.90 µg/mL (Helmin and Brenneisen, 1992).

Blood levels in intoxicated drivers have ranged from 110–590 ng/mL (Bost, 1988). There is one case report of a 13-month old child who ingested a capsule of MDMA, containing between 50 to 150 mg of drug. The child developed a typical hyperadrenergic syndrome with fever, tachycardia, hypertension, and convulsions. Serum MDMA measured approximately 90 minutes after ingestion was 700 ng with 100 ng of MDA detected at the same time (Russell et al., 1992).

There is tremendous overlap between recreational and toxic levels. In seven patients who died of MDMA toxicity, blood levels ranged from 110 ng/mL–1260 ng/mL. Levels in five patients who survived serious bouts of toxicity were from 200–970 ng, while levels in five car-accident victims were from 50–340 ng/mL (Bedford et al., 1992; Henry et al., 1992).

Rat liver and brain microsomes are capable of metabolizing MDA, via demethylation, to dihydroxyamphetamine and MDMA, to dihydroxymethamphetamine. In both locations, the conversion is cytochrome P450-dependent. Both of the metabolites can be further oxidized to form quinone or semiquinones that can react with sulfhydryl groups. The presence of these latter compounds could account for the known toxic effects of MDMA on serotonergic neurons (Hiramatsu et al., 1990; Lin et al., 1992). Other routes have been observed in experimental animals (N-demethylation, O-dealkylation, deamination, and conjugation) (Steele et al., 1994). A substantial percentage of a given dose appears unchanged in the urine where it can be detected with screening immunoassays such as the EMIT®-d.a.u. monoclonal test (Poklis et al., 1993). Sensitive HPLC methods for MDMA quantitation also exist (Michel et al., 1993).

MDMA shares the same properties as other amphetamines, acting on both the heart and the central nervous system, with increased release of catecholamines (including serotonin), and prevention of reuptake (Abbott and Concar, 1992). Neurotoxicity in animals is manifested by damage to serotonergic neurons. In the rat model, even one dose results in degeneration of serotonin-containing neurons. Animals treated with massive and repeated doses, while showing initial damage, do eventually recover, and at one year after treatment have no apparent lesions (Battaglia et al., 1987). There is considerable interspecies variation in the response to MDMA. The monkey is much more sensitive to the MDMA's serotonin-depleting effects than is the rat (Ricaurte et al., 1985; Barnes, 1988). Whether the results of animal studies can be generalized to humans remains unclear. Neurotoxicity in rats seems to be solely due to the S-(+) form of MDMA (Lim et al., 1993). The amount of this isomer formed by humans is not known.

No brain lesions have been demonstrated in humans, but chronic paranoid psychosis has been reported in MDMA abusers (Schifano, 1991; Creighton et al., 1991; Williams et al., 1993; McGuire et al., 1994). The experience in Europe is that MDMA abuse may result in a diverse group of psychiatric syndromes, including toxic psychosis. Psychotic symptoms in the MDMA users appear to be no different from symptoms seen in individuals with psychosis from any other cause. Clinically, there is no evidence that humans ever develop typical symptoms of serotonin depletion (disorders of sleep, mood, appetite). It has even been suggested that MDMA toxicity may be the result of too much, rather than too little, serotonin (Padkin, 1994). "Serotonin syndrome," also referred to as the "indolamine syndrome," was first recognized in depressed patients being treated with monoamine oxidase inhibitors and tryptophan. The patients became confused, and simultaneously developed ataxia, restlessness, lower-extremity hyperreflexia, and diaphoresis — symptoms very much like those seen in individuals with MDMA toxicity (Ames and Wirshing, 1993; Bodner et al., 1995).

On the other hand, at least one preliminary study found that humans previously exposed to MDMA have lower concentrations of 5-HIAA in their spinal fluid than non-drug-using controls. When compared to normals, MDMA users had 26% less 5-HIAA, and since the 5-HIAA content of the spinal fluid is believed to reflect the activity of central serotonergic neurons, the results suggest the presence of at least impaired function, if not morphologic changes (McCann et al., 1994). The situation is analogous to the problems with fenfluramine. It is a definite neurotoxin in animals, but no pathology has been reported in the 50 million plus users who have taken it for diet control (Grob et al. 1990).

In spite of very widespread use, reports of adverse effects in the United States have been rare. However, a number of fatalities have been described in the British literature, and from the data that has been presented, it appears that the increased toxicity seen in the U.K. is, at least partly, a function of how the drug is used (Chadwick et al., 1991; Campkin and Davies, 1992;

Screaton et al., 1992; Fahal et al., 1992; Henry, 1992). Almost all of the case reports from England involve young people who develop hyperthermia, rhabdomyolysis, renal failure, and disseminated intravascular coagulation (Brown and Osterloh, 1987; Chadwick et al., 1991; Campkin and Davies, 1992; Screaton et al., 1992; Henry et al., 1992; Singarajah and Lavies, 1992; Satchell and Connaughton, 1994).

Common to almost all the cases is the fact that, after taking the drug, the victims danced for many hours in hot, poorly ventilated clubs. There is evidence, however, that rhabdomyolysis in MDMA users may sometimes be the result of direct drug toxicity (Lehmann et al., 1995). Two cases of reversible aplastic anemia have also been described, further reinforcing the notion that MDMA, or some contaminant introduced during its production, is inherently toxic (Marsh et al., 1994). Urinary retention is a much less serious, but certainly distressing, disorder associated with MDMA use. Because MDMA is both an α and β adrenergic agonist, it may disrupt the innervation of the bladder neck and produce urinary retention (Bryden et al., 1995). Intracranial hemorrhage has also been reported (Hughes et al., 1993).

That such cases are rarely encountered in the United States probably has to do with the fact that American users tend to take the drug while they are alone, or at small gatherings, and that they do not do anything to generate more heat over and above that generated by MDMA's disruption of serotonin metabolism. The situation is likely to change in the near future, as "rave" parties, where participants use MDMA and dance all night, have become increasingly popular in the United States.

In animal studies, chronic treatment with MDMA causes testicular atrophy and prostatic hypertrophy (Frith et al., 1987). That abnormality has not been observed in humans, but many of the same disorders associated with cocaine and methamphetamine use have occurred in MDMA users. MDMA-related subarachnoid hemorrhage and ruptured berry aneurysm have been described (Gledhill et al., 1993), and so has keratopathy (O'Neill and Dart, 1993). Some of the deaths appear to have been secondary to malignant rhythm disturbances. Autopsy information about MDMA-related deaths is very spotty. Dowling described a case of a man with high-grade multivessel disease, who collapsed and died at the wheel of his car. His blood level was 0.95 mg/L, and autopsy was otherwise unremarkable (Dowling et al., 1987). Suarez described a 34-year old individual with Wolf-Parkinson-White syndrome, and an MDMA blood level of 0.2 mg%, who died of a cardiac arrhythmia. Findings at autopsy were unremarkable except for the heart which had areas of patchy fibrosis (Suarez and Riemersma, 1988).

Other deaths manifested fairly classic amphetamine/catecholamine toxicity with hyperadrenergic symptoms, including fever, tachycardia, and hypertension, as well as rhabdomyolysis, renal failure, and disseminated intravascular coagulation (Chadwick et al., 1991; Campkin and Davies, 1992). One such patient died after taking an undetermined amount of MDMA (only a qualitative toxicology screen was done). No microscopic findings were reported, and the general autopsy disclosed diffuse pulmonary and cerebral edema with "evidence of a generalized hemorrhagic diathesis" (Simpson and Rumak, 1981). Another individual survived in spite of developing fever, tachycardia, and pulmonary edema, apparently brought on by only 150 mg (twice a normal dose) (Brown et al., 1987). MDMA can precipitate death by misadventure. One intoxicated individual electrocuted himself (Dowling et al., 1987). Of course the presence of the drug might also be just an accidental finding. Dowling described one asthmatic with a blood MDMA of 1.1 mg/L, and autopsy findings of severe chronic lung disease.

Reports from England have also described patients with severe hepatitis. Liver damage seems to have been the result of an idiosyncratic reaction to MDMA or to some contaminant ingested along with it. In the cases that have been reported to date, all of the standard tests for hepatitis have been negative. A liver biopsy in one case showed florid changes with both portal and lobular necrosis. There was an inflammatory infiltrate containing mostly monocytes and there were substantial numbers of eosinophils. Liver biopsy, in another case, showed extensive necrosis concentrated in the periportal areas. The infiltrate was comprised of plasma cells and lymphocytes with only an occasional eosinophil. In both of the biopsied cases, recovery was uneventful.

4.2.8 MDEA (3,4-methylenedioxyethamphetamine, Eve)

MDEA appeared on the market shortly after MDMA. It is a close relative of MDMA, with essentially the same actions. It was banned in 1985 along with MDMA. Neither the clinical pharmacology, nor toxicology, of this compound have been studied. There is one reported fatality in an individual with an enlarged heart and some non-specific histologic changes. The subject's blood contained 2.0 mg/L of MDEA.

4.2.9 4-MAX (U4Euh, EU4EA, U4EA, 4-methylaminorex, aminorex)

4-MAX and 4-methylaminorex belong to a group of compounds known as oxazolines. Aminorex was sold in Europe by McNeil Laboratories during the 1960s under the brand names Menocil® and Apiquel®. It was promoted for appetite suppression and weight reduction, but had to be withdrawn from the market when its use was linked with the development of fatal pulmonary hypertension. The first reports of 4-methylaminorex abuse were from Florida during the mid-1980s, but since then, sporadic seizures have occurred across the country. On the street, it is sometimes called "ice" or "blue ice." Instead of being sold under its own name, it is often misrepresented as methamphetamine. Because it is relatively simple to synthesize, it has the potential to become a low-cost substitute for cocaine or methamphetamine (World Health Organization, 1991). 4-methylaminorex was classified as a Schedule I substance in April 1989. No deaths or emergency room visits were attributed to 4-MAX in the 1990 DAWN report.

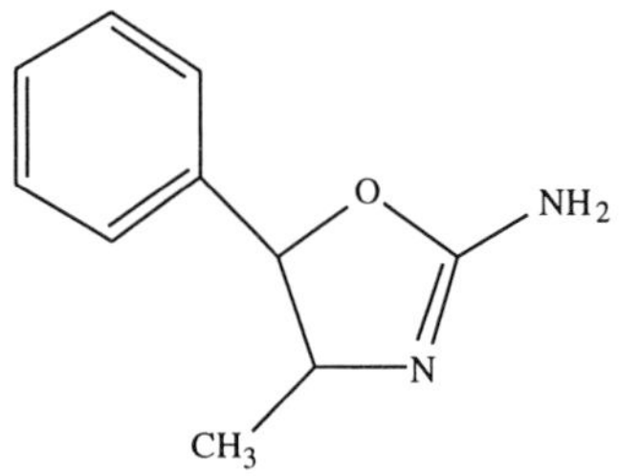

Figure 4.2.9   Aminorex molecule. 4-methylaminorex differs from MDMA and other ring-substituted amphetamines. It is classified as an oxazoline and has a side chain substitution that resembles pemoline, a potent stimulant.

The cis-(+)isomer is the form found in most clandestine drug laboratories. It is synthesized in a one-step reaction by condensing phenylpropanolamine with cyanogen bromide. It could also be produced starting with norpseudoephedrine. Both phenylpropanolamine and norpseudoephedrine are unrestricted and easily available. In laboratory experiments, 4-MAX produces the same effects as the other amphetamines, causing substantial increases in brain dopamine release and decreases in tryptophan hydroxylase activity (Hanson et al., 1992). When it was discovered that aminorex had lethal side effects, all work with it and related compounds stopped. Current clinical research is all but nonexistent. In animal trials, 4-MAX seems to be more epileptogenic than the other compounds in this class (Hanson et al., 1991), but otherwise it would be logical to suppose that 4-methylaminorex shares common mechanisms of toxicity with the rest of the amphetamines.

Pharmacokinetic studies of aminorex were done before sophisticated methods became available, and the pharmacokinetics of 4-MAX have been barely studied. Aminorex absorption is relatively rapid. A single 15-mg oral dose produces peak plasma concentration of 40 µg/mL at two hours. Concentrations decline slowly after that, dropping to 5 µg/mL at 24 hours. The reported half-life for aminorex in humans is 7.7 hours. Studies have not been done on 4-MAX, but the similarities to aminorex are so great that it should behave in much the same way. Most of a given dose is eliminated unchanged in the urine (World Health Organization, 1991).

Detecting 4-MAX in blood or body fluids is problematic, because neither aminorex nor 4-MAX are detectable with the routinely used screening tests. None of the currently available radioimmunoassays (RIA), fluorescence polarization assays (TDX), or enzyme multiplied immunoassays (EMIT) for amphetamines cross-react with the oxazolines. Detection with chromatographic or spectrophotometric techniques is not a problem, but since most medical examiners and all workplace testing programs screen with immunoassays, the presence of the oxazolines is likely to go undetected. Blood and urine levels have been measured in one fatality. The 4-MAX concentration was 21 µg/mL in the blood and 12.3 µg/mL in the urine (World Health Organization, 1991).

4.2.10 Other MDMA homologs

The 2-butanamine-2-homolog of MDMA (N-methyl-1-(3,4-methylenedioxyphenyl)-2-butanamine) has been produced by clandestine chemists in Germany. Use of the drug is said to result in a pleasant introspective state, devoid of hallucinogenic effects. Identification of the drug is straightforward, but nothing is known of its pharmacologic or metabolic effects (Rösner and Junge, 1994).

4.2.11 "Kat" (2-methylamino-1-phenylpropan-1-one,"Jeff," 2-(methylamino)-propiophenone; α-(methylamino) propiophenone; α-N-methylaminopropiophenone; N-methylcathinone; methylcathinone; AL-464; AL-422; AL-463; UR1432, "Cat")

Kat was first discovered many years ago, but reports of abuse, initially from the former U.S.S.R, only began to appear in the early 1990s. In the 1950s, the Parke Davis company considered marketing methcathinone as an appetite suppressant, and in 1957 filed for a patent on the production process. In subsequent studies, Parke Davis chemists discovered that only the *l*-form was active, but with storage, especially in basic solution, the pure *l*-form rapidly converted into a racemic mixture. Because of the active form's limited shelf life, Parke Davis never proceeded to human testing, but it appears that the clandestine chemists are using the synthetic route specified in the original Parke Davis patent.

Kat is synthesized directly from ephedrine by oxidation with potassium permanganate. In the United States, clandestine chemists have traditionally opted to reduce ephedrine and make methamphetamine. But the oxidative route is much simpler. The required chemicals (battery acid, sodium dichromate, lye, paint thinner, and epsom salts) are much easier to come by without attracting notice, and cookbook recipes are being sold on the street and over the Internet.

Methcathinone has all of the characteristics of an amphetamine, including the ability to cause the release of dopamine from the rat caudate nucleus (Glennon et al., 1987). A number of deaths have been attributed to "Jeff" overdoses in the former U.S.S.R, but nothing is known of the pathology or clinical pharmacology of this agent (Zhingel et al., 1991). A recent report described the clinical findings in four alleged cases treated in a midwestern hospital, but blood and urine levels were not measured (Emerson et al., 1993). Symptoms in the four subjects were generally indistinguishable from those of amphetamine toxicity. In two cases, substantial amounts of ephedrine were also detected, suggesting that the clandestine chemist responsible had not carried the reaction to completion. According to DEA reports, Kat is used in binges lasting two to six days. It is usually taken by nasal insufflation, but can be taken orally or injected, with the average dose of roughly 100 mg taken as often as every hour (Federal Register, 1993).

Between June 1991 and August 1993, 27 clandestine laboratories were seized, all in Michigan and Wisconsin. Since then, production has expanded, and seizures reported in the south and western portions of the United States. Although it is occasionally passed off as methamphetamine, Kat is usually represented as a form of synthetic khat. Methcathinone has recently been classified as a Schedule I drug (Anon., Department of Justice, 1993).

References

Abbott, A. and Concar, D. (1992). A trip into the unknown. New Scientist, 1836: 30–34.

Ames, D. and Wirshing, W. (1993). Ecstasy, the serotonin syndrome, and neuroleptic malignant syndrome — a possible link? JAMA, 269: 869–870.

Anon. (1898). Paradise or inferno. Br Med J, 1: 390.

Anon. (1993). Department of Justice, Drug Enforcement Administration, 21 CFR Part 1308, Schedules of controlled substances temporary placement of methcathinone into Schedule 1. Federal Register, 58(80): 25788–25789.

Anon. (1994a). Department of Justice, Drug Enforcement Administration, 21 CFR Part 1308, Schedules of controlled substances temporary placement of 4-bromo-2,5-dimethoxyphenethylamine into Schedule 1. Federal Register, 59(4): 671–673.

Anon. (1994b). Drug intelligence report: 4-Bromo-2,5-dimethoxyphenethylamine. Microgram, 27(12): 410.

Barnes, D. (1988). New data intensify the agony over Ecstasy. Science, 239: 864–866.

Barron, F., Jarvik, M., and Bunnell, S. (1964). The hallucinogenic drugs. Sci Am, 210: 29–37.

Battaglia, G., Yeh, S., and DeSouza, E. (1988). MDMA-induced neurotoxicity: parameters of degeneration and recovery of brain serotonin neurons. Pharmacol Biochem Behav, 29: 269–274.

Bedford, A., Schwartz, R., and Dawling, S. (1992). Accidental ingestion of "Ecstasy" (3,4-methylenedioxymethylamphetamine). Arch Dis Child, 67: 1114–1115.

Bodner, R., Lynch, T., Lewis, L. et al. (1995). Serotonin syndrome. Neurology, 45: 219–223.

Bohn, G. (1981). Illegally manufactured 2,5-dimethoxy-4-bromoamphetamine in connection with a fatal intoxication. Toxichemistry, 14: 140–141.

Bost, R. (1988). 3,4-methylenedioxymethamphetamine (MDMA) and other amphetamine derivatives. J Foren Sci, 33(2): 576–587.

Bowen, J., Davis, G., Kearney, T., and Bardin, J. (1983). Diffuse vascular spasm associated with 4-bromo-2,5-dimethoxyamphetamine ingestion. JAMA, 249: 1477–1479.

Brown, C. and Osterloh, J. (1987). Multiple severe complications from recreational ingestion of MDMA ('Ecstasy'). JAMA, 258(6): 780–781.

Bryden, A., Rothwell, A., and O'Reilly, P. (1995). Urinary retention with misuse of Ecstasy. Br Med J, 310(6978): 504.

Buhrich, N., Morris, G., and Cook, G. (1983). Bromo-DMA: the Australian hallucinogen? Australia and New Zealand J Psych, 17(3): 275–279.

Campkin, T. and Davies, U. (1992). Another death from Ecstasy. J R Soc Med, 85(1): 61.

Chadwick, I., Curry, P., Linsley, A. et al. (1991). Ecstasy, 3,4-methylenedioxymethamphetamine (MDMA), a fatality associated with coagulopathy and hyperthermia. J Royal Soc Med, 84(6): 371.

Charalampous, K., Orengo, A., Walker, K., and Kinross-Wright, J. (1964). Metabolic fate of β-(3,4,5-trimethoxyphenyl)-ethylamine (mescaline) in humans: isolation and identification of 3,4,5-trimethoxyphenylacetic acid. J Pharm Exp Ther, 145: 242–246.

Charalampous, K., Walker, K., and Kinross-Wright, J. (1966) Metabolic fate of mescaline in man. Psychopharmacologia, 9: 48–63.

Chesher, G. (1990). Designer drugs — the "whats and the whys." Med J Aust, 153(3): 157–161.

Cimbura, G. (1972). 3,4-methylenedioxyamphetamine (MDA): analytical and forensic aspects of fatal poisoning. J Forensic Sci, 17: 329–333.

Cimbura, G. (1974). PMA deaths in Ontario. Can Med Assoc J, 110: 1263–1267.

Clark, C., Noggle, F., DeRuiter, J., and Andurkar, S. (1994). GC-MS analysis of products, intermediates and by-products in the synthesis of MDA from isosafrole. Microgram, XXVII: 188–199.

Creighton, F., Black, D., and Hyde, C. (1991). "Ecstasy" psychosis and flashbacks. Br J Psych, 159: 713–715.

Dal Cason, T. (1990). An evaluation of the potential for clandestine manufacture of 3,4-methylenedioxyamphetamine (MDA) analogs and homologs. J Forensic Sci, 35: 675–697.

Davis, W., Hatoum, H., and Waters, I. (1987). Toxicity of MDA (3,4-methylenedioxyamphetamine) considered for relevance to hazards of MDMA (Ecstasy) abuse. Alcohol and Drug Res, 7: 123–134.

Delliou, D. (1980) Bromo-DMA: new hallucinogenic drug. Med J Aust, 1: 83.

Delliou, D. (1983). 4-Bromo-2,5-dimethoxyamphetamine: psychoactivity, toxic effects and analytical methods. Forensic Sci Int, 21: 259–267.

Dowling, G., McDonough, E., and Bost, R. (1987). "Eve" and "Ecstasy": a report of five deaths associated with the use of MDEA and MDMA. JAMA, 257: 1615–1617.

Drug Enforcement Administration (1993). Final rule: schedule of Controlled Substances; placement of methcathinone into Schedule I. Federal Register 58 FR-53404.

Eisner, B. (1989). *Ecstasy, the MDMA story.* Berkeley: Ronin Publishing.

Emerson, T. and Cisek, J. (1993). Methcathinone: a Russian designer amphetamine infiltrates the rural midwest. Ann Emerg Med, 22: 1897–1903.

Fahal, I., Sallomi, D., Yaqoob, M., and Bell, G. (1992). Acute renal failure after "Ecstasy." Br Med J, 305: 29.

Frith, C., Chang, I., Lattin, D. et al. (1987). Toxicity of 3,4-methylenedioxymethamphetamine in the dog and rat. Fund Appl Toxicol, 9: 110–119.

Gledhill, J., Moore, D., Bell, D., and Henry, J. (1993). Subarachnoid hemorrhage associated with MDMA abuse. J Neurol Neurosurg Psych, 56: 1036–1037.

Glennon, R., Yousif, M., Naiman, N., and Kalix P. (1987). Methcathinone: a new and potent amphetamine-like agent. Pharm Biochem Behav, 26: 547–551.

Grob, C., Bravo, G., and Walsh, R. (1990). Second thoughts on 3,4-methylenedioxymethamphetamine (MDMA) neurotoxicity. Arch Gen Psychiatry, 47: 288.

Grob, C., Bravo, G., Walsh, R., and Liester, M. (1992). The MDMA-neurotoxicity controversy: implications for clinical research with novel psychoactive drugs. J Nerve Ment Dis, 180: 355–356.

Gunn, J., Gurd, M., and Sachs, I. (1939). The action of some amines related to adrenaline: methoxy-phenylisopropylamines. J Physiol, 95: 485–500.

Hanson, G., Bunker, C., Johnson, M. et al. (1992). Response of monoaminergic and neuropeptide systems to 4-methylaminorex: a new stimulant of abuse. Euro J Pharm, 218: 287–293.

Hanson, G., Johnson, M., Bush, L. et al. (1992). Behavioral and neurochemical re-
sponses to 4-methylaminorex: a new stimulant of abuse. In L. Harris (Ed.).
Committee for problems of drug dependency, 1991 Annual Conference. NIDA
Research Monograph 119, Washington, D.C.: U.S. Government Printing Office.

Hardman, H., Haavik, C., and Seevers, M. (1973). Relationship of the structure of
mescaline and seven analogs to toxicity and behavior in five species of laboratory
animals. Toxicol and Appl Pharmacol, 25(2): 299–309.

Helmin, H. and Brenneisen, R. (1992). Determination of psychotropic phenylalky-
lamine derivatives in biological matrices by high-performance liquid chromatography with photodiode-array detection. J Chromotography, 593: 87–94.

Hel Henry, J., Jeffreys, K., and Dawling, S. (1992). Toxicity and deaths from 3,4-
methylenedioxymethamphetamine ("ecstasy"). Lancet, 340: 384–387.

Henry, J. (1992). "Ecstasy" and the dance of death: severe reactions are unpredictable.
Br Med J, 305: 5–6.

Hermle, L., Fünfgeld, M., Oepen, G. et al. (1992). Mescaline-induced psychopatho-
logical, neuropsychological, and neurometabolic effects in normal subjects: experimental psychosis as a tool for psychiatric research. Biol Psych, 32: 976–991.

Hiramatsu, M., Kumagai, Y., Unger, S., and Cho, A. (1990). Metabolism of methylenedioxymethamphetamine: formation of dihydroxymethamphetamine and a
quinone identified as its glutathione adduct. J Pharmacol Exp Ther, 254: 521–527.

Hoffer, A. and Osmond, H. (Eds.). (1967). *The hallucinogens*. New York: Academic
Press.

Hollister, L. (1967). Chemical Psychoses. Springfield, IL: Charles Thomas, 17–18.

Hughes, J., McCabe, M., and Evans, R. (1993). Intracranial hemorrhage associated
with ingestion of "Ecstasy." Arch Emerg Med, 10: 372–374.

Kapadia, G. and Fayez, M. (1970) Peyote constituents: chemistry, biogenesis, and
biological effects. J Pharm Sci, 59: 1699–1727.

Karch, S. (1987). Resuscitation-induced myocardial necrosis. Am J Forensic Med and
Path, 8(1): 3–8.

Lehmann, E., Thom, C., Croft, D. et al. (1995). Delayed severe rhabdomyolysis after
taking ecstasy. Post Grad Med, 71(833): 186–187.

Lewin, T. and Henning, R. (1888). *Anhalonium Lewinii*. Therapeutic Gazette, 231–237.

Lim, H., Su, Z., and Foltz, R. (1993). Stereoselective dispostiion: enantioselective
quantitation of 3,4-(methylenedioxy)methamphetamine and three of its metabolites by gas chromatography/electron capture negative ion chemical ionization
mass spectrometry. Bio Mass Spect, 22: 403–411.

Lin, L., Kumagai, Y., and Cho, A. (1992). Enzymatic and chemical demethylenation
of (methylenedioxy)amphetamine and (methylenedioxy)methamphetamine by
rat brain microsomes. Chem Res Toxicol, 5: 401–406.

Lukaszewski, T. (1979). 3,4-methylenedioxyamphetamine overdose. Clin Toxicol, 15:
405–409.

Mannich, C. and Jacobsohn, W. (1910). Hydroxy phenylalkylamines and dihydrox-
yphenalkylamines. Berichte, 43: 189.

Marquardt, G., DiStefano, V., and Ling, L. (1978). Pharmacological and toxicological
effects of β-3,4-methylenedioxyamphetamine isomers. Toxicol Appl Pharmacol,
45: 675–683.

Marsh, J., Abboudi, Z., Gibson, F. et al. (1994). Aplastic anaemia following exposure
to 3,4-methylenedioxymethamphetamine "Ecstasy." Br J Heme, 88: 281–285.

McCann, U., Ridenour, A., Shaham, Y. et al. (1994). Serotonin neurotoxicity after (±)
3,4-methylenedioxymethamphetamine (MDMA; "Ecstasy"): a controlled study
in humans. Neuropsychopharmacol, 10(2): 129–138.

McGuire, P., Cope, H., and Fahy, T. (1994). Diversity of psychopathology associated with use of 3,4-methylenedioxymethamphetamine ("Ecstasy"). Br J Psych, 165: 391–395.

Metzer, W. (1989). The experimentation of S. Weir Mitchell with mescal. Neurology, 39: 303–304.

Michel, R., Rege, A., and George, W. (1993). High-pressure liquid chromatography/electrochemical detection method for monitoring MDA and MDMA in whole blood and other biological tissues. J Neurosci Methods, 50: 61–66.

Mitchell, S. (1896). Remarks on the effects of *Anhalonium lewinii* (the mescal button). Br Med J, 2: 1625–1629.

Mokrasch, L. and Stevenson, I. (1959). The metabolism of mescaline with a note on correlations between metabolism and psychological effects. J Nerve Ment Dis, 129: 177–183.

National Institute on Drug Abuse. (1993a). Annual Emergency Room Data. Data from the Drug Abuse Warning Network. Statistical Series, Number 13-B. Rockville, MD, U.S. Department of Health and Human Services.

National Institute on Drug Abuse. (1990b). Annual Medical Examiner Data. Data from the Drug Abuse Warning Network. Statistical Series, Number 10-B. Rockville, MD, U.S. Department of Health and Human Services.

Nichols, G., Davis, G., Corrigan, C., and Ransdell, J. (1990). Death associated with abuse of a "designer drug." Kentucky Med Assn J, 88(November): 600–603.

Nichols, D., Hoffman, A., Oberlender, P. et al. (1986). Derivatives of 1-(1,3-benzodioxol-5-yl)-2-butanamines: representatives of a novel therapeutic class. J Med Chem, 29: 2009–2015.

Oepen, G., Fuenfgeld, M., Harrington, A. et al. (1989). Right hemisphere involvement in mescaline-induced psychosis. Psychiatry Research, 29(3): 335–336.

O'Neill, D. and Dart, J. (1993). Methylenedioxyamphetamine ("Ecstasy")-associated keratopathy. Eye, 7: 805–806.

Padkin, A. (1994). Treating MDMA toxicity. Anesthesia, 49(3): 259

Poklis, A., Mackell, M., and Drake, W. (1979). Fatal intoxication from 3,4-methylenedioxyamphetamine. J Forensic Sci, 24: 70–75.

Poklis, A., Fitzgerald, R., Hall, K. et al. (1993). EMIT®-d.a.u. monoclonal amphetamine/methamphetamine assay. II. Detection of methylenedioxyamphetamine (MDA) and methylenedioxymethamphetamine (MDMA). Forensic Sci Int, 59: 63–70.

Prentiss, D. and Morgan, F. (1893). *Anhalonium lewinii* (mescal buttons): study of the drug with special reference to its physiological action upon man, with report of experiments. Ther Gazette, 11: 577–585.

Ramos, J., Fitzgerald, R., and Poklis, A. (1988). MDMA and MDA cross reactivity observed with Abott TDx amphetamine/methamphetamine reagents. Clin Chem, 34(5): 991.

Ratcliffe, B. (1974). Editorial: MDA. Clin Toxicol, 7(4): 409–411.

Reed, D., Cravey, R., and Sedgwick, P. (1972). A fatal case involving methylenedioxyamphetamine. Clin Toxicol, 5: 3–6.

Reynolds, P. and Jindrich, E. (1985) A mescaline associated fatality. J Analyt Toxicol, 9(4): 183–184.

Ricaurte, G., Bryan, G., Strauss, L. et al. (1985). Hallucinogenic amphetamine selectively destroys brain serotonin nerve terminals. Science, 229: 986–988.

Rösner, P. and Junge, T. (1994). N-methyl-1-(3,4-methylenedioxyphenyl)-2-butanamine, a representative of a new class of street drugs. Microgram, 27(12): 411–418.

Satchell, S. and Connaughton, M. (1994). Inappropriate antiduretic hormone secretion and extreme rises in serum creatinine kinase following MDMA ingestion. Br J Hosp Med, 51: 495.

Schifano, F. (1991). Chronic atypical psychosis associated with MDMA ("Ecstasy") abuse. Lancet, 338(8778): 1335.

Screaton, G., Cairns, H., Sarner, M. et al. (1992). Hyperpyrexia and rhabdomyolysis after MDMA ("Ecstasy") abuse. Lancet, 33: 677–678.

Shulgin, A., Sargent, T., and Naranjo, C. (1973). Animal pharmacology and human psychopharmacology of 3-methoxy-4,5-methylenedioxyphenylisopropylamine (MMDA). Pharmacology, 10: 12–18.

Shulgin, A. (1977). Profiles of psychedelic drugs: STP. J Psychedelic Drugs, 9: 171–172.

Shulgin, A. (1981). Profiles of psychedelic drugs: DOB. J Psychedelic Drugs, 13: 99.

Shulgin, A. (1986). The background and chemistry of MDMA. J Psychoact Drugs, 18: 291–304.

Simpson, D. and Rumak, B. (1981). Methylenedioxyamphetamine: clinical description of overdose, death and review of pharmacology. Arch Intern Med, 141: 1507–1509.

Singarajah, C. and Lavies, N. (1992). An overdose of Ecstasy, a role for dantrolene. Anaesthesia, 47: 686–687.

Smythies, J., Johnston, V., Bradley, R. et al. (1967). Some new behavior-disrupting amphetamines and their significance. Nature, 216(October 14): 128–129.

Snyder, S., Failace, L., and Hollister, L. (1967). 2,5-dimethoxy-4-methyl-amphetamine (STP): a new hallucinogenic drug. Science, 158: 669–670.

Steele, T., McCann, U., and Ricuarte, G. (1994). 3, 4-methylenedioxymethamphetamine (MDMA, "Ecstasy"): pharmacology and toxicology in animals and humans. Addiction, 89: 539–551.

Suarez, R. and Riemersma, R. (1988). "Ecstasy" and sudden cardiac death. Am J For Med and Pathol, 9(4): 339–341.

Verebey, K., Alrazi, J., and Jaffe, J. (1988). The complications of "Ecstasy" (MDMA). JAMA, 259(11): 1649–1650.

Verweij, A. (1990) Clandestine manufacture of 3,4-methylenedioxymethylamphetamine (MDMA) by low pressure reductive amination. A mass spectrometric study of some reaction mixtures. Forensic Sci Int, 45: 91–96.

Williams, H., Meagher, D., and Galligan, P. (1993). M.D.M.A. ("Ecstasy"); a case of possible drug-induced psychosis. Irish J Med Sci, 162(2): 43–44.

Winek, C., Collom, W., and Bricker, J. (1981). A death due to 4-bromo-2,5-dimethoxyamphetamine. Clin Toxicol, 18: 267–271.

World Health Organization (1991). Information manual designer drugs. World Health Organization, Vienna, 103–119.

Zhingel, K., Dovensky, W., Crossman, A., and Allen, A. (1991). Ephedrone: 2-methylamino-1-phenylpropan-1-one (Jeff). J Forensic Sci, 36(3): 915–920.

4.3 Phenylalkylamines

4.3.1 Simple tryptamines

4.3.1.1 DMT (N,N-dimethyltryptamine)

DMT is also a component of South American hallucinogenic snuffs. It can be isolated from both old and new world plants, and even European mushrooms. DMT is not active when taken orally and must either be smoked or injected. DMT is usually sold on the black market as a brownish solid material that smells like mothballs. Users cut off small pieces and smoke them by placing them at the end of a cigarette, often a marijuana cigarette. DMT is sometimes referred to as the "businessman's high" because a single inhalation will produce a five to ten minute trip that is entirely gone by 30 minutes (Chamakura, 1993).

Nothing is known about the toxicology of kinetics of smoked DMT; however, controlled double blind studies with intravenously administered drug have been done with experienced hallucinogen users. With doses of 0.2 and 0.4 mg/kg (which are fully hallucinogenic), effects are experienced almost instantly, peaking within two minutes, and disappearing in 20 to 30 minutes. Measured blood levels corresponded to the subjective effects of the drug. Peak levels varied widely from subject to subject and ranged from 32–204 ng after a 0.4 mg/kg dose. Hallucinogenic drugs like DMT are serotonergic agonists, or at least partial agonists, and, in addition, have adrenergic and dopaminergic properties, which explains why a number of hormonal, autonomic, and cardiovascular changes were also observed. Pupils dilated, and levels of cortisol, prolactin, corticotropin, growth hormone, and β-endorphin, all increased in a dose-dependent manner. These values returned to near baseline within 30 minutes. Similar changes were observed for heart rate and blood pressure. Body temperature also rose, although that change lagged slightly behind the others (Strassman and Qualls, 1994).

4.3.1.2 Bufotenine (5-hydroxy-N,N-dimethyl-tryptamine)

Bufotenine shares structural and mass spectral similarities with psilocybin and is a potent hallucinogen. It is the active ingredient in the South American hallucinogenic snuffs described by early Amazon explorers more than 400 years ago (Monardes, 1574). Archaeologic evidence indicates that the use of bufotenine-containing snuff goes back several thousand years (Torres et al., 1991). In spite of its ancient origins, the drug received little attention until a California wildlife instructor was arrested in 1994 for the possession of bufotenine which he had collected from four pet toads. At about the same time, police from Australia began to encounter people smoking the dried skin of the Australian cane toad. Occasional samples of bufotenine began appearing at crime laboratories (Chamakura, 1993), and the process of "toad smoking" began to receive extensive publicity in the lay press (Gallagher, 1994).

Bufotenine was first purified in 1934. It occurs naturally in a number of different plants and animals. It is present in at least four different species of toads, and not just in their skin. The digitalis-like component of the poison can be detected in toad plasma and internal organs (Lichtstein et al., 1993). Bufotenine is also found in mushrooms, plant leaves, stems, and even some plant seeds (Chamakura, 1993). It can also be found in Asian herbal remedies prepared in China from either dried toad skins or from milking the parotid secretions. The toad product containing medications is called *Chan-Su*. It is used topically to treat various skin ailments. Toad products are also added, in minute amounts, to other Asian proprietary mixtures in hopes of strengthening the heart. *Chan-Su* can be legally prescribed by herbalists practicing in the United States.

Confiscated samples of bufotenine have been described as resinous, reddish brown cubes, reminiscent of root beer barrel candies that have been sucked on (Chamakura, 1993; Vohlken, 1993). It is believed that abusers shave off some of the resin and smoke it at the end of a cigarette. The dose used is not known, and resultant blood levels have never been measured. A fairly extensive literature on bufotenine's botany and chemistry now exists, but essentially nothing is known of its pharmacokinetics or pharmacodynamics.

The toxicologic studies that have been done are difficult to interpret. Toad secretions contain at least two different pharmacologically-active classes of compounds: a group of steroid derivatives called bufogenins, and bufotoxins which resemble cardiac glycosides. At least one of these glycosides is also a potent vasoconstrictor, and its effects are not entirely blocked by antidigoxin antibodies (Bagrov et al., 1993). A second group of basic components includes epinephrine, norepinephrine, serotonin, and bufotenine. Dogs poisoned with toad secretions develop drooling, seizure activity, cyanosis, and cardiac arrhythmias (Palumbo and Perri, 1975). The hemodynamic effects, at least, seem to be due to the combined effects of the glycosides and catecholamines (Ojiri et al., 1991).

Human toad poisoning does occur, although death is rare. A 1986 case report described a child who developed status epilepticus after mouthing a toad (Hitt and Ettinger, 1986). Profound drooling, seizure activity, arrhythmias, and cyanosis have all been described in *Chan-Su* users (Chern et al., 1991; Kwan et al., 1992; Yei and Deng, 1993). Elevated digoxin levels may be seen in individuals who ingest toad venom, and the symptoms in the *Chan-Su* users probably occur not from bufotenine, but from the cardiac glycosides ingested along with the bufotenine (Chern et al., 1991; Cheung et al., 1989; Kwan et al., 1992; Lin et al., 1989).

4.3.1.3   Psilocybin (4-phosphoryl-N,N-dimethyltryptamine)

4.3.1.3.1   History.   Psilocybin-containing mushrooms were probably used by the Aztecs, but until the 1960s they aroused little interest outside of Mexico. The name psilocybin is derived from the Greek roots "psilo" meaning bald and "cybe" meaning head, presumably because of the shape of the mushrooms from which the compounds are derived. The molecule's structure was not even established until 1958, when the active principle of these mushrooms was isolated by Albert Hoffman at Sandoz Pharmaceuticals. Hoffman had succeeded in synthesizing LSD just a few years earlier. For some time, Sandoz marketed pure psilocybin under the brand name Indocybin® (Stafford, 1982).

Psilocybin can be found in three different genera of mushrooms: *Psilocyba*, *Panelous*, and *Concybe*. All three varieties grow naturally in the northwestern and southeastern portions of the United States. Related or identical forms grow wild in Central and South America as well as Southeast Asia and India. Large quantities are cultivated for illegal distribution. The most common species is *Psilocybe cubensis.* It grows wild in the manure of cattle, water buffalo, and other ruminants, including deer, and possibly kangaroos.

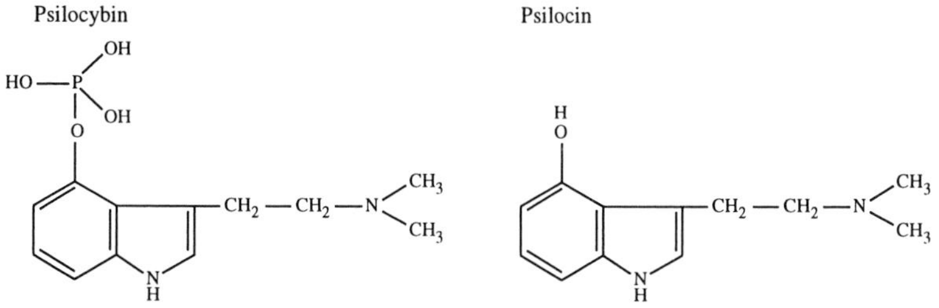

Figure 4.3 Psilocybin and psilocin molecules.

In Southeast Asia, farmers collect droppings from these animals and systematically grow the fungi in disused rice paddies (Allen and Merlin, 1992).

All three genera contain the tryptophan derivatives psilocybin (4-phosphoryloxy-N-N-dimethyltryptamine) and psilocin (4-hydroxyl-N, N-dimethyltryptamine). *Psilocybe cubensis* is generally the preferred cultivar, and on average yields 10 mg of psilocybin per gram of fresh mushroom, which is equal to an average dose. Psilocin is 1.5 times more potent than psilocybin, but because the latter oxidizes more slowly than the former, both contribute almost equally to the mushroom's effect (Leikin, Krantz, and Zellkanter, 1989). During the early 1980s, growing kits complete with spores were advertised in magazines. They are now illegal (Schwartz and Smith, 1988).

Identifying wild *Psilocyba* is difficult and can be dangerous. Psilocybin-containing mushrooms grow side by side with the poisonous *Galerina autumnalis*. The two can be separated by the fact that Galerina species have rust brown colored spores while the spores of Psilocybe species are gray to lilac. Some, but not all, species of *Psilocybe* mushrooms can be distinguished from some poisonous mushrooms by the fact that, when cut, they will oxidize and turn blue within 30 to 60 minutes. Unfortunately, some poisonous mushrooms can do the same thing. As a result, pathologists are much more likely to encounter cases of mushroom poisoning than they are to encounter psilocybin-associated medical problems!

4.3.1.3.2   Chemical constants. Psilocybin is 3-[2-(dimethylamino)ethyl]-1 H-indol-4-ol dihydrogen phosphate ester. Its formula is $C_{12}H_{17}N_2O_4P$ with a molecular weight of 284.27. It is composed of 50.7% carbon, 6% hydrogen, 9.9% nitrogen, 22.5% oxygen, and 10.9% phosphorus. The melting point is variable, depending on how it was crystallized. Psilocin, the 4-hydroxy analog of psilocybin, is formed by metabolic dephosphorylation. It is also contained in hallucinogenic mushrooms, but in much smaller amounts. Psilocin is the active form within the central nervous system and, on a weight for weight basis, is much more potent than psilocybin. Its formula is $C_{11}H_{16}N_2O$ with a molecular weight of 204.27. It forms plate-like crystals and has a melting point of 173–176°C (Budavari et al., 1988).

4.3.1.3.3   Metabolism and tissue levels. Controlled human studies are nonexistent. Pharmacokinetic studies in rats, which may or may not be relevant to man, suggest that 50% of a given dose will be absorbed from the stomach, and 65% will be excreted in the urine, with another 20% appearing in the bile and stool. Most of the excretion occurs in the first eight hours but, in the rat at least, labeled drug may appear in the urine for as long as a week (Aboul-Enein, 1974). Tissue levels have not been reported in humans.

4.3.1.3.4   *Clinical findings.* Symptoms consistent with sympathetic stimulation have been described. A 30-year old case report describes the death of a 6-year old child who developed hyperthermia and status epilepticus after ingesting an undetermined number of mushrooms (McCawley et al., 1962). A review of 27 patients with "magic mushroom" poisoning found that mydriasis and hyperreflexia were as common as disorders of perception, and that all of the individuals recovered uneventfully (Peden et al., 1981). A paper published in 1983 reviewed 318 cases reported to Poison Control Centers, and found increasing use, but no serious toxicity (Francis and Murray, 1983). Since then no other cases have been reported. It seems probable that any deaths that do occur are likely to be accidental, usually as a result of drug-induced confusion. In times of shortage, dealers may misrepresent LSD or PCP as psilocybin, producing a somewhat puzzling clinical picture.

4.3.2   Beta carbolines

4.3.2.1   Harmaline

Harmine and harmaline are the active ingredients in some of the hallucino-genic snuffs used by South American Indians. They are only two of many naturally occurring alkaloids found in *Peganum harmala*, also known as Syrian rue, the traditional source of the characteristic red dye used in Turkish carpet (Furst, 1985). *Peganum harmala* is a perrenial herbaceous plant found not only in the Amazon basin, but also in North Africa and the American Southwest (Bahri and Vhemli, 1991). *Peganum harmala* is just one of at least eight plant families, some old world, some new, that contain harmine and harmaline, β-carboline derivatives thought to be capable of inhibiting tryp-tophane hydroxylase and monoamine oxidase. They are profoundly hallu-cinogenic. In the new world, *Banisteriopsis,* a malpighiaceous tropical genus, is the main source of the psychoactive snuff. Very little is known about their metabolism or potential toxicity.

A 200 ml sample of Daime, a ritual herbal potion used in the Amazon, was found to contain 298 mg of harmine, 278 mg of tetrahydroharmine, and 106 mg of DMT (Liwszyc et al., 1992). Based on a limited number of animal studies, harmaline and its derivatives do not appear to be particularly toxic; the LD_{50} in rats is 120 mg/kg. Autopsies of cattle that consumed large amounts of harmaline-containing shrubs have disclosed only passive vis-ceral congestion (Bailey, 1979). Studies in humans have not been reported.

Harmaline is closely related to ibogaine, a compound thought to have potent anti-addictive properties. Preclinical trials with both harmaline and ibogane have shown that, in high doses, both compounds are capable of causing Purkinje cell degeneration, possibly due to the release of excitatory amino acids (O'Hearn and Molliver, 1993).

4.3.3 Alpha-methyltryptamines

4.3.3.1 5-MeO-DMT (5-Methoxy-N,N-dimethyltryptamine)

MeO-DMT is a potent hallucinogen closely related to bufotenine (5-hydroxy-N,N-dimethyltryptamine). It is also found in some toad species (Weil and Davis, 1994). Other than the fact that it is a potent $5HT_2$ antagonist (Gudelsky et al., 1994), and the fact that it is only effective when smoked, virtually nothing is known about its toxicology in humans.

4.3.3.2 Alpha-ethyltryptamine

Also known as Etryptamine and Monase, α-ethyltryptamine was first marketed in 1961 as an antidepressant under the brand name Monase®. It was subsequently withdrawn from the market when it was found to be neurotoxic. Illicit use has caused several deaths in Germany and Spain (Anon, 1994) and at least one death in the United States. Its potency is considered to be comparable to that of DMT (Glennon, 1993; Strassman and Qualls, 1994; Morano et al., 1993).

Drug studies done by the Upjohn Company, when it was marketing Monase®, found that it was rapidly absorbed and widely distributed. It is metabolized via 6-hydroxylation, eliminated mainly by the kidneys, and has an estimated plasma half-life of 8.2 hours. The only reported fatality in the United States involved a 19-year old woman who took two tablets of what she thought was MDMA. Within a few hours, the woman became disoriented, vomited, and collapsed. The principal autopsy findings were pulmonary edema and terminal aspiration. Epicardial petichae were noted, but could have been the result of attempted resuscitation. The only drug detected was α-ethyltryptamine. The concentration in heart blood was 5.6 mg/L, with 2.4 mg/L in the vitreous, 18.3 mg/L in the liver, 24 mg/L in the kidneys, and 22 mg/L in bile (Morano et al., 1993).

References

Aboul-Enein, H. (1974). Psilocybin: a pharmacological profile. Am J Pharm, 146: 91–95.

Allen, J. and Merlin, M. (1992). Psychoactive mushroom use in Koh Samui and Koh Pha-Ngan, Thailand. J Ethnopharm, 35: 205–228.

Anon. (1994). α-ethyltryptamine. Microgram, 27(11): 367–368.

Bagrov, R., Roukoyatkina, N., Fedorova, D. et al. (1993). Digitalis-like and vasoconstrictor effects of endogenous digoxin-like factor(s) from the venom of Bufo marinus toad. Euro J Pharm, 234(2–3): 165–172.

Bahri, L. and Vhemli, R. (1991). Vet Hum Toxicol, 33(3): 276–277.

Bailey, M. (1979). Major poisonous plant problems in cattle. Bovine Pract, 14: 169–175.

Budavari, S., O'Neil, M., Smith, A., and Henckelman, P. (Eds.) (1988). *The Merck Index: an encyclopedia of chemicals, drugs and biologicals.* Eleventh edition. Rahway, NJ: Merck and Company, Inc., NJ.

Chamakura, R. (1993). Bufotenine. Microgram, 26(8): 185–192.

Chamakura, R. (1994). Tryptamines. Microgram, 27: 316–321.

Chern, M., Ray, C., and Wu, D. (1991). Biologic intoxication due to digitalis-like substance after ingestion of cooked toad soup. Am J Cardiol, 67: 443–444.

Cheung, K., Hinds, J., and Duffy, P. (1989). Detection of poisoning by plant-origin cardiac glycoside with the Abbott TDx Analyzer. Clin Chem, 35(2): 295–297.

Francis, J. and Murray, V. (1983). Review of enquiries made to the NPIS concerning psilocybe mushroom ingestion, 1978–1981. Hum Toxicol, 2: 349–352.

Furst, P. (1985). *Hallucinogens and culture*. Novato, CA: Chandler and Sharp.

Gallagher, L. (1994). Smoking toad. New York Times Magazine. 48–49.

Glennon, R. (1993). MDMA-like stimulus effects of α-ethyltryptamine and the α-ethyl homolog of DOM. Pharm Biochem Behav, 46: 459–462.

Gudelsky, G., Yamamot, B., and Nash, J. (1994). 3,4-methylenedioxymethamphet-amine-induced dopamine release and serotonin neurotoxicity by 5-HT2 receptor agonists. Euro J Pharm, 264(3): 325–330.

Hitt, M. and Ettinger, D. (1986). Toad toxicity (letter). N Engl J Med, 314: 1517.

Leikin, J., Krantz, A., and Zellkanter, M. (1989). Clinical features and management of intoxication due to hallucinogenic drugs. Med Toxicol Adverse Drug Exp, 4(5): 324–350.

Lichtstein, D., Gati, I., and Ovadia, H. (1993). Digitalis-like compounds in the toad Bufo viridis: interactions with plasma proteins. J Cardiovas Pharm, 22(Suppl. 2): S102–105.

Lin, C., Cheng, M., Chen, K. et al. (1989). A digoxin-like immunoreactive substance and atrioventricular block induced by a Chinese medicine "Kyushin." Jpn Circ J, 53: 1077–1080.

Liwszyc, G., Vuori, E., Rasanen, I. et al. (1992). Daime — a ritual herbal potion. J Ethnopharm, 36: 91–92.

McCawley, E., Brummett, R. et al. (1962). Convulsions from Psilocybe mushroom poisoning. Proc West Pharmacol Soc, 5: 27–33.

Monardes, N. (1574). Primera y segunda y tercera partes de la historia medicinal de las cosas que se traen de nuestras Indias Occidentales que sirven en medicena. Sevilla, A. Escrivano.

Morano, R., Spies, C., Walker, F., and Plank, S. (1993). Fatal intoxication involving etryptamine. J. Forensic Sci, 38: 721–725.

O'Hearn, E. and Molliver, M. (1993). Degeneration of purkinje cells in parasagittal zones of the cerebellar vermis after treatment with ibogaine or harmaline. Neurosci, 55: 303–310.

Ojiri, Y., Noguchi, K., and Sakanashi, M. (1991). Effects of a senso (toad venom) containing drug on systemic hemodynamics, cardiac function and myocardial oxygen consumption in anesthetized doges. Am J Chinese Med, 19(1): 17–31.

Palumbo, N. and Perri, S. (1975). Experimental induction and treatment of toad poisoning in the dog. J Am Vet Med Assoc, 167: 1000–1005.

Peden, N., Macaulay, K., and Bisset, A. (1981). Clinical toxicology of "magic mushroom" ingestion. Postgraduate Med J, 57: 543–545.

Schwartz, R. and Smith, D. (1988). Hallucinogenic mushrooms. Clin Peds, 27(2): 70–73.

Stafford, P. (1982). *Psychedelics encyclopedia*, revised edition. Los Angeles, Boston: J. P. Tarcher, Inc.

Strassman, R. and Qualls, C. (1994). Dose-response study of N,N-dimethyltryptamine in humans. Arch Gen Psychiat, 51: 85–97.

Torres, C., Repke, D., and Chan, R. (1991). Snuff powders from pre-historic San Pedro de Atacama; chemical and contextual analysis. Curr Anthro, 32: 640–665.

Vohlken, B. (1993). Bufotenine and psilocin, mass spectral distinctions. Microgram, 26: 233–234.

Weil, A. and Davis, W. (1994). *Bufo alvarius*: a potent hallucinogen of animal origin. J Ethnopharm, 41(1–2): 1–8.

4.3.4   Ergolines

4.3.4.1   Lysergic acid diethylamine

4.3.4.1.1   History.   Albert Hoffman synthesized LSD in 1938. He had been working as a research chemist at Sandoz Laboratories in Basel, where his chief interest was the chemistry of ergot. He isolated lysergic acid from ergot and then combined it with various amines via peptide linkages. Hoffman was trying to produce chemical agents that lacked some of ergot's toxic side effects, but which might have use as circulatory or respiratory stimulants. In that goal, at least, he was successful. He synthesized Methergine®, which is still used today to stop uterine bleeding after birth. During the course of his experiments, Hoffman created a series of related compounds. The twenty-fifth substance he produced was d-lysergic acid diethylamine (LSD-25). When tested on laboratory animals, the results were disappointing.

For five years, Hoffman worked on other projects, but in April of 1943 he decided to re-evaluate LSD-25. The hallucinogenic experience which

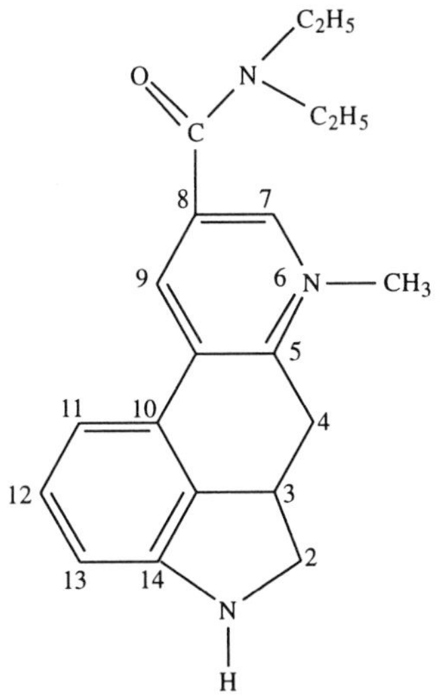

Figure 4.3.4.1   LSD-25. LSD-25 was produced by Albert Hoffman at Sandoz Laboratories. He had isolated lysergic acid from ergot and was trying to make a chemical agent that would act as a circulatory stimulant. LSD-25 was the 25th compound that he produced.

ensued when he accidentally ingested some LSD led to the start of the
modern "psychedelic" age (Hoffman, 1970). After further studies, Sandoz
eventually marketed LSD as Delysid®, recommending, among other things,
that psychiatrists try it on themselves so they could find out first-hand what
the subjective experiences of a schizophrenic were like (Ulrich and Patten,
1991).

LSD was never a great commercial success, but its availability fostered
research into the chemical origins of mental illness. None of the theories
proposed during the 50s and 60s proved correct, but these theories eventually did lead to more modern research into serotonin metabolism and receptor research. The theories also led to some rather bizarre experiments by the
Central Intelligence Agency. It was believed that LSD had great potential for
mind control. To verify that theory, the CIA mounted a special operation
called MK-ULTRA. Prostitutes were used to lure businessmen to brothels
where they were secretly dosed with LSD and their behavior observed. The
experiments were unsuccessful.

The psychedelic age began in the early 1960s when Timothy Leary under-
took his researches with psilocybin at Harvard. In 1961, he tried LSD and was
so altered by the experience that he dropped his psilocybin studies and began
researching the effects of LSD. Leary was forced to leave Harvard in 1962, but
by that time the media had launched the psychedelic age to the tune of Leary's
anthem: "Tune in, Turn on, Drop out." LSD was finally outlawed by the federal
government in 1965. The outlawing of LSD use, coupled with questionable
studies demonstrating chromosomal damage as a consequence of LSD use,
led to a rapid decline in its popularity (Ulrich and Patten, 1991). Sporadic
reports from around the country indicate there is renewed interest in LSD
use, but the seizure of a clandestine LSD laboratory is a distinctly rare event.
Over the past few years there has been some fluctuation in the price of LSD.
The average price on the street for one "hit" ranges from $1 to $10. At wholesale (more than 1,000 "hits"), prices range from 35 cents to $3.50 per dose
(National Narcotics Intelligence Consumers Committee, 1994).

LSD is usually available at the same "rave" parties where MDMA is
sold. However, the doses used today are only a fraction of what was taken
in the 1960s, and that may explain why current reports of toxicity are uncommon. The other reason that reports are uncommon may have to do with
difficulties in detecting LSD. Urine concentrations are rarely much above
2–3 ng/mL. Such low levels are near the limits of detection for most methodologies, and, until quite recently, no screening tests existed. However,
sensitive immunoassays for LSD have now been developed by several different manufacturers, and routine screening for LSD should soon be possible.
Only then will the true incidence of LSD use be known.

4.3.4.1.2   Chemical constants and drug manufacture.   LSD is 9,10-
didehydro-N-diethyl-6-methylergoline-8β-carboxamide. It is also referred to
as LSD-25 because it was the 25th derivative of lysergic acid that Hoffman
synthesized. Its formula is $C_{20}H_{25}N_3O$, with a molecular weight of 323.42. It
is composed of 74.3% carbon, 7.8% hydrogen, 13% nitrogen, and 5% oxygen.

When crystallized from benzene, it forms pointed prisms with a melting point of 80–85°C.

Clandestine chemists have two options when it comes to producing LSD. Alkaloids, related to LSD, can be extracted from the seeds of plants such as morning glories, and then further processed to make LSD. The Hawaiian baby woodrose is the preferred seed, since it contains nearly 7 mg of alkaloid per gram of seeds (Smith, 1981). Alternatively, *Claviceps purpurea* can be cultured with yields of ergotamine as high as 4 g/L. If starter fungus cannot be purchased commercially, it can be found growing on top of rye grass, near the seed-bearing area. Growing large quantities of fungus is technically demanding, and probably not done very often.

The result in either case is an assortment of different lysergic acid molecules, each linked to different amide groups. The amide is hydrolyzed off and used as the starting point for the synthesis of LSD. The synthesis utilizes a number of fairly toxic and potentially explosive chemicals, including hydrazine, trifluoroacetic acid, and diethylamine. The dangerous nature of the business may account for the infrequency with which LSD labs are discovered.

4.3.4.1.3   Tissue levels and metabolism. During the 1960s, the standard street dose was between 100–300 μg (Cohen, 1984). This small amount of LSD can be impregnated in almost any medium, including sugar cubes and chewing gum. Much smaller quantities of LSD are being used today than in the past. Blotter acid sold today typically contains LSD in concentrations that range from 20–80 μg (Nelson et al., 1992). A recurring urban myth claims that children may be exposed to the drug by applying temporary (water soluble) tattoos. While in theory that may be possible, especially with a dose of only 20 mg, in fact this occurrence has never been reported.

Absorption is rapid and almost complete. LSD circulates in the blood mostly bound to protein and has an estimated half-life of 2.5 hours. Human volunteers given 2 μg/kg intravenously had plasma levels of 6–7 ng/mL 30 minutes later. After that, the level gradually declined with an apparent half-life of 175 minutes (Aghajanian and Bing, 1964). When a single oral dose of 160 μg was given, the peak blood level was 9 ng/mL, and the calculated half-life was almost identical (180 minutes) to the half-life seen after intravenous administration (Upshall and Wailling, 1972). When 50 μg were given to a volunteer, LSD was detectable three days after ingestion at a cutoff level of less than 1 ng (Vu-Duc, 1991). Levels have been measured in emergency room patients with LSD intoxication. Blood samples were obtained at various times between 2 and 11 hours after ingestion, and levels were found to range from 0.5–1.9 ng/mL (McCarron et al., 1990). Urine concentrations in the same patients were between 0.2 and 7.7 ng/mL. Serum levels in other cases of severe intoxication have been remarkably similar, ranging between 2 and 4 ng/mL (Baselt and Cravey, 1989). Tissue levels have not been measured in humans.

4.3.4.1.4   Clinical syndromes. LSD usage results in somatic, perceptual, and psychic symptoms that seem to follow each other in a fairly predictable order. Physiologic effects are, however, minimal and unpredictable. The clinical changes produced by LSD seem to be indistinguishable from those produced by mescaline. It has been suggested that changes in pulse rate, respiration, and blood pressure seen with LSD use are probably just the result of varying anxiety levels (Klepitz and Racy, 1973). In the past there were frequent reports of acute panic reactions (Barnett, 1972), "flashbacks" (Moskowitz, 1971), and homicides while under the influence (Klepitz and Racy, 1973). Lapses of judgment resulting in self-injury can also occur, but the incidence of such events also seems to be decreasing. There have been no reports of fatalities due directly to LSD effects, and no reported autopsy studies.

   4.3.4.1.5   Detection. Since the half-life of LSD is relatively short and the amounts ingested quite small, detection is a problem. Urine concentrations reach sub-nanogram levels within a few hours after ingestion. There are problems with most of the currently used detection techniques. Since LSD is not one of the "NIDA 5," and since reported workplace incidents have been rare, there is a general feeling that the additional expense involved in screening for LSD would not be justified. With the advent of EMIT® tests for LSD, screening will, no doubt, become much more widespread.

4.4   Other agents

4.4.1   Phencyclidine

4.4.1.1   Historical aspects

Phencyclidine (1-(1)-phenylcyclohexyl piperidine, or PCP) was discovered by pharmacologists at Parke-Davis in 1956 (Greifenstein et al., 1958). Sold as an intravenous anesthetic called Sernyl® (Collins et al., 1960), phencyclidine offered a number of advantages over other surgical anesthetics. In recommended doses, it produced neither respiratory nor cardiovascular depression and, at least in animals, it appeared to be devoid of cellular toxicity (Chen and Weston, 1960). Unfortunately, human use had to be discontinued because 10–20% of patients became delirious and unmanageable for many hours after surgery (Greifenstein et al., 1958).

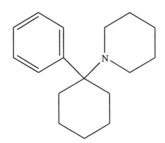

Figure 4.4.1   Phencyclidine molecule. The preferred route in clandestine labs starts with condensation of 1-phenylcyclopentylamine with pentamethylene dibromide. The ethyl ether and other volatile solvents used in the process give off a distinctive odor that often gives away the location of the laboratory.

Still, it was a good veterinary anesthetic and it continued in use until production was discontinued in 1979. Recreational abuse was first reported in California during the late 1960s, but the drug soon developed a reputation for causing anti-social, violent behavior (Fauman et al., 1976). Abuse was prevalent during the 1970s and early 1980s, but during the last 10 years illicit use of PCP has markedly decreased, while the price at wholesale has increased. The DAWN report for 1993 lists 196 PCP-related deaths, amounting to 2.6% of all drug-related deaths for that year (Substance Abuse Humans Services Agency, 1995). During that same interval, only four deaths were attributed to LSD usage.

Phencyclidine's mode of action is probably the most complex of any abused drug, and is highly dependent on the amount of drug taken (Gao et al., 1993). At low doses, PCP binds to its own receptor in the NMDA channel and produces only mild inebriation. At higher doses, the effects begin to resemble those of methamphetamine.

PCP blocks dopamine uptake, and on a weight-per-weight basis, is nearly as potent a reuptake blocker as the amphetamines. PCP also causes the release of stored catecholamines, but in this respect, at least, it is much less potent than methamphetamine (Johnson and Jones, 1990; Yang et al., 1991). In the rat model, PCP has a biphasic course of action. High doses lead to an initial increase in brain glucose metabolism at three hours, followed by a decrease at 24 hours, with return to normal at 48 hours. Low doses cause no initial change, but glucose metabolism is depressed at 24 hours, and remains that way for some time (Gao et al., 1993). PCP also inhibits ATP-sensitive K^+ channels in both heart and brain, increasing the inward Ca^{2+} current and blocking the outward K^+ current (Kokoz et al., 1994).

PCP has become the subject of intense interest in the scientific community. There is strong evidence that PCP, and other related compounds, protect against the effects of cerebral ischemia (Olney et al., 1987). PCP binds with high affinity to membrane receptors located in the NMDA receptor (N-methyl-D-aspartate) complex (Su, 1991). The fact that PCP competitively binds at the NMDA receptor complex is of interest, because it is stimulation of this complex that mediates the neurotoxic events responsible for tissue damage in stroke (Nuglisch et al., 1991). Some PCP derivatives, such as MK-801, show even more neuroprotective activity than PCP. Binding in the NMDA complex probably does not explain the behavioral effects of PCP, because PCP also binds the sigma receptor.

Sigma receptors are found not just in the central nervous system, but also on membranes from endocrine, immune, and peripheral tissues (Su, 1991). Their stimulation is thought to be responsible for many of the unpleasant side effects associated with opiate use, and could possibly explain why *in vitro* studies have shown that lymphocyte function is depressed after exposure to relatively low doses of PCP (Thomas et al., 1993). In addition to PCP, cocaine, pentazocine, dextromethorphan, and even anabolic steroids, all bind sigma receptors, which may explain certain similarities in the behavioral effects of these drugs.

Whatever the mechanism for PCP's behavioral and psychological effects, death appears to be a consequence of respiratory and cardiac depression. In the dog model of extreme PCP intoxication, death results when convulsions are followed by respiratory failure and cardiac failure that is secondary to hypoxia, hyperpyrexia, and acidosis. If the animals are paralyzed, convulsions and hyperthermia are prevented, but respiratory and cardiac depression still occur. At the highest doses, death seems to be entirely due to myocardial depression (Davis et al., 1991). These results can be extrapolated to humans only with great caution, because reports of massive overdose (blood level > 1,800 ng/mL) in humans do not mention myocardial compromise (Jackson, 1989).

4.4.1.2 Physical constants

Phencyclidine has a molecular weight of 243, and its hydrochloride form has a melting point range of 234° to 236°C. It is water-soluble with a pK_a of 8.5. It is a tertiary amine and its most important physical property, at least as far as toxicity is concerned, is its lipid solubility. PCP is extremely lipophilic and is rapidly shifted from the bloodstream into adipose tissue and the brain.

4.4.1.3 Clandestine laboratories

In clandestine labs, the preferred route of synthesis involves condensation of 1-phenylcyclopentylamine with pentamethylene dibromide (Kalir et al., 1969). Other routes are possible and many different analogs have been detected in street samples. PCP is sold in bulk either in liquid or powder form. Street drug may be anywhere from 50–100% pure. The ethyl ether and other volatile solvents used in the production process give off a distinctive odor that often gives away the location of the laboratory. The fumes are also quite explosive, making illicit PCP production a risky affair.

Most of the U.S. PCP supply is manufactured by Los Angeles-based street gangs. Their affiliates then distribute the drug around the country. Six clandestine PCP laboratories were seized in 1993, compared to four in the preceding year, and 21 in 1988. Street prices have risen over the years, but have leveled off recently. In 1976, the price on the street was $1–$3 dollars per hit (Lundberg, Gupta, and Montgomery, 1976). Now, depending on which area of the country, individual cigarettes saturated with PCP cost from $5 to more than $50. One gallon of illicit PCP sells for $5,000–$10,000 in Los Angeles, and even more elsewhere. The national range for one ounce of powder is $500–$1,200 per ounce (National Narcotics Intelligence Consumers Committee, 1994).

4.4.1.4 Routes of administration

PCP can be smoked, snorted, injected, or swallowed. Cigarettes soaked in PCP were very popular during the 1980s. In some areas of the country, PCP-laced cigarettes are called "Sherms," because the cigarette preferred for soaking purposes was produced by a company called Nat Sherman. Parsley leaves soaked in PCP are an occasionally-used alternative. Studies on human volunteers who smoked 100 μg of (^{3}H)-phencyclidine indicate that most smoked PCP is absorbed. Peak blood levels occur 15 to 20 minutes after smoking, but there is a second peak, suggesting delayed release from the lungs. The maximum concentration achieved in this particular smoking study was 1.5 ng/mL. The mean half-life of the smoked PCP was 24 hours ± 7 hours (Cook et al., 1982a). Oral absorption is nearly as good as intravenous administration. Volunteers given 1 mg orally had average PCP concentrations of 2.7 ng/mL. Plasma concentrations after 1 mg given intravenously were 2.9 ng/mL. Peak plasma levels after oral dosing were at 2.5 hours, although levels were near maximal at 1.5 hours. After both oral and intravenous administration, there follows a 1–2 hour plateau period, where plasma levels remain relatively stable (Cook et al., 1982b).

Some skin absorption does occur, and can result in positive urine tests, possibly at levels exceeding NIDA cutoffs. In one study a crime lab chemist was found to have a PCP level of 28 ng/mL (Pitts et al., 1981). Just how relevant all of these measurements are to the problems of clinical intoxication is not entirely clear. The amounts used for the volunteer studies are probably very small when compared to the amounts taken by abusers. When PCP was first introduced as a legal anesthetic, sophisticated techniques for measuring blood levels were not available. Now that such techniques exist, ethical considerations prevent the administration of PCP in quantities that accurately reflect street practices.

4.4.1.5 Metabolism

PCP is extensively metabolized, and less than 10% is excreted unchanged in the urine (Woodworth et al., 1985; Wall et al., 1981). Recovery of PCP and its metabolites in urine and feces is incomplete. Hydroxylated derivatives, accounting for less than 50% of a total dose, can be recovered from the urine. At the same time, unchanged PCP can be found in saliva and sweat, suggesting that some elimination may occur by these routes (Cook et al., 1982b).

Phencyclidine is metabolized by hydroxylation on position 4 of the cyclohexane ring and/or on the piperidine moiety. Both of the resulting metabolites are pharmacologically inactive. The metabolites then undergo glucoronidation, and are excreted in the urine. Since PCP is a weak base, acidification of the urine enhances its excretion. In the past, PCP overdoses were given ammonium chloride or ascorbic acid, in hopes of increasing excretion and minimizing toxicity, but this approach was eventually found to be ineffective. On the other hand, continuous gastric suction has proved a useful treatment because PCP is excreted into the stomach, setting up a pathway for gastroenteric recirculation (Aniline and Pitts, 1982).

The window for detection of PCP in the urine is variable. In experimental animals, the half-life for PCP is only three to five hours (Woodworth, Owens, and Mayersohn, 1985), but in humans it is much longer. After oral administration, the terminal half-life may approach 24 hours, which means that PCP should still be detectable in the blood for five days, and for at least as long in the urine. NIDA cutoffs require the presence of at least 25 ng/mL before a measurement may be reported as positive.

4.4.1.6   Tissue levels

PCP levels during clinically apparent intoxication, and at autopsy, have been extensively reported. Intoxication is not apparent with blood levels lower than 3 ng/mL, but otherwise clinical correlations between blood levels and physical findings, except for systolic blood pressure, are generally poor (Bailey et al., 1978b). In 70 cases where PCP was deemed a factor in the death, 90% of the cases had blood levels ranging from 10–300 ng/mL (Budd and Liu, 1982). In a smaller series of 5 PCP-related deaths and 10 cases of intoxication, levels at autopsy ranged from 8–2,100 ng/mL. The 10 individuals with clinical evidence of intoxication had plasma levels ranging from <10 ng up to 812 ng/mL (Bailey et al., 1978a). The PCP blood levels which result from a given dose may vary depending on what other drugs are used at the same time. In a dog model of PCP intoxication, concurrent administration of PCP with marijuana results in higher blood and brain levels of PCP than when PCP is used alone. Alcohol, on the other hand, does not exert this effect (Godley et al., 1991). This synergy may explain why PCP and marijuana are frequently detected in the same urine specimens. PCP appears in saliva, and levels there appear to correlate well with blood levels (McCarron et al., 1984).

4.4.1.7   Interpreting blood and tissue levels

PCP blood and urine measurements are of historical interest only. They prove that the individual in question did, at one time, take PCP. The clinical and forensic importance of isolated blood and urine levels is impossible to determine. PCP is rapidly extracted from the blood by brain and fatty tissues which then slowly release PCP back into the circulation. In one animal study, PCP levels in adipose tissue were 13 times higher than brain levels and 20 times higher than blood levels (James and Schnoll, 1976). Continued slow release from these depots can occur over an extended period of time. PCP also makes its way back into the circulation after being reabsorbed from the gastric contents entering the small bowel. Measurable levels may persist for months (Aniline and Pitts, 1982). NIDA guidelines call for screening and confirmation tests with a 25 ng/mL cutoff, thereby significantly reducing the time frame for detectability. If the cutoff was reduced by one-half, the period during which PCP could be detected might be lengthened by a period of weeks! Controlled studies on the limits of detection have not been published, but in one case report, a police chemist who had daily contact with PCP still had a blood level of 70 ng/mL six months after leaving the laboratory (Pitts et al., 1981). PCP remains stable in stored urine specimens for long periods of time. There is almost no change in PCP concentration after three months of cold storage, and one-half of the initial concentration of PCP will still be present after six months (Hughes et al., 1991). Since PCP is no longer marketed, either as a human or veterinary anesthetic, its presence can only be explained by illicit use.

Episodes of fatal PCP intoxication, as opposed to homicides and trauma deaths where PCP is an incidental finding, are uncommon (Noguchi and Nakamura, 1978; Poklis et al., 1990). Tolerance to PCP is seen in animals, and almost certainly in man. It has been argued that tolerance in humans is proven by the fact that blood levels in patients dying directly from PCP's effects overlap with the blood levels seen in individuals with accidental deaths (Poklis et al., 1990; Bailey, 1979). This same phenomenon can be seen in cocaine-related deaths, and probably in all other stimulant-related fatalities.

A case report from 1989 is of some interest. A man swallowed two balloons full of PCP and promptly lapsed into a coma. The particulars of his history, however, were unknown to his physicians until he passed the two balloons, one ruptured, while he was still comatose on day 11. His maximum blood level on the third hospital day was 1,879 ng/mL. His blood level at the time he passed the two balloons was not recorded, but the level in his cerebrospinal fluid was 245 ng/mL, and the blood level the day before was nearly 1,000 ng/mL (Jackson, 1989). Maternal/fetal relationships have not been studied in depth, but the limited number of studies that have been published have shown not only that PCP crosses the placenta with ease, but also that the fetus concentrates the drug and usually has higher levels than the mother (Aniline and Pitts, 1982).

4.4.1.8   Toxicity by organ system

4.4.1.8.1   Neurologic disorders. The limited number of autopsy studies that have been reported make no mention of neuropathologic changes. Whether this reflects a lack of toxicity or just limited numbers of observations remains to be seen. All of the arylhexylalkyamines that have been tested, including MK-801, ketamine, and tiletamine, produce acute changes in rat brains. Vacuolization of neurons in the posterior cingulate and retrosplenial cortices can be seen within four hours of subcutaneously injecting 1 mg/kg of PCP. There is some evidence that the changes resolve, and tolerance to the effects develops, with repeated usage (Olney et al., 1989; Gao et al., 1993). There is also evidence that PCP, though not MK-801, can cause damage to Purkinje cells of the cerebellar virmus (Nakki et al., 1995). It is conceivable that these transient changes could account for behavioral disorders that are seen in human PCP users. There is no proof, however, one way or the other. Fatal status epilepticus has been reported (McCarron, 1981; Kessler et al., 1974), but these cases are difficult to interpret, because PCP, and related compounds such as MK-801, have anticonvulsant properties (Balster, 1987).

4.4.1.8.2   Renal disorders. In one series of 1,000 PCP intoxicated patients, 2.2% had rhabdomyolysis, and three of these patients had renal failure requiring dialysis (McCarron, 1981). Most instances of renal failure appear to be in deeply comatose patients suffering from drug-induced seizures (Hoogwerf et al., 1979; Fallis et al., 1982; Cogen et al., 1978; Cho et al., 1989).

4.4.2   Dextromethorphan

Dextromethorphan is the dextro-isomer of the codeine analog, levorphanol. It is the active ingredient in numerous over-the-counter remedies. More than

Table 4.4.2 Blood and Tissue Levels in 70 Fatal Cases
of PCP Intoxication

Blood	Urine	Liver	Bile	Brain	Kidney
100–2,400	100–7,600	100–7,820	100–1,690	30–710	400–900

Concentrations are in ng/mL. Adapted from Budd and Liu.

50 dextromethorphan-containing remedies are listed in the current PDR. In low doses, dextromethorphan causes neither depression nor euphoria. It is, nonetheless, an effective cough suppressant. Dextromethorphan has abuse potential because it binds to opiate sigma receptors (Klein and Musacchio, 1989). Sigma receptors are thought to be directly involved in the development of both tolerance and dependence in opiate abusers. One of dextromethorphan's metabolites, dextorphan, also binds to the NMDA receptor (Craviso and Musacchio, 1983; Szekely et al., 1991). Clinical reports suggest that when high doses are consumed (>600 mg/day), the effects are similar to those produced by phencyclidine (Schadel and Sellers, 1992).

When dextromethorphan is taken as a recreational drug, it is usually in the form of an alcohol-containing cough syrup (Dodds and Revi, 1967; Murray and Brewerton, 1993; Wolfe and Carvati, 1995), although there is one report of a man who snorted powdered dextromethorphan (Flemming, 1986). Most case reports have described symptoms consistent with toxic psychosis, but some fatalities have been reported (Rammer et al., 1988; Craig, 1992). In several instances, symptoms were said to have improved after treatment with narcotic antagonists, although improvement did not occur until many hours later, and doubt exists as to the efficacy of such treatment (Pender and Parks, 1991).

Dextromethorphan is metabolized both by O- and N-demethylation. O-demethylation is the most important route, and in man, the process occurs in the liver, catalyzed by cytochrome P4502D6 (Bochner et al., 1994). The gene responsible for producing the enzyme is located on human chromosome 22. Considerable polymorphism exists for this enzyme, and 7%–10% of the Caucasian population lacks the enzyme entirely (Schmid et al., 1985; Relling et al., 1991; Marshall et al., 1992). Deficient individuals cannot produce dextorphan. As a consequence, deficient individuals are, presumably, protected from PCP-like effects, even after taking large doses of dextromethorphan.

Routine toxicologic screening tests will not detect dextromethorphan; the anti-opiate antibodies used in both the EMIT® and FPIA® systems do not recognize the dextromethorphan molecule (Kintz and Mangin, 1992). Nonetheless, fatalities appear to be rare, and autopsy findings are poorly characterized. Postmortem toxicologic findings have been described in three patients (Rammer et al., 1988; Kintz and Mangin, 1992). High concentrations of dextromethrophan are found in the liver. Liver/blood ratios have fallen into a very broad range, from just over 2 to nearly 70. Reported blood levels have been from 3.3 mg/L–9.2 mg/L.

References

Aghajanian, G. and Bing, O. (1964). Persistence of lysergic acid diethylamide in the plasma of human subjects. Clin Pharm Ther, 5: 611–614.

Aniline, O. and Pitts, F. (1982). Phencyclidine (PCP): a review and perspectives. CRC Crit Rev Toxicol, 10: 145–177.

Bailey, D. (1979). Phencyclidine abuse: clinical findings and concentrations in biological fluids after nonfatal intoxication. Am J Clin Path, 72: 796–799.

Bailey, D., Shaw, R., and Guba, J. (1978a). Phencyclidine abuse: plasma levels and clinical findings in casual users and in phencyclidine-related deaths. J Analyt Toxicol, 2: 233–237.

Bailey, D., Shaw, R., and Guba, J. (1978b). Phencyclidine abuse: plasma levels and clinical findings in phencyclidine-related deaths. J Analyt Toxicol, 2: 233–237.

Balster, R. (1987). The behavioral pharmacology of phencyclidine. *Psychopharmacology: the third generation of progress.* New York: Raven Press.

Barnett, B. (1972). Diazepam treatment for LSD intoxication. Lancet, II(270).

Baselt, R. and Cravey, R. (1989). *Disposition of toxic drugs and chemicals in man.* Chicago, London: Year Book Medical Publishers, 470–473.

Bochner, F., Smogy, A., and Chen, Z. (1994). Dextromethrophan metabolism in rat: interstrain differences and the fate of individually administered oxidative metabolites. Xenobiotica, 24: 543–552.

Budd, R. and Liu, Y. (1982). Phencyclidine concentrations in postmortem body fluids and tissues. J Toxicol Clin Toxicol, 19(8): 843–850.

Chen, G. and Weston, J. (1960). The analgesic and anesthetic effect of 1-(1-phenylcyclohexyl)piperidine HCL on the monkey. Anesth Analg, 39: 132–137.

Cho, A., Hiramatsu, M., Pechnick, R., and Di Stefano, E. (1989). Pharmacokinetic and pharmacodynamic evaluation of phencyclidine and its decadeutero variant. J Pharm and Exp Ther, 250: 210–215.

Cogen, F., Rigg, Z., Simmons, J., and Domino, E. (1978). Phencyclidine associated acute rhabdomyolysis. Ann Intern Med, 88: 210–212.

Cohen, S. (1984). The hallucinogens and the inhalants. Psych Clin N Amer, 7: 681–688.

Collins, V., Gorospe, C., and Rovenstine, E. (1960). Intravenous nonbarbiturate, nonnarcotic analgesics: preliminary studies. I. Cyclohexylamines. Anesth Analg, 39: 302–306.

Cook, C., Brine, B., Quin, B. et al. (1982a). Phencyclidine and phenylcyclohexene disposition after smoking phencyclidine. Clin Pharmacol Ther, 31(5): 635–641.

Cook, C., Brine, D., Jeffcoat, R. et al. (1982b). Phencyclidine disposition after intravenous and oral doses. Clin Pharm Ther, 31(5): 625–634.

Craig, D. (1992). Psychosis with Vicks Formula 44-D® abuse. Can Med Assoc J, 146: 1199–1200.

Craviso, G. and Musacchio, J. (1983). High-affinity dextromethorphan binding sites in guinea pig brain II: competition experiments. Mol Pharm, 23: 629–640.

Davis, W., Hackett, R., Obrosky, K., and Waters, I. (1991). Factors in the lethality of IV phencyclidine in conscious dogs. Gen Pharmacol, 22(4): 723–728.

Dodds, A. and Revi, E. (1967). Toxic psychosis due to dextromethorphan. Med J Aust, 2: 231.

Fallis, R., Aniline, O., Pitts, F., Jr., and Weiner, L. (1982). Massive phencyclidine intoxication. Arch Neurol, 39: 316.

Fauman, B., Aldinger, G., Fauman, M., and Rosen, P. (1976). Psychiatric sequelae of phencyclidine abuse. Clin Toxicol, 9: 529–537.

Flemming, P. (1986). Dependence on dextromethorphan hydrobromide. Br Med J, 293: 597–598.

Gao, X., Shirakawa, O., Du, F. et al. (1993). Delalyed regional metabolic actions of phencyclidine. Euro J Pharm, 241: 7–15.

Godley, P., Moore, E., Woodworth, J., and Fineg, J. (1991). Effects of ethanol and delta-9-tethrahydrocannabinol on phencyclidine disposition in dogs. Biopharmaceutics and Drug Disp, 12: 189–199.

Greifenstein, F., Devault, M., Yoshitake, J., and Gajewski, J. (1958). A study of 1-arylchclohexamine for anesthesia. Anesth Analg, 37: 283–294.

Hoffman, A. (1970). Notes and documents concerning the discovery of LSD. Agents Actions, (Jan/Feb): 148–181.

Hoogwerf, B., Kern, J., Bullock, M., and Comty, C. (1979). Phencyclidine-induced rhabdomyolysis and acute renal failure. Clin Toxicol, 14: 47–53.

Hughes, R., Hughes, A., Levine, B., and Smith, M. (1991). Stability of phencyclidine and amphetamines in urine specimens. Clin Chem, 37(12): 2141–2142.

Jackson, J. (1989). Phencyclidine pharmacokinetics after a massive overdose. Ann Intern Med, 111: 613–615.

James, S. and Schnoll, S. (1976). Phencyclidine: tissue distribution in the rat. Clin Toxicol, 2: 573–582.

Johnson, K. and Jones, S. (1990). Neuropharmacology of phencyclidine: basic mechanisms and therapeutic potential. Am Rev Pharmacol Toxicol, 30: 707–750.

Kalir, A., Sadeh, S., Karoly, H. et al. (1969). 1-phenylcycloalkylamine derivatives, II. J Med Chem, 12: 473.

Kessler, G., Demers, L., Berlin, C. et al. (1974). Phencyclidine and fatal status epilepticus. N Engl J Med, 291: 979.

Kintz, P. and Mangin, P. (1992). Toxicological findings in a death involving dextromethorphan and terfenadine. Am J Forensic Med Pathol, 13: 351–352.

Klein, M. and Musacchio, J. (1989). High affinity dextromethorphan binding sites in guinea pig brain: effect of sigma ligands and other agents. J Pharmacol Exp Ther, 251: 207–215.

Klepfisz, A. and Racy, J. (1973). Homicide and LSD. JAMA, 223: 429–430.

Kokoz, Y., Alekseev, A., Povzun, A. et al. (1994). Anaesthetic phencyclidine, blocker of the ATP-sensitive potassium channels. Fed Euro Biochm Soc Letters, 337: 277–280.

Kwan, T., Paiusco, A., and Kohl, L. (1992). Digitalis toxicity caused by toad venom. Chest, 102: 949–950.

Lundberg, G., Gupta, R., and Montgomery, S. (1976). Phencyclidine: patterns seen in street drug analysis. Clin Toxicol, 9: 503–511.

McCarron, M., Schuylze, B., Thompson, G. A. et al. (1981). Acute phencyclidine intoxication: clinical patterns, complications and treatments. Ann Emerg Med, 10: 290–297.

McCarron, M., Wallberg, C., Soares, S. et al. (1984). Detection of phencyclidine usage by radioimmunoassay of saliva. J Analyt Toxicol, 8: 197–201.

McCarron, M., Walberg, C., and Baselt, R. (1990). Confirmation of LSD intoxication by analysis of serum and urine. J Analyt Toxicol, (May/June): 165–167.

Moskowitz, D. (1971). Use of haloperidol to reduce LSD flashbacks. Milit Med, 136: 754–756.

Murray, S. and Brewerton, T. (1993). Abuse of over-the-counter dextromethorphan by teenagers. South Med J, 86(10): 1151–1153.

Nakki, R., Koistinaho, J., Sharp, F. et al. (1995). Cerebellar toxicity of phencyclidine. J Neurosci, 15(3): 2097–2109.

National Narcotics Intelligence Consumers Committee (1994). The NICC Report 1993, The supply of illicit drugs to the United States. Drug Enforcement Administration, Arlington, VA (DEA-94066).

Nelson, C. and Foltz, R. (1992). Determination of lysergic acid diethylamide (LSD), iso-LSD, and n-dimethyl-LSD in body fluids by gas chromatography/tandem mass spectrometry. Anal Chem, 64: 1578–1585.

Noguchi, T. and Nakamura, G. (1976). Phencyclidine-related deaths in Los Angeles County, 1976. J Forensic Sci, 23: 503–507.

Nuglisch, J., Rischke, R., and Krieglstein, J. (1991). Preischemic administration of flunarizine or phencyclidine reduces local cerebral glucose utilization in rat hippocampus seven days after ischemia. Pharmacology, 42(6): 333–339.

Olney, J., Labruyere, J., and Price, M. (1989). Neurotoxic effects of phencyclidine. Science, 244: 1360–1362.

Olney, J., Price, M., Salles, K. et al. (1987). MK-801 powerfully protects against N-methyl aspartate neurotoxicity. Eur J Pharmacol, 141: 357–361.

Pender, E. and Parks, B. (1991). Toxicity with dextromethorphan-containing preparations: a literature review and report of two additional cases. Ped Emerg Care, 7: 163–165.

Pitts, F., Allen, R., Aniline, O., and Yago, L. (1981). Occupational intoxication and long-term persistence of phencyclidine (PCP) in law enforcement personnel. Clin Toxicol, 18(9): 1015–1020.

Poklis, A., Graham, M., and Magin, D. (1990). Phencyclidine and violent deaths in St. Louis, Missouri: a survey of Medical Examiners cases from 1977 to 1986. Am J Drug Alcohol Abuse, 16(3 and 4): 265–274.

Rammer, L., Holmgren, P., and Sandler, H. (1988). Fatal intoxication by dextromethorphan: a report of two cases. Forensic Sci Int, 37: 233–236.

Relling, M., Cherrie, J., Schell, M. et al. (1991). Lower prevalence of the desbrisoquin oxidative poor metabolizer phenotype in American black vs. white subjects. Clin Pharmacol Ther, 50: 308–313.

Schadel, M. and Sellers, E. (1992). Psychosis with Vicks Formula 44D®. Can Med Assoc, 147: 843–844.

Schmid, B., Bircher, J., Preisig, R. et al. (1985). Polymorphic dextromethorphan metabolism: co-segration of oxidative O-demethylation with desbrisoquin hydroxylation. Clin Pharm Ther, 38: 618–624.

Smith, M. V. (1981). *Psychedelic chemistry.* Pt. Townsend, WA: Loompanics Unlimited.

Su, T.-P. (1991). Review. Sigma receptors, putative links between nervous, endocrine and immune systems. Eur J Biochem, 200: 633–642.

Substance Abuse and Mental Health Services Administration. (1995). Annual Medical Examiner Data. Data from the Drug Abuse Warning Network. Statistical Series, Number 10-B. Rockville, MD, U.S. Department of Health and Human Services.

Szekely, J., Sharpe, L., and Jaffe, J. (1991). Induction of phencyclidine-like behavior in rats by dextrorphan, but not dextromethorphan. Pharm Biochem Behav, 40: 381–386.

Thomas, P., House, R., and Bhargava, H. (1993). Phencyclidine exposure alters *in vitro* cellular immune response parameters associated with host defense. Life Sci, 53: 1417–1427.

Ulrich, R. and Patten, B. (1991). The rise, decline and fall of LSD. Persp Biol and Med, 34(4): 561–578.

Upshall, D. and Wailing, D. (1972). The determination of LSD in human plasma following oral administration. Clin Chim Acta, 36: 67–73.

Vu-Duc, T., Vernay, A., and Casalanca, A. (1991). Detection of lysergic acid diethy-lamine in human urine: elimination, screening and analytical confirmation. Sch-weizerische Medizinische Wochenschrift (French), 121(50): 1887–1890.

Wall, M., Brine, D., Jeffcoat, A. et al. (1981). Phencyclidine metabolism and disposition in man following a 100 µg intravenous dose. Res Comm in Substance Abuse, 2: 161–172.

Wolfe, T. and Caravati, M. (1995). Massive dextromethorphan ingestion and abuse. Am J Emerg Med, 13: 174–176.

Woodworth, J., Owens, S., and Mayersohn, M. (1985). Phencyclidine (PCP) disposi-tion kinetics in dogs as a function of dose and route of administration. J Pharm Exp Ther, 234: 654–661.

Yang, Q., Moroji, T., Takamatsu, Y., Hagino, Y., and Okuwa, M. (1991). The effects of intraperitoneally-administered phencyclidine on the central nervous system — behavioral and neurochemical studies. Neuropeptides, 19(2): 77–90.

chapter five

Narcotics

5.1 Introduction

5.1.1 Prevalence of opiate-related morbidity

Medical examiners participating in the federally sponsored DAWN (Drug Abuse Warning Network) program reported 5,876 opiate-related deaths in 1993, a 15% increase from 1992, and a 65% increase from the 3,403 narcotic-related deaths reported in 1990 (Substance Abuse & Mental Health Services Administration, 1995). Heroin toxicity now accounts for nearly half of all drug-related deaths, compared to one-third in 1990 (National Institute on Drug Abuse, 1990). Toxicity from the other opiates was much less frequent than from heroin. Table 5.1.1 lists the other agents that were encountered in the United States during that same time period.

Table 5.1.1 Deaths from Narcotic Analgesics in 1994 (DAWN Report)

Drug	Number of Mentions	Percentage of Mentions
Heroin/Morphine	3,981	47.3
Codeine	1,170	13.9
Methadone	367	4.4
D-Propoxyphene	351	4.2
Hydrocodone	116	1.4
Meperidine	36	0.45
Oxycodone	38	0.45
Hydromorphone	19	0.2
Fentanyl	16	0.2

A total of 20,156 drug-related deaths were reported in the DAWN survey for 1994. Of these, 3,981 (19.7%) were due to cocaine, and 3,522 (17.4%) were due to heroin. There was essentially no significant change in the number of deaths attributed to other narcotic agents.

5.1.2 Classifications of narcotic agents

Opiate-related toxicity may be due to: (1) direct effects of the drug or its metabolites, (2) direct effects of adulterants or expients injected along with the drug, or (3) infectious, mechanical, or life-style complications associated with the practices of drug abuse. Earlier schemes classified opiates on the basis of their source, as either naturally occurring (morphine or codeine), semisynthetic, morphine-based (heroin or hydromorphone), semisynthetic thebane-based (oxymorphone or oxycodone), or purely synthetic (meperidine or pentazocine) (Inturrisi, 1982). This classification, while possibly of some interest to forensic chemists, does little to explain the mechanisms of toxicity. Others classify members of this group as being opiates or opioids, the former term being reserved for peptides that are derived from the morphine molecule that stereospecifically bind to opioid receptors, while the latter is used to describe non-peptide agents binding at the same sites. The most useful way to classify these drugs is by the receptors to which they bind.

The body produces endogenous pain-relieving substances that have molecular structures similar to that of morphine. These substances, called endorphins or enkephalins, along with exogenous opiates such as morphine, bind to opioid receptors located in the brain, and throughout the body. Depending on which receptor is activated, the result may be, among other things, analgesia, dysphoria, or respiratory depression. Five basic classes of opioid receptors have been discovered. They have been given Greek names based on the type of drugs that binds to them.

The mu receptor is so named because morphine binds to it. Other molecules that bind at this same site are called mu agonists, not only because they bind to the same receptor, but also because they cause the same effects as morphine. The effects associated with mu receptors activation are supraspinal analgesia, euphoria, moderate sedation, and respiratory depression. Two subtypes of Mu receptors have been identified. Analgesia results from the activation of the Mu 1 receptor. Opiate side effects, such as respiratory depression, miosis, constipation, urinary retention, and euphoria, are associated with the Mu 2 receptor (Shook, Watkins, and Canaporesi, 1990; Pasternak, 1988 and 1993).

Table 5.1.2 lists the principal receptor types and the effects that can be anticipated when they are stimulated (Lipman, 1990).

Table 5.1.2   Principal Opiate Receptor Types

Receptor Type	Result of Stimulation
Mu 1	Supraspinal analgesia
Mu 2	Respiratory depression, sedation, bradycardia
Kappa	Spinal analgesia, sedation
Sigma	Dysphoria, psychomotor stimulation, tachycardia

Morphine also binds to Kappa, Delta, and Sigma receptors. Activation of Kappa prevents the transmission of pain over spinal pathways. Kappa activation can cause many of the same side effects as Mu stimulation, but generally respiratory depression is less marked. Pentazocine is the best known of the drugs binding at the Kappa receptor. Delta receptors also produce spinal analgesia. Their ability to produce analgesia, and side effects, is midway between those of Kappa and Delta receptors.

Sigma receptor activation does not relieve pain, but it does cause dysphoria, hallucinations, and most of the undesirable effects associated with the clinical use of morphine. Epsilon receptors avidly bind beta-endorphin, but their clinical significance remains to be determined (Poole et al., 1992).

With a few notable exceptions (such as propoxyphene, which, in addition to being a Mu agonist, is also a potent local anesthetic), direct opiate toxicity is due to mu receptor activation. While there may be some important clinical differences between Mu agonists, there is little to distinguish the direct toxic effects of one from another. For that reason, the pathologic changes attributable to opiate abuse are considered here as a group. Pharmacokinetic and toxicologic data are supplied for the 10 agents cited most frequently in the DAWN reports. Toxicity from the other opiates is too rare to be characterized.

Though it would be logical to suppose that opiate addiction is, in some way, mediated by changes in opiate receptors, that appears not to be the case. No consistent change in the number of opiate receptors has ever been demonstrated (Nestler, 1992). There is, however, an emerging consensus that postreceptor mechanisms are in some way involved, especially in the class of intracellular messengers referrred to as G-proteins. These proteins act as links between cell membrane receptors and intracellular effector systems such as the formation of cyclic AMP. In man and animal alike, acute doses of heroin and morphine cause basal levels of cyclic AMP in the brain to fall, but chronic treatment produces compensatory increases throughout the chain of enzymes involved in the cyclic AMP system (Escriba et al., 1994). There is mounting evidence that up-regulation of cyclic AMP and other intracellular systems may be the common mechanism underlying both the process of tolerance and dependence (Busquets et al., 1995).

References

Busquets, X., Escriba, P., Sastre, M. et al. (1995). Loss of protein kinase C-ab in brain of heroin addicts and morphine-dependent rats. J Neurochem, 64(1): 247–252.

Escriba, P., Sastre, M., and Garcia-Sevilla, J. (1994). Increased density of guanine nucleotide-binding proteins in the postmortem brain of heroin addicts. Arch Gen Psych, 51: 494–501.

Inturrisi, C. (1982). Narcotic drugs. Med Clin North Am, 66: 1061–1071.

Lipman, A. (1990). Clinically relevant differences among the opioid analgesics. Am J Hosp Pharm, 47(Suppl. 1): S7–S13.

National Institute on Drug Abuse (1990). Annual Medical Examiner Data. Data from the Drug Abuse Warning Network. Statistical Series, Number 10-B. Rockville, MD, U.S. Department of Health and Human Services.

Nestler, E. (1992). Molecular mechanisms of drug addiction. J Neurosci, 12(7): 2439–2450.

Pasternak, G. (1988). Multiple morphine and enkephalin receptors and the relief of pain. JAMA, 259: 1362–1367.

Pasternak, G. (1993). Pharmacological mechanisms of opioid analgesics. Clin Neuropharm, 16(1): 1–18.

Poole, J. and Jahr, H. (1992). Opiate receptors: a review of analgesic properties and pharmacological side effects. J Louisiana State Med Soci, 144(3): 106–108.

Shook, J., Watkins, W., and Canaporesi, E. (1990). Differential roles of opioid receptors in respiration, respiratory disease, and opiate-induced respiratory depression. Am Rev Respir Dis, 142: 895–909.

5.2   History of opiate abuse

5.2.1   Origins in antiquity

Opium poppies can be seen on coins and in drawings that antedate written mentions in the Greek literature by at least 1,000 years (Kritikos and Papadaki, 1967). Homer and Hesiod discussed the medicinal merits of poppies, and writings from the classical period of ancient Greece frequently mentioned the same subject. In Greece the poppy was called *opion*. The term was derived from the word for juice (*opos*). Translated into Latin, *opion* becomes *opium*. For the ancients, the poppy symbolized sleep, occasionally everlasting. The cup given to Socrates contained the standard solution used at the time for purposes of euthanasia and suicide: a mixture of hemlock

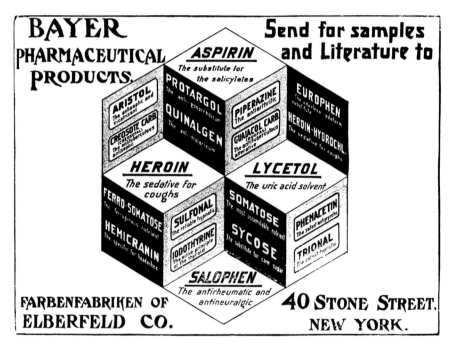

Figure 5.2.1   Heroin. First marketed as a cough suppressant, it was especially recommended for the treatment of tuberculosis. Bayer began selling heroin in 1898. The name derives from the German for "great" or "heroic." Courtesy of the National Library of Medicine.

and opium. Opium was known, but used sparingly in Europe during the Middle Ages, possibly because medieval surgeons seemed to have been largely indifferent to the suffering of their patients (Kramer, 1979).

5.2.2   Introduction to Europe and Asia

During the Renaissance, opium's popularity increased. This was partially due to the efforts of Philippus Aureolus Theophrastus Bombast von Hohenheim, a.k.a. Paracelsus (1490–1540). Paracelsus recognized that, no matter what the cause of a disease, sleep and pain relief were part of the cure; thus, Paracelsus medicated his patients with formulas that contained opium. He prescribed opium in a host of different formulations, calling one of the formulations "laudanum" (from the Latin, "something to be praised"). Laudanum was comprised of one-fourth opium, to which was added henbane juice, crushed pearls and coral, "bone of the heart of a stag, bozar stone, amber, musk, and essential oils." As an alternative preparation, Paracelsus used opium in combination with orange and lemon juice, frogs' sperm, cinnamon, cloves, ambergris, and saffron (Macht, 1915). Somewhat more streamlined versions of laudanum were used well into the 19th century (Lewin, 1931). In much the same way that Freud later enthusiastically recommended the use of cocaine as a panacea (Freud, 1884), Sydenham (1624–1689) argued that opium was the drug of choice for a range of conditions, not all of them painful (Sydenham, 1848). Thomas Dover, a ship's doctor and one of Sydenham's students, earned his place in history for two contributions: he rescued the real Robinson Crusoe, and he created a powdered opium formulation that became an immensely popular home remedy. Dover's Powder was still used in the early 1900s.

Medical writers began to discuss opiate toxicity as early as 1700. Terry (Terry and Pallens, 1928) quotes an English physician who claimed to have successfully separated opium's "noxious quality" from its "palliative" and "curative" actions, thereby avoiding the complications associated with excessive opium use. That physicians over-relied on opium should not be surprising: opium worked. It improved the conditions for which it was prescribed. It relieved pain, calmed stomachs, and suppressed coughs. Until the 20th century, such efficacy could be claimed for few other drugs. Because opium was widely available and widely used, it was inevitable that many would become addicted (Haller, 1989).

In 1803 Sertürner began his experiments with opium, trying to separate its components. In 1805 he published a report announcing that he had isolated an alkaline base in opium called *morphium*. He continued his research on *morphium* for many years, frequently using himself as a subject; at one point he nearly died of an overdose. His discovery of morphine was certainly important clinically, but his discovery also marked a sea change in the way chemists thought about the chemicals contained in plants. Prior to the discovery of morphine, it was universally held that plants could only produce products that were acid or, at most, neutral. It was believed that only metallic compounds could be alkaline. Sertürner discovery changed all of that. In relatively rapid succession, hundreds of other potent plant alkaloids, including quinine and cocaine, were isolated (Macht, 1915). Commercial morphine production began not long after morphine's isolation. The founder of England's Royal Pharmaceutical Society, Thomas Morson, started refining and selling morphine in 1821. Merck of Darmstad began wholesale production at about the same time (Berridge, 1987).

Addiction and abuse were major problems by the dawn of the 19th century, although there is some evidence to suggest that morphine addiction (as opposed to opium eating) may not have been all that widespread (Kramer, 1979). Patent medications, such as Dover's Powder, and other "cordials," "carminatives," or "soothing syrups," were nothing more than tincture of opium combined with flavorings and ample amounts of alcohol. Case reports describing "morphia" toxicity were being published with some regularity by the late 1830s.

Perhaps because he was an active proselytizer for opium consumption, the best known addict of that period was DeQuincey. He had first used opium to treat a toothache, but he rapidly developed a formidable habit. At one point he was consuming more than 20 grams (not grains) per day (De Quincey, 1822). While he was only one of many addicts to be found within London's artistic community, he was opium's most vocal advocate, having written, among other things, that "happiness might now be bought for a penny, and carried in the waistcoat pocket." DeQuincey's *Confessions of an English Opium Eater* was first published in 1821, and a revised, considerably enlarged, second edition was published in 1856. That same year, Elizabeth Barrett Browning published her acclaimed narrative poem, *Aurora Leigh*. Although Browning was also addicted, and the poem was highly autobiographical, she never argued that much good came from the habit (Bishop, 1994). This probably explains why DeQuincey's name is synonymous with drug use and Browning's is not.

Opium and Islam were introduced into China by Arab traders during the Tang Dynasty (618–907 A.D.). At first, the Chinese used opium only for medicinal purposes. The *Pen Tsao Kang Mu*, a materia medica published in 1590, nearly 1,000 years after opium was first introduced into China, makes absolutely no mention of addiction or abuse (Way, 1982). Opium was only taken orally, and then only for treatment of pain and diarrhea. Opium smoking, which probably originated in Java, began nearly a millennium later. The first mentions of opium smoking in China are from the 16th century, occurring at just about the same time the Portuguese were introducing the Chinese to tobacco. Over the next two centuries, the popularity of opium smoking steadily increased. In 1880, for reasons having more to do with an increasing balance of trade deficit than concerns with abuse, Emperor Chin Ching banned opium importation. The East India Company ignored the ban and continued to smuggle large amounts of opium into China. In 1839, the Chinese government finally decided to take active measures against opium importation. The measures prompted England to declare a war that China promptly lost. Customs figures from 1881 show that opium imports into China were in excess of 6 million kilograms per year, enough to supply one

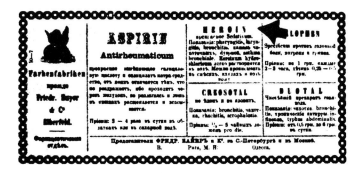

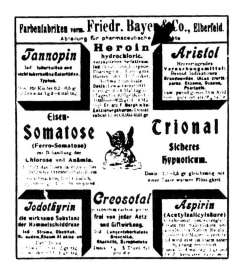

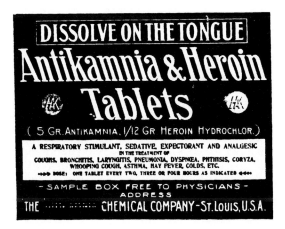

Figure 5.2.2 **Heroin.** Because of its effectiveness, heroin and heroin-containing products were not difficult to market. Many different formulations were sold in Europe and in the United States. Reprinted from the Bulletin on Narcotics, 1967.

million smokers. In spite of numerous conventions and treaties, addiction remained a major problem in China until the habit was suppressed by Mao Tse-tung in the early 1960s.

There are some striking historical parallels in the evolution of opium and cocaine abuse. Thousands of years of coca leaf chewing in South America caused few social, and no detectable medical, problems for the Incas. However, as soon as purified cocaine became widely available in Europe, there were huge increases in the amount of cocaine used. As the amount used increased, so did toxicity (Karch, 1989). Taking small amounts of opium orally was medically effective and, at worst, a benign indulgence. Much of orally-administered opium is inactivated on its first pass through the liver, so this route of ingestion has some built-in safeguards. Smoking opium is another matter entirely. When smoked, much more morphine gets into the body, blood levels rise more quickly, and there is no "first pass" effect. The net result is that when opium is smoked, the dosage is effectively multiplied. Not surprisingly, serious toxicity and addiction results.

Chinese laborers are said to have introduced opium smoking into the United States, but opium was already popular in America long before the Chinese immigration. In 1844 the New York City coroner held six inquests regarding opium-related deaths and 23 inquests on deaths related to laudanum (Woodman and Tidy, 1877). According to U.S. Government figures, over five million pounds of opium were imported into the United States from 1850 to 1877. This figure does not take into account opium which was smuggled in to avoid taxation, and opium which was cultivated domestically. Opium was produced in California, Arizona, and the New England states (Brecher, 1973). Like their European counterparts, American physicians couldn't have practiced without opium. A survey done in Boston in 1888 disclosed that, of 10,000 prescriptions dispensed by 35 pharmacies, 15% contained opium and 78% contained opiates (Way, 1982). Whatever the problems associated with opium abuse, they very likely would have been manageable had the hypodermic syringe not become available in the 1870s, and had heroin not been introduced at the turn of the century.

5.2.3   *Invention of the hypodermic syringe*

In 1855, a Scottish physician, Alexander Wood, published an account of his experiments injecting large numbers of people with opium (Wood, 1855). He injected tincture of opium and, although his original intent was to achieve something akin to a nerve block, he quickly realized that injected morphine was being carried throughout the body. In the course of his experiments, Wood managed to addict his wife to intramuscular morphine. She probably was the first woman to die of an injected narcotic overdose (Terry and Pellens, 1928).

Wood may have received most of the credit, but the idea of injecting people with narcotics had been around for hundreds of years before Wood was born. Christopher Wren, the famous architect and professor of astronomy at Gresham College, Oxford, was also a physician. According to the

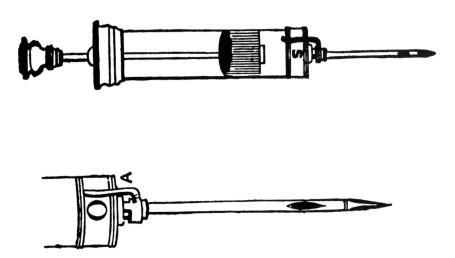

Figure 5.2.3 Hypodermic syringes. Commercial production of syringes began just before the Civil War. Initially, opiates were injected only subcutaneously. The intravenous injection of morphine and heroin did not become common practice until the 1920s. Courtesy of the National Library of Medicine.

history of the Royal Society, Wren injected dogs with intravenous opium in 1656. Using a quill attached to a small bladder, he injected lean animals with easily visible veins. There were no fatalities. Wren was so encouraged by his preliminary studies that the following year, he tried the same experiment on a man. An ambassador to the Court of St. James volunteered the services of a "delinquent servant." The volunteer was injected with an emetic which made him faint. Other experiments were even less successful, and this area of research was ignored for nearly 100 years (Terry and Pellens, 1928).

Wood's publication prompted others to experiment with the parenteral injection of many different drugs, but narcotics attracted the most interest, and injection of narcotics soon became standard practice. Hypodermic syringes were said to have been in great demand and short supply during the U.S. Civil War (Billings, 1905), although the shortage couldn't have been all that severe, since many of the veterans became addicts. Addiction, as a problem in America, was slower to evolve than in Europe, but by the 1870s, "morphism" was rampant in both the old and new world. The lag time may have been partially due to the fact that hypodermic injection did not catch on as quickly in the United States as in Europe.

Even though addiction was common, neither the mechanism of opiate action, nor the process of addiction were even remotely understood. It was widely thought, for instance, that using morphine injections, as opposed to "eating opium," minimized the probability of addiction (Anstie, 1868; Howard-Jones, 1972). Accordingly, treatment modalities for addiction were simplistic to the extreme. Freud's *Über coca*, published in 1884 (Freud, 1884), reflects the thinking of many during that period. Because cocaine's effects seemed to be so opposite to morphine's, Freud concluded that cocaine would be a logical treatment for "morphinism." Some prominent physicians, including Erlenmeyer (Erlenmeyer, 1885), disagreed, but Freud's notions were widely accepted, and a large group of patients became addicted simultaneously to cocaine and morphine. It is only quite recently, since the discovery of opiate receptors and neurotransmitters, that rational approaches to narcotic addictions have been formulated.

5.2.4   Synthesis of heroin

The other key development in the history of narcotic addiction was the synthesis of heroin. In 1874, C.R.Wright, a researcher at St. Mary's Hospital in London, boiled anhydrous morphine with acetic anhydride and produced a series of acetylated morphine derivatives (Eddy, 1953). One of the derivatives was diacetyl morphine (although the nomenclature was different at the time). He sent samples to an associate at Owens College, London, who assayed the substance for biological activity. The ability of the drug to decrease respiratory rate and blood pressure was quickly noted. For reasons that are not clear, the discovery created very little interest. In 1898, Strube published a paper outlining his favorable results when he had used heroin to treat patients with tuberculosis. He found that the drug effectively relieved severe coughs and allowed patients to sleep. Perhaps more important, he claimed to have observed no ill effects (Strube, 1898). The Bayer Company in Eberfeld, Germany, began commercial production of heroin in 1898.

Bayer had been producing pharmaceuticals since 1889, but the really profitable market for alkaloids (morphine, quinine, cocaine) was largely dominated by other companies such as Merck, Knoll, and Boehringer. Bayer's lead chemist, Felix Hoffman, synthesized heroin on August 21, 1897, just two weeks after he produced aspirin! Bayer pharmacologists began experimenting with both codeine and heroin, carrying out a number of tests on themselves, animals, and their employees. The Bayer chemists concluded, quite mistakenly, that heroin produced less respiratory depression than codeine. Based on those findings, Bayer began production, marketing heroin as a safer, more potent, cough suppressant (deRidder, 1994).

Whatever the medical profession believed about heroin, it was warmly received by the underground. By 1920 heroin addiction was such a problem that the A.M.A. House of Delegates voted to prohibit its importation, manufacture, and sale. Legitimate heroin production in the United States ceased after 1924, although low levels of illegal imports persisted. Interestingly, it seems that no one thought to inject heroin intravenously until the early 1920s. The dating is suggested by the fact that the first report describing typical track marks was not published until 1929 (Biggam, 1929). The outlawing of production, along with international treaties and conventions, but most especially the advent of World War II, led to sharp reductions in clandestine imports. In 1950, there were fewer than 40 heroin seizures within the United States.

Interest in heroin resurfaced with the advent of the Vietnam War, but was temporarily eclipsed by a general disinterest in sedative hypnotics, and a superimposed cocaine pandemic. Heroin use, at least when judged by the amount of illicit heroin now being confiscated, is again increasing. During 1990, the most recent year for which statistics are available, narcotic analgesics accounted for 57% of all drug-related deaths, with 1,976 of the deaths directly attributable to heroin abuse. By comparison, cocaine was responsible for 43% of the drug-related deaths reported to the federal government (National Institute on Drug Abuse, 1990).

5.2.5   The first pathology studies

The first autopsy describing both cerebral and pulmonary congestion was that of a New Yorker who died of laudanum overdose. It was reported by a Dr. Lee in 1852 (Woodman and Tidy, 1877). Autopsy findings in a second narcotic overdose were published in 1862. A young woman drank "gin mixed with a shilling's worth of laudanum." She quickly became comatose and intense meiosis was noted. Autopsy disclosed cerebral congestion; however, the lungs were unremarkable (Slater, 1862). A forensics text from 1877 mentions that "congestion of the lungs and of the vessels of the brain" are typically seen in opiate-related deaths, but cautioned that the findings at autopsy were "neither certain nor characteristic" (Woodman and Tidy, 1877). Understanding of the problem advanced very little until Helpern and Rho published their paper, "Deaths from Narcotism — Incidence, Circumstances, and Postmortem Findings" in 1966 (Helpern and Rho, 1966). In addition to carefully describing the epidemiology of the disease, the authors systematically described all of the signs that have come to be classically associated with narcotism, including pulmonary edema, portal adenopathy, and track marks. Since then, opiate receptors have been discovered and other disorders, such as heroin-associated nephropathy (Rao et al., 1974) and leukoencephalopathy (Wolters et al., 1982), have been described. Nonetheless, our basic understanding of the pathologic changes produced by narcotic abuse has advanced very little. During the three years that have elapsed since the first edition of this book, fewer than a dozen histologic or anatomic studies of narcotic abuse have been published!

References

Anstie, A. (1868). The hypodermic injection of remedies. Practitioner, 1: 32–41.

Berridge, V. (1987). *Opium and the people. Opiate use in nineteenth-century England.* New Haven and London: Yale University Press.

Biggam, A. (1929). Malignant malaria associated with the administration of heroin intravenously. Trans Royal Soc Trop Med and Hyg, 23: 147–153.

Billings, J. (1905). Medical reminiscences of the Civil War. Trans Coll Phys Phil, xxvii: 115–121.

Bishop, K. (1994). Drugs and art — Thomas DeQuincey and Elizabeth Barrett Browning. J Royal Soc Med, 87: 128–131.

Brecher, E. (1973). *Licit and illicit drugs; the Consumers Union report on narcotics, stimulants, depressants, inhalants, hallucinogens, and marijuana — including caffeine, nicotine, and alcohol.* Boston: Little Brown.

DeQuincy, T. D. (1822). *Confessions of an English opium eater.* London: Taylor and Hessey.

deRidder, M. (1994). Heroin: new facts about an old myth. J Psychoactive Drug, 26(1): 65–68.

Eddy, N. (1953). Heroin (diacetylmorphine): laboratory and clinical evaluation of its effectiveness and addiction liability. Bull Narcotics, 5: 39–44.

Erlenmeyer, A. (1885). Cocaine in the treatment of morphinomania. J Ment Sci, 31: 427–428.

Freud, S. (1884). Über coca. Wien Centralblatt für die ges Therapie, 2: 289–314.

Haller, J. (1989). Opium usage in nineteenth century therapeutics. Bull NY Acad Med, 65(5): 591–607.

Helpern, M. and Rho, Y. (1966a). Deaths from narcotics in New York City. NY State Med J, 66: 2391–2408.

Helpern, M. and Rho, Y. (1966b). Deaths from narcotism — incidence, circumstances, and postmortem findings. J Forensic Sci, 11(1): 1–16.

Howard-Jones, N. (1972). The origins of hypodermic medication. Sci Am, 96–102.

Karch, S. (1989). The history of cocaine toxicity. Hum Pathol, 20(11): 1037–1039.

Kramer, J. (1979). Opium rampant: medical use, misuse, and abuse in Britain and the West in the 17th and 18th centuries. B J Addict, 74: 377–389.

Kritikos, P. and Papadaki, S. (1967). The history of the poppy and of opium and their expansion in antiquity in the Eastern Mediterranean area. Bull Narc, 19(4): 5–10.

Lewin, L. (1931). *Phantastica: narcotic and stimulating drugs; their use and abuse.* New York: E. P. Dutton and Company.

Macht, D. (1915). The history of opium and some of its preparations and alkaloids. JAMA, 64(6): 477–481.

Macht, D. (1916). The history of intravenous and subcutaneous administration of drugs. JAMA, 66: 856–860.

National Institute on Drug Abuse. (1990). Annual Medical Examiner Data. Data from the Drug Abuse Warning Network. Statistical Series, Number 10-B. Rockville, MD, U.S. Department of Health and Human Services.

Rao, T., Nicastri, A., and Friedman, E. (1974). Natural history of heroin associated nephropathy. N Engl J Med, 290: 19–23.

Slayter, C. (1862). Poisoning by opium and gin: fatal result. Lancet, 1(March 29): 326.

Strube, G. (1898). Mittheilung über therapeutische Versuche mit Heroin. Berl Klinische Wochenschrift, 38: 38.

Sydenham, T. (1848). *The works of Thomas Sydenham, M.D.* Translated from the Latin edition of *Dr. Greenhil; with a life of the author* by R. G. Latham. London: The Sydenham Society.

Terry, C. and Pellens, M. (1928). *The opium problem.* New York: Committee on Drug Addictions, Bureau of Social Hygiene, Inc.

Way, E. (1982). History of opiate use in the Orient and the United States. Opioids in mental illness: theories, clinical observations, and treatment possibilities. Ann NY Acad Sci, 398: 12–23.

Wolters, E., Wijngaarden, G., Stam, F. et al. (1982). Leucoencephalopathy after inhaling "heroin" pyrolysate. Lancet, ii: 1233–1237.

Wood, A. (1855). New method of treating neuralgia by the direct application of opiates to painful spots. Edinburgh Med and Surg J, 82: 265.

Woodman, W. and Tidy, C. (1877). *Forensic medicine and toxicology.* Philadelphia: Lindsay and Blakiston.

5.3   Cultivation and manufacture

5.3.1   Botanic considerations

From the end of World War II until the late 1980s, opium production was confined to two primary areas: Southeast and Southwest Asia. Sometime during the early 1990s, South American cocaine cartels began cultivating poppies in remote, mountainous regions of northwestern Mexico, Columbia, Venezuela, and even Guatemala. Mexican opium, and the heroin produced from it, is distinguishable from opium products raised in other parts of South Amercia. Government experts now recognize four distinct opium producing areas: Southeast and Southwest Asia, South America, and Mexico.

Mexican output reached substantial levels by the early 1990s, and "black tar" Mexican heroin now accounts for much of the market in California and the Western United States. Opium production has also begun in the Central Asian republics of the old U.S.S.R. The old Silk Road, running from Europe to China, has been resurrected, except now opium, not silk, is being bartered. Opium produced in Afghanistan is smuggled into Tajikistan and Uzbekistan, where it is either refined locally into heroin, or sent on to Russia for further refining. Most of the Silk Road production appears destined for Europe, with European heroin seizures having increased from 8 tons in 1993 (Specter, 1995) to over 16 tons in 1994. Growing conditions in all four areas share common characteristics, though very little specific information is available about Central Asian production.

There are six genera in the Papaveraceae family, and within the genus there are six distinct species. *Papaver somniferum* is commonly cultivated as the "opium" poppy, but the wild growing *Papaver setigerum* also contains significant amounts of morphine. Over the years, many hybrids have been developed, but describing a generic "poppy" is difficult, if not impossible. Flowers may be single or double, with variation in both shape and color. Blossoms may be white, red, pink, purple, crimson, and many shades in between. The capsules, from which the juice is extracted, also vary in shape and alkaloid content. There can be two, three, or more capsules on a plant. Height is also variable, and may range from 30–150 centimeters or more (Anon, 1953).

The poppy is an annual plant. It grows in almost any climate, but does best in warm, temperate areas. It cannot be grown in areas that are subject to frost. When grown in humid regions, the poppy is vulnerable to infection by a range of fungal and plant parasites. Poppies grow well in average soil, but the soil requires treatment with manure or chemical fertilizers. Plants take two to three weeks to germinate, and two months to fully develop. After a field has been weeded and thinned out, as many as 15 plants can be grown in a square meter. After the plant flowers, and the petals have fallen off, the capsule continues to ripen for another two weeks, at which time the latex can be harvested. The entire cycle takes less than three months.

Harvesting is a two-step process. First, the capsule is incised, allowing the sap to run out and then solidify. Twelve hours after the capsule has been incised, the latex is harvested. Incising the capsule is a delicate operation: if the incision is too deep, the latex will run down the inside of the plant and be lost to harvest. Farmers prefer to do the incising at sunrise or sunset. That allows the latex to exude and solidify for 8–14 hours. The caked latex is then scraped off the capsule using a dull blade. The yield per acre depends on many variables. Historically, the yield in Turkey and the Mediterranean is said to be 10 kg of opium per hectare. Yields in India are said to be higher. Yields in the newer fields being established in South America, and in the Central Asian republics, have yet to be determined.

Over 20 different alkaloids have been identified in opium, but only three are of any significance: morphine, codeine, and thebaine. Thebaine has almost no morphine-like activity of its own, but it can be used to manufacture other narcotic agents. Hundreds of semisynthetic derivatives, referred to as Bentley Compounds, have been synthesized from thebaine, and many of these do have narcotic effects. A few of the derivatives, such as etorphine, have 1,000 times the activity of morphine. Morphine is the principal alkaloid found in opium. It constitutes between 8–19% of air-dried opium. Reported ranges for codeine content are from 1.25–3.4% (Anon, 1963).

Poppy seeds sold for cooking and baking purposes may contain very substantial amounts of morphine and codeine. In one study, the morphine content was found to be anywhere from 7.3–60.1 μg/gm of seed, while the codeine content ranged from 6.1–29.8 μg/gm (Hasegawa et al., 1992). It is hardly surprising that the urine of people eating poppy seeds tests positive on opiate screening tests!

Estimated world production of opium in 1994 was 3,400 metric tons. More than half (2,132 tons) was produced in Southeast Asia (Burma, Laos, Thailand), followed by Southwest Asia with 1,100 tons (Afghanistan and Pakistan), and South America and Mexico, where totals were estimated to be 60 tons.

5.3.2 *Manufacture*

Heroin can be manufactured directly from opium, or from semipurified morphine. The route utilized depends mostly on the availability of the precursors. Morphine and opium are both sold on the illicit market, and the availability of one or the other depends largely on local conditions.

The clandestine separation of morphine from crude opium involves three separate steps. A kilogram of opium is dissolved in 2 liters of water along with 200 gm of lime, and the resultant solution poured through a coarse filter. Then, 250 gm of ammonium chloride is added to the filtrate, causing morphine base to slowly precipitate out. The morphine is collected on a fine cloth filter and then washed with water. The crude morphine is then mixed with charcoal and with either hydrochloric or sulfuric acid. The mixture is filtered and ammonium hydroxide is added to the filtrate, causing purified morphine to precipitate out. The precipitate is collected by filtration and allowed to dry in room air.

Table 5.3.2.1 Adulterants Found in Heroin from Mexico, South
America, Southeast Asia, and Southwest Asia. Numbers Indicate the
Percentage of Samples Found to Contain Each of the Adulterants

Adulterant	Southeast Asia	Southwest Asia	Mexican	America
Quinine	36	30	27	18
Diphenhydramine	17	3	20	—
Caffeine	22	8	—	8
Acetaminophen	21	8	1	6
Procaine	4	14	—	23
Cocaine	2	3	3	6
Lidocaine	1	3	4	6

Based on data supplied by the Drug Enforcement Administration. Table
shows the percentage of specimen from that area containing a particular
adulterant. Other compounds are occasionally seen, but they are encountered
so infrequently that no pattern is discernible.

In the second phase of production the dried morphine is added to acetic
anhydride and the mixture is refluxed at a constant temperature for five
hours. After the mixture has been allowed to cool, it is neutralized with
sodium carbonate. The crude heroin that precipitates out is filtered and
washed with water.

In the final stage of production, heroin is purified by redissolving the
crude heroin in boiling water that contains citric acid and charcoal. The
mixture is filtered and purified, and heroin is precipitated by the addition
of sodium carbonate. If the lab wants to produce the hydrochloride form
instead of heroin base, the heroin is redissolved in acetone, and hydrochloric
acid is added to the solution.

Depending on market demand, clandestine chemists will sometimes
synthesize morphine, instead of opium. Production begins by dissolving one
kilogram of opium in two liters of water and adding 200 gm of slaked lime,
500 mL of alcohol, and 500 mL of ether. The resultant solution is then filtered
through a cloth, leaving crude morphine on the cloth. This material is further

Table 5.3.2.2 Diluents Found in Heroin from Mexico,
South America, Southeast Asia, and Southwest Asia

Dilutent	Southeast Asia	Southwest Asia	Mexican	South America
Lactose	46	43	39	33
Mannitol	65	73	6	67
Starch	21	19	6	27
Dextrose	5	3	—	6

Other compounds are so infrequently seen that no pattern is discernible.

Note: Numbers indicate the percentage of samples found to contain each of the adulterants.

purified and decolorized by refluxing it with 2 liters of dilute sulfuric acid and 250 gm of charcoal for about half an hour. This solution is then filtered and ammonium hydroxide added to the filtrate. The off-white colored, semi-purified morphine that precipitates out is dried in room air. Hardened dried morphine granules are rubbed against a hard surface to produce a powder (Narayanaswami, 1985).

In the past there have been reports of clandestine laboratories synthe-sizing methadone, but at present, fentanyl and its analogs are the only narcotics synthesized clandestinely, and then not very often. The infrequency of this occurrence probably has to do with the fact that the synthesis of fentanyl is more difficult than that of other illicit chemicals such as meth-amphetamine and phencyclidine. At least three different synthetic routes are possible. The most popular route involves the use of norfentanyl or 3-methyl-norfentanyl intermediates. These are produced from 1-benzyl-4-poperidone by reductive amination with aniline, then acetylation and hydrogenation to form norfentanyl. Fentanyl and its analogs are then manufactured by alky-lating the piperidine nitrogen.

The DEA estimates that total heroin production in Southeast Asia in 1994 was 177 tons, with another 111 tons being produced in Southwest Asia, and 6 tons in Mexico and South America (National Narcotics Intelligence Con-sumers Committee, 1994). Total production in the newly independent central Asian republics is difficult to estimate, but some feel that production in those regions may add another 10% to world totals (Drug Enforcement Adminis-tration, 1994).

5.3.3 Sample analysis

There are, of course, ways to make pure morphine containing no other alkaloids, but these methods are not routinely used by clandestine labs. Thus, the ratio of heroin to acetylcodeine in illicit heroin is nearly the same as the ratio of morphine to codeine in the illicit morphine that was used to produce the heroin in the first place. Studies have shown that the ratio of heroin to acetylcodeine in an illicit heroin sample may be used to identify that sample's country of origin. The ratio is fairly high for samples emanating from Afghanistan (20.9:1), and quite low for specimens coming from China (6.38:1) (Lim and Chow, 1978; Narayanaswami, 1985). However, in the final analysis, the ratio of heroin to 6-acetylmorphine and morphine is more an indicator of clandestine lab proficiency than country of origin (O'neil and Pitts, 1992).

Substances carried over from the original plant or from opium are referred to as adulterants. Substances added with the intent of altering the character of the heroin in some way are also called adulterants. Included in this group are compounds such as quinine, caffeine, and diphenhydramine. The term, diluent, is reserved for those substances, devoid of physiologic effects, that are added to increase the bulk of the final product. As illustrated in Tables 5.3.2.1 and 5.3.2.2, heroin produced in different regions can be characterized by the adulterants and diluents that have been added. In the past, three types of product could be identified; illicit heroin samples from Southeast Asia, Southwest Asia, and Mexico all had distinctive profiles. Within the last two years, enough samples have been seized to allow the characterization of a fourth type of heroin being produced in South America.

During the mid-1990s, the average purity of heroin sold on the streets increased dramatically, from 24.5% in 1990 to 35.8% in 1993. Samples coming from South America had the highest purity, averaging 59.3%. Southwest Asian heroin was, on average, 47.2% pure, followed by Southeast Asian (32.2%), and Mexican (27.8%). The purity of heroin sold on the streets varies widely from city to city. The average for the entire United States in 1993 was 35.8%, at an average cost of $1.47 per milligram. But, in Miami the price was higher ($2.00) and the purity lower (only 8%). In Philadelphia, samples were almost 75% pure, and the price only $.51 (Drug Enforcement Administration, 1994). Heroin sold in the Western states is primarily of Mexican origin, while heroin sold on the East coast comes mainly from Southeast Asia. Heroin from Southwest Asia (India, Iran, and Pakistan) is sold mainly in the East and Midwest, and has an average purity somewhere between that of heroin sold on either of the two coasts.

The type of material added as diluents varies from region to region, and from time to time, depending on local conditions and on the preferences of the illicit manufacturer. French chemists have noted rather drastic shifts in the composition of seized specimens. They report that during the late 1980s, caffeine and mannitol were the most frequently used diluents. But by 1991, caffeine and mannitol had been almost entirely replaced by paracetamol (Chaudron-Thozet et al., 1992). Specimens from Southeast Asia are usually diluted with mannitol or lactose. Most of the diluents and adulterants are relatively non-toxic, although recently confiscated specimens of Mexican "black tar" have been encountered that contained xylazine, an anesthetic used by veterinary surgeons (Anon, 1993).

If present in sufficient concentrations, xylazine may be quite toxic. In animal models it causes increased pulmonary capillary permeability and sudden onset pulmonary edema (Amouzadeh et al., 1991). Human data is sparse, but one case report described a 36-year old veterinarian who died within a few hours of injecting himself with xylazine. Levels in blood, brain, kidney, liver, and lung were 0.2, 0.4, 0.6, 0.9, and 1.1 mg/kg (or mg/L), respectively (Poklis et al., 1985).

References

Amouzadeh, H., Sangiah, S., Qualls, C. et al. (1991). Xylazine-induced pulmonary edema in rats. Tox Appl Pharm, 108: 417–427.

Anon (1953). The opium poppy. Bull Narc, V(3) (July–September): 9–12.

Anon (1963). The opium alkaloids. Bull Narc, V(3) (July–September): 13–14.

Anon (1993). Xylazine. Microgram, XXVI: 193.

Chaudron-Thozet, H., Girard, J., and David, J. (1992). Analysis of heroin seized in France. Bull Narc, XLIV(1): 29–33.

Drug Enforcement Administration (1992). Domestic monitor program. A quarterly report on the source areas, cost, and purity of retail-level heroin, January-March, 1991. DEA #92006.

Drug Enforcement Administration, Strategic Intelligence Section. (1994). The newly independent states; a special assessment and country briefs. Washington, D.C.

Hasegawa, M., Maseda, C., Kagawa, M. et al. (1992). Morphine and codeine in poppy seed and poppy seed food. Jpn J Toxicol Environ Health, 38: 192–195.

Lim, H. and Chow, S. (1978). Heroin abuse and a gas chromatographic method for determining illicit heroin samples in Singapore. J Forensic Sci, 23(2): 319–328.

Narayanaswami, K. (1985). Parameters for determining the origin of illicit heroin samples. Bull Narc, 37(1): 49–62.

National Narcotics Intelligence Consumers Committee (1994). The NICC report 1993: The supply of illicit drugs to the United States, Drug Enforcement Administration, DEA-94066.

O'neil, P. and Pitts, J. (1992). Illicitly imported heroin products (1984 to 1989) — some physical and chemical features indicative of their origin. J Pharm Pharmacol, 44(1): 1–6.

Poklis, A., Mackell, M., and Case, M. (1985). Xylazine in human tissues and fluids in a case of fatal drug abuse. J Analyt Toxicol, 234–237.

Specter, M. (1995). Opium finds its silk road in chaos of Central Asia. New York Times. 1.

5.4   Individual narcotic agents

5.4.1   Morphine

Morphine was isolated from opium by Setürner in 1805. More than 120 years passed before Sir Robert Richardson characterized morphine's chemical structure in 1927, and total synthesis was only accomplished in 1952. The time lag between morphine's discovery and its chemical characterization is paralleled by the slow evolution in understanding its metabolism and mechanism of action. The principal site of metabolism is the liver, but because the total body clearance of morphine is higher than hepatic flow (Säwe et al., 1985), questions still remain about extrahepatic metabolism. Other questions remain about the usefulness of blood and tissue levels measured during the 1970s and early 1980s. These measurements were made using radioimmunoassays that have since been shown to be unreliable when compared with figures obtained by specific high-performance liquid chromatography (Aherne and Littleton, 1985; Hanks et al., 1988) or GC/MS.

5.4.1.1   General considerations

Morphine's elimination is best described as a biphasic process. During an initial phase, lasting only a few minutes, morphine is rapidly distributed throughout the tissues with the highest blood flow. During a second phase, morphine is quickly converted to its principal metabolite, morphine-3-glucuronide (M3G), and somewhat more slowly to smaller amounts of morphine-6-glucuronide (M6G). The second phase takes from one to eight hours, with two hours as the most widely accepted value (Brunk and Delle, 1974; Dahlström and Paalzow, 1978, 1979; Säwe et al., 1981; Murphy and Hug,

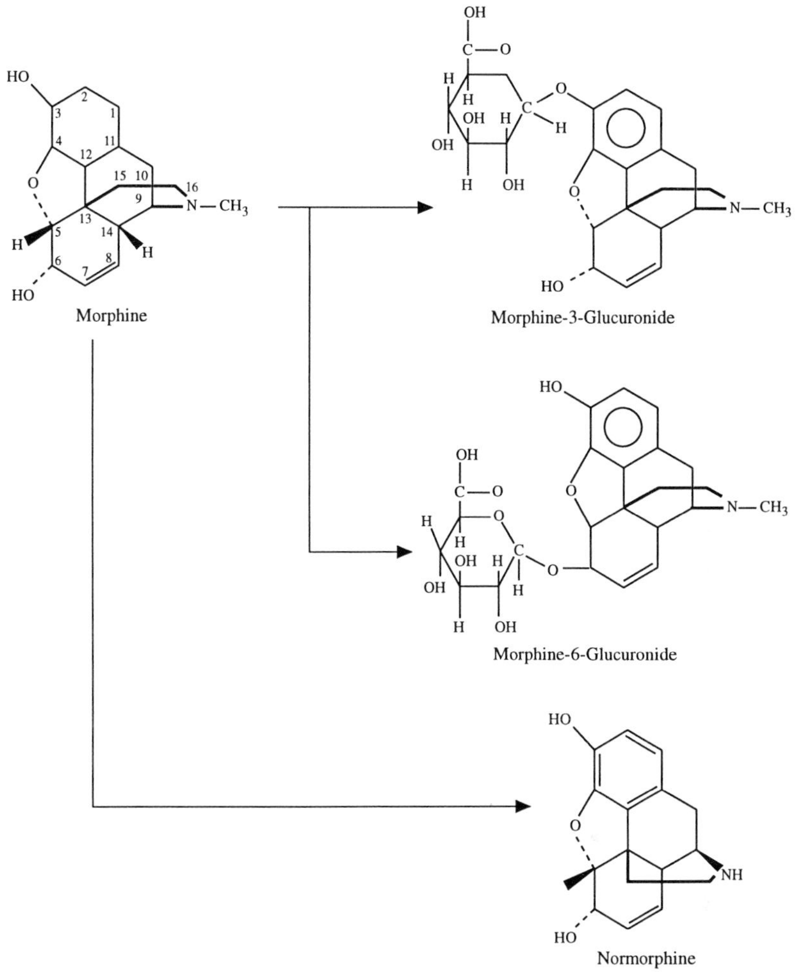

Figure 5.4.1   Basic elements of morphine metabolism.

1981). Conversion of morphine to the 3-glucuronide form is rapid. Within six minutes after intravenous injection, there is more metabolite than morphine circulating in the bloodstream. Both of the metabolites are highly ionized and lipophilic (Carrupt et al., 1991), and they readily cross the blood-brain barrier (Portnoy, 1991; Morland et al., 1995).

The most recent studies in normal volunteers who were given intravenous morphine showed an initial distribution half-life to be five minutes, and the terminal elimination phase, 1.7 hours. This means that morphine will be present in measurable quantities in the plasma for between four to six hours. The fact that M6G is pharmacologically active, and possibly more potent than morphine itself, has only recently been appreciated. The notion that conjugation is the same as detoxification is widely accepted, but not always true. Usually the process of conjugation alters the shape of the original molecule so that it cannot effectively interact with its intended receptor. However, in the case of morphine, glucuronidation at the 6 position increases the affinity of morphine for binding at the μ receptors (Mulder, 1992).

The terminal half-life of M3G is 3.9 ± 1.5 hours, while that of M6G is only 2.6 ± 0.69 hours (Osborne et al., 1990). Human studies are lacking, but in animals, M3G blocks the effects of both morphine and M6G at the μ receptor (Smith, 1990). Whether a similar process occurs in humans is not clear, but it has been suggested that differences in the absolute concentrations of morphine, M3G, and M6G at μ receptors in the spinal cord may be what determines the degree of analgesia (Bowsher, 1993).

The half-life of M6G can, however, rise to over 50 hours in individuals with renal failure. Other morphine metabolites have also been identified, but their importance has yet to be assessed. One metabolite of potential interest is normorphine. Modest amounts are formed after parenteral administration, but when morphine is taken orally, large amounts are produced. This compound is both psychoactive and neurotoxic.

Studies of morphine's metabolism have been hampered by inadequate assay techniques. Until recently, radioimmunoassay was the most widely used method for quantitating morphine in blood and biological fluids. The problem with this approach is that the antibodies used to detect morphine are relatively non-specific, and significantly crossreact with morphine metabolites. Plasma morphine measurements made with this technique reflect the presence of two or three different compounds, some of them psychoactive and some not. Measuring plasma half-life, or correlating these levels with specific behavioral effects, toxicity, or lethality, is difficult, if not impossible.

Recently, the techniques of gas chromatography and high-performance liquid chromatography with mass spectrometry have been adapted to simultaneously measure morphine and its metabolites. Simultaneous measurements of morphine, morphine-3, and morphine-6 glucuronide have been made in heroin addicts and in heroin-related deaths (Aderjan et al., 1995). Since M6G/morphine and M3G/morphine ratios depend, at least partially, on the time elapsed from when the drug was taken, knowledge of these ratios should give substantially more information about drug use in relation to time of death.

Once morphine enters the bloodstream, it is quickly distributed throughout the body to the areas with the highest blood flow. High morphine levels can be measured in lung, kidney, liver, spleen, and muscle (Brunk and Delle, 1974; Stanski et al., 1978). Morphine and its metabolites also quickly cross the blood-brain and placental barriers. One-third of a given dose circulates protein-bound (Spector and Vessell, 1971), so that abnormalities of protein binding, such as would be seen in hepatic failure or malignancies, can alter the degree of protein binding and, indirectly, lead to higher circulating levels of free morphine (Säwe, 1986).

Only minimal quantities of morphine are excreted unchanged in the urine. In humans, roughly 70% of a given dose is converted to glucuronide (57% M3G, 10% M6G) (Hasselström and Säwe, 1993) and then excreted via the kidneys. Less than 10% of a given dose is excreted unchanged in the urine. Elimination of unchanged morphine is not affected by renal failure. On the other hand, elimination of the glucuronides is affected by renal failure, and since M6G is psychoactive, patients with renal failure may become toxic due to the presence of accumulated metabolite (Ball et al., 1985). Most morphine is disposed of by glucuronidation. Pathways for ethereal sulfate formation and other oxidative pathways are also known to exist. Most of these biotransformations occur in the liver, but in humans, as much as 38% undergoes glucuronidation elsewhere, probably in the kidney. In animal species, and in the human fetus, the intestinal mucosa may also be an important site of transformation (Laitinen et al., 1975; Iwamato and Klassen, 1977; Pacifici and Rane, 1982), but that is not the case in adult humans (Mazoit et al., 1990).

Opiate receptor studies have shown that the 3-position in the morphine moiety must remain accessible for a molecule to have opiate activity. Since the carbon 3 position is open in the M6G molecule, it is not surprising that this metabolite has analgesic effects in its own right (Osborne et al., 1988). Viewed in this light, data from earlier studies distinguishing between free and conjugated morphine levels becomes impossible to interpret, since there are at least two morphine conjugates, and one is psychoactive.

Other controversies about the metabolism and excretion of morphine remain unresolved. One is whether or not morphine is converted to codeine. Whether or not the presence of codeine in a urine specimen can rightly be taken as proof of morphine or heroin abuse is an important issue. The results of earlier studies suggested that, at least in chronic opiate abusers, the conversion occurred (Boerner et al., 1975). The most recent studies, using gas chromatography/mass spectrometry, indicate that the conversion does not occur (Mitchell et al., 1991; Cone et al., 1991b). The demonstration of codeine in the urine after giving morphine or heroin is probably explained by the presence of codeine impurities present even in pharmaceutical grade morphine (Cone et al., 1991a). The presence of codeine in a urine or blood specimen is proof only that codeine, and not any other drug, was ingested.

Within the last few years it has become increasingly clear that morphine undergoes enterohepatic circulation. In seven healthy volunteers given 5 mg doses of morphine intravenously, 57.3% of the dose was converted to M3G, 10.4% to M6G, and 10.9% appeared unchanged in the urine, leaving 20.8% of the original morphine unaccounted for (Hasselström and Säwe, 1993). Studies of fecal excretion indicate that this route may account for between 7% and 10% of a given dose in chronic users (Hanks et al., 1988), and it is also known that morphine glucuronides excreted in the bile can be deconjugated by bacteria in the gut and then reabsorbed through the intestinal mucosa. In the ewe, at least, M3G is actually synthesized by the gut (Millne et al., 1993).

As a consequence, morphine glucuronides will continue to appear in the urine for days after the drug was last used, even in healthy individuals without liver or kidney disease. It will continue to be excreted in the urine for as long as there is morphine to be excreted in the bile. Concentrations of unchanged morphine in bile may reach extremely high levels. In one study of narcotic-related deaths, the average concentration of morphine in the bile was 312 mg/L (Chan et al., 1986). In Gottschalk and Cravey's series of 119 cases, the median level of morphine in the bile was 33.7 mg/L (Gottschalk and Cravey, 1980). It is not known with any certainty just how long it takes an addict to clear morphine from the enterohepatic circuit, but it is reasonable to suppose that heroin abusers might test positive for quite sometime after the drug was last taken. This possibility must be taken into account when interpreting drug abuse screening tests. Similar considerations may apply to an individual returning to work after a prolonged hospital stay.

5.4.1.2   Absorption and routes of administration

Almost all of the opiates are well absorbed, no matter the route of administration. However, not all opiates are equally well absorbed. Morphine levels after varying routes of administration have been measured, but mostly in healthy volunteers, or in cancer patients. There have been very few studies where large amounts of drug have been given to addicts and tolerant subjects.

5.4.1.2.1   *Intravenous.*   A 10-mg bolus given to healthy volunteers undergoing elective surgery results in a peak blood level of 200–400 ng/mL five minutes after injection (Berkowitz et al., 1975). Whether or not similar results would be obtained in tolerant addicts is not known. In a more recent study comparing the pharmacokinetics of smoked and intravenous heroin, measurements were made in two subjects; in one subject, peak concentrations ranged from 72 ng/mL after a 10 mg dose, and 401 ng/mL after a 20 mg dose. In a second subject 3 mg produced a peak level of 64 ng/mL, while 6 mg gave a peak of 315 ng/mL. Levels rapidly declined thereafter and reached limits of detection within 30 minutes of injection (Jenkins et al., 1994).

5.4.1.2.2   *Subcutaneous.*   Absorption via the subcutaneous route, and after intramuscular injection, is almost as rapid as the intravenous route. After either route, morphine blood levels peak at 10–20 minutes, somewhat longer than after intravenous injection, but not so much longer as to have much clinical significance. The pharmacokinetics for both routes are nearly the same as after intravenous injection, and plasma levels comparable to those seen after intravenous use can be achieved after subcutaneous injection. That may explain why, in the past, subcutaneous injection (known as "skin popping") enjoyed considerable popularity among some groups of abusers. This practice, and the skin lesions commonly associated with it, seem to be less common today than in the past. It may be that "skin popping" is being replaced by smoking.

5.4.1.2.3   *Oral.*   Morphine is absorbed completely from the small intestine, and peak plasma levels occur after 30–90 minutes, but resultant peak plasma levels are only one-tenth as high as after giving the same amount parenterally. Bioavailability is significantly reduced because of first-pass metabolism in the liver. The degree to which morphine is subject to extraction and metabolism by the gastrointestinal tract can be affected by a number of factors, including age, liver disease, gender, food effects, disease states, and genetic polymorphism (Tam, 1993). Because of these effects, less than a quarter of a given dose may finally enter the bloodstream (Brunk and Delle, 1974).

The oral route was popular among the "Opium Eaters" of the 17th and 18th centuries, when distribution was unregulated and prices were low. Today, it is an impractical route for abusers because it costs too much. In the case of cancer patients who have access to legally supplied morphine, oral administration is a mainstay in the management (Hoskin et al., 1989; Osborne et al., 1990; Gourlay et al., 1986).

Oral overdose, intentional or accidental, can occur (Fisher et al., 1987; Breheny et al., 1993). The most recent case involved an intentional overdose with an unspecified number of time release morphine capsules (MS Contin®, Pharmacia). In addition to profound respiratory depression, the patient subsequently developed rhabdomyolysis and renal failure. Initial levels of morphine, M6G and M3G, roughly 36 hours after ingestion, were 57 ng/mL, 154 ng/mL, and 798 ng/mL, respectively.

5.4.1.2.4 Rectal. Plasma levels after rectal administration are somewhat higher than after oral morphine, but are much less than after parenteral (Ellison and Lewis, 1984). This route does not seem to be particularly popular among abusers, at least when compared to the rectal use of cocaine, which is a fairly common practice. One reason may be that rectal administration of morphine significantly reduces first-pass exposure in the liver, resulting in decreased hepatic transformation of morphine to its pharmacologically active metabolite, morphine-6-glucuronide (Babul and Darke, 1993).

When 0.6 mg/kg of morphine was given to women undergoing cancer treatment, there was considerable variation between individuals, but peak concentrations of 31–75 ng/mL were reached at between 45–120 minutes (Westerling et al., 1982). Fatalities have been reported at levels that were not much higher, and seizures, particularly in neonates, have been reported at levels that were much lower. Morphine-induced seizures have occurred at levels as low as 9 ng/mL (Koren et al., 1983). One report described a postoperative death, from cerebral plasma levels after rectal administration. A child who died of respiratory arrest after being treated with multiple 4-mg morphine suppositories had a morphine blood level of 94 ng/mL when measured 4 hours after death (Gourlay and Boas, 1992). Rectal absorption of morphine is variable. Different studies have shown rectal bioavailability to be anywhere from 12–61% (Westerling et al., 1982; Lindahl et al., 1981). Pharmacologic manipulation of the morphine medium can improve absorption and result in levels comparable to oral administration. If the carrier medium is acidified, then the percentage of non-ionized drug increases, as does absorption.

5.4.1.2.5 Intranasal. Heroin and morphine can both be used intranasally, but the transnasal absorption of morphine is poor, at least when compared to other agents such as cocaine. At the turn of the century, probably up through the mid 1920s, as many people took heroin by nasal insufflation as by injection. Today's abusers seem to have rediscovered this effective route. Goverment surveys report that the practice of heroin snorting has become increasingly popular on the "club" circuit, and as heroin prices continue to fall, this route can be expected to become increasingly popular. The pharmacokinetics of intranasal and intramuscular heroin have been compared in one study. Peak heroin concentrations, after either intranasal or intramuscular (IM) administration, occur within five minutes. Resultant blood levels after 6 mg dose of heroin, by either route, are on the order of 30–40 ng/mL. The mean elimination half-life after intranasal administration was found to be 5.4 minutes ± 4.5 minutes vs. 4.2 minutes ± 0.12 minutes after intramuscular administration.

Concentrations of 6-acetylmorphine peaked at 5–10 minutes after administration by either route, with peak levels of 22.6 ng/mL after a 6 mg dose. The elimination half-life was longer for 6-acetylmorphine than for heroin: 10.8 ± 8.4 minutes after intranasal compared to 11.4 minutes ± 5.4 minutes after IM dosing with 6 mg. Once the heroin had been converted to morphine, the half-life for morphine following intranasal administration ranged from 90 ± 96 minutes (6 mg dose intranasally) to 168 ± 216 (12 mg dose intranasally) vs. only to 66 ± 6.5 minutes after 6 mg IM (Mo and Way, 1996; Jenkins et al., 1993).

5.4.1.2.6   Inhalation.   Opium smoking has never been scientifically studied, but the pharmacokinetics of heroin smoking have recently been characterized (Jenkins et al., 1994). It appears that the bioavailability of smoked heroin is variable and unpredictable. Heroin can be detected in the blood within one minute of smoking. Peak levels after smoking 10.6 mg/L were 299 ng/mL in one subject, and 108 ng/mL in another. Blood level rapidly declined to limits of detection (under 1 ng/mL) within 30 minutes of smoking. Levels of 6-acetylmorphine peak 1–2 minutes after peak heroin levels. Morphine levels rise and fall more slowly. In this study the estimated half-lives of heroin, 6-monoactyl-morphine, and morphine were 3.3 minutes, 5.4 minutes, and 18.8 minutes, respectively. In general, these results are comparable to those observed after intravenous administration. Reports from Europe suggest that the practice of smoking heroin "freebase" is increasingly popular. The melting point of heroin is much higher than that of cocaine, so preparing freebase heroin is more complicated than making crack cocaine, which probably explains why the practice is not more common.

5.4.1.2.7   Skin.   Morphine is not sufficiently fat-soluble to be absorbed though the skin in quantities sufficient to produce psychological effects. Other opioids, particularly fentanyl and sulfentanyl, and also meperidine, are well absorbed via this route. Since these other agents are also much more potent than morphine or heroin, transdermal application is quite practical. Time-release patches containing fentanyl are now for sale, and are even beginning to appear on the black market (Calis et al., 1992).

5.4.1.2.8 Maternal/fetal. It has been recognized for more than a century that mothers can transfer morphine to their children in breast milk (Anon, 1861). Depending on the degree of lipid solubility, narcotic agents passively diffuse across the placenta. Fetal uptake after maternal dosing with heroin has been studied in the Rhesus monkey using ^{11}C-heroin and positron tomography. Peak levels in the placenta were reached within a few minutes of administration. Peak maternal levels were twice the fetal level, but by one hour, fetal blood levels were higher than maternal levels. Concentrations of labeled morphine in the liver quickly rise and quickly fall (Hartvig et al., 1989). Once the narcotic agents are taken up by the fetus, they are metabolized and excreted. They may be detected in the amniotic fluid (Rurak, Wright, and Axelson, 1991), or in specimens of hair or meconium (Graham et al., 1989; Little et al., 1989).

The results of animal studies suggest that morphine metabolites, chiefly morphine-3-glucuronide, also enter the amniotic fluid, but much more slowly than morphine itself. After 12 hours of continuous infusion of morphine-3-glucuronide, fetal concentrations may amount to less than half of those observed in the mother (Gerdin et al., 1990).

5.4.1.3 Tissue disposition. The volume of distribution for morphine is over 3 L/kg (Goodman and Gilman, 1990), which means that less than 2% of a given dose is to be found circulating in the blood. Morphine is rapidly distributed throughout the body, and resultant tissue concentrations reflect the relative blood flow. The time it takes morphine to redistribute, and the final tissue concentrations that are observed when redistribution is completed, are altered by age (Chan et al., 1975). Concentrations in skeletal muscle never reach those of the blood or other tissues, but muscle is an important storage site for opiates, just by virtue of its sheer bulk. Morphine is not as highly lipophilic as some agents, such as fentanyl, so it tends not to accumulate in fat. Morphine crosses the blood-brain barrier, but not so freely as compounds like heroin and codeine which possess an aromatic hydroxyl group at the C3 position. Morphine tissue disposition does not appear to be altered by the concomitant use of sympathomimetic agents such as ephedrine and phenylpropanolamine (Dambisya et al., 1992). Whether this is also true for methamphetamine and cocaine is not known.

Simultaneous measurement of heroin and its metabolites has only recently become possible. With the advent of efficient extraction procedures for the recovery of heroin, 6-acetylmorphine, and morphine from postmortem tissues (Goldberger et al., 1994), a clearer picture of heroin toxicity may yet emerge. However, only a limited number of such measurements have been reported. In the older literature, measurements of tissue concentrations from both heroin and morphine overdoses are generally reported together. Since heroin is rapidly converted to 6-acetylmorphine and then to morphine, such extrapolation seems permissible.

Extreme caution must be exercised in the interpretation of postmortem morphine measurements, especially in the case of blood. Morphine, like digoxin, and other drugs with large volumes of distribution, almost certainly undergoes postmortem redistribution, with morphine moving from various tissues into blood. Since only 2% of the morphine present is actually circulating in the blood, the release of only 1% more from deep tissue stores would be enough to double measured postmortem tissue concentrations. No human studies of redistribution have been reported, but in animal studies, measured levels of free morphine more than doubled during the first 24 hours after death. Measurement of free morphine may also be falsely elevated by-products of putrification that cross-react with the antibodies used to measure morphine (Koren and Klein, 1992).

The other difficulty in interpreting postmortem measurements has to do with differences in the volume of distribution for morphine and its glucuronides. The volume of distribution for morphine is more than 10 times that of either M3G or M6G. In contrast to free morphine, which diffuses into tissues throughout the body, almost all the conjugated morphine is to be found circulating in the blood. That being the case, measurements of total morphine circulating in the blood are relatively meaningless (Aderjan et al., 1995).

5.4.1.3.1   Blood.   Blood levels of morphine in seven different autopsy series have ranged from 10 ng/ mL (Richards et al., 1976) to 2,800 ng/mL (Felby et al., 1974). Various ranges have been reported for free morphine levels, and in some cases values as high as 8,000 ng/mL have been observed (Reed et al., 1977; Gottschalk and Cravey, 1980; Hine et al., 1982; Cravey, 1985; Chan et al., 1986; Sawyer et al., 1988; Steentoft et al., 1988; Steentoft et al., 1989; Kintz et al., 1989). Using newer techniques, heroin, 6-acetylmorphine, and morphine levels in two overdose deaths were 0, 11.3, and 16.2, 207.8, and 81.7 ng, respectively (Goldberger et al., 1994). Body packers dying from ruptured drug packets may have heroin and morphine levels > 100,000 ng/m (Joynt and Mikhael, 1985). Using those same techniques (solid phase extraction coupled with gas chromatograpy/mass spectrometry) to analyze blood samples in 21 heroin-related deaths, heroin levels were 0 in every case. Mean 6-acetylmorphine levels were 9.9 ng/mL (range 0–82.9), while mean free morphine levels were 222 ng/mL (range 11.2–1,277 ng/mL).

Generalizing from these results is extremely difficult for at least three reasons. Firstly, all of the observations were made before it became apparent that M6G was metabolically active. Secondly, many of the measurements were made using immunoassays that cross-react with metabolites. Thirdly, there is the problem of tolerance. Opiate abusers become extremely tolerant to opiate-induced respiratory depression, but this tolerance is rapidly lost (Harding-Pink and Fryc, 1988). Even the presence of track marks and other stigmata is not proof that the deceased was tolerant at the time of death, since these signs do not rapidly regress when the drug is discontinued. Except for confirming that the decedent was, in fact, abusing opiates, quantitation of blood levels helps very little in determining the cause of death. Spiehler analyzed multiple variables common to 200 morphine-induced fatalities, using an artificial intelligence program. The study results suggested that the most useful parameters for diagnosis of overdose deaths were blood unconjugated morphine levels, blood total morphine, and liver total morphine.

Spiehler found that the most reliable predictor for overdose death was the presence of unconjugated morphine levels that were greater than 240 ng/mL (Spiehler and Brown, 1987; Spiehler, 1989), but recent discoveries about the metabolic activity of M6G have considerably diminished the value of free morphine and total morphine concentrations' determination. Measurement of the M6G/morphine ratio may be a much more useful indicator. In a 1995 study of heroin intoxication, and heroin-related deaths, M6G/morphine ratios < 2 were found to be a reliable indicator that the distribution of heroin was not complete. Much higher ratios were observed in living patients who were only intoxicated with heroin (Aderjan et al., 1995).

5.4.1.3.2   Brain.   Only a handful of blood-brain ratio measurements have been reported. In the three heroin users described by Kintz, the blood-brain ratios were 13, 0.24, and 1.5, with tissue concentrations ranging from 0.005 mg/kg to 0.089 mg/kg of wet brain (Kintz et al., 1989). In Goldberg's report, CSF and brain levels of 6-acetylmorphine were much higher than levels in blood, liver, lung, and kidney. One individual had a blood 6-acetylmorphine of 11.3 ng/m compared to levels of 58 ng/mL in the CSF and 158 ng/mL in brain. In a second case, blood levels were 16.2 ng/mL, while levels in the CSF and brain were 38.5 and 53.6 ng/mL, respectively (Goldberger et al., 1994). The concentration ratio of blood morphine to the morphine levels in other tissues varies so widely that calculating the ratios is of little use. However, in one reported study, blood/CSF ratios appear to be fairly stable (2.74 ± 1.69). In 89% of the cases, morphine levels were lower in the CSF than in the blood. Measurement of CSF may prove to be a useful diagnostic tool, but not until more data has been accumulated (Whaba et al., 1993).

5.4.1.3.3   Liver.   Morphine concentrations have been measured in several series. In the 10 cases analyzed by Felby, the mean was 3.0 mg/kg and the range was 0.4–18 mg/kg (Felby et al., 1974). The two cases reported by Chan had levels of 7.0 and 2.9 mg/kg in the liver. In another series of 20 narcotic-related deaths, liver concentrations of free morphine ranged from 0.039–0.55 mg/kg with an average value of 0.21 mg/kg . The average blood levels in those same individuals were 0.099 mg/L (Levine et al., 1994).The corresponding biliary concentrations in these last two cases were nearly 30 times higher than the blood levels (312 mg/L and 248 mg/L, respectively) (Chan et al., 1986). In other series, the differential between liver and bile has not been quite so striking. Kintz found bile levels of 0.087–0.363 mg/L in the bile, while concentrations were 0.067–1.424 mg/kg in the liver. The differences have to do partly with the amount taken before death, and partly with the chronicity of use (Kintz et al., 1989).

Concentrations of free morphine in the liver may be quite substantial; that appears not to be the case for heroin. In two patients where heroin and its metabolites were measured, no heroin or 6-acetylmorphine was detected in samples from the liver, even though brain concentrations were 158 ng/mL in one case and 54 ng/mL in another (Goldberger et al., 1994).

Quantitation of hepatic morphine levels is a particulary useful approach in the case of exhumations. In such cases, blood and urine are unlikely to be available; however, soft tissue will be, and formalyn embalming does not interfere with the extraction and measurement of free morphine (Levine et al., 1994).

5.4.1.3.4   Lymph nodes.   One of the classic autopsy findings in narcotic addicts is the presence of enlarged hepatic lymph nodes. Whether or not the enlargement is the result of some toxic effect exerted by morphine itself, or the contaminants injected with it, is not known. Nonetheless, lymph nodes concentrate morphine and, in some cases, nodes taken at autopsy may have higher concentrations of morphine than either blood or bile. In the only systematic study published, levels ranged from 0.03–0.87 mg/100 grams of tissue (Nakamura and Choi, 1983).

5.4.1.3.5   Other biofluids.   Like cocaine, heroin and morphine can be detected in saliva, but results must be interpreted with some cautions, since the oral or intranasal use of these drugs may result in very high saliva levels due to contamination of the oral cavity (Wang et al., 1994). Simultaneous measurement of morphine in saliva, plasma, and urine disclosed that urine concentrations of morphine were 100 times greater than the levels measured in saliva, and 16 times higher than levels in the plasma (Cone, 1990). Following an oral dose of 30 mg of codeine, saliva levels were 120 ng/mL three hours later (Sharp et al., 1983). Saliva/plasma ratios for the naturally occurring opiates have not been determined with any accuracy, but similar levels are measured in both fluids (Schramm, 1992). Because of its increased lipid solubility, heroin appears in saliva much more quickly than morphine (Cone, 1994), but neither compound is likely to be detectable in saliva for much more than 12 hours.

On the other hand, the correlations between saliva and plasma levels appear to be excellent in the case of methadone (saliva/plasma ratio is about 0.5), and probably for other synthetic opiates as well. One hour after administration, the saliva hydromorphone concentration is the same as that in plasma (Ritschel, 1987).

Cerebrospinal fluid levels peak three hours after a dose of morphine is given intramuscularly, and at equilibrium, the ratio of CSF to plasma is very nearly 1:1. The elimination half-life of morphine from CSF is the same as the elimination half-life of morphine from the blood (Nordberg, 1984). Measurements were made in patients undergoing lumbar myelography, one and one-half hours after they had been given 10 mg IM doses of morphine. The CSF levels of morphine, M6G, and M3G were 8.8 ng/mL, 35 ng/mL, and 55 ng/mL, respectively (Laizure et al., 1993). CSF morphine levels higher than 20 ng/mL are thought to be consistent with narcotic-induced fatal respiratory depression (Logan and Lüthi, 1994). In the only study published to date, the measurement of free morphine in vitreous humor and CSF appeared to be a very promising approach. In 22 cases where comparisons could be made, the blood/vitreous ratio was 6.4 ± 4, with vitreous concentrations lower than blood concentrations 95% of the time (Wahba and Winek, 1993).

5.4.1.3.6 Urine. Most of a given dose of morphine is excreted in the urine after it has been converted to glucuronide. In previously reported autopsy studies, urine concentrations of conjugated morphine have ranged from 100 ng/mL to 120,000 ng/mL (Säwe, 1986). The observed concentration depends largely on the volume of urine that is allowed to collect between measurements (Cone, 1990). In 29 victims of heroin overdose, the blood/urine ratio for morphine was 2.53 ± 5.45, but the range is so wide (0.006–25.2) that drawing any sort of inference is almost impossible (Wahba et al., 1993).

5.4.1.4 Excretion and detectability

Since the half-life of morphine is under two hours, measurable levels are unlikely to be detected after 12 hours have passed. The half-lives of the glucuronides are nearly twice that of morphine. The excretion of morphine and its glucuronides is predominantly renal. Over 85% of a given dose can be recovered in the urine within 24 hours of administration. Less than 10% of the excreted material will be unchanged morphine; 50–60% will be morphine-3-glucuronide; and 15% will be in the form of other metabolites such as morphine-6-glucuronide and normorphine. Given current levels of sensitivity, morphine or its metabolites should be detectable for at least 48 hours after administration. Since morphine also undergoes enterohepatic circulation and can reach high concentrations in the gall bladder with chronic use, it would not be surprising if very small amounts, certainly well below the NIDA cutoffs, could be excreted for days after the drug was last used.

Racial and interethnic differences must also be considered. Controlled studies have demonstrated that Chinese subjects have a higher clearance rate for morphine than Caucasians, primarily beause they form more glucuronide than Caucasians, and they do it faster. Whether or not these difference will have a bearing on drug detection is not clear, but the differences certainly can have clinical significance. In non-tolerant subjects, equal doses of morphine produce more respiratory depression and a greater drop in blood pressure in Caucasians than in Chinese (Zhou et al., 1993).

5.4.2   Heroin

Heroin is a synthetic morphine derivative. It was first marketed by Bayer in 1898. It is produced by the acetylation of morphine's two hydroxyl groups. Once in the body, heroin is very rapidly converted by deacetylation to 6-acetylmorphine, and then to morphine. Conversion to 6-acetylmorphine is completed within 10–15 minutes. The complete conversion of heroin to morphine is completed within a few hours. In the United States and Europe, intravenous injection is the preferred route of administration, but heroin can

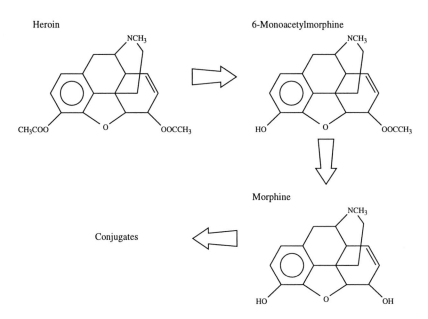

Figure 5.4.2   Heroin metabolism. Heroin is rapidly deacylated to 6-monoacetylmorphine, and then to morphine.

be smoked and "snorted" (nasal insufflation). Both routes are becoming more popular.

Heroin can be heated on a piece of folded tin foil and the fumes inhaled, or it can be inhaled into the nose, sometimes through a straw. In Hong Kong, heroin used for this purpose was often dyed red, and as the fumes rise from the foil they can be imagined to have the undulating shape of a dragon's tail, explaining why the practice is called "chasing the dragon." Alternatively, the lighted end of a cigarette can be dipped in powdered heroin and then smoked. In order to keep the heroin from falling off the end of the cigarette, the smoker has to hold his head tilted backwards. The heroin can also be mixed into the contents of a cigarette. None of these routes is particularly effective. Studies have been done in addicts that compared urinary excretion after heroin was administered by injection, volatilization, and by smoking in the form of a cigarette. The mean percentage of morphine recovered after injection was 68%, after volatilization it was 26%, and after cigarette smoking it was only 14%. The pharmacokinetics of heroin smoking and "snorting" are discussed in Sections 5.4.1.2.5 and 5.4.1.2.6.

5.4.2.1   Tissue distribution

Even though 6-acetylmorphine is a unique heroin metabolite, it has a very short half-life and usually is not quantitated. That situation may change now that it is possible to simultaneously determine heroin and its metabolites, but for the moment, toxicologic investigations of opiate-related deaths continue to rely on measurements of free morphine concentrations in blood, liver, urine, and bile (Steentoft et al., 1988; Felby et al., 1974; Reed et al., 1977;

Table 5.4.2.1 Tissue Levels
from 5 Cases of Acutely Fatal
Heroin Overdose

Tissue	Range
Blood	0.06–0.90
Urine	0.21–6.60
Bile	0.09–1.25
Stomach contents	0.01–0.03
Lung	0.09–0.18
Liver	0.07–0.29
Kidney	0.01–1.18
Heart	0.09–0.10
Spleen	0.11–0.95
Brain	0.01–0.10
Vitreous humor	0.03–0.35
Testicle	0.03–0.09
Muscle	0.01–0.04

Values are in mg/L or mg/kg.
Urine and bile specimens were
hydrolyzed to free morphine
from its conjugate. Adapted from
Kintz et al., 1989.

Sawyer et al., 1988). Like cocaine, heroin and 6-acetylmorphine are rapidly excreted in sweat, which may prove to be a useful matrix for analysis (Cone et al., 1994). Separate measurements of morphine-6-glucuronide in drug-related deaths still have not been made, because it has only recently become apparent that M6G exerts opiate effects in its own right.

In only one study of heroin-related deaths have simultaneous measurements of morphine levels in multiple organs been made (Table 5.4.2.1). The observed values for morphine concentrations in those cases were comparable to those reported in two decedants where heroin, 6-acetylmorphine, and free morphine were measured simultaneously (Goldberger et al., 1994). As is true in cases of cocaine body packers, tissue levels in heroin body packers with ruptured packets of drug in their gastrointestinal tract may reach astronomic levels. A woman who had swallowed a number of packets containing 25% heroin was found to have a 6-acetylmorphine level of 184,000 ng/mL. Morphine and codeine levels were equally impressive (120,000 ng /mL and 1,700 ng/mL) (Joynt and Mikhael, 1985).

5.4.2.2 Excretion and detectability

Since the conversion of heroin to morphine is so rapid, the probability of detecting heroin in either blood or urine is quite small. Once the conversion to morphine is complete, the limits of detection are the same as for morphine itself (see above).

Testing for opiates in urine is a problem. Poppy seeds are widely eaten, and they contain morphine and codeine. On the other hand, poppies do not contain heroin. Thus individuals who eat poppy seeds may well be found to have codeine or morphine in their urine. Poppy seed eaters will not have detectable levels of 6-acetylmorphine (6-MAM). The latter compound is seen only in the blood or urine of individuals who have taken heroin. Small amounts of 6-MAM may also be ingested directly as contaminants present in heroin, which had been introduced during the clandestine refining process (O'neil and Pitts, 1992).

The identification of 6-MAM in the urine is relatively simple (Hanisch and Meyer, 1993), but the presence or absence of 6-MAM cannot be used to reliably separate innocent poppy seed ingestion from heroin abuse, because 6-MAM is only detectable for a few hours. If it is absent from a suspect's specimen, that may only mean that heroin use occurred more than three or four hours earlier. In the absence of 6-MAM, separating innocent poppyseed ingestion from heroin abuse can be difficult, and is a real problem for medical review officers. In the past they have had to rely on detecting confirmatory evidence of drug abuse, such as track marks.

Recently it has been shown that 6-MAM is deposited within the hair matrix, where it is stable for many months. The same is true for morphine-6-glucronide. It has been suggested that the demonstration of 6-MAM in hair might be another conclusive way to prove that an individual had been using heroin (Cone et al., 1991b; Rothe and Pragst, 1995). But heroin samples can also contain 6-MAM. That means that the presence of 6-MAM, like the presence of heroin itself, may be the result of external contamination (as in a customs officer who confiscates a large quantity of heroin).

5.4.3   Codeine

5.4.3.1   General considerations

Codeine is one of the naturally occurring alkaloids found in opium. Depending on where the poppies are grown, samples of opium may contain from 0.7% to 2.5% codeine. Codeine was first isolated from opium by Robiquet in 1832, 27 years after Sertürner isolated morphine. Most of the codeine that is consumed in antitussive and analgesic mixtures is of semisynthetic origin, produced by the methylation of morphine. The DAWN report lists 501 codeine-related deaths in 1990. Tons of this compound are consumed annually, but very important questions about codeine metabolism and toxicity remain unanswered. There is, for instance, some evidence that codeine's pain-relieving properties, which are about one-fifth of morphine's, arise from the fact that it is converted to morphine (Sanfilippo, 1948). More important, at least so far as investigations of toxicity are concerned, is the fact that substantial variation exists in an individual's ability to metabolize codeine (Yue et al., 1991; Yue et al., 1991; Chen et al., 1991).

The major metabolic pathways for codeine are glucuronidation and demethylation, but most of a given dose is converted to codeine-6-glucuronide, an inactive metabolite. Much smaller amounts may be converted to norcodeine, which is believed to be psychoactive (Fraser et al., 1960). It has only recently become apparent that, depending on an individual's genetic

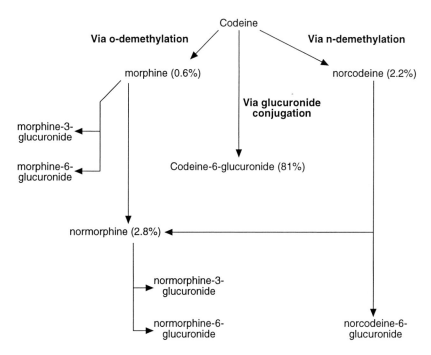

Figure 5.4.3.1   Human metabolism of codeine.

makeup, significant amounts of codeine may be shunted to pathways yielding pharmacologic active products. N-demethylation produces norcodeine
that is converted to glucuronide or to normorphine. The O-demethylation
route is much more important, because it leads to the production of morphine. Codeine that has been converted to morphine is, in turn, converted
to morphine-3-glucuronide or morphine-6-glucuronide. All of these compounds are excreted in the urine, where somewhat less than 90% of a single
dose can be recovered within 48 hours, mostly as codeine-6-glucuronide
(Chen et al., 1991). The important consideration here is that codeine metabolism yields three different compounds with known psychoactivity: morphine, normorphine, and morphine-6-glucuronide.

5.4.3.2   Routes of administration

Pharmacokinetic studies of codeine's fate have been published, but the radioimmunoassays used very likely produced spuriously high concentrations of
codeine in the plasma and urine (Chen et al., 1991). Similar considerations
apply to many of the earlier studies on the fate of morphine. Measurements
in healthy volunteers given a 50-mg oral dose of codeine show a plasma
half-life of 2.4–3.2 hours (Yue et al., 1991; Yue et al., 1991; Chen, 1991). When
measured with high-pressure liquid chromatography, peak blood levels after
an oral dose of 50 mg in healthy, normal metabolizers averaged 140 ng/mL
(Yue et al., 1991b). A second study, also using HPLC, yielded similar results
(Chen et al., 1991). Interestingly, the peak concentration of codeine in the

saliva is nearly three times that measured in the blood, even though the half-life in both fluids is approximately 3.2 hours (Chen et al., 1991). Resultant blood levels after alternate routes of administration have not been reported.

5.4.3.3 Role of genetic polymorphism

After oral dosing, plasma levels of codeine glucuronide are 5–10 times higher than codeine levels. After chronic dosing, the pharmacokinetics of both codeine and its principal metabolite, codeine-6-glucuronide, are unchanged, even though chronic usage seems to have no effect. The genetic makeup of an individual does change, however, both in terms of analgesic properties and toxic effects.

Table 5.4.3.3 Effects of Genetic Polymorphism on Codeine Metabolism

Drug	Hydroxylators	Non-hydroxylators
Codeine	411 ± 219	239 ± 60
C6G	4090 ± 3380	3890 ± 949
NC	48 ± 26	48 ± 13
NCG	108 ± 44	146 ± 8
M3G	186 ± 121	9.1 ± 8.2
M6G	41 ± 23	non-detectable
NM	41 ± 33	non-detectable
M	27 ± 23	non-detectable

Values are in nmol/dL. All measurements are from healthy volunteers who had been previously screened for the ability to hydroxylate debrisoquine. Data derived from Yue et al., 1991.

Codeine metabolism is under monogenic control. The ability to form morphine-6-glucuronide, morphine, and norcodeine from codeine can be predicted by an individual's ability to hydroxylase debrisoquine (debrisoquine phenotype). Approximately 10% of Caucasians, and a much larger percentage of Chinese, are poor hydroxylators. The majority of Caucasians, referred to as extensive hydroxylators, convert 6% of a given dose of codeine by demethylation and subsequent conjugation, eventually producing small amounts of morphine. Plasma levels of morphine-6-glucuronide, normorphine, and morphine peak at levels that are about one-tenth the peak codeine level (see Table 5.4.3.3). In poor hydroxylators, much less than 0.5% is metabolized in this manner, and no morphine, morphine-6-glucuronide, or morphine is detectable in the plasma.

The forensic significance of these observations needs further elaboration, but it should be apparent that some individuals will have more psychoactive material in their bloodstreams than simple measurements of morphine or codeine levels would indicate. The obverse is also true. Individuals likely to be slow hydroxylators should have little or no morphine detectable in their blood if the only drug taken was codeine.

Interpreting the presence of small amounts of codeine and morphine in urine specimens is something of a problem. It had been thought that small amounts of morphine were metabolically converted to codeine, but in fact, that is not the case. The codeine detected in urine gets there because it is present in morphine in trace amounts, even in pharmaceutical grade morphine preparations. Thus, the presence of codeine should not be presumed to be evidence of anything except the ingestion of codeine. The presence of trace amounts of morphine, on the other hand, can be accounted for by the metabolic conversion of codeine to morphine. Before accepting such an explanation, some attempt should be made to determine whether that individual is, in fact, capable of such a metabolic conversion. Fully 10% of the Caucasian population, and a much larger proportion of the Asian population, may not be capable of metabolic conversion, and in those cases the presence of morphine may be evidence for the use of morphine or heroin.

5.4.3.4   Codeine tissue disposition

Data on codeine's tissue distribution is sparse and difficult to interpret in light of what is now known about the role of active metabolites, such as morphine and morphine-6-glucuronide. Almost all the reports in the literature are from the 1970s, before the role of genetic variation was recognized, and before the importance of metabolically active glucuronides was appreciated.

Table 5.4.3.4   Tissue Levels in Reported Cases of Codeine Overdose Deaths

	Blood	Bile	Liver	Kidney	Urine
Codeine	2.8 (1–8.8)	17.6 (5–43)	6.8 (0.6–45)	11.7 (2.3–36)	103.8 (29–229)
Morphine	0.2 (0–0.5)	37.6 (3–117)	1.5 (0–6.3)	2 (0.3–5.2)	19.6 (0–58)

Data adapted from Baselt and Cravey.

5.4.3.5   Excretion and detectability

The elimination half-life of both codeine and its main metabolite, codeine-6-glucuronide, is slightly over three hours. Both compounds should be detectable in the bloodstream for more than 12 hours, but less than 24 hours. Urinary excretion of codeine may be longer than that of morphine.

5.4.4   Methadone

The 1994 DAWN survey reported 367 methadone-related deaths, amounting to 4.1% of all reported narcotic deaths for that year. The percentage of deaths due to methadone has been gradually declining since 1990 (7.5% in 1990). The decline is unexplained, but may have to do with the relatively slow increase in the total number of methadone maintenance programs and with the availability of methadone on the black market. Methadone belongs to a class of compounds referred to as diphenylpropylamine derivatives. Drugs in this class have the general formula which, at first glance, bears little

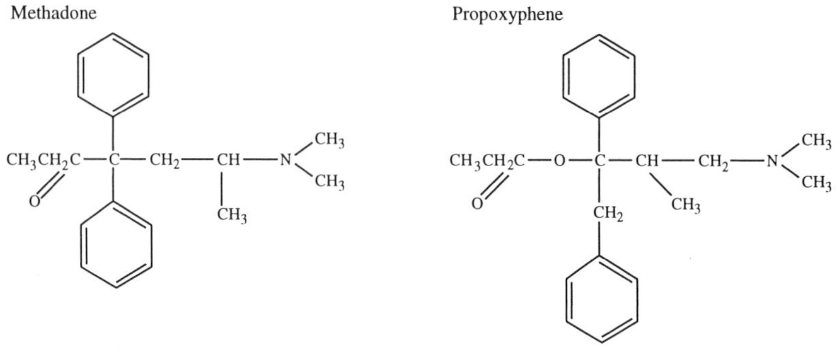

Methadone   Propoxyphene

Figure 5.4.4 Methadone and propoxyphene. Even though it is not obvious, the methadone molecule contains the same basic structures as all the other morphine related analgesics. Propoxyphene is a derivative of morphine.

relationship to the basic morphine molecule, but which, in fact, contains the same basic structures common to morphine analgesics. Methadone is supplied as a racemic mixture, but almost all of the opiate activity is due to the *l* form.

Until 1965, when it was introduced as a maintenance drug for heroin addicts, methadone enjoyed little popularity, probably because, in some individuals, its half-life can exceed 50 hours. Today, it is the drug of choice for the treatment of heroin addiction, and is frequently prescribed to cancer patients. It has been suggested that methadone treatment may even normalize depressed immune function in heroin addicts (Novick et al., 1989); however, this notion has been disputed (Mazzone et al., 1994; Carballo-Diéguez et al., 1994). The question is still unresolved. If methadone does reverse long term heroin-related immunosuppression, it may have more to do with the improved life-style and decreased number of intravenous injections in treated addicts than with any direct effect of methadone (McLachlan et al., 1993).

5.4.4.1   General considerations

Drawing conclusions about the toxicity of a given dose of methadone, or of a particular methadone blood level, without additional historical and clinical information, is impossible. Tolerant individuals may take doses of methadone that would induce fatal respiratory depression in naive users. In one study, heroin addicts treated with doses ranging from 180 mg to 260 mg/day experienced no adverse effects (Walton, 1978). On the other hand, the average dose taken by ten newly enrolled former addicts was only 57 mg/day, but they still died of respiratory depression, with mean blood levels of 600 ng/mL. In other studies characterizing methadone-related deaths, average blood levels ranged from 200 ng/mL (Worm and Kringsholm, 1993) to nearly 1,000 ng/mL (Robinson and Williams, 1971; Norheim, 1973; Kreek, 1973; Segal and Catherman, 1974; Manning et al., 1976; Kreek, 1988; Drummer et al., 1992).

Nonetheless, recent studies on methadone kinetics have shown that: (1) there is fairly good correlation between the dose given and the resultant plasma level (Wolff and Hay, 1991; Wolff et al., 1991); (2) addicts are likely to complain of withdrawal symptoms if their blood level drops much below 50 ng/mL (Wolff et al., 1992); and, (3) clients treated with higher doses are less likely to test positive for opiates than clients treated with lower doses or placebo (Strain et al., 1993). In one recent study, patients receiving 40 mg/day were found to be more than twice as likely to use heroin as those receiving 80 mg/day (Caplehorn et al., 1993).

There is evidence that the best results, both in terms of prevention of HIV seroconversion and preventing heroin use, are seen when a patient takes at least 90 mg/day (Lorimer and Schmid, 1992), and when plasma levels exceed 100 ng/mL (Holmstrand et al., 1978; Tennant, 1987). Ultimately, however, methadone dosages must be individualized to account for individual variations in tolerance and dependency (Wolff and Hay, 1994). Since methadone is a potent respiratory depressant, and since methadone treatment is ineffective if doses are too low, there is an emerging consensus that therapeutic drug monitoring should be an integral component of all methadone treatment programs.

5.4.4.2 Routes of absorption and pharmacokinetics

Oral absorption of methadone is excellent, and when compliance is good, there is a very good correlation between the dose administered and the plasma level that results. Over the range of 3–100 mg, plasma methadone concentrations increase by 263 ng/mL for every milligram of methadone per kilogram of body weight administered (Wolff et al., 1991). This same, nearly linear, concentration increase is also observed in saliva, although the peak levels are somewhat higher and the half-life somewhat longer (Wolff and Hay, 1991).

The results of intravenous methadone injections have been studied in cancer patients. In one case, a 10-mg bolus produced a peak plasma level slightly above 500 ng/mL immediately after injection, falling to below 100 ng/mL at one hour (Inturrisi et al., 1987). In a group of addicts maintained on methadone, saliva levels were found to be somewhat higher than simultaneously measured blood levels (Wolff and Hay, 1991). Levels, after the less common routes of administration, have not been measured. Once in the body, methadone is transformed via N-demethylation to a group of metabolites, all of which are inactive.

Blood levels in methadone maintainence patients, even compliant ones, may vary considerably. In one study, values ranged from 20–1,308 ng/mL with a mean concentration of 451.4 ± 306 ng/mL (Lorimer and Schmid, 1992). Scandinavian researchers, however, found that levels in methadone maintenance patients were about 100 ng/mL, compared to levels of 200–300 ng/mL in methadone fatalities. There is wide individual variation in its half-life, with reported values ranging from 13–58 hours (Goldstein, 1991; Inturrisi, 1972).

In the only recent study of steady-state methadone pharmacokinetics in opioid addicts, a single compartment model was found to apply. Increases in plasma methadone levels can be detected 15–30 minutes after oral administration. The volume of distribution was quite large (6.7 liters per kilogram), and the clearance rate quite slow (3.1 ml/minute/kilogram). The observed elimination half-life of 26.8 hours was much lower than earlier estimates (Wolff et al., 1993).

Methadone clearance is altered when it is taken with other drugs. In theory, some of these interactions could lead to toxicity, but when alcohol and methadone are taken together, they enhance each other's metabolism, so that the most likely outcome of this combination is the onset of withdrawal symptoms (Kreek, 1988). Similarly, when methadone and cocaine are taken together, is a relatively frequent occurrence, methadone plasma levels decrease, apparently because the cocaine accelerates methadone excretion (Tennant and Shannon, 1995).

5.4.4.3 Autopsy findings
Individuals in methadone maintenance programs are likely to have some cutaneous stigmata of past intravenous heroin abuse. Since all opiates are respiratory depressants, bronchopneumonia would not be a surprising finding. Chronic persistent hepatitis is a frequent finding in methadone-related deaths. Inflammatory infiltrates, without evidence of necrosis, are commonly seen in the portal triads of heroin abusers (see Section 5.10.3). Opiate abusers enrolled in methadone programs are very likely to be infected with hepatitis-C, with or without histologic changes.

Table 5.4.4.3   Dosage and Tissue Levels in 10 Methadone-Related Deaths

Dosage Range	Blood Level	Liver Level	Urine Concentration
45–70 mg/day	260–2,500 ng/mL	670–5,500 ng/mL	15,000–116,000 ng/mL

Adapted from Drummer et al., 1992.

5.4.4.4 Tissue levels
Tissue levels, using various techniques, have been measured in about 50 cases, most of them in the early 1970s (Robinson and Williams, 1971; Norheim, 1973; Segal and Catheman, 1974; Manning et al., 1976; Drummer et al., 1992). Methadone tends to concentrate in the liver, but often blood levels equal or exceed hepatic levels when measured at autopsy. In the most recent study, blood and liver concentrations were measured in individuals whose methadone dosage was known (Drummer et al., 1992).

The concentrations observed in fatal cases overlap the methadone concentrations that have been observed in patients participating in methadone maintenance programs (Garriott et al., 1973; Robinson and Williams, 1971). Given the degree of overlap, it is difficult, if not impossible, to distinguish between overdose and maintenance on the basis of toxicology testing alone (Baselt and Cravey, 1989). If tissue levels of methadone metabolites are high, it suggests chronic use, but the breakdown rate of methadone metabolites postmortem has not been characterized.

5.4.4.5   Maternal-fetal considerations

Maternal methadone levels correlate significantly with neonatal plasma methadone levels, at least during the first day of life. It also has been observed that the severity of central nervous system signs of withdrawal correlate with the rate of decline in the infant's plasma methadone levels (Doberczak, Kandall, and Friedman, 1993). In a group of 21 neonates with symptoms of withdrawal, mean maternal methadone levels 16 hours after delivery were 183 ng/mL ± 118 ng, while the mean plasma levels in a sample drawn from the infants at the same time was 26 ng/mL ± 8 ng. Methadone levels decreased in the infants at the average rate of 0.2 ± 0.3 ng/mL/hour.

5.4.5   Propoxyphene

5.4.5.1   General considerations

Chemists have used manipulations of the methadone molecule to create a series of related analgesics, the most important of which is propoxyphene. Unlike methadone, which is a potent analgesic, propoxyphene has only mild analgesic properties. In spite of that, it is widely prescribed, and overdose has been associated with large numbers of fatalities (Soumerai et al., 1987). Three hundred fifty-one propoxyphene-related fatalities were reported in the 1994 DAWN survey, accounting for 4% of reported opiate-related deaths, and less than 1.6 of all reported drug-related fatalities for that year (Substance Abuse and Mental Health Services Administration, 1995). Propoxyphene is particularly toxic because, in addition to exerting the usual respiratory depressant effects common to all μ agonist narcotics, propoxyphene and its principal metabolites also act as local anesthetics, with potent membrane stabilizing effects.

Intravenous propoxyphene abuse has been all but eliminated by reformulating the drug. Essentially, all cases of toxicity are now due to oral ingestion. It is absorbed rapidly out of the gastrointestinal tract (Flanagan et al., 1984; Gibson et al., 1980; Young, 1983), with peak plasma concentrations occurring within one to two hours after a single oral dose. Peak concentrations of propoxyphene, itself, are usually not very high, because the drug undergoes extensive first-pass metabolism in the liver where it is oxidized to norpropoxyphene. Peak propoxyphene levels after a single 65-mg dose in healthy young volunteers ranged from 260–900 ng/mL with a mean of 590 ng/mL. In this same group, the half-life ranged from 6.4–26.4 hours, with a mean of 13 hours. Simultaneous measurements of nordexpropoxyphene showed peak levels ranging from 510–2,140 ng/mL with a mean of 1,950 ng/mL. The half-life for the metabolites is much longer than that of the parent compound, with a mean value of 22.2 hours.

There are no detectable differences between the sexes, but age has definite effects on how propoxyphene is metabolized. The half-life for both parent compound and metabolite is more than twice as long in the elderly than the young. The half-life of dextropropoxyphene in the young is only

13 hours, but it rises to over 35 hours in the elderly. Similarly, the half-life for norpropoxyphene in young adults is approximately 22 hours, but it rises to over 40 hours in the elderly (Flanagan, Ramsey, and Jane, 1984). This pattern is not unique, and is often encountered with drugs that undergo hepatic oxidation, and then renal elimination. The prolonged course of excretion in the elderly may have some bearing on reported cases of toxicity, since norpropoxyphene has the same membrane stabilizing properties as propoxyphene itself (Nickander et al., 1984).

Excretion is also prolonged in the elderly and individuals with liver impairment. In the latter group, first-pass oxidation can be reduced in increased levels of propoxyphene causing to accumulate in the circulation. Since both parent and metabolite have equal membrane stabilizing ability, there probably is no increase in cardiotoxicity, though the opiate effects of propoxyphene may be exaggerated (Giacomini et al., 1980). There is some evidence that, when used with ethanol, first-pass transformation is decreased and higher blood levels of propoxyphene result (Orguma and Levy, 1981), but this effect is modest. When large numbers of propoxyphene-related deaths are analyzed, consistent correlations between propoxyphene and alcohol levels have not been demonstrated (Theilade, 1989).

5.4.5.2   Tissue distribution

Propoxyphene is highly lipid soluble, and very large amounts can be sequestered in fat tissue. Fatalities were frequent during the mid-1970s, and levels at autopsy have been reported for hundreds of cases (Caplan, Thompson, and Fisher, 1977; McBay 1976; Finkle et al., 1981; Finkle et al., 1976; Baselt et al., 1975; Cravey, Shaw, and Nakamura, 1974). In the past, it was generally assumed that serious toxicity was associated with levels greater than 1 mg/L, and fatalities associated with levels of over 2 mg/L. But, as with all opiates, there is tremendous overlap, and fatalities have occurred at much lower levels while, at the same time, higher values have been observed as incidental findings.

Even though blood and tissue levels have been measured and reported many times, the results of a recent study suggest that postmortem measurements are unpredictable, and that measured concentrations depend entirely on the area in the body where the blood samples are drawn (Yonemitsu and Pounder, 1992). Multiple blood and tissue samples from four different individuals who had died after overdosing with dextropropoxyphene and paracetamol were analyzed after taking samples from various sites within each cadaver. Then the sampling was repeated at 24 and 48 hours. In every case, the lowest blood levels were observed in peripheral blood samples. When the levels in the peripheral blood measured 3.5 mg/L, the concentration in the aorta was 1.9 grams/L, nearly 55 times higher! When blood was drawn from the pulmonary artery, the propoxyphene concentration increased two-fold at 24 hours and three-fold at 48 hours. When repeat samples were drawn from the inferior vena cava, there were variable increases in measured blood levels. In one individual, there was a seven-fold increase over 24 hours.

Given the wide variations in values that can be measured in the same individual, drawing any conclusion from quantitative propoxyphene levels would appear to be very risky. For forensic purposes, it may be more useful to look at the individual's electrocardiogram. Truly toxic propoxyphene levels will produce some fairly distinctive EKG changes (Whitcomb et al., 1989), and these might reveal more about the cause of death than quantitation of blood levels.

Thus, in a group of 29 patients who committed suicide by taking propoxyphene orally, the median total level of propoxyphene was 9.4 mg/L vs. a total of only 2.2 mg/L in accident victims (Kaa and Dalgaard, 1989). In another study, propoxyphene and norpropoxyphene levels were measured in a group of opiate addicts who were being maintained on propoxyphene instead of methadone. They received, on average, 800–1,600 mg of propoxyphene napsylate daily for anywhere from 13–50 months. Serum propoxyphene levels ranged from 127–1,070 mg/L and norpropoxyphene levels measured from 814–2,638 ng/mL, while the ratio of the two compounds ranged from 0.1 to 0.4. Since these levels are well in excess of what was believed to be toxic levels, it is obvious that tolerance occurs, and at very significant levels (Hartman et al., 1988).

5.4.5.3 Excretion and detectability

Propoxyphene is not a "NIDA drug." Furthermore, none of the current standard immunologic screening tests for opiates react with propoxyphene to any significant degree, so it would not even be detected on a standard NIDA urine-screening test (Cone et al., 1992). Nonetheless, it remains present in the urine for very long periods of time, and given a half-life of 22 hours for norpropoxyphene, the drug or its metabolite, should still be detectable in the bloodstream for more than four days after the last dose was taken. The window of detectability in the urine may be longer.

5.4.5.4 Mechanisms of toxicity

Propoxyphene-induced respiratory depression is treated effectively with opiate antagonists. But most patients who reach the hospital die of cardiotoxicity, and cardiotoxicity is not reversed with naloxone. Evidence for propoxyphene-induced cardiotoxicity includes electrocardiographic changes such as QRS prolongation, bundle branch block, and, in extreme cases, asystole. Myocardial contractility decreases and, as a result, cardiac output and blood pressure both drop. Neither treatment with beta adrenergic agents, nor pacing, have proven very effective (Whitcomb et al., 1989). All of these electrophysiologic changes can be accounted for by propoxyphene's ability to block the inward sodium current (I_{Na}). The orderly sequence of depolarization is disrupted, conduction is delayed across the myocardium, and insufficient calcium enters the myocytes, preventing them from contracting maximally. The same thing happens in cases of cocaine toxicity, which is hardly surprising, since cocaine is also a local anesthetic agent that binds to receptors controlling the I_{Na} channel. The reason that this type of toxicity is more evident in the case of propoxyphene is probably related to relative receptor affinity at the site of the sodium influx channel.

5.4.6   Fentanyl and other synthetic agents

5.4.6.1   General considerations

Fentanyl is a mu-agonist, a synthetic phenylpiperidine derivative closely related in structure to meperidine (Demerol®). It is not detected by routine drug screen test, and fentanyl-related deaths are not tabulated in the DAWN survey. It was first introduced into clinical practice in the early 1960s. On a weight-for-weight basis, fentanyl is 50 to 100 times more potent than morphine. Other fentanyl-related compounds, however, may be much more potent. The cis-isomer of 3-methylfentanyl, which has been manufactured by clandestine laboratories in the Russian Federation, is thought to be 5,500 times more potent than morphine (Sorokin, Semkin, and Savilov, 1994).

Most reported fentanyl-related deaths have been in males (78%) with a mean age of 32.5 years ± 6.7 years. The age range and sex distribution are not very different from the typical heroin overdose victims, 80% of whom are males with a mean age of 40. Unlike heroin users, who are often found on the street, fentanyl overdoses usually occur at home, in the bedroom or bath. Like heroin-related deaths, 60% of the time the deceased are found with paraphernalia at their side. Otherwise, autopsy findings are the same as in heroin overdose. Mean lung weights are 726 grams.

The first two fentanyl-related deaths were reported in 1979. In both cases the deceased had died with their paraphernalia at their sides, and at autopsy both were noted to have needle tracks and pulmonary edema. Surprisingly, toxicologic tests on both bodies and on the injection paraphernalia were negative for opiates. Six additional deaths occurred before it was finally determined that the individuals had overdosed on α-methylfentanyl (Kram, 1981; Allen, Cooper, and Kram, 1981). During the last decade, there have been over 100 additional deaths from fentanyl or one of its illicitly produced homologs (Allen et al., 1981; Henderson, 1991). Sporadic cases occur almost exclusively in medical personnel with access to pharmaceutical fentanyl. However, a large number of cases occasionally occur in clusters, with out-

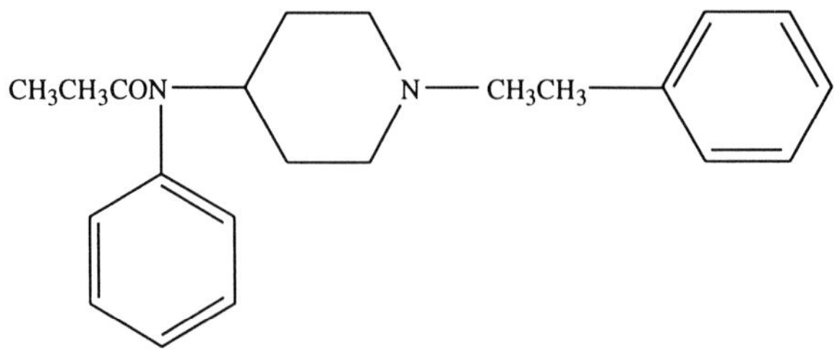

Figure 5.4.6   Fentanyl molecule.

breaks having been reported in New York City and Philadelphia. These outbreaks are the result of clandestine production of fentanyl or one of its analogs. In February of 1991, heroin mixed with fentanyl, selling for $10 a bag, suddenly appeared on the streets in New York, resulting in the hospitalization of 200 victims, and at least 22 deaths. Literally, hundreds of different fentanyl analogs can be synthesized and detection is difficult. At least 12 different analogs are known to have been sold on the illicit drug market (World Health Organization, 1990).

Fentanyl sedation may prove particularly risky in elderly individuals undergoing diagnostic procedures. Through mechanisms that are not entirely understood, fentanyl and related conjoiners cause rigidity of the thoracic musculature, referred to as "wooden chest syndrome" (Jackson, 1994). The increased tone may make ventilation difficult, and is said to pose a significant danger in endoscopic procedures, especially when they involve the elderly. With a dose of 3.9 µg/kg, 4% of those undergoing fentanyl anesthesia develop the syndrome — but not until a total of 250 µg is given. If high doses are given (500–900 µg) over 60 to 90 seconds, the syndrome may be particularly severe. An additional problem associated with fentanyl and sufentanil anesthesia is the disruption of cerebrovascular autoregulation. When these agents are given to patients with head trauma, significant elevations in intracranial pressure occur (DeLima, 1993).

5.4.6.2   Routes of absorptions

The fentanyls are mostly used intravenously. After an oral dose of 15 µg/kg, peak plasma concentrations in healthy volunteers were 3.0 ng/mL. Peak plasma levels after giving that same amount intravenously were almost ten times higher; however, the terminal elimination half-life is approximately seven hours in either case (Streisand et al., 1991). Other studies have shown that loss of consciousness occurs at levels of 34 ± 7 ng/mL (Lunn et al., 1979), but respiratory depression may be detected at levels as low as 1–5 ng/mL (Fung and Eisele, 1980; Andrews et al., 1983). The preponderance of evidence, however, suggests that respiratory depression occurs in the 2–3 ng/mL range (Cartwright et al., 1983). The minimal effective plasma concentration to produce analgesia averages 0.63 ± 0.25 ng/mL, but there is considerable variation in sensitivity from individual to individual (Gourlay et al., 1988).

In the Rhesus monkey, which appears to parallel human responses quite well, 4 µg/kg given intravenously results in a plasma fentanyl concentration of 2.7 ± 0.9 ng/mL. A dose of 64 µg/kg results in a blood level of 43.4 ± 26.0 ng/mL. These animals become apneic at blood levels over 40 ng/mL (Nussmeier et al., 1991).

Fentanyl can be smoked or snorted. There are reports that clandestine labs sometimes manufacture two forms of the drug, one for "shooters" and one for "snorters" (World Health Organization, 1990). In either case, small amounts of fentanyl are mixed with very large amounts of mannitol, lactose, and occasionally, heroin. There are no published studies on absorption by non-traditional routes such as rectal, vaginal, or nasal application. One report described a 36-year old man who scraped the contents of a fentanyl patch onto a piece of aluminum foil, heated the foil with a cigarette lighter, and then inhaled the smoke. He collapsed and died after one inhalation. Femoral blood measured at autopsy contained 2.6 ng/mL of fentanyl, with 6 ng/mL in heart blood, 3.3 ng/mL in vitreous, and 122 ng/g in the liver (Marquardt and Tharratt, 1994).

Because fentanyl is lipophilic and of low molecular weight, it is readily absorbed through the skin. Transdermal delivery systems are now marketed in the United States and Europe. The degree of absorption depends on where the patch is placed and varies from person to person. Measurements indicate that 46%–66% of a given dose applied to the skin will be absorbed. After applying a patch, serum levels are undetectable for two hours, then rise gradually for 12–14 hours, reaching a steady state at 24 hours. Studies done on surgical patients show mean levels ranging from 0.3 ng/mL to 2.7 ng/mL at various times after patch application (Calis et al., 1992). Patches have already been diverted to the illicit market and are now available on the streets.

Fentanyl is also well absorbed when taken orally. Fentanyl-containing raspberry-colored lozenges on a plastic handle are now being used to pre-medicate children before anesthesia. Fentanyl is rapidly absorbed through the buccal mucosa with additional, albeit slower, absorption occurring in the gastrointestinal tract. Plasma concentrations peak in 20 minutes, and may reach levels of 3–4 ng/mL in children treated with the maximum recom-mended dose (Anon, 1994). The efficacy of the oral route is supported by at least one case report of fentanyl dependence associated with the oral ingestion fentanyl preparations intended for intravenous injection (Hays et al., 1992).

5.4.6.3   Metabolism and excretion

After an initial rapid uptake by lung and fat, fentanyl is slowly released with a mean terminal half-life of 2–4 hours in healthy volunteers, and anywhere from 2.5–8 hours in surgical patients (Mather, 1983). It is metabolized in the liver and transformed by N-dealkylation to norfentanyl (Goromaru et al., 1981). The conversion is rapid, and within 30 minutes of intravenous admin-istration, metabolite concentration is higher than fentanyl concentration (McClain and Hug, 1980). Other metabolites, primarily despropionfentanyl, are also formed, and less than 10% of a given dose is excreted in the urine (Schleimer et al., 1978). Approximately 50% of a given dose is eliminated in the urine within the first eight hours, and 85% will be recovered in the urine within 72 hours (World Health Organization, 1990; McClain and Hug, 1980; Silverstein et al., 1993).

Urinary excretion patterns, for both fentanyl and sufentanyl, have been studied in surgical patients. Unchanged fentanyl can be detected in all patients during the immediate postoperative period, and in 40% of patients at 24 hours (Silverstein et al., 1993; Schwartz et al., 1994). Norfentanyl, on the other hand, can be detected in all patients at 48 hours, and in >50% of patients at 96 hours. Despropionlfentanyl could not be detected in any of the samples. The window of detectablity is much shorter for sufentanyl. After five hours it was undetectable in the urine of patients given up to 1,000 μg of sufentanyl during surgery.

Radioimmunoassay screening kits for the detection of fentanyl, sufentanyl, and alfentanyl are commercially available. GC/MS quantitation, using *n*-chlorobutane extraction, has now been developed and is capable of reliably measuring fentanyl and sufentanyl with a detection limit approaching 0.5 ng/mL (Schwartz et al., 1994). Procedures have also been described for simple extraction of fentanyl using commercially available extraction tubes and GC/MS. Although the limit of detection is not as low as limits attained using other methodologies, the technique is particularly useful for verifying that medical personnel are actually discarding fentanyl-, and not saline-, filled syringes (Kingsbury et al., 1995).

5.4.6.4   *Tissue levels*

All of the fentanyls are highly lipid soluble and they distribute widely throughout the body (Hess, Hertz, and Friedel, 1972; Hess, Stiebler, and Hertz, 1972). Fentanyl's relatively short duration of action is, in fact, explained by rapid lipid uptake. In animal studies, high levels are achieved quickly in well perfused tissues such as lung, kidney, heart, and brain. Approximately 3%–4% of an intravenous dose will be secreted into the gastric juice where there is minimal reabsorption (Stoeckle et al., 1979). Fentanyl tissue/blood partition coefficients have been measured in the rat model, and there is good evidence to suggest that tissue distribution in this model reflects the distribution pattern seen in humans. The values in Table 5.4.6.4.1 were measured after a 6-hour infusion. Levels in the liver and brain were four times higher than in the plasma. Levels measured in the stomach can be misleading because, as previously mentioned, fentanyl is actively secreted into the stomach (Stoeckel, 1979; Björkman, 1990).

In Henderson's series of 112 deaths from illicit fentanyl preparations, fentanyl concentrations in blood ranged from 0.2 ng/mL to > 50 ng/mL, and urine concentrations ranged from 0.2 to > 800 ng/mL. If the few individuals with extremely high levels are excluded, the mean fentanyl level at autopsy was 3.0 ± 3.1 ng/mL in the blood and 3.9 ± 4.3 ng/mL in the urine.

Table 5.4.6.4.1   Steady State
Tissue/Blood Partition
Coefficients for Fentanyl in Rats
After a 6-hour Infusion

Organ/Tissue	Relative Level
Plasma	1
Brain	4
Liver	4
Heart	5
Stomach	14
Kidneys	14
Lungs	15
Pancreas	24
Fat	30

Adapted from Björkman et al., 1990.

Table 5.4.6.4.2   Blood Levels in Fentanyl-
Related "Overdose" Deaths and Levels
Seen in Anesthetized Patients Dying
of Surgical Complications

	Deaths from Fentanyl Overdose	Deaths at Surgery
Blood	11–233 ng/mL	5–45 ng/mL
Brain	20–194 ng/mL	18–85 ng/mL
Liver	28–1,000 ng/mg	41–158 ng/mg

Adapted from McGee et al., 1992.

In the handful of deaths due to fentanyl citrate (the pharmaceutical grade product used as an intravenous anesthetic), blood concentrations have ranged from 3–27 ng/mL (Garriott, 1973; Rodriguez et al., 1984; Garriot et al., 1984; Matejezyk, 1988).

McGee et al. compared blood and tissue levels in seven overdose deaths with fentanyl levels observed in anesthetized patients dying at surgery (McGee et al., 1992). In most cases the overdose deaths had levels that were 5 to 10 times higher than levels in anesthetized patients. The plasma level required to produce effective analgesia in surgical patients is 1–3 ng/mL, but there is wide interpatient variability. Values in this range can also be associated with severe respiratory depression, but the relationship between fentanyl and carbon dioxide levels is inconsistent (Lehmann, Freier, and Daub, 1982). Respiratory depression is observed in human volunteers when levels are between 2–3 ng/mL (Cartwright et al., 1983). Effects of the illicit fentanyl homologs have never been assessed in humans.

As is true in all opiate-related deaths, other drugs are frequently detected. In nearly 40% of the fentanyl-related deaths, alcohol is also present, frequently at high levels. In 20% of the cases, cocaine was also detected. At one time, most fentanyl-related deaths were reported from California. That is no longer true. Increasingly, cases are now being reported from the East Coast. Supplies of this drug remain quite limited. Of 3,000 blood samples submitted to Henderson's reference laboratory at the University of California, only 112 were positive for fentanyl or one of its known illicit analogs: alpha-methylfentanyl, paraflurofentanyl, 3-methylfentanyl, and thienmylfentanyl (Henderson, 1991).

5.4.7   Other opiates

Other opiates are abused with some frequency, but the associated incidence of untoward events is quite low. These other agents cause fewer than 2% of the deaths and fewer than 2% of the emergency-room visits reported to the DAWN survey (Substance Abuse and Mental Health Services Administration, 1995). These drugs are not reliably detected by the immunologic screening tests used to detect morphine and codeine (Cone et al., 1992), and under NIDA rules, the presence of these drugs would not be reported. (Most

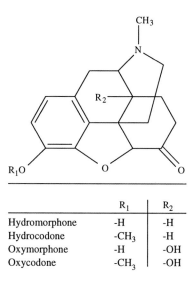

	R_1	R_2
Hydromorphone	-H	-H
Hydrocodone	-CH$_3$	-H
Oxymorphone	-H	-OH
Oxycodone	-CH$_3$	-OH

Figure 5.4.7.1 Synthetic opiates produced by substitution at position R_1 and R_2.

federally regulated drug programs only test for the "NIDA five" drugs: cocaine, phencyclidine, marijuana, methamphetamine, and morphine. Even if propoxyphene were detected, reporting its presence would not be allowed. Different rules apply to the nuclear and transportation industries.)

5.4.7.1 Hydromorphone (Dilaudid®)

Hydromorphone is a semisynthetic opiate, the hydrogenated ketone derivative of morphine. On a weight-per-weight basis, it is 7–10 times more potent than morphine (Mahler and Forest, 1975), but otherwise it shares most of morphine's properties. Hydromorphone has been available for many years, but it has recently become popular in the management of chronic pain syndromes. It can be prepared in more concentrated aqueous solutions than morphine. In spite of its potency, and persistent strong underground demand for this drug, it is seldom associated with toxicity. Of the 5,685 opiated-related deaths reported in the 1994 DAWN survey, only 19 (0.2% of all cases) were due to hydromorphone.

Hydromorphone is well absorbed by all routes. After an intravenous injection, more than 90% is cleared from the plasma and redistributed into tissue stores within 10 minutes of injection. This is almost exactly the same result after giving intravenous morphine, and methadone (Hill et al., 1991). Elimination of the drug then depends on how fast it diffuses back into the bloodstream. The average elimination half-life is three hours, but there is very substantial intersubject variation. In the most recently published study, a 40-µg/kg bolus given intravenously produced average blood levels of 7 ng/mL at 15 minutes, 5 ng/mL at 30 minutes, and 4 ng/mL at one hour. The kinetics are not dose-dependent. Humans mainly excrete the 3-glucuronide (Cone, Phelps, and Gorodetzky, 1977). Less than 6% of a given dose is excreted unchanged in the urine. The 6-hydroxy metabolite is probably

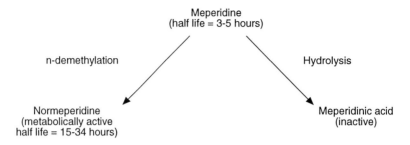

Figure 5.4.7.2 Meperidine metabolism. The metabolite normeperidine has about half the analgesic potency of meperidine and is also neurotoxic. Normeperidine's half-life is much longer than meperidine's, and toxic levels may accumulate in individuals with renal impairment.

not produced in man. Older measurements of blood and tissue levels are difficult to interpret, because the radioimmunoassays that were used cross-react with the glucuronide metabolites, resulting in final concentrations that were probably falsely high. Most of the urine screening tests now on the market detect hydromorphone, although some do not (Smith et al., 1995).

Hydromorphone is a mu-agonist and produces all of the classic symptoms of opiate intoxication. The minimum plasma concentration necessary to relieve severe pain is 4 ng/mL (Ridenberg et al., 1988). Studies in abusers have not been made. There is a paucity of autopsy data and no evidence to suggest that hydromorphone abuse causes any unique pathologic alterations. Since oral tablets are often crushed and injected, angiothrombotic lung disease could be a sequela of long-term use, but this has not been substantiated.

5.4.7.2 Hydrocodone (Hycodan®, Tussend®, Tussionex®)

This compound is structurally almost identical with codeine, the only difference being a =O group substitution for a hydroxyl group at position 6. Alone or in combination with other drugs, hydrocodone was responsible for 45 deaths in 1990. Since then the number of hydrocodone-related deaths has declined, and the DAWN survey no longer lists them in a separate category. Hydrocodone is well absorbed from the gastrointestinal tract, and according to Baselt it has a half-life of 3.8 hours. Hydrocodone is converted to hydromorphone (Cone et al., 1978), and rapidly cleared from the urine, with peak metabolite levels measured at roughly eight hours. In the urine, it is detectable by most of the widely used screen tests for opiates (Smith et al., 1995). Hydrocodone is also a mu-agonist capable of causing respiratory depression and death. As is true for hydromorphone, there is almost no autopsy information available, but there is no reason to suppose that this drug causes lesions any different from the other opiate agents.

5.4.7.3 Oxycodone (Tylox®, Percodan®)

Oxycodone is a semisynthetic derived from codeine. It has an elimination half-life of 2–5.5 hours (Pöyhiä et al., 1991). A dose of 4.5 mg given orally results in blood levels of 9–37 ng (Renzi and Tam, 1979), with urine concentrations of its O-demythelated metabolite peaking in under eight hours, and falling to under 300 ng in 24–48 hours (Smith et al., 1995). Therapeutic blood levels are less than 100 ng/mL. Its potency and duration of action are comparable to that of morphine. Detection of oxycodone abuse is problematic, because it is cleared from the urine so rapidly. The window for detection using TDx® and EMIT® testing is under 24 hours. In some test systems, because of the antibody used for detection, oxycodone will remain undetected (Smith et al., 1995).

Only 42 deaths from oxycodone were mentioned in the 1993 DAWN survey, but its toxicity may be greater than those numbers suggest. A recent report from Australia described nine oxycodone-related deaths, most in polydrug abusers (Drummer et al., 1994). Femoral blood concentrations ranged from 600–1400 ng/mL with a mean of 900 ng/mL. No unique autopsy findings were noted.

5.4.7.4 Oxymorphone (Numorphan®)

Oxymorphone is a semisynthetic opioid with pure mu-agonist properties, and a potency that is seven to ten times as great as morphine. In 1990, it accounted for less than 0.2% of all narcotic-related fatalities. By 1993, the number of reported cases had fallen to such low levels that oxymorphone is no longer listed as a separate category in the DAWN survey. The true incidence of oxymorphone abuse is impossible to gauge since it is not detected by the most widely used urine screening tests (Smith et al., 1995). More recently, this agent has seen increasing use as an intravenous anesthetic agent. Since it is capable of producing profound respiratory depression for over five hours after administration, more fatalities may be anticipated (Patt, 1988).

5.4.7.5 Meperidine (Demerol®, Pethidine®)

A synthetic phenylpiperidine derivative, meperidine is the only member of this class known to cause toxicity or death with any regularity. In 1994, meperidine accounted for 0.5% of narcotic-related deaths (36 deaths vs. 3,552 for heroin) (Substance Abuse Mental Health Administration, 1995) reported in the United States. On a weight-for-weight basis, meperidine has only one-sixth the analgesic potency of morphine. Unlike the naturally occurring opiates, meperidine in large doses can be neurotoxic. This toxicity is manifested as muscle twitching or convulsions (Boros et al., 1984; Morisy and Platt, 1986; Hershey, 1983). Meperidine-induced neurotoxicity is not reversed by opiate antagonists, but meperidine-induced respiratory depression is reversed. There are reports in the literature of prolonged narcosis, especially in elderly patients receiving high doses (Chan et al., 1975).

Meperidine is well absorbed by all conventional routes of administration. Peak plasma levels occur one to two minutes after intravenous administration, and within one hour after it is given orally. After intravenous administration there is extensive first-pass uptake of meperidine (as is true for most, but not all, of the other opiates) by the lung. Measurements have shown that as much as 75% of a given dose of meperidine is taken up in the lung during the first pass. The drug is then released back into the circulation at a variable rate (Roerig et al., 1987). Meperidine is also rapidly and transiently taken up by the myocardium, which may partly account for its known negative inotropic effects (Huang et al., 1994). This first-pass phenomenon does not occur with morphine or heroin. After oral dosing, maximum plasma levels are seen from 0.5–1.5 hours later (Pond et al., 1981).

Meperidine is hydrolyzed in the liver to form meperidinic acid (Asatoor et al., 1963; Pond et al., 1981). N-demethylation leading to the formation of normeperidine has also been documented. Normeperidine is metabolically active. It has about one-half the analgesic potency of meperidine, but is several times more neurotoxic (Siek, 1978; Miller and Anderson, 1984). It also has a much longer half-life (Pond et al., 1981). Under normal circumstances the half-life of meperidine is three to five hours (Koska et al., 1981; Mather et al., 1975), but the clearance rate depends somewhat on the amount given. In individuals with extensive liver disease, meperidine is metabolized more slowly. The half-life of meperidine in such cases can be as long as 11 hours (Pond et al., 1981). There is also evidence that chronic heroin users may metabolize meperidine more slowly than non-drug users and, as a result, they may develop higher blood levels (Houghton et al., 1993).

When large doses of meperidine are administered, normeperidine accumulates in the plasma in substantial quantities (Koska et al., 1981). In normal individuals, the terminal half-life of normeperidine is anywhere from 15–34 hours, but in individuals with renal impairment it may be three or four days. Thus toxicity, when it occurs, may be prolonged (Szeto et al., 1977). In control studies, 5% of a given dose was excreted unchanged in the urine. One-quarter of the dose will be excreted as meperidinic acid or normeperidinic acid.

Like all the opiates, meperidine and normeperidine distribute widely throughout the body. Meperidine blood levels measured at autopsy in the six cases reported by Siek ranged from 4,300 ng/mL–12,000 ng/mL. Hepatic levels were twice the blood levels in patients who were intravenous users, but only one-half the blood level if the individual had taken the meperidine orally. Clinical evidence of normeperidine toxicity is seen with levels ranging from 425–1,900 ng/mL, with normeperidine to meperidine ratios of 0.79–5.4 (Szeto et al., 1977). Even higher ratios have been observed. In the autopsy case reported by Jiraki, an addict with end-stage renal failure was found to have a meperidine blood level of only 60 ng/mL, while at the same time his normeperidine level was 3,000 ng/mL (Jiraki, 1992).

5.4.7.6   Pentazocine (Talwin®)

Pentazocine differs from the other agents discussed in that it is both a narcotic agonist and antagonist. It is active at Kappa and Delta receptor sites, but antagonizes effects at the mu-receptor site. It has less than half the potency of morphine. While there is no question that pentazocine (Talwin®) can be abused, the practice is extremely uncommon. No pentazocine-related deaths were noted in the DAWN survey for 1990, and pentazocine accounted for fewer than 0.2% of all drug-related emergency-room visits in that same year (Substance Abuse and Mental Health Services Administration, 1995). The low incidence of reports may well have to do with the fact that the oral form of pentazocine has been reformulated by the manufacturer and now contains the opiate antagonist, naloxone.

Earlier discussions of pentazocine abuse emphasized the high incidence among medical professionals, and the fact that pentazocine was often used with other drugs, especially alcohol, and the antihistamine, tripelennamine (Ellenhorn and Barceloux, 1988). In some areas, this latter combination was especially popular among pregnant women. One of the older pentazocine tablets crushed together with 2 tripelennamine tablets would be dissolved in water and injected (Carlson, 1982). The combination was referred to as "T's and Blues." That pattern of usage also seems to have changed, as evidenced by the fact that the most recent DAWN report contains no mention of pentazocine use in conjunction with any other drug.

With the exception of a tendency to produce myositis and fibrosis (Oh et al., 1975; Schiff and Kern, 1977; DeSchepper and Degryse, 1980), long-term parenteral abuse of the drug results in the same set of complications produced by the long-term parenteral abuse of any other opiate (King and Betts, 1978). Unlike other opiates, pentazocine causes increased release of epinephrine from the adrenals (Fukumitsu et al., 1991) and elevates circulating catecholamines. That may explain why high doses increase both heart rate and blood pressure, a rather dangerous combination for individuals with preexisting coronary artery disease (Alderman et al., 1972). The results of these experimental studies raise the possibility that, in pentazocine-related deaths, there might be anatomic findings consistent with catecholamine toxicity, such as contraction band necrosis. Such alterations are yet to be reported, but it is not clear if they have ever been systematically sought.

Peak pentazocine blood levels occur 15 minutes to one hour after intramuscular administration, but after oral administration peak levels may not be reached for several hours. Oral administration can produce levels that are almost as high as those seen after intramuscular injection. The peak level after a 75-mg dose given orally averages 160 ng/mL (Berkowitz, 1969). Peak levels after 45 mg intramuscularly were 140 ng/mL. Five to 10 minutes after a 30-mg intravenous dose, blood levels as high as 1,000 ng/mL may be seen (Agurell et al., 1974). Baselt states that plasma levels in fatalities range from 1–5 mg/L (Baselt, 1989), but patients have survived with blood levels as high as 9 mg/L (Stahl and Kasser, 1983). The same difficulties apply to the interpretation of pentazocine levels as apply to any opiate. Tolerance occurs, and without knowledge of the individual's past history, attributing a specific event or outcome to an isolated toxicologic finding is impossible.

Pentazocine's terminal half-life is between two and four hours (Berkowitz, 1969), but there is considerable variation from individual to individual. Very high levels can also be measured in the brain, where the concentration may exceed that found in the blood. High levels are also seen in the liver, bile, and kidney (Pittman, 1973). There is extensive first-pass metabolism in the liver, where both oxidation and glucuronidation occur. Less than 10% of a given dose is excreted unchanged (Pittman, 1970).

References

Aderjan, R., Hofmann, S., Schmitt, G., and Skopp, G. (1995). Morphine and morphine glucuronides in serum of heroin consumers and in heroin-related deaths determined by HPLC with native fluorescence detection. J Analyt Toxicol, 19: 163–168.

Agurell, S., Boréus, L., Gordon, E. et al. (1974). Plasma and cerebrospinal fluid concentrations of pentazocine in patients; assay by mass fragmentography. J Pharm Pharmacol, 26: 1–8.

Aherne, G. and Littleton, P. (1985). Morphine-6-glucuronide, an important factor in interpreting morphine radioimmunoassays. Lancet, ii: 210–211.

Alderman, E., Barry, W., Graham, A., and Harrison, D. (1972). Hemodynamic effects of morphine and pentazocine differ in cardiac patients. N Engl J Med, 287: 623–627.

Allen, A., Cooper, D., and Kram, T. (1981). "China White": α-methylfentanyl. Microgram, 14(3): 26–32.

Andrews, C. and Prys-Roberts, C. (1983). Fentanyl — a review. Clin Anaesthesiol, 1: 97–122.

Anon (1861). A new theory of poisoning. Lancet, i: 93.

Anon (1994). Oral transmucosal fentanyl citrate. Med Letter, 36(918): 24–25.

Asatoor, A., London, D., Milne, M., and Simenhoff, M. (1963). The excretion of pethidine and its derivatives. Br J Pharm, 20: 285–298.

Babul, N. and Darke, A. (1993). Disposition of morphine and its glucuronide metabolites after oral and rectal administration: evidence of route specificity. Clin Pharm Ther, 54(3): 286–292.

Ball, M., McQuay, H., Moore, M. et al. (1985). Renal failure and the use of morphine in intensive care. Lancet, 1: 784–786.

Baselt, R. and Cravey, R. (1989). Disposition of toxic drugs and chemicals in man, 3rd edition. Chicago, IL: Year Book Medical Publishers.

Baselt, R., Wright, J., Turner, J., and Cravey, R. (1975). Propoxyphene and norpropoxyphene tissue concentrations in fatalities associated with propoxyphene hydrochloride and propoxyphene napsylate. Arch Tox, 34: 145–152.

Berkowitz, B., Ngai, S., Yang, J. et al. (1975). The disposition of morphine in surgical patients. Clin Pharm Ther, 17: 629–635.

Berkowitz, B., Asling, J., Way, E. et al. (1969). Relationship of pentazocine plasma levels to pharmacological activity in man. Clin Pharm Ther, 10: 320–328.

Björkman, S., Stanski, D., Verotta, D., and Harashima, H. (1990). Comparative tissue concentration profiles of fentanyl and alfentanil in humans predicted from tissue/blood partition data obtained in rats. Anesthesiology, 72: 865–873.

Boerner, U., Abbott, S., and Roc, R. (1975). The metabolism of morphine and heroin in man. Drug Metab Rev, 4: 39–73.

Boros, M., Chaudhry, I., Nagashima, H. et al. (1984). Myoneural effects of pethidine and droperidol. Br J Anesth, 56: 195–202.

Bowsher, D. (1993). Paradoxical pain. When metabolism and morphine are in the wrong ratio. Br Med J, 306: 473–474.

Breheny, F., McDonagh, T., Hackett, L. et al. (1993). Disposition and clinical effects of morphine, morphine-6-glucuronide and morphine-3-glucuronide following an intentional overdose of slow release oral morphine in a patient with renal failure. Drug Invest, 6(5): 291–293.

Brunk, F. and Delle, M. (1974). Morphine metabolism in man. Clin Pharm Ther, 16: 51–57.

Calis, K., Kohler, D., and Corso, D. (1992). Transdermally-administered fentanyl for pain management. Clin Pharm, 11:22–36.

Caplan, Y., Thompson, B., and Fisher, R. (1977). Propoxyphene fatalities: blood and tissue concentrations of propoxyphene and norpropoxyphene and a study of 115 medical examiner cases. J Analyt Toxicol, 1: 27–35.

Caplehorn, J., Bell, J., Kleinbaum, D. et al. (1993). Methadone dose and heroin use during maintenance treatment. Addiction, 88: 119-124.

Carballo-Diéguez, A., Sahs, J., Goetz, R. et al. (1994). The effect of methadone on immunological parameters among HIV-positive and HIV-negative drug users. Am J Drug Alcohol Abuse, 230(3): 317–329.

Carlson, C. (1982). The drug victim too often the same: The fetus. JAMA, 248: 409–410.

Carrupt, P., Testa, B., Bechalany, A. et al. (1991). Morphine-6-glucuronide and morphine-3-glucronide as molecular chameleons with unexpected lipophilicity. J Med Chem, 34: 1272–1275.

Cartwright, P., Prys-Roberts, C., Gill, K. et al. (1983). Ventilatory depression related to plasma fentanyl concentrations during and after anesthesia in humans. Anesth Analg, 62: 966–974.

Chan, K., Kendall, M., Mitchard, M., and Well, W. (1975). The effect of age on plasma pethidine concentrations. Br J Clin Pharm, 2: 297–302.

Chan, S., Chan, E., and Kaliciak, H. (1986). Distribution of morphine in body fluids and tissues in fatal overdose. J Forensic Sci, 31(4): 1487–1491.

Chen, Z., Somogyi, A., Reynolds, G., and Bochner, F. (1991). Disposition and metabolism of codeine after single and chronic doses in one poor and seven extensive metabolizers. Br J Clin Pharm, 31: 381–390.

Cone, E., Phelps, B., and Gorodetzky, C. (1977). Urinary excretion of hydromorphone and metabolites in humans, rats, dogs, guinea pigs, and rabbits. J Pharm Sci, 66: 1709–1713.

Cone, E., Darwin, W., Gorodetzky, C. et al. (1978). Comparative metabolism of hydrocodone in man, rat, guinea pig, rabbit, and dog. Drug Metab Dispos, 6: 488–493.

Cone, E. (1990). Testing human hair for drugs of abuse. I. Individual dose and time profiles of morphine and codeine in plasma, saliva, urine, and beard compared to drug-induced effects on pupils and behavior. J Analyt Toxicol, 14: 1–7.

Cone, E., Welch, P., Paul, B., and Mitchell, J. (1991a). Forensic drug testing for opiates, III. Urinary excretion rates of morphine and codeine following codeine administration. J Analyt Toxicol, 15: 161–166.

Cone, E., Welch, P., Mitchell, J., and Paul, B. (1991b). Forensic drug testing for opiates: I. Detection of 6-acetylmorphine in urine as an indicator of recent heroin exposure; drug assay and considerations and detection times. J Analyt Toxicol, 15: 1–7.

Cone, E., Dickerson, S., Pau, B., and Mitchell, J. (1992). Forensic drug testing for opiates. IV. Analytical sensitivity, specificity, and accuracy of commercial urine opiate immunoassays. J Analyt Toxicol, 16: 72–78.

Cone, E., Millsgrove, M., Jenkins, A. et al. (1994). Sweat testing for heroin, cocaine, and metabolites. J Analyt Toxicol, 18: 298–305.

Cravey, R., Shaw, R., and Nakamura, G. (1974). Incidence of propoxyphene poisoning. A report of fatal cases. J Forensic Sci, 19: 72–80.

Cravey, R. (1985). An unusually high blood morphine concentration in a fatal case. J Analyt Toxicol, 9: 237–239.

Dahlström, B. and Paalzow, L. (1978). Pharmacokinetic interpretation of the enterohepatic recirculation and first-pass elimination of morphine in the rat. J Pharmacokinet Biopharm, 6: 505–529.

Dambisya, Y., Chan, K., and Wong, C. (1992). Dispositional study of opioids in mice pretreated with sympathomimetic agents. J Pharm Pharmacol, 44: 687–690.

DeLima, L. (1993) Cerebrovascular autoregulation may be the probable mechanism responsible for fentanyl- and sufentanil-induced increases in intracranial pressure in patients with head trauma. Anesthesiology, 79: 186–187.

De Schepper, A. and Degryse, H. (1990). Imaging findings in a patient with pentazocine-induced myopathy. Am J Roent, 154: 343–344.

Doberczak, T., Kandall, S., and Friedman, P. (1993). Relationships between maternal methadone dosage, maternal-neonatal methadone levels, and neonatal withdrawal. Obstet Gynecol, 81(6): 936–946.

Drummer, O., Opeskin, K., Syrjanen, M., and Cordner, S. (1992). Methadone toxicity causing death in 10 subjects starting on a methadone maintenance program. Am J Forensic Med Pathol, 13: 346–350.

Drummer, O., Syrjanen, M., Phelan, M. et al. (1994). A study of deaths involving oxycodone. J Forensic Sci, 39(4): 1069–1075.

Ellenhorn, M. and Barceloux, D. (1988). *Medical toxicology: the diagnosis and treatment of human poisoning* (1st ed.). New York: Elsevier, 734.

Ellison, N. and Lewis, G. (1984). Plasma concentrations following single doses of morphine sulfate in oral and rectal suppository. Clin Pharm, 3: 614–617.

Felby, S., Christensen, H., and Lund, H. (1974). Morphine concentrations in blood and organs in cases of fatal poisoning. Forensic Sci, 3: 77–81.

Finkle, B., Caplan, Y., Garriott, J. et al. (1981). Propoxyphene in postmortem toxicology 1976–1978. J Forensic Sci, 26: 739–757.

Finkle, B., McCloskey, K., Kiplinger, G., and Bennett, I. (1976). A national assessment of propoxyphene in postmortem medicolegal investigation, 1972–1975. J Forensic Sci, 21: 706–742.

Fisher, A., Hanna, M., and Rhodes, S. (1987). Spinal level analgesia after morphine overdose? Lancet, 1: 573.

Flanagan, R., Ramsey, J., and Jane, I. (1984). Measurement of dextropropoxyphene and nordextropropoxyphene in biological fluids. Hum Toxicol, 3: 103S–114S.

Fraser, H., Isbel, H., and Van Horn, G. (1960). Human pharmacology and addiction liability of norcodeine. J Pharm Exp Ther, 129: 172–177.

Fukumitsu, K., Sumikawa, K., Hayashi, Y. et al. (1991). Pentazocine-induced catecholamine efflux from the dog perfused adrenals. J Pharm Pharmacol, 43: 331–336.

Fung, D. and Eisele, J. (1980). Narcotic concentration-respiratory effect curves in man. Anesthesiology, 53: S397.

Garriott, J., Sturner, W., and Mason, M. (1973). Toxicologic findings in six fatalities involving methadone. Clin Toxic, 6: 163–173.

Garriott, J., Rodriguez, R., and DiMaio, V. (1984). A death from fentanyl overdose. J Analyt Toxicol, 8: 288–289.

Gerdin, E., Gabrielsson, J., Lindberg, B. et al. (1990). Disposition of morphine-3-glucuronide in the pregnant Rhesus monkey. Pharmacol Tox, 66: 185–189.

Giacomini, K., Giacomini, J., Gibson, T., and Levy, G. (1980). Propoxyphene and norpropoxyphene plasma concentrations after oral propoxyphene in cirrhotic patients with and without surgically-constructed portacaval shunt. Clin Pharm Ther, 28: 417–424.

Gibson, T., Giacomini, K., Briggs, W. et al. (1980). Propoxyphene and norpropoxyphene plasma concentrations in anephric patients. Clin Pharm Ther, 27: 665–670.

Goldberger, B., Cone, E., Grant, T. et al. (1994). Disposition of heroin and its metabolites in heroin-related deaths. J Analyt Toxicol, 18: 22–28.

Goldstein, A. (1991). Measuring compliance in methadone maintenance patients: use of a pharmacologic indicator to estimate methadone plasma levels. Clin Pharm Ther, 50: 199–207.

Goodman, L. and Gilman, S. (1990). *The pharmacological basis of therapeutics.* New York: Macmillan.

Goromaru, T., Furuta, T., Baba, S. et al. (1981). Metabolism of fentanyl in rats and man. Anesthesiology, 55: A173.

Gottschalk, L. and Cravey, R. (1980). *Toxicological and pathological studies in psychoactive drug-involved deaths.* Davis, CA: Biomedical Publications.

Gourlay, G., Cherry, D., and Cousins, M. (1986). A comparative study of the efficacy and pharmacokinetics of oral methadone and morphine in the treatment of severe pain in patients with cancer. Pain, 25: 297–312.

Gourlay, G., Kowalski, S., Plummer, J. et al. (1988). Fentanyl blood concentration analgesic response relationship in the treatment of postoperative pain. Anesth Analg, 67: 329–337.

Gourlay, G. and Boas, R. (1992). Fatal outcome with use of rectal morphine for postoperative pain control in an infant. Br Med J, 304: 766–777.

Graham, K., Koren, G., Klein, J. et al. (1989). Determination of gestational cocaine exposure by hair analysis. JAMA, 262(23): 3328–3330.

Greene, M., Luke, J., and DuPont, R. (1974). Opiate overdose deaths in the District of Columbia. Part II — methadone-related deaths fatalities. J Forensic Sci, 19: 575–584.

Hanisch, W. and Meyer, L. (1993). Determination of the heroin metabolite 6-monoacetylmorphine in urine by high-performance liquid chromatography with electrochemical detection. J Analyt Toxicol, 17: 48–50.

Hanks, G., Hoskin, P., Aherne, G. et al. (1988). Enterohepatic circulation of morphine. Lancet, I: 469.

Harding-Pink, D. and Fryc, O. (1988). Risk of death after release from prison: a duty to warn. Br Med J, 297: 596.

Hartman, B., Miyada, D., Pirkle, H. et al. (1988). Serum propoxyphene concentrations in a cohort of opiate addicts on long-term propoxyphene maintenance therapy. Evidence for drug tolerance in humans. J Analyt Toxicol, 12: 25–29.

Hartvig, P., Lindberg, B., Lilja, A. et al. (1989). Positron emission tomography in studies on fetomaternal disposition of opioids. Dev Pharm Ther, 12: 74–80.

Hasselström, J. and Säwe, J. (1993). Morphine pharmacokinetics and metabolism in humans. Enterohepatic cycling and relative contribution of metabolites to active opioid concentrations. Clin Pharmacokinet, 24(4): 344–354.

Hays, L., Stillner, V., and Littrell, R. (1992). Fentanyl dependence associated with oral ingestion. Anesthesiology, 77: 819–820.

Henderson, G. (1991). Fentanyl-related deaths: demographics, circumstances, and toxicology of 112 cases. J Forensic Sci, 236: 422–433.

Hershey, L. (1983). Meperidine and central neurotoxicity. Ann Intern Med, 98: 548–549.

Hess, R., Hertz, A., and Friedel, K. (1972). Pharmacokinetics of fentanyl in rabbits in view of the importance for limiting the effect. J Pharm Exp Ther, 179: 474–484.

Hess, R., Stiebler, G., and Herz, A. (1972). Pharmacokinetics of fentanyl in man and the rabbit. Euro J Clin Pharm, 4: 135–141.

Hill, H., Coda, B., Tanaka, A., and Schaffer, R. (1991). Multiple-dose evaluation of intravenous hydromorphone pharmacokinetics in normal human subjects. Anesth Analg, 72: 330–336.

Hine, C., Wright, J., Allison, D. et al. (1982). Analysis of fatalities from acute narcotism in a major urban area. J Forensic Sci, 27: 372–384.

Holmstrand, J., Anggard, E., and Gunne, L. (1978). Methadone maintenance plasma levels and therapeutic outcome. Clin Pharm Ther, 23: 175–180.

Hoskin, P., Hanks, G., Aherne, G. et al. (1989). The bioavailability and pharmacokinetics of morphine after intravenous, oral, and buccal administration in healthy volunteers. Br J Clin Pharm, 27: 499–505.

Houghton, I., Aun, C., and Chan, K. (1993). Pethidine pharmacokinetics in a heroin addict: a case report. J Clin Pharm Ther, 18: 139–140.

Huang, Y., Upton, R., and Mather, L. (1994). The pharmacokinetics of meperidine in the myocardium of conscious sheep. Anesth Analg, 79: 987–992.

Inturrisi, C. and Verebely, K. (1972). The levels of methadone in the plasma in methadone maintenance. Clin Pharm Ther, 13: 633–647.

Inturrisi, C., Colburn, W., Kaiko, R. et al. (1987). Pharmacokinetics and pharmacodynamics of methadone in patients with chronic pain. Clin Pharm Ther, 41: 392–401.

Iwamato, K. and Klassen, C. (1977). First-pass effect of morphine in rats. J Pharm Exp Ther, 200: 236–244.

Jackson, F. (1994). Fentanyl and the wooden chest. Gastroenterology, 106: 820–824.

Jenkins, A., Keenan, R., Henningfield, J. et al. (1994). Pharmacokinetics and pharmacodynamics of smoked heroin. J Analyt Toxicol, 18: 317–330.

Jenkins, A., Oyler, J., and Cone, E. (1995). Comparison of heroin and cocaine concentrations in saliva with concentrations in blood and plasma. J Analyt Toxicol, 19: 359–374.

Jiraki, K. (1992). Lethal effects of normeperidine. Am J Forensic Med and Pathol, 13: 42–43.

Joynt, B. and Mikhael, N. (1985). Sudden death of a heroin body packer. J Analyt Toxicol, 9: 238–241.

Kaa, E. and Dalgaard, J. (1989). Fatal dextropropoxyphene poisonings in Jutland, Denmark. Zeitschrift für Rechtsmedizin, 102: 107–115.

King, A. and Betts, T. (1978). Abuse of pentazocine. Br Med J, 2: 21.

Kingsbury, D., Makowski, G., and Stone, J. (1995). Quantitative analysis of fentanyl in pharmaceutical preparations by gas chromatography-mass spectrometry. J Analyt Toxicol, 19: 27–29.

Kintz, P., Mangin, P., Lugnier, A., and Chaumont, A. (1989). Toxicological data after heroin overdose. Hum Toxicol, 8: 487–489.

Koren, G., Butt, W., Pape, K., and Chiryanga, H. (1983). Morphine-induced seizures in newborn infants. Vet Hum Toxicol, 27: 519–520.

Koren, G. and Klein, J. (1992). Postmortem redistribution of morphine in rats. Ther Drug Monitor, 14: 461–463.

Koska, A., Kramer, W., Romagnoli, A. et al. (1981). Pharmacokinetics of high dose meperidine in surgical patients. Anesth Analg, 60: 8–11.

Kram, T., Cooper, D., and Allen, A. (1981). Behind the identification of China White. Analyt Chem, 53(12): 1379A–1386A.

Kreek, M. (1973). Plasma and urine levels of methadone: comparison following four medication forms used in chronic maintenance treatment. NY State J Med, 73: 2773–2777.

Kreek, M. (1988). Medical complications in methadone patients. Ann NY Acad Sci, 311: 110–134.

Laitinen, L., Kanto, J., Vapaavuori, M., and Viljanen, M. (1975). Morphine concentrations in plasma after intramuscular injection. Br J Anaesth, 47: 1265–1267.

Laizure, S., Miller, J., Stevens, R. et al. (1993). The disposition and cerebrospinal fluid penetration of morphine and its two major glucuronidated metabolites in adults undergoing lumbar myelogram. Pharmacotherapy, 13(5): 471–475.

Lehmann, K., Freier, J., and Daub, D. (1982). Fentanyl-pharmacokinetics and postoperative respiratory depression. Anaesthesia, 31: 111–118.

Levine, B., Wu, S., Dixon, A. et al. (1994). An unusual morphine fatality. Forensic Sci Int, 65: 7–11.

Lindahl, S., Olsson, A., and Thomson, D. (1981). Rectal premedication in children. Anesthesia, 36: 376–379.

Little, B., Snell, L., Klein, V., and Gilstrap, III, L. (1989). Cocaine abuse during pregnancy: maternal and fetal implications. Obstet Gynecol, 73(2): 157–160.

Logan, B. and Lüthi, R. (1994). The significance of morphine concentratons in the cerebrospinal fluid in morphine-caused deaths. J Forensic Sci, 39(3): 699–706.

Lorimer, N. and Schmid, R. (1992). The use of plasma levels to optimize methadone maintenance treatment. Drug Alcohol Depend, 30: 241–246.

Lunn, J., Stanley, T., Eisele, J. et al. (1979). High dose fentanyl anesthesia for coronary artery surgery: plasma fentanyl concentrations and influence of nitrous oxide on cardiovascular responses. Anest Analg, 58: 390–395.

Mahler, D. and Forrest Jr., W. (1975). Relative analgesic potencies of morphine and hydromorphone in postoperative pain. Anesthesiology, 42: 602–607.

Manning, T., Bidanset, S., Cohen, B. et al. (1976). Evaluation of Abuscreen for methadone. J For Sc, 21: 112–120.

Marquardt, K. and Tharratt, S. (1994). Inhalation abuse of fentanyl patch. Clin Toxicol, 32(1): 75–78.

Matejczyk, R. (1988). Fentanyl-related overdose. J Analyt Toxicol, 12: 236–238.

Mather, L. (1983). Clinical pharmacokinetics of fentanyl and its newer derivatives. Clin Pharmacokinet, 8: 422–426.

Mather, L., Tucker, G., Pflug, A. et al. (1975). Meperidine kinetics in man. Clin Pharm Ther, 17: 21–30.

Mazoit, J., Sandouk, P., Scherrmann, J., and Roche, A. (1990). Extrahepatic metabolism of morphine occurs in humans. Clin Pharm Ther, 48: 613–618.

Mazzone, A., Mazzucchelli, I., Fossati, G. et al. (1994). Granulocyte defects and opioid receptors in chronic exposure to heroin or methadone in humans. Int J Immunopharmac, 16(11): 958–967.

McBay, A. (1976). Propoxyphene and norpropoxyphene concentrations in blood and tissues in cases of fatal overdose. Clin Chem, 22: 1319–1321.

McClain, D. and Hug, C. (1980). Intravenous fentanyl kinetics. Clin Pharm Ther, 28: 106–114.

McGee, M., Marker, E., Jovic, M., and Stajic, M. (1992). Fentanyl related deaths in New York City. Annual Meeting American Academy of Forensic Science. New Orleans, LA: February, 1992.

McLachlan, C., Crofts, N., Wodak, A. et al. (1993). The effects of methadone on immune function among injecting drug users: a review. Addicition, 88: 257–263.

Miller, J. and Anderson, H. (1984). The effect of N-demethylation on certain pharmacologic actions of morphine, codeine and meperidine in the mouse. J Pharmacol Exp Ther, 112: 191–196.

Milne, R., Sloan, P., McLean, C. et al. (1993). Disposition of morphine and its 3- and 6-glucuronide metabolites during morphine infusion in the sheep. Dru Metab Disp, 21(6): 1151–1156.

Mitchell, J., Paul, B., Welch, P., and Cone, E. (1991). Forensic drug testing for opiates. II. Metabolism and excretion rate of morphine in humans after morphine administration. J Analyt Toxicol, 15: 49–53.

Mo, B. and Way, E. (1966). An assessment of inhalation as a mode of administration of heroin by addicts. J Pharm and Exp Ther, 154: 142–151.

Morisy, L. and Platt, D. (1986). Hazards of high dose meperidine. JAMA, 255: 467–468.

Morland, J., Alkana, R., Paulsen, R. et al. (1995). Morphine-6-glucuronide: a possible mediator of acute effects related to morphine dependence. CPDD 1995 57th Annual Meeting, June 10–15, 1993, Scottsdale, Arizona.

Mulder, G. (1992). Pharmacological effects of drug conjugates: is morphine 6-glucuronide an exception? Trends Pharm Sci, 131: 302–303.

Murphy, M. and Hug, C. (1981). Pharmacokinetics of intravenous morphine in patients anesthetized with enflurane-nitrous oxide. Anesthesiology, 54: 187–192.

Nakamura, G. and Choi, J. (1983). Morphine in lymph nodes of heroin users. J Forensic Sci, 28(1): 249–250.

National Institute on Drug Abuse (1990b). Annual Medical Examiner Data. Data from the Drug Abuse Warning Network. Statistical Series I, Number 10-B. Rockville, MD: U.S. Department of Health and Human Services.

Nickander, R., Emmerson, J., Hynes, M. et al. (1984). Pharmacologic and toxic effects in animals of dextropropoxyphene and its major metabolite, norpropoxyphene: a review. Hum Toxicol, 3: 13S–36S.

Nordberg, G. (1984). Pharmacokinetic aspects of spinal morphine analgesia. Acta Anaesth Scand, 28(Suppl. 79): 7–38.

Norheim, G. (1973). Methadone in autopsy cases. Z Rechtsmed, 73: 219–224.

Novick, D., Ochshorn, M., Ghali, V. et al. (1989). Natural killer cell activity and lymphocyte subsets in parenteral heroin abusers and long-term methadone maintenance patients. J Pharm Exp Ther, 250: 606–610.

Nussmeier, N., Benthuysen, J., Steffey, E. et al. (1991). Cardiovascular, respiratory, and analgesic effects of fentanyl in unanesthetized Rhesus monkeys. Anesth Analg, 72: 221–226.

Oguma, T. and Levy, G. (1981). Acute effect of ethanol on hepatic first-pass elimination of propoxyphene in rats. J Pharm Exp Ther, 219: 7–13.

Oh, S., Rollins, J., and Lewis, I. (1975). Pentazocine-induced fibrous myopathy. JAMA, 231: 271–273.

O'neil, P., and Pitts, J. (1992). Illicitly imported heroin products (1984 to 1989) — some physical and chemical features indicative of their origin. J Pharm Pharmacol, 44(1): 1–6.

Osborne, R., Joel, S., Trew, D., and Slevin, M. (1988). Analgesic activity of morphine-6-glucuronide. Lancet, I: 828.

Osborne, R., Joel, S., Trew, D., and Slevin, M. (1990). Morphine and metabolite behavior after different routes of morphine administration: demonstration of the importance of the active metabolite morphine-6-glucuronide. Clin Pharm Ther, 47: 12–19.

Pacifici, G. and Rane, A. (1982). Renal glucuronidation of morphine in the human fetus. Acta Pharm Toxicol, 50: 155–160.

Patt, R. (1988). Delayed postoperative respiratory depression associated with oxymorphone. Anesth Analg, 67: 403–404.

Pittman, K. (1970). Human metabolism of orally administered pentazocine. Biochem Pharm, 19: 1833–1836.

Pittman, K. (1973). Pentazocine in Rhesus monkey. Plasma and brain after parenteral and oral administration. Life Sci, 12: 131–143.

Pond, S., Tong, T., Benowitz, N. et al. (1981). Presystemic metabolism of meperidine to normeperidine in normal and cirrhotic subjects. Clin Pharm Ther, 30: 183–188.

Portnoy, R., Kahn, E., Layman, M. et al. (1991). Chronic morphine therapy for cancer pain: plasma and cerebrospinal fluid morphine and morphine-6-glucuronide concentrations. Neurology, 41: 1457–1461.

Pöyhiä, R., Olkkola, K., Seppäläm, T. et al. (1991). The pharmacokinetics of oxycodone after intravenous injection in adults. Br J Clin Pharm, 32: 516–518.

Reed, D., Spiehler, V., and Cravey, R. (1977). Two cases of heroin-related suicide. Forensic Sci, 9(1): 49–52.

Reidenberg, M., Goodman, H., Erle, H. et al. (1988). Hydromorphone levels and pain control in patients with severe chronic pain. Clin Pharm Ther, 44: 376–382.

Renzi, N. and Tam, J. (1979). Quantitative GLC determination of oxycodone in human plasma. J Pharm Sci, 68: 43–45.

Richards, R., Reed, D., and Cravey, R. (1976). Death from intravenously administered narcotics: a study of 114 cases. J Forensic Sci, 21: 467–482.

Ritschel, W., Parab, P., Denson, D. et al. (1987). Absolute bioavailability of hydromorphone after peroral and rectal administration in humans: saliva/plasma ratio and clinical effects. J Clin Pharm, 27: 647–653.

Robinson, A. and Williams, F. (1971). The distribution of methadone in man. J. Pharm Pharmacol, 23: 353–358.

Roerig, D., Kotrly, K., Vucins, E. et al. (1987). First-pass uptake of fentanyl, meperidine, and morphine in the human lung. Anesthesiology, 67: 466–472.

Rothe, M. and Pragst, F. (1995). Solvent optimization for the direct extraction of opiates from hair samples. J Analyt Toxicol, 19: 236–240.

Rurak, D., Wright, M., and Axelson, J. (1991). Drug disposition and effects in the fetus. J Dev Physiol, 15: 33–44.

Sanfilippo, G. (1948). Contributo sperimenteale all'ipotesi della semtilazione della codeina nell'organismo. I. Influenza della dose sull'assuefazione alla codeina. II. Assuefazione alla codeina ottenuta con somministrazione prolungata di morfina. Boll Soc Ital Biol Sper, 24: 723–726.

Säwe, J. (1986). High dose morphine and methadone in cancer patients. Clinical pharmacokinetic considerations of oral treatment. Clin Pharmacokinet, 11: 87–106.

Säwe, J., Dahlstrom, B., Paalzow, L., and Rane, A. (1981). Morphine kinetics in cancer patients. Clin Pharm Ther, 30: 629–635.

Säwe, J., Kager, L., Svensson, J., and Rane, A. (1985). Oral morphine in cancer patients: *in vivo* kinetics and *in vitro* hepatic glucuronidation. Br J Clin Pharm, 19: 495–501.

Sawyer, W., Waterhouse, G., Doedens, D., and Forney, R. (1988). Heroin, morphine, and hydromorphone determination in postmortem material by high performance liquid chromatography. J Forensic Sci, 33: 1146–1155.

Schiff, B. and Kern, A. (1977). Unusual cutaneous manifestations of pentazocine addiction. JAMA, 238: 1542–1543.

Schleimer, R., Benjamini, E., Eisle, J., and Henderson, G. (1978). Pharmacokinetics of fentanyl as determined by radioimmunoassay. Clin Pharm Ther, 23(2): 188–194.

Schramm, W., Smith, R., Craig, P., and Kidwell, D. (1992). Drugs of abuse in saliva: a review. J Analyt Toxicol, 16: 1–9.

Schwartz, J., Garriott, J., Sommerset, J. et al. (1994). Measurements of fentanyl and sufentanil in blood and urine after surgical application. J Forensic Med Pathol, 15(3): 236–244.

Segal, R. and Catherman, R. (1974). Methadone — a cause of death? J Forensic Sci, 19: 64–71.

Sharp, M., Wallace, S., Hindmarsh, K., and Peel, H. (1983). Monitoring saliva concentrations of methaqualone, codeine, secobarbital, diphenhydramine and diazepam after single oral doses. J Analyt Toxicol, 7: 11–14.

Siek, T. (1978). The analysis of meperidine and normeperidine in biological specimens. J Forensic Sci, 23: 6–13.

Silverstein, J., Rieders, M., McMullin, M. et al. (1993). An analysis of the duration of fentanyl and its metabolites in urine and saliva. Anesth Analg, 76: 618–621.

Smith, M., Hughes, R., Levine, B. et al. (1995). Forensic drug testing for opiates. VI. Urine testing for hydromorphone, hydrocodone, oxymorphone, and oxycodone with commercial opiate immunoassays and gas chromatography-mass spectrometry. J Analyt Toxicol, 19: 18–26.

Sorokin, V., Semkin, E., and Savilov, A. (1994). Expert examination of 3-methylfentanyl. Microgram, 27(7): 221–224.

Soumerai, S., Avorn, J., Gortmaker, S., and Hawley, S. (1987). Effect of government and commercial warnings on reducing prescription misuse: the case of propoxyphene. Am J Public Health, 77: 1518–1523.

Spector, S. and Vesell, E. (1971). Disposition of morphine in man. Science, 174: 421–422.

Spiehler, V. (1989). Computer-assisted interpretation in forensic toxicology: morphine-involved deaths. J Forensic Sci, 34(5): 1104–1115.

Spiehler, V. and Brown, R. (1987). Unconjugated morphine in blood by radioimmunoassay and gas chromatography/mass spectrometry. J Forensic Sci, 32: 906–916.

Stahl, S. and Kasser, I. (1983). Pentazocine overdose. Ann Emerg Med, 12: 28–31.

Stanski, D., Greenblatt, D., and Lowenstein, E. (1978). Kinetics of intravenous and intramuscular morphine. Clin Pharm Ther, 24: 52–59.

Steentoft, A., Worm, K., and Christensen, H. (1988). Morphine concentrations in autopsy material from fatal cases after intake of morphine and/or heroin. J Forensic Sci, 28: 87–94.

Steentoft, A., Kaa, E., and Worm, K. (1989). Fatal intoxications in the age group 15–34 years in Denmark in 1984 and 1985. A forensic study with special reference to drug addicts. Zeitschrift für Rechtsmedizin, 103: 93–100.

Stoeckle, H., Hengstmann, J., and Schüttler, J. (1979). Pharmacokinetics of fentanyl as a possible explanation for recurrence of respiratory depression. Br J Anesth, 51: 741–745.

Strain, E., Stitzer, M., Liebson, I. et al. (1993). Methadone dose and treatment outcome. Drug Alchol Depend, 33: 105–117.

Streisand, J., Varvel, J., Stanski, D. et al. (1991). Absorption and bioavailability of oral transmucosal fentanyl citrate. Anesthesiology, 75: 223–229.

Substance Abuse and Mental Health Services Administration. (1995). Annual Emergency Room Data. Data from the Drug Abuse Warning Network. Statistical Series I, Number 13-B. Rockville, MD: U.S. Department of Health and Human Services.

Svensson, J., Rane, A., Säwe, J., and Sjöqvist, F. (1982). Determination of morphine, morphine-3-glucuronide, and (tentatively) morphine-6-glucuronide in plasma and urine using ion-pair high-performance liquid chromatography. J Chromatogr, 230: 427–432.

Szeto, H., Inturrsi, C., Houde, R. et al. (1977a). Accumulation of normeperidine, an active metabolite of meperidine in patients with renal failure or cancer. Ann Intern Med, 86: 738–741.

Szeto, H., Inturrisi, C., Houde, R. et al. (1977b). Accumulation of norpemeridine, an active metabolite of meperidine, in patients with renal failure or cancer. Ann Intern Med, 86: 738–741.

Tam, Y. (1993). Individual variation in first-pass metabolism. Clin Pharmacokinet, 25(4): 300–328.

Tennant, F. (1987). Inadequate plasma concentrations in some high-dose methadone maintenance patients. Am J Psych, 144: 1349–1350.

Tennant, F. and Shannon, J. (1995). Cocaine abuse in methadone maintenance patients is associated with low serum methadone concentrations. J Addict Dis, 14: 67–74.

Theilade, M. (1989). Death due to dextropropoxyphene: Copenhagen experiences. Forensic Sci Int, 40: 143–151.

Wahba, W., Winek, C., and Rozin, L. (1993). Distribution of morphine in body fluids of heroin users. J Analyt Toxicol, 17: 123–124.

Walton, R., Thornton, T., and Whal, G. (1978). Serum methadone as an aid in managing methadone maintenance patients. Int J Addict, 13: 689–694.

Wang, W., Darwin, W., and Cone, E. (1994). Simultaneous assay of cocaine, heroin and metabolites in hair, plasma, saliva and urine by gas chromatography-mass spectrometry. J Chromatog B, Biomed Appl

Westerling, D., Lindahl, S., Andersson, K. et al. (1982). Absorption and bioavailability of rectally administered morphine in women. Eur J Clin Pharm, 23: 59–64.

Whitcomb, D., Gilliam III, F., Starmer, C., and Grant, A. (1989). Marked QRS complex abnormalities and sodium channel blockade by propoxyphene reversed with lidocaine. J. Clin Invest, 84: 1629–1636.

Wolff, K. and Hay, A. (1991). Methadone in saliva. Clin Chem, 37(7): 1297–1298.

Wolff, K., Hay, A., Raistrick, D. et al. (1991). Measuring compliance in methadone maintenance patients: use of a pharmacologic indicator to estimate methadone plasma levels. Clin Pharm Ther, 50: 199–207.

Wolff, K., Hay, A., and Raistrick, D. (1992). Plasma methadone measurements and their role in methadone detoxification programs. Clin Chem, 38: 420–425.

Wolff, K. and Hay, A. (1994). Plasma methadone monitoring with methadone maintenance treatment. Drug Alcohol Depend, 36: 69–71.

Wolff, K., Hay, A., Raistrick, D. et al. (1993). Steady-state pharmacokinetics of methadone in opioid addicts. Eur J Clin Pharm, 44: 189–194.

World Health Organization (1990). *Fentanyl analogs. Information manual on designer drugs.* Geneva: World Health Organization.

Worm, K. and Kringsholm, B. (1993). Methadone and drug addicts. Int J Leg Med, 106: 119–123.

Yonemitsu, K. and Pounder, D. (1992). Postmortem toxico-kinetics of co-proximol. Int J Leg Med, 104: 347–353.

Young, R. (1983). Dextropropoxyphene overdosage: pharmacological considerations and clinical management. Drugs, 26: 70–79.

Yue, Q., Svensson, J., Alm, C. et al. (1989). Codeine O-demethylation co-segregates with polymorphic debrisoquine hydroxylation. Br J Clin Pharm, 28: 639–645.

Yue, Q., Hasselström, J., Sevensson, J., and Säwe, J. (1991). Pharmacokinetics of codeine and its metabolites in Caucasian healthy volunteers: comparisons between extensive and poor hydroxylators of debrisoquine. Br J Clin Pharm, 31: 635–642.

Yue, Q., Svensson, J., Sjöqvist, F., and Säwe, J. (1991). A comparison of the pharma-
    cokinetics of codeine and its metabolites in healthy Chinese and Caucasian
    extensive hydroxylators of debrisoquine. Br J Clin Pharm, 31: 643–647.
Zhou, H., Sheller, J., Nu, H. et al. (1993) Ethnic differences in response to morphine.
    Clin Pharm Ther, 54: 507–513.

5.5   Interpreting tissue and blood levels

5.5.1   Introduction

Whenever there is an investigation of a drug-related death or injury, two
important questions arise: How much drug was present, and was it responsible for the outcome? Toxicology testing can answer the first question, but
not the second. Whether or not a specific blood level caused death, morbidity,
or even significant impairment depends not only on the findings at autopsy,
but also on what is observed at the scene, and on the individual's past
medical and drug history (Stafford et al., 1983; Harding-Pink and Frye, 1991).
In poisoning cases, information may be available from many sources, including the emergency room, and the physicians who attended the patient in the
past. Valuable historical information is almost always available, and in some
cases, such historical sources can provide information not obtained at
autopsy. This is especially true in cases of advanced decomposition, and
where the individual is HIV seropositive (Harding-Pink and Frye, 1991).

There are other situations where only the first question is at issue. Workplace drug testing is done only to determine whether or not a certain drug
is present; whether impairment and disability are present is irrelevant.
Answering the first question can be more complex than it appears, because
chemical testing does not always yield unequivocal results.

5.5.2   Clinical profile of opiate abusers

More often than not, postmortem examinations of opiate users are unrevealing. Anatomic findings are often non-specific and may be entirely absent.
Toxicology findings may not be particularly helpful either. There is no way
to assess tolerance after death, so even high total morphine blood levels do
not conclusively establish morphine as the cause of death. A thorough clinical history and scene investigation may be more revealing than any autopsy
finding. The clinical history is particularly important. Opiate tolerance rapidly disappears; addicts recently released from jail are at particular risk
(Harding-Pink and Fryc, 1988).

Heroin abusers share certain characteristic features. Particulars may vary
from location to location, but in each locale a fairly typical profile emerges.
If the death is thought to be opiate related, the profile of the deceased should
not be totally at odds with the expected profile for the area. In San Francisco,
the median age of autopsied heroin abusers is 38 years (±8), and the victims
are overwhelmingly male (5:1). In spite of San Francisco's large Asian population, victims in drug-related deaths, both heroin and cocaine, are predominantly white (75%). More than one-third of the deceased are found in tran-

sient's hotels, usually in bed. Drug paraphernalia are found at the scene at least 40% of the time, and at least 40% of the victims have one or more tattoos (unpublished data, San Francisco Medical Examiners Office).

The picture applies to heroin abusers only, and then only in a particular locale. As documented in the most recent DAWN report, drug use characteristics vary widely from city to city. In Norfolk, Virginia, for example, women accounted for more than half of the drug-related deaths. In Europe, heroin-related deaths tend to occur in much younger individuals (Penning et al., 1993; Keul et al., 1993). In San Francisco, deaths in men outnumbered deaths in women by nearly five to one (Substance Abuse and Mental Health Services Administration, 1995). The type of drug is also important. In Munich, heroin is most often the culprit in drug-related deaths (Penning et al., 1993), but in most areas of the United States cocaine-related deaths are still more common than those due to heroin. Fentanyl-related deaths, for example, are more likely to occur in private homes. Deaths due to fentanyl are more likely in employed individuals, who are less likely to be tattooed (Henderson, 1991).

On occasion, the clinical profile of the deceased may reveal more about the manner of death than any findings at autopsy, especially if the clinical profile of the deceased is greatly at variance with the normally expected pattern for the area. Deaths due to polypharmacy, where opiates constitute only one component, may present a confusing picture, but there is often a history of psychiatric disorder.

5.5.3 Testing urine

The procedures followed for drug testing in the workplace are somewhat different from those followed by the medical examiner. If the testing is done under Federal rules, screening for opiates must be done with a test that can differentiate specimens that contain more than 300 ng/mL from those that do not. Because the body metabolizes codeine to morphine, both can appear in the urine at the same time. It then becomes a question of determining whether the origin of the drug was licit or illicit. The most widely used screening tests (TDx® Opiates, Abuscreen® Radioimmunoassay for Morphine, and Emit®-d.a.u.) all cross-react with other opiates besides morphine, but the Coat-A-Count® for Morphine in Urine is highly selective for free morphine (Cone et al., 1992).

The accurate interpretation of urine opiate testing results usually requires quantitation of the amount of codeine and morphine present. Poppy seed ingestion ensures the presence of both codeine and morphine in the urine. A prescription for codeine could explain the presence of some, but not massive amounts of, morphine in the urine. After oral dosing with codeine, 5–15%, and possibly more, will be excreted in the urine as free or conjugated morphine (Moffat et al., 1986; Gjerde and Morland, 1991). It has been suggested that, when GC-MS analysis shows: (1) a morphine concentration greater than 5,000 ng, and codeine concentrations in excess of 300 ng/mL; or (2) morphine-to-codeine ratios of less than 2; or (3) 6-acetyl morphine is detected, then the findings are the result of heroin ingestion (ElSohly and Jones, 1989). However, many experts feel that measuring ratios is an unreliable way to determine which drug was used.

Heroin use can explain the presence of both morphine and codeine in the urine, because heroin is rapidly converted to morphine and because heroin is often contaminated with small amounts of codeine (Yong and Lik, 1977). The evidence is convincing that in humans, morphine is not metabolized to codeine (Mitchell et al., 1991). The best way to prove heroin use is to detect 6-acetyl morphine, but the half-life of this compound is so short that this option is rarely available. Even without being able to detect 6-acetyl morphine, heroin use will result in substantial levels of morphine that, even allowing for a 300-ng/mL cutoff, will be detectable for several days.

Codeine-containing cough syrups (one syrup sold in Japan and Southeast Asia is responsible for a large percentage of positive tests at the Army's testing lab in Hawaii), and poppyseed-containing pastries, both cause positive urine tests for opiates. Poppy seeds contain both morphine and codeine, and very high levels can be seen if substantial amounts (several teaspoons) are eaten (ElSohly et al., 1990; Ketchum et al., 1990; Selavka, 1991). Things become a bit confusing if the tested individual has a prescription for codeine and also claims to have eaten poppy seeds. In that case his urine might well have more morphine than codeine in it, even if he were not abusing drugs!

The general characteristics of the commercial opiate assays are such that semisynthetic opiates are unlikely to be detected. The EMIT® test for morphine, for instance, cross-reacts well with codeine, but hardly at all with oxymorphone or oxycodone. The Roche Abuscreen® test cross-reacts with codeine, but not with 6-acetyl morphine, hydromorphine, hydrocodone, oxymorphone, or oxydocodone (Mitchell et al., 1991). Since none of these latter compounds are metabolized to codeine or morphine, they will not be detected on routine urine screens, and, even if they were, they could not be reported out under current Substance Abuse and Mental Health Administration testing guidelines (which only permit the reporting of morphine or codeine).

5.5.4   Testing blood

Opiate abusers become tolerant of the opiate's respiratory depressant effects. The fact that tolerance occurs makes interpretation of blood levels difficult. In cases of acute overdose, where death is obviously due to respiratory depression or pulmonary edema, blood levels have ranged anywhere from 100 to 2,800 ng/mL (Felby et al., 1974; Richards et al., 1976; Reed et al., 1977; Moffat et al., 1986; Logan et al., 1987; Sawyer et al., 1988; Steentoft et al., 1988; Kintz et al., 1989). All of these reported values were measured before it was appreciated that morphine-6-glucuronide was as metabolically active as morphine itself. Thus the range of reported values in these cases is very broad, and probably not very accurate. The same value may be associated with death in one individual and minimal symptoms in another. Even though fatalities have often been associated with codeine levels of over 500 ng/mL, a recent case report describes a man arrested for erratic driving who was found to have a codeine level of 8,600 ng/mL! Final determinations as to the mode and manner of death cannot be made on the basis of toxicological data alone.

5.5.5   Interpreting test results

Even in cases where the results of testing appear to be straight-forward, the results must not be considered in isolation. Examination of the death scene may reveal findings that can confirm or cast doubt on the toxicology results. Helpern was one of the first to point out that there was a sameness about heroin-related deaths. More often than not the heroin user is found on the street, or in an alley, injecting himself and dying in isolation (Helpern, 1972). His paraphernalia is likely to be at his side and, in some instances, the needle may still be in his arm. More than three-quarters of the victims are males, mostly in their mid-twenties (Louria et al., 1967; Cherubin, 1967; Froede and Stahl, 1971; Wetli, Davis, and Blackbourne, 1972). Under such circumstances, if the blood morphine level were found to be quite low, then an examiner would be justified in wondering if heroin overdose were really the cause of death. Conversely, if a well-dressed, middle-aged woman was found dead in a doorway, with no injection apparatus, but with high levels of morphine, then the examiner would, again, be justified in wondering if opiate overdose was all that was going on.

The situation is quite different in fentanyl-related deaths where the victim is usually found at home, in his bedroom (Henderson, 1991). The individual is still most likely to be a man, but the average age at death is 32.5 years, older than in heroin users who tend to be in their mid-twenties and tend not to die in their own home, or the home of a friend or relative. Heroin-related deaths are much more likely to occur on the streets. Nearly one-third of fentanyl deaths occur in employed individuals, many of them professionals, while heroin-related deaths are more frequent in the unskilled and the unemployed. The probability of finding drug paraphernalia is about the same (>60%) in both fentanyl and heroin-related deaths. In both cases, if there are other individuals present at the time of death, it is likely they will make every effort to remove any evidence of illicit drug use.

Historical information is also important because deaths in opiate abusers are more likely to occur when they have been abstinent for some time. It is important to establish whether the individual has just been released from jail or a detoxification program (Harding-Pink and Fryc, 1988). Another important historical finding is whether or not the individual used alcohol. This combination is notoriously lethal, but the mechanism is unexplained. In Ruttenber's large series of 505 heroin-related deaths, those who had not been drinking had higher morphine levels in their blood and bile (500 ng/mL and 7,500 ng/mL) than those individuals who had been drinking (levels of 300 ng/mL and 3,000 ng/mL). These findings suggest that opiate abusers who also use alcohol are occasional users, with lower levels of tolerance, placing them at greater risk for overdose (Ruttenber et al., 1990).

The findings at autopsy may or may not be helpful in opiate-related deaths. If the lungs are frothy, weigh 2,000 grams, and the morphine blood level is 1,000 ng/mL, then the diagnosis is obvious. But pulmonary edema is not present in every case of heroin overdose, blood levels much lower than 1,000 ng/mL can cause respiratory depression, and there may be no cutaneous stigmata (Kintz et al., 1989). Indeed, death from narcotism has been diagnosed in cases where the blood morphine level was zero (Richards, Reed, and Cravey, 1976). Furthermore, even if there were some known, dependable, relationship between a given morphine blood level and a specific effect, levels measured at autopsy probably do not correspond to levels measured in life. Morphine levels may even vary depending on the location in the body from which the blood sample is obtained. That certainly is the case in cocaine-related deaths (Hearn et al., 1991). There is evidence from animal studies that significant increases in blood morphine can be detected within minutes of death, and continue for days afterwards (Sawyer and Forney, 1988).

The results of toxicological testing cannot be considered in isolation. Other than the fact that the drug was taken, not much else can be inferred from a single blood level. The notion that the likelihood of death can be determined by consulting a reference table, if it was ever valid, certainly is no longer so. Quantitative measurement of drugs at autopsy is only of value when the results are combined with evidence obtained by thoroughly examining the death scene, reviewing the deceased's history, and examining the body. The final diagnosis depends on appropriately weighing all these factors. In 1972, Helpern wrote that "a diagnosis of an acute death from narcotic addiction is more reliably arrived at from the investigation of the circumstances under which the body is found and the findings of the complete postmortem examination than from the toxicologic analysis, which has proved revealing in less than half the cases." The passage of twenty years has produced no evidence to contradict Helpern's original impression.

References

Cherubin, C. (1967). The medical sequelae of narcotic addiction. Ann Intern Med, 67: 23–33.

Cone, E., Dickerson, S., Paul, B., and Mitchell, J. (1992). Forensic drug testing for opiates. IV. Analytical sensitivity, specificity, and accuracy of commercial urine opiate immunoassays. J Analyt Toxicol, 16: 72–78.

ElSohly, H., ElSohly, M., and Stanford, D. (1990). Poppy seed ingestion and opiates urinalysis: a closer look. J Analyt Toxicol, 14(September/October): 308–310.

Felby, S., Christensen, H., and Lund, A. (1974). Morphine concentrations in blood and organs in cases of fatal poisoning. Forensic Sci, 3: 77–81.

Froede, R. and Stahl, C. (1971). Fatal narcotism in military personnel. J Forensic Sci, 16(2): 199–218.

Gjerde, H. and Morland, J. (1991). A case of high opiate tolerance: implications for drug analyses and interpretations. Int J Leg Med, 104(4): 239–240.

Harding-Pink, D. and Fryc, O. (1988). Risk of death after release from prison: a duty to warn. Br Med J, 297: 596.

Harding-Pink, D. and Fryc, O. (1991). Assessing death by poisoning: does the medical history help? Med Sci Law, 31: 69–75.

Hearn, W., Keran, E., Wei, H., and Hime, G. (1991). Site-dependent postmortem changes in blood cocaine concentrations. J Forensic Sci, 36(3): 673–684.

Helpern, M. (1972). Fatalities from narcotic addiction in New York City. Incidence, circumstances, and pathologic findings. Hum Pathol, 3(1): 13–21.

Henderson, G. (1991). Fentanyl-related deaths: demographics, circumstances, and toxicology of 112 cases. J Forensic Sci, 2: 422–433.

Ketchum, C., Stabler, T., Upton, K., and Robinson, C. (1990). Positivity rate of urine opiate tests following ingestion of poppy seeds. Clin Chem, 36(6): 1026.

Keul, H., Schäfer, V., Lörcher, U. et al. (1993). Preliminary results of an interdisciplinary survey of drug victims. Forensic Sci Int, 62: 147–149.

Kintz, P., Mangin, P., Lugnier, A., and Chaumont, A. (1989). Toxicological data after heroin overdose. Hum Toxicol, 8: 487–489.

Logan, B., Oliver, J., and Smith, H. (1987). The measurement and interpretation of morphine in blood. Forensic Sci Int, 35: 189–195.

Louria, D., Hensle, T., and Rose, J. (1967). The major medical complications of heroin addiction. Ann Int Med, 67: 1–22.

Mitchell, J., Paul, B., Welch, P., and Cone, E. (1991). Forensic drug testing for opiates. II. Metabolism and excretion rate of morphine in humans after morphine administration. J Analyt Toxicol, 15: 49–53.

Moffat, A., Jackson, J., Moss, M., and Widdop, B. (1986). *Clarke's isolation and identification of drugs in pharmaceuticals, body fluids, and postmortem material.* London: The Pharmaceutical Press.

Penning, R., Fromm, E., Betz, P. et al. (1993). Drug death autopsies at the Munich Institute of Forensic Medicine (1981–1992). Forensic Sci Int, 62: 135–139.

Reed, D., Spiehler, V., and Cravey, R. (1977). Two cases of heroin-related suicide. Forensic Sci, 9(1): 49–52.

Richards, R., Reed, D., and Cravey, R. (1976). Death from intravenously administered narcotics: A study of 114 cases. J Forensic Sci, 21: 467–482.

Ruttenber, A., Kalter, H., and Santinga, P. (1990). The role of ethanol abuse in the etiology of heroin-related death. J Forensic Sci, 35: 891–900.

Sawyer, W. and Forney, R. (1988). Postmortem disposition of morphine in rats. Forensic Sci Int, 38: 259–273.

Sawyer, W., Waterhouse, G., Doedens, D., and Forney, R. (1988). Heroin, morphine, and hydromorphone determination in postmortem by high performance liquid chromatography. J Forensic Sci, 33: 1146–1155.

Selavka, C. (1991). Poppy seed ingestion as a contributing factor to opiate-positive urinalysis results: the Pacific perspective. J Forensic Sci, 36(3): 685–696.

Stafford, D., Prouty, R., and Anderson, W. (1983). Current conundrums facing forensic pathologists and toxicologists. Am J Forensic Med Pathol, 4: 103–104.

Steentoft, A., Worm, K., and Christensen, H. (1988). Morphine concentrations in autopsy material from fatal cases after intake of morphine and/or heroin. J Forensic Sci, 28: 87–94.

Substance Abuse and Mental Health Administration. (1995). Annual Medical Examiner Data. Data from the Drug Abuse Warning Network. Rockville, MD, U.S. Department of Health and Human Services.

Wetli, C., Davis, J., and Blackbourne, B. (1972). Narcotic addiction in Dade County, Florida — an analysis of 100 consecutive autopsies. Arch Pathol, 93: 330–343.

Yong, L. and Lik, N. (1977). The human urinary excretion pattern of morphine and
    codeine following the consumption of morphine, opium, codeine and heroin.
    Bull Narc, 29: 45–74.

5.6   Dermatologic sequelae of opiate abuse

There are dermatologic sequelae associated with all types of intravenous
drug abuse, but skin lesions are more common in opiate, than in stimulant,
abusers. This is somewhat surprising, because stimulant abusers inject much
more frequently than do opiate abusers. Some of the difference has to do
with the properties of the drugs themselves. Stimulants, for instance, do not
cause histamine release and therefore they seldom are associated with pruritus or excoriations. For the most part, the higher incidence of cutaneous
complications seen in intravenous opiate abusers can be explained by the
adulterants and expients injected along with the opiates.

5.6.1   Fresh puncture sites

Recent injection sites are usually present, although in sophisticated users
these marks may be difficult to find. While not quite as dramatic as finding
a needle still in the user's arm, the presence of dried blood on the surface
of the skin surrounding a puncture is considered almost equally strong
evidence that sudden death occurred following an injection (Hirsch, 1972).
The antecubital fossa is the most common location, but punctures may be
detected at the wrist, under a watch band, or between the toes. The presence
of injection tracks may be confirmed by making a skin incision immediately
adjacent to the suspected site. This will reveal the presence of small subcutaneous hemorrhages that occur after venipuncture (Helpern, 1972). Alternatively, a single longitudinal incision can be made on the flexor surface of
the arm from midbiceps to distal forearm, and the subcutaneous tissues
exposed by either blunt or sharp dissection (Hirsch, 1972). Subcutaneous
hemorrhage will not be evident in every case, but chemical analysis of tissue
around the needle track often yields evidence of the drug injected. As the
practice of "snorting" becomes more popular (it appears that fear of AIDS
has sparked increased interest in this route), the situation may well arise
where there are no track marks to be seen. If there is even the remotest
suspicion that a narcotic was used, the nasal cavity should be examined and
then swabbed with saline for toxicology testing.

5.6.2   Atrophic scarring

Novice abusers, and the occasional experienced abuser who cannot find a
vein, will inject subcutaneously, usually on the flexor aspect of the arm.
Absorption of heroin is fairly good by this route, but the deposition of
expients in the subcutaneous tissue eventually leads to the development of
oval or irregularly shaped lesions that may measure 1–3 cm. These lesions
are slightly depressed and often hyperpigmented. Most of these lesions are

located at the site of healed abscesses, but they may be produced without preceding abscess formation. These lesions have been recognized for more than a half century, but the dermatopathology remains poorly characterized and the etiology unclear. Early workers suggested that they were a direct result of heroin's effect on the skin (Light and Torrance, 1929), but adulterants or infectious agents are just as likely to be the cause. It may be the pH of the solution, rather than the drug itself, that determines whether tissue injury occurs (Pollard, 1973). Microscopic examination of healed atrophic lesions usually reveals subcutaneous fibrosis. Foreign body granulomas may or may not be present, but birefringent material, such as talc or starch crystals, is likely to be seen (Hirsch, 1972).

5.6.3 Abscess and ulcerations

Abscesses are common and result from infection at the injection site (Orangio et al., 1984; Webb and Thadepalli, 1979; Minkin and Cohen, 1967). Lesions are found mostly on the extensor surfaces and lateral aspects of the arms and hands, but they may also be seen almost anywhere on the body. Injection into the subclavian area and the femoral triangle can lead to life-threatening infections (Pace et al., 1984). Similar complications occur after injection into the intercostal vessels (Gyrtrup, 1989). Active ulcers have a punched-out configuration and indurated borders surrounding a floor of granulation tissue. There is nothing to distinguish the appearance of injection site abscesses from any other sort of soft tissue abscess. In the past, the organisms most commonly encountered were various species of *staphylococci* and *streptococci* (Sapira, 1968), but many different gram-negative organisms have also been cultured and polymicrobial infections are not uncommon (Webb and Thadepalli, 1979). In the most recent study, which is more than 10 years out of date, *Staphylococcus aureus* and beta-hemolytic *streptococci* were found to be the most common cause of soft tissue infections in parenteral drug abusers, but enteric gram negative aerobes and oral flora were also common (Orangio et al., 1984).

Most of the material injected is adulterant. Depending on the part of the country, an assortment of different chemicals may be used to "cut" the heroin. Commonly encountered agents include lactose, mannitol, procaine, and quinine. These compounds predominate, but substances such as methaqualone, caffeine, and phenobarbitone (Oneil and Pitts 1992) (see Tables 5.3.2.1 and 5.3.2.2) can also be encountered. Most of the compounds added to adulterate heroin are not very soluble in water. When these insoluble materials extravasate out into the area surrounding an injection site, foreign-body reactions occur. Even if the material does not extravasate, repeated injections can lead to the formation of needle "tracks" (see Section 5.7.4).

5.6.4 "Track" marks

This lesion was first described in 1929. It was observed in a heroin addict who had contracted malaria from intravenous injections (Biggam, 1929). The author who first described them thought that the lesions resembled railroad tracks. Lesions are linear, indurated, and hyperpigmented. What the tracks will look like, and how rapidly they will form, depends on what is being injected. The expients found in illicit cocaine and methamphetamine are usually water soluble, so "track" marks are an uncommon finding in this group of abusers (Wetli, 1987). Paregoric, on the other hand, causes an intense sclerotic reaction, and when paregoric injecting was popular in the 1960s, addicts ran out of peripheral veins so quickly they resorted to injecting themselves in the neck and groin (Lerner and Oerther, 1966). Heroin, even in its adulterated form, is less sclerotoxic than paregoric, but prolonged use will eventually cause thickening and sclerosis of the subcutaneous veins.

The skin overlying the affected veins becomes hyperpigmented, probably as a result of the underlying chronic inflammatory process (Vollum, 1970). The degree of hyperpigmentation depends largely on the individual's coloration, and not necessarily on how long the addict has been injecting himself. Discoloration of the area can also be the result of inadvertent tattooing. Addicts may try to sterilize their needles with a match flame. This causes small amounts of soot to be deposited on the outside of the needle, and this soot is carried into the skin at the time of injection. Addicts have traditionally tried to conceal these marks by tattooing, or even by burning themselves in the hopes of scarring the whole area.

The histologic appearance of sclerotic veins varies (Schoster and Lewis, 1968). There may be only fibrous thickening of the vein wall, consistent with a low-grade, chronic inflammatory process. In other instances, thrombophlebitis, sterile or septic, may occur. The results are hard to predict. Helpern even commented that on occasion the veins repeatedly used by addicts "show less evidence of closure by thrombosis than the veins of patients subjected to repeated punctures by physicians for medical purposes" (Helpern, 1972).

5.6.5   Tattoos

Tattoos are sometimes used to conceal the scars and track marks associated with intravenous drug abuse, though that hardly explains the frequency of this finding in addict subpopulations. The practice derives its name from the Tahitian word "tatau" which means "the results of tapping," the process in which tattoos were applied. The practice dates back to antiquity. Tattoos have been found on Egyptian mummies from the Eleventh Dynasty, making the practice at least 4,000 years old (Sperry, 1991). Tattoos are applied in jail using the "melted-toothbrush" technique. Any pointed object, such as a bedspring or matchbook staple, can be used as a needle. The end of a plastic toothbrush is then melted in a flame and the smoky residue collected. The residue is mixed with soap and water to form an ink (Martinez and Wetli, 1989).

Chronic abusers sometimes apply tattoos in order to obscure old track marks, but most of the time tattoos are applied for other reasons, usually while the individual is in jail. In the past, much significance was attributed to the design and location of tattoos. Symbols on the thumb webbing were popularly said to indicate criminal specialties. The results of more recent studies suggest that hand-web tattoos probably have significance only in the prison where they are applied (Martinez and Wetli, 1989). In some specific subpopulations, such as the Marielitos, tattoos may represent religious symbols or themes, but these interpretations are not generalizable to other subgroups.

5.6.6 "Puffy" hands

Lymphedema is sometimes seen in chronic users. The condition was first described in the 1960s. Both hands become smooth and slightly edematous with obliteration of the normal anatomic landmarks. Pitting edema is absent. In contrast to the changes seen in the hands of myxedematous patients, the skin in addicts with "puffy" hands is thin and smooth. The skin on the volar aspect of the forearm will be normal, even though evidence of repeated injections can be seen in both antecubital fossa (Abeles, 1965; Ritland and Butterfield, 1973).

5.6.7 Necrotizing fascitis

Necrotizing fascitis was first described over 120 years ago. As commonly used, the term refers to a severe infection of the superficial fascia and subcutaneous tissue. At least initially, the infection does not involve the overlying skin (Wojno and Spitz, 1989). There have been no controlled studies, but it has been suggested that this disorder may be more prevalent in cocaine users (Webb and Thadepalli, 1979; Wetli, 1987; Sperry and McFeely, 1987). In the absence of drug abuse, necrotizing fascitis is usually seen in diabetics, or patients with severe atherosclerosis, but the infectious process can be initiated by surgery, or even minor trauma. Individuals taking non-steroidal anti-inflammatory drugs are said to be at increased risk (Rimailho, 1987).

Once infection becomes established, necrosis rapidly spreads through fascia and subcutaneous tissues. The overlying skin looks normal until very late in the course of the disease, and the underlying muscle is usually not involved either (Tehrani and Ledingham, 1977). Hematogenous seeding may occur, involving organs throughout the body. Even purulent myocarditis has been reported as a complication. The fact that the overlying skin looks normal may delay the diagnosis and lead to a fatal outcome (Wojno and Spitz, 1989). At first it was thought that gram positive aerobes were the causative agent, but in more recently reported cases, the etiology was polymicrobial. In the two heroin users described by Webb the causative organisms were *Enterobacter* and *Proteus*.

5.6.8 Histamine-related urticaria

Skin excoriations are common, but it is not clear if the skin excoriations are the result of narcotic-induced pruritus or psychologic disorder (Young and

Rosenberg, 1971). Histamine release in narcotic abusers is not a true, IgE mediated, allergic response (Hermens et al., 1985; Paton, 1957). Opiates act, in some undetermined fashion, directly on mast cells to produce histamine release. The amount of histamine released depends on the dose of opiate administered. In one series more than 20% of the patients receiving post operative opiates developed urticaria (Withington et al., 1993). In some instances, the amount of histamine liberated can be large enough to cause hypotension in addition to erythema and tachycardia. Not all narcotics are associated with histamine release. Substantial elevations in plasma histamine can be seen after dosing with intravenous morphine and meperidine, and diacetylmorphine (heroin) but not after treatment with fentanyl or sufentanil (Flacke et al., 1987; Withington et al., 1993).

5.6.9   Fungal lesions

Candida infections of the mouth, esophagus, upper airway, and lungs are recognized as "indicator" diseases for AIDS. The prevalence of oral thrush in AIDS patients is 40–90%. The prevalence of esophageal involvement is much lower, only 4–14% (Redfield et al., 1986; Tavitian et al., 1986). As a rule, in AIDS patients *C. albicans* infections are limited to the mucosa. Disseminated disease does not occur in AIDS patients unless they are also heroin addicts or have some other similar risk factor (steroid therapy, indwelling catheters, severe granulocytopenia) (Drouhet and Dupont, 1991).

Candida-related febrile septicemia with cutaneous involvement is a disorder that is confined to heroin addicts. The syndrome was first encountered in 1981 when a cluster of cases occurred in Paris (Drouhet et al., 1981). Subsequently, hundreds of additional cases were reported across Europe and Australia, though only sporadic cases have been reported in the United States (Yap et al., 1981). Epidemiologists eventually linked the outbreak to the use of poorly soluble heroin which had been exported from Iran ("brown" heroin). This particular variety of heroin was poorly soluble and could not be dissolved for injection unless users acidified the mixture by adding lemon juice or some other acidifying agent (Mellinger et al., 1982). Researchers found that even bottled lemon juice could be contaminated with *C. Albicans* found on the addicts' skin (Bisbe et al., 1992). A significant majority of the cases have been due to a single strain of *Candida* (serotype A, biotype 153/7) (Shankland and Richardson, 1988). Hundreds of cases have now been reported. Subcutaneous lesions have been noted in 75–100%, of the cases, occular involvement in approximately 60%, and osteoarticular involvement in 20–50% of the cases (Dupont and Drouhet, 1985; Bisbe et al., 1992).

In a typical case, symptoms occur within 2–24 hours after the last heroin injection. Chills, fever, headache, and profuse diaphoresis quickly follow. Within one to three days, patients develop disseminated folliculitis and scalp nodules. Any hair-bearing area may be involved, but the scalp is the most common site (Dupont and Drouhet, 1985). Painful cutaneous nodules, usually measuring less than 1 cm, erupt quite suddenly. As many as 100 of these nodules may be present, and it is said that the scalps of these individuals feel like "a sack of marbles." Smaller pustules may be seen adjacent to the nodules. The pustules strongly resemble lesions produced by staphylococcal or streptococcal infection, but microscopic examination discloses yeast and filaments of *C. albicans*. Biopsy of the follicular nodules is more likely to be diagnostic than blood cultures. Gomori-methenamine-silver staining will reveal bifurcated filaments of *C. albicans* mixed with an intense, mixed inflammatory infiltrate (Drouhet and Dupont, 1991).

Since the initial reports were first published, others have appeared describing the same syndrome after injecting methadone-containing syrup diluted with orange juice (Scheidegger et al., 1993), and after injecting buprenorphine tablets diluted in lemon juice (Scheidegger and Frei, 1989), and even in intravenous methamphetamine abusers (Mohri et al., 1991).

5.6.10 Miscellaneous cutaneous abnormalities

Other skin disorders are occasionally seen, but none with sufficient frequency to be of any diagnostic value. Sapira described a rosette of cigarette burns around the neck. After self-injecting with opiate, the abuser may fall asleep with a cigarette in his mouth, and burn his anterior chest when his head falls forward (Sapira, 1968). Other lesions reflect usage patterns that were unique to a specific time and place and are as much historical curiosities as anything else. In the late 1800s, when opium smoking was still popular, the presence of cauliflower ears (swelling of the auricles) was considered almost pathognomonic for opium use. They were the result of lying for long periods on opium beds with hard wooden pillows (Owens and Humphries, 1988).

References

Abeles, H. (1965). The puffy-hand sign of drug addiction. N Engl J Med, 273: 1167.

Biggam, A. (1929). Malignant malaria associated with administration of heroin intravenously. Trans Royal Soc Trop Med and Hyg, 23(2): 147–153.

Bisbe, J., Miro, J., Latorre, X. et al. (1992). Disseminated candidiasis in addicts who use brown heroin: report of 83 cases and review. Clin Infect Dis, 15: 910–923.

Clemons, K., Shankland, G., Richardson, M., and Stevens, D. (1991). Epidemiologic study by DNA typing of a candida-albicans outbreak in heroin addicts. J Clin Microbiol, 29: 205–207.

Drouhet, E., Dupont, B., Lapressle, C. et al. (1981). Nouvelle pathologie: candidose folliculaire et nodulaire avec des localisations osteo-articulaires et oculaires au cours des septicemies a Candida albicans chez les heroinomanes. Bull de la Société Francaise de Mycologie Med, 10: 179–183.

Drouhet, E. and Dupont, B. (1991). Candidasis in heroin addicts and AIDS — new immunologic data on chronic mucocutaneous candidosis. Candida and Candidamycosis, 50: 61–72.

Dupont, B. and Drouhet, E. (1985). Cutaneous, ocular, and osteoarticular candidasis in heroin addicts: new clinical and therapeutic aspects in 38 patients. J Infect Dis, 152: 577–591.

Flacke, J., Flacke, W., Bloor, B. et al. (1987). Histamine release by four narcotics: a double blind study in humans. Anesth Analg, 66: 723–730.

Frank, R. (1987). Drugs of abuse: data collection systems of DEA and recent trends. J Analyt Toxicol, 11: 237–241.

Gyrtrup, H. (1989). Fixing into intercostal vessels: a new method among drug addicts. Br J Addict, 84: 945–946.

Helpern, M. (1972). Fatalities from narcotic addiction in New York City. Incidence, circumstances, and pathologic findings. Hum Pathol, 3(1): 13–20.

Hermens, J., Ebertz, J., Hanifin, J., and Hirshman, C. (1985). Comparison of histamine release in human skin mast cells induced by morphine, fentanyl, and oxymorphone. Anesthesiology, 62: 124–129.

Hirsch, C. (1972). Dermatopathology of narcotic addiction. Hum Pathol, 3(1): 37–53.

Lerner, A. and Oerther, F. (1966). Characteristics and sequelae of paregoric abuse. Ann Intern Med, 65: 1019–1030.

Light, A. and Torrance, E. (1929). Opium addiction — physical characteristics and physical fitness of addicts during administration of morphine. Arch Intern Med, 43: 326–334.

Martinez, R. and Wetli, C. (1989). Tattoos of the Marielitos. Am J Forensic Med and Pathol, 10(4): 315–325.

Mellinger, M., DeBeauchamp, O., Gallen, C. et al. (1982). Epidemiological and clinical approach to the study of candidiasis caused by *Candida albicans* in heroin addicts in the Paris region: analysis of 35 observations. Bull Narc, 34: 61–81.

Minkin, W. and Cohen, H. (1967). Dermatologic complications of heroin addiction. Report of a new complication. N Engl J Med, 277: 473–475.

Mohri, S., Naito, S., and Nakajima, H. (1991). Immunohistochemically-proved endothrix *Candida* growth in folliculitis barbae candidomyceta in a methamphetamine addicted patient. J Mycologie Med, 1(4): 296–299.

O'neil, P. and Pitts, J. (1992). Illicitly imported heroin products (1984 to 1989) — some physical and chemical features indicative of their origin. J Pharm Pharmacol, 44(1): 1–6.

Orangio, G., Pitlick, S., Latta, P. et al. (1984). Soft tissue infections in parenteral drug abusers. Ann Surg, 199: 97–100.

Owens, D. and Humphries, M. (1988). Cauliflower ears, opium, and Errol Flynn. Br Med J, 297: 643–644.

Pace, B., Doscher, W., and Margolis, I. (1984). The femoral triangle — a potential death trap for the drug abuser. NY State J Med, 84: 596–598.

Paton, W. (1957). Histamine release by compounds of simple chemical structure. Pharmacol Rev, 9: 269–328.

Pollard, R. (1973). Surgical implications of some types of drug dependence. Br Med J, 1: 784–787.

Redfield, R., Wright, D., and Tramont, E. (1986). Walter Reed staging classification for HTLV-III/LAV infection. N Engl J Med, 314: 131–132.

Rimailho, A. (1987). Fulminant necrotizing fasciitis and nonsteroidal anti-inflammatory drugs. J Infect Dis, 155: 143–146.

Ritland, D. and Butterfield, W. (1973). Extremity complications of drug abuse. Am J Surg, 126: 639–648.

Sapira, J. (1968). The narcotic addict as a medical patient. Am J Med, 45: 555–588.

Scheidegger, C. and Frei, R. (1989). Disseminated candidasis in a drug addict not using heroin. J Infect Dis, 159: 1007–1008.

Scheidegger, C., Pietrzak, J., and Frei, R. (1993). Methadone diluted with contaminated orange juice or raspberry syrup as a potential source of disseminated candidiasis in drug users. Eur J Clin Microbiol Infect Dis, 12: 229–231.

Shuster, M. and Lewis, M. (1968). Needle tracks in narcotic addicts. NY State J Med, 68: 3129–3134.

Sperry, K. and McFeely, P. (1987). Medicolegal aspects of necrotizing fascitis of the neck. J Forensic Sci, 32: 273–281.

Sperry, K. (1991). Tattoos and tattooing. Am J Forensic Med and Pathol, 12(4): 313–319.

Tavitian, A., Raufman, J., and Rosenthal, L. (1986). Oral candidasis as a marker for esophageal candidasis in the Acquired Immunodeficiency Syndrome. Ann Intern Med, 104: 54–55.

Tehrani, M. and Ledingham, I. (1977). Necrotizing fascitis. Postgrad Med J, 53: 237–242.

Vollum, D. (1970). Skin lesions in drug addicts. Br Med J, 2: 647–650.

Webb, D. and Thadepalli, H. (1979). Skin and soft tissue polymicrobial infections from intravenous abuse of drugs. West J Med, 130: 200–204.

Wetli, C. (1987). Fatal reactions to cocaine. *Cocaine: a clinician's handbook*. A. M. Washington and M. S. Gold (Eds.). New York, London: Guilford Press.

Withington, D., Patrick, J., and Reynolds, F. (1993). Histamine release by morphine and diamorphine in man. Anaesthesia, 48: 26–29.

Wojno, K. and Spitz, W. (1989). Necrotizing fascitis: a fatal outcome following minor trauma. Am J Forensic Med and Pathol, 10(3): 239–241.

Yap, S., Ravitch, M., and Pataki, K. (1981). En bloc chest wall resection for candidal costochondritis in a drug addict. Ann Thorac Surg, 31: 182–187.

Young, A. and Rosenberg, F. (1971). Cutaneous stigmas of heroin addiction. Arch Derm, 104: 80–86.

5.7 Cardiovascular disorders

5.7.1 Introduction

The frequency of heart disease in opiate abusers is not known. Except for endocarditis, and the various complications associated with HIV infection, it is not even clear that heart disease is any more frequent among opiate abusers than it is in controls (Kringsholm and Christoffersen, 1987). In Siegel and Helpern's classic paper on the "Diagnosis of death from intravenous narcotism," heart disease is not even mentioned (Siegel et al., 1966), nor were any significant cardiac abnormalities noted in Wetli's study of 100 consecutively autopsied narcotic abusers (Wetli et al., 1972). When Louria analyzed the discharge diagnosis of addicts admitted to Bellevue Hospital's general medicine service, the incidence of endocarditis was under 10% and no other cardiac disorders were noted (Louria et al., 1967). At the other extreme is the comprehensive study by Dressler and Roberts. They analyzed 168 drug-related deaths and found the incidence of cardiac abnormalities approached 100% (Dressler and Roberts, 1989b)!

Interpreting the older studies, and some of the newer ones, is difficult. The phrase "narcotic addict" has never been used consistently. Often, it has

Table 5.7.1   Types of Cardiac Lesions Found
in 168 Opiate Abusers

Disorder	Percentage
Cardiomegaly	68
Endocarditis (active or healed)	48
Coronary artery disease	21
Congenital	11
Acquired valvular disease	10
Myocardial disease	8

These figures are based on the report by Dressler
and Roberts, published before HIV infection was
widespread.

been applied to any sort of intravenous drug abuse, even though the effects
of sympathomimetics are manifestly different from those of opiates. In early
studies, chemical confirmation of the diagnosis was lacking. The diagnosis
of opiate abuse was based solely on clinical findings. Even after toxicologic
screening first became available, the limits of detection were far higher than
they are today. Another confounding factor is that almost all of the studies,
old and new, were uncontrolled. The very high frequency of cardiac lesions
reported by Dressler and Roberts cannot be generalized. Their study was
uncontrolled, and many of the 168 cases they examined had been referred
to the National Heart, Lung and Blood Institute, presumably because the
original prosecutors suspected that cardiopulmonary abnormalities were
present. Only one controlled study has compared the cardiopulmonary
pathology in opiate-related deaths with the findings in a group of age-
matched controls. Many changes could be identified in the opiate users'
lungs, but the hearts of the addicts differed in no significant way from those
of the controls (Kringsholm and Christoffersen, 1987).

The observed frequency of a particular cardiac lesion depends on the
pattern of drug abuse within the population being studied. When Rajs
reviewed the cardiac pathology in a group of 25 intravenous drug users, he
found contraction band necrosis, fibrosis, and inflammatory infiltrates (Rajs
and Falconer, 1979), but amphetamine abuse was common in the population
he studied, and the changes that he observed are consistent with that fact.
In some areas, especially Europe, the injection of pills meant for oral use is
still a fairly common practice. In those localities, granulomatous lung disease
and pulmonary hypertension are common. The spectrum of cardiac lesions
seen at autopsy is likely to reflect that fact. An increasing number of drug-
related deaths are due to violence, and not to any direct opiate-mediated
effect or medical complication of opiate abuse. The frequency of incidental
cardiac lesions in addicts dying of trauma has never been tabulated.

The lesions most likely to be seen in the hearts of opiate abusers are
listed in decreasing frequency in Table 5.7.1. No data has been compiled
since HIV infection became widespread, and there is no doubt that a very
significant percentage of HIV-positive opiate abusers will have lesions and

Table 5.7.2 Cardiac Findings in AIDS
Patients at Autopsy, in Order of Frequency

1. Pericardial effusion
2. Right ventricular hypertrophy
3. Infiltrates
4. Opportunistic infection
5. Kaposi's sarcoma
6. Nonbacterial thrombotic endocarditis

Adapted from Lewis, 1989.

opportunistic infections as a consequence of their disease. Similarly, in areas where mixed opiate-stimulant abuse is prevalent, changes associated with catechol toxicity, such as contraction band necrosis and myocardial fibrosis, are likely to be superimposed on any of the changes secondary to opiate abuse (Rajs and Falconer, 1979).

5.7.2 Pathology associated with HIV infection

In some areas of the United States more than one-half of all intravenous drug abusers carry the HIV virus. The true percentage of intravenous heroin abusers who die from AIDS, rather than some complication of their drug abuse, is not known. Whatever the number, it is not inconsiderable. Given that fact, and the fact that endocarditis is the only cardiac disorder unequivocally associated with intravenous opiate abuse, it is highly probable that any myocardial lesion encountered in the heart of an intravenous heroin user is due to HIV infection, or an opportunistic infection related to HIV infection.

Pericardial effusion is the cardiac lesion most commonly seen in AIDS patients. One-third of the patients dying of AIDS have effusions, with or without pericarditis (Lewis, 1989), and the probability is that the effusion will not have been symptomatic during life. The second most common AIDS-related abnormality is right ventricular hypertrophy. Right ventricular hypertrophy is not particularly surprising in drug abusers who are likely to have both angiothrombotic lung disease from their drug abuse and AIDS-related fibrotic interstitial lung disease at the same time. In Lewis's autopsy series of AIDS patients, mononuclear infiltrates were present in the myocardium of 10% of the patients, but none had evidence of healed or active myocarditis. Clinical experience suggests that the incidence of opportunistic infection, especially disseminated cryptococcosis and CMV infections, is also high, and usually unsuspected during life. Kaposi's sarcoma involving the myocardium, and even the epicardial coronary arteries, has been observed in a small percentage of cases.

5.7.3 Endocarditis

After HIV infection, endocarditis is the only other cardiac disorder with a clearly higher incidence among intravenous drug abusers than in the population at large. There has been surprisingly little research with any bearing on what, exactly, makes the intravenous drug user more susceptible to valvular infection. Autopsy evidence suggests that most (>80%) vegetations occur on previously normal valves (Dressler and Roberts, 1989a). However, recently published echocardiographic studies, comparing the valves of intravenous heroin users having no clinical evidence of endocarditis with the valves of healthy controls, have demonstrated tiny areas of thickening on both the mitral and tricuspid valves (Pons-Lladó et al., 1992). This finding is consistent with the notion that some type of endothelial trauma must occur to allow the deposition of the microscopic thrombi that appear to constitute the first stage of infection.

It has always been emphasized that addicts are prone to right-sided infection. While there is no question that the tricuspid and pulmonic valves are involved more often in addicts than in the general population, it is also true that in some series addicts actually have left-sided involvement more often than right (Dressler and Roberts, 1989a; Hubbell et al., 1981). The origin of the infectious agent has also been a matter of some dispute. Addicts do not use sterile techniques. Needles may be contaminated and the injected material unsterile. The injection site, especially if it is in the groin, may be colonized with pathogenic organisms. Thus there are a number of possible sources for infection. With the exception of *Candida* infection (Drouhet and Dupont, 1991), studies have failed to link the heroin itself, or the paraphernalia used, with the infectious organism (Tuazon, 1974). More often than not, the infectious organism is derived from either the addict's normal surface flora (Tuazon et al., 1974), or from a preexisting infection such as cellulitis or suppurative thrombophlebitis.

Platelet deposition, for whatever cause, damages valvular epithelium, exposing the matrix of subendothelial connective tissue below, allowing the further deposition of fibrin and platelet thrombi. The resulting vegetations are friable, white or tan, and most likely to be found along the line of valve closure. Bacterial vegetations tend to arise on the atrial aspect of the atrioventricular valves and on the ventricular surfaces of the aortic and pulmonary valves. With time they may proliferate and involve the opposite side of the valve, or spread to the chordae tendinae or onto the parietal pericardium. The lesions ulcerate, and the ulcerations seen in acute endocarditis tend to be larger and deeper than those associated with subacute disease (Silber, 1987).

The size of vegetations is variable. Their size, color, and appearance depend on the type of infectious agent. Fungal lesions tend to be larger and bulkier than bacterial vegetations and are more likely to cause valvular insufficiency and embolization. *Streptococcal* vegetations grow more slowly than *Staphylococcal* vegetations, but they may get to be much larger. Much smaller sterile vegetations may be seen in up to 2% of patients coming to autopsy. Such small, sterile lesions are classified as nonbacterial thrombotic endocarditis (marantic endocarditis or NBTE), and there is a particularly strong association with carcinoma and general cathexia (Angrist and Oka,

1963). On microscopic examination, NBTE lesions are seen to be composed of amorphous material that is free of bacteria. On rare occasions, one of the larger sterile vegetations can dislodge, enter the circulation, and cause infarction. Marantic endocarditis is seen in AIDS patients, and so is to be anticipated in intravenous drug abusers.

Depending on how much fibrin has been deposited, the color of the vegetations can range from white to tan or gray. On microscopic examination, there is no confusing the lesions of marantic endocarditis with those of infectious endocarditis. Masses of fibrin, platelets, and polymorphonuclear leukocytes can be seen surrounding colonies of bacteria located directly on the valve's surface. Necrotic areas of valve are surrounded with a mixed cellular infiltrate that often includes giant cells. In older lesions capillary proliferation occurs, along with the formation of granulation tissue (Saphir, 1960). Fibrous tissue eventually proliferates over the vegetations, the necrotic material becomes organized, and eventually endothelialized. Healed lesions are often calcified.

The pattern of valvular involvement is different in drug abusers than in the population at large, and so are the symptoms. In Dressler and Robert's series of 80 autopsied addicts with infectious endocarditis, the tricuspid valve was involved almost half the time. Within the general population, tricuspid valve involvement is seen less than 5% of the time in subacute cases, and less than 15% of the time in acute endocarditis (Lerner and Weinstein, 1966; Johnson et al., 1975; El-Khatib et al., 1976; Reisberg, 1979; Pelletier and Petersdorf, 1977; Pankey, 1962). Table 5.7.3.1 compares the frequency of involvement in addicts with the frequency seen in the general population. There is some evidence that the likelihood of infection depends upon the pressure to which the valve is subjected (Lepeschkin, 1952), so the high incidence of low-pressure valve disease in addicts is puzzling and unexplained. Equally difficult to explain is the fact that a significant incidence of right-sided involvement has been reported in some non-drug using populations (Grover et al., 1991).

Table 5.7.3.1   Frequency of Valve Involvement
in Addicts Vs. General Population

Site	Addicts	General (recent)
Left-sided	41%	85%
Aortic	23%	15–25%
Mitral	19%	30–45%
Right–sided	30%	5–20%
Tricuspid	29%	1–15%
Pulmonic	1%	<1%
Right and Left	16%	5–10%

Data for addict population derived from Dressler and Roberts. Data for general population derived from published clinical studies.

There is no satisfactory explanation for why the spectrum of organisms attacking the right heart should be so different, and so much more virulent, than the group of agents that infect the mitral and aortic valves. *Staphylococcus aureus* is the predominant organism infecting right-sided valves, while 60–80% of the time, the causative organism on the left is a *Streptococcus Viridians* sps. 60–80% (Weinberger et al., 1990). The predominant organisms in addicts and the general population are compared in Table 5.7.3.2.

Table 5.7.3.2 Pathogens Reported in Addicts with
Infectious Endocarditis, Compared with Pathogens
Observed in Non-Addicted Populations
(Summary of Published Studies)

Pathogen	% Addicts	% Non-Addicts
Streptococci	15%	65%
Viridians (β-hemolytic)	<5%	35%
Group D	<5%	25%
Staphylococcus aureus	50–80%	25%
Pseudomonas aeruginosa	10–40%	<5%
Polymicrobial	10–20%	<1%

Infection with multiple organisms is uncommon on the left, but polymicrobial involvement of the tricuspid valve is becoming more prevalent, especially among intravenous drug abusers. Until recently, polymicrobial infection was a distinctly rare entity. In one retrospective study of nearly 1,000 patients seen from 1951 to 1966 there was only one case (Weinstein and Rubin, 1973). In more recent reports the incidence has been closer to 8% (Levine et al., 1986). As many as 7 different organisms may be involved at one time, and since many of these organisms are quite fastidious, all may not be diagnosed by routine laboratory methods (Adler et al., 1991).

Right-sided involvement produces symptoms that are more pulmonary than cardiac. Dislodged vegetations frequently embolize to the lung, producing multiple segmental infiltrates, especially in the lower lobes (Chan et al., 1989). Tricuspid vegetations can, on occasion, grow quite large and may even interfere with valve function. Papillary rupture, on the other hand, produces relatively few symptoms on the right because of the low intracavitary pressure (Conway, 1969). Aneurysm of the sinus of Valsalva may result when infection dissects into the valve ring. This process is most often seen in cases of *staphylococcal* infection. *Staphylococcal* infections may also extend outward from the ring, and in addition to ring abscess, infection may also involve the interventricular septum (Conde et al., 1975; Rawls et al., 1968). Lethal arrhythmia can result. Extension of the infection outward may result in purulent pericarditis or even cardiac rupture.

Purulent pericarditis is seen in nearly 20% of all cases of endocarditis, and need not be the result of a large abscess rupturing (Silber, 1987). Smaller abscesses may be scattered throughout the myocardium, and even though abscess formation is more common in cases of acute endocarditis, it may be seen in subacute cases as well. Abscesses may be subendocardial or subperi-cardial, but are most likely to be found in the left ventricle (Arnett and Roberts, 1976). A spectrum of other myocardial alterations, short of frank abscess formation, can also be seen. In acute cases, there may be cloudy swelling of the myocytes, hemorrhage, or even tiny areas of infarction. Small infarcts occur in subacute cases where small emboli obstruct distal branches of the coronary arteries (Saphir et al., 1950).

The peripheral sequelae of valve infection have changed little since Osler described them in the Gulstonian Lectures in 1885 (Osler, 1885). The periph-eral complications associated with endocarditis in addicts differ in no sig-nificant way from the same complications when they occur in the general population. Many of the extracardiac manifestations are the result of arterial embolization of the friable vegetations. Mycotic aneurysm is the result of septic emboli, most of which occur at the bifurcation of medium-size arteries (Katz et al., 1974). This process is especially common in the brain, but can also occur elsewhere. In the kidneys, septic emboli can cause infarction, especially when *Staphylococcus* is the etiology. Glomerulonephritis is seen in more than half of the patients, and is the result of immune complex depo-sition (Bell, 1932; Gutman et al., 1972). In addition to the classic focal embolic changes seen in the kidneys of patients with endocarditis, diffuse prolifera-tive glomerulonephritis may also be seen. In these latter cases there is strong evidence for an immune-related etiology. It may well be that other peripheral lesions, such as Roth spots and even Osler's nodes, have an immune etiology (Bayer and Theofilopoulos, 1990).

At autopsy, if there is any suspicion that the patient was suffering from infectious endocarditis, aseptic technique should be used to ensure the col-lection of uncontaminated material. The major vessels should be clamped before removing the heart from the body. An area on the surface of the heart adjacent to the affected valve (e.g., entrance through the posterior right atrial wall would give access to the tricuspid valve) should then be seared and the center of the area incised with a sterile scalpel, allowing direct access to the valve which can be sampled and cultured. If such an approach is not fol-lowed, the samples obtained may well be contaminated, but even then, the cultures are probably worth the effort. Hearts should not be placed in for-malin prior to sectioning, because then it becomes impossible to rule out the presence of infected vegetations. Smears should be made of the vegetations. In addition to routine gram stains, slides should also be stained for fungi (Gomori stain) and acid-fast organisms. Even if no organisms are apparent on the stains, some material should still be cultured, since in partially treated cases the organism may lose the ability to take stain (Atkinson and Virmani, 1991).

5.7.4   *Other myocardial disorders*

Myocardial fibrosis is also a frequent finding in drug abusers' hearts. Certain patterns of fibrosis play a role in the generation of malignant rhythm disor-ders and sudden cardiac death (Strain et al., 1983; Karch and Billingham,

1986; Lecomte et al., 1992). Microfocal fibrosis is most typically seen in stimulant abusers (Rajs and Falconer, 1979; Tazelaar et al., 1987), where it is the result of healing contraction band necrosis. The occurrence of myocardial fibrosis in opiate abusers, particularly if it is perivascular in location, probably represents a healed bout of endocarditis. Of course, healed myocarditis may also result in fibrosis, but there is no evidence to suggest that this disease is any more frequent in addicts than it is in the rest of the population. Larger zones of fibrosis are likely to represent healed areas of ischemia infarction. This process too, may also be related to healed endocarditis, as emboli may cause infarction in some of the smaller coronary artery branches (Silber, 1987).

There is some evidence that myocardial hypertrophy is a concomitant of chronic heroin abuse (Karch et al., 1995a). Cardiac enlargement in intravenous abusers with lung disesase is to be expected; however, the findings of preliminary studies suggest that modest degrees of enlargement occur, even in the absence of lung disease. Similar changes have been observed in the hearts of cocaine abusers (Karch et al., 1995b) and in experimental animals treated with cocaine (Besse et al., 1994). Cocaine activates a number of myocardial genes, and heroin may well exert similar effects.

5.7.5 Miscellaneous disorders

Fever in intravenous drug users is usually not the result of endocarditis. Pneumonia has been found to be the underlying cause in 26% of the cases, followed by cellulitis in 19%, with endocarditis responsible less than 10% of the time (O'Connor et al., 1994). Another possible cause is "cotton fever," a benign syndrome occasionally seen in intravenous narcotic abusers (Thompson, 1975). Heroin injectors who filter their "fix" through a wad of cotton may be injecting themselves with limited amounts of endotoxin. Cotton plants are heavily colonized with gram-negative bacteria, especially *E. agglomerans* (Rylander and Lundholm, 1978) Endotoxin released by *E. agglomerans* may activate pulmonary macrophages and neutrophils, and activation of those cells promotes the release of other chemicals causing fever and leucokocytosis (Ferguson et al., 1993). The same phenomenon occurs in cotton workers who inhale the endotoxin which floats freely in the air of cotton mills (Rylander, 1987). Unfortunately, there is no effective way to immediately identify patients who have injected themselves with limited amounts of preformed endotoxin, and those who have actually innoculated themselves with *E. agglomerans* or other bacterial agents. Since the latter group are at risk for sepsis or endocarditis, prudence dictates that patients presenting with "cotton fever" should have blood cultures drawn and then be treated, at least initially, with empiric antibiotic therapy.

Intravenous heroin abusers have abnormal, atherogenic lipid profiles (Maccari et al., 1991). Whether the incidence of coronary artery disease in heroin addicts is any different from that in age-matched controls is not known. Dressler and Roberts found significant coronary artery disease

(>75% narrowing) in 8% of their referral cases (Dressler and Roberts, 1989b), but this observation has not been confirmed. In fact, no mention of coronary artery disease is made in any published autopsy series (Helpern and Rho, 1966; Siegel et al., 1966; Louria et al., 1967; Froede and Stahl, 1971; Wetli et al., 1972).

References

Adler, A., Blumberg, E., Schwartz, D. et al. (1991). Seven-pathogen tricuspid endocarditis in an intravenous drug abuser. Chest, 99: 490–491.

Angrist, A. and Oka, M. (1963). Pathogenesis of bacterial endocarditis. JAMA, 183: 249–252.

Arnett, E. and Roberts, W. (1976). Prosthetic valve endocarditis. Clinicopathologic analysis of 22 necropsy patients with comparison of observations in 74 necropsy patients with active infective endocarditis involving natural left-sided cardiac valves. Am J Cardiol, 38: 281–292.

Atkinson, J. and Virmani, R. (1991) Infective endocarditis: changing trends and general approach for examination. In R. Virmani, J. Atkinson, and J. Fenoglio (Eds.). *Cardiovascular pathology.* Philadelphia: W. B. Saunders Company.

Bayer, A. and Theofilopoulos, A. (1990). Immunopathogenetic aspects of infective endocarditis. Chest, 97: 204–212.

Bell, E. (1932). Glomerular lesions associated with endocarditis. Am J Pathol, 8: 639–663.

Besse, S., Assayag, P., Latour, C. et al. (1994). Myocardial effects of acute and chronic cocaine treatment. Circulation, 90(4, Part 2): I–580.

Chan, P., Ogilby, J., and Segal, B. (1989). Tricuspid valve endocarditis. Am Heart J, 117(5): 1140–1145.

Conde, C., Meller, J., Donoso, E. et al. (1975). Bacterial endocarditis with ruptured sinus of Valsalva and aorticocardiac fistula. Am J Cardiol, 35: 912–917.

Conway, N. (1969). Endocarditis in heroin addicts. Br Heart J, 31: 543–545.

Dressler, F. and Roberts, W. (1989a). Infective endocarditis in opiate addicts: analysis of 80 cases studied at necropsy. Am J Cardiol, 63: 1240–1257.

Dressler, F. and Roberts, W. (1989b). Modes of death and types of cardiac diseases in opiate addicts: analysis of 168 necropsy cases. Am J Cardiol, 64: 909–920.

Drouhet, E. and Dupont, B. (1991). Candidasis in heroin addicts and AIDS — new immunologic data on chronic mucocutaneous candidasis. Candida and Candidamycosis, 50: 61–72.

El-Khatib, R., Wilson, F., and Lerner, A. (1976). Characteristics of bacterial endocarditis in heroin addicts in Detroit. Am J Med Sci, 271: 197–201.

Ferguson, R., Feeny, C., and Chirurgi, V. (1993). Enterobacter agglomerans-associated "cotton fever." Arch Int Med, 153: 2381–2382.

Froede, R. and Stahl, C. (1971). Fatal narcotism in military personnel. J Forensic Sci, 16(2): 199–218.

Grover, A., Anand, I., Varma, J. et al. (1991). Profile of right-sided endocarditis: an Indian experience. Int J Cardiol, 33: 83–88.

Gutman, R., Striker, G., Gilliland, B., and Cutler, R. (1972). The immune complex glomerulonephritis of bacterial endocarditis. Medicine, 51: 1–25.

Helpern, M. and Rho, Y. (1966). Deaths from narcotism in New York City. NY State Med J, 66: 2391–2408.

Hubbell, G., Cheitlin, M., and Rappaport, E. (1981). Presentation, management, and follow-up evaluation of infective endocarditis in drug addicts. Am Heart J, 102: 85–94.

Johnson, D., Rosenthal, A., and Nadas, A. (1975). A forty-year review of bacterial endocarditis in infancy and childhood. Circulation, 51: 581–588.

Karch, S. and Billingham, M. (1986). Myocardial contraction bands revisited. Hum Pathol, 17: 9–13.

Karch, S., Green, G., and Young, S. (1995). Myocardial hypertrophy and coronary artery disease in male cocaine users. J Forensic Sci, 40: 591–595.

Katz, R., Goldberg, H., and Selzer, M. (1974). Mycotic aneurysm. Arch Intern Med, 134: 939–942.

Kringsholm, B. and Christoffersen, P. (1987). Lung and heart pathology in fatal drug addiction. A consecutive autopsy study. Forensic Sci Int, 34: 39–51.

Lecomte, D., Fornes, P., and Nicolas, G. (1992). Isolated myocardial fibrosis as a cause of sudden cardiac death and its possible relation to myocarditis. Presented at Annual Meeting of the American Academy of Forensic Sciences. New Orleans, LA. February 20, 1992.

Lepeschkin, E. (1952). On the relation between the site of valvular involvement in endocarditis and the blood pressure resting on the valve. Am J Med Sci, 224: 318–319.

Lerner, P. and Weinstein, L. (1966). Infective endocarditis in the antibiotic era (pts 1 through 4). N Engl J Med, 274: 199–206.

Levine, D., Crane, L., and Zervos, M. (1986). Bacteremia in narcotic addicts at the Detroit Medical Center: II. Infectious endocarditis: a prospective comparative study. Rev Infect Dis, 8: 374–396.

Lewis, W. (1989). AIDS: cardiac findings from 115 autopsies. Prog Cardiovasc Dis, 32: 207–215.

Louria, D., Hensle, T., and Rose, J. (1967). The major medical complications of heroin addiction. Ann Int Med, 67: 1–22.

Maccari, S., Bassi, C., Zanoni, P., and Plancher, A. (1991). Plasma cholesterol and triglycerides in heroin addicts. Drug Alcohol Depend, 29(2): 183–187.

O'Connor, P., Samet, J., and Stein, M. (1994). Management of hospitalized intravenous drug users: role of the internist. Am J Med, 96: 551–558.

Osler, W. (1885). Gulstonian lectures on malignant endocarditis. Lancet, 1: 415–418; 459–464; 505–508.

Pankey, G. (1962). Acute bacterial endocarditis at the University of Minnesota Hospitals, 1939–1959. Am Heart J, 64: 583–591.

Pelletier, L. and Petersdorf, R. (1977). Infective endocarditis: a review of 125 cases from the University of Washington Hospitals. Medicine, 56: 287–313.

Pons-Lladó, G., Carreras, F., Borras, X. et al. (1992). Findings on Doppler echocardiography in asymptomatic intravenous heroin users. Am J Cardiol, 69(3): 238–241.

Rajs, J. and Falconer, B. (1979). Cardiac lesions in intravenous drug addicts. Forensic Sci Int, 13: 193–209.

Rawls, W., Shuford, W., Logan, W. et al. (1968). Right ventricular outflow tract obstruction produced by a myocardial abscess in a patient with tuberculosis. Am J Cardiol, 21: 738–745.

Reisberg, B. (1979). Infective endocarditis in the narcotic addict. Prog Cardiovasc Dis, 22: 193–204.

Rylander, R. and Ludholm, M. (1978). Bacterial contamination of cotton and cotton dust and effects on the lungs. Br J Ind Med, 35: 204–207.

Rylander, R. (1987). The role of endotoxin for reactions after exposure to cotton dust. Am J Ind Med, 12: 687–697.

Saphir, O. (1960). *Endocarditis. Pathology of the heart.* Springfield, IL: Charles C. Thomas.

Saphir, O., Katz, L., and Gore, I. (1950). The myocardium in subacute bacterial endocarditis. Circulation, 1: 1155–1167.

Siegel, H., Helpern, M., and Ehrenreich, T. (1966). The diagnosis of death from intravenous narcotism, with emphasis on the pathologic aspects. J Forensic Sci, 11(1): 1–16.

Silber, E. (1987). Infective endocarditis, in *Heart disease.* 2nd edition. New York: Macmillan, 1192–1219.

Strain, J., Grose, R., Factor, S., and Fisher, J. (1983). Results of endomyocardial biopsy in patients with spontaneous ventricular tachycardia but without apparent structural heart disease. Circulation, 68(6): 1171–1181.

Tazelaar, H., Karch, S., Billingham, M., and Stephens, B. (1987). Cocaine and the heart. Hum Pathol, 18: 195–199.

Thompson, B. (1975). Medical complications of heroin addiction. Ariz Med, 32: 798–801.

Tuazon, C., Hill, R., and Sheagren, J. (1974). Microbiologic study of street heroin and injection paraphernalia. J Infect Dis, 129(3): 327–329.

Weinberger, I., Rotenberg, Z., Zacharovitch, D. et al. (1990). Native valve infective endocarditis in the 1970s vs. the 1980s: underlying cardiac lesions and infecting organisms. Clin Cardiol, 13: 94–98.

Weinstein, L. and Rubin, R. (1973). Infective endocarditis — 1973. Prog Cardiovasc Dis, 16: 239–274.

Wetli, C., Davis, J., and Blackbourne, B. (1972). Narcotic addiction, Dade County, Florida — an analysis of 100 consecutive autopsies. Arch Pathol, 93: 330–343.

5.8 Pulmonary disorders

5.8.1 Noninfectious complications

5.8.1.1 Respiratory failure and pulmonary edema

In the 1850s, narcotic-related pulmonary edema was first described by a Dr. Lee, from New York City. Lee described both cerebral edema and pulmonary congestion in a man dying from a laudanum overdose (Woodman and Tidy, 1877). There is a general presumption that pulmonary edema in heroin abusers is in some way related to the respiratory depression, and respiratory failure, but the pathophysiology of this condition is far from clear. All opiates exert direct effects on brain stem respiratory centers, resulting in decreased responsiveness of the respiratory centers to increased levels of PCO_2. When enough drug is given, the respiratory drive disappears.

There is no way an addict can know the potency of the drug he is using. If the sample should be less adulterated than usual, fatal respiratory depression may supervene. Purity on the street is highly variable, but at anything less than 3% purity, withdrawal symptoms are likely. Addicts who have been abstinent for some time are particularly at risk, since they will have lost their tolerance. This situation is not uncommon in addicts who have been incarcerated and then returned to the streets (Harding-Pink and Fryc, 1988).

Autopsy findings in typical cases reveal pulmonary congestion of varying degrees, but there need not always be florid pulmonary edema. Some addicts die with needles still in their arms (Siegel et al., 1966). Such deaths are believed to be the result of acute respiratory depression, even though the maximal effects of intravenous narcotics on the brain stem are not seen for several minutes (Sanford and Gilman, 1990).

The edema fluid in these cases is rich in protein, and agonal respiratory efforts will cause the fluid to froth up, much like beaten egg whites. In extreme cases, congealed froth is seen in the mouth and nares. In one series, the average weight of the right and left lungs was 830 grams and 790 grams, respectively (Levine and Grimes, 1973). Siegel reported an average total weight of 1,400 grams for both lungs. The changes are lobular in distribution, with areas of congestion and edema alternating with other areas of air trapping and acute emphysematous change. The posterior lower lobes are most severely affected, especially if gastric aspiration has also occurred. Depending on the severity of the process, histologic examination may reveal a spectrum of changes. In less severe cases, the only abnormality found will be widening of the interstitial spaces, especially around the bronchi and extraalveolar vessels (Pietra, 1991). In more extreme cases, the alveolar spaces are flooded with protein-rich fluid (Gottlieb and Boylen, 1974).

If there is enough time for hypoxic heart failure to occur, blood vessels in the nose and pharynx rupture, giving a pink tinge to the edema fluid. After 24 hours, hyaline membranes will be visible in the alveoli. They are composed of necrotic alveolar cell debris, mixed with the protein-rich edema fluid deposited on the alveolar walls. This phase is followed by a recovery phase. During this final phase, the cut surface of the lung will be firm and brownish, suggesting the diagnosis of pneumonia. Type II alveolar cells and fibroblasts proliferate and the fibrinous exudate in the alveoli is replaced by granulation tissue.

The results of repeated long-term opiate use are readily apparent when the lungs of intravenous narcotic abusers are compared to age- and sex-matched controls (Rajs, Härm, and Ormstad, 1984). Alveolar septa are thickened, fibrotic, and hypercelullar. Hemosiderin-laden macrophages can often be seen in the alveolar walls and even in the lamina of the alveoli and respiratory passages. If any one morphologic finding in the lung is typical of narcotic drug abuse, it is the presence of iron-containing macrophages in the lung.

Why some individuals should develop florid pulmonary edema and others not is unexplained. It has been argued that heroin has direct toxic effects on pulmonary capillaries, or even the heart, leading to hypoxic-induced heart failure (Menon, 1965; Silber and Clerkin, 1959). A role for altered capillary permeability is suggested by the fact that the protein content of the edema fluid is almost twice that of serum (Katz et al., 1972). Other theories that have been proposed include acute allergic reactions to heroin, the presence of contaminants in the heroin, histamine release, or some centrally mediated effect (Silber, 1959). Current thinking favors a mechanism similar to that in high-altitude sickness: respiratory depression leads to hypoxia which, in turn, causes increased capillary permeability and fluid extravasation into the alveoli (Duberstein and Kaufman, 1971).

5.8.1.2 *Emphysema*

Emphysematous changes are occasionally seen in the subset of intravenous abusers who inject medications meant for oral use. The process may involve both the upper (Goldstein et al., 1986; Paré et al., 1979; Paré and Fraser, 1989) and lower lobes (Smeenk et al., 1990). In extreme cases involvement may be panacinar (Groth et al., 1972). Usually, the upper lobes show the most damage. Intravenous drug abusers with emphysema are in their late 30s, which distinguishes them from those whose emphysema is due to smoking or alpha-1-antitrypsin deficiency, where victims tend to be much older.

Emphysematous changes are more common in stimulant abusers than in individuals taking opiates (Schmidt et al., 1991; Guenter et al., 1981). There is an experimental model where symptomatic bullae result from the coalescence of smaller bullae (Strawbridge, 1960; Guenter et al., 1981). The smaller bullae could be a manifestation of septic emboli damaging the capillary beds, or possibly even a result of granuloma formation (Thomashow et al., 1977), but proof is lacking. A more recent explanation for emphysematous changes is pneumocystisis infection. The healing process in such infections may lead to pneumatoceles that are discovered only at a later date.

5.8.1.3 *Needle and mercury emboli*

Attempts at central vein injection may sometimes result in needle fragments embolizing to the lung. These events are usually not fatal, but the x-ray appearance can be quite frightening (Shapiro, 1941; Lewis and Henry, 1985; Angelos, Sheets, and Zych, 1986). In the late 1980s several reports were published that described the picture seen when mercury was injected intravenously (Murch, 1989). According to street lore, such injection increased athletic ability and sexual prowess. There have been no recent reports and no autopsy studies. Chest x-rays of these individuals show striking metallic opacities outlining the pulmonary vascular bed and the apex of the right ventricle!

5.8.1.4 *Foreign body granulomas*

Foreign particle embolization is frequent in intravenous drug abusers, but clinical symptoms related to the practice are uncommon, and granuloma formation is an inconsistent finding at autopsy (Helpern and Rho, 1966; Sapira, 1968; Gottlieb and Boylen, 1974; Glassroth et al., 1987). Granulomas form when intravenous abusers repeatedly inject themselves with aqueous suspensions of pharmaceutical preparations designed to be taken orally. Heroin has been available since the turn of the century, and morphine for nearly 200 years, but pulmonary granulomatosis in drug users was first described in 1950 (Spain, 1950). The time lapse suggests that the injection of oral medications is a relatively recent innovation.

In some cases, cotton fibers are the culprit. Some addicts load their syringes by drawing up the liquid through a cotton ball; small fibers of cotton are drawn up at the same time. Most granulomas are due to magnesium

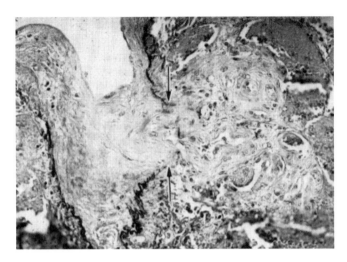

Figure 5.8.1.4   Thromboembolic arteriopathy. Repeated injection of particulate material can lead to pulmonary hypertension. Organizing and recanalizing thrombi in
drug abusers can look very much like the plexiform lesions of primary pulmonary
hypertension. The plexiform lesions of primary pulmonary hypertension, such as the
above, are typically seen only at the branch points of stenotic small arteries. Lesions
are composed of a complex network of small blood vessels and proliferating mytofi-
broblasts. Courtesy of Giuseppe Pietra, Director, Division of Anatomic Pathology,
Hospital of the University of Pennsylvania.

trisilicate (talc), because talc is widely used in the pharmaceutical industry
as a filler. The amount of active ingredient in most pills is often quite small,
so talc is added to create a pill of manageable size. When injected, talc
particles become trapped in the pulmonary arterioles and capillaries, producing acute focal inflammation and thrombosis. The reported incidence of
talc-containing granulomas ranges from 15% (Hopkins, 1972) to as high as
90% in some series. The tissue reaction to cotton is about the same as the
response to talc. The lesions seen are determined by the general pattern of
abuse within the population being studied. If the injection of crushed pills
is common, then so will be the incidence of foreign-body granulomas
(Tomashefski and Hirsch, 1980; Kringsholm and Christofferson, 1987). Fungal spores can also cause granulomatous disease. The soil saprophyte *Scopulariopsis brumptii* was found to be the cause of hypersensitivity pneumonitis
in at least one addict (Grieble et al., 1975), and analysis of confiscated heroin
samples has shown the presence of many different fungal varieties.

Whether the offending agent is talc, cotton, corn starch, or cellulose, the
clinical course and pathologic findings are much the same. Trapped particles
cause microthrombosis, and granulomas form. Some of the trapped material
may migrate into the perivascular space where the process is repeated, and
more granulomas form. If the process is ongoing, a reduction in the size of
the pulmonary bed occurs, and pulmonary hypertension can result. Associ-

Table 5.8.1.4.1 Characteristics of Birefringent Materials Found in the Lungs of
Intravenous Drug Users

Substance	Shape	Size	PAS Staining
Talc	needle shaped	5–15 μm	negative
Potato starch	Maltese cross, eccentric center	20–200 μm	positive
Maize starch	Maltese cross, concentric	10–30 μm	positive
Microcrystalline cellulose	elongated rod	25–200 μm	positive
Cotton fibers	irregular	variable	negative

Talc and cellulose are frequently seen in conjunction with granulomatous reactions, but other agents are not. Adapted from Kringsholm and Christoffersen, 1987.

ated anatomic changes include medial hypertrophy, and eccentric/concentric intimal fibrosis. The tissue diagnosis can be confusing, because organizing and recanalizing thrombi seen in intravenous drug users can appear very much like the plexiform lesions of primary pulmonary hypertension. The two conditions can be distinguished by the fact that plexiform lesions are typically seen only at the branching points of stenosed small arteries (Pietra et al., 1989).

Microcrystalline cellulose, a depolymerized form of cellulose, is also used as a filler and binder in the manufacture of oral medications. Cellulose crystals measure anywhere from 20–90 μm and are a good deal larger than talc or cornstarch crystals. The larger size of these crystals explains granuloma formation in the larger elastic pulmonary arteries, and even the right ventricle. Corn starch granulomas are particularly associated with the injection of oral pentazocine and secobarbitol preparations (Newell et al., 1988). They can be identified by their distinctive Maltese-cross pattern visible with the polarizing microscope, and by the fact that they stain as carbohydrates (Tomashefski and Hirsch, 1980). The presence of birefringent material in the interstitium is consistent with a long standing process, while material confined to the media of vessels is consistent with more recent use.

5.8.1.5 Injuries of the great vessels

Adulterants and expients mixed with illicit heroin can provoke an inflammatory reaction. As a result, peripheral veins become sclerotic, and abusers must use central veins for access. The two most popular sites are the vessels of the groin (Pace, Doscher, and Margolis, 1984) and neck (Lewis et al., 1980) (the "groin hit" and the "pocket shot"). The neck vessels are especially hard for the abuser to inject himself, and for a fee, other addicts will do the injecting. The results are predictable. Pneumothorax is a frequent occurrence, as is hemothorax from laceration to one of the great vessels (Lewis et al., 1980; Douglass and Levison, 1986). Pyohemothorax (Zorc et al., 1988) and pseudoaneurysm (Navarro et al., 1984; Johnson et al., 1984; McCarroll and Roszler, 1991) are also seen. In Europe, the use of intercostal vessels seems to be a popular alternative to neck injections. Reported complications include both pneumothorax and infection (Gyrtrup, 1989).

5.8.2　Infectious complications

5.8.2.1　Aspiration pneumonia

The combination of depressed cough reflex and decreased level of consciousness, in conjunction with a general tendency to retain secretions, favors aspiration (Cherubin, 1967). If the aspirated stomach contents are of very low pH, acute chemical pneumonitis will result. If there is much particulate matter present, then acute airway obstruction is possible. Pneumonitis, in such cases, is usually a result of infection with gram-negative and anaerobic organisms. Aspiration pneumonia in narcotics abusers is not any different from aspiration pneumonia in alcoholics or in people debilitated with chronic disease.

5.8.2.2　Community-acquired pneumonia

Even before the HIV epidemic, intravenous drug abusers were at increased risk for pneumonia, and for infections in general (Cherubin, 1971; Harris and Garret, 1972; Hussey and Katz, 1950; Moustoukas et al., 1983; Scheidegger and Zimmerli, 1989). If opiate users had normal immune function, which they do not (Novick et al., 1989), the injection of unsterilized material through contaminated syringes would still cause a transient septicemia. The number of HIV-infected individuals in some areas is already over 50% (Quinn et al., 1989). HIV-positive intravenous drug users are much more prone to develop community-acquired pneumonia and tuberculosis than are their HIV-negative counterparts (Selwyn et al., 1988). When HIV-positive individuals get community-acquired pneumonia, their clinical course is said to be more severe (Hind, 1990).

Among HIV-infected patients, including those without AIDS, the increased rate of infection can be quite striking. In one study, the annual attack rate for *Streptococcus pneumoniae* was only 0.7–2.6/1,000 in the general population, compared to 21/1,000 in asymptomatic HIV-infected intravenous abusers (Selwyn et al., 1988). There is nothing to distinguish community-acquired pneumonia among intravenous heroin abusers from their non-infected counterparts, but there is evidence that infections may be more severe and the mortality higher (Chaisson, 1989). Opportunistic lung infections in HIV(+) intravenous drug abusers are similar in frequency and type to those seen in other HIV(+) subgroups (Neidt and Schinella, 1985; Ambros et al., 1987).

Eosinophilic pneumonia appears to be more common in cocaine users and crack smokers (see Section 1.11.3.3) than in heroin addicts, but the process does occur. Diffuse pulmonary infiltrates with eosinophilic of bronchoalveolar fluid has been described and appears to be the result of an IgE mediated hypersensitivity reaction (Brander and Tukianinen, 1993).

5.8.2.3　Fungal pneumonia

Pulmonary fungal infections occur even in HIV-negative intravenous drug users (Rosenbaum et al., 1974; Mellinger et al., 1983; Collignon and Sorrel, 1983; Orangio et al., 1984). Street heroin is often contaminated with a fungal species, and percipitins to *Aspergillus*, *Micropolyspora faeni*, and *Thermoacti-*

nomyces vulgaris are frequently found in intravenous abusers (Smith et al., 1975). The preponderance of evidence suggests that most of the fungi found in illicit drug samples are there largely because of airborne contamination introduced when the users prepare their fix. The presence of specific fungi cannot be used to identify the origin of a sample, though some types of heroin seem to contain more contaminants than others (Domínguez-Vilches et al., 1991). Analysis of several outbreaks of fungal pneumonia among addicts suggests that the cause of infection was contaminated paraphernalia, including preserved lemon juice which is used to prepare the heroin injection (Clemons et al., 1991). Some types of heroin (Mexican Brown) are poorly soluble in water and can only be dissolved after they have been acidified. The two most popular agents for acidifying are lemon juice and vinegar. *Candida* species are present as contaminants of the lemon rind. Infected patients most often present with lobar pneumonia. In a high percentage of cases peripheral nodules, with or without cavitation, may be seen. Lung abscess and empyema may also develop (Mellinger et al., 1983). Hilar and mediastinal adenopathy can be a prominent finding that resolves over the course of weeks or months. Pleural effusions are seen in about 20% of cases, and pleural thickening may result (Lazzarin et al., 1985).

Disseminated candida infections have a rapid onset a few hours after injecting. The infection may be manifest as a self-limiting lobar pneumonia or as a generalized infection, with endocarditis, chorioretinitis, and hepatitis, with and without soft tissue abscesses. Occasionally the septicemia is manifested only as an isolated endopthalmitis (Shankland, Richardson, and Dutton, 1986). Repeat showers of emboli cause mycotic aneurysms of the pulmonary arteries, but these are usually asymptomatic and are only incidentally found at autopsy. Histologic diagnosis can sometimes be made by examination of scalp biopsy specimens which will show infiltration of the hair follicles with chronic inflammatory cells and *Candida albicans*.

5.8.2.4 *Tuberculosis and melioidosis*

There is an increased incidence of tuberculosis in both HIV positive and negative opiate abusers. Even without HIV infection, chronic heroin abuse is associated with a depressed immune response (Helpern and Rho, 1966; Brown et al., 1974; Reichman et al., 1979; Novick et al., 1989; Hendrickse, 1989). The clinical course and pathologic findings are the same as in any other patients with tuberculosis. Pulmonary melioidosis (due to *Pseudomonas pseudomallei*), which can resemble tuberculosis on x-ray, also occurs in narcotics addicts (Cooper, 1967). The diagnosis can be made by sputum culture.

5.8.2.5 *Septic pulmonary emboli*

Septic pulmonary emboli are not an infrequent finding in intravenous abusers. Recurrent emboli of infected material may be due to infected bone or soft tissue at the injection site, septic thrombophlebitis, or even endocarditis. The most probable source is vegetations on the tricuspid valve (Wendt et al., 1964) and in fact, recurrent septic pulmonary emboli must raise the possibility of tricuspid vegetations.

5.8.2.6   Anterior mediastinitis

Mediastinitis, secondary to soft-tissue infection in the chest wall, has recently been described in HIV-positive heroin users. In one case, the initial infection was sternoclavicular, and in another infection was sternochondrial. In both cases, the infectious agent was *S. aureus*, and in both cases the infection of the anterior mediastinum caused sepsis and vascular compromise. Soft-tissue infections of the chest wall are relatively common among intravenous drug abusers, but spread to the mediastinum is not. Invasion of the mediastinum in these cases likely was a consequence of HIV infection.

References

Ambros, R., Lee, E., Sharer, L. et al. (1987). The acquired immunodeficiency syndrome in intravenous drug abusers and patients with a sexual risk: clinical and post-mortem comparisons. Hum Pathol, 18: 1109–1114.

Angelos, M., Sheets, C., and Zych, P. (1986). Needle emboli to lung following intravenous drug abuse. J Emerg Med, 4: 391–396.

Brander, P. and Tukianinen, P. (1993). Acute eosinophilic pneumonia in a heroin smoker. Euro Respir J, 6: 750–752.

Brown, S., Stimmel, B., Taub, R. et al. (1974). Immunologic dysfunction in heroin addicts. Arch Intern Med, 134: 1001–1006.

Chaisson, R. (1989). Bacterial pneumonia in patients with human immunodeficiency virus infection. Semin Respir Infect, 4: 133–138.

Cherubin, C. (1967). The medical sequelae of narcotic addiction. Ann Intern Med, 67: 23–33.

Cherubin, C. (1971). Infectious disease problems of narcotic addicts. Arch Intern Med, 128: 309–313.

Clemons, K., Shankland, G., Richardson, M., and Stevens, D. (1991). Epidemiologic study by DNA typing of a *Candida albicans* outbreak in heroin addicts. J Clin Microbiology, 29(1): 205–207.

Collignon, P. and Sorrel, T. (1983). Disseminated candidiasis: evidence of a distinctive syndrome in heroin abusers. Br Med J, 287: 861–862.

Cooper, E. (1967). Melioidosis. JAMA, 200: 337–339.

Domínguez-Vilches, E., Durán-González, R., Infante, F., and Luna-Maldonado, A. (1991). Mycontamination of illicit samples of heroin and cocaine as an indicator of adulteration. J Forensic Sci, 36(3): 844–856.

Douglass, R. and Levison, M. (1986). Pneumothorax in drug users. An urban epidemic? Amer Surg, 52: 377–380.

Duberstein, J. and Kaufman, D. (1971). A clinical study of an epidemic of heroin intoxication and heroin-induced pulmonary edema. Am J Med, 51: 704–714.

Glassroth, J., Adams, G., and Schnoll, S. (1987). The impact of substance abuse on the respiratory system. Chest, 91: 596–602.

Goldstein, D., Karpel, J., Appel, D. et al. (1986). Bullous pulmonary damage in users of intravenous drugs. Chest, 89: 266–269.

Gottlieb, L. and Boylen, T. (1974). Pulmonary complications of drug abuse. West J Med, 120: 8–16.

Grieble, H., Rippon, J., Maliwan, N., and Daun, V. (1975). Scopulariopsosis and hypersensitivity pneumonitis in an addict. Ann Intern Med, 83: 326–329.

Groth, D., Mackay, G., Crable, J., and Cochran, T. (1972). Intravenous injection of talc in a narcotics addict. Arch Pathol, 94: 171–178.

Guenter, C., Coalson, J., and Jacques, J. (1981). Emphysema associated with intravascular leukocyte sequestration. Comparison with papain-induced emphysema. Am Rev Respir Dis, 123: 79–84.

Gyrtrup, H. (1989). Fixing into intercostal vessels: a new method among drug addicts. Br J Addict, 84: 945–946.

Harding-Pink, D. and Fryc, O. (1988). Risk of death after release from prison: a duty to warn. Br. Med J, 297(6648): 596.

Harris, P., and Garret, R. (1972). Susceptibility of addicts to infection and neoplasia. N Engl J Med, 287: 310.

Helpern, M. and Rho, Y. (1966). Deaths from narcotics in New York City. NY State Med J, 66: 2391–2408.

Hendrickse, R., Maxwell, S., and Young, R. (1989). Aflatoxins and heroin. Br Med J, 299: 492–493.

Hind, C. (1990). Pulmonary complications of intravenous drug misuse. 1. Epidemiology and non-infective complications. Thorax, 45(11): 891–898.

Hopkins, G. (1972). Pulmonary angiothrombotic granulomatosis in drug offenders. JAMA, 221: 909–911.

Hussey, H. and Katz, S. (1950). Infections resulting from narcotic addiction. Am J Med, 9: 186–193.

Johnson, J., Lucas, C., Ledgerwood, A., and Jacobs, L. (1984). Infected venous pseudoaneurysm: a complication of drug addiction. Arch Surg, 119: 1097–1098.

Katz, S., Aberman, A., Frand, U. et al. (1972). Heroin pulmonary edema. Evidence for increased pulmonary capillary permeability. Am Rev Resp Dis, 106: 472–474.

Kringsholm, B. and Christoffersen, P. (1987). The nature and the occurrence of birefringent material in different organs in fatal drug addiction. Forensic Sci Int, 34: 53–62.

Lazzarin, A., Uberti-Foppa, C., Gaslli, M. et al. (1985). Pulmonary candidiasis in a heroin addict: some remarks on its etiology and pathogenesis. Br J Addict, 80: 103–104.

Levine, S. and Grimes, E. (1973). Pulmonary edema and heroin overdose in Vietnam. Arch Pathol, 95(5): 330–332.

Lewis, J., Groux, N., Elliott, J. et al. (1980). Complications of attempted central venous injections performed by drug abusers. Chest, 74: 613–617.

Lewis, T. and Henry, D. (1985). Needle embolus: a unique complication of intravenous drug abuse. Ann Emerg Med, 14: 906–908.

McCarroll, K. and Roszler, M. (1991). Lung disorders due to drug abuse. J Thorac Imaging, 6(1): 30–35.

Mellinger, M., DeBeauchamp, O., Gallien, G. et al. (1982). Epidemiological and clinical approach to the study of candidiasis caused by *Candida albicans* in heroin addicts in the Paris region: analysis of 35 observations. Bull Narc, 34: 61–68.

Menon, N. (1965). High-altitude pulmonary edema: a clinical study. N Engl J Med, 273: 66–73.

Moustoukas, N., Nichols, R., Smith, J. et al. (1983). Contaminated street heroin — relationship to clinical infections. Arch Surg, 118: 746–749.

Murch, C. (1989). Quicksilver heart. Br Med J, 299: 1056.

Navarro, C., Dickinson, P., Kondlapoodi, P., and Hagstrom, J. (1984). Mycotic aneurysms of the pulmonary arteries in intravenous drug addicts. Am J Med, 76: 1124–1131.

Neidt, G. and Schinella, R. (1985). Acquired Immunodeficiency Syndrome: clinicopathologic study of 56 autopsies. Arch Pathol Lab Med, 109: 727–734.

Newell, G., Reginato, A., Auerbach, D. et al. (1988). Pulmonary granulomatosis secondary to pentazocine abuse mimicking connective tissue diseases. Am J Med, 85: 890–892.

Novick, D., Ochshorn, M., Ghali, V. et al. (1989). Natural killer cell activity and lymphocyte subsets in parenteral heroin abusers and long-term methadone maintenance patients. J Pharm and Exp Ther, 250(2): 606–610.

Orangio, G., Pitlick S., Latta, P. et al. (1984) Soft tissue infections in parenteral drug abusers. Ann Surg, 199: 97–100.

Pace, B., Doscher, W., and Margolis, I. (1984). The femoral triangle — a potential death trap for the drug abuser. NY State Med J, 84: 596–598.

Paré, J., Fraser, R., Hogg, J. et al. (1979). Pulmonary mainline granulomatosis: talcosis of intravenous methadone abuse. Medicine, 58: 229–239.

Paré, J. and Fraser, R. (1989). Long-term follow-up of drug abusers with intravenous talcosis. Am Rev Respir Dis, 139: 233–241.

Pietra, G. (1991). Pathologic mechanisms of drug-induced lung disorders. J Thorac Imaging, 6(1): 1–7.

Pietra, G., Edwards, W., Kay, J. et al. (1989). Histopathology of primary pulmonary hypertension. A qualitative and quantitative study of pulmonary blood vessels from 58 patients in the National Heart, Lung, and Blood Institute Primary Pulmonary Hypertension Registry. Circulation, 80: 1198–1206.

Quinn, T., Zacarias, F., St. John, P., and St. John, R. (1989). HIV and HTLV-1 infections in the Americas: a regional perspective. Medicine, 68: 189–209.

Rajs, J., Härm, T., and Ormstad, K. (1984). Postmortem findings of pulmonary lesions of older datum in intravenous drug addicts. Virchows Arch, 402: 405–414.

Reichman, L., Felton, C., and Edsall, J. (1979). Drug dependence, a possible new risk factor for tuberculosis disease. Arch Intern Med, 139: 337–339.

Rosenbaum, R., Barber, J., and Stevens, D. (1974). *Candida albicans* pneumonia: diagnosis by pulmonary aspiration, recovery without treatment. Am Rev Respir Dis, 109: 373–378.

Sanford, L. and Gilman, A. (1990). *Goodman and Gilman's the pharmacologic basis of therapeutics*. Eighth edition. New York: Pergamon Press.

Sapira, J. (1968). The narcotic addict as a medical patient. Am J Med, 45: 555–588.

Scheidegger, C. and Zimmerli, W. (1989). Infectious complications in drug addicts: seven-year review of 269 hospitalized narcotics abusers in Switzerland. Rev of Inf Dis, 11(3): 486–493.

Schmidt, R., Glenny, R., Godwin, J. et al. (1991). Panlobular emphysema in young intravenous Ritalin® abusers. Am Rev Respir Dis, 143: 649–656.

Selwyn, P., Feingold, A., Hartel, D. et al. (1988). Increased risk of bacterial pneumonia in HIV-infected intravenous drug users without AIDS. AIDS, 1: 267–272.

Shankland, G., Richardson, M., and Dutton, G. (1986). Source of infection in *Candida endopthalmitis* in drug addicts. Br Med J, 292: 1106–1107.

Shapiro, S. (1941). Passage of a hollow needle into the venous blood stream to the heart, through the cardiac wall, and into the thorax. Am Heart J, 22: 835–838.

Siegel, H., Helpern, M., and Ehrenreich, T. (1966). The diagnosis of death from intravenous narcotism, with emphasis on the pathologic aspects. J Forensic Sci, 11(1): 1–16.

Silber, R. and Clerkin, E. (1959). Pulmonary edema in acute heroin poisoning: report of four cases. Am J Med, 27: 187–192.

Smeenk, F., Serlie, J., Vanderjagt, E., and Postmus, P. (1990). Bullous degeneration of the left lower lobe in a heroin addict. Eur Resp J, 3(10): 1224–1226.

Smith, W., Wells, I., Glauser, F., and Novey, H. (1975). High incidence of precipitins in sera of heroin addicts. JAMA, 232: 1337–1338.

Spain, D. (1950). Patterns of pulmonary fibrosis as related to pulmonary function. Ann Intern Med, 33: 1150–1163.

Strawbridge, H. (1960). Chronic pulmonary emphysema (an experimental study). III. Experimental pulmonary emphysema. Am J Pathol, 37: 391–407.

Thomashow, D., Summer, W., Soin, J. et al. (1977). Lung disease in reformed drug addicts: diagnostic and physiologic correlations. Johns Hopkins Med J, 141: 1–8.

Tomashefski, J. and Hirsch, C. (1980). The pulmonary vascular lesions of intravenous drug abuse. Human Pathol, 11: 133–145.

Wendt, V., Puro, H., Shapiro, J. et al. (1964). Angiothrombotic pulmonary hypertension in addicts. JAMA, 188: 755–757.

Woodman, W. and Tidy, C. (1877). *Forensic medicine and toxicology.* Philadelphia: Lindsay and Blakiston, 337–342.

Zorc, T., O'Donnell, A., Holt, R. et al. (1988). Bilateral pyopneumothorax secondary to intravenous drug misuse. Chest, 93: 645–647.

5.9   Gastrointestinal disorders

5.9.1   Introduction

Although there is some evidence to suggest that heroin may be directly hepatotoxic (de Araújo et al., 1990), most of the changes seen in the livers of opiate abusers are secondary in nature. These changes can be divided into several groups, depending on the underlying mechanism. The most commonly encountered pattern is that of hepatic and generalized visceral congestion. Portal fibrosis is also fairly common, its presence signifying previous viral infection. Foreign body granulomas are uncommon, but when they occur they are due to the intravenous injection of pills meant for oral use. None of these alterations are unique to opiate abusers, although the presence of enlarged nodes in the porta hepatis is almost diagnostic for chronic narcotism.

5.9.2   Bowel disease

Narcotics decrease gut motility, resulting in severe constipation or obstipation. At autopsy, much of the colon may be distended with hard feces. The other bowel disease associated with narcotics is the "body packer" syndrome. This disorder was first noted in a cocaine courier by Suarez in 1977 (Suarez et al., 1977). Since that time, this mode of smuggling has been widely adapted (Pinsky, Ducas, and Ruggere, 1978; Sinner, 1981; Wetli and Mittleman, 1981; Gheradi et al., 1988; Roberts et al., 1986). Smugglers, known as "mules," ingest anywhere from 20–100 rubberized packets that contain multiple gram quantities of drug. At first the packets were made from condoms or balloons, or the fingers of surgical gloves. Now more care is devoted to the packaging, not only because the packets occasionally rupture and kill the courier, but also because the earlier packets were too easy to see on x-ray. Detection can be avoided by minimizing the contrast difference between the packets and the surrounding feces. To this end, more sophisticated smug-glers may drink mineral oil to further reduce the contrast between the pack-ets and the bowel contents. Even if they are difficult to see with plain films, packets can be easily demonstrated using CT scanning (Vanarthros et al., 1990). Urine testing is often positive, even if none of the packets rupture, because the rubber wrapping acts as a semipermeable membrane through which small amounts of the packet's contents gradually diffuse and enter the bloodstream (Gheradi et al., 1988).

5.9.3   Liver disorders

When death is due to acute narcotic overdose, the liver is, more often than not, enlarged and congested. In typical cases, the liver may weigh over 2,000 grams. Cut sections will be hyperemic. The other abdominal organs are also likely to be congested. Since these changes often occur in conjunction with pulmonary edema, it seems likely that the congestion is due to acute cardiac decompensation, although the issue has never been investigated satisfacto-rily, and it is far from proven that heroin-induced pulmonary edema is a consequence of heart failure.

Experimental models for heroin and opiate toxicity are virtually nonex-istent. However, one study did review histologic and ultrastructural changes in liver sinusoids of otherwise healthy heroin users and found that a signif-icant increase in sinusoidal wall surface occurs (de Araújo et al., 1990). The increase is due to hypertrophy of the sinusoidal cells and results in fibrosis within the space of Disse. It is not clear whether these changes represent damage, or possibly some protective adaptation. No further studies have been published.

5.9.3.1   Porta hepatis adenopathy

Enlargement of lymph nodes that are located in direct proximity of the liver is common, and nearly diagnostic for chronic intravenous heroin abuse. The exact incidence of these changes has never been tabulated, but some have placed it at over 75% (Edland, 1972). The porta hepatis, subpyloric, and peripancreatic lymph nodes, along with the cystic node at the neck of the gallbladder, and other nodes located along the common duct, may all be involved. Not infrequently the gastroduodenal and pancreatoduodenal nodes will also be enlarged. These nodes are gray, firm, sharply demarcated, and the degree of enlargement may be striking. Nodes measuring as much as 2 cm across are not uncommon. Microscopic examination of these nodes shows only a nonspecific pattern of reticuloendothelial hyperplasia. A puz-zling aspect of this abnormality is why, even though systematic autopsies have been done on opiate abusers for nearly 150 years, this common abnor-mality was not recognized until Siegel and Helpern published their paper in 1966 (Siegel et al., 1966), and their findings were reconfirmed by Wetli in 1972 (Wetli et al., 1972).

There are at least three possible explanations for this type of adenopathy, but they are all unproven. Node enlargement could be a reaction to the injection of particulate material. In one series, birefringent material was found in 39% of nodes from confirmed addicts (Kringsholm and Christof-fersen, 1987). Another possible explanation is recurrent infection. Changes consistent with nonspecific reactive hepatitis are found more than half the time in known drug users (Paties et al., 1987), and deep abdominal lym-phadenopathy can also be seen in HIV infection, though usually only in individuals with overt AIDS and secondary malignancy (Subramanyam et al., 1985; Cassani et al., 1993). Finally, there is the possibility that morphine, itself, might exert some direct effect on lymph nodes causing them to enlarge. Morphine is easily detectable in nodes draining the portal areas, and in most cases the concentration of morphine is greater in the nodes than it is in the blood. Lymph node morphine concentrations measuring anywhere from 300 ng/mL to over 8,000 ng/mL have been recorded (Nakamura and Choi, 1983). Whether lymph node enlargement is the result of some direct opiate effect has been a matter of conjecture for more than 50 years. The first paper suggesting the direct hepatotoxicity of heroin was published in 1935 (Balta-ceano and Visilu, 1935).

5.9.3.2 Non-specific alterations

Inflammation of the portal tracts is usually a constant finding in long-term intravenous drug abusers. In one series, the incidence was over 92% (Paties et al., 1987). The pattern of inflammation seen in addicts is commonly referred to as "triadiatis." There is a predominantly lymphocytic infiltrate, with fairly frequent plasma cells. On occasion, neutrophils may also be seen, but these infiltrates are usually devoid of eosinophils (Kaplan, 1963; Siegel et al., 1966; Edland, 1972).

Table 5.9.3.2 Frequency of Hepatic Lesions in 150 Randomly Selected Drug Addicts

Lesion	Percentage
Steatosis	70%
Portal Fibrosis	47%
Portal Flogosis	93%
Piecemeal Necrosis	46%
Lymphoid Follicles	40%
Plasma Cells	34%
Acidophil Bodies	23%
Viral Antigens	16%
Bile Duct Proliferation	6%
Bridging Necrosis	5%
Granulomas	2%
Birefringent Material	<1%
Mallory's Hyaline	abs

Patients had mean age of 23.3 years and were predominantly male (86%). Adapted from Paties.

Lobular inflammation is almost as common as "triadiatis" (85%), but necrosis is less common (46%) and tends to be widely scattered. The changes in addicts are easily distinguishable from those seen in alcoholics, since there are no centrolobular lesions, no Mallory's hyaline, and only rare neutrophils. True bridging necrosis is also uncommon in these individuals. Infiltrates in areas of necrosis are composed mainly of monocytes. Steatosis, which earlier workers believed was uncommon, can be found over 70% of the time. The fatty accumulations may be microvesicular, macrovesicular, or mixed.

Hepatic foreign body granulomas are uncommon, since most injected contaminants are trapped in the pulmonary vascular bed and never enter the systemic circulation. Whether or not birefringent material will be found in the liver or hepatic nodes depends, in large part, on the population being studied. If the population of addicts is injecting pills meant for oral consumption, then the probability of finding birefringent material is greater. Of course, foreign bodies can be widely disseminated if there is a septal defect and a shunt, and there are occasional reports of users with widespread, systemic, granulomas (Riddick, 1987).

5.9.3.3 Hepatitis

In Paties' series of 150 addicts published in 1987, changes consistent with chronic active hepatitis were found in 24% of cases, and acute hepatitis was diagnosed in 12%. Most of these individuals had one or more viral antigens demonstrable with immunohistochemical techniques. In acute cases, scattered foci of parenchymal cell loss with acidophilic necrosis and swelling will be seen throughout the parenchyma, along with proliferating reticuloendothelial cells and mononuclear infiltrates. During the last ten years, the prevalence of both hepatitis B and C in intravenous drug abusers seems to have increased considerably; two-thirds of injecting drug users in Victoria, Australia were found to be seropositive for hepatitis C (Crofts et al., 1993), while nearly one-third of the addicted patients tested in Greece had viral markers for hepatitis B (Dalekos et al., 1993). In California, polymerase chain reaction testing was used to measure the frequency of hepatitis C infection in heroin addicts attending a methadone clinic. Fifty-five of sixty-one patients (90%) had detectable viral DNA (Tennant and Moll, 1995).

In non-drug abusing populations, hepatitis B is, as a rule, a mild disease with a fatality rate of less than 2%, even among those requiring hospitalization. In addicts, fulminant hepatitis is much more frequent (Sheinbaum et al., 1974), probably a consequence of concurrent Delta virus-hepatitis B confection. In the United States, at least, Delta virus infection is mainly associated with parenteral drug abuse, but small numbers of cases are seen in the same groups that are at increased risk for hepatitis B (Lettau et al., 1987).

5.9.3.4 HIV infection and AIDS

For a variety of reasons, nearly two-thirds of AIDS patients have hepatomegaly and abnormal liver function tests. The abnormalities may be a consequence of alcoholism, or of previously existing viral hepatitis, or even a manifestation of opportunistic infections or opportunistic tumors. Liver disease can also be a complication of sepsis, malnutrition, or drug therapy (Schneiderman, 1988). The longer an individual has had AIDS, the higher the probability that histologic changes will be seen in the liver and opportunistic infection will be present. High levels of alkaline phosphase should raise the suspicion of *M. avium-intracellulare* infection, with multiple granulomas obstructing the terminal branches of the biliary tree (Glasgow et al., 1985). In these cases, diagnosis is often made more easily and rapidly by demonstrating mycobacteria on biopsy than by culture (Cappell et al., 1990). Besides tuberculosis, other opportunistic infections that have been reported include cytomegalovirus, *Cryptococcus neoformans*, and type 2 herpes simplex virus, to name but a few (Schneiderman, 1988; Devars du Mayne et al., 1985).

Elevation in total bilirubin in addition to elevation of alkaline phosphase suggests the presence of intrahepatic lymphoma (Schneiderman, 1988). Kaposi's sarcoma, non-Hodgkin's lymphoma, and malignant fibrosarcoma all occur in AIDS patients (Reichert et al., 1983). Interestingly, HIV infected patients, like anabolic steroid abusers, may develop peliosis. This is a condition of unknown origin, characterized by the presence of many small, cystic, blood-filled areas, usually in the liver, but occasionally in the lungs or other organs. These blood-filled lesions are found randomly scattered throughout the liver, often in association with foci of hepatocellular necrosis. The condition was first recognized in conjunction with tuberculosis, but the connection with anabolic steroid abuse has been recognized for some time (Taxy, 1978; Bagheri and Boyer, 1974). The mechanism by which these lesions are formed is unknown. One theory is that these lesions may represent a transitional step preceding the more recognizable endothelial changes seen in Kaposi's sarcoma (Devars du Mayne et al., 1985). Others have speculated that in AIDS patients, Kaposi's sarcoma and peliosis are both manifestations of a system-wide vascular stimulation initiated by unknown causes (Devars du Mayne et al., 1985). The results of the most recent study raise the possibility that peliosis may be the result of an infectious process, related to, or possibly the same as, bacillary angiomatosis, a lesion usually found only in individuals with HIV infection (Leong et al., 1992). The bacilli responsible for bacillary angiomatosis have staining and histologic similarities with the bacilli known to cause cat scratch disease, but whether infection with this agent is responsible for all cases of peliosis remains to be seen. Whatever the explanation, there is nothing to distinguish the changes seen in steroid abusers from the changes seen in AIDS patients, and in both groups the presence of these lesions can be symptomatic.

5.9.3.5 *Hepatic amyloidosis*

Hepatic deposition of amyloid protein occurs in both primary and secondary amyloidosis, and intravenous drug abusers with hepatic amyloid often are HIV infected. When hepatic amyloid deposition occurs in heroin and cocaine abusers it is almost invariably a consequence of the chronic supprative skin lesions resulting from poor hygiene and repeated subcutaneous heroin injection. In heroin addicts the type of amyloid deposited is unpredicatable and of no diagnostic value.

References

Bagheri, S. and Boyer, J. (1974). Peliosis hepatis associated with androgenic-anabolic steroid therapy. Ann Intern Med, 81: 610–618.

Baltaceano, G. and Visiliu, C. (1935). Intoxication of hepatic cells by diacetylmorphine and its effects on bile. Can Royal Soc Biol, 120: 229–244.

Cappell, M., Schwartz, M., and Biempica, L. (1990). Clinical utility of liver biopsy in patients with serum antibodies to the Human Immunodeficiency Virus. Am J Med, 88: 123–130.

Cassani, F., Costigliola, P., Zoli, M. et al. (1993). Abdominal lymphadenopathy detected by ultrasonography in HIV-1 infection: prevalence and significance. Scan J Infect Dis, 25: 221–225.

Crofts, N., Hopper, J., Bowden, D. et al. (1993). Hepatitis-C virus infection among a cohort of Victorian injecting drug users. Med J Australia, 159: 237–241.

de Araújo, M., Gerard, F., Chossegros, P. et al. (1990). Vascular hepatotoxicity related to heroin addiction. Virchows Arch, 417: 497–503.

de Araújo, M., Gérard, F., Chossegros, P. et al. (1993). Cellular and matrix changes in drug abuser liver sinusoids: a semiquantitative and morphometric ultrastructural study. Virchow Archiv, 422: 145–152.

Dalekos, G., Manoussakis, N., Zervou, E. et al. (1993). Immunological and viral markers in the circulation of anti-HIV negative heroin addicts. Euro J Clin Invest, 23: 219–225.

Devars du Mayne, J., Marche, C. et al. (1985). Hepatic involvement in Acquired Immune Deficiency Syndrome: a study of 20 cases. Presse Med, 14: 1177–1180.

Edland, J. (1972). Liver disease in heroin addicts. Hum Pathol, 3(1): 75–84.

Gheradi, R., Baud, F., Leporc, P., and Marc, B. (1988). Detection of drugs in the urine of body-packers. Lancet, 1(May 14): 1076–1077.

Glasgow, B., Anders, K., Layfield, L. et al. (1985). Clinical and pathologic findings of the liver in the Acquired Immune Deficiency Syndrome (AIDS). Am J Clin Pathol, 83: 582–588.

Kaplan, K. (1963). Chronic liver disease in narcotics addicts. Am J Dig Dis, 8: 402–410.

Kringsholm, B. and Christoffersen, P. (1987). Lymph-node and thymus pathology in fatal drug addiction. Forensic Sci Int, 34: 245–254.

Leong, S., Cazen, R., Yu, G. et al. (1992). Abdominal visceral peliosis associated with bacillary angiomatosis. Ultrastructural evidence for endothelial destruction by bacilli. Arch Pathol Lab Med, 116: 866–871.

Lettau, L., McCarthy, J., Smith, M. et al. (1987). Outbreak of severe hepatitis due to Delta and Hepatitis B viruses in parenteral drug abusers and their contacts. New Engl J Med, 317: 1256–1261.

Nakamura, G. and Choi, J., (1983). Morphine in lymph nodes of heroin users. J Forensic Sci, 28(1): 249–250.

Osick, L., Lee, T., Pedemonte, M. et al. (1993). Hepatic amyloidosis in intravenous drug abusers and AIDS patients. J Hepatology, 19: 79–84.

Paties, C., Peveri, V., and Falzi, G. (1987). Liver histopathology in autopsied drug addicts. Forensic Sci Int, 35: 11–26.

Pinsky, M., Ducas, J., and Ruggere, M. (1978). Narcotic smuggling: the double condom sign. J Can Assoc Radiol, 29: 78–81.

Reichert, C., O'Leary, T., Levens, D. et al. (1983). Autopsy pathology in the Acquired Immune Deficiency Syndrome. Am J Pathol, 112: 357–382.

Riddick, L. (1987). Disseminated granulomatosis through a patent foramen ovale in an intravenous drug user with pulmonary hypertension. Am J Forensic Med and Pathol, 8(4): 326–333.

Roberts, J., Price, D., Goldfrank, L., and Hartnett, L. (1986). The bodystuffer syndrome: a clandestine form of drug overdose. Am J Emerg Med, 4: 24–27.

Schneiderman, D. (1988). Hepatobiliary abnormalities of AIDS. Gastroenterol Clin North Am, 17: 615–630.

Sheinbaum, A., Damus, K., Michael, T., and Gitnick, G. (1974). Acute fulminant hepatitis: a clustering of cases. Arch Intern Med, 134: 1093–1094.

Siegel, H., Helpern, M., and Ehrenreich, T. (1966). The diagnosis of death from intravenous narcotism, with emphasis on the pathologic aspects. J Forensic Sci, 11(1): 1–16.

Sinner, W. (1981). The gastrointestinal tract as a vehicle for drug smuggling. Gastrointest Radiol, 198(6): 319–323.

Suarez, C., Arango, A., and Lester, J. (1977). Cocaine-condom ingestion. JAMA, 238: 1391–1392.

Subramanyam, B., Balthazar, E., Horii, S. et al. (1985). Abdominal lymphadenopathy in intravenous drug addicts: sonographic features and clinical significance. Am J Radiol, 144: 917–920.

Taxy, J. (1978). Peliosis: a morphologic curiosity becomes an iatrogenic problem. Hum Pathol, 9: 331–340.

Tennant, F. and Moll, D. (1996). Seroprevalence of hepatitis A, B, C, and D markers and liver function abnormalities in intravenous heroin addicts. J Addict Dis, 14: 35–49.

Vanarthos W., Aizpuru, R., and Lerner, H. (1990). CT demonstration of ingested cocaine packets. Am J Radiol, 155: 419–420.

Wetli, C., Davis, J., and Blackbourne, B. (1972). Narcotic addiction in Dade County, Florida — an analysis of 100 consecutive autopsies. Arch Pathol, 93: 330–343.

Wetli, C. and Mittleman, R. (1981). The body packer syndrome; toxicity following ingestion of illicit drugs packaged for transportation. J Forensic Sci, 26: 492–500.

5.10 Renal disorders

5.10.1 Introduction

Chronic intravenous narcotic use can cause renal disease, although the factors determining individual susceptibility remain poorly understood. Symptomatic individuals are almost always middle-aged hypertensives with variable degrees of proteinuria, hematuria, and pyuria. These abnormalities merely represent a final common pathway for a very diverse group of disorders. In the past, focal segmental glomerulosclerosis was the most frequent cause of nephrotic syndrome in addicts. It appears that morphine may have a direct role on mesangial cell growth and expansion. Opiate receptors have been found on mesangial cells and, at least in tissue culture, their proliferation appears to be stimulated by exposure to morphine (Singhal et al., 1992). Today, in some populations, renal amyloidosis is the predominant histopathologic lesion. Table 5.10.1 lists the more common renal disorders that have been identified in narcotic abusers.

Table 5.10.1   Renal Disorders Associated with
Opiate Abuse

Focal glomerulosclerosis
Membranoproliferative glomerulonephritis
Renal amyloidosis
Necrotizing angiitis with renal involvement
Interstitial nephritis
Acute tubular necrosis due to rhabdomyolysis

5.10.2 Acute renal failure due to nontraumatic rhabdomyolysis

Rhabdomyolysis was first observed in narcotic users just over 20 years ago
(Richter et al., 1971), but cases have been reported regularly since then
(Schreiber et al., 1971; Penn et al., 1972; Dolich, 1973; Koffler et al., 1976; Rao
et al., 1978; Akmal and Massry, 1983; Blain et al., 1985; DeGans et al., 1985;
Curry et al., 1989; Otero et al., 1992). Rhabdomyolysis accounts for much of
the renal disease seen in addicts. Most cases of rhabdomyolysis are caused
by a combination of factors including hypotension, fluid imbalance, and
pressure necrosis. The result is muscle destruction and the liberation of myoglobin into the bloodstream. However, as Richter observed, the syndrome
can occur in patients who are neither comatose, nor subject to muscle compression, and in those cases it seems likely that mycotoxic adulterants play
a role. Whatever the etiology, rapid onset of oliguria is followed by azotemia,
acidosis, hypophosphatemia, hyperuricemia, and all the other electrolyte and
chemical disorders associated with renal failure. Since the condition is rarely
fatal, these patients do not come to autopsy, or even biopsy. There is no reason
to suppose that the histologic changes are in any way different from those
encountered in cases due to traumatic rhabdomyolysis.

5.10.3 Secondary amyloidosis

The first reports of amyloidosis in heroin abusers were published in 1978
(Jacob et al., 1978). Since then it has become apparent that the incidence of
renal amyloid in heroin addicts is significantly higher than the incidence of
amyloid found at autopsy in the general population (Dubrow et al., 1985).
Furthermore, the incidence seems to be increasing. Amyloid is more common
in older, long-term abusers. Those affected suffer from massive proteinuria,
with or without azotemia. Over 90% of addicts with renal amyloid have had
clinical evidence of repeated skin infections with suppurative cutaneous
lesions (Neugarten et al., 1986; Menchel et al., 1983; Meador et al., 1979; Jacob
et al., 1978). Most of the reported cases have been from New York City, raising
the possibility that some local practice has a role. It has been suggested that
subcutaneous injecting, and the inevitable chronic skin infections that result,
are the cause (Dietrick and Russi, 1958; Campistol et al., 1988). Renal amyloid
is hardly unique to heroin users and a proven mechanism in these patients
is still wanting (Maury and Teppo, 1982). Routine light microscopy with

hematoxylin eosin, or PAS staining, shows large amounts of eosinophilic material within the glomerulus. Confirmation that the material is, in fact, amyloid, can be obtained by Congo red staining, or by using polarizing microscopy. Amyloid has a typical apple-green birefringence. Electron microscopy shows amyloid fibrils.

5.10.4 Heroin associated nephropathy (HAN) and other glomerular disorders

The possibility that opiate abuse might cause renal damage was recognized even before the advent of intravenous heroin (Light and Torrance, 1929). It has been known for many years that long-term heroin users can develop a relentlessly progressive variety of nephrotic syndrome, unresponsive to therapy, terminating in renal failure within a few months to a few years (Rao et al., 1978; Cunningham et al., 1983; Dubrow et al., 1985). Consistent with the general pattern that has been observed in other types of drug toxicity (Sanders and Marshall, 1989a), the predominant histologic alteration in intravenous heroin users is focal segmental glomerulosclerosis (Grishman et al., 1976; Sanders and Marshall, 1989b; Stachura, 1985).

Table 5.10.4.1 Differentiating HAN from HIV

Heroin Associated Nephropathy	HIV
Mesangial hypercellularity	Mesangial hypocellularity
Interstitial infiltrates present	Interstitial infiltrates absent
Interstitial fibrosis prominent	Interstitial fibrosis absent

IgM and C3 complement protein can both be identified in abnormal segments of the glomerulus, and electron microscopic studies show fusion of the foot processes (Treser et al., 1974). The mechanism for these changes is not clear, and appropriate animal models are lacking. Rats given high doses of heroin develop interstitial disease (Stachura, 1985), but that pattern of injury does not reflect what is seen in human heroin users. Glomerulosclerosis has not been reproduced in an animal model. Because the human lung filters out foreign bodies before they ever reach the kidneys, granulomatous interstitial nephritis is not seen in addicts either. The underlying mechanism for the changes observed in humans is thought to involve increased glomerular capillary permeability (May et al., 1986), possibly from chronic immune complex deposition (Sanders and Marshall, 1989a). What causes those changes is an open question; however, the process may well be related to the adulterants injected along with the heroin. Recent epidemologic studies in New York, where the incidence of HAN was very high, have found sharp decreases in reported new cases. The decrease corresponds almost exactly with increases in the purity and availability of street drug, as monitored by the Drug Enforcement Agency, and decreases in the price for heroin (Friedman and Rao, 1995).

Whatever the cause, progression of the lesions ultimately leads to glomerular destruction and symptomatic renal disease. Lesions consist primarily of intracapillary deposits of eosinophilic, PAS positive material involving isolated or multiple segments of the glomerulus.

HIV infection, even in the absence of opiate abuse, can cause a picture very similar to that seen in HAN. Without actually demonstrating the presence of virus, distinguishing HAN from HIV may be impossible. However, there are some features that can be used to distinguish the two groups. Tissue from the heroin abusers usually shows marked interstitial fibrosis and interstitial infiltrates of lymphocytes and plasma cells. Bowmans capsule may be markedly thickened, and mesangial hypercellularity may also be a feature. Focal segmental glomerulosclerosis in AIDS patients, on the other hand, is usually devoid of cellular infiltrates, even when there is supervening opportunistic infection, and there is mesangial hypocellularity. In contrast to heroin abusers, AIDS patients generally do not have interstitial fibrosis. Nonetheless, specialized electron microscopic studies or even gene probes may be required to confirm the diagnosis (Chander et al., 1987)

Other infectious diseases can also involve the glomerulus, either directly or indirectly. Many heroin injectors with endocarditis are found to have focal or diffuse glomerulonephritis as a result of circulating antigen-antibody complex deposition (Rao et al., 1978). The deposition of immune complexes causes diffuse proliferative changes and even classic crescent formation. Most reported cases are in the older literature, and occurred in individuals with *Staphylococcal* endocarditis (Gutman et al., 1972; Louria, 1967). The true incidence of glomerulonephritis in addicts has never been established, but reports are uncommon. In Sapira's autopsy study, the incidence of chronic glomerulonephritis in known addicts was 8% (Sapira et al., 1970). More recent experience suggests that the incidence of acute disease may be much lower. In most cases of endocarditis, renal embolization with infarction is probably more common than immune complex deposition, but these lesions rarely cause significant disease.

Hepatitis B and C infections may also cause glomerulopathy. Membranous nephropathy associated with chronic hepatitis B surface antigenemia is a well recognized entity (Cunningham et al., 1980). Chronic hepatitis C infection, thought to be present in up to 80% of chronic intravenous drug injectors, may be associated with mixed cryoblobulinemia which, in turn, may result in glomerulonephritis (Ramos et al., 1994).

5.10.5 *Necrotizing angiitis*

A polyarteritis-like syndrome in intravenous drug abusers was first reported by Citron in 1970 (Citron et al., 1970). As originally described, medium-sized and small arteries in most organs, as well as the arterioles in the brain, were involved. The elastic arteries, capillaries, and veins were all spared. Acutely there was fibrinoid necrosis of the media and intima, with prominent infiltrates of eosinophils and lymphocytes. Occlusive thrombi were also described. The subacute process was marked by intimal proliferation and luminal narrowing, with saccular aneurysms, especially at vessel bifurcations. There is very little evidence that such a disorder ever occurs in opiate abusers. Most of the patients described by Citron were intravenous amphetamine abusers, or polydrug abusers taking combinations of amphetamine with other drugs. Of the patients Citron studied, none that used only heroin developed the syndrome. There have been no reports in heroin users since.

References

Akmal, M. and Massry, S. (1983). Peripheral nerve damage in patients with nontraumatic rhabdomyolysis. Arch Intern Med, 143: 835–836.

Blain, P., Lane, R., Bateman, D., and Rawlins, M. (1985). Opiate-induced rhabdomyolysis. Hum Toxicol, 4: 71–74.

Campistol, J., Montoliu, J., Soler-Amigo, J. et al. (1988). Renal amyloidosis with nephrotic syndrome in a Spanish subcutaneous heroin abuser. Nephrol Dial Transplant, 3: 471–473.

Chan, Y., Wong, P., and Chow, T. (1990). Acute myoglobinuria as a fatal complication of heroin addiction. Am J Forensic Med and Pathol, 11(2): 160–164.

Chander, P., Soni, A., Suri, A. et al. (1987). Renal ultrastructural markers in AIDS-associated nephropathy. Am J Pathol, 126: 513–526.

Citron, B., Helpern, M., McCarron, M. et al. (1970). Necrotizing angiitis associated with drug abuse. N Engl J Med, 283(19): 1003–1011.

Crofts, N., Hopper, J., Bowden, D. et al. (1993). Hepatitis C virus infection among a cohort of Victorian injecting drug users. Med J Australia, 159: 237–241.

Cunningham, E., Brentjens, J., Zielezny, M. et al. (1980). Heroin nephropathy. A clinicopathologic and epidemiologic study. Am J Med, 68: 47–53.

Cunningham, E., Zielezny, M., and Venuto, R. (1983). Heroin-associated nephropathy, a nationwide problem. JAMA, 250: 2935–2936.

Curry, S., Chang, D., and Connor, D. (1989). Drug and toxin-induced rhabdomyolysis. Ann Emerg Med, 18: 1068–1084.

DeGans, J., Stam, J., and Van Wijngaarden, G. (1985). Rhabdomyolysis and concomitant neurological lesions after intravenous heroin abuse. J Neurol Neurosurg Psychiatr, 48: 1957–1959.

Dietrick, R. and Russi, S. (1958). Tabulation and review of autopsy findings in fifty-five paraplegics. JAMA, 166: 41–44.

Dubrow, A., Mittman, N., Ghali, V. et al. (1985). The changing spectrum of heroin-associated nephropathy. Am J Kidney Dis, 5: 36–41.

Friedman, E. and Rao, T. (1995). Disappearance of uremia due to heroin-associated nephropathy. Am J Kidney Dis, 25: 689-693.

Grishman, E., Churg, J., and Porush, J. (1976). Glomerular morphology in nephrotic heroin addicts. Lab Invest, 35: 415–424.

Gutman, R., Striker, G., Gilliland, B., and Cutler, R. (1972). The immune complex glomerulonephritis of bacterial endocarditis. Medicine, 51: 1–25.

Jacob, H., Charytan, C., Rascoff, J. et al. (1978). Amyloidosis secondary to drug abuse and chronic skin suppuration. Arch Intern Med, 138: 1150–1151.

Koffler, A., Friedler, R., and Massry, S. (1976). Acute renal failure due to nontraumatic rhabdomyolysis. Ann Intern Med, 85: 23–28.

Light, A. and Torrance, E. (1929). Opium addiction — physical characteristics and physical fitness of addicts during administration of morphine. Arch Intern Med, 43: 326–334.

Louria, D., Hensle, T., and Rose, J. (1967). The major medical complications of heroin addiction. Ann Int Med, 67: 1–22.

Maury, C. and Teppo, A. (1982). Mechanism of reduced amyloid-A-degrading activity in serum of patients with secondary amyloidosis. Lancet, 2: 234–237.

May, D., Helderman, J., Eigenbrodt, E., and Silva, F. (1986). Chronic sclerosing glomerulopathy (heroin-associated nephropathy) in intravenous T's and blues abusers. Am J Kid Dis, 8: 404–409.

Meador, K., Sharon, Z., and Lewis, E. (1979). Renal amyloidosis and subcutaneous drug abuse. Ann Intern Med, 91: 565–567.

Menchel, S., Cohen, D., Gross, E. et al. (1983). AA protein related renal amyloidosis in drug addicts. Am J Pathol, 112: 195–199.

Neugarten, J., Gallo, G., Buxbaum, J. et al. (1986). Amyloidosis in subcutaneous heroin abusers ('Skin Poppers' Amyloidosis'). Am J Med, 81: 635–640.

Otero, A., Esteban, J., Martine, J., and Cejudo, C. (1992). Rhabdomyolysis and acute renal failure as a consequence of heroin inhalation. Nephron, 62: 245.

Penn, A., Rowland, L., and Fraser, D. (1972). Drugs, coma, and myoglobinuria. Arch Neurol, 26: 336–343.

Ramos, A., Vinhas, J., and Carvalho, M. (1994). Mixed cryoglobulinemia in a heroin addict. Am J Kidney Dis, 23(5): 731–734.

Richter, R., Challenor, Y., Pearson, J. et al. (1971). Acute myoglobinuria associated with heroin addiction. JAMA, 216: 1172–1176.

Sanders, M. and Marshall, A. (1989a). Acute and chronic toxic nephropathies. Ann Clin Lab Sci, 19(3): 216–220.

Sapira, J., Bal, J., and Penn, H. (1970). Causes of death among institutionalized narcotic addicts. J Chron Dis, 22: 733–742.

Schreiber, S., Liebowitz, M., Bernstein, L. et al. (1971). Limb compression and renal impairment (crush syndrome) complicating narcotic overdose. N Engl J Med, 284: 368–369.

Singhal, P. C., Gibbons, N., and Abramovici, M. (1992). Long term effects of morphine on mesangial cell proliferation and matrix synthesis. Kidney International, 41(6): 1560–1570.

Sreepeda Rao, T., Nicastri, A., and Friedman, E. (1977). Renal consequences of narcotic abuse. Adv Nephrol, 7: 261–290.

Stachura, I. (1985). Renal lesions in drug addicts. Pathology Annual, 20(2), 83–99, New York: Appleton-Century-Crofts.

Treser, G., Cherubin, C., Lonegran, E. et al. (1974). Renal lesions in narcotic addicts. Am J Med, 57: 687–694.

van den Hoek, J., van Haastrecht, H., Goudsmit, J. et al. (1990). Prevalence, incidence and risk factors of hepatitis C virus infection among drug users in Amsterdam. J Infect Dis, 162: 823–826.

5.11 Neuropathology

5.11.1 Introduction

When the first reports of heroin toxicity were published at the turn of the century, opiates were thought to be neurotoxic. Creutzfeldt, Nissl, and other pioneers argued that they could see unique pathologic changes in the brains and spinal cords of narcotics abusers (Nissl, 1897; Creutzfeldt, 1926). Fatty

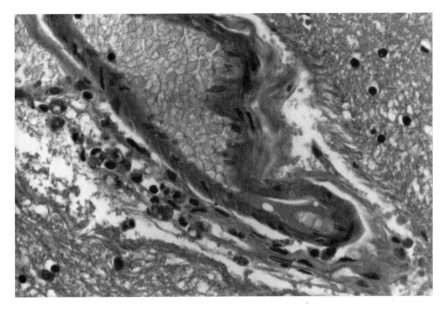

Figure 5.11.1 Hemosiderin laden macrophages. This micrograph is from the brain of an HIV negative heroine addict. Similar cells are often seen in the lungs. In both locations they appear to be the result of repeated intravenous injections of particulate material. Courtesy of Professor Françoise Gray, Départment de Pathologie, Hôpital Henri Mondor, Creteil, France.

Table 5.11.1 Neuropathologic
Complications of Narcotic Abuse

1. Hypercapnic hypoxia
       Cerebral edema
       Venous congestion
       Focal hemorrhage
2. Infections
       Complications of endocarditis
       Complications of HIV infection
          Encephalopathy
          Opportunistic infections
          Opportunistic tumors
       Phycomycosis
3. Spongiform encephalopathy
4. Transverse myelopathy
5. Peripheral neuropathy
6. Rhabdomyolysis
7. Stroke
8. Necrotizing angiitis
9. Parkinsonism

degeneration, particularly of neurons in the deeper layers of the frontal cortex and Ammon's horn, was thought to be diagnostic for morphinism. Subsequent studies have shown that the changes observed were either non-specific or artifactual. In the 1950s it was argued that heroin abusers were uniquely prone to infarction of the basal ganglia (Jervis and Joyce, 1948; Strassmann et al., 1969; Pearson et al., 1972). The nonspecific nature of this finding is also now appreciated. With the exception of perivascular pigment deposition within macrophages, which probably is the result of repeated intravenous injection of foreign material (Gray et al., 1992), no one lesion is diagnostic for narcotic abuse. Nonetheless, drug abusers do subject their nervous systems to a variety of insults, and some of these insults do produce lesions. The better-known neuropathologic complications of narcotic abuse are listed in Table 5.11.1.

5.11.2 Hypoxic encephalopathy

Deaths from acute opiate toxicity are usually associated with cerebral edema, meningeal congestion, and flattening of the gyri (Pearson and Richter, 1975; Adelman and Aronson, 1969; Levine and Grimes, 1973). As a rule these deaths occur so rapidly that morphologic evidence of cellular injury is not apparent. With longer periods of survival, characteristic patterns of tissue necrosis emerge. The injuries seen are not so much a result of hypoxia, but rather a result of the arterial hypotension that ensues because of the hypoxia (Brierley, 1972).

In almost all cases there will be terminal changes such as nerve cell ischemia and vascular congestion (Slater, 1862; Gray, 1992), but, under certain circumstances, the pattern of injury may reveal a great deal about the clinical events that preceded death. A major abrupt decrease in systemic blood pressure typically produces necrosis in the arterial boundary zones between the major arteries. The area most frequently involved is the parieto-occipital region. If the drop in blood pressure is more gradual and of longer duration, then laminar necrosis may be seen. This lesion is most prominent in the deeper layers of the cortex and cerebellum. A pattern of continuous necrosis, often accentuated in arterial border zones, may also be observed. The Purkinje cells of the cerebellum are particularly vulnerable to injury, as are the cells of Sommer's sector, located in the hippocampus (Adams et al., 1966; Brierley, 1972). Some time must elapse before these patterns become apparent. If death occurs within 3–6 hours, the probability of detecting anything but chronic changes is small. With the passage of more time, typical eosinophilic degenerative changes become apparent in scattered neurons. The cells of the caudate and putamen may or may not be involved. If changes are to be detected in those nuclei, then sampling from multiple sites will be required.

Chronic hypoxic episodes from repeated overdoses result in necrosis and scarring of the hippocampus, though the finding is hardly unique to narcotic abuse. And, of course, acute lesions may be superimposed on preexisting chronic or subacute changes. Thus, parietal-occipital lesions may be seen along with areas of laminar necrosis, suggesting an initial acute hypotensive episode followed by prolonged hypotension and decreased cerebral flow, a sequence not uncommon in heroin addicts.

5.11.3 Infectious diseases

5.11.3.1 Complications of endocarditis

Narcotics abusers get infectious diseases because of their unhealthy life styles, because their sterile injection technique is not good, and because chronic opiate use causes immunosuppression. This combination of factors occasionally leads to some very bizarre infections, such as mucormycosis. Such infections are uncommon, and are not major causes of morbidity. On the other hand, septicemia and endocarditis are fairly common, and both disorders have neurologic sequelae. In fact, the incidence of neurologic complications from subacute endocarditis has changed hardly at all since the introduction of antibiotics (Ziment, 1969).

Vegetations on the aortic and tricuspid valves can shed, producing disseminated microabscesses throughout the central nervous system. Small lesions center around septic emboli that lodge in terminal vessels, producing cerebral infarction (Grindal et al., 1978). In more severe cases, foci of metastatic suppuration may be seen throughout the leptomeninges, but intracranial hemorrhage secondary to the rupture of a mycotic aneurysm is a relatively uncommon event (Jones et al., 1969). The main sites of infection are the capillaries and small venules. They are usually surrounded by perivascular collections of polymorphonuclear leukocytes. Microabscesses do not produce severe or focal symptoms, and their presence may often be masked by other, more obvious disease processes (Adams et al., 1984).

5.11.3.2 Complications of HIV infection

Many intravenous drug abusers are HIV-infected, and most HIV-infected patients have central nervous system abnormalities detectable at autopsy. The AIDS-associated disorders can be divided into three groups: (1) AIDS encephalopathy, due to the direct effects of the virus itself, (2) opportunistic viral, fungal, parasitic, and bacterial infections, and (3) opportunistic neoplastic processes, particularly primary brain lymphoma.

The most frequently seen abnormality in the brains of AIDS patients is atrophy with diffuse or focal lesions in the white matter. There is pallor of the myelin, and necrosis is prominent in the centrum semiovale. There may also be diffuse or focal neuronal loss in the caudate and putamen (Navia et al., 1986; Petito et al., 1986). In cases where there is diffuse white matter damage, multifocal microgranulomatous lesions and multinucleated giant cells can be seen. Immunohistochemical techniques will almost invariably demonstrate the presence of the virus itself (Budka, 1991).

Cytomegalovirus (CMV) infection is also common. Evidence of infection is apparent in one-quarter of all autopsied AIDS cases (Petito et al., 1986), but these patients often have minimal symptoms during life. Infection is evidenced by the presence of microglial nodules. Viral inclusions may or may not be obvious, but the presence of the virus can be detected with immunohistochemical techniques (Magello et al., 1987).

Toxoplasmosis infection is much less common than CMV infection, but it is more likely to produce symptomatic disease (Navia et al., 1986). In life, the diagnosis is made with CT scanning. It typically shows hypodense lesions with ring contrast enhancement. Serologic testing confirms the diagnosis. The findings at autopsy will depend on how long the disorder has been present, and whether it has been under treatment. Early on, there will be poorly demarcated foci of necrosis with surrounding edema and mixed inflammatory infiltrates. There may or may not be evidence of arteritis. The diagnosis of toxoplasmosis is confirmed by the demonstration of extracellular tachyzoites and bradyzoite containing cysts. In longer-standing cases, organization of the necrotic material occurs and well-demarcated areas of coagulation necrosis can be seen. In long-standing cases, cysts and tachyzoites may be very hard to find.

The principal opportunistic neoplasm seen in AIDS patients is high-grade B cell lymphoma. The diagnosis is often difficult to make, especially in individuals who are already suffering from opportunistic infections (So et al., 1986; Gill et al., 1985). Diffusely infiltrating masses may be seen that are indistinguishable from any other sort of glioma. Alternatively, lesions may consist of small necrotic foci that can be confused with microabscesses. A variegated picture is seen microscopically, and malignant cells are likely to be mixed in with benign inflammatory infiltrates.

5.11.3.3 *Primary phycomycosis*

This fungal infection is usually associated with poorly controlled diabetes, or the presence of some disorder, such as leukemia or severe burns, that depresses immunity. A handful of reports have linked phycomycosis to intravenous drug abuse, usually in heroin users (Chmel and Grieco, 1973; Hameroff et al., 1970; Kasantikul et al., 1987; Masucci et al., 1982; Adelman and Aronson, 1969; Micozzi and Wetli, 1985; Pierce et al., 1982; Wetli et al., 1984). Infection begins in the nasal cavities and then, by invasion of the turbinates and the veins that drain them, infection extends into the paranasal sinuses, eventually reaching the orbital area. In other instances the infection reaches the brain by a hematogenous route. It may be that the brain supplies a particularly conducive environment in which the fungus can grow. Whatever the route of infection, the result is edema, proptosis, and ultimately destruction of the trigeminal and facial nerves. At least in drug addicts, the disease follows a fulminant course. Most patients die within two weeks of onset. Diagnosis in life may require brain biopsy, because fungi are not detected in the cerebrospinal fluid. CT scanning may be suggestive, but it is not diagnostic. Lesions are usually multiple, symmetric, and involve the basal ganglia. Material removed at surgery or autopsy is composed of aggregates of macrophages, lymphocytes and multinucleated giants cells. Even routine H and E staining will show the broad, branching, nonseparate fungal mycelia (Schwartz, 1982).

5.11.3.4 *Spongiform leukoencephalopathy*

The classification of this disorder is somewhat obscure. It has never been established whether its etiology is toxic or infectious. In 1982, an epidemic outbreak of spongiform leukoencephalopathy occurred in the Netherlands. Nearly 50 patients were involved, and the only factor common to all those affected was that they were addicts who smoked heroin. In most cases the disorder ran a two to three month course. In the initial stages, motor restlessness and apathy with obvious cerebellar signs rapidly gave way to hypertonic hemiplegia or even quadriplegia. In some cases, patients developed myoclonic jerks or choreoathetoid movements. Onset of hemiplegia seemed to mark a turning point in the progression of the disease. Half the patients stabilized or improved, while the other half progressed to a final, fatal stage with central pyrexia, spastic paresis, and akinetic mutism. These individuals died of respiratory failure (Wolters et al., 1982). Since then other cases have occurred in England, Germany, and Spain (Sempere et al., 1991; Haan et al., 1983; Wolters et al., 1982; Hugentobler and Waespe, 1990; Roulet et al., 1992; Shiffer et al., 1985), and Holland (Tan et al., 1994) though not in the United States.

All patients had obvious edema with flattening of the convolutions and brain weights of 1,380–2,560 grams. In all cases, microscopic examination showed damaged white matter filled with vacuoles. In some areas the vacuoles had coalesced to form larger cavities. Around the cavities could be

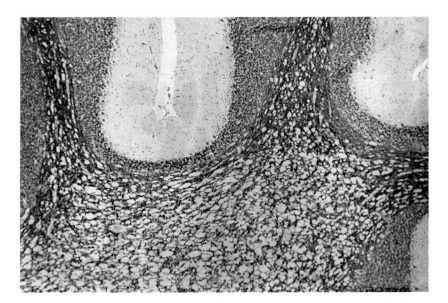

Figure 5.11.3.4 Spongiform leukoencelopathy. Seen only in heroin smokers. Histologically, lesions are indistinguishable from Jacob Creutzfield Disease. Courtesy of Dr. E. Ch. Wolters, Academisch Ziekenhuis, Vrije Universiteit, The Netherlands.

seen a fine network of attenuated myelin. The number of oligodendroglia was reduced, but no myelin breakdown products were evident. Inflammatory cells were also absent. Electron microscopy done in several cases showed multivacuolar degeneration of the oligodendroglia, with swollen mitochondria and distended endoplasmic reticulum. Light microscopic examination did not disclose it, but the electron micrographs showed abnormalities of the myelin lamellae and axoplasm, which also contained swollen, abnormal mitochondria.

The changes in these individuals are easily distinguishable from those seen in AIDS-associated leukoencephalopathy, where there is obvious evidence of demyelination, often with aggregates of microglial nodules. In addition, AIDS leukoencephalopathy is associated with changes in the microvasculature, including mural thickening, pleomorphism of the endothelial cells, and prominent perivascular collections of HIV-positive monocytes and multinucleated cells. AIDS can also be associated with very severe vacuolar changes, but these changes are confined to the posterior columns of the spinal cord (Petito et al., 1985). Toxicologic evaluation of all patients has been unremarkable, and chemical analysis of samples of local heroin used by the addicts showed only the usual adulterants: caffeine, lidocaine, procaine, phenobarbital, and methaqualone. None of these agents have ever been shown to be neurotoxic.

5.11.3.5 Transverse myelitis

This rare entity was first described in 1926. Its etiology also remains undetermined, but its occurrence has been noted in conjunction with a heterogeneous group of disorders, including viral infections, AIDS, systemic lupus erythematosus, smallpox vaccination, trauma, extreme physical exertion, and heroin abuse. The association with heroin abuse was first noted in 1968 (Richter and Rosenberg, 1968). Since the index report, transverse myelitis has been observed on a number of occasions (Schein et al., 1971; Rodriguez et al., 1972; Thompson and Waldman, 1970; Pearson et al., 1972; Hall and Karp, 1973). Judging from the number of recent reports, the incidence of this disorder seems to be decreasing.

The patients first described by Richter had not been taking heroin for a number of months, and they developed neurologic symptoms only after they began injecting heroin again. In all of the cases, onset of symptoms was quite rapid, ranging anywhere from a few hours to a few days. Victims developed flaccid paralysis and complete sensory loss ascending from the lower extremities to thoracic or even cervical levels. In the addict subpopulation, at least, fairly rapid improvement seems to be the norm, though there were usually residual deficits. Myelography in acute cases is unremarkable (Arlazoroff et al., 1989) and the disorder is sufficiently uncommon so that patients have yet to be evaluated with NMR or CT scanning. Cerebrospinal fluid analysis has also been unremarkable. Autopsy studies are rare, but when they have been done, the only findings have been extensive, but non-specific necrosis.

At first, transverse myelitis was thought to be the result of anterior spinal artery occlusion, but when more cases were studied, it became evident that the circulation in other territories could also be involved. Even ventral pontine disease has been observed (Hall and Karp, 1973). This disorder is the result of an isolated vascular accident within the spinal cord, but, at least in the case of narcotics abusers, it is not clear whether that accident is the result of thromboembolic phenomena, some sort of inflammatory vascular disease, or a toxic manifestation due to some contaminant injected along with the heroin. The most interesting new development in this regard is the recognition that heroin administration can increase or decrease blood flow to specific areas of the brain. Whether the decrease is ever large enough to produce neurologic symptoms remains to be determined (Fuller and Stein, 1991).

5.11.3.6 Peripheral neuropathy

Peripheral nerve lesions occur in addicts for a number of reasons. Unsterile injections may lead to local infection with nerve involvement, as can the injection of toxic adulterants. Neuropathy associated with rhabdomyolysis is a well-recognized entity. Nerve injury may be an indirect result of elevated compartment pressure, or a direct result of ischemia that can occur if compartment pressures rise high enough. Unperceived pressure or traction can also cause plexus or peripheral nerve injuries, even without muscle swelling (Kaku and Yuen, 1990). There is evidence to suggest that all of these mechanisms come into play (Schreiber et al., 1971; Pearson et al., 1972; Penn et al., 1972; Sheehan and Jabre, 1995). In addition, HIV-positive patients are subject to peripheral and autonomic neuropathies, probably due to direct invasion by the virus, though it has also been suggested that an autoimmune etiology might be possible (Villa et al., 1992).

Nerve injuries in narcotics addicts have been documented with electrophysiologic testing, but there have been no autopsy studies (Akmal and Massry, 1983). The mechanism in these cases has never been elucidated, but toxic or allergic reactions seem likely candidates, because there have been cases of lumbar plexus involvement where pressure or traction are obviously not factors (Jacome, 1982; Challenor et al., 1973; Greenwood, 1974).

5.11.3.7 Rhabdomyolysis

Heroin had been available for nearly 70 years before anyone ever observed that abusing it could cause acute myoglobinuria (Richter et al., 1971; Schreiber et al., 1971; Greenwood, 1974; D'Agostino and Annett, 1979; Jacome, 1982; DeGans et al., 1985; Penn et al., 1972; Grossman et al., 1974; Koffler et al., 1976; Nicholls et al., 1982; Gibb, 1985; Hecker and Friedli 1988; Strohmaier et al., 1991). The incidence of rhabdomyolysis in heroin users is not known with any precision, but judging by the number of cases reported in the literature, rhabdomyolysis may be occurring more often than is generally appreciated.

In some instances, the cause of muscle injury is obvious: pressure necrosis from the weight of the patient's own body while the individual is lying comatose (Schreiber et al., 1971). But not very many of the reported cases can be explained in this fashion (Chan et al., 1990). There are even cases with unequivocal evidence of concurrent cardiac necrosis, where the etiology could hardly have been pressure necrosis (Schwartzfarb et al., 1977). In such cases, a direct effect of heroin or of an adulterant seems to be responsible. The notion that heroin is directly myotoxic is supported by animal studies showing degenerative changes in rat soleus muscle after intraperitoneal heroin administration (Peña et al., 1993). Lesions produced in this model included hypercontraction of muscle fibers and disruption of the sarcoplasmic reticulum. Eosinophils were frequently observed around the degenerating fibers, suggesting that muscle destruction might be the result of a hypersensitivity reaction.

Patients usually complain of muscle weakness, pain, and swelling that begins several hours to several days after using heroin. The muscles of the lower limbs are involved more often than the upper limbs. Associated neurologic complaints and neuropathies of various sorts have been reported in conjunction with heroin-induced rhabdomyolysis (DeGans et al., 1985). Diagnosis in these cases is usually suggested by the presence of muscle swelling and elevated creatinine phosphokinase levels. However, muscle swelling need not always be evident, and the presence of myoglobin in the serum is, at best, an unreliable indicator because myoglobin is rapidly cleared from the plasma. Early on, laboratory tests will disclose marked elevations of creatinine phosphokinase and aldolase. Some individuals may complain of dark urine, and about half will go on to develop full-blown renal failure, with typical laboratory findings.

5.11.3.8 Stroke

Occasional reports of stroke in heroin users have been published, but the incidence seems to be lower now than it was 20 years ago. In most cases the etiology is obscure. Twenty years ago, it was thought that the re-exposure of addicts to heroin after a period of abstinence might lead to vascular hypersensitivity reactions, but the theory has never been substantiated (Rumbaugh et al., 1971; Ostor, 1977; Citron et al., 1970; Woods and Strewler,

Table 5.11.3.8 Possible Etiologies for
Stroke in Opiate Abusers

Thromboembolism
Thrombocytopenia
Vasculitis
Septic emboli
Hypotension
   Secondary to arrhythmia
   Secondary to decreased cardiac output
   Secondary to peripheral vasodilation
Positional vascular compression

1972; Caplan et al., 1982). Necrotizing angiitis (see Section 5.11.3.9) can certainly cause cerebral infarction, but there is rarely evidence for this disorder, and the apparent decline in its incidence, in general, suggests that it may have been the result of some toxic contaminants mixed with the heroin (King et al., 1978; Citron et al., 1970). As often as not, angiographic studies will be normal (Herskowitz and Gross, 1973; Olson and Winther, 1990). Table 5.11.3.8 lists additional mechanisms that can cause stroke in opiate abusers. The same mechanisms that cause stroke in stimulant abusers could also cause stroke in opiate abusers, but vasospasm seems unlikely in opiate users, since opiates share no common pharmacologic mechanisms with stimulants, and do not (except for pentazocine) cause elevations in circulating catecholamines.

A likely mechanism in many cases of stroke is positional vascular compression. The most recently published case involved a 35-year old addict with dense hemiparesis. Regional flow studies demonstrated severe hyperemia of the entire carotid territory on the affected side, but normal vessels on angiography. Such localized hyperemia is often seen following restoration of flow in stroke patients (Caplan, Hier, and Banks, 1982), and after cerebral spasm (Voldby et al., 1985). Generalized hyperemia is more likely to be observed after global ischemia. Stroke in these patients may have been the result of an unfortunate set of circumstances. Large doses of narcotic lead to hypotension, decreased respiration, and generalized cerebral ischemia. If the carotid artery is then compressed, by lying in the wrong way, perfusion might be lowered beneath some critical level and stroke could occur in an already ischemic brain (Olson and Winther, 1990). In the absence of experimental evidence such an explanation is speculative, but it could well account for an occasional infarct.

Hemorrhagic stroke in heroin abusers is the result of a deranged clotting mechanism, as might be encountered in cases of fulminant hepatitis or in individuals with AIDS-associated thrombocytopenia (Brust and Richter, 1976). Rupture of a mycotic aneurysm, or underlying AV malformation is also possible, but extremely uncommon. This is in contrast to hemorrhagic stroke in cocaine users, where victims commonly bleed from a preexisting malformation or aneurysm.

5.11.3.9 Necrotizing angiitis

Reports of a polyarteritis-like disorder in intravenous drug abusers were first published in the late 1960s. Traditionally, this disorder has been acknowledged to be a complication of intravenous drug abuse (see Section 5.11.5). Most of the patients described in the original report by Citron were intravenous amphetamine abusers, or polydrug abusers taking combinations of amphetamine and other drugs (Citron et al., 1970). None of Citron's patients who limited themselves to heroin abuse had the syndrome, and only one other case of arteritis in opiate abusers has been reported (King, 1978).

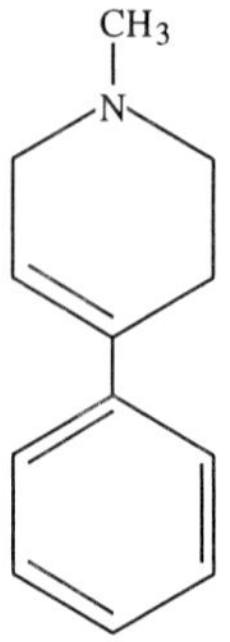

Figure 5.11.3.10   MPTP. 1-Methyl-4-phenyl-1,2,3,6-tetrahydropyridine (MPTP) molecule.

5.11.3.10 Parkinsonism

MPPP is a potent meperidine analog. When it is synthesized by clandestine chemists, inattention to detail occasionally results in the production of a neurotoxic by-product, known as MPTP. Taken in sufficient quantity, MPTP can produce all the classic symptoms of Parkinsonism, including resting tremor, rigidity, bradykinesia, and postural instability. At least three isolated outbreaks of recognized MPTP toxicity have been reported.

The first reported case of Parkinsonism in a MPPP user occurred in 1979 (Davis et al., 1979) and involved a graduate student who had been synthesizing and intravenously injecting MPPP for a period of six months. Just before he became symptomatic he had modified his synthetic methods, and later analysis by authorities disclosed that he had actually produced a mixture of MPPP and MPTP. His symptoms responded well to treatment, but he died of an unrelated drug overdose some two years later. Detailed neuropathologic examination of his brain disclosed degenerative changes within the substantia nigra that were confined to zona compacta. A marked astrocytic response and focal glial scarring were present, along with abundant collections of extraneuronal melanin pigment.

A second cluster of patients was reported in 1983. Four patients bought what they thought was "synthetic heroin" and, within a matter of days, developed striking features of parkinsonism. Analysis of material injected by these individuals showed they had been using mixtures of MPTP and MPPP (2.5–3.2% MPTP, 0.3–27% MPPP) (Langston et al., 1983). Since that original report, an additional 22 cases with less florid symptoms have been identified, all stemming from exposure to product from the same clandestine lab that had been operating in Northern California (Tetrud et al., 1989). The results of follow-up epidemiologic studies indicate that, during the three-year period from 1982–1985, over 500 individuals were exposed to MPTP, probably all from the same clandestine lab (Ruttenber, 1991).

Additional cases stemming from exposure to products from other sources were reported in 1983 and 1984. The first case was in a non-drug abusing chemist exposed to MPTP at work. He developed classic symptoms of Parkinsonism that responded to treatment. The last reported case was in a polydrug-abusing chemist who responded to initial treatment, but who died of unrelated causes 2 years later. This individual preferred to snort his drug, but his Parkinsonian symptoms were no less severe than those of the intravenous users. When he accidentally drowned, examination of his brain was perfunctory, and the substantia nigra was not examined (Wright et al., 1984).

Other than the fact that different age groups are involved (average age in the 30s vs. average age in the 60s), there is little to distinguish parkinsonism occurring after MPTP exposure from Parkinsonism in the general population. Initial symptoms may be mild or quite severe, though there is some evidence to suggest that tremor is somewhat less common in the drug abusers.

It is an open question whether additional new cases are likely to be encountered. Only sporadic seizures of samples containing MPTP have been reported. The most recent of these were in 1985, the same year when production of MPTP was made illegal. A closely related analog of MPTP called PEPTP (1,2-phenylethyl-1,2,5,6-tetrahydropyridine) can be generated as a by-product of PCP production, and may well possess the same neurotoxicity as MPTP, but no cases of Parkinsonism attributable to PCP contamination have been reported to date.

References

Adams, J., Brierley, J., Connor, R. et al. (1966). The effects of systemic hypotension upon the human brain: clinical and neuropathological observations in 11 cases. Brain, 89: 235–268.

Adams, J., Corsellis, J., and Duchen, L. (1984). *Greenfield's neuropathology*, 4th Edition, New York: John Wiley and Sons, 1126.

Adelman, L. and Aronson, S. (1969). The neuropathologic complications of narcotics addiction. Bull New York Acad Med, 45(2): 225–234.

Akmal, M. and Massry, S. (1983). Peripheral nerve damage in patients with nontraumatic rhabdomyolysis. Arch Intern Med, 143: 835.

Arlazoroff, A., Klein, C., Blumen, N., and Ohry, A. (1989). Acute transverse myelitis, a possible vascular etiology. Med Hypothesis, 30: 27–30.

Brierley, J. (1972). The neuropathology of brain hypoxia. *Scientific foundations of neurology*. M. Critchley (Ed.). Philadelphia: F. A. Davis Company.

Brust, J. and Richter, R. (1976). Stroke associated with addiction to heroin. J Neurol Neurosurg Psychiatry, 39: 194–199.

Budka, H. (1991). The definition of HIV-specific neuropathology. Acta Pathol Jpn, 41: 182–191.

Caplan, L., Hier, D., and Banks, G. (1982). Current concepts of cerebrovascular disease-stroke and drug abuse. Stroke, 13: 869–872.

Challenor, Y., Richter, R., Bruun, B., and Pearson, N. (1973). Nontraumatic plexitis and heroin addiction. JAMA, 225: 958–965.

Chan, Y., Wong, P., and Chow, T. (1990). Acute myoglobinuria as a fatal complication of heroin addiction. Am J Forensic Med and Pathol, 11: 160–164.

Chmel, H. and Grieco, M. (1973). Cerebral mucormycosis and renal aspergillosis in heroin addicts without endocarditis. Am J Med Sci, 266: 225–231.

Citron, B., Helpern, M., McCarron, M. et al. (1970). Necrotizing angiitis associated with drug abuse. N Engl J Med, 283: 1003–1011.

Creutzfeldt, H. (1926). Histologischer befund bei Morphinismus mit Morphium-und Veronalvergiftung. Ztsch fdg Neurologie u Psychiatrie, 101: 97–108.

D'Agostino, R. and Arnett, E. (1979). Acute myoglobinuria and heroin snorting. JAMA, 241: 277.

Davis, G., Williams, A., Markey, S. et al. (1979). Chronic parkinsonism secondary to intravenous injection of meperidine analogs. Psychiatry Res, 1: 249–254.

DeGans, J., Stam, S., and Van Wijngaarden, R. (1985). Rhabdomyolysis and concomitant neurological lesions after intravenous heroin abuse. J Neurol Neurosurg Psychiatr, 48: 1057–1059.

Fuller, S. and Stein, E. (1991). Effects of heroin and naloxone on cerebral blood flow in the conscious rat. Pharmacol Biochem Behav, 40(2): 339–344.

Gibb, W. and Shaw, I. (1985). Myoglobinuria due to heroin abuse. J Royal Soc Med, 78: 862–863.

Gill, P., Levine, A., Meyer, P. et al. (1985). Primary central nervous system lymphoma in homosexual men: clinical, immunologic, and pathologic features. Am J Med, 78: 742–748.

Gray, G., Lescs, M., Keohane, C. et al. (1992). Early brain changes in HIV infection: neuropathological study of 11 HIV seropositive, non-AIDS cases. J Neuropath and Exp Neurol, 51: 177–185.

Greenwood, R. (1974). Lumbar plexitis and rhabdomyolysis following abuse of heroin. Postgrad Med J, 50: 772–773.

Grindal, A., Cohen, R., Saul, R. et al. (1978). Cerebral infarction in young adults. Stroke, 9: 39–42.

Grossman, R., Hamilton, R., Morse, B. et al., (1974). Nontraumatic rhabdomyolysis and acute renal failure. N Engl J Med, 291: 807–811.

Haan, J., Müller, E., and Gerhard, L. (1983). Spongiöseleukodystrophie nach drogenmisbrauch. Nervenartz, 54: 489–490.

Hall, J. and Karp, H. (1973). Acute progressive ventral pontine disease in heroin abuse. Neurology, 23: 6–7.

Hameroff, S., Eckholdt, J., and Lindenberg, R. (1970). Cerebral phycomycosis in a heroin addict. Neurology, 20: 261–265.

Hecker, E. and Friedli, W. (1988). Plexusläsionen, Rhabdomyolyse und Heroin. Schweiz med Wschr, 118: 1982–1988.

Herskowitz, A. and Gross, E. (1973). Cerebral infarction associated with heroin sniffing. South Med J, 66: 778–784.

Hugentobler, H. and Waespe, W. (1990). Leukoenzephalopathie nach inhalation von Heroin-Pyrolypsat. Schweiz Med Wochenschr, 120: 1801–1905.

Jacome, D. (1982). Neurogenic bladder, lumbosacral plexus neuropathy, and drug-associated rhabdomyolysis. J Urol, 127: 994.

Jensen, R. and Olsen, T. (1990). Severe non occlusive ischemic stroke in young heroin addicts. Acta Neurol Scand, 81: 354–357.

Jervis, G. and Joyce, F. (1948). Barbiturate-opiate intoxication with necrosis of the basal ganglia of the brain. Arch Pathol, 45: 319–326.

Jones, H., Siekert, R., and Geraci, J. (1969). Neurologic manifestations of bacterial endocarditis. Ann Intern Med, 71: 21–28.

Kaku, D. and So, Y. (1990). Acute femoral neuropathy and iliopsoas infarction in intravenous drug abusers. Neurology, 40(40): 1317–1318.

Kasantikul, V., Shuangshoti, S., and Taecholarn, C. (1987). Primary phycomycosis of the brain in heroin addicts. Surg Neurol, 28: 468–472.

King, J., Richards, M., and Tress, B. (1978). Cerebral arteritis associated with heroin abuse. Med J Aust, 2: 444–445.

Koffler, A., Friedler, R., and Massry, S. (1976). Acute renal failure due to nontraumatic rhabdomyolysis. Ann Intern Med, 85: 23–28.

Kreek, M., Dodes L., Kane, S. et al. (1972). Long-term methadone maintenance therapy: effects on liver function. Ann Intern Med, 77: 598–602.

Langston, J., Ballard, P., Tetrud, J., and Irwin, I. (1983). Chronic parkinsonism in humans due to a product of meperidine-analog synthesis. Science, 219: 979–980.

Levine, S. and Grimes, E. (1973). Pulmonary edema and heroin overdose in Vietnam. Arch Pathol, 95(5): 330–332.

Masucci, E., Fabara, J., Sain, N., and Kurtzke, J. (1982). Cerebral mucormycosis (phycomycosis) in a heroin addict. Arch Neurol, 39: 304–306.

McDonough, R., Madden, J., Falek, A. et al. (1980). Alteration of T and null lymphocyte frequencies in the peripheral blood of human opiate addicts. *In vivo* evidence for opiate receptor sites on T lymphocytes. J Immunol, 125: 2539–2543.

Micozzi, M. and Wetli, C. (1985). Intravenous amphetamine abuse, primary cerebral mucormycosis and acquired immunodeficiency. J Forensic Sci, 30: 504–510.

Morgello, S., Cho, E., Nielsen, S. et al. (1987). Cytomegalovirus encephalitis in patients with Acquired Immunodeficiency Syndrome: an autopsy study of 30 cases and a review of the literature. Hum Pathol, 18: 289–297.

Navia, B., Cho, E., Petito C., and Price, R. (1986). The AIDS dementia complex: II Neuropathology. Ann Neurol, 19: 525–535.

Navia, B., Petito, C., Gold, J. et al. (1986). Cerebral toxoplasmosis complicating the Acquired Immune Deficiency Syndrome: Clinical and neuropathological findings in 27 patients. Ann Neurol, 19: 224–238.

Nicholls, K., Niall, J., and Moran, J. (1982). Rhabdomyolysis and renal failure. Med J Aust, 2: 387–389.

Nissl, F. (1897). Die Hypothese der specifischen Nervenzellenfunction. Allg. Ztschr f Psychiatrie, 54: 1–107.

Ostor, A. (1977). The medical complications of narcotic addiction. Med J Aust, 1: 497–499.

Pearson, J., Challenor, Y., Baden, M., and Richter, R. (1972). The neuropathology of heroin addiction. J Neuropath and Exp Neurol, 31(1): 165–166.

Pearson, J. and Richter, R. (1975). Neuropathological effects of opiate addiction. *Medical aspects of drug abuse.* New York, Evanston, San Francisco, London: Harper and Row.

Peña, J., Luque, E., Aranda, C. et al.,(1993). Experimental heroin-induced myopathy: ultrastructural observations. J Submicrosc Cytol Pathol, 25: 279–284.

Penn, A., Rowland, L., and Fraser, D. (1972). Drugs, coma, and myoglobinuria. Arch Neurol, 26: 336–343.

Petito, C., Cho, E., Lemann, W. et al. (1986). Neuropathology of acquired immunodeficiency syndrome (AIDS): an autopsy review. J Neuropathol Exp Neurol, 45: 635–646.

Petito, C., Navia, B., Cho, E. et al. (1985). Vacuolar myelopathy pathologically resembling subacute combined degeneration in patients with the acquired immunodeficiency syndrome. N Engl J Med, 312: 874–879.

Pierce, P., Solomon, S., Kaufman, L. et al. (1982). Zygomycetes brain abscesses in narcotic addicts with serological diagnosis. JAMA, 248: 2881–2882.

Richter, R., Challenor, Y., Pearson, J. et al. (1971). Acute myoglobinuria associated with heroin addiction. JAMA, 216: 1172–1176.

Richter, R. and Rosenberg, R. (1968). Transverse myelitis associated with heroin addiction. JAMA, 206: 1255–1257.

Rodriguez, E., Smokvina, M., Sokolow, J., and Grynbaum, B. (1972). Encephalopathy and paraplegia occurring with use of heroin. NY State Med J Med, 71: 2879–2880.

Roulet Perez, E., Maeder, P., Rivier, L., and Deonna, T. (1992). Toxic leucoencephalopathy after heroin ingestion in a 2-year old child. Lancet, 340: 729.

Rumbaugh, C., Bergeron, T., Fang, H., and McCormick, R. (1971). Cerebral angiographic changes in the drug abuse patient. Radiology, 101: 335–344.

Ruttenber, A. (1991). Stalking the elusive designer drugs: techniques for monitoring new problems in drug abuse. J Addict Dis, 11(1): 71–87.

Sapira, J. (1968). The narcotic addict as a medical patient. Am J Med, 45: 555–588.

Schawarz, J. (1982). Progress in pathology: the diagnosis of deep mycosis by morphologic methods. Hum Pathol, 13: 519–533.

Schein, P., Yessayan, L., and Mayman, C. (1971). Acute transverse myelitis associated with intravenous opium. Neurology, 21: 101–102.

Schiffer, D., Brignolio, F., Giordana, M. et al. (1985). Spongiform encephalopathy in addicts inhaling pre-heated heroin. Clin Neuropathol, 4: 174–180.

Schreiber, S., Liebowitz, M., Bernstein, L. et al. (1971). Limb compression and renal impairment (crush syndrome) complicating narcotic overdose. N Engl J Med, 284: 368–369.

Schwartzfarb, L., Singh, G., and Marcus, D. (1977). Heroin-associated rhabdomyolysis with cardiac involvement. Arch Intern Med, 137: 1255–1257.

Sempere, A., Posada, I., Ramo, N., and Caabello, A. (1991). Spongiform leukoencephalopathy after inhaling heroin. Lancet, 338: 320.

Sheehan, T. and Jabre, J. (1995). Dorsal ulnar sensory neuropathy in a heroin user. Muscle and Nerve, 18: 559.

Slayter, W. (1862). Poisoning by opium and gin: fatal result. Lancet, 1: 326.

So, Y., Beckstead, J., and Davis, R. (1986). Primary central nervous system lymphoma in Acquired Immune Deficiency Syndrome: a clinical and pathological study. Ann Neurol, 20: 566–572.

Strassmann, G., Sturner, W., and Helpern, M. (1969). Gehirnschädigungen ins besondere linsenkernerweichungen bei Heroinsüchtigen nach Barbituratvergiftung, Spättod nach Erhängen und Herzstillstand in der Narkose Beitr Gerichtl Med, 25: 236–242.

Strohmaier, A. and Friedrich, M. (1991). Rhabdomyolyse und plexusläsion nach Heroinintoxikation. Radiologe, 31: 95–97.

Tan, T., Algra, P., Valk, J. et al. (1994). Toxic leuckoencephalopathy after inhalation of poisoned heroin: MR findings. Am J Nuc Res, 15: 175–178.

Tetrud, J., Langston, J., Garbe, P., and Ruttenber, A. (1989). Mild parkinsonism in persons exposed to 1-methyl-4-phenyl-1,2,3,6-tetrahydropyridine (MPTP). Neurology, 39(11): 1483–1487.

Thompson, W. and Waldman, M. (1970). Cervical myelopathy following heroin administration. J Med Soc NJ, 67: 223–224.

Villa, A., Foresti, V., and Confalonieri, F. (1992). Autonomic nervous system dysfunction associated with HIV infection in intravenous heroin users. AIDS, 6: 85–89.

Voldby, B., Enevoldsen, E., and Jensen, F. (1985). Regional CBF, intraventricular pressure, and cerebral metabolism in patients with ruptured intracranial aneurysms. J Neurosurg, 62: 48–58.

Wetli, C., Weiss, S., Cleary, T., and Gyori, F. (1984). Fungal cerebritis from intravenous drug abuse. J Forensic Sci, 29: 260–268.

Wolters, E., Wijngaarden, G., Stam, F. et al. (1982). Leukoencephalopathy after inhaling heroin pyrolysate. Lancet, ii: 1233–1237.

Woods, B. and Strewler, G. (1972). Hemiparesis occurring six hours after intravenous heroin injection. Neurology, 22: 863–866.

Wright, J., Wall, R., Perry, T., and Paty, D. (1984). Chronic parkinsonism secondary to intranasal administration of a product of meperidine-analog synthesis. N Engl J Med, 310: 325.

Ziment, I. (1969). Nervous system complications in bacterial endocarditis. Am J Med, 47: 593–607.

5.12 Hormonal and immune alterations

Heroin abusers are subject to a number of hormonal alterations, mostly involving sexual and reproductive functions. Studies have demonstrated decreased levels of both testosterone and leutinizing hormone with testicular atrophy and impotence (Mirin et al., 1980). Hyperprolactinemia has also occurred in chronic opiate abusers. Compared to non-drug using controls, long-term heroin users have decreased levels of parathyroid hormone and decreased levels of testosterone. As a consequence, they have abnormal bone and mineral metabolism, with decreased vertebral bone density (Pedrazzoni et al., 1993). The etiology of these changes is not at all clear, but there is some evidence that opiates may act directly on the pituitary. Pituitary volume in healthy men addicted to both heroin and cocaine is, when assessed by MRI imaging, nearly twice as great as volume observed in healthy controls (Teoh et al., 1993).

Host resistance to most pathogens is reduced by opiate abuse. Long before the advent of HIV, heroin addicts were known to have higher rates of opportunistic infection and cancer than the population at large (Sapira, 1968; Harris and Garret, 1972). Studies done in the early 1900s demonstrated the effects of morphine on lymphocytes (Achard et al., 1909; Terry and Pellens, 1928). With the advent of intravenous narcotic abuse, sometime in the mid 1920s, other abnormalities of the immune system were first described. These included generalized lymphadenopathy (Halpern and Rho, 1966), elevated serum immunoglobins (Kreek et al., 1972), lymphocytosis (Sapira, 1968), and abnormal T-cell rosette formation (McDonough et al., 1980).

The life-style of addicts is, no doubt, partially responsible for some of the abnormalities that have been observed. Chronic infection with viruses other than HIV may also contribute. Several reports have described very high rates of both hepatitis B and C infection. In Victoria, Australia, for example, 68% of injecting drug users are hepatitis infected (Crofts et al., 1993), and similarly high rates have been reported from California (Tennant and Moll, 1995). Increased production of non-organ specific auto-antibodies is detectable in most hepatitis C infected drug abusers, presumably in response to some product produced by the viruses (Dalekos et al., 1993).

The other reason for immunologic abnormalities in heroin abusers is that morphine (but possibly not methadone) alters immune function via centrally-mediated effects on neurons in the periaqueductal gray matter (Weber and Pert, 1989). Opiates interact with receptors throughout the entire neuroimmune system. Opiate receptors are also found in the periphery, on the surfaces of the two major classes of lymphocytes. Among the better known immunologic abnormalities in narcotic abusers are (1) decreased cutaneous sensitivity, (2) decreased mitogen responsiveness (Brown et al., 1974), and depressed levels of T cells as determined by the ability to form E-type rosettes with sheep red blood cells (Wybran et al., 1979; McDonough et al., 1980; Donohoe et al., 1987). It was the discovery that many of these abnormalities could be reversed with naloxone that led to the discovery that opiate receptors were located on lymphocytes.

The ability of opiates to alter lymphocyte function is important because lymphocytes, in addition to compromising a major component of the immune system, also have a role in the regulation of macrophages, mast cells and granulocytes. Regulation is accomplished by the release of compounds such as prostaglandins, complement, cytokines, and lymphokines. Release of these compounds is in turn modulated by the neuroendocrine axis. The resultant changes in immune response depend on whether or not opiate exposure is acute or chronic, since animals chronically exposed to opiates become tolerant to the initial immunologic effects (Donohoe, 1991).

In addition to the indirect control of mast cell function by cytokine release, opiates can also bind directly to specific receptor sites on the mast cell membranes (Fjellner and Hagermark, 1982). One result of such binding is histamine release that can lead to bronchospasm, hives, and flushing. Opiate-induced histamine release has occasionally been referred to as "pseudoallergy." IgG class antibodies to morphine and other opiates have been demonstrated in man, but it is not known if the presence of these antibodies has any clinical significance (Biagini et al., 1992; Biagini et al., 1990). IgE-type opiate antibodies have not been identified, at least in humans. Most addicts have elevated serum immunoglobulins, especially IgM. The elevations are thought to be a consequence of repeatedly injecting antigenic material (Millian and Cherubin, 1971). The changes revert when heroin use is discontinued (Cushman, 1980). Some of these IgM antibodies are specific for morphine and codeine. In two separate studies, IgM antibodies were detected in 50–60% of addicts tested (Gamaleya et al., 1993; Gamaleya, 1993).

Current research is centered on the possible role of opiates as cofactors in HIV infection. Comparisons of HIV seronegative intravenous narcotic users with seronegative, rehabilitated methadone users and normals have shown that natural killer activity is significantly reduced in the heroin users when compared to activity measured in methadone maintenance patients and controls. Measurements made in these same individuals show higher absolute numbers of CD2, CD3, CD4, and CD8-positive cells (Novick et al., 1989). Similar changes have been observed in mice chronically treated with morphine. Mice treated with opiates have increased numbers of CD4 cells in the spleen and thymus (Arora et al., 1990). Measurements in heroin users

Table 5.12   Immune Abnormalities in
Opiate Abusers

Depressed E-rosette formation (*in vitro*)
Depressed cutaneous sensitivity
Depressed mitogenic response
Elevated CD4 cells
Elevated CD4/CD8 ratio
Elevated levels of CD4 receptors
Elevated neopterin levels
Elevated soluble interleukin 2 receptors
Elevated gamma interferon levels

Adapted from Pillai et al., 1991.

have confirmed the presence of increased numbers of CD4+/T cells. Since the CD4 antigen is the receptor which the HIV virus uses to get into T cells, the presence of increased numbers of CD4 cells in narcotic abusers may favor HIV infection (Pillai et al., 1991). The observation is of clinical significance, since it has also been shown that long-term methadone maintenance normalizes lymphocyte function (Novick et al., 1989).

The possibility also exists that opiates may interfere with HIV replication. Kappa-type opiate receptors are thought to modulate immune responses within the brain. HIV replication occurs mainly within microglia. When opiate agonists bind Kappa receptors located on the surface of the microglia, replication of HIV within the cell is inhibited (Chao, 1995).

Immune thrombocytopenic purpura occurs in HIV-seropositive individuals (Marti et al., 1993). Like other HIV-infected patients, the spleens of these individuals are enlarged, often to well over 300 grams, although the spleen is not enlarged in non-HIV infected patients with idiopathic thrombocytopenic purpura. Lymphoid follicles in the white pulp are increased in size, but fewer macrophages and ceroid histiocytes will be seen than in the spleens of normal individuals, or patients with idiopathic thrombocytopenic purpura (Marti et al., 1993).

References

Achard, C., Bernard, H., and Gagneux, C. (1909). Action de la morphine sur les propriétés leucocytaires: leuco-diagnostic du morphinisme. Bull et Mem Soc Med Hosp Paris, 28: 958–966.

Arora, L., Fride, E., Petitto, J. et al. (1990). Morphine induced immune alterations *in vivo*. Cell Immunol, 126: 343–353.

Biagini, R., Klincewicz, S., Henningsen, G. et al. (1990). Antibodies to morphine in workers occupationally exposed to opiates at a narcotics-manufacturing facility and evidence for similar antibodies in heroin abusers. Life Sci, 47: 897–908.

Biagini, R., Bernstein, D., Klincewicz, S. et al. (1992). Evaluation of cutaneous responses and lung function from exposure to opiate compounds among ethical narcotics-manufacturing workers. J Allerg Clin Immunol, 89(1): 108–118.

Brown, S., Stimmel, B., Taub, R. et al. (1974). Immunologic dysfunction in heroin addicts. Arch Int Med, 134: 1001–1006.

Chao, C., Gekker, G., Sheng, W. et al. (1995). Kappa opioid receptors in human microglia: suppression of HIV-1 replication. Problems of Drug Dependence 1995: Proceedings of the 56th Annual Scientific Meeting, The College on Problems of Drug Dependence. Rockville, MD, National Institutes on Drug Abuse. In press.

Crofts, N., Hopper, J., Bowden, D. et al. (1993). Hepatitis C virus infection among a cohort of Victorian injecting drug users. Med J Aust, 159: 237–241.

Cushman, P. (1980). The major medical sequelae of opioid addiction. Drug Alcohol Depend, 5: 239–254.

Dalekos, G., Manoussakis, N., Zervou, E. et al. (1993). Immunological and viral markers in the circulation of anti-HIV negative heroin addicts. Euro J Clin Invest, 23: 219–225.

Donohoe, R. (1991). Immune effects of opiates in test tubes and monkeys. Problems of Drug Dependence, 1990: Proceedings of the 52nd Annual Scientific Meeting of the Committee on Problems of Drug Dependence. Rockville, MD, NIDA Research Monograph Series, 105: 103–108.

Donohoe, R., Bueso-Ramos, C., Donohoe, F. et al. (1987). Mechanistic implications of the findings that opiates and other drugs of abuse moderate T cell surface receptors and antigenic markers. Ann NY Acad Sci, 496: 711–721.

Fjellner, B. and Hägermark, Ö. (1982). Potentiation of histamine-induced itch and flare responses in human skin by the enkephalin analog FK-33-824, beta-endorphin, and morphine. Arch Derm Res, 274: 29–37.

Gamaleya, N. (1993). Antibodies to drugs as indicators of chronic drug use. An alternative to toxicological hair analysis. Forensic Sci Int, 63: 285–293.

Gamaleya, N., Tagliaro, F., Pasrshin, A. et al. (1993). Immune response to opiates: new findings in heroin addicts investigated by means of an original enzyme immunoassay and morphine determinations in hair. Life Sci, 53: 95–105.

Harris, P. and Garret, R. (1972). Susceptibility of addicts to infection and neoplasia. N Engl J Med, 287: 310.

Helpern, M. and Rho, Y. (1966). Deaths from narcotism in New York City. NY State Med J, 66: 2391–2408.

McDonough, R., Madden, J., Falek, A. et al. (1980). Alteration of T and null lymphocyte frequencies in the peripheral blood of human opiate addicts: *in vivo* evidence for opiate receptor sites on T lymphocytes. J Immunol, 125: 2539–2543.

Marti, M., Feliu, E., Campo, E. et al. (1993). Comparative study of spleen pathology in drug abusers with thrombocytopenia related to Human Immunodeficiency Virus infection and in patients with idiopathic throbocytopeni purpura. A morphometric, immunohistochemical and ultrastructural study. Am J Clin Path, 100–105.

Millian, S. and Cherubin, C. (1971). Serologic investigations in narcotic addicts. Am J Clin Pathol, 56: 693–698.

Mirin, S., Meyer, R., Mendelson, J. et al. (1980). Opiate use and sexual function. Am J Psych, 137: 909–915.

Novick, D., Ochshorn, M., Ghali, V. et al. (1989). Natural killer cell activity and lymphocyte subsets in parenteral heroin abusers and long-term methadone maintenance patients. J Pharm and Exp Ther, 250(2): 606–610.

Pedrazzoni, M., Vescovi, P., Maninetti, L. et al. (1993). Effects of chronic heroin abuse on bone and mineral metabolism. Acta Endocrinol, 129: 42–45.

Pillai, R., Nair, B., and Watson, R. (1991). AIDS, drugs of abuse and the immune system: a complex immunotoxicological network. Arch Toxicol, 65: 609–617.

Sapira, J. (1968). The narcotic addict as a medical patient. Am J Med, 45: 555–588.

Tennant, F. and Moll, D. (1995). Determination of hepatitis C carrier prevalence in heroin addicts by polymerase chain reaction analysis: correlation with liver function abnormalities. Problems of Drug Dependence 1995: Proceedings of the 56th Annual Scientific Meeting, The College on Problems of Drug Dependence. NIDA Research Monograph 162, Washington, D.C.; U.S. Government Printing Office.

Teoh, S., Mendelson, J., Woods, B. et al. (1993). Pituitary volume in men with concurrent heroin and cocaine dependence. J Clin Endocrin Metab, 76(6): 1529–1532.

Terry, C. and Pellens, M. (1928). The opium problem. New York: Committee on Drug Addictions in collaboration with the Bureau of Social Hygiene, Inc.

Weber, R. and Pert, A. (1989). The periaqueductal gray matter mediates opiate-induced immunosuppression. Science, 245: 188–190.

Wybran, J., Appelboom, T., Famaey, J., and Govaerts, A. (1979). Suggestive evidence for receptors for morphine and methionine-enkephalin on normal human blood lymphocytes. J Immunol, 123: 1068–1070.

5.13 Bone and soft tissue disorders

5.13.1 Introduction

Fibrous myopathy is a known complication of chronic pentazocine abuse, and meperidine abuse (Levine and Engle, 1975; von Kemp et al., 1989). There is evidence that it may also be associated with repeated injections of heroin (Russ et al., 1994). Nonetheless, most bone and soft tissue disorders seen in opiate abusers are infectious in origin. Infectious complications are, in fact, the main reason that drug abusers are hospitalized (White, 1973; Cherubin, 1967). Directly or indirectly, especially if HIV infection is included, infectious complications account for the majority of deaths. In the past such exotic infections as malaria and tetanus were common. These disorders have been replaced by endocarditis, hepatitis, and HIV infection, but much more mundane conditions such as cellulitis, soft tissue abscess, and septic thrombophlebitis are the conditions which most often bring the abuser to medical attention. There is also evidence that the relative reduction in testosterone produced by chronic opiate abuse may lead to altered bone metabolism and decreased trabecular bone mass (Pedrazzoni et al., 1993).

5.13.2 Bone and joint infection

In most instances, the source of bone and soft tissue infections is either the solution used to dissolve the drug or the abuser's own skin flora (Tuazon et al., 1974). Once introduced into the body, the infection may spread locally or hematogenously. The pattern of sites most frequently infected, and the organism responsible for the infection, appears to be changing. In the past, the skeletal sites most frequently infected were the vertebral column and sternoarticular joints (Waldvogel and Vasey, 1980; Covelli et al., 1993). In more recent studies the extremities, especially the left knee (Chandrasekar and Narula, 1986), were found to be involved much more than the sternoarticular joint. The shift seems to be due to the fact that more addicts are injecting themselves in the groin, and the fact that infection is most likely to occur in the structures closest to the injection site. Since most individuals are right handed, the left side is most frequently injected.

In early studies, *P. aeruginosa* was responsible for most (more than 80%) of the joint and bone infections in intravenous drug abusers (Waldvogel and Vasey, 1980; McHenry et al., 1975). The results of studies published in the mid 1980s indicate that a shift to a gram positive organism has occurred (Chandrasekar and Narula, 1986; Ang-Fonte et al., 1985; Dreyfuss et al., 1992), but any number of organisms may be responsible. Infectious discitis caused by *Enterobacter cloacae* has been described in both HIV+ and HIV– intravenous drug users (Marce et al., 1993). Infections with *Candida* are increasingly frequent, but it is not obvious that the increase has anything to do with HIV infection.

Except in addicts, infections of the cervical spine are rare in adults. While rare in the past, infection of the upper spine is becoming more common, and the infectious agent is, more often than not, *staphylococcus*. Just as addicts are using the large vessels in the groin, they are also injecting into the great veins of the neck, introducing *staphylococcus* from their skin (Endress et al., 1990). In life, CT scanning will show an inflammatory reaction about the carotid sheath with prevertebral soft-tissue masses adjacent to the areas of bone destruction.

Candida bone infections, on the other hand, almost never involve the cervical spine. They occur with increased frequency in intravenous abusers and in patients with indwelling venous catheters. The route of *Candida* infection, in these cases, is hematogenous. Just why the blood supply should favor the lower lumbar spine is not obvious, but almost all cases of *Candida* osteomyelitis have involved the lower lumbar area. Infection spreads into the endplate of the vertebral body, which is supplied by ventral branches of the spinal arteries. *C. albicans* is the responsible agent in two-thirds of the cases (Almekinders and Greene, 1991; Lafont et al., 1994)

Tuberculosis is occurring with increased frequency in addicts, especially those that are HIV-seropositive. Extrapulmonary involvement, with or without obvious lung lesions, is seen in 15% of cases (Alvarez and McCabe, 1984), and in many of these the extrapulmonary site involved is osteoarticular, usually the vertebral bodies and their intervertebral discs. Involvement of the bony arch usually produces a compression syndrome. Fortunately, involvement of the arch is rare, but it has been reported in intravenous heroin users (Mallolas, 1988).

5.13.3 Soft tissue infections

Though skin and soft tissue infections are common among intravenous abusers, there is nothing to distinguish their appearance from similar lesions in non-drug users. The bacteriology of these infections is somewhat controversial, with conflicting results being reported from different centers. In one series, most infections were polymicrobial, and only 19% had isolates of *S. aureus*, the remainder being anaerobes, including clostridia and *Bacteroides spp.* (Webb and Thadepalli, 1979). Other series have also described polymicrobial infections, with *S. aureus* present in almost every case, along with enteric gram negative aerobes and oropharyngeal organisms (Orangio et al., 1984). *E. corrodens*, a gram negative anaerobe, part of the normal flora in the mouth, is occasionally seen when addicts use their saliva to dilute or dissolve their drug for injection (Brooks et al., 1979).

5.13.4 Fibrous myopathy of pentazocine abuse

Woody infiltration, cutaneous ulcers, and abnormal pigmentation can be seen surrounding areas of repeated pentazocine injection. Clinically the syndrome is marked by limitation of motion, neuropathic symptoms, and even muscle and joint contractures (Oh et al., 1975). The contractures and neuropathic symptoms are secondary to nerve damage and reflex sympathetic dystrophy (Roberson and Dixon, 1983; Hertzman et al., 1986).

The syndrome may be the result of a foreign body reaction, with crystallization of the drug within the muscle (Levin, 1975; Oh, 1975). This possibility is suggested by the fact that birefringent crystals have been demonstrated in the areas of most intense induration (Adams et al., 1983). Myocytes are destroyed and replaced with dense, fibrotic tissue. Inflammatory infiltrates may or may not be present. Dystrophic calcification may be so marked that it sometimes can be detected by CT scanning or sonography.

References

Adams, E., Horowitz, H., and Sundstrom, W. (1983). Fibrous myopathy in association with pentazocine. Arch Intern Med, 143: 2203–2204.

Almekinders, L. and Greene, W. (1991). Vertebral *candida* infections — a case report and review of the literature. Clin Orthop, 267: 174–178.

Alvarez, S. and McCabe, W. (1984). Extrapulmonary tuberculosis revisited: a review of experience at Boston City and other hospitals. Medicine, 63: 25–55.

Ang-Fonte, G., Rozboril, M., and Thompsons, G. (1985). Changes in nongonococcal septic arthritis: drug abuse and methicillin-resistant *Staphylococcus aureus*. Arthritis Rheum, 28: 210–213.

Brooks, G., O'Donoghue, J., Rissing, J. et al. (1979). *Eikenella Corrodens*. A recently recognized pathogen: infections in medical-surgical patients in association with methylphenidate abuse. Medicine, 53(5): 325–342.

Chandrasekar, P. and Narula, A. (1986). Bone and joint infections in intravenous drug abusers. Rev Infect Dis, 8(6): 904–911.

Cherubin, C. (1967). The medical sequelae of narcotic addiction. Ann Intern Med, 67: 23–33.

Covelli, M., Lapadula, G., Pipitone, N. et al. (1993). Isolated sternoclavicular joint arthritis in heroin addicts and/or HIV-positive patients; three cases. Clin Rheumatol, 12(3): 422–425.

Dreyfuss, D., Djedaini, K., Bidault-Lapomme, C. et al. (1992). Nontraumatic acute anterior mediastinitis in two HIV-positive heroin addicts. Chest, 101: 583–585.

Endress, C., Guyot, D., Fata, J., and Salciccioli, G. (1990). Cervical osteomyelitis due to IV heroin use: radiologic findings in 14 patients. Am J Radiol, 155: 333–335.

Hertzman, A., Toone, E., and Resnik, C. (1986). Pentazocine-induced myocutaneous sclerosis. J Rheumatol, 13: 210–214.

Lafont, A., Olivé, A., Gelman, M. et al. (1994). *Candida albicans* spondylodiscitis and vertebral osteomyelitis in patients with intravenous heroin drug addiction. Report of 3 new cases. J Rheumatol, 21: 953–956.

Levin, B. and Engel, W. (1975). Iatrogenic muscle fibrosis. JAMA, 234: 621–624.

Louis, E., Bodner, R., Challenor, Y. et al. (1994). Focal myopathy induced by chronic intramuscular heroin injection. Muscle Nerve, 17: 550–552.

Marce, S., Antoine, J., Schaeverbeke, T. et al. (1993). *Enterobacter cloacae* vertebral infection in a heroin addict with HIV infection. Ann Rheumatic Dis, 52: 695–696.

McHenry, M., Alfidi, R., Wilde, A., and Hawk, W. (1975). Hematogenous osteomyelitis: a changing disease. Clevel Clin Q, 42: 125–153.

Mollalas, J., Gatell, J., Rovira, M. et al. (1988). Vertebral arch tuberculosis in two human immunodeficiency virus-seropositive heroin addicts. Arch Intern Med, 148: 1125–1127.

Oh, S., Rollins, J., and Lewis, I. (1975). Pentazocine-induced fibrous myopathy. JAMA, 231: 271–273.

Orangio, G., Pitlick, S., Latta, P. et al. (1984). Soft tissue infections in parenteral drug abusers. Ann Surg, 199: 97–100.

Pedrazzoni, M., Vescovi, P., Maninetti, L. et al. (1993). Effects of chronic heroin abuse on bone and mineral metabolism. Acta Endocrinol, 129: 42–45.

Roberson, J. and Dimon, J. (1983). Myofibrosis and joint contractures caused by injections of pentazocine. J Bone Joint Surg, 65A: 1007–1009.

Tuazon, C., Hill, R., and Sheagren, J. (1974). Microbiologic study of street heroin and injection paraphernalia. J Infect Dis, 129: 327–329.

van Kemp, K., Herregodts, P., Duynslaeger, L. et al. (1989). Muscular fibrosis due to chronic intramuscular administration of narcotic analgesics. Acta Clin Belg, 44: 383–387.

Waldvogel, F. and Vasey, H. (1980). Osteomyelitis: the past decade. N Engl J Med, 303: 360–370.

Webb, D. and Thadepalli, H. (1979). Skin and soft tissue polymicrobial infections from intravenous abuse of drugs. West J Med, 130: 200–204.

White, A. (1973). Medical disorders in drug addicts: 200 consecutive admissions. JAMA, 223: 1469–1471.

chapter six

Anabolic steroids

6.1   Introduction

Anabolic steroids are synthetic compounds structurally related to testosterone, the male sex hormone. Testosterone has two different effects on the body: it promotes the development of secondary male sexual characteristics (androgenic effects), and it accelerates muscle growth (anabolic effects). The hormonal basis for male sexual characteristics was discovered by Berthold in 1849. He observed that the male characteristics of roosters disappeared when they were castrated, and reappeared when the testes were implanted in the abdomen. Berthold correctly deduced that the testes were secreting something into the blood that controlled the development of male traits. In 1930, another scientist, from the same medical school in Göttingen where Berthold had made his original discovery, succeeded in isolating 15 mg of a compound with anabolic activity from 25,000 liters of policemen's urine. The compound was named androsterone for three reasons: it was virilizing (*andro*, Greek for male), the nucleus of its molecule was like that of cholesterol's ("ster" for sterol), and it contained a ketone group ("one"). A few years later testosterone was crystallized from bull testes (testo = testis) and its chemical structure characterized (Kochakian, 1990).

When experimenters in the 1940s were finally able to synthesize testosterone, they were disappointed to find that it had minimal effect when given orally. Subsequent research demonstrated that testosterone's positive effects on nitrogen balance and muscle growth could, at least partially, be separated from its androgenic effects. In the process of trying to separate the androgenic from the anabolic effects, it was observed that substitutions, at the 17-position, produced orally-absorbed compounds that had anabolic effects with only a fraction of testosterone's androgenic effects. Further manipulations of the testosterone molecule at the 17-position have led to the production of a series of "anabolic" steroids that are active when taken orally.

No agent is purely anabolic. All so-called "anabolic steroids" exert androgenic effects, and the only difference between agents is the proportion of anabolic to androgenic effects that are produced. When commercially prepared anabolic steroids became available just before World War II, they were used to promote healing and speed recovery. It quickly became appar-

aging without wasting...

supportive oral anabolic therapy • potent • well-tolerated

With advancing age, weakness and weight loss may indicate a "wasting" of dietary protein due to poor protein metabolism. A potent, well-tolerated anabolic agent plus a diet high in protein can make a remarkable difference. Patients show a notable increase in strength, vigor and sense of well-being. There is marked improvement in appetite, measurable weight gain. The natural anabolic processes are helped in the utilization of dietary protein for tissue building and other vital functions.

WINSTROL® brand of STANOZOLOL

...a new oral anabolic agent, combines high anabolic activity with outstanding tolerance. Although its androgenic influence is extremely low*, women and children should be observed for signs of slight virilization (hirsutism, acne or voice change), and young women may experience milder or shorter menstrual periods. These effects are reversible when dosage is decreased or therapy discontinued. Patients with impaired cardiac or renal function should be observed because of the possibility of sodium and water retention. Liver function tests may reveal an increase in BSP retention, particularly in elderly patients, in which case therapy should be discontinued. Although it has been used in patients with cancer of the prostate, its mild androgenic activity is considered by some investigators to be a contraindication.

Dosage in adults, *usually 1 tablet t.i.d.;* young women, *1 tablet b.i.d.;* children (school age), *up to 1 tablet t.i.d.;* children (pre-school age), *½ tablet b.i.d. Shows best results when administered with a high protein diet. Available as scored tablets of 2 mg. in bottles of 100.*

*The therapeutic value of anabolic agents depends on the ratio of anabolic potency to androgenic effect. This anabolic androgenic ratio of Winstrol is especially great because it combines high potency with low androgenic activity.

Winthrop

Winthrop Laboratories, New York, N. Y.

Figure 6.1 Anabolic steroids. When these agents first became available, they were often used for indications that are no longer considered acceptable today. This advertisement is from a 1961 issue of JAMA.

ent that these drugs also had the ability to alter mood, and they were used to treat depression (Bahrke et al., 1990). It is alleged that steroids were given to German stormtroopers to increase both strength and hostility. The notion that steroids might improve physical performance is attributed to Boje, who published his ideas in 1939 (Boje, 1939). Table 6.2.1.1 lists the anabolic steroids most commonly abused today. There is a thriving black market for these drugs, with much clandestine production and importation. Analysis of confiscated samples has shown wide variation in steroid content. Many products are falsely labeled.

Athletes use steroids because they believe steroids will improve their performance. Specifically, it has been claimed that steroid use (1) increases lean body mass, (2) increases strength, (3) increases aggressiveness, and (4) leads to a shorter recovery time between workouts. There is some evidence to support all of these claims, particularly the increases in strength (Plymate and Friedl, 1992), but rigidly controlled studies have never been done, nor are they likely to be. Athletes use doses of steroids that most physicians consider dangerous. Ethical considerations prevent physicians from participating in "megadose" steroid studies. Anecdotal reports suggest that East German scientists have done many of the requisite studies, but the results have never been published.

The steroid-abusing subculture recognizes three patterns of steroid use. These are referred to as stacking, cycling, and pyramiding. "Stacking" refers to the practice of using several different steroid preparations at once. The hope is that maximal anabolic effects will be achieved while, at the same time, the androgenic effects are minimized. "Cycling" describes a pattern of usage where combinations of drugs are taken in alternating six to twelve week cycles. The rationale here is that the practice will prevent tolerance from occurring. "Pyramiders" start with low doses of the drug and gradually increase the amount of drug taken over several weeks, tapering off entirely before a competition. Not uncommonly, serious steroid abusers combine all three approaches.

The real incidence of steroid abuse in general, and as a cause of medical problems, in particular, is hard to evaluate. The DAWN report for 1994 contains no mention of steroid-related deaths or emergency room visits (Substance Abuse Mental Health Services Administration, 1995). On the other hand, results of the National Household Survey on Drug Abuse indicate that more than 1,000,000 Americans are current or former users, with more than 300,000 having used steroids within the last year. The median age for the users is 18 years. Among older users at least, steroid abuse was associated with the abuse of other drugs (Yesalis et al., 1993).

Single case reports of steroid-related deaths and vascular disease have increased, but are still uncommon. Multiple surveys have confirmed steroid abuse in at least 7% of high-school-aged males and 1% of females. When an announced drug-testing program was initiated by the National Collegiate Athletic Association, steroid use was detected in fewer than 1% of the athletes, but when the International Olympic committee performed surprise, non-punitive, testing in 1984–1985, approximately 50% of those tested were positive for steroids (Yesalis et al., 1990)! Comparable rates of abuse have been observed in the United Kingdom. In a recent survey, 7.7% of 1,669 gym-goers admitted to recent steroid abuse (Anon, 1993).

6.2   Pharmacology

6.2.1   Synthesis and metabolism

Testosterone is synthesized in the testes and adrenal glands, but only about 5% originates in the adrenals. It is a 19-carbon molecule synthesized from cholesterol. Cholesterol is produced from acetate stored in the testes, not from circulating cholesterol bound to low-density lipoprotein. Conversion from cholesterol to pregnenolone occurs in the mitochondria. From there the pregnenolone is transported to the endoplasmic reticulum, where a three-step synthesis converts it to testosterone. Once it is produced, testosterone is immediately released into the circulation. It has been estimated that a normal adult male produces 6 mg of testosterone per day.

Once testosterone is released into the bloodstream, approximately 50% of it circulates, tightly-bound to the sex-hormone-binding globulin (SHBG), which is a glycoprotein produced in the liver. Much smaller amounts circulate loosely-bound to albumin. The bond between albumin and testosterone is so weak that for practical purposes it can be considered unbound. Free testosterone seems to enter cells by simple diffusion. Once it does, it binds to a steroid receptor in the cytosol that is transported to the nucleus, where it initiates DNA transcription. Because the testosterone bound to SHBG is so tightly-bound, it probably never enters cells. For that reason, changes in the concentration of SHBG must be considered when measuring total testosterone blood levels, since they may drastically affect the observed half-life of the drug. Half-life values reported in the literature have ranged anywhere from 10–100 minutes.

When testosterone is given orally, nearly half of it will be metabolized on the first pass through the liver, so very large oral doses are required to produce any therapeutic effect. Agents such as methyltestosterone are not as extensively metabolized by the liver, which is why they can be used orally. There are two pathways in the liver by which testosterone is broken down into a series of 17 ketosteroids. The latter are excreted in the urine, along

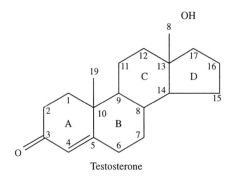

Testosterone

Figure 6.2.1   Testosterone. Testosterone is rapidly degraded by the liver when it is given orally. Modifications at the 17-position, such as esterification of the β hydroxyl group, prevent hepatic breakdown and allow the drug to be given orally.

with much larger amounts of 17 ketosteroids that are produced in the adrenal cortex. About 90% of a dose of testosterone is excreted in the urine either as the glucuronic or sulfuric acid conjugates. Approximately 6% is excreted unconjugated in the feces, and small amounts of glucuronide may appear in the bile. Less than 250 µg/day of testosterone appears unchanged in the urine. For testing purposes, most programs monitor the ratio of testosterone to epitestosterone that is excreted in the urine. In healthy young men, this ratio is known to be less than 2:1, but the International Olympic Committee accepts any value of less than 6:1 as normal.

Table 6.2.1.1 Commercially Available
Steroid Preparations

Injectable agents:
  Deca-Durbolin (Nandrolone decanoate)
  Depo-Testosterone (Testosterone cypionate)
  Delatestryl (Testosterone enanthate)
  Durabolin (Nandrolone phenpropionate)
  Oreton (Testosterone propionate)
  Primobolan (Methenolone enanthate)
Oral agents:
  Anadrol-50 (Oxymetholone)
  Anavar (Oxandrolone)
  Dianabol (Methandrostenolone)
  Halotestin (Fluoxymesterone)
  Maxibolin (Ethylestrenol)
  Metandren (Methyltestosterone)
  Nibal (Methenolone acetate)
  Nilevar (Norethandrolone)
  Winstrol (Stanozolol)

6.2.2   Black market steroids and steroid contaminants

The Anabolic Steroids Control Act of 1990 became effective in February 1991, but since that time, anabolic steroids have increasingly been smuggled into the United States. Much of the product reaching the U.S. has been legally manufactured in Europe, but diverted into the American black market. The quality and quantity of smuggled product are often misrepresented, placing users at some risk.

Gamma hydroxybutyric acid (GHB) is, not infrequently, represented as a steroid, or mixed into illicit steroid preparations. GHB is a depressant that, in some European countries, is used as an adjunct in anesthesia. Bodybuilders in the U.S. are said to have started abusing GHB during the early 1990s, probably because the drug was thought to promote the release of growth hormone. The average dose is thought to be only a few grams. Large doses can cause nausea, vertigo, seizures, and respiratory depression (Auerbach, 1990). GHB is relatively easy to synthesize, and recipes for home production continue to circulate in the underground press (Krawczseniuk, 1993). No toxicologic data is avaialble.

6.3 Legitimate clinical indications

In males, the only legitimate indication for androgen is replacement therapy when, for whatever reason (trauma, congenital), there is testicular failure. Androgens are occasionally used to treat women who have metastatic breast cancer with bone involvement. Steroids classified as anabolic agents, such as stanozolol (Winstrol®), are indicated only for use in the treatment of hereditary angioedema. Compounds that exert both androgenic and anabolic effects are also indicated for the treatment of deficient red cell production, as occurs in acquired aplastic anemia and myelofibrosis. Methyltestosterone is occasionally sold in combination with estrogens (Premarin®) for the relief of symptoms associated with menopause.

6.4 Steroid-related disorders

6.4.1 Liver disease

Elevated liver enzymes have been observed in steroid-abusing athletes, but since exercise itself can be associated with some enzyme changes (depending on when the sample is drawn in relation to exercise), it is hard to be sure if any connection exists at all (Graham and Kennedy, 1990). The connection between peliosis hepatis and steroid use is much firmer. The evidence that anabolic steroid use can cause hepatic adenomas is convincing, but evidence for hepatoma and other malignancies is not as strong, especially given the enormous number of people taking these drugs.

6.4.1.1 Peliosis hepatis

This obscure disorder has been recognized for well over 100 years. Histologically, its appearance is characterized by the presence of scattered, small, cystic, blood-filled lakes scattered throughout the liver. Some of the cysts may be lined with epithelium while others are not (Kalra et al., 1976). These collections of blood often abut on zones of hepatocellular necrosis. The lungs may also be involved in the same process, as may the entire reticuloendothelial system. Lesions have been described in the spleen, lymph nodes, and bone marrow (Kent and Thompson, 1961; Taxy, 1978).

Peliosis was first described in tuberculosis patients (Zak, 1950), but over the years, reports have been published linking peliosis to many other conditions. The connection between anabolic steroids and peliosis was first noted in 1952 (Burger and Marcuse, 1952). Since then, it has been reconfirmed on many occasions. In one series of 38 patients with peliosis, 27 had hematologic disorders and all 27 had been treated with 17 alpha-alkyl substituted steroids (Boyer, 1978). In an autopsy study of patients with aplastic anemia, one-third of the patients treated with steroids had peliosis. Only 3% of the patients who had not been treated with steroids had peliosis (Wakabayashi et al., 1984). Other studies have confirmed the steroid connection (Friedl, 1990). Testosterone, and the testosterone esters, have not been implicated. In all of the steroid/peliosis case reports, 17-alkylated androgens have been the responsible agents.

Peliosis is not easily diagnosed in life. If studied, patients with peliosis will have abnormal liver scans (Lowdell and Murray-Lyon, 1985), but since they are mostly asymptomatic, the probability that they will be scanned is small. Patients with peliosis occasionally bleed to death from these lesions (Bagheri and Boyer, 1974; Nadell and Kosek, 1977; Taxy, 1978), or die of hepatic coma, but since most of them were gravely ill with other disorders, it is hard to determine what prompted the fatal event. More recently, peliosis has been described in AIDS patients, where the lesions may be confused with Kaposi's sarcoma (Czapar et al., 1986).

At first, it was believed that peliosis was congenital (Zak, 1950); however, that explanation seems unlikely, especially since cows with peliosis (St. George's disease) have been cured simply by change of pasture (Graham and Kennedy, 1990). Another explanation was suggested by Paradinas, who, after analyzing biopsy material from individuals with peliosis, suggested that the 17-alkylated androgens induce hepatocyte hyperplasia. If the hyperplasia is marked, then the hepatocytes can obstruct venous drainage, and perhaps also the bile canaliculi (Paradinas et al., 1977). The problem with this theory is that it does not explain how some of the cysts come to have an endothelial lining. The results of the most recent study on the subject suggest that peliosis may be the result of an infectious process related to, or possibly the same as, bacillary angiomatosis, a lesion usually found only in individuals with HIV infection (Leong et al., 1992). The bacilli responsible for bacillary angiomatosis have staining and histologic similarities with the bacilli known to cause cat scratch disease, but whether infection with this agent is responsible for all cases of peliosis remains to be seen.

6.4.1.2   Cholestasis

The 17-alpha-alkyl substituted steroids can cause cholestatic jaundice. Bile accumulates in the canaliculi, but without evidence of inflammation or necrosis (Foss and Simpson, 1959). There are many cases of cholestasis in the literature, and the connection with steroid abuse seems clear (Foss and Simpson, 1959; Westaby et al., 1977; Lucey and Moseley, 1987), however, the frequency with which it occurs is not clear. Different estimates have placed the incidence of cholestasis at anywhere from less than 1% to at least 17% (Friedl, 1990). Several deaths from cholestatic jaundice have been attributed to steroids, but they occurred in elderly, debilitated patients, and the evidence of causality is far from convincing (Friedl, 1990). Based on animal studies, the mechanism for bile accumulation appears to involve a disruption of the microfilaments within the hepatocytes that reduces the ability of the cells to transport bile (Phillips et al., 1978). A case report published in 1994 described severe cholestasis and jaundice in a non-C17 alkylated steroid (testosterone propionate) raising the possibility that cholestasis may not be confined only to users of oral agents (Yoshida et al., 1994).

6.4.1.3   Hepatic tumors

A clear association exists between the use of C-17 alkylated androgens and hepatic tumors. Hepatocellular adenomas, similar in many ways to the adenomas that arise in the livers of women taking birth control pills, are not uncommon, even in men who are not steroid abusers. Judging from the number of reports, the incidence is 1% to 3% among the 17 alkylated androgen users (Friedl, 1990). The difficulty of assessing the frequency of the lesion is that, like peliosis, hepatocellular adenomas are usually silent, only coming to medical attention when adenomas are found incidentally at autopsy, or when they rupture and cause hemoperitoneum (Bruguera, 1975; Lesna et al., 1976; Paradinas et al., 1977; Boyd and Mark, 1977; Hermandez-Nieto et al., 1977; Bird et al., 1979; Westaby et al., 1983; Creagh et al., 1988).

Adenomas have the same appearance in both androgen and birth-control users. They are comprised of sheets of cells that look like normal hepatocytes. There are, however, some differences. One important difference is that androgen-related adenomas tend to be larger. Adenomas in steroid users range in size from a few millimeters to several centimeters in diameter. Androgen-related adenomas often form bile-containing acini, and absent a history of androgen abuse, acini formation is usually considered to be histologic evidence of malignancy. Adenomas, in steroid users, may also display other features which are suspect for malignancy, such as bizarre nuclei and even rare mitoses (Creagh et al., 1988). The benign nature of most of these lesions is confirmed by their sharply demarcated margins, their failure to metastasize, the absence of demonstrable alpha feto protein, and the absence of associated cirrhosis (the most frequent setting for hepatocellular carcinoma). The fact that adenomas regress when androgens are discontinued also argues against their malignant nature (Friedl, 1990). Nonetheless, hepatocellular carcinoma has been reported in C-17 substituted androgen users (Overly et al., 1984), so the possibility for conversion from adenoma to carcinoma cannot be ruled out (Boyd and Mark ,1977).

Like peliosis, hepatic adenomas can be difficult to diagnose in life. Liver function tests may well be normal (Westaby et al., 1983), and the distribution of these lesions can be patchy (Bagheri and Boyer, 1974a; Westaby et al., 1977), so that percutaneous biopsy may well miss the lesions. There are proven instances where nodular hyperplasia resulted in portal hypertension, even in the face of a normal biopsy (Stromeyer and Ishak, 1981). This possibility is confirmed by one report of bleeding varices in a steroid abuser, where the biopsy was negative and there were no other risk factors or findings to account for the bleeding (Winwood, Robertson, and Wright, 1990).

6.4.2   Cardiovascular disease

Myocardial infarction, sudden arrhythmic death, and stroke have all been described in young steroid abusers. There are many good reasons why that should be, including the fact that highly conditioned athletes, the individuals most likely to abuse steroids, do not have anatomically normal hearts to

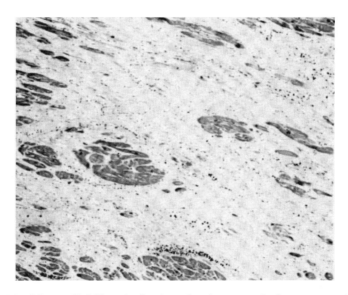

Figure 6.4.2   Myocardial fibrosis. Section of an interventricular septum taken from a steroid-abusing weight lifter who died of an arrythmia. There is no extensive myocardial fibrosis which probably accounts for the occurrence of the arrythmia. Original magnification 60×. Courtesy of Dr. Renu Virmani, Chairman, Department of Cardiovascular Pathology, Armed Forces Institute of Pathology.

begin with (Huston et al., 1985), and the fact that anabolic androgens have direct effects on cardiac growth, on myocyte metabolism (Kinson et al., 1991; Melchert et al., 1992; Kochakian and Welder, 1993; Tseng et al., 1994), and on platelet function (Halushka et al., 1993). Relevant animal studies are almost entirely lacking and very few case reports have been published. But the results of animal studies confirm that testosterone increases thromboxane A_2 receptor density (Halushka et al., 1993), which could easily lead to infarction. Myocardial hypertrophy and fibrosis are easily produced in the rat model (Tseng et al., 1994), and either one could supply the substrate for arrhythmic sudden death. Whether these same changes actually occur with any regularity in steroid abusers remains to be seen. One echocardiographic study of steroid-using weight lifters found no evidence of left ventricular hypertrophy (Thompson et al., 1992). The problem with echocardiographic studies is that they are unlikely to detect small increases in ventricular mass, even though a small increase may be all that is required as a substrate for sudden cardiac death.

The first documented steroid-related infarct was reported in 1988. Angiography showed no lesions, but the patient was hyperlipidemic and had evidence of increased platelet aggregation (McNutt et al., 1988). Another case associated with hyperlipidemia was reported in 1989 (Graham and Kennedy, 1990). A third case with thrombotic occlusion of both the left main and left anterior descending coronary arteries was briefly described in 1991 (Ferenchick, 1991). A fourth case with thrombus of the left anterior descending artery was reported in a 25-year old steroid-abusing weight lifter with no other associated risk factors. At the time of infarction, he had very low antithrombin III activity, but levels quickly returned to normal once steroid abuse had been discontinued (Huie, 1994).

Infarction has also been reported in a weight lifter who was abusing aspirin and testosterone simultaneously (Ferenchick and Adelman, 1992). Arterial thrombosis manifested as saddle pulmonary embolus in a steroid-abusing weight lifter has been described (Montine and Gaede, 1992). Another paper recounts the clinical history of a 32-year old with "cardiomyopathy" and stroke (Mochizuki and Richter, 1988). Since the last patient did not undergo angiography or biopsy, the diagnosis of cardiomyopathy remains in question. The autopsy findings in other recent cases of sudden arrhythmic death, however, have in fact demonstrated prominent myocardial fibrosis (Luke et al., 1991; Kennedy and Lawrence, 1993), not unlike the changes that have been described in the hearts of stimulant abusers' (Karch and Billingham, 1988).

If, in fact, steroid abusers are more prone to thrombosis and infarction than the rest of the population, it may be explained by the 50% decrease in high-density lipoprotein levels that has been documented in some steroid-abusing athletes. At the same time, low-density lipoprotein levels increase by more than 36% (Glazer, 1991). Hyperlipidemia, in turn, initiates a train of events, all of which have unfavorable effects on the vascular system. There is even evidence that hypercholesteremia potentiates coronary-artery response to epinephrine (Rosendorff et al., 1981). Hyperlipidemia leads to hyperinsulinemia (Friedl et al., 1989), and hyperinsulinemia is known to be associated with accelerated atherogenesis (Ducimetriere et al., 1980). Hyperlipidemia also favors increased platelet aggregation (Sano et al., 1983). The problem with implicating lipids as the cause of thrombosis in the steroid-abusing subpopulation is that different steroids have different effects on the lipid profile (Thompson et al., 1989). In some instances, the effect may even be beneficial (Maciejko et al., 1983), but since the steroid abusers themselves rarely know what drug they are taking, determining cause-and-effect relationships is nearly impossible.

Even though only one case of "cardiomyopathy" has been described, the argument for steroid-induced alterations in the myocardium is strong and could conceivably account for some cases of sudden death in athletes. In experimental studies, guinea pigs and rats treated with methandrostenolone predictably develop myocyte necrosis, cellular edema, and mitochondrial swelling (Behrendt and Boffin, 1977; Appell et al., 1983). Clinical echocardiographic studies have yielded conflicting results as to whether anabolic steroids counteract the improvement of cardiac performance that results from endurance training (Takala et al., 1991), but there is no question that animals given steroids have morphologic alterations in their hearts, and that these alterations are different from those produced by exercise alone (Appell et al., 1983). In beagles, anabolic steroids modulate the increased collagen production normally seen in the hearts of animals that have undergone endurance training (Takala et al., 1991). In murine peripheral muscle, anabolic steroid administration results in mitochondrial disruption and, most importantly, a decrease in myocyte capillary supply. Decreases also occur in the total number of mitochondria present when compared to muscle fibers from animals not treated with steroids (Tesch, 1987; Soares and Duarte, 1991).

If similar subcellular changes occur in human hearts, it could explain the histologic picture recently described in one case report (Luke et al., 1991). The authors described the findings in a 21-year old, previously healthy, steroid-abusing (nandrolone and testosterone) weight lifter who died of cardiac arrest. In addition to renal hypertrophy and hepatosplenomegally, there was biventricular hypertrophy with chamber dilatation. The heart weighed 530 grams, but the valves and coronary arteries were entirely normal. Sectioned myocardium showed extensive fibrosis, especially in the subendocardium and the central parts of the left ventricle and intraventricular septum. One area of fibrosis measured more than 8 cm across. Microscopic sections disclosed small foci of necrosis with sparse neutrophilic and round cell infiltrates. In some of these small foci of necrosis, myocytes with contraction band necrosis were evident. A similar case with widespread patchy fibrosis and occasional lymphocytic foci has been reported from Australia (Kennedy and Lawrence, 1993) and another with extensive fibrosis and severe atherosclerosis from Denmark (Lyngberg, 1991). While there is no way to rule out occult myocarditis in this particular individual, the similarities to catechol toxicity are quite striking (Reichenbach and Benditt, 1970).

Several mechanisms could explain fibrosis in these cases. If muscle fiber hypertrophy is not accompanied by proportionate increases in blood supply, small areas of infarction may result. When these areas of infarction heal, they are replaced by fibrosis. Alternatively, it has been known for many years that steroids can also cause contraction band necrosis (Karch and Billingham, 1986). It is even conceivable that steroid use might in some way produce catecholamine elevation, but studies are lacking. Whatever the cause, fibrotic material has conduction properties quite unlike those of normal muscle, and areas of fibrosis may later provide the anatomic substrate for lethal reentrant arrhythmias. However, until more autopsy material becomes available, the mechanism for sudden death in these individuals remains speculative.

6.4.3   Neurologic disorders

Cases of cerebral thrombosis have been reported (Mochizuki and Richter, 1988; Frankle et al., 1988), but they are decidedly rare events. Psychiatric disturbances are, on the other hand, relatively common, and steroid-related psychosis has been used as a defense in several murder trials. One study of 41 self-admitted steroid abusers found that 22% of those interviewed had affective disorders and 12% had episodes of frank psychosis (Pope and Katz, 1988). Another study described three men, none with previous psychiatric histories, who committed violent crimes, including murder, while they were taking steroids. In each instance, anabolic steroids were thought to have played a role, and in all three cases, the men returned to their normal premorbid personalities when the steroids were withdrawn (Pope and Katz,

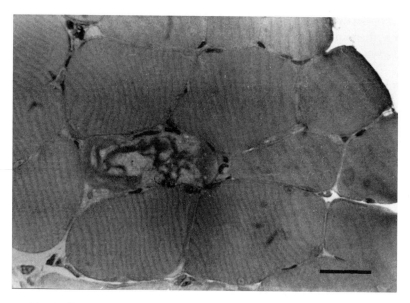

Figure 6.4.3.1   Degenerating muscle in steroid treated rat. The peripheral muscle of rat treated with nandrolone decanoate and forced to exercise. Microscopic analysis discloses focal necrosis; degenerating fibers intermingled with normal appearing fibers (scale bar = 50 μm). Morphometric analysis of these same fibers shows decreased numbers of capillaries when compared to controls. Courtesy of Dr. J. M. Soares, Faculty of Sport Sciences, University of Porto, Porto, Portugal.

Figure 6.4.3.2   Steroid induced mitochondrial damage in rat. Electron micrographs of rats chronically treated with nandrolone show mitochondrial swelling and disruption very similar to what is seen in the hearts of animals exposed to high levels of catecholamines (scale bar = 2 μm). Courtesy of Dr. J. M. Soares, Faculty of Sport Sciences, University of Porto, Porto, Portugal.

1990). Other case reports have described domestic violence attributable to steroid abuse (Schulte et al., 1993).

At least two controlled studies have confirmed the findings suggested in the case reports and retrospective studies. In one study, methyltestosterone in high (240 mg/day) and low (40 mg/day) doses was given to 20 volunteers over a number of days. The subjects were not steroid users, and were not involved in any athletic training. The low dose regimen produced no measurable effects on mood or behavior, but the high dose did cause changes including euphoria and sexual arousal, as well as irritability, mood swings, and confusion. One of the 20 subjects experienced an acute manic episode and a second became hypomanic (Su et al., 1993). In a second study, psychiatric and physical findings were compared in 88 steroid-abusing athletes and 68 others who were not steriod users (Pope, 1994). The steroid users had more frequent gynecomastia, decreased mean testicular length, and higher cholesterol/HDL ratios than non-users. More importantly, 23% of the steroid abusers reported symptoms consistent with major mood disorders such as mania, hypomania, or major depression.

As yet, no jury has been willing to accept a "steroid defense" (Moss, 1988), but the role of steroid abuse in the case of individual violent crimes is well worth considering. There is a firm physiologic basis for arguing that psychiatric disturbances can result from steroid abuse. Along with PCP and cocaine, steroids bind with the sigma receptor (Su, 1991). This receptor is located in nonsynaptic regions of plasma membranes in the central nervous system, and peripherally in endocrine and immune tissues. Binding to the sigma receptor is believed to be the explanation for cocaine's dysphoric effects (Sharkey et al., 1988), and possibly for progesterone-related mood disturbances seen during the menstrual cycle (Bäckström et al., 1989). Since PCP also binds at the sigma receptor site, it should hardly be surprising that steroids binding to these same receptors should cause behavior changes.

6.4.4   Musculoskeletal disease

Surprisingly little is known about the effects of steroid abuse on the musculoskeletal system, and not that much more is known about the effect of endogenously-produced hormone on muscle mass and strength. One study compared muscle strength and hormone levels in middle aged and elderly men and women. In men, the effects of aging were minimal, but in women, aging was associated with decreased testosterone levels, decreased muscle mass, and decreased strength (Häkkinen and Pakarinen, 1993).

Mice chronically treated with anabolic steroids have abnormal tendons. The collagen fibrils, which under normal circumstances are neatly aligned and symmetric, become crimped, fragmented, and frayed (Mincha, 1986a; Mincha, 1986b). Stress testing shows that the tensile strength of the fibers is reduced. Light microscopic examination of tendons from these experimental animals shows no evident abnormalities, although electron microscopy will disclose alterations in the size of the collagen fibrils (Miles et al., 1992). These alterations may explain the occasional report of steroid-related tendon rupture (Hill et al., 1983; Kramhoft and Solgaard, 1986; Laseter and Russell, 1991). Avascular necrosis of the femoral heads, similar to that seen with long-term glucocorticoid therapy, has also been reported, but it is not clear that the phenomenon is due to anabolic steroid abuse. It could just as easily be an idiosyncratic reaction (Pettine, 1991). Exercise-conditioned animals given anabolic steroids have reduced numbers of capillaries per muscle fiber, while at the same time the amount of fatty and connective tissue in their muscles increases (Soares and Duarte, 1991). The relative decrease in the number of capillaries per fiber means that there is inefficient exchange of respiratory gases and substrates in the hypertrophied muscles. The typical histologic picture in these animals is patchy fiber necrosis. Degenerating fibers are surrounded by fibers which have normal morphology. Similar control studies in humans are lacking.

6.4.5   Detecting steroid abuse

Medical review officers must correlate laboratory data with physical findings in the diagnosis of narcotic abuse, and the situation is not dissimilar in cases of steroid abuse. A clinical profile of typical steroid abusers can be drawn, and reference to it is often helpful when the history is unclear. Typical findings are shown in Table 6.4.5. Testosterone blood levels remain poorly characterized, and cannot be used to detect abuse. A recent study measured mean testosterone levels in conditioned athletes both before and after exercising. Resting levels were 16–17 nmol/dL. After an intense period of strength training, levels increased by 27%. Testosterone levels increased even more after endurance training (37%), but after both types of training levels returned to normal within a few hours (Jensen et al., 1991).

Because blood tests that detect steroid abuse are not yet reliable, and because they are invasive, steroid detection programs rely entirely on the results of urine testing. Competitive athletes, who know they are subject to testing rarely use oral anabolic agents, because it is widely known that such agents can be detected for weeks after their last use. Largely for that reason, the use of injectable testosterone has become more and more popular. The easiest way to detect testosterone abuse is to measure the ratio of testosterone to epitestosterone (17 alpha-hydroxy-4-androsten-3-one) in the urine. The exact role of this hormone is not clear, but *in vitro* studies suggest that epitestosterone has androgen-counteracting activity, and may be involved in the prostatic hypertrophy associated with advancing age, and possibly even with body hair distribution (Stárka, 1993).

Epitestosterone is secreted by human adrenal, testes, and ovaries, but it is not produced from testosterone. It is poorly metabolized by man, and at least 50% of injected epitestosterone can be recovered unchanged in the urine (Wilson and Lipsett, 1966). In adults, but not necessarily during prepuberal development (Raynaud et al., 1993), roughly equal concentrations of test-

Table 6.4.5 Profile of a Steroid Abuser

Social
Recent changes in friends, acquaintances
Obsession with health, exercise, weight lifting
Spends most of time in gyms or health clubs
Takes large amounts of vitamins and food supplements
Very high calorie intake
Does not abuse other drugs because of concern with leading a
"healthy life style"

Physical
Rapid weight gain and muscle development
Increased body hair, deepening of voice
Acne (both sexes)
Hair loss (both sexes)
Breast enlargement (males)
Testicular atrophy
Difficulty urinating
Elevated blood pressure
Complaints of stomach upset
Jaundice
Edema of extremities

Mental Changes
Increased aggression
Hyperactivity, irritability
Auditory hallucinations
Paranoid delusions
Manic episodes
Depression and anxiety
Panic disorders
Suicidal thoughts

Laboratory Findings
Decreased HDL cholesterol
Decreased luteinizing hormone
Decreased follicle stimulating hormone
Decreased thyroid stimulating hormone
Decreased thyroid hormones
Elevated liver enzymes
Increased hematocrit
Increased LDL cholesterol
Increased triglycerides
Increased glucose

Adapted from Narducci et al.: Anabolic steroids, a review of the clinical
toxicology and diagnostic screening. Clinical Toxicology, 28(3): 287–310.

osterone and epitestosterone are excreted in the urine of both women and men. Under normal conditions the production of epitestosterone is relatively constant and independent of testosterone production. Thus, abnormally high ratios of testosterone to epitestosterone are generally considered by the International Olympic Committee (IOC) and other sports federations and organizations as proof of exogeous testosterone administration.

In normal young men, the testosterone/epitestosterone ratio is less than 3:1 and is probably closer to 1:1 (Dehennin, 1993). However, the IOC, and other official sports bodies, accept any ratio of less than 6:1 as normal. In practice, that means that an athlete who wants to take steroids can do so with relative impunity, since modest doses of testosterone will not alter the ratio sufficiently to lead to disqualification (Dehennin and Matsumoto, 1993). There are even reports of testosterone abusers who titrate their dose. One week after an injection, they have their T/E ratio measured. If the ratio is still low enough, they can increase their dosage.

Because such large sums of money are involved, considerable effort is expended to find new ways to beat steroid testing programs. One of the newest approaches is to inject epitestosterone along with testosterone (Dehennin, 1994b), thereby keeping the ratio of the two compounds within accepted limits. The only problem with this approach is that the absolute amount of epitestosterone in the urine will be abnormally high. As a result, the IOC has recently banned epitestosterone use and ruled that any specimen found to contain more than 150 ng/mL of epitestosterone is suspect. The IOC is also experimenting with other ways of detecting testosterone abuse, such as measuring the ratio of testosterone to 17 alpha-hydroxyprogesterone (Carlström et al., 1992; Catlin and Cowan, 1992; Wheeler, 1993).

In spite of the permissive ratio selected by the IOC, biologic false positives are possible. In 1992 there was a report of a college football player who vehemently denied testosterone abuse, but who nonetheless was found to have persistent ratios as high as 1:10 (Baylis et al., 1992). When biological false positives do occur, it is probably a result of abnormal testicular epitestosterone secretion or the abnormal breakdown of epitestosterone once it is produced (Raynaud et al., 1992; Dehennin, 1994). Many approaches have been suggested for separating abusers from biologic false positives. One way is to administer ketoconazole. A side effect of treatment with this antifungal agent is that it inhibits testosterone production (by inhibiting 17 alpha hydroxylase and 17,20 lyase activity). If testosterone levels are high because ketaconazole has been injected, it will not cause levels to drop. On the other hand, if an innocent athlete with a T/E ratio > 6 is given ketoconazole, one would expect a steep drop in testosterone levels, and a concomitant decrease in the T/E ratio. This has proven to be the case when ketaconazole was given to athletes with high ratios (Kieman et al., 1993; Oftebro et al., 1994).

The results in a recent case decided by the appeals board of the International Amateur Athletic Federation may mean that testing protocols for testosterone will undergo some changes in the near future. A woman runner was suspended when she was found to have a T/E ratio > 40. Her urine sample had been stored at room temperature for two days and had a pH of

8.5 at the time of testing. Experts retained by the runner carried out a series of experiments showing that at high pH ranges, bacteria in the urine may convert testosterone precursors to testosterone. There is also evidence that the reverse process can occur, so whether or not bacteria in the urine make a positive result more or less likely is hard to say. It may be that, in the future, samples to be tested for testosterone will also have to be cultured to prove that they are bacteria-free.

References

Anon. (1993). Anabolic steroid use. Lancet, 341(May 29): 1407.

Appell, H., Heller-Umpfenbach, B., Feraud, M., and Weicker, H. (1983). Ultrastructural and morphometric investigations on the effects of training and administration of anabolic steroids on the myocardium of guinea pigs. Int J Sports Med, 4: 268–274.

Auerbach, S. (1990). Multistate outbreak of poisonings associated with illicit use of gamma hydroxy butyrate. MMWR, 39: 861–863.

Bäckström, T., Sanders, D., Leask, R. et al. (1989). Mood, sexuality, hormones, and the menstrual cycle II. Hormone levels and their relationship to the premenstrual syndrome. Psychosom Med, 45(6): 503–507.

Bagheri, S. and Boyer, J. (1974). Peliosis hepatis associated with androgenic-anabolic steroid therapy. Ann Intern Med, 81: 610–618.

Bahrke, M., Yesalis, C., and Wright, J. (1990). Psychological and behavioral effects of endogenous testosterone levels and anabolic-androgenic steroids among males. Sports Med, 10(5): 303–337.

Baylis, B., Chan, S., and Przybylski, P. (1992). A case of naturally high urinary ratio of testosterone to epitestosterone. 44th Annual Meeting of the American Academy of Forensic Sciences.

Behrendt, H. and Boffin, H. (1977). Myocardial cell lesions caused by an anabolic hormone. Cell Tissue Res, 181: 423–426.

Bird, D., Vowles, K., and Anthony, P. (1979). Spontaneous rupture of a liver cell adenoma after long-term methyl testosterone: report of a case successfully treated by emergency right hepatic lobectomy. Br J Surg, 66: 212–213.

Boje, O. (1939). Doping. Bull Hlth Org League Nations, 8: 439–469.

Boyd, P. and Mark, G. (1977). Multiple hepatic adenomas and a hepatocellular carcinoma in a man on oral methyl testosterone for 11 years. Cancer, 40: 1765–1770.

Boyer, J. (1978). Androgenic-anabolic steroid-associated peliosis hepatis in man — a review of 38 reported cases. *Advances in pharmacology and therapeutics*. Volume 8. Drug-action modifications, comparative pharmacology. Oxford: Pergamon Press.

Bruguera, M. (1975). Hepatoma associated with androgenic steroids. Lancet, i: 1295.

Burger, R. and Marcuse, P. (1952). Peliosis hepatis: report of a case. Am J Clin Pathol, 22: 569–573.

Carlström, K., Palonek, E., Garle, M. et al. (1992). Detection of testosterone administration by increased ratio between serum concentrations of testosterone and 17 alpha-hydroxyprogesterone. Clin Chem, 38: 1770–1784.

Catlin, D. and Cowan, D. (1992). Detecting testosterone administration. Clin Chem, 38: 1685–1686.

Creagh, T., Rubin, A., and Evans, D. (1988). Hepatic tumors induced by anabolic steroids in an athlete. J Clin Pathol, 41: 441–443.

Czapar, C., Weldon-Linne, M., Moor, D., and Rhone, D. (1986). Peliosis hepatis in the acquired immunodeficiency syndrome. Arch Pathol Lab Med, 110: 611–613.

Dehennin, L. (1994). On the origin of physiologically high ratios of urinary testosterone to epitestosterone; consequences for reliable detection of testosterone administration by male athletes. J Endocrin, 142: 353–360.

Dehennin, L. and Matsumoto, A. (1993). Long-term administration of testosterone enanthate to normal men: alterations of the urinary profile of androgen metabolites potentially useful for detection of testosterone in sport. J Steroid Biochem Molec Biol, 44(2): 179–189.

Ducimetriere, P., Eschwere, E., Papoz, L. et al. (1980). Relationship of plasma insulin levels to the incidence of myocardial infarction and coronary heart disease mortality in a middle-aged population. Diabetologia, 19: 205–210.

Ferenchick, G. (1991). Anabolic/androgenic steroid abuse and thrombosis — is there a connection? Med Hypotheses, 35(1): 27–31.

Ferenchick, G. and Adelman, S. (1992). Myocardial infarction associated with anabolic steroid use in a previously healthy 37-year old weight lifter. Am Heart J, 124: 507–508.

Foss, G. and Simpson, S. (1959). Oral methyltestosterone and jaundice. Br Med J, 1: 259–263.

Frankle, M., Eichberg, R., and Zachariah, S. (1988). Anabolic androgenic steroids and a stroke in an athlete: case report. Arch Phys Med Rehabil, 69(8): 632–633.

Friedl, K. (1990). Reappraisal of the health risks associated with the use of high doses of oral and injectable androgenic steroids. Anabolic Steroid Abuse. Rockville, MD: National Institute on Drug Abuse.

Friedl, K., Jones, R., Hannan, C., and Plymate, S. (1989). The administration of pharmacological doses of testosterone or 19-nortestosterone to normal men is not associated with increased insulin secretion or impaired glucose tolerance. J Clin Endocrinol Metab, 68: 971–975.

Glazer, G. (1991). Atherogenic effects of anabolic steroids on serum lipid levels. A literature review. Arch Intern Med, 151(10): 1923–1925.

Graham, S. and Kennedy, M. (1990). Recent developments in the toxicology of anabolic steroids. Drug Safety, 5(6): 458–476.

Häkkinen, A. and Pakarinen, A. (1993). Muscle strength and serum testosterone, cortisol and SHBG concentrations in middle-aged and elderly men and women. Acta Physiol Scand, 148: 199–207.

Halushka, P., Masuda, A., and Matsuda, K. (1993). Regulation of thrombaxane A_2 receptors by testosterone: implications for steroid abuse and cardiovascular disease. Transactions of the American Clinical and Climatological Association, 105: 95–103.

Hernandez-Nieto, L., Bruguera, M., Bombi, S. et al. (1977). Benign liver cell adenoma associated with long term administration of an androgenic anabolic steroid (methandienone). Cancer, 40: 1761–1764.

Hill, J., Suker, J., Sachs, K., and Brigham, C. (1983). The athletic polydrug abuse phenomenon. A case report. Am J Sports Med, 11: 269–271.

Huie, M. (1994). An acute myocardial infarction occurring in an anabolic steroid user. Med Sci Sports Exerc, 26(4): 408–413.

Huston, T., Puffer, J., and Rodney, W. (1985). The athletic heart syndrome. N Engl J Med, 313(1): 24–31.

Jensen, J., Oftebro, H., Breigan, B. et al. (1991). Comparison of changes in testosterone concentrations after strength and endurance exercise in well-trained men. Eur J Appl Physiol, 63(6): 467–471.

Kalra, T., Mangla, J., and DePapp, E. (1976). Benign hepatic tumors and oral contraceptive pills. Am J Med, 61: 871–877.

Karch, S. and Billingham, M. (1988). The pathology and etiology of cocaine-induced heart disease. Arch Pathol Lab Med, 112: 225–230.

Karch, S. and Billingham, M. (1986). Myocardial contraction bands revisited. Hum Pathol, 17: 9–13.

Kennedy, M. and Lawrence, C. (1993). Anabolic steroid abuse and cardiac death. Med J Aust, 158: 346–347.

Kent, G. and Thompson, J. (1961). Peliosis hepatis: involvement of reticuloendothelial system. Arch Pathol Lab Med, 72: 658–664.

Kieman, A., Oftebro, H., Walker, C. et al. (1993). Potential use of ketoconazole in a dynamic endocrine test to differentiate between biological outliers and testosterone use by athletes. Clin Chem, 39(9): 1796–1798.

Kinson, G., Lyberry, R., and Hebert, B. (1991). Influences of anabolic androgens on cardiac growth and metabolism in the rat. Can J Physiol Pharmacol, 69: 1698–1704.

Kochakian, C. (1990). History of anabolic-androgenic steroids. Anabolic Steroid Abuse. Rockville, MD: National Institute on Drug Abuse.

Kochakian, C. and Welder, A. (1993). Invited review: anabolic-androgenic steroids: in cell culture *in vitro*. Cell Dev Biol, 29a: 433–438.

Kramhoft, M. and Solgaard, S. (1986). Spontaneous rupture of the extensor pollicis longus tendon after anabolic steroids. J Hand Surg, 11B: 87.

Krawczeniuk, A. (1993). The occurrence of gamma hydroxybutyric acid (GHB) in a steroid seizure. Microgram, XXVI(7): 160–162.

Laseter, J. and Russell, J. (1991). Anabolic steroid-induced tendon pathology — a review of the literature. Med Sci Sports Exerc, 23(1): 1–3.

Leong, S., Cazen, R., Yu, G. et al. (1992). Abdominal visceral peliosis associated with bacillary angiomatosis. Ultrastructural evidence for endothelial destruction by bacilli. Arch Pathol Lab Med, 116: 866–871.

Lesna, M., Spencer, I., and Walker, W. (1976). Liver nodules and androgens. Lancet, i: 1124.

Lowdell, C. and Murray-Lyon, I. (1985). Reversal of liver damage due to long term methyltestosterone and safety of non-17a-alkylated androgens. Br Med J, 291: 636.

Lucey, M. and Moseley, R. (1987). Severe cholestasis associated with methyltestosterone: a case report. Am J Gastroenterol, 82: 461–462.

Luke, J., Farb, A., Virmani, R., and Sample, R. (1991). Sudden cardiac death during exercise in a weight lifter using anabolic androgenic steroids: pathological and toxicological findings. J. Forensic Sci, 35(6): 1441–1447.

Lynberg, K. (1991). Myocardial infarction and death of a bodybuilder after using anabolic steroids. Ugeskritt for Laeger, 153(8): 587–588.

Maciejko, J., Holmes, D., Kottke, B. et al. (1983). Apolipoprotein A-I as a marker of angiographically-assessed coronary-artery disease. N Engl J Med, 309: 385–389.

McNutt, R., Ferenchick, G., Kirlin, P., and Hamlin, N. (1988). Acute myocardial infarction in a 22-year old world class weight lifter using anabolic steroids. Am J Cardiol, 62(1): 164.

Melchert, R., Herron, T., and Welder, A. (1992). The effect of anabolic-androgenic steroids on primary myocardial cell cultures. Med Sci Sports Exer, 24(2): 206–212.

Miles, J., Grana, W., Egle, D. et al. (1992). The effect of anabolic steroids on the biomechanical and histological properties of rat tendon. J Bone Joint Surg [Am], 74A(3): 411–422.

Mincha, H. (1986a). Organization of collagen fibrils in tendon: changes induced by anabolic steroid. I. A morphometric and sterologic analysis. Virchows Arch (B), 52: 87–89.

Mincha, H. (1986b). Organization of collagen fibrils in tendon: changes induced by anabolic steroid. I. Functional and ultrastructural studies. Virchows Arch (B), 52: 75–86.

Mochizuki, R. and Richter, K. (1988). Cardiomyopathy and cerebrovascular accident associated with anabolic-androgenic steroid use. Physician Sportsmed, 16: 109–114.

Montine, T. and Gaede, J. (1992). Massive pulmonary embolus and anabolic steroid abuse. JAMA, 267(17): 2328–2329.

Moss, D. (1988). And now the steroid defense? Am Bar Assn J, (October 1): 22.

Nadell, J. and Kosek, J. (1977). Pelosis hepatis: 12 cases associated with oral androgen therapy. Arch Pathol Lab Med, 101: 405–410.

Oftebro, H., Jensen, J., Monwinckle, P. et al. (1994). Establishing a ketoconazole suppression test for verifying testosterone administration in the doping control of athletes. J Clin Endocrin Metab, 78: 973–977.

Overly, W., Dankoff, J., Wang, B., and Singh, U. (1984). Androgens and hepatocellular carcinoma in an athlete. Ann Intern Med, 100(1): 158–159.

Paradinas, F., Bull, T., Westaby, D., and Murray-Lyon, I. (1977). Hyperplasia and prolapse of hepatocytes into hepatic veins during long term methyltestosterone therapy: possible relationships of these changes to the development of peliosis hepatis and liver tumors. Histopathology, 1: 225–226.

Pettine, K. (1991). Association of an anabolic steroids and avascular necrosis of femoral heads. Am J Sports Med, 19(1): 96–98.

Phillips, M., Oda, M., and Funatsu, K. (1978). Evidence for microfilament involvement in norethandrolone-induced intrahepatic cholestasis. Am J Pathol, 93: 729–744.

Pope, H. and Katz, D. (1988). Affective and psychotic symptoms associated with anabolic steroid use. Am J Psychiatry, 145(4): 487–490.

Pope, H. and Katz, D. (1990). Homicide and near homicide by anabolic steroid users. J Clin Psych, 51: 28–31.

Pope, H. (1994). Psychiatric and medical effects of anabolic-androgenic steroid use. Arch Gen Psych, 51: 375–382.

Plymate, S. and Friedl, K. (1992). Anabolic steroids and muscle strength. Ann Intern Med, 116(3): 270.

Raynaud, E. et al. (1992). False-positive cases in detection of testosterone doping. Lancet, 340: 1468–1469.

Raynaud, E., Audran, M., Pagés, J. et al. (1993). Determination of urinary testosterone and epitestosterone during pubertal development: a cross-sectional study in 141 normal males. Clin Endocrin, 38: 353–359.

Reichenbach, D. and Benditt, E. (1970). Catecholamines and cardiomyopathy. Hum Pathol, 1(1): 125–150.

Rosendorff, C., Hoffman, J., Verner, E. et al. (1981). Cholesterol potentiates the coronary artery response to norepinephrine in anesthetized and conscious dogs. Circ Res, 48(3): 320–329.

Sano, T., Motomiya, T., and Yamazaki, H. (1983). Influence of lipids on platelet activation *in vivo*. Thromb Res, 31: 675–684.

Schulte, H., Hale, M., and Boyer, M. (1993). Domestic violence associated with anabolic steroid abuse. Am J Psych, 150(2): 348.

Sharkey, J., Glen, K., Wolfe, S., and Kuhar, K. (1988). Cocaine binding at sigma receptors. Euro J Pharmacol, 149: 171–174.

Soares, J. and Duarte, J. (1991). Effects of training and an anabolic steroid on murine red skeletal muscle — a stereological analysis. Acta Anat, 142(2): 183–187.

Stárka, L. (1993). Epitestosterone — a hormone or not. Endocrin Reg, 27: 43–48.

Stromeyer, F. and Ishak, K. (1981). Nodular transformation of the liver: a clinico-pathologic study of 30 cases. Hum Pathol, 12: 60–71.

Su, T. (1991). Review: Sigma receptors. Putative links between nervous, endocrine and immune systems. Euro J Biochem, 200: 633–642.

Su, T., Pagliaro, M., Schmidt, P. et al. (1993). Neuropsychiatric effects of anabolic steroids in male normal volunteers. JAMA, 269: 2760–2764.

Substance Abuse and Mental Health Services Administration. (1995). Annual Medical Examiner Data. Data from the Drug Abuse Warning Network. Rockville, MD: U.S. Department of Health and Human Services.

Takala, T., Ramo, P., Kiviluoma, K. et al. (1991). Effects of training and anabolic steroids on collagen synthesis in dog heart. Eur J Appl Physiol, 62(1): 1–6.

Taxy, J. (1978). Peliosis: a morphologic curiosity becomes an iatrogenic problem. Hum Pathol, 9: 331–340.

Tesch, P. (1987). Acute and long-term metabolic changes consequent to heavy-resistance exercise. Med Sport Sci, 26: 67–89.

Thompson, P., Cullinane, E., Sady, S. et al. (1989). Contrasting effects of testosterone and stanozolol on serum lipoprotein levels. JAMA, 261: 1165–1168.

Thompson, P., Sadaniantz, A., Cullinane, E. et al. (1992). Left ventricular function is not impaired in weight lifters who use anabolic steroids. J Am Coll Cardiol, 19: 278–282.

Tseng, Y., Rockhold, R., Hoskins, B. et al. (1994). Cardiovascular toxicities of nandrolone and cocaine in spontaneously hypertensive rats. Fund Appl Toxicol, 22: 113–121.

Wakabayashi, T., Onda, H., Tada, T. et al. (1984). High incidence of peliosis hepatis in autopsy cases of aplastic anemia with special reference to anabolic steroid therapy. Acta Pathol Jpn, 34: 1079–1086.

Westaby, D., Ogle, S., Paradinas, F. et al. (1977). Liver damage from long-term methyl-testosterone. Lancet, ii: 261–263.

Westaby, D., Portmann, B., and Williams, R. (1983). Androgen-related primary hepatic tumors in non-Fanconi patients. Cancer, 51: 1947–1952.

Wheeler, M. (1993). Methods for the detection of testosterone abuse in athletes. Clin Endocrin, 38: 351–352.

Wilson, H. and Lipsett, M. (1966). Metabolism of epitestosterone in man. J Clin Endocrin Metab 26: 902–914.

Winwood, P., Robertson, D., and Wright, R. (1990). Bleeding oesophageal varices associated with anabolic steroid use in an athlete. Postgrad Med J, 66: 864–865.

Yesalis, C., Anderson, W., Buckley, W., and Wright, J. (1990). Incidence of the non-medical use of anabolic-androgenic steroids. Anabolic Steroid Abuse. Rockville, MD: National Institute on Drug Abuse. 97–112.

Yesalis, C., Kennedy, N., Kopstein, A. et al. (1993). Anabolic-androgenic steroid use in the United States. JAMA, 270(10): 1217–1221.

Yoshida, E., Erb, S., Scudamore, C. et al. (1994). Severe cholestasis and jaundice secondary to an esterified testosterone, a non-C17 alkylated anabolic steroid. J Clin Gastroenterol, 18(3): 268–271.

Zak, F. (1950). Peliosis hepatis. Am J Pathol. 26: 1–15.

chapter seven

Organic solvent and aerosol abuse

The prevalence of inhaled solvent abuse, at least as measured by emergency room visits and medical examiner reports, is increasing. Compared to other abused drugs, however, the practice remains relatively uncommon. In 1994 there were 33 cocaine-related deaths for every one attributed to inhalant and solvent abuse (Substance Abuse and Mental Health Services Agency, 1995). Hundreds, perhaps thousands, of commercial and household products contain solvents that potentially may be abused. Unfortunately, the toxicity associated with their abuse remains poorly characterized. Case reports describing medical complications related to chronic solvent abuse have been reported from most major industralized countries. But in the absence of any systematic studies, the frequency of medical complications in these abusers remains unknown.

7.1   General considerations

Solvent abuse is not a new problem. Reports of recreational solvent inhalation date back to World War I. Ether abuse was popular in England during the 1890s, and deaths from recreational chloroform abuse were first reported even earlier. The practice did not become widespread in the United States until the late 1950s. Solvent abuse is also said to be common in both Japan and Europe (Anon, 1988), but the true incidence of the problem is difficult to assess. In the late 1970s, national surveys of high school seniors found that solvent abuse had been tried on at least one occasion by 10–13% of the respondents. The same surveys also disclosed that, in addition to glues and solvents, abuse of amyl and butyl nitrates had become fairly common (Smart, 1986).

Most solvent abusers are between the ages of 13 and 15, with male users outnumbering females 4:1 (Anon, 1988); however, tremendous variation exists within specific subgroups. Among the Indians living in the Southwestern United States, solvent abuse is more common among women than men (May, 1995). Adult abusers are occasionaly encountered, especially in rural communities, and in locations where individuals have ready access to the appropriate chemicals (Flanagan and Ives, 1994).

The reported frequency of medical complications among solvent abusers, and the general popularity of solvent abuse, varies greatly from location to location. In England, in 1991, for example, a total of 122 solvent abuse deaths were reported (Flanagan and Ives, 1994). During that same period 56 deaths were reported in the United States. *Since the population of the United States is roughly 10 times that of the United Kingdom, the death rate in the United Kingdom is nearly 20 times higher than that in the United States!*

All of the drugs in this group are highly soluble in lipids. They rapidly enter the central nervous system, and once there act as depressants. In this regard they share some characteristics with other depressants such as barbiturates, benzodiazepines, and alcohol (Evans and Balster, 1991). Whether or not they also share the ability to produce dependence is a matter of some dispute (Miller and Gold, 1991; Flanagan and Ives, 1994), but the results of animal studies certainly suggest that solvent abusers can become physically dependent (Evans and Balster, 1993).

Psychatric, neurologic, renal, and hepatic disorders have all been described in solvent abusers, but the primary risk associated with solvent abuse has always been sudden death. A recent study from England analyzed the patterns and mechanisms of death in a series of 1,237 solvent abusers over a 20 year period. Deaths were divided into four different groups, according to the type of solvent involved: (1) aerosol propellants, (2) gas fuels, (3) chlorinated and other types of solvents, and (4) solvents from adhesives. As illustrated in Table 7.1, the proportion of deaths due to direct toxicity, aspiration, and asphyxia were remarkably similar in all the groups except for adhesive solvents (most often toluene). In the latter group, trauma was the most frequent cause of death, suggesting that impairment of judgment is somewhat more likely with the adhesive solvents.

7.2   Absorption and tissue disposition

Not all solvents are abused. In order to have abuse potential, a compound must be sufficiently volatile to be inhaled, which explains why petroleum distillates, such as kerosene and ethylene glycol, have such low abuse potential. On the other hand, toluene, the solvent most often used in contact adhesives, is highly volatile and frequently abused. Table 7.2 lists some of the more commonly abused agents.

How a particular product is abused depends largely on the boiling range of the solvent. For toluene-containing contact adhesives, the preferred route is to pour the products into a plastic bag, gather the ends of the bag together, and hold the top of the bag over the mouth and nose (the practice is called "huffing"). Plastic bags can also be used to collect propellants from aerosol cans. More volatile agents, like gasoline, are simply sniffed from soaked rags (Flanagan and Ives, 1994). Toluene is eliminated by hepatic conjugation and by renal excretion as hippuric acid. Toluene is very lipophilic, and when it is inhaled, it is rapidly taken up by the brain and by fat stores elsewhere in

Table 7.2 Commonly Abused Solvents*

A. Aerosol Propellants (air fresheners, deodorant spray, hair spray)
    Dimethyl ether
    Butane
    Halogenated fluorocarbons
        Bromochlorodifluoromethane (from fire extinguishers)
        Carbon tetrachloride
        Ethyl chloride
        Perchloroethylene
        Trichloroethylene
B. Gas Fuels (disposable cigarette lighters)
    Propane
    Butane
    Liquid petroleum gas
C. Chlorinated Solvents (commercial dry cleaning/degreasing agents)
    Carbon tetrachloride
    Dichloremethane
    Methanol
    Tetrachloroethylene
    Toluene
D. Solvents from Adhesives (also paints, nail polish, varnish remover)
    Acetone
    Butane
    Cyclohexanone
    Toluene
    Xylene

* Partial list of agents that may be responsible for inhalant abuse toxicity, grouped
by pattern of toxicity. Agents from group A are more likely to be associated with
traumatic injuries and death. Agents from the other three groups are more likely
to manifest direct toxicity.

the body. After rapid initial uptake, it is slowly released over a considerable
period of time.

7.3   Clinical syndromes

7.3.1   Neurologic disorders

Of the neurologic alterations described in chronic solvent abusers, most are
associated with aliphatic and aromatic hydrocarbons, particularly toluene.
An acute syndrome of nausea, abdominal pain, impaired judgment, altered
consciousness, and seizures is well recognized (Watson, 1982). The acute and
long-term effects of other agents in this category are less well-known. Transient neurologic symptoms certainly occur with the use of amyl nitrite and
related compounds, but there are no reports of permanent neurologic
sequelae.

   The first reports of toluene-related neurologic disorder were published
more than 30 years ago (Grabski, 1961; Kelly, 1975). In chronic toluene abuse,
cerebellar signs predominate, and patients present with ataxia, tremor, and

nystagmus (Rosenberg et al., 1988a). However a variety of disorders may occur, ranging from relatively minor degress of cognitive dysfunction and poor performance in school (Hormes et al., 1986; Fornazzari et al., 1983), to much more serious disorders with signs of pyramidal damage. Cerebral and cerebellar atropy have both been described (Hormes et al., 1986), as has cranial nerve injury (Fornazzari et al., 1983). Some users, particularly adult abusers, may present with a disorder mimicking Guillian-Barré syndrome (Streicher et al., 1981).

In most cases, symptoms disappear, or at least improve, when exposure to the solvent stops. In some cases, however, symptoms persist; seizure disorders and cognitive impairment are not infrequent (Bryne, 1991). Chronic toluene users may also be prone to the development of paranoid psychosis, with schizophrenic symptoms that may be atypical; in one series, several of the toluene users had visual hallucinations.

Only a limited number of morphologic studies have been published (Escobar and Aruffo, 1980; Rosenberg et al., 1988b), but the available evidence suggests that when symptoms persist, widespread demylination has occurred. In the three cases described by Kornfeld et al., the essential features of the disorder were severe, but spotty loss of myelin, but with relatively mild degress of axonal loss and gliosis. A constant histologic feature was the presence of macrophages filled with PAS-positive granules, and the absence of any foamy macrophages. The histologic appearance, in these three cases at least, was not that different from the picture seen in adrenoleukodystrophy (Kornfeld et al., 1994).

7.3.2   Renal disease

Urinary complaints, particularly hematuria, are said to be common (Streicher et al., 1981). Glomerulonephritis may complicate chronic solvent abuse (Streicher et al., 1981), although the actual incidence of these complications appears to be quite low. Disorders of the renal tubules have been more frequently reported (Taher et al., 1974; Fischman and Oster, 1979; Moss et al., 1980; Voigts and Kaufman, 1983). Toluene, and possibly some of the other agents, appears to damage the distal tubule, decreasing the ability to excrete hydrogen ions. The resultant hyperchloremic acidosis may be symptomless, or it may lead to profound muscle weakness from hypokalemia (Fischman et al., 1979).

Renal tubular changes may also lead to hypercalcuria and stone formation (Kroeger et al., 1980); however, it appears that stones may also form in chronic solvent abusers with normal renal tubular function (Kaneko et al., 1992). This suggests that chronic solvent abuse should be considered in the differential diagnosis when evaluating juveniles with kidney stones.

7.3.3   Gastrointestinal disease

In contrast to gastrointestinal symptoms, which are frequent in solvent abusers, true disease is uncommon. Centrolobular necrosis was first described in solvent abusers nearly 30 years ago (Baerg and Kimberg, 1970), and more recently, fulminant hepatic failure has also been reported (McIntyre and Long, 1992). There have been no other reports, and surveillance studies, done by occupational medicine researchers, have found no evidence for subclinical alterations in liver or kidney function among workers with long-term trichloroethylene exposure (Rasmussen et al., 1993). Interestingly, experimental studies have shown that the simultaneous administration of methamphetamine enhances carbon tetrachloride hepatotoxicity (Roberts et al., 1994). In theory, a solvent abuser who was taking amphetamines might be at increased risk. In practice, solvent abusers are hardly ever found to be abusing other drugs at the same time.

7.3.4   Cardiovascular disease

Sudden cardiac death is the most important disorder associated with solvent abuse. Except for trauma-related deaths in adhesive solvent abusers, direct toxicity, manifested as ventricular fibrillation or profound myocardial depression, is thought to account for most deaths in individuals abusing aerosol propellants, gas fuels, and most solvents. A number of different mechanisms, involving both direct and indirect mechanisms, are possible.

Trichlorethylene, like halothane, sensitizes the myocardium to catecholamine stimulation. Once the myocardium has been sensitized, arrhythmias may be set off by any event causing the releases of catecholamines. Exercise, sexual activity, or fleeing the police all could provide a surge of epinephrine sufficient to precipitate an arrhythmia (Bass, 1970; Reinhardt et al., 1973; Carlton, 1976; Kobayashi et al., 1982). Whether exposure to these agents also sensitizes coronary artery receptors, and produces spasm, is not known. However, cases of myocardial infarction in solvent abusers have been described (Cunningham et al., 1987).

Direct toxicity is also possible, but only limited studies with trichloroethylene have been reported. The results of those studies suggest that trichloroethylene is a myocardial depressant. Like halothane, trichloroethylene, and probably other halogenated solvents as well, reduces calcium levels with the cytosol of myocytes (Hoffman et al., 1992). Since the force of contraction depends on intracytosolic calcium levels reaching a certain critical set point, decreased availability of calcium within the cardiac myocytes translates into decreased force of contraction. Whether depression is ever profound enough to cause ischemia and sudden death has never been proven clinically.

When death is associated with amyl nitrate abuse, several mechanisms are possible; amyl nitrate inhalation causes significant, occasionally fatal, amounts of methemoblobin to be produced (Horne, 1975; Guss, 1985; Sarvesvaran et al., 1992). Alternatively, vasodilation and intense vagal stimulation could also lead to arrhythmias and sudden death.

Still other mechanisms for sudden death in solvent abusers are possible. If solvent concentrations in the brain reach sufficiently high levels, fatal respiratory depression could result, although establishing such a sequence at autopsy would be difficult, if not impossible. Much more likely, at least in the large series reported from the United Kingdom, is vomiting with aspiration. Flanagan and Ives reported that aspiration was the cause of death in 20–30% of all solvent-related sudden deaths (Flanagan and Ives, 1994).

References

Anon. (1988). Complications of chronic volatile substance abuse. Lancet, 431–432.

Baerg, R. and Kimberg, D. (1970). Centrilobular hepatic necrosis and acute renal failure in "solvent sniffers." Ann Intern Med, 73: 713–720.

Bass, M. (1970). Sudden sniffing death. JAMA, 212: 2075–2079.

Carlton, R. (1976). Flurocarbon toxicity: deaths and anaesthetic reactions. Ann Clin Lab Sci, 6: 411–414.

Cunningham, S. (1987). Myocardial infarction and primary ventricular fibrillation after glue sniffing. Br Med J, 294: 739–740.

Escobar, A. and Aruffo, C. (1980). Chronic thinner intoxication: clinico-pathologic report of a human case. J Neurol Neurosurg Psych, 43: 986–994.

Evans, E. and Balster, R. (1991). CNS depressant effects of volatile organic solvents. Neurosci Biobehav Rev, 15: 233–241.

Fischman, C. and Oster, J. (1979). Toxic effects of toluene: a new cause of high anion gap metabolic acidosis. JAMA, 241: 171–174.

Flanagan, R. and Ives, R. (1994). Volatile substance abuse. Bull Narc, XLVI: 49–78.

Fornazzari, L., Wilkinson, D., Kapur, B. et al. (1983). Cerebellar, cortical and functional impairment in toluene abusers. Acta Neurol Scand, 67: 319–329.

Grabski, D. (1961). Toluene sniffing producing cerebellar degeneration. Am J Psych, 118: 461–462.

Guss, P., Normann, S., and Manoguerra, A. (1985). Clinically significant methaemoblobinemia from inhalation of isobutylnitrite. Am J Emerg Med, 3: 46–47.

Hoffmann, P., Breitenstein, M., and Toraason, M. (1992). Calcium transients in isolated cardiac myocytes are altered by 1,1,1-trichloroethane. J Mol Cell Cardiol, 24: 619–629.

Hormes, J., Filley, C., and Rosenberg, N. (1986). Neurologic sequelae of chronic solvent vapor abuse. Neurology, 36: 698–702.

Horne, M., Waterman, M., and Simon, L. (1979). Methaemoblobinemia from sniffing butylnitrite. Ann Intern Med, 91: 417–418.

Kaneko, T., Koizumi, T., Takezaki, T. et al. (1992). Urinary calculi associated with solvent abuse. J Urol, 147: 1365–1366.

Kelly, T. (1975). Prolonged cerebellar dysfunction associated with paint sniffing. Peds, 56: 605–606.

Kobayashi, H., Hobara, T., Hirota, H. et al. (1982). Sensitization of dog myocardium to epinephrine by 1,1,1-trichloroethane. Jpn J Ind Health, 24: 450–454.

Kornfeld, M., Moser, M., Moser, H. et al. (1994). Solvent vapor abuse leukoencephalopathy. Comparison to adrenoleukodystrophy. J Neurpath Exp Neurol, 53: 389–398.

May, P. (1995). Overview of inhalant abuse problems among human populations in the western United States. Presented at the Fifty-Seventh Annual Scientific Meeting, College on Problems of Drug Dependence, Scottsdale, AZ, June 12, 1995.

McIntyre, A. and Long, R. (1992). Fulminant hepatic failure in a "solvent abuser." Postgrad Med J, 68: 29–30.

Miller, N. and Gold, M. (1991). Organic solvent and aerosol abuse. Am Fam Phys, 44: 182–199.

Moss, A., Gabow, P., Kaehny, W. et al. (1980). Fanconi's syndrome and distal renal tubular acidosis after glue sniffing. Ann Intern Med, 92: 69–70.

Rasmussen, K., Brogren, C., and Sabroe, S. (1993). Sub-clinical affection of liver and kidney function and solvent exposure. Int Arch Occup Environ Health, 64: 445–448.

Reinhardt, G., Mullin, L., and Maxfield, M. (1973). Epinephrine-induced cardiac arrhythmia potential of some common industrial solvents. J Occup Med, 15: 953–955.

Roberts, S., Harbison, R., and James, R. (1994). Methamphetamine potentiation of carbon tetrachloride hepatotoxicity in mice. J Pharm Exp Ther, 271(2): 1057–1951.

Rosenberg, N., Kleinschmidt-DeMasters, B., Davis, K., et al. (1988). Toluene abuse causes diffuse central nervous system white matter changes. Ann Neurol, 23(23): 611–614.

Rosenberg, N., Spitz, M., Filley, C. et al. (1988). Central nervous system effects of chronic toluene abuse — clinical, brain stem evoked response and magnetic imaging studies. Neurotoxicol Teratol, 10: 485–489.

Sarvesvaran, E., Fysh, R., and Bowen, D. (1992). Amyl nitrite related deaths. Med Sci Law, 32(3): 267–269.

Smart, R. (1986). Solvent use in North America: aspects of epidemiology, prevention, and treatment. J Psychoactive Drug, 18: 87–96.

Streicher, H., Gabow, P., Moss, A. et al. (1981). Syndromes of toluene sniffing in adults. Ann Intern Med, 94: 758–762.

Substance Abuse and Mental Health Administration. (1995). Annual Medical Examiner Data. Data from the Drug Abuse Warning Network. Rockville, MD: U.S. Department of Health and Human Services.

Taher, S., Anderson, R., McCartney, R. et al. (1974). Renal tubular acidosis associated with toluene "sniffing." N Engl J Med, 290: 765–768.

Voigts, A. and Kaufman, C. (1983). Acidosis and other metabolic abnormalities associated with paint sniffing. South Med J, 76: 443–447.

Watson, J. (1982). Solvent abuse, presentation and clinical diagnosis. Hum Tox, 1: 249–256.

Webb, J. (1996). A sporting chance. New Scientist, March 23, 1996.

Appendix

Predicted Normal Heart Weight (g) as a Function of
Body Height in 392 Women and 373 Men*

Body height		Women			Men		
(cm)	(in)	L95	P	U95	L95	P	U95
130	51	133	204	314	164	232	327
132	52	135	207	319	167	236	333
134	53	137	210	324	170	240	338
136	54	139	214	329	173	243	344
138	54	141	217	334	175	247	349
140	55	143	220	338	178	251	355
142	56	145	223	343	181	255	361
144	57	147	226	348	184	259	366
146	57	149	229	353	187	263	372
148	58	151	232	358	189	267	378
150	59	153	236	363	192	271	383
152	60	155	239	368	195	275	389
154	61	157	242	372	198	280	395
156	61	159	245	377	201	284	400
158	62	161	248	382	204	288	406
160	63	163	251	387	207	292	412
162	64	165	254	392	209	296	417
164	65	167	258	397	212	300	423
166	65	169	261	401	215	304	429
168	66	171	264	406	218	308	435
170	67	173	267	411	221	312	440
172	68	176	270	416	224	316	446
174	69	178	273	421	227	320	452
176	69	180	277	426	230	324	458
178	70	182	280	431	233	328	463
180	71	184	283	435	235	332	469
182	72	186	286	440	238	336	475
184	72	188	289	445	241	341	481
186	73	190	292	450	244	345	487
188	74	192	295	455	247	349	492
190	75	194	299	460	250	353	498
192	76	196	302	465	253	357	504
194	76	198	305	469	256	361	510
196	77	200	308	474	259	365	516
198	78	202	311	479	262	369	522
200	79	204	314	484	265	374	527
202	80	206	318	489	268	378	533
204	80	208	321	494	271	382	539

Predicted Normal Heart Weight (g) as a Function of
Body Height in 392 Women and 373 Men*(continued)

Body height		Women			Men		
(cm)	(in)	L95	P	U95	L95	P	U95
206	81	210	324	499	274	386	545
208	82	212	327	508	276	394	557
210	83	214	330	508	279	394	557

* P = predicted normal heart weight; L95 = lower 95% confidence limit; U95 = upper 95% confidence limit.

This monogram is reproduced from the Mayo Clinic Proceedings (Kitzman, D. et al. Age-related changes in normal human
hearts during the first 10 decades of life. Part II (Maturity):
A quantitative anatomic study of 765 specimens from subjects
20 to 99 years old, Mayo Clin Proc, 63: 1237–1246, 1988).
Observed heart weight should be compared to predicted
heart weight in all cases, not just those where drug abuse is
suspected. Variations of more than 10% are very likely to be
clinically significant, but not apparent if only wall thickness
is determined. Percentage-based formulas (e.g., .4% of body
weight for men and .45% for women) are approximations
only, and not nearly so accurate or reliable.

Index

A

Abscesses, 349
Absinthe, 177–180
  clinical and autopsy studies, 179–180
  history, 177–180
Abuscreen® Radioimmunoassay for
    Morphine, 343
Accelerated atherogenesis, 418
Acetaminophen, presence in cocaine, 98
Acetaminophen poisoning, 139
Acetic anhydride, 295
6-Acetylmorphine, 311
Acidifying agent, 352
Acidophil bodies, 377
Acini formation, 416
Acquired aplastic anemia, 414
ACTH secretion, 164
Action potential
  amplitude, 104
  duration, 106
Acute respiratory distress syndrome, 234
Acute tubular necrosis, 156, 382
"Adam", see MDMA
Ad-Din, Gaguib, 190
Adenosine receptors, 186
Adenyl cyclase, 65
Adrenal medulla, 91, 163
α-Adrenergic agonist, 232
α-Adrenergic blockade, 91
α_1-Adrenergic receptors, 65
α-Adrenergic stimulation, and coronary
    artery contraction, 108
Adrenoleukodystrophy, 434
Adulterants, 281, 296
Adventitial mast cells, 89
AEME, see Anhydroecgonine methylester
Aerosol abuse, organic solvent and, 431–437
  absorption and tissue disposition, 432–433
  clinical syndromes, 433–436
    cardiovascular disease, 435–436

gastrointestinal disease, 434–435
    neurologic disorders, 433–434
    renal disease, 434
  general considerations, 431–432
Affective disorders, 419
After-depolarizations, 108
Age, effect of on propoxyphene metabolism,
    319
Agitated delirium, see Cocaine
AIDS, 99, 130
  encephalopathy, 389
  leukoencephalopathy, 392
    myocardiae disease and, 99
    renal lesions in patients with, 159
Airway hyperresponsiveness, 125
Akathisia, 151
AL-422, see Kat
AL-463, see Kat
AL-464, see Kat
Alcohol, relationship to cocaine, 41–42
Alcohol, relationship to PCP, 274
Alcohol intoxication, 48
Alcoholism, rhabdomyolysis and, 221
Alfentanyl, 325
Alkaline phosphatase, 379
Alkaloid, 177, 183
17-Alkylated androgens, 415
Allergic granulomatosis angitis, 98
Alles, Gordon, 199, 247
Allocaine, 15
Alveolar hemorrhage, 129
Amazon, 2
Amide local anesthetic, 107
Aminopyrine, 98
Aminorex, 253
  fumarate, 217
  lethal side effects of, 254
  molecule, 254
Ammon's horn, 388
Amniotic fluid, 61, 305
Amphetamine(s), see Stimulants, synthetic

Amyl nitrite, 433
Amyloid
   angiopathy, 149
   protein, 379
Anabolic effects, 409
Anabolic steroid abusers, 379
Anabolic Steroids Control Act of 1990, 413
Anadrol-50, 413
Anatomic substrate, 105
Anatoxin, 42
Anavar, 413
Androgenic effects, 409
Androsterone, 409
Aneurysm of sinus of Valsalva, 360
ANF, see Atrial naturetic factor
Anhalonium Lewinii, 241
Anhydroecgonine methyl ester
            (methylecgonidine), 42
Anterior communicating artery, 148
Anterior mediastinitis, 372
Anterior spinal syndrome, 145
Anthracosis, pulmonary, 128
Anti-adrenergic measures, 220
Antiplatelet antibodies, 166
Antipsychotic drugs, 112
Antithrombin activity, in steroid abusers, 418
α-1-Antitrypsin, 367
α-1-Antitrypsin deficiency, 217
Antitussive, 248
Aortic dissection, 100
Apaches, use of peyote, 242
Apiquel®, 253
Aplastic anemia, 252
Appetite suppression, 218
Arecoline, 42
Aromatic hydrocarbons, 433
Arrhythmia, 69, 74, 98, 105, 173, 186, 187, 213, 233, 394
Arterial boundary zones, 388
Arterial embolization, 361
Arteriovenous malformation, 149
Aschenbrant, 190
Ascorbic acid, 98
Aspergillus, 370
Aspiration pneumonia, 370
Asprin acid, 98
Aspirin metabolites, interfering with EMIT®
            assay, 212
Asystole, 105
Asystolic arrest, 104
Atherosclerosis, accelerated, 101
ATPase, 92
Atrial naturetic factor (ANF), mRNA for, 104–105
Atrial naturetic hormone, 92
Atrioventricular valves, 358

Atrophic scarring, 348
Australian cane toad, 261
Autopsy, catecholamine measurements at, 20
AV malformation, 395
Avascular necrosis of femoral heads, 422

B

Bacillary angiomatosis, 379, 415
Bacteroides spp., 407
Bailey, 5
Barium contrast studies, Dx of body packing
            and, 26
Barotrauma, cocaine use and, 126
Basal ganglia, 144, 220
Baudelaire, absinthe and, 178
Bayer, 284, 290
β blockers, 220
B cell lymphoma, 390
BEG, see benzoylecogonine
Bentley Compounds, 294
Benzodrex®, 201, 213, 214, 217, 219
Benzedrine®, 199
Benzocaine, 98
Benzodiazepines, 98
Benzoic acid, 13, 14
Benzoylecgonine, 13, 21, 22, 24, 29, 29, 36–41, 43, 48, 49, 52–53, 55, 57–61, 114, 145, 146, 172
Bicarbonate, 20, 23, 99
Bile canaliculi, 415
Bile duct proliferation, 377
Biofluids, 308
Biological Society of Paris, 4
Biopsy specimens, 74
Biotransformation, 60
Birefringent material, 377
Biventricular hypertrophy, 419
Black sputum, in crack smokers, 129
Black tar, Mexican heroin, 293, 297
Bleeding times, 197
Bleeding varices, 416
β blockade, 71
Blood brain barrier, 52, 299
Blood/CSF ratios, for morphine, 307
Blotter paper, 246
Blue ice, 253
Body packer syndrome, 5, 25, 26, 48, 173
Boerhave, 1
Bolivia, 13
Bone and joint infection, 405
Boric acid, 98
Bowel
   disease, 375
   infarction, 86
Bowman's capsule, 157, 384

Brain death, 68, 109
Brain
  baboon model, 71
  concentrations of cocaine in, 52–53, 112
  concentrations of morphine in, 307
  homogenates, 29
Breast
  feeding, transmission of
          methamphetamine by, 209
  milk, 60, 208, 305
Bridging necrosis, 377, 378
British Medical Journal, 3
Bromocriptine, 113
4-Bromo-2,5-dimethoxyamphetamine, see
          DOB
4-Bromo-2,5-dimethoxyphenethylamine, see
          Nexus
Bromo-DMA, 246
Bronchi, 366
Bronchiolitis obliterans, 124
Bronchopneumonia, 318
Bronchospasm, 402
Brown fat, 58
Browning, Elizabeth Barrett, opium use by,
          286
Brush border membrane, 168
Bufogenins, 262
Bufotenine, 241
  ancient origins of, 261
  appearance of, 262
  Australian use of, 261
  poisoning from, 262
Bufotoxins, 262
Bullae formation, 217
Burroughs Wellcome Company, 199

C

Caffeine, 28, 98, 180–187, 296
  athletic performance, affect on, 181–182
  autopsy findings, 187
  blood levels, 186–187
  chemical constants and tissue disposition,
          183–184
  clinical studies of caffeine, 184–186
  consumption, European, 181
  consumption, U.S., 180, 181
content, of commonly consumed beverages
          and medications, 181
  disease, links to, 183, 186–187
  history, 180–183
  metabolism
    cystic fibrosis, and, 185
Calcium
  channel, 67, 70
    blockade, 70, 220

  regulation, 36
  overload, 71, 74, 187
Camphophenique®, 180
Camphor, 179–180
  in over-the-counter remedies, 180
  toxicity, 180
  as treatment for depression, 179–180
Candida bone infections, 406
Candida infections, 352
Carbonaceous pigment, 129
Carbon dioxide levels, 326
Carboxylesterase systems, 38
Cardiac arrest, 3
Cardiac conduction abnormalities, 42
Cardiac lesion, in opiate abusers, 356–357
Cardiac myocyte contraction, 69, 72
Cardiac output, 107
Cardiac rupture, 360
Cardiomegally, 112
Cardiomyopathy, 5, 96, 105, 108, 215
Cardiotoxicity, 321
Carminatives, 286
"CAT," see ephedrone
Catecholamine(s), 49, 137, 185, 209, 331
  excess, 20, 168, 169, 173
  -induced necrosis, 55, 96, 106
  lesions, with PPA use, 234
  metabolism, 163, 207
  toxicity, 67–70, 84, 96, 131, 158, 217
Catechol-o-methyl transferase, 65
Cathinone, 192
Cat scratch disease, 379
Caudate, 388
CBN, see Contraction band necrosis
C3 complement, 383
CD4 antigen, 403
CD4+ cells, 166
CD8+ cells, 166
Cellulitis, 82, 362, 405
Cellulose granulomas, 131
Central Intelligence Agency, mind control
          experiments and, 268
Central retinal infarction, 145
Centrolobular lesions, 378
Cerebellar atrophy, 434
Cerebellum, 219
Cerebral edema, 247, 388
Cerebral glucose metabolism, 144
Cerebral infarction, 144
Cerebral ischemia, 271
Cerebral perfusion, 144
Cerebral spinal fluid (CSF), 52
Cerebral vasculitis, 83, 146
Cerebrospinal fuid, 308
c-fos, 95, 143
Chan-Su, 261

Chaparé, 11–12
Chasing the dragon, 310
Chemical pneumonitis, 370
n-Chlorobutane extraction, 325
Chloroform abuse, 431
Chloroform, use in mescaline preparation, 243
Chlorpromazine, 211
Cholestasis, 415
Cholesterol, 412
Cholinesterase, 37, 38, 39
Choreoathetoid movements, 391
Choreoathetosis, 151
Chorioretinitis, 371
Chromosomal damage, LSD use and, 268
Chromosome 22, 276
Chronic paranoid psychosis, 251
Chronic persistent hepatitis, 318
Churg-Strauss syndrome, 98
CIA, involvement with LSD, 268
Cigarette burns, rosette of, 353
Cigarettes, 89, 91
Cinnamoylcocaine, 13
Ciprofloxacin, 185
Circulating lymphocytes, a and b receptors located on, 162
c-jun, 95
C^{11}-labeled cocaine, 41, 51
Clandestone laboratories, 272
Claviceps purpurea, 269
Clobenzorex, 211
Clostridia, 407
c-myc, 95
Coagulative myocytolysis, 70
Coat-A-Count® for Morphine, 343
Cobalt poisoning, 68
Coca
    Boerhave, mentions of, 1
    chewers, 1, 125
    Coca-Cola® flavoring and, 11
    crop yields, 12
    cultivation of, 11–13
    definition of, 1
    Hooker, Sir William, translations of articles on, 1
    Monardes, Nicolas B., accounts of, 1
    paste, 13
    plantation, 12–13
    Poeppig, Edward, observations of use, 1
    toxicity from leaf, 6
    von Tschudi, Johan, observations of, 1
Cocaethylene, 28, 29, 38, 39–42, 49, 52, 55, 58, 138
    in hair samples as proof of cocaine use, 57
    in tissue samples as proof of cocaine use, 42

Cocaine, 1–175
    adulterants found in, 98
    alcohol, relationship to, 41–42
    anesthetic, use as, 3, 5, 7, 21, 104, 109
    -associated agitated delirium, 4, 49, 102, 110–114
        racism in early reports of, 4
    -associated pneumomediastinum, 126
    -associated seizures, 109
    -associated sudden death, 49
    autopsy studies of cocaine-related deaths, 4, 8–9, 36, 171–174
    baboon testing, 54–55
    binding sites for, 28
    binging, 2
    blood levels, 18, 19, 21, 23, 24, 25, 26, 34–35, 43, 48–50, 54, 55, 58, 100, 172, 173
    cardiac toxicity and, 103
    cardiac transplant, cocaine use affect on, 97
    catecholamine
        contraction band necrosis and sudden death, 73–74
        general considerations, 64–67
        histopathology of catecholamine toxicity, 70–73
        measurement, at autopsy, 20
        metabolism, cocaine's effect on, 20, 64–77
        surge of, 113
        toxicity, 65, 67–70, 125
    chewing, peak blood levels after, 18
    Coca-Cola®, content in, 3
    cocaine tissue disposition, 51–64
        adrenals, 56
        biofluids, 58–61
            amniotic fluid, 6
            breast milk, 60
            saliva, 58–59
            spinal fluid, 60
            urine, 60–61, see also Urine
            vitreous humor, 59
        brain, 52–54
        fat, 58
        hair, 57–58
        heart, 54–55
        kidneys, 56
        liver, 55–56
    CT scan, for detection, 26
    detoxification, 59, 60
    diastomers, 15
    Dr. Tucker's Asthma Specific, content in, 4
    drug constants, 17–18
    Egyptian mummies, detection of use in, 1
    elimination clearance of, 34
    epidemiologic data, 77–78

/epinephrine
    combinations, 20
    paste, 20
external markers of cocaine abuse, 78–82
    cocaine tracks, 79–80
    crack eye, 80
    crack hands, 81
    crack keratitis, 80–81
    crack thumb, 81
    dental erosions, 81
    perforated nasal septum, 79
    terminal seizures, evidence of, 81
euphoria, 48
"ewe" model, 27
extraction, 13–16
fetal metabolism of, 43
gastrointestinal absorption of, 25
half-life of, 34
heart rate, effect on, 41
"high," 107
history, 1–9
hydrochloride, 4, 14, 18, 22, 41, 81
immune system, effect on, 165–167
-induced coronary artery spasm, 90
-induced heart block, 107
-induced seizures, 150–151
interpreting cocaine blood levels,
        48–51
/lidocaine, 20
Magnon's symptom, 4
maternal/fetal considerations, 25, 27–66,
        136, 137, 168–169
metabolism, 34–47
    cocaine disposition, 34–43
    fetal metabolism, 43
morphine addiction treatment and, 8
"mules," 25
muriate, 18
N-formyl, 14
organ donation by abusers, 159
paste production, 13–16
paste smoking, 14
pharmaceutical grade, 42, 58
placenta concentrations, 29
post-mortem levels, 36, 48, 52, 55, 56, 59
pregnancy, use during, 22, 27–29, 168–169
prevalence of cocaine-related morbidity, 10
price of, 16
psychiatric syndromes and, 143–144
purification of, 2
purity of, 16
receptors, 51
refining, 15
-related deaths, 5, 6, 10, 14, 102, 127,
        171–174
    accidental vs. suicide, 173

renal disease, 156–159
renal levels, post-mortem, 56
routes of administration, 18–34
    dermal absorption, 22–23
    gastrointestinal absorption, 25–27
    genital application, 22
    inhalation, 23–25
    intranasally, 37, 41, 88
    intravenous use, 21–22, 99
        risk of HIV and, 21–22, 99, 130
    leaf chewing, 18
    "pocket shooters," 131
    "skin popping," 82–83
    smoking, 14
    snorting, 4, 18–19
    subcutaneous injection, 79, 82–83
    surgical application, 20–21
scleroderma, relationship to, 83–84
SIDS, relationship to, 25
smuggling, 22
snorting, peak blood levels after, 18
sudden death and, 73, 89, 102–106
sudden infant death syndrome,
        relationship to, 25
surgical application, peak blood levels
        after, 18
synthesis of, 15
total synthesis of, 15
toxicity
    early reports of, 3, 4, 6
    organ system, classified by, 82–171
        cardiovascular system, 83–114
            acute chatecolamine-related effects
                and, 107
            aorta and peripheral vessels,
                100–102
            chronic cocaine effects on, 107
            coronary artery disease and,
                84–90
            coronary artery spasm and, 90–92
            myocardial diseases and,
            sudden cardiac death and, 102
        gastrointestinal disorders, 135–140
        hepatic disease and, 137
        ischemic injuries, 135
        hematologic abnormalities,
                161–162
        hormonal alterations, 163–165
        immune system abnormalities,
                165–167
        neurologic disorders, 142–151
            cerebral infarction, 144
            cerebral vasculitis, 146
            cocaine-related stroke, 142
            movement disorders, 152
            psychiatric syndromes, 143

seizures, 150–151
    subarachnoid and intraventricular
        hemorrhage, 148
    pregnancy interactions, 168–169
    pulmonary disease, 124–131
        barotrauma and, 126
        inflammatory disease and, 125
        parenchymal disease and, 127
        vascular adaptations and, 130
    renal disease, 156–159
    skin, 82–83
    umbilical cord blood, presence in, 29
    urine levels, 5, 20–22, 24, 28, 35, 36, 59–61
    vin Mariani, content in, 2
    volume of distribution of, 34
    x-ray, for detection of body packing, 26
    withdrawal from, 59
Codeine, 281, 282
    conversion, from morphine, 301
    -6-glucuronide, 314, 315
    excretion and detectability, 315
    impurities, 301
    metabolism, role of genetic polymorphism
        on, 314
    routes of administration, 313
    tissue disposition, 315
Coffee
    coffee houses, 182
    disease, links to, 183
    origins of drinking, 182
Collagen
    fibrils, 421
    mRNA for, 105
    production, induced by cocaine, 174
Colombia, 13, 14
Commanches, use of peyote, 242
Compulsive behavior, 219
Conduction block, 107
Conduction system, 214
Confessions of an English Opium Eater, 286
Congestive cardiomyopathy, 71
Conjugation, 206
Consumptive coagulopathy, 221
Continuous gastric suction, in treatment of
        PCP ingestion, 273
Contraction band necrosis, 4, 93, 173, 174, 187,
        356
    conditions associated with, 68
    early reports of, 70
    sudden death and, 73, 104
Convulsions, 329
Coquero, 2
Cord blood, 29, 61
Cordials, 286
Corn starch, 98, 130, 216
Coronary artery spasm, 21, 90

Cortical necrosis, 127
Cotinine, 28
Cotton
    fever, 362
    fibers, 216, 369
Cough suppressant, 290
Crack, 23
    cocaine, 6
    dancing, 151
    exposure in children through smoke, 25
    eye, 80
    hands, 81
    keratitis, 80
    pellets, 25
    pipe, 129
    rocks, 23
    smoking, 23–25, 35, 99, 129, 136
        vasospasm caused by, 130–131
    thumb, 81
Cryptococcus, 99
Cryptococcus neoformans, 379
Crystal lab, 14
CSF, see Cerebral spinal fluid
CT scanning, Dx of body packing and, 26
Cutaneous complications, 348
Cutaneous sensitivity, 402
Cutaneous stigmata, 318
Cutaneous ulcers, 79
Cyclic AMP, 65, 66, 283
Cycling pattern, of steroid abuse, 411
Cytochrome P450, 250
Cytochrome P4502D6, 276
Cytokine production, 166
Cytokines, 402
Cytomegalovirus, 99, 379
Cytomegalovirus infection, 389

D

Daime, 264
Dallas criteria, 99
DAWN (Drug Abuse Warning Network), 10,
        201, 241, 242, 270, 281, 312, 315,
        319, 326, 327
DEA (Drug Enforcement Agency), 58, 202,
        247, 253, 255, 296, 383
Deamination, 206
Death in custody, 112
Debrisoquine, 314
Deca-durbolin
Defibrillation, 68
Degas, absinthe and, 178
Delatestryl, 413
Delirium
    agitated, 102, 110
    cocaine-associated agitated, 4, 49

Delta receptors, 282, 330
Delta virus, 378
Delusions, 219
Delysid®, 268
Demerol®, 329
Depo-testosterone, 413
Deprenyl®, 210
DeQuincey, 286
Derivitizing agent, 212
Designer amphetamines, 243
Despropionfentanyl, 324
Detectability, 309
Detection of drug use
    blood, see specific drug entries
    caliometric technique, 5
    CT scan, 26
    EMIT® d.a.u. monoclonal immunoassay,
            23, 211, 212, 250, 254, 270, 329
    gas chromatography, 5, 53, 300
    hair, see Hair
    Helmsing's technique, 5
    meconium, 61
    "NIDA 5," 270, 327
    PET scanning, 5, 54, 55
    radioimmunoassays, 254, 300, 349
    solid phase extraction, 53
    TDx®, 329
    urine, see Urine, see also specific drug
            entries
Dexfenfluramine, 217, 218
Dextroamphetamine, 199
Dextromethorphan, 271
    abuse of, 276
    blood levels, 276
    liver levels, 276
    over-the-counter remedies, presence in,
            275–276
    screening for, 276
Dextrose, 98, 295
Diabetes, 351
Diacetyl morphine, 290
Dianabol, 413
Dibucaine numbers, 39
Diethylamine, 269
Digitalis, 261
Digoxin, 305
Dilaudid®, 222, 327
Diluents, definition, 296
N,N-Dimethyltryptamine, see DMT
Diphenhydramine, 98, 296
Diphenylpropylamine derivatives, 315
Disseminated cryptococcosis, 357
Disseminated intravascular coagulation, 112
dl-cocaine, 15
D1-like receptors, 112
D2-like receptors, 112

DMT (N,N-dimethyltryptamine)
    blood levels, 261
    routes of administration, 260–261
DOB (4-bromo-2,5-dimethoxyamphetamine),
            241, 246
DOD cutoffs, 21
DOM (methyl-2,5-dimethoxyamphetamine),
            241, 245
Dopamine, 66
    antagonists, 113, 164
    binding sites for, 28
    reuptake, 40
    transporter, 109
Dopaminergic agents, 113
Dover, Thomas, 285
Dover's Powder, 285
Doxepin, 211
D-Propoxyphene, 281
D1 Receptors, 112, 113
D2 Receptors, 112, 113
D3 Receptors, 112
D4 Receptors, 112, 113
D5 Receptors, 112
Dr. Tucker's Asthma Specific, 4
Drowning, 68, 70
Drug
    abuse, polydrug, 130, 131
    contaminants, 65
    -related death, 78, 173
        while in police custody, 113
    toxicity, rhabdomyolysis and, 221
Dumas, Alexander, 2
Durabolin, 413

E

E. allgolerans, 362
Early expression genes, 95
East India Company, 286
Ecgonine, 13, 37
Ecgonine methyl ester (EME), 36–39, 41, 57,
            59, 60
Echocardiographic studies, 92, 358
Echocardiography, 105
E. corrodens, 407
Ecuador, 13
Edeleano, 199
Edema fluid, 366
Edison, Thomas, 2
Effective refractory period, 106
Eldepryl®, 210
Electrocution, 68
Eli Lilly, 201
Ellis, Havelock, 243
Embolism, 145
Emde, 199

EME, see Ecgonine methyl ester
Emit®-d.a.u., 343
EMIT® d.a.u. monoclonal immunoassay, 23,
        211, 212
Empathogen, 249
Emphysema, 367
Empyema, 371
Endocarditis, 99, 355
Endomyocardial biopsies, 86
Endoplasmic reticulum, 67, 392
Endopthalmitis, 371
Endorphins, 282
Endoscopic procedures, fentanyl and, 323
Endothelial injuries, 5
Endothelial trauma, 358
Endothelin-1, 168
Endotoxin, 362
Enkephalins, 282
Enterobacter cloacae, 406
Entero-hepatic circulation, of morphine,
        301
Environmental cocaine exposure, 24
Eosinophilic infiltrates, 97–98
Eosinophilic leukemia, 98
Eosinophilic myocarditis, 98
Ephedrine, 98, 177, 194–198, 199, 203, 204
    chemistry and metabolism, 196
    clinical studies, 196–197
    false positive drug tests, caused by, 212
    history, 194–195
    obstetrical use of, 197
    plasma levels of, 196
    synthesis for Kat production, 255
    teas, 195
    urine levels of, 196
    World War II, use during, 195
Ephedrone, 177
Epilepsy, sudden death and, 109
Epileptogenic foci, 109
Epinephrine, 20, 21, 55, 65, 68, 69, 80, 91, 137
Epsilon receptors, 283
Ergotism, 246
Erlenmeyer, 290
Erythroxylum coca Lam, 11
Erythroxylum–coca novogranatense var.
            truxillense (Rusby) Plowman, 11
Erythroxylum–coca var. Plowman, 11
Erythroxylum novogranatense Hieron, 11
Ethylestrenol, 413
α-Ethyltryptamine, 265
Etorphine, 294
Etryptamine, 265
Euphoria, cocaine and, 48
"Eve," see MDEA
Exhumations, 308
Extensive hydroxylators, of codeine, 314

External contamination, 58
Extrapulmonary tuberculosis, 406

F

Facial nerves, 390
False negatives, 58
Fasciculus retroflexus, 143
Fatty acid ethyl ester synthetase, 39
Fatty degeneration, 388
Femoral triangle, 126, 349
Fenfluramine, see Stimulants, Synthetic
Fentanyl, 304
    blood levels, 323, 324, 325, 326
    citrate, 325
    detection of, 323
    labs, 323
    lozenges, 324
    patch, 324
    -related deaths, 322, 323,, 345
        geographic clusters of, 322–323
    routes of administration, 323
Ferdinand, Archduke, 2
Fever, in intravenous drug abuse, 362
Fibrinoid necrosis, 86
Fibrocystic disease, 183
Fibrosis, 71, 331, 356
Fibrous myopathy, 405, 407
Fixation artifact, 74
Flow abnormalities, in cocaine user's brain,
        146
Fluoxymesterone, 413
Foamy macrophages, 434
Focal glomerulosclerosis, 159, 381, 382
Focal hemorrhages, 108
Focal interstitial fibrosis, 97
Focal segmental glomerulosclerosis, 383
Focal subendocardial hemorrhage, 214
Folliculitis, 352
Foreign body granulomas, 216, 349, 367
Formalyn embalming, 308
Forskal, Peter, 190
Freebase cocaine, 17, 22, 23, 24
Free radical
    formation, 221
    injuries, 68
French Wine Cola, 3
Freud, 3, 285, 289–290
Fulminant hepatitis, 378
Fungal spores, 368

G

Galerina autumnalis, 263
Gamma hydroxybutyric acid (GHB), 413
Gamma interferon, 166

Gastrointestinal disorders, 135
GC/MS quantitation, 325
Gene expression, 143
General cathexia, 358
Generalized lymphadenopathy, 401
Genital application of cocaine, 22
GHB, see Gamma hydroxybutyric acid
Giant cell arteritis, 101
Giant cells, 147, 220
Gilles de la Tourette syndrome, exacerbated
      by crack use, 151
Glioma, 390
Global ischemia, 395
Glossitis, coca chewing and, 125
Glucuronidation, 301
Glycogen sparing, 182
Gomori stain, 361
Göttingen, 2
G-protein, 65, 92, 112, 283
Granulocytopenia, 352
Granulomas, 377
Granulomatous lung disease, 356
Groin hit, 369
Growth hormone, 413
Guillain, Georges, 4
Guillian-Barré syndrome, 434
Gut motility, 375
Gynecomastia, 421

H

Hair
  bleaching, 58
  color, 57
  follicles, 57
  samples, 28
  testing, 24, 29, 57–58, 168, 206
Hallucinations, 4, 219
Hallucinogenic snuffs, 264
Hallucinogens, 241–280
  addiction to, 241
  common features of, 241
  definition of, 241
  ergolines, 267–270
  other agents, 270–280
    dextromethorphan, 275–276
    phencyclidine, 270–275
  phenylalkylamines, 260–270
    alpha-methyltryptamines, 265
    beta carbolines, 264–265
    simple tryptamines, 260–264
      bufotoneine, 261–262
      DMT, 260–261
      psilocybin, 262–264
  phenylethylamine derivatives, 241–245
    mescaline, see Mescaline

-related deaths, 241
substituted amphetamines, 245–256
  4-MAX, 253–254
  DOB, 246–247
  DOM, 241, 245–246, 247
  Kat, 255–256
  MDA, 247–249
  MDEA, 253
  MDMA, 241, 247, 248, 249–253
  MDMA homologs, 255
  Nexus, 247
  PMA, 246
  TMA, 245
Halotestin, 413
HAN, see Heroin associated nephropathy
Harmaline, 241, 264–265
Harmine, 264–265
Harrison Narcotic Act of 1914, 6, 178
Hawaiian baby woodrose, 269
Hawaii, ice labs in, 202
Head circumference, 169
Heart
  block, unidirectional, 103
  transplantation, 71
Heat
  rhabdomyolysis and, 221
  shock proteins, 213
Helmsing, 5
Helpern, Milton, 291
Hemiplegia, 391
Hemlock, 284
Hemolytic-uremic syndrome, 156, 158
Hemorrhagic stroke, 395
Hemosiderin-laden macrophages, 128, 129,
    366
Hemothorax, 126, 369
Henning, 242
Hepatic adenomas, 414
Hepatic amyloidosis, 379
Hepatic coma, 415
Hepatic esterases, 36
Hepatic failure, effects of on morphine
    metabolism, 300
Hepatic insufficiency, 185
Hepatic lymph nodes, 308
Hepatic oxidation, 55, 320
Hepatitis B, 378
Hepatitis C, 378
Hepatocellular adenomas, 416
Hepatocellular carcinoma, 416
Hepatocellular necrosis, 137
Hepatosplenomegally, 419
Hepatotoxicity, 135, 221, 375
Heptaflurobutyric anhydride (HFBA), 212
Herbal teas, containing ephedrine, 195
Hereditary angiodema, 414

Heroin, 281
  adulterants found in, 98
  associated nephropathy (HAN), 291, 383
  body packers, 311
  as cough suppressor, 290
  dilutants found in, 295, 297
  elimination clearance of, 34
  excretion and detectability of, 310
  external markers of, 78
  freebase, 304
  gastrointestinal absorption of, 25
  half-life of, 34
  manufacture of, 294
  purity, 297
  routes of administration
    inhalation of fumes, 310
    intravenous, 302
    oral, 302
    rectal, 303
    smoking, 304, 310
    snorting, 304
    subcutaneous, 302
  synthesis of, 290
  thrombocytopenic purpura in abusers of,
      161
  tissue distribution, 310
  toxicity, in drug-related deaths, 281
  Vietnam war, resurgence during, 290
  volume of distribution of, 34
HFBA, see Heptaflurobutyric anhydride
5-HIAA, in spinal fluid, 251
High-density lipoprotein levels, 418
Hiropon, 202
His-Purkinje system, 107
Histamine
  in atherosclerosis, 89
  -related urticaria, 351
  release, 348
Histoplasmosis, 99
HIV, 21, 81, 130, 139, 159, 161, 162, 166, 168,
      317, 355, 357–361, 401
HIV+, myocarditis and, 99
Hives, 402
Hoffman, Albert, 262, 267
Hoffmann, Felix, 290
Hogtied victims, 110
Homovanillic acid, 218
Hooker, Sir William, 1
HUS, see Hemolytic-uremic syndrome
Hyaline membranes, 129, 366
Hycodan®, 328
Hydrazine, 269
Hydrocodone, 281, 328
Hydromorphone, 281, 282, 327
Hydroxylation, 206
Hygrine, 13

Hypercapnic hypoxia, 387
Hyperchloremic acidosis, 434
Hyperemia, at autopsy, 4
Hypereosinophilia, 71
Hyperfrontal pattern, 244
Hyperinsulinemia, 418
Hyperlipidemia, 417
Hyperprolactinemia, 163, 401
Hyperpyrexia, in methamphetamine abuse,
      212
Hypersensitivity
  myocarditis, vs. toxic myocarditis, 98
  pneumonitis, 368
Hyperthermia, 102, 110, 157
Hypodermic syringes, 288–290
Hypokalemia, rhabdomyolysis and, 221
Hypotension, as possible cause of stroke, 394
Hypothalamic temperature center, 221
Hypothalamus, 113
Hypoxic encephalopathy, 388
Hypoxic heart failure, 366

I

Ibogaine, 264
ICD-9 classification system, 172
Ice, 196, 202, 253
Ice smokers, 81, 205, 215
Idiopathic long QT, 92
IgG class antibodies, 402
IgM antibodies, 402
Immune abnormalities, in opiate abusers,
      403
Immunoassays, 29
Impairment, 210
Impotence, 401
Impulse conduction, 67
INa channel, 321
Indian shamans, 242
Indicator diseases, 352
Indocybin®, 262
Indolamine syndrome, 251
Indoylalkylamines, 241
Infections, 387
Infectious discitis, 406
Injectable agents, 413
Injection tracks, 348
Inositol, 98
Inotropic effects of cocaine, 42
Insulin levels, 209
Interethnic differences, in drug metabolism,
      309
Interleukin-2, 166
International Olympic Committee, 196, 411
Interstitial edema, 215
Interstitial fibrosis, 129, 214

Interventricular septum, 360, 417
Intervertebral discs, 406
Intimal fibrosis, 217, 369
Intimal hyperplasia, myocardial infarction
    and, 84
Intraalveolar hemorrhages, due to
    fenfluramine, 217
Intracellular calcium, 66
Intracerebral hemorrhage, 68, 70, 148
Intrahepatic lymphoma, 379
Intrauterine anoxia, 209
Intravenous propoxyphene abuse, 319
Intraventricular hemorrhage, 148
Intraventricular hemorrhage in newborn,43
Intussesception, 136
IOC, see International Olympic Committee
Iodine crystals, 204
Ischemia, 69
Ischemic colitis, 135
Ischemic necrosis, 96
Isoproterenol, 214, 68

J

Jacobsohn, first synthesis of MDA, 247
Jamaica, 23
Japan, ice labs, 202
Jatlow, 5
Jaundice, 415
"Jeff," see Kat

K

Kaposi's sarcoma, 99, 357
Kappa receptors, 282
Kappa receptor sites, 330
Kat (methylcathinone)
    abuse in U.S.S.R., 255
    deaths from, 255
    siezures of clandestine labs, 256
    synthesis of, 255
Ketamine, 275
Ketoconazole, 424
Khat, 190, 247
    -associated psychosis, 193
    chemistry and clinical studies, 192
    chewing, 190
    history of, 190
    revenue from, 191–192
    social use, 190
    urine levels of, 192
    use in Africa, 190–192
Kindling, 150
Kiowa, use of peyote, 242
Köller, 3
Koran, prohibition of intoxicants, 182

L

Labor, duration of, 168
Lactose, 98, 295
Laminar necrosis, 127, 388
Langendorf preparations, 187
La Paz, 11
Lateral medullary syndrome, 145
Laudanum, 285, 291
LDL uptake, 89
Lead
    contamination of cocaine, 14
    poisoning, 203
Leary, Timothy, 268
Left heart blood, 211
Left ventricular hypertrophy, sudden cardiac
    death and, 105
Left ventricular mass, 92, 105
Lemon juice, 352
Leukoderma, coca chewing and, 125
Leukotriene C4, 89
Leukotriene D4, 89
Leutinizing hormone, 401
Levodopa, 113
Levorphanol, 275
Lewin, 182, 242
Lidocaine, 20, 98, 104, 165
Ligand binding, 112
Lipid
    peroxidation, 43, 137
    profiles, 362
Lipolysis, 182
Liver, concentrations of morphine in, 307
Local anesthetic, 3, 21
Lophora williamsii, 241
"love drug," see MDA
LSD, see Lysergic acid diethylamine
LSD-25, see Lysergic acid diethylamine
Lumbar myelography, 308
Lymphadenopathy, 82
Lymphangitis, 82
Lymph nodes, 308
Lymphocyte
    function, 271
    infiltrates, 214
    proliferation, 165
    receptor, 66
Lymphoid follicles, 377
Lysergic acid, 267
Lysergic acid diethylamine (LSD), 241, 246,
    247, 262, 264
    chemical constants and manufacture of,
        268–269
    CIA involvement with, 268
    chromosomal damage related to use, 268
    clinical syndromes of, 269

comparisons to schizophrenia, 268
detection of, 270
outlaw by federal government, 268
"rave" parties and, 268
serotonin metabolism and, 268
synthesis of 264
Timothy Leary and, 268
tissue levels and metabolism of, 269
urine concentrations of, 268

M

"Magic mushroom" poisoning, 264
Magnesium trisilicate, 368
Magnon, Valentine, 4, 178
Ma Huang, 195
Maier, 5
Maize starch, 369
Malignancies, 300
Malignant fibrosarcoma, 379
Mallory's hyaline, 377, 378
Maltese cross, 130, 369
Manet, absinthe and, 178
Manganese contamination of cocai, 14
Mannich, first synthesis of MDA, 247
Mannitol, 98, 295
MAO inhibitor, 210
Mao Tse-tung, 288
Marantic endocarditis, 358
Marfan's syndrome, 100
Mariani, Angelo, 2, 178
Marielitos, 351
Marijuana, and PCP, 274
Massive overdose, 150
Mast cells, in opiate abusers, 352
Maternal drug use, see under individual
    drugs
Maternal/fetal cocaine ratios, 25, 28
M. avium-intracellulare, 379
4-MAX (4-methylaminorex), 253–254
    blood levels of, 254
    difficulty of detection, 254
    pulmonary hypertension, links to, 253
    urine levels of, 254
Maxibolin, 413
Mayo Clinic nomogram, 95–96, 174, 439
McNeil Laboratories, 253
MDA (3,4-methylenedioxyamphetamine),
    218
    arrhythmias and, 248
    -associated sudden death, 248
    autopsy studies and, 248
    blood levels of, 248
    tachycardia and, 247, 248
MDEA (3,4-methylenedioxyetham-
    phetamine), 253

MDM, see MDMA
MDMA (3,4-methylenedioxymethylamphet-
    amine), 218, 245, 249
    blood levels of, 250
    detection of, 250
    hepatitis, links to, 253
    psychiatric use of, 249
    production of, 250
    "rave" parties and, 252
    -related deaths, 252
    serotonin depletion and, 251
    toxicity of, 250
    urine levels of, 250
    U.S. Army involvement with, 249
MDP-2-P, 248
Meconium, 29, 305
Meconium testing, 61, 168
Medial hypetrophy, 217
Medial thickening, 86
Mediastinal adenopathy, 371
Medical personnel, 322
Melioidosis, 371
Membrane
    potentials, 67
    receptors, 271
Membranoproliferative glomerulonephritis,
    382
Menocil®, 253
Mentholatum®, 180
5-MeO-DMT, 265
Meperidine, 281, 304
Meperidine-induced neurotoxicity, 329
Meperidinic acid, 330
Merck, 247
Merck of Darmstad, 286
Mescaline, 241
    blood levels, 244
    brain levels, 244
    chemical preparation of, 243–244
    clinical syndromes of, 244
    confusion caused by, 244
    history of, 241
    metabolism of, 240, 244
    origins of, 242–243
    pathologic findings, 244
    peyote buttons and, 242
        Native Americans, use by, 242
Metandren, 413
Methadone, 281
    autopsy findings, 318
    blood levels of, 316
    clearance, 318
    heroin addicts, use in treatment of, 317
    maternal/fetal considerations, 319
    overdose, 318
    routes of absorption, 317–318

pharmacokinetics, 317–318
-related deaths, 315
tissue levels, 318
Methamphetamine, see Stimulants, synthetic
Methandrostenolone, 413, 418
Methanol, 202
Meth cooks, 203
Methedrine®, 199
Methemoglobinemia, 162
Methenolone
    acetate, 413
    enanthate, 413
Methergine®, 267
Methodone levels, neonatal, 319
2-Methylamino-1-phenylpropan-1-one, see
        Kat
4-Methylaminorex, see 4-MAX
Methylcathinone, see Kat
Methyl-2,5-dimethoxyamphetamine, see
        DOM
Methylecgonine, 13
Methyl ecgonine ester, 36
Methylene-dioxyamphetamine, 217
3,4-Methylenedioxyamphetamine, see MDA,
        218
3,4-Methylenedioxyethamphetamine, see
        MDEA
3,4-Methylenedioxymethylamphetamine, see
        MDMA
3-Methylfentanyl, 322
α-Methylfentanyl, 322
Methylnorfentanyl, 296
Methylphenidate, 208, 216
Methyltestosterone, 412, 413, 414
α-Methyltryptamines, 265
Mexico, ephedrine imports from, 204
Microabscesses, 389
Microcrystalline cellulose, 130, 216, 369
Microfocal fibrosis, 73, 174
Microgranulomatous lesions, 389
Micropolyspora faeni, 370
Microsomal fraction, 39
Microthrombi, 92
Milk production, in khat chewing women,
        193
Mitchell, S. Weir, 242–243
Mitochondria, 94, 215
Mitogen responsiveness, 402
Mitral valve leaflets, 214
MK-ULTRA, 268
Monardes, Nicolas B., 1
Monase, 265
Monilial keratitis, 81
Monoamine uptake inhibitors, 165–166
Mononuclear infiltrate, 71, 108, 357
Mood elevation, cocaine and, 48

Morning glories, 269
Morphine, 281, 282
    absorption and routes of administration of,
        302
    blood, 306
    brain, 307
    inhalation, 304
    intranasal, 303
    intravenous, 302
    liver, 307
    lymph nodes, 308
    maternal/fetal, 305
    oral, 302
    other biofluids, 308
    rectal, 303
    skin, 304
    subcutaneous, 302
    tissue disposition, 305
    urine, 309
    addiction, 3
    biphasic process of, 298–300
    blood levels, 298, 306
    binding sites for, 28
    crude, 295
    elimination clearance of, 34
    excretion and detectability, 309
    -3-glucuronide, 298, 301, 303, 305, 307
    -6-glucuronide, 298, 301, 303, 305,
        307, 314
    half-life of, 34
    levels, conjugated, 301
    moiety, 301
    volume of distribution of, 34
Morphism, 289
Morson, Thomas, 286
Movement disorders, 151
MPPP, 396
MPTP, 396
Mu agonists, 282
Mucormycosis, 389
Munich, drug-related deaths in, 78
Mu receptor, 282
Muscle ischemia, rhabdomyolysis and,
        221
Mycobacteria, 99
Mycotic aneurysm, 131, 361
Mycotoxic adulterants, 382
Myelofibrosis, 414
Myocardial calcification, 169
Myocardial diseases, 92
    AIDS-related, 99
Myocardial fibrosis, 83, 95, 214, 233, 417
Myocardial hypertrophy, in cocaine users, 92,
        174
Myocardial infarction, 68, 105, 416
    amphetamine-related, 215

cocaine and, 20
   lesions and, 84, 86, 102, 187
   intimal hyperplasia and, 84
Myocardial perfusion, 54
Myocardium, 173, 330
Myocyte(s), 4
   hypertrophy, 92
   metabolism, 417
Myofibrillar apparatus, 71
Myofibrillar degeneration, 70
Myofilament Ca2+ responsiveness, 42
Myofilaments, 67
Myoglobin, 382
Myoglobinuria, 158
Myometrial contraction, 168
α Myosin, mRNA for, 105
β Myosin, mRNA for, 105
Myositis, 331

N

Nagi, Nagayoshi, 194
Nails, methamphetamine found in, 206
Naloxone, 321
Nandrolone, 419
   decanoate, 413
   phenpropionate, 413
Narcosis, prolonged, 329
Narcotic antagonists, 276
Narcotics, 281–408
   abuse, 130
   bone and soft tissue disorders, 405–407
     bone and joint infection, 405–406
     fibrous myopathy of pentazocine abuse,
       407
   soft tissue infections, 407
   cardiovascular disorders, 355–363
     endocarditis, 357–361
     miscellaneous disorders, 362–363
     other myocardial disorders, 361–362
     pathology associated with HIV
       infection, 357
   classifications of narcotic agents, 282–283
   cultivation and manufacture, 293–297
     botanic considerations, 293–294
     manufacture, 294–296
     sample analysis, 296–297
   dermatologic sequelae of opiate abuse,
     348–353
   abscess and ulcerations, 349
   atrophic scarring, 348–349
   fresh puncture sites, 348
   fungal lesions, 352–353
   histamine-related urticaria, 351–352
   miscellanous cutaneous abnormalities,
     353

     necrotizing fascitis, 351
     puffy hands, 351
     tattoos, 350–351
     track marks, 349–350
   gastrointestinal disorders, 375–379
     bowel disease, 375–376
     liver disorders, 376–379
   history of opiate abuse, 284–291
     first pathology studies, 291
     introduction to Europe and Asia,
       285–288
     invention of hypodermic syringe,
       288–290
     origins in antiquity, 284–285
     synthesis of heroin, 290–291
   hormonal and immune alterations,
     401–403
   individual narcotic agents, 298–331
     codeine, 312–315
     fentanyl and other synthetic agents,
       322–326
     heroin, 309–312
     methadone, 315–319
     morphine, 298–309
     other opiates, 326–331
     propoxyphene, 319–322
   injections of, 21
   interpreting tissue and blood levels,
     342–346
     clinical profile of opiate abusers,
       342–343
     interpreting test results, 345–346
     testing blood, 344–345
     testing urine, 343–344
   neuropathology, 386–397
     hypoxic encephalopathy, 388–389
     infectious diseases, 389–397
   prevalence of opiate-related morbidity, 281
   pulmonary disorders, 365–372
     infectious complications, 370–372
     noninfectious complications, 365–369
   rhabdomyolysis and, 156
   renal disorders, 381–385
     acute renal failure due to nontraumatic
       rhabdomyolysis, 382
     heroin associated nephropathy, 383–384
     necrotizing angitis, 384–385
   secondary amyloidosis, 382–383
Nasal septum perforation, 124
National Collegiate Athletic Association, 411
National Institute on Drug Abuse, see NIDA
National Transportation Safety Board, ruling
     of drug intoxication as cause of
     crash, 50
Native American Church, 242
Naturally occurring opiates, 282

NBTE, see Nonbacterial thrombotic
    endocarditis
N-demethylation, of codeine, 313
Necrotizing angiitis, 148, 382, 384, 387, 395
Necrotizing enterocolitis, 136
Necrotizing fascitis, 351
Necrotizing vasculitis, 220
Needle fragments, 367
Needle and mercury emboli, 367
Neonatal jaundice, 169
Nephrotic syndrome, 159, 381
Nephrotoxicity, 156
Nerve block, 288
Neurogenic pulmonary edema, 128
Neuroleptic malignant syndrome, 110
Neurotransmitter, 65
New World plants, 1
Nexus (4-bromo-2,5-dimethoxyphene-
    thylamine), 247
Niacinamide, 98
Nibal, 413
Nicotine, 1
NIDA cutoffs, 21, 29, 50, 273
NIDA testing programs, 211, 212, 321, 327
Niemann, Albert, 2
Nilevar, 413
Nitric oxide, 90
Nitrogen balance, 409
NMDA, 271
NMDA receptor, 271
Nonbacterial thrombotic endocarditis
    (NBTE), 357, 358
Non-Hodgkin's lymphoma, 379
Non-steroidal anti-inflammatory drugs, 351
Noradrenaline, 218
Norcocaethylene, 40
Norcocaine, 15
    alcohol, relationship to, 41
    concentrations in samples, 14, 57
    hepatotoxicity, 14
    maternal/fetal considerations, 28, 29
    nitroxide, 42, 43, 56
Norcodeine, 312
Norephedrine, 196, 206, 232
Norepinephrine, 65–66, 68, 69, 86, 88, 107,
    166, 168, 214, 218
    myocarditis, 96
    synthesis of, 68
    transporter, 55, 56
Norethandrolone, 413
Norfentanyl, 296, 324
Normeperidine, 330
Normorphine, 300
Norpropoxyphene, 319, 320
Numorphan®, 329
Nursing, 209

O

Obstipation, 375
Occult myocarditis, 419
O-demethylation, of codeine, 313
Ogata, 199
Oligodendroglia, 392
Opiate(s)
    abuse, 65, 128
    abusers, clinical profile of, 342–343
    addiction, 8, 283
    binding sites, 282
    blood testing, 344
    dermatologic dequelae of abuse, 348
        abscess and ulcerations, 349
        atrophic scarring, 348–349
        fresh puncture sites, 348
        fungal lesions, 352–353
        histamine-related urticaria, 351
        miscellaneous cutaneous abnormalities,
            353
        puffy hands, 351
        tattoos, 350
        track marks, 349–350
    history of, 284–290
    interpreting test results, 345
    -related deaths, 127, 291
    side effects of, 282
    synthetic, 308
    toxicity, 281, 283
    urine testing, 343–344
Opioid receptors, 282
Opioids, 282
Opium
    addicts, 1
    blood levels, 288
    cultivation and manufacture, 293–297
        world production of, in metric tons, 294
    Eaters, 303
    eating, 286
    first death from injected overdose, 288
    injections, 288–290
    introduction to China, 286, 288
    manufacture of, 294
    poppies, 284, 293
        harvesting of, 293
    smoking, 288, 304
Opportunistic infections, 357, 389
Opportunistic neoplastic processes, 389
Opportunistic tumors, 378
Oral agents, 413
Oral thrush, 352
Organophosphate insecticide, 39
Osler, 361
Osler's nodes, 361
Oteton, 413

Oxandrolone, 413
Oxazolines, 254
Oxidative cocaine metabolism, 137
Oxycodone, 281, 282, 328
Oxygen demand, 69
Oxymetholone, 413
Oxymorphone, 282, 329

P

P. aeruginosa, 406
Paget-Schroetter syndrome, 101
PAI-1, see Plasminogen activator inhibitor
Panacinar emphysema, 216, 367
Papaver somniferum, 293
Papillary muscles, 214
Papillary rupture, 360
Paracelsus, 285
Paramethoxyamphetamine, see PMA
Parathyroid hormone, 401
Paraxanthine, 183, 184
Paregoric, 350
Parenchymal disease, 127
Parke Davis and Company, 3, 255, 270
Parkinsonism, 151, 387, 396
Parsley leaves, 272
Pasqua Rosee, 182
Paste lab, 13
Pathy myocardial fibrosis, 108
PCP, see Phencyclidine
Peliosis, 379
Peliosis hepatis, 414
Pemberton, John Styth, 3
Pemoline®, 221–222, 254
Pen Tsao Kang Mu, 286
Pentazocine, 271, 330, 369
Peoppig, Edward, 1
Percodan®, 328
Perforated nasal septum, 79
Performance
    effects of cocaine on, 143
    improvement, 182
Periacqueductal gray matter, 402
Periarteritis nodosa, 148
Pericardial effusion, 357
Pericarditis, 357
Periodate degradation, 212
Peripancreatic lymph nodes, 376
Peripheral neuropathy, 387
Periportal inflammation, 137
Perivascular pigment deposition, 388
Permanganate oxidation, 14
Pernod, Henri-Louis, 177
Peru, 1, 13
Pethidine®, 329
Petichae, 248

PET scanning, see Detection of drug use
Peyote buttons, 242
Pharmaceutical Gazette, 190
Phenactin, 98
Phencyclidine
    alcohol and, 274
    blood levels of, 273, 274
    clandestine labs, 272
    glucose metabolism and, 271
    historical aspects of, 270–272
    interpreting blood and tissue levels,
        274
    Los Angeles gangs and, 272
    marijuana and, 274
    metabolism of, 273, 274
    physical constants, 272
    -related deaths and, 271
    routes of administration and, 272
    skin absorption of, 273
    street prices of, U.S., 272
    tissue levels of, 274
    toxicity by organ system, 275
        neurologic disorders, 275
        Renal disorders
    urine levels of, 273, 274
    violent behavior and, 271
Phenmetrazine, see Stimulants, synthetic
Phenoformin, 217
Phenteramine, 211
Phenylalkylamines, 241
Phenylisopropylamine, 199
Phenylpiperidine, 322
Phenylpropanolamine, 68, 98, 202, 213, 214
Phenyl-2-propanone (P2P), 203
Pheochromocytoma, 70
Phosphodiesterase inhibitors, 185
Phosphoinositol, 65
Phospholipase-C, 65, 92
Physical agitation, 110
Physical constants, 272
Piecemeal necrosis, 377
Piperidine moiety, 273
Pisacocas, 13
Pituitary, 401
Pizzi, Enrique, 2
Placenta, 27
    metabolism of cocaine by, 43
Placenta praevia, 168
Plains Indians, 242
Plaque rupture, 89
Plasma
    BEG detection in, 49, 58
    cells, 377
    cholinesterase, 36, 37, 38, 55, 186
    cocaine levels in, 58
    half-life, 205

Plasminogen activator inhibitor (PAI-1), 145, 162
Platelet
  aggregation, 84
  function, 417
  responsiveness, 145
Pleural effusions, 371
Plexiform lesions, 216
Pliny, 194
PMA (paramethoxyamphetamine), 246
Pneumocystitis, 99, 367
Pneumomediastinum, 124
Pneumonia, community-acquired, 125
Pneumothorax, 125, 369
Pocket shooters, 131
Pocket shot, 369
Poeppig, Edward, 1
Polyarteritis nodosa, 98, 220
Polymicrobial infections, 349
Polymicrobial valve infection, 360
Ponderax®, 237
Pondimin®, 211, 237
Pontine hemorrhage, 102
Poor hydroxylators, of codeine, 314
Pope Leo XIII, 2
Poppy seeds, 294, 343
Portal adenopathy, 291
Portal fibrosis, 375, 377
Portal flogosis, 377
Portal hypertension, 416
Positional vascular compression, as possible cause of stroke, 394
Posterior communicating artery, 148–149
Posterior wall thickness, 92
Postganglionic nerve endings, 65
Post-mortem redistribution, 306
Postreceptor mechanisms, 283
Potassium
  efflux channels, 106
  permanganate, 15, 255
Potato starch, 369
PPA, see Phenylpropanolamine; Stimulants, synthetic
P2P, see Phenyl-2-propanone
PR interval, 107
Preeclampsia, 168
Preexisting lesions, 69
Pregnancy, 209
Pregnenolone, 412
Preludin®, 211
Premarin®, 414
Pressure necrosis, s382
Primary phycomycosis, 390
Primobolan, 413
Proarrhythmic effect, of cocaine, 107
Procaine, 98

Progesterone-related mood disturbances, 421
Progressive pulmonary hypertension, 217
Prolactin levels, 163
Proliferative glomerulonephritis, 361
Propoxyphene, 283
  blood levels of, 320
  detectability of, 321
  excretion of, 320
  intravenous use, elimination of, 319
  levels, post-mortem, 320
  -related deaths, 319
  tissue distribution, 320
  toxicity, electrocardiogram in, 321
  toxicity, mechanism of, 321–322
Propylhexedrine, 201, 213, 214, 217, 219
Prostaglandin D2, 89
Prostaglandins, 402
Prostatic hypertropy, 252
Protein binding, 300
Pruritus, 352
Pseudoallergy, 402
Pseudoaneurysm, 131, 369
Pseudoephedrine, 213
Pseudomembranous colitis, 136
Pseudomonas pseudomallei, 371
Psilocybe cubensis, 262
Psilocybin, 241
  chemical constants, 263
  clinical findings, 264
  history of, 262
  metabolism and tissue levels, 263
  mushrooms for production of, 262–263
Psilocybin-containing mushrooms, 262
Psychadelic age, 268
Psychiatric disturbances, 419
Psychosis, cocaine and, 110
Puffy hands, 351
Pulmonary anthracosis, 128
Pulmonary artery, 211
Pulmonary capillary permeability, 297
Pulmonary edema, 124, 127, 187, 291, 322, 365
Pulmonary emboli, 125
Pulmonary fibrosis, 216
Pulmonary granulomas, 214
Pulmonary hypertension, 130, 214, 253, 356
Pure Food and Drug Act of 1906, The, 5–6
Purkinje cell degeneration, 265
Purkinje cells, 275
Purulent myocarditis, 351
Purulent pericarditis, 360
Putamen, 388
Pyramiding pattern, of steroid abuse, 411
Pyrolysis products of cocaine, 36

Q

QRS interval, 107
QT interval, 107
QT prolongation, 91
QTc interval, 107
Quadriplegia, 391
Quinidine, 104
Quinine, 98, 286, 296

R

Rate-pressure product, 88
"Rave" parties, see MDMA; LSD
α Receptors, 162
α2 Receptors, 65–66, 69, 234
β Receptors, down-regulation of, 66, 161
β1 Receptors, 65–66
β2 Receptors, 65–66
Rectal application of cocaine, 22
Reductive amination, 203
Reinforcement, 180
Renal amyloid, 382
Renal amyloidosis, 382
Renal artery arteriosclerosis, 157
Renal blood flow, cocaine and, in fetus,
        43
Renal cocaine levels, 56
Renal cortex, 56
Renal disease, 220
Renal failure, 112
   in cocaine abuse, 158
   effects of on morphine metabolism, 300
Reperfusion, 68
Reproductive functions, in heroin abusers,
        401
Respiratory arrest, 110
Respiratory depression, 282, 308
Resting membrane potential, 104
Reticuloendothelial hyperplasia, 376
Retroviral infection, 166
Rexall, 201
Rhabdomyolysis, 112, 156, 220, 221, 252, 275,
        382, 387
Richardson, Sir Robert, 298
Right heart blood, 211
Right ventricular hypertrophy, 357
Ring abscess, 360
Ring contrast enhancement, 390
Ritalin®, 208, 216, 221–222
Ritalinic acid, 208
Robiquet, 312
Royal Botanical Gardens at Kew, 1
Royal Pharmaceutical Society, 286
Russian Federation, 322

S

Saccular aneurysms, 148
Saddle nose deformity, 4
Saddle pulmonary embolus, 418
Saliva, 58
Saliva/plasma ratios, 308
Sandoz Pharmaceuticals, 262, 267
Schizophrenia, 219
Scleroderma, cocaine use and, 82–83
Scopulariopsis brumptii, 368
Seay, Edward, 231
Secobarbitol, 369
Second messengers, 67
Secondary amyloidosis, 382
Secondary male sexual characteristics, 409
Seizures, 109, 150
Selegiline, 210
Semisynthetic opiates, 282
Septal perforation, 4
Septic emboli, 361, 394
Septic pulmonary emboli, 371
Septic shock, 221
Septic thrombophlebitis, 405
Sernyl®, 270
Serotonin, 88
   binding sites for, 28
   levels with amphetamine use, 218
   levels with fenfluramine use, 237, 239
   levels with MDMA use, 251
   metabolism with LSD, 268
   Nexus, interactions with, 247
   transporter, 109, 168
   toxicity, 217
Sertürner, opium experiments of, 285–286,
        298, 312
Setürner, 298
Sex-hormone-binding globulin, 412
Shabu, 195, 202
Sherms, 272
Sidestream cocaine exposure, 24
Sigma receptors, 219, 271, 282, 421
Signal transduction, 73
Silk Road, 293
SIDS, related to cocaine use, 25
Sinusoidal wall surface, in heroin abusers,
        376
Skeletal muscle, 305
Skin
   absorption, of PCP, 273
   excoriations, in heroin abusers, 351
   flora, 405
   popping, 82
Sloan's Liniment®, 180
Smith, Kline and French, 199, 201

Snorting cocaine, 18
Socrates, 284
Sodium channel
    blockade, 104
    inward, 42
Soft tissue abscess, 405
Solvent abuse, 431
Sommer's sector, 388
Soothing syrups, 286
Space of disse, 376
Spinal epidural hematoma, 150
Spinal fluid, 60
Spongiform encephalopathy, 387
Spongiform leukoencephalopathy, 391
Sputum, black, 129
Squibb, 201
St. George's disease, 415
Stacking pattern, of steroid abuse, 411
Stanozolol, 413, 414
Staphylococcal vegetations, 358
Starch, 295
Starch granules, 130
Starvation, 68
Status epilepticus, 109, 150, 275
Steatosis, 377, 378
Stellate ganglion, 91
Sternoarticular joints, 406
Sternoclavicular infection, 372
Steroid
    -related deaths, 411
    -related psychosis, 419
    therapy, 68
Steroids, anabolic, 409–429
    legitimate clinical indications, 414
    pharmacology, 412–414
        black market steroids and steroid
            contaminants, 413–414
        synthesis and metabolism, 412–413
    steroid-related disorders, 414–424
        cardiovascular disease, 416–419
        detecting steroid abuse, 422–424
        liver disease, 414–416
        musculoskeletal disease, 421–422
        neurologic disorders, 419–421
Stevenson, Robert Louis, 2
Stigmata, 306
Stimulants, naturally occurring, 177–198
    absinthe, 177–180
        clinical and autopsy studies, 179–180
        history, 177–178
    caffeine, 180–187
        athletic performance, affect on,
            181–182
        autopsy findings, 187
        blood levels, 186–187

chemical constants and tissue
        disposition, 183–184
    clinical studies of caffeine, 184–186
    consumption, European, 181
    consumption, U.S., 180, 181
    content, of commonly consumed
            beverages and medications, 181
    disease, links to, 183, 186–187
    history, 180–183
ephedrine, 194–198
    chemistry and metabolism, 196
    clinical studies, 196–197
    history, 194–195
khat, 190–194
    chemistry and clinical studies, 192–193
    history, 190–192
Stimulants, synthetic
    amphetamine and methamphetamine
        abuse of, 201
        alcohol consumption and, 206
        environmental exposure to, 209
        "ewe" model, 209
        early medical use of, 199–201
        -associated deaths, 210, 211
        blood levels, 205, 206, 209, 210
        chemistry, 205
        contraction band necrosis and, 68
        cost and toxicity of, vs. cocaine, 6
        demethylation of, 207
        designer, 218, 243
        drug testing for, 211
        "high," vs. cocaine, 202
        history, 199–203
        illicit manufacture, 202, 203–204
        interpreting amphetamine levels,
            210–212
        maternal/fetal considerations, 208, 209
        mercury levels in, 203
        metabolism, 205–208
        nasal inhalers, use in, 199, 201
        obesity and, 200, 218
        -related psychosis, 218–219
        routes of administration, 205
        saliva levels of, 205
        snorting, 215
        stroke and, 218, 219–220
        tissue disposition, 208–210
        toxicity by organ system, 212–222
            cardiovascular, 213–215
            central nervous system and, 218–220
            hepatic disease and, 221–222
            pulmonary toxicity, 216
            renal disease and, 220–221
            sudden death and, 213
        toxicity, episodes of in U.S., 203

urine levels, 206, 208, 210
World War II, use during, 201
fenfluramine, 202, 211, 217, 218, 237–239
  blood and tissue levels, 238–239
  drug constants, 238
  historical aspects, 237–238
  metabolism, 238
  overdose-related deaths and, 238
  serotonin levels and, 239, 239
  toxicity by organ system, 239
    cardiopulmonary, 239
    neurological, 239
  urine levels and, 238
phenylpropanolamine, 68, 98, 202, 213, 214, 230–237
  blood levels, 232
  caffeine, interactions with, 232
  chemistry, 231
  consumption, U.S., 230
  historical aspects, 230–231
  metabolism, 232–233
  stroke and, 233–234
  toxicity by organ system, 233–237
    cardiac disease, 234
    gastrointestinal disorders, 234
    neurologic disease, 233–234
    pulmonary disease, 234
    renal disease, 234
  weight loss, use in, 230–231
Stomatitis, coca chewing and, 125
STP, 245, 247
Strain's series, 108
Streptococcal vegetations, 358
Striatal reward centers, 143
Striato-limbic hyperactivity, 244
Striatum, 52
Stridor, in crack smokers, 126
Stroke, 387, 416
  in opiate abusers, 394
  perinatal, 43
  phenylpropanolamine-related, 219
  subarachnoid hemorrhage and, 102
Subarachnoid hemorrhage, 148
Subclavian vein, blood samples from, 48
Subcutaneous drug injection, 82
Subcutaneous fibrosis, 349
Subendocardial hemorrhages, 74
Substantia nigra, 219, 396
Sudafed®, 213
Sudden arrhythmic death, 416
Sudden cardiac death, 102
Sudden death, 69
Sudden infant death syndrome, related to cocaine use, 25
Sugar cubes, 247

Sulfentanyl, 304
Supraclavicular fossa, 126
Surgical application of cocaine, 20
Sweat, methamphetamine found in, 206
Sydenham, 285
Sympathetic axis, 91
Sympathetic nerve terminals, 58
Sympathetic stimulation, 264
Synaptic cleft, 213
Synthetic opiates, 282, 308

T

Tachyzoites, 390
Tajikistan, 293
Takayasu's disease, 101
Talc, 130, 368, 369
Talc granulomas, 131
Talwin®, 330
Tang Dynasty, 286
Tattoos, 350
TDx® Opiates, 343
Tendon rupture, 421–422
Terminal seizures, 81
Terpenes, 179
Testicular atrophy, 164, 252, 401
Testosterone, 401, 409
  cypionate, 413
  enanthate, 413
  /epitestosterone ratio, 413
  levels, in chronic cocaine abusers, 164
  propionate, 413
Tetracaine, 98
Thebaine, 294
Thein, 183
Theobromine, 183
Theophylline, 184, 185
Theriaki, 8
Thermoactinomyces vulgaris, 371
Thienmylfentanyl, 326
Thrombi, 358
Thrombocytopenia, as possible cause of stroke, 394
Thrombocytopenic purpura, 161, 403
Thromboembolic arteriopathy, 216, 368
Thromboembolism, as possible cause of stroke, 394
Thrombophlebitis, 101
Thrombotic microangiopathy, 158
Thromboxane A2 receptor density, 417
Thrombus formation, 88
Thujone, 179
Tiletamine, 275

TMA (2,4,5-trimethoxyamphetamine), 245
Toads, for production of Bufotenine, 261
"Toad smoking," 261
Tolerance, 26, 210
Tolerance, to PCP, 274
Toluene, 433
Torases-de pointes, 91–92
Total bilirubin, 379
Toulouse-Lautrec, absinthe and, 178
Toxicity, see cocaine
Toxic myocarditis, 98
Toxoplasmosis, 99, 390
Track marks, 291, 306, 349
Transdermal delivery, of fentanyl, 324
Transesterification of cocaine with alcohol, 39
Transverse myelopathy, 387
Triadiatis, 377
Tricuspid valve, 359
Trifluoroacetic acid, 269
Trimethobenzamide, 211
3,4,5-Trimethoxybenzeneethanamine, see Mescaline
2,4,5-Trimethoxyamphetamine, see TMA
Tripelennamiune, 331
Tropacocaine, 13
Tropine, 13
Tryptamines, simple, 260
Tryptophan hydroxylase, 143
T suppressor cell activity, 166
Tuberculosis, 371
Tubular lesions, 157
Tussend®, 328
Tussionex®, 328
Tylox®, 328
Type II alveolar cells, 366
Type 2 herpes simplex virus, 379
Tyrosine hydroxylase, 73, 143, 218

U

U4Euh, see 4-MAX
U4EA, see 4-MAX
Über Coca, 3, 178, 289
Urinary retention, 252
Urine, 60
    detection of cocaine in, 5, 20, 21, 22, 24, 28, 35, 36, 59, 60–61
    detection of methamphetamines in, 206, 208, 210
    detection of morphine in, 300, 309
    testing, in workplace, 343–344
Uterine bleeding, 267

Uterine blood flow, 28
Uteroplacental blood flow, 168
Uzbekistan, 293

V

Vacuolization of neurons, 275
Vagina, concealment of drugs in, 22
Valsalva maneuver, 126
Valvular heart disease, 99
van Gogh, absinthe and, 178
Vascular adaptations, 130
Vascular endothelium, 90
Vascular spasm, 246
Vasculitis, 145, 219
Vasculitis, as possible cause of stroke, 394
Vasopressors, 86
Vasospasm, 28
Vaughn, James, 190
Vegetations, 358
Ventricular arrhythmias, 69
Ventricular fibrillation, 105
Ventricular modeling, 105
Ventricular tachycardia, 107, 186
Verne, Jules, 2
Vertebral bone density, 401
Vertebral column, 406
Vicks®, 208, 211
Vicks Vaporub®, 180
Vin Mariani, 2
Viral antigens, 377
Viral inclusions, 390
Viral infection, in cocaine user, 166
Virchow, 182
Visceral congestion, 214, 375
Vitreous humor, 59, 309
Volatile sovents, methamphetamine production and, 202
Volume of distribution, of morphine, 305
von Scherzer, Carl, 2
von Tschudi, Johan, 2

W

Wayamine®, 211
Wegner's granulomatosis, 124
White matter filled with vacuoles, 391
WHO, see World Health Organization
Williams, Edward, 4
Winstrol, 413
Wöhler, Carl, 2
Wolff-Parkinson-White syndrome, 105
Wood, Alexander, 288
Wooden chest syndrome, 323

Woods, 5
World Health Organization (WHO), 10
Wormwood, 177
Wren, Christopher, 288
W. S. Merrell, 201
Wyeth, entry into amphetamine market, 201

X

Xanthine(s), 184
  derivatives, 177
  oxidase, 185
XTC, see MDMA
Xylazine, death from, 297

Y

Yemen, 190
Yield per acre, of opium, 294
Yungas, 11

Z

Zanchevski, Vasili, 4
Z-band remnants, 71, 97
Zona compacta, 396
Zone-3 necrosis, 139
Zone-1 type injury, 139